CRIME AGAINST WOMEN

CRIME AGAINST WOMEN

UDAI VEER

ANMOL PUBLICATIONS PVT. LTD.
NEW DELHI - 110 002 (INDIA)

ANMOL PUBLICATIONS PVT. LTD.
4374/4B, Ansari Road, Daryaganj
New Delhi - 110 002
Ph.: 23261597, 23278000
Visit us at: www.anmolpublications.com

Crime Against Women

First Published, 2004

ISBN 81-261-1876-8

PRINTED IN INDIA

Published by J.L. Kumar for Anmol Publications Pvt. Ltd., New Delhi - 110 002 and Printed at Mehra Offset Press, Delhi.

Contents

Preface

Women are said to be the better half of the society and are supposed to enjoy all privileges and comforts, at par with men. But, the reality is not that beautiful. Despite all the sloganeering, tall claims and official schemes, women in our social fabric are very much vulnerable to all sorts of threats, dangers and even fatal assaults. Their honour and dignity is always the target of unwanted elements in the society.

All women-lib activists are in action, a strong movement for feminine rights is in full swing and the law of land is always there to protect them, yet women are molested, dishonoured and robbed of their dignity almost every day, in our society.

Truly speaking, women are subjected to all sorts of torture and violence, which can be thought of. From the confinement of the four walls of the house to place of work and public places, the women are victims of tyranny.

This small but comprehensive and exclusive book deals with all aspects of violence, which is let loose against women by their family members, colleagues and even the custodians of law. It covers all aspects and dimensions of the crimes, committed against women.

The editor is confident of the acceptance of this research-based work by scholars and academics, as a sincere and serious effort in an area, where more works of similar nature are required, in order to create an awakening regarding women's issues and their genuine problems.

— Editor

ONE

Introduction

One of the directive principles of state policy prescribes that the state should direct its policy towards securing equal pay for equal work for both men and women. Although the directive principles are fundamental in the governance of the country and are to be applied in enacting legislation, they are not judicially enforceable. In this context, one of the provisions of the Constitution is of special significance. After having laid down that the state shall not discriminate against any citizen on grounds of sex, among other things, it provides that nothing in this article shall prevent the state from making any special provision for women and children. So there is a Constitutional provision in India permitting the state to discriminate in favour of women, if such discrimination is found necessary.

Child marriage, especially of the female infant, was common; widow marriage was prohibited, even if she succeeded in escaping from the funeral pyre of her deceased husband where she was expected to be burnt alive; a divorce was generally looked down upon and her remarriage was socially disapproved. If some of these attitudes still persist it is not because legislation has lagged behind, but because law has not succeeded in playing its role of social engineering and changing certain deeply-rooted social attitudes. During the last two decades a number of laws were adopted with a view to ensuring equality of status and opportunity for women. But it appears that in practice this equality eludes the Indian woman's grasp.

In what follows an attempt is made to examine some of the more important legislation enacted by the Central legislature in

India to ameliorate certain unhappy conditions in which women, particularly Hindu women, found themselves. Occasionally, there is talk about ameliorating the conditions of Muslim women, but political consideration stand in the way of doing anything substantial towards that end. Muslim personal laws are considered to be part of the religion of Islam and government generally considers it necessary not to interfere directly in matters regarded as religious.

With a view to preventing child marriages, especially the giving away of infant girls in marriage, the Child Marriage Restraint Act was passed in 1929 declaring it an offence for a man to marry a girl under fifteen years of age. Any person who performs a marriage where the bridegroom is below 18 years or the bride below 15 years commits an offence, as also parents or guardians of the bridegroom or the bride.

This socially motivated legislation has been made relatively ineffective by stating that a marriage celebrated in violation of the stipulation regarding age would nevertheless be valid. The same restrictions regarding marriageable age are found in the Hindu Marriage Act, 1955. There is a Dowry Prohibition Act also in the Indian statute book which prohibits the giving or taking dowry. But this again is ineffective in practice mainly because any dowry given may be construed as "presents" which are not prohibited by law if made at the time of marriage. In the case of both these statutes the teeth of the legislation are practically blunted both by loopholes within the law and by the resistance of social structures and attitudes to change. Certain conservative section of the community regard child marriage a good, if not a proper, thing and would prefer to pay a fine rather than keep their infant sons and daughters unmarried.' A large number of young men and their parents consider dowry a legitimate stepping stone to higher rungs in the social ladder, and possibly a passport to domestic comfort if not happiness.

Two years before the adoption of the Hindu Marriage Act, which inter alia provided of or divorce, the Special Marriage Act, 1954 was enacted. There is a provision in the Special Marriage Act for obtaining a decree of divorce by mutual consent, provided the parties have lived separately for a year and three years have elapsed since the date of marriage. Apart from the common grounds on which either party to the marriage may obtain dissolution of a marriage performed or registered under the Act, the wife may sue the husband for divorce on the ground that he has committed rape, sodomy or bestiality. Persons married under the Act with the result that they would now be governed by its provisions.

Those who marry under the Act or whose marriages are registered under it are, in matters of inheritance, governed by the Indian Succession Act, 1925. When a man to whom the Indian Succession Act applies dies leaving a widow and lineal descendants, the widow is entitled to one third of the property of the deceased and the lineal descendants to two-thirds. Under the Act, in the case of Christians, a widow in the absence of lineal descendants will get the entire property of the husband, provided its value does not exceed Rs. 5,000. If it does, she will receive Rs. 5,000 and a share in what remains along with the kindred of the deceased according to the specific rules laid down in the Act. Some persons, especially women, prefer to be married under the Special Marriage Act because of its beneficial provisions regarding divorce and interstate succession. We shall advert to this later.

It may be said in general that the right of a wife to obtain a divorce in India is much more restricted than that of the husband under customary law; however, in certain Hindu communities, as also among most tribal groups, it is possible for the husband and the wife to obtain divorce without resource course to court.

They are only required to follow some customary practice, like making a declaration before the elders of the community or the headman of the tribe that they no longer desire their marital relationship to continue. It is well known that among Muslims, while the husband can unilaterally and without assigning any reason divorce his wife by pronouncing *talaq* (that is by uttering the words, "I divorce you") three times, the wife has to get a judicial pronouncement of divorce on specified grounds.

It is, however, possible for the wife to have the power of divorce delegated too her by the husband at the time of entering into the marriage contract. For instance, it may be stipulated that if he takes a second wife, she should have the option of repudiating her marriage. Such delegation is, however, uncommon. Considering the fact that the Constitution makes provision for equality of the sexes, it may be desirable to give judicial recognition to *fasaq* by means of which a Muslim wife may unilaterally repudiate her marriage. An opportunity for such recognition was lost when the Kerala High Court in 1975 ruled that the right of Muslim women to obtain divorce is exclusively governed by the Dissolution of Muslim Marriages Act, 1939 and that it is not permissible to go beyond it.

The divorce provisions of the Hindu Marriage Act, 1955 maintain equality of the sexes in the matter of grounds for divorce. The Act applies to Hindus, Buddhists, Jains and Sikhs. In the provisions of the Indian Divorce Act, which applies to Christians there is some discrimination between the sexes in the matter of grounds for divorce. A single isolated act of adultery on the part of the wife is a valid ground for granting a divorce on the petition of the husband but, if a wife has to be successful in her petition for divorce, she has generally to prove against her husband not only adultery, but also an additional ground such as desertion or cruelty.

Commission or rape, sodomy or bestiality by the husband can also be ground for obtaining a decree of divorce. This Act was modeled after English enactments for matrimonial reliefs adopted about the middle of the last century. Over a hundred years later, the United kingdom prescribed by legislation a single valid ground for divorce, that is, irretrievable breakdown of marriage.

If in 1869 the idea was that Indian Christians would do well to follow in the footsteps of the British in obtaining matrimonial reliefs, is there any valid reason to assume that they should be governed by rules different from those applicable to the British after the passage of a century. If irretrievable breakdown of marriage is made the only ground for judicial declaration of divorce applicable to all communities and religious groups in India there will be equality of treatment not only between men and women but also between various religious groups.

Perhaps one has to wait for the adoption of a uniform civil code for such unification of laws. In the meantime, the Indian Divorce Act could be amended making grounds for divorce identical for both men and women, preferably adopting the provision regarding irretrievable breakdown of marriage as the sole ground of divorce as laid down in the (British) Divorce Referm Act. 1969.

During the pendency of a suit under the Indian Divorce Act, a wife may apply for alimony and the court may grant an amount not exceeding one-fifth of the husband's average net income. While passing a decree for divorce or judicial separation, the court may order the husband to pay a lump sum or make periodical payments for life to the wife, taking into account her fortune, the means of the husband and the conduct of the parties.

There are similar provisions for the benefit of the wife in the Parsi Marriage and Divorce Act, 1936. The spirit of equality envisaged in the Constitution finds clear expression in the Hindu Marriage Act, 1955. It makes provision for the grant of expenses of matrimonial suits and a monthly allowance for the support of either spouse during the pendency of legal proceedings, provided the spouse applying for the expenses and allowances has not sufficient income to support himself or herself.

The Act also has a provision for making an order for permanent alimony or maintenance in favour of either of the spouses. On remarriage the spouse loses his or her right to maintenance. Further, if the recipient of the alimony is the wife, she is required to remain chaste; if maintenance is granted to the husband, he is enjoined from having sexual relations with any other woman.

In spite of the provisions for divorce contained in the Act of 1955, it is not often that recourse is to them : this is because Hindu social values in general are opposed to the concept of divorce. As Kapadia puts it, "the principle of divorce is alien to the social pattern" with the result that "the norm accepted by law has not been accepted in practice". Whereas prior to 1955, divorce was considered absolute anathema by women of the higher castes, after the passing of the Act, it is the women of the upper classes and higher castes as well as the rich and educated in urban areas who petition the courts for divorce. Probably, the illiterate women in the rural areas do not even know that there are legal provisions for divorce apart from those enshrined in the customary law of certain communities or tribes.

Marriage under the Special Marriage Act has the effect of making the provisions of the Indian Succession Act applicable to the parties. These provisions were more beneficial to women, be they Hindus, Muslims Indian Christians of Pondicherry or Indian

Christians in those areas of Kerala which formerly comprised the princely states of Travancore and Cochin, provided they were not governed by matrilineal custom. Before the adoption of the Hindu succession Act in 1956, when a woman succeeded to the divided property of a deceased Hindu male, she took only a limited interest. A woman was denied her legal capacity in a Hindu joint family.

The Hindu Succession Act, 1956, which applies to Hindus, Buddhists, Jains and Sikhs determines the their on the basis of consanguinity or affinity without any discrimination on the ground of sex. It gives a woman full ownership in the property inherited or acquired by her. The widow, the mother and the daughter now not only inherit property along with the son but also take an equal share with him. A Parsi woman takes only half the share that her brother gets in their father's property. A similar half share is the lot of Muslim women as well. Though the Indian Succession Act is generally applicable to Christians, there are various regions in the country where the Act is not applied.

There are also certain Christian Communities to which it not made applicable. Certain tribal Christian communities and those who follow matriliny are outside the purview of the Act. As the Act is not extended to the Union Territory of Pondicherry, Indian Christians in the territory are governed by traditional Hindu law (that is, Hindu law as it was in force in the region before certain changes were effected by the Indian Parliament in 1955 and 1956) in the matter of inheritance with all the disadvantages and disabilities which that law imposed on women.

In the erstwhile princely states of Travancore and Cochin, there are in operation local enactment relating to succession among Christians which appear to discriminate against women. Under the Travancore Christian Succession Regulation, 1916 the share of the widow in the estate of the husband is a life interest, terminable on her death or remarriage, except where she gets the whole estate in the absence of certain specified relatives of her deceased husband.

Under the Cochin Christian Succession Act, 1921 the widow gets share equal to two-thirds of the share of a son if the deceased is survived by a son or lineal descendants of a son. The Travancore Regulation seems to discriminate against daughters who can take only one-fourth of the value of the share of a son or Rs. 5,000 whichever is less. The Regulation does not apply to the small body of Indian Christians in the taluk of Neyyattinkara of the erstwhile princely state who follow Marumakkathayam (matrilineal descent).

The Roman Catholic Christians of the Latin rite and certain non-Catholic Christens living in a few southern taluks of Travancore follow their customary usage, and among them male and female heirs of an intestate share equally in his property. Under the Travancore Regulation, the maternal relatives are excluded from succeeding to the intestate if there are paternal relatives surviving him, whereas in the Cochin Act no maternal relatives are included among the heirs.

The areas where these two enactments are still in force are remarkable for a high female literacy rate and a large number of highly educated women. Nevertheless the fact remains that these women, if they happen to .be Christians to whom these enactments apply, have a right to only a quarter of the share of a brother in the property of their deceased father. Would these educated women and their literate sisters think of reverting to matriliny which was once prevalent in these areas? At the moment they do not appear to be eager to effect any change.

The Hindu Minority and guardianship Act, 1956 also bestowed a few additional rights on Hindu women. It provides that though the father may appoint by will a guardian for his minor children, any such appointment will not take effect during the lifetime of the mother if she survives the father. It will take effect only on her death, provided she has not appointed a guardian by her own will. A Hindu mother is entitled to act as the natural guardian of her minor children if the father ceases to be a Hindu or renounces the world by becoming a hermit or ascetic. The Hindu widow and the Hindu mother, entitled to act as natural guardians of their minor children, are empowered under the Act to appoint guardians for them by will.

In 1956 substantial changes were effected in the law of adoption applicable to Hindus. The Hindu Adoption and Maintenance Act, 1956 has invested the Hindu woman with certain rights of adoption which she had not enjoyed before. Previously an adoption could only be to a male but, under the Act, a woman is competent to adopt to herself a son or a daughter.

Again, under the Act, a married man cannot, except under certain special circumstances, make an adoption without the consent of his wife. Under the earlier law her consent was immaterial but under the present law, her consent is unnecessary only when she has renounced the world or has ceased to be Hindu or has been judicially declared to be of unsound mind. A Hindu woman who is not of unsound mind and who is not a minor is now competent to adopt a son as well as a daughter, provided she is a spinster, divorcee, or widow or one whose husband has finally renounced the world or has ceased to be a Hindu or has been judicially declared to be of unsound mind. In general, during coverture it is only the husband who can adopt. If the woman wants to adopt a son, she should not have a Hindu son, son's son or son's son's son living at the time of the adopted should be younger to her by at least twenty one years.

If she intends adopting a daughter, an essential condition is hat she should have no Hindu daughter or son's daughter living at the time of the adoption. Corresponding requirements have also to be observed by the man who wishes to adopt a son or daughter.

The wife has a right to maintenance for life. She may not forfeit this right even if she lives separately from her husband on certain specific grounds such as the husband's cruelty, desertion, keeping a concubine or having another wife, his suffering from a virulent form of leprosy, his conversion to another religion or any other cause justifying her living separately. She, however, forfeits her right to maintenance if she is unchaste or ceases to be a Hindu.

The Factories Act, 1948 empowers state governments to prohibit employment of women in dangerous operations. A few enactments lay down the general rule that women should not be permitted to work between 7 p.m and 6 a.m., but this rule is relaxable in certain circumstances. Provisions for maternity benefits for women have been incorporated in the Employees, State Insurance Act, 1948 and a number of state enactments. While maternity benefit in coal mines is governed by the Maternity Benefit Act, 1961 women workers in factories and plantations are entitled to maternity leave according to the maternity benefit enactments of different states. Both the Factories Act, 1948 and the Plantations Labour Act, 1951 make it obligatory for factories and plantation employing not less than fifty women to provide creches. In spite of these statutory benefits and the Constitutional directive regarding equal pay for equal work, women agricultural labourers generally get 10 to 60 per cent less in wages than men for the same work. It is not infrequent that, when the husband becomes a "bonded labourer" for the landlord or the labour contractor, the wife also becomes similarly "bonded" with the not unusual result that she is made vulnerable exploitation including trafficking for immoral purposes.

Only 13 per cent of Indian women, according to the 1971 Census, may be regarded as workers, i.e. those who are engaged in some form of economic activity. About 80 per cent of these working women are engaged in agriculture. Only 12 per cent of the total employees in central and state administrative services and public sector undertakings are women. This may not be unrelated to their education or lack of it.

Only 18 per cent of India women are literate. Though one of the directive principles of the Constitution requires the state to provide free and compulsory education for all children under 14 years of age the directive is generally followed with callous disregard of its spirits and its significance for the country. Coupled with the general apathy to women's education, this indifference to put in practice a Constitutional directive results in greater social and economic deprivation for girls than for boys.

At the primary school level while 97 out of 100 boys attend school, the corresponding figure for girls is 62. Further, out of 100 girls who enter the first grade only 26 go up to the fifth grade. It is only about 2 per cent of women who are able to benefit by the opportunities provided for higher education. In 1971-72, 36 girls only were under instruction at various levels of education compared to a hundred boys. If in 1971 about 18 per cent of women were literate, this may appear to compare well with only 8 per cent literacy for women on the eve of independence in 1947, but an increase of 10 per cent in the not too short span of about three decades is hardly something that should make us complacent.

There are certain other types of social legislation which seek to protect interests and benefits that are of special concern to women. The Suppression of Immoral Traffic in Women and Girls Act. 1956, as its title indicates, is intended to protect helpless women and girls from a typical mode of exploitation not altogether unknown in the country. The same year saw the enactment of another piece of social legislation: the Women's and Children's institutions (Licensing) Act, 1956. This was later on superseded by the Orphanages and Other Charitable Homes (Supervision and Control) Act, 1960.

The object of the enactment was to regulate the activities of these institutions and to prescribe a proper standard to which the treatment and the training of the inmates should conform. Such a measure was found necessary because, while there are many good and properly-managed charitable institutions, there are many others run with the objective of exploitation as their main and sustaining inspiration.

The Medical Termination of Pregnancy Act, 1971 may also be mentioned in the context of social legislation relative to women. The enactment seeks, among other things, to protect women's interests. It has a few provisions which, it is clear, were enacted with the sufferings of women in the legislator's mind. It provides that a pregnancy may be terminated where the length of the pregnancy does not exceed twenty weeks, if two medical practitioners are of the opinion that the continuance of the pregnancy would involve a risk to the life of the pregnant woman or of grave injury to her physical or mental health. Two explanations are offered in the enactment itself of what constitutes grave injury to the mental health of the pregnant woman. The first explanation reads: when any pregnancy is alleged by the pregnant woman to have been caused by rape, the anguish caused by such pregnancy shall be presumed to constitute a grave injury to the mental health of the pregnant woman.

In this case the "anguish" is perhaps palpable. The second explanation is more intriguing in that "anguish" is given an extended application. It states:

Where a pregnancy occurs as a result of failure of any device or method used by any married woman or her husband for the purpose of limiting the number of children, the anguish caused by such unwanted pregnancy may be presumed to constitute a grave injury to the mental health of the pregnant woman. Though the promotional slant of the government's family planning programme may be perceptible in this explanation, it is evident that Parliament cannot be blamed for any lack of solicitude for the largest minority in the country.

This solicitude may be even more evident in another provision of the Act which stipulates that in determining whether the continuance of a pregnancy would involve grave risk to the health of a pregnant woman, account may be taken of her actual or reasonably foreseeable environment. This enactment has been hailed as "a major landmark in India's social legislation", and "a far-reaching measure assuring the women of India freedom from undesirable and unwanted pregnancies.

From a study of the ameliorative legal provisions relating to women and the actual situation in which they find themselves, it is clear that something more than legislation is required. Perhaps that first thing to be attempted is to make women aware of their rights, however this is done. It is also necessary to change the attitudes of both men and women, of society in general, to social objectives sought to be achieved by legislation. A radical change in the attitudes of women induced by an awareness of their rights, which are constitutionally guaranteed and legally protected will be the first step in the complex process of transforming the social structure so that women may enjoy full equality with men in every sphere of life.

Convention on the elimination of all forms of discrimination against women

The states parties to the present Convention,

Noting that the Charter of the United Nations reaffirms faith in fundamental human rights, in the dignity and worth of the human person and in the equal rights of men and women,

Noting that the Universal Declaration of Human Rights affirms the principle of the inadmissibility of discrimination and proclaims that all human beings are born free and equal in dignity and rights and that everyone is entitled to all the rights and freedoms set forth therein, without distinction of any kind including distinction based on sex,

Noting that the States Parties to the International Covenants of Human Rights have the obligation to ensure the equal rights of men and women to enjoy all economic, social cultural, civil and political rights,

Considering the international conventions concluded under the auspices of the United Nations and the specialized agencies promoting equality of rights of men and women,

Noting also the resolutions, declarations and recommendations adopted by the United Nations and the specialized agencies promoting equality of rights of men and women,

Concerned, however, that despite these various instruments, extensive discrimination against women continues to exist,

Recalling that discrimination against women violates the principles of equality of rights and respect for human dignity, is an obstacle to the participation of women, on equal terms with men, in the political, social, economic and cultural life of their countries, hampers the growth of the prosperity of society and the family and makes more difficult the full development of the potentialities of women in the service of their countries and of humanity,

Concerned that in situations of poverty women have the least access to food, health, education, training and opportunities for employment and other needs,

Convinced that the establishment of the new international economic order based on equity and justice will contribute significantly towards the promotion of equality between men and women,

Emphasizing that the eradication of apartheid, all forms of racism, racial discrimination, colonialism, neo-colonialism, aggression, foreign occupation and domination and interference in the internal affairs of States is essential to the full enjoyment of the rights of men and women,

Affirming that the strengthening of international peace and security, the relaxation of international tension, mutual cooperation among all States irrespective of their social and economic systems, general and complete disarmament, in particular nuclear disarmament under strict and effective international control, the affirmation of the principles of justice, equality and mutual benefit in relations, among countries and the realization of the right of peoples under alien and colonial domination and foreign occupation to self-determination and independence, as well as respect for national sovereignty and territorial integrity, will promote social progress and development and as a consequence, will contribute to the attainment of full equality between men and women,

Convinced that the full and complete development of a country, the welfare of the world and the cause of peace require the maximum participation of women of equal terms with men in all fields,

Bearing in mind the great contribution of women to the welfare of the family and to the development of society, so far not fully recognized, the social significance of maternity and the role of both parents in the family and in the upbringing of children, and aware that the role of women in procreation should not be a basis for discrimination but that the upbringing of children requires a sharing of responsibility between men and women and society as a whole,

Aware that a change in the traditional role of men as well as the role of women in society and in the family is needed to achieve full equality between men and women,

Determined to implement the principles set forth in the Declaration on the Elimination of Discrimination against Women and, for that purpose, to adopt the measures required for the elimination of such discrimination in all its forms and manifestations, Have agreed on the following

Article I: For the purposes of the present Convention, the term "discrimination against women" shall mean any distinction, exclusion or restriction made on the basis of sex which has the effect or purpose of impairing or nullifying the recognition, enjoyment or exercise by women, irrespective of their marital status, on a basis of equality of men and women, of human rights and fundamental freedoms in the political, economic, social, cultural, civil or any other field.

Article 2: States Parties condemn discrimination against women in all its forms, agree to pursue by all appropriate means and without delay a policy of eliminating discrimination against women and, to this end, undertake:

(a) To embody the principle of the equality of men and women in their national constitutions or other appropriate legislation if not yet incorporated therein and to ensure, through law and other appropriate means, the practical realization of this principle;

(b) To adopt appropriate legislative and other measures, including sanctions where appropriate, prohibiting all discrimination against women;

(c) To establish legal protection of the rights of women on an equal basis with men and to ensure through competent national tribunals and other public institutions the effective protection of women against any act of discrimination;

(d) To refrain from engaging in any act or practice of discrimination against women and to ensure that public authorities and institutions shall act in conformity with this obligation;

(e) To take all appropriate measures to eliminate discrimination against women by any person, organization or enterprise;

(f) To take all appropriate measures, including legislation, to modify or abolish existing laws, regulations, customs and practices which constitute discrimination against women;

(g) To repeal all national penal provisions which constitute discrimination against women.

Article 3: States Parties shall take in all fields, in particular in the political, social, economic and cultural fields, all appropriate measures, including legislation, to ensure the full development and advancement of women, for the purpose of guaranteeing them the exercise and enjoyment of human rights and fundamental freedoms on a basis of equality with men.

Article 4

1. Adoption by States Parties of temporary special measures aimed at accelerating de fact equality between men and women shall not be considered discrimination as defined in the present Convention, but shall in no way entail as a consequence, the maintenance of

unequal or separate standards; these measures shall be discontinued when the objectives of equality of opportunity and treatment have been achieved.

2. Adoption by States Parties of special measures, including those measures contained in the present Convention, aimed at protecting maternity shall not be considered discriminatory.

Article 5: States Parties shall take all appropriate measures:

(a) To modify the social and cultural patterns of conduct of men and women, with a view to achieving the elimination of prejudices and customary and all other practices which are based on the idea of the inferiority or the superiority of either of the sexes or on stereotyped roles for men and women;

(b) To ensure that family education includes a proper understanding of maternity as a social function and the recognition of the common responsibility of men and women in the upbringing and development of their children, it being understood that the interest of the children is the primordial consideration in all cases.

Article 6: States Parties shall take all appropriate measures, including legislation, to suppress all forms of traffic in women and exploitation of prostitution of women.

Article 7: States Parties shall take all appropriate measures to eliminate discrimination against women in the political and public life of the country and, in particular, shall ensure to women, on equal terms with men, the right:

(a) To vote in all elections and public referenda and to be eligible for election to all publicly elected bodies;

(b) To participate in the formulation of government policy and the implementation thereof and to hold public office and perform all public functions at all levels of government;

(c) To participate in non-governmental organizations and associations concerned with the public and political life of the country.

Article 8: States Parties shall take all appropriate measures to ensure to women, on equal terms with men and without any discrimination, the opportunity to represent their Governments at the international level and to participate in the work of international organizations.

Article 9

1. States Parties shall grant women equal rights with men to acquire, change or retain their nationality. They shall ensure in particular that neither marriage to an alien nor change of nationality by the husband during marriage shall automatically change the nationality of the wife, render her stateless or force upon her the nationality of the husband.
2. States Parties shall grant women equal rights with men with respect to the nationality of their children.

Article 10: States Parties shall take all appropriate measures to eliminate discrimination against women in order to ensure to them equal rights with men in the field of education and in particular to ensure, on a basis of equality of men and women

(a) The same conditions for career and vocational guidance, for access to studies and for the achievement of diplomas in educational establishments of all categories in rural as well as in urban areas; this equality shall be ensured in pre-school, general, technical, professional and higher technical education, as well as in all types of vocational training;

(b) Access to the same curricula, the same examinations, teaching staff with qualifications of the same standard and school premises and equipment of the same quality;

(c) The elimination of any stereotyped concept of the roles of men and women at all levels and in all forms of education by encouraging coeducation and other types of education which will help to achieve this aim and, in particular, by the revision of textbooks and school programmes and the adaptation of teaching methods;

(d) The same opportunities to benefit from scholarships and other study grants;

(e) The same opportunities for access to programmes of continuing education, including adult and functional literacy programmes, particularly those aimed at reducing, at the earliest possible time, any gap in education existing between men and women;

(f) The reduction of female student dropout rates and the organization of programmes for girls and women who have left school prematurely;

(g) The same opportunities to participate actively in sports and physical education;

(h) Access to specific educational information to help to ensure the health and well-being of families, including information and advice on family planning.

Article 11

1. States Parties shall take all appropriate measures to eliminate discrimination against women in the field of employment in order to ensure, on a basis of equality of men and women the same rights in particular;

    (a) The right to work as a right of all human beings.

    (b) The right to the same employment opportunities, including the application of the same criteria for selection in matters of employment;

    (c) The right to free choice of profession and employment, the right to promotion, job security and all benefits and conditions of service and the right to receive vocational training and retraining, including apprenticeships, advanced vocational training and recurrent training;

    (d) The right to equal remuneration, including benefits, and to equal treatment in respect of work of equal value, as well as equality of treatment in the evaluation of the quality of work;

    (e) The right to social security, particularly in cases of retirement, unemployment, sickness, invalidity and old age and other incapacity to work, as well as right to paid leave;

(f) The right to protection of health and to safety in working conditions, including the safeguarding of the function of reproduction.

2. In order to prevent discrimination against women on the grounds of marriage or maternity and to ensure their effective right to work, States Parties shall take appropriate measures:

   (a) To prohibit, subject to the imposition of sanctions, dismissal on the grounds of pregnancy or of maternity leave and discrimination in dismissals on the basis of marital status;

   (b) To introduce maternity leave with pay or with comparable social benefits without loss of former employment, seniority or social allowances;

   (c) To encourage the provision of the necessary supporting social services to enable parents to combine family obligations with work responsibilities and participation in public life, in particular through promoting the establishment and development of a network of child-care facilities;

   (d) To provide special protection to women during pregnancy in types of work proved to be harmful to them.

3. Protective legislation relating to matters covered in this Article shall be reviewed periodically in the light of scientific and technological knowledge and shall be revised, repealed or extended as necessary.

Article 12

1. States Parties shall take all appropriate measures to eliminate discrimination against women in the field of health care in order to ensure, on a basis of equality of men and women, access to health care services, including those related to family planning.

2. Notwithstanding the provisions of paragraph 1 of this Article, States Parties shall ensure to women appropriate services in connection with pregnancy,

confinement and the post-natal period, granting free services where necessary, as well as adequate nutrition during pregnancy and lactation.

Article 13: States Parties shall take all appropriate measures to eliminate discrimination against women in other areas of economic and social life in order to ensure, on a basis of equality of men and women, the same rights, in particular:

(a) The right to family benefits;

(b) The right to bank loans, mortgages and other forms of financial credit;

(c) The right to participate in recreational activities, sports and all aspects of cultural life.

Article 14

1. States Parties shall take into account the particular problems faced by rural women and the significant roles which rural women play in the economic survival of their families, including their work in the non-monetized sectors of the economy, and shall take all appropriate measures to ensure the application of the provisions of the present convention to women in rural areas.
2. States Parties shall take all appropriate measures to eliminate discrimination against women in rural areas in order to ensure, on a basis of equality of men and women, that they participate in and benefit from rural development and, in particular, shall ensure to such women the right:

   (a) To participate in the elaboration and implementation of development planning at all levels;

   (b) To have access to adequate health care facilities, including information, counselling and services in family planning;

   (c) To benefit directly from social security programmes;

   (d) To obtain all types of training and education, formal and non-formal, including that relating to functional literacy, as well as, inter alia, the benefit of all community and extension services, in order to increase their technical proficiency;

(e) To organize self-help groups and co-operatives in order to obtain equal access to economic opportunities through employment or self-employment;

(f) To participate in all community activities;

(g) To have access to agricultural credit and loans, marketing facilities, appropriate technology and equal treatment in land and agrarian reform as well as in land resettlement schemes;

(h) To enjoy adequate living conditions, particularly in relation to housing, sanitation, electricity and water supply, transport and communications.

Article 15

1. States Parties shall accord to women equality with men before the law.
2. States Parties shall accord to women, in civil matters, a legal capacity identical to that of men and the same opportunities to exercise that capacity. In particular, they shall give women equal rights to conclude contracts and to administer property and shall treat them equally in all stages of procedure in courts and tribunals.
3. States Parties agree that all contracts and all other private instruments of any kind with a legal effect which is directed at restricting the legal capacity of women shall be deemed null and void.
4. States Parties shall accord to men and women the same rights with regard to the law relating to the movement of persons and the freedom to choose their residence and domicile.

Article 16

1. States Parties shall take all appropriate measures to eliminate discrimination against women in all matters

relating to marriage and family relations and in particular shall ensure, on a basis of equality of men and women:

(a) The same right to enter into marriage;

(b) The same right freely to choose a spouse and to enter into marriage only with their free and full consent;

(c) The same rights and responsibilities during marriage and at its dissolution;

(d) The same rights and responsibilities as parents, irrespective of their marital status, in matters relating to their children; in all cases the interests of the children shall be paramount;

(e) The same rights to decide freely and responsibly on the number and spacing of their children and to have access to the information, education and means to enable them to exercise these rights;

(f) The same rights and responsibilities with regard to guardianship, wardship, trusteeship and adoption of children, or similar institutions where these concepts exist in national legislation; in all cases the interests of the children shall be paramount;

(g) The same personal rights as husband and wife, including the right to choose a family name, a profession and an occupation;

(h) The same rights for both spouses in respect of the ownership, acquisition, management, administration, enjoyment and disposition of property, whether free of charge or for a valuable consideration.

2. The betrothal and the marriage of a child shall have no legal effect, and all necessary action, including legislation, shall be taken to specify a minimum age for marriage and to make the registration of marriages in an official registry compulsory.

Article 17

1. For the purpose of considering the progress made in the implementation of the present Convention, there shall be established a Committee on the Elimination of Discrimination against Women (hereinafter referred to as the Committee) consisting, at the time of entry into force of the Convention, of eighteen and, after ratification of or accession to the Convention by the thirty-fifth State Party, of twenty-three experts of high moral standing and competence in the field covered by the Convention. The experts shall be elected by States Parties from among their nationals and shall serve in their personal capacity, consideration being given to equitable geographical distribution and to the representation of the different forms of civilization as well as the principal legal systems.
2. The members of the Committee shall be elected by secret ballot from a list of persons nominated by States Parties. Each Party may nominate one person from among its own nationals.
3. The initial election shall be held six months after the date of the entry into force of the present Convention. At least three months before the date of each election, the Secretary General of the United Nations shall address a letter to the States Parties inviting them to submit their nominations within two months. The Secretary General shall prepare a list in alphabetical order of all persons thus nominated, indicating the States Parties which have nominated them, and shall submit it to the States Parties.
4. Elections of the members of the Committee shall be held at a meeting of States Parties convened by the Secretary General at United Nations Headquarters. At that meeting, for which two thirds of the States Parties shall constitute a quorum, the persons elected to the Committee shall be those nominees who obtain the largest number of votes and an absolute majority of the

votes of the representatives of States Parties present and voting.

5. The members of the Committee shall be elected for a term of four years. However, the terms of nine of the members elected at the first election shall expire at the end of two years; immediately after the first election the names of these nine members shall be chosen by lot by the Chairman of the Committee.
6. The election of the five additional members of the Committee shall be held in accordance with the provisions of paragraphs 2,3 and 4 of this article, following the thirty-fifth ratification or accession. The terms of two of the additional members elected on this occasion shall expire at the end of two years, the names of these two members having been chosen by lot by the Chairman of the Committee.
7. For the filling of casual vacancies, the State Party whose expert has ceased to function as a member of the Committee shall appoint another expert from among its nationals, subject to the approval of the Committee.
8. The members of the Committee shall, with the approval of the General Assembly, receive emoluments from United Nations resources on such terms and conditions as the Assembly may decide, having regard to the importance of the Committee's responsibilities.
9. The Secretary-General of the United Nations shall provide the necessary staff and facilities for the effective performance of the functions of the Committee under the present Convention.

Article 18

1. States Parties undertake to submit to the Secretary General of the United Nations, for consideration by the Committee, a report on the legislative, judicial, administrative or other measures which they have adopted to give effect to the provisions of the present Convention and on the progress made in this respect:

(a) Within one year after the entry into force for the State concerned;

(b) Thereafter at least every four years and further whenever the Committee so requests.

2. Reports may indicate factors and difficulties affecting the degree of fulfilment of obligations under the present Convention.

Article 19

1. The Committee shall adopt its own rules of procedure.
2. The Committee shall elect its officers for a term of two years.

Article 20

1. The Committee shall normally meet for a period of not more than two weeks annually in order to consider the reports submitted in accordance with article 1 S of the present Convention.
2. The meetings of the Committee shall normally be held at United Nations Headquarters or at any other convenient place as determined by the Committee.

Article 21

1. The Committee shall, through the Economic and Social Council, report annually to the General Assembly of the United Nations on its activities and may make suggestions and general recommendations based on the examination of reports and information received from the States Parties. Such suggestions and general recommendations shall be included in the report of the Committee together with comments, if any, from States Parties.

2. The Secretary General of the United Nations shall transmit the reports of the Committee to the Commission on the status of Women for its information.

Article 22: The specialized agencies shall be entitled to be represented at the consideration of the implementation of such provisions of the present Convention as fall within the scope of their activities. The committee may invite the specialized agencies to submit reports on the implementation of the Convention in areas falling within the scope of their activities.

Article 23: Nothing in the present Convention shall affect any provisions that are more conducive to the achievement of equality between men and women which may be contained:

(a) In the legislation of a State Party; or

(b) In any other international convention, treaty or agreement in force for that State.

Article 24: States Parties undertake to adopt all necessary measures at the national level aimed at achieving the full realization of the rights recognized in the present Convention.

Article 25

1. The present Convention shall be open for signature by all States.
2. The Secretary-General of the United Nations is designated as the depositary of the present Convention.
3. The present Convention is subject to ratification. Instruments of ratification shall be deposited with the Secretary-General of the United Nations.
4. The present Convention shall be open to accession by all States. Accession shall be effected by the deposit of an instrument of accession with the Secretary General of the United Nations.

Article 26

1. A request for the revision of the present Convention may be made at any time by any State Party by means of a notification in writing addressed to the Secretary-General of the United Nations.
2. The General Assembly of the United Nations shall decide upon the steps, if any, to be taken in respect of such a request.

Article 27

1. The present Convention shall enter into force on the thirtieth day after the deposit with the Secretary General

of the United Nations of the twentieth instrument of ratification or accession.

2. For each State ratifying the present Convention or acceding to it after the deposit of the twentieth instrument of ratification or accession, the Convention shall enter into force on the thirtieth day after the date of the deposit of its own instrument of ratification or accession.

Article 28

1. The Secretary General of the United Nations shall receive and circulate to all States the text of reservations made by States at the time of ratification or accession.
2. A reservation incompatible with the object and purpose of the present Convention shall not be permitted.
3. Reservations may be withdrawn at any time by notification to this effect addressed to the Secretary-General of the United Nations, who shall then inform all States thereof. Such notification shall take effect on the date on which it is received.

Article 29

1. Any dispute between two or more States Parties concerning the interpretation or application of the present Convention which is not settled by negotiation shall, at the request of one of them, be submitted to arbitration. If within six months from the date of the request for arbitration, the Parties are unable to agree on the organization of the arbitration, any one of those parties may refer the dispute to the International Court of Justice by request in conformity with the statute of the Court.
2. Each State Party may at the time of signature or ratification of the present Convention or accession thereto declare that it does not consider itself bound by paragraph 1 of this article. The other States Parties shall not be bound by that paragraph with respect to any State Party which has made such a reservation.

3. Any State Party which has made a reservation in accordance with paragraph 2 of this article may at any time withdraw that reservation by notification to the Secretary General of the United Nations.

Article 30: The present Convention, the Arabic, Chinese. English, French, Russian and Spanish texts of which are equally authentic, shall be deposited with the Secretary-General of the United Nations.

In Witness Whereof the undersigned, duly authorized, have signed the present Convention.

Declaration on the Elimination of Discrimination against Women

The General Assembly,

Considering that the peoples of the United Nations have, in the Charter, reaffirmed their faith in fundamental human rights, in the dignity and worth of the human person and in the equal rights of men and women,

Considering that the Universal Declaration on Human Rights asserts the principle of non-discrimination and proclaims that all human beings are born free and equal in dignity and rights and that everyone is entitled to all the rights and freedoms set forth therein without distinction of any kind, including any distinction as to sex,

Taking into account the resolutions, declarations, conventions and recommendations of the United Nations and the specialized agencies designed to eliminate all forms of discrimination and to promote equal rights for men and women,

Concerned that, despite the Charter of the United Nations the Universal Declaration of Human Rights, the International Covenants on Human Rights and other instruments of the United Nations and the specialized agencies and despite the progress made in the matter of equality of rights, there continues to exist considerable discrimination against women,

Considering that discrimination against women is incompatible with human dignity and with the welfare of the family and of society, prevents their participation, on equal terms with men, in the political, social, economic and cultural life of their countries and is an obstacle to the full development of the potentialities of women in the service of their countries and of humanity,

Bearing in mind the great contribution made by women to social, political, economic and cultural life and the part they play in the family and particularly in the rearing of children,

Convinced that the full and complete development of a country, the welfare of the world and the cause of peace require the maximum participation of women as well as men in all fields,

Considering that it is necessary to ensure the universal recognition in law and in fact of the principle of equality of men and women, Solemnly proclaims this declaration:

Article 1: Discrimination against women, denying or limiting as it does their equality of rights with men, is fundamentally unjust and constitutes an offence against human dignity.

Article 2: All appropriate measures shall be taken to abolish existing laws, customs, regulations and practices which are discriminatory against women, and to establish adequate legal protection for equal rights of men and women, in particular

(a) The principle of equality of rights shall be embodied in the constitution or otherwise guaranteed by law;

(b) The international instruments of the United Nations and the specialized agencies relating to the elimination of discrimination against women shall be ratified or acceded to and fully implemented as soon as practicable.

Article 3: All appropriate measures shall be taken to educate public opinion and to direct national aspirations towards the eradication of prejudice and the abolition of customary and all other practices which are based on the idea of the inferiority of women:

Article 4: All appropriate measures shall be taken to ensure to women on equal terms with men, without any discrimination:

(a) The right to vote in all elections and be eligible for election to all publicly elected oodles;

(b) The right to vote in all public referenda;

(c) The right to hold public office and to exercise all public functions.

Such rights shall be guaranteed by legislation.

Article 5: Women shall have the same rights as men to acquire, change or retain their nationality. Marriage to an alien shall not automatically affect the nationality of the wife either by rendering her stateless or by forcing upon her the nationality of her husband.

Article 6

1. Without prejudice to the safeguarding of the unity and the harmony of the family, which remains the basic unit of any society, all appropriate measures, particularly legislative measures, shall be taken to ensure to women, married, or unmarried, equal rights with men in field of civil law, and in particular:
   (a) The right to acquire, administer, enjoy, dispose of and inherit property, including property acquired during marriage;
   (b) The right to equality in legal capacity and the exercise thereof;
   (c) The same rights as men and with regard to the law on the movement of persons.
2. All appropriate measures shall be taken to ensure the principle of equality of status of the husband and wife, and in particular:
   (a) Women shall have the same right as men to free choice of a spouse and to enter into marriage only with their free and full consent;
   (b) Women shall have equal rights with men during marriage and at its dissolution. In all cases the interest of the children shall be paramount;
   (c) Parents shall have equal rights and duties in matters relating to their children. In all cases the interest of the children shall be paramount.
3. Child marriage and the betrothal of young girls before puberty shall be prohibited, and effective action, including legislation, shall be taken to specify a

minimum age for marriage and to make the registration of marriages in an official registry compulsory.

Article 7: All provisions of penal codes which constitute discrimination against women shall be repealed.

Article 8: All appropriate measures, including legislation, shall be taken to combat all forms of traffic in women and exploitation of prostitution of women.

Article 9: All appropriate measures shall be taken to ensure to girls and women, married or unmarried, equal rights with men in education at all levels, and in particular:

(a) Equal conditions of access to, and study in educational institutions of all types, including universities and vocational, technical and professional schools;

(b) The same choice of curricula, the same examinations, teaching staff with qualifications of the same standard, and school premises and equipment of the same quality, whether the institutions are co-educational or not;

(c) Equal opportunities to benefit from scholarships and other study grants;

(d) Equal opportunities for access to programmes of continuing education, including adult literacy programmes;

(e) Access to educational information to help in ensuring the health and well-being of families.

Article 10

1. All appropriate measures shall be taken to ensure to women, married or unmarried, equal rights with men in the field of economic and social life, and in particular:

   (a) The right, without discrimination on grounds of marital status or any other grounds, to receive vocational training, to work, to free choice of profession and employment, and to professional and vocational advancement;

   (b) The right to equal remuneration with men and to equality of treatment in respect of work of equal value;

(c) The right to leave with pay, retirement privileges and provision for security in respect of unemployment, sickness, old age or other incapacity to work;

(d) The right to receive family allowances on equal terms with men.

2. In order to prevent discrimination against women on account of marriage or maternity and to ensure their effective right to work, measures shall be taken to prevent their dismissal in the event of marriage or maternity and to provide paid maternity leave, with the guarantee of returning to former employment, and to provide the necessary social services, including child-care facilities.

Recommendation on consent to marriage, minimum age for marriage and registration of marriages

The General Assembly, recognizing that the family group should be strengthened because it is the basic unit of every society, and that men and women of full age have the right to marry and to found a family, that they are entitled to equal rights as to marriage and that marriage shall be entered into only with the free and full consent of the intending spouses, in accordance with the provisions of article 16 of the Universal Declaration of Human Rights, Recalling its resolution 843(IX) of 17 December 1954,

Recalling further article 2 of the Supplementary Convention on the Abolition of Slavery, the Slave Trade, and Institutions and Practices Similar to Slavery of 1956, which makes certain provisions concerning the age of marriage, consent to marriage and registration of marriages,

Recalling also that Article 13, paragraph lb. of the Charter of the United Nations provides that the General Assembly shall make recommendations for the purpose of assisting in the realization of human rights and fundamental freedoms for all without distinction as to race, sex, language or religion,

Recalling likewise that, under Article 64 of the Charter, the Economic and Social Council may make arrangements with the Members of the United Nations to obtain reports on the steps taken to give effect to its own recommendations and to recommendations on matters falling within its competence made by the General Assembly,

1. Recommends, that, where not already provided by existing legislative or other measures, each Member State should take the necessary steps, in accordance with its constitutional processes and its traditional and religious practices, to adopt such legislative or other measures as may be appropriate to give effect to the following principles:

Principle I

(a) No marriage shall be legally entered into without the full and free consent of both the parties, such consent to be expressed by them in person, after due publicity and in the presence of the authority competent to solemnize the marriage and of witnesses, as prescribed by law,

(b) Marriage by proxy shall be permitted only when the competent authorities are satisfied that each party has, before a competent authority and in such manner as may be prescribed by law, fully and freely expressed consent before witnesses and not withdrawn such consent.

Principle II:

Member States shall take legislative action to specify a minimum age for marriage, which in any case shall not be less than fifteen years of age; no marriage shall be legally entered into by any person under this age, except where a competent authority has granted a dispensation as to age, for serious reasons, in the interest of the intending spouses.

Principle III :

All marriages shall be registered in an appropriate official register by the competent authority.

2. Recommends that each Member State should bring the Recommendations on Consent to Marriage, Minimum Age for Marriage and Registration of Marriages contained in the present resolution before the authorities competent to enact legislation or

to take other action at the earliest practicable moment and, if possible, not later than eighteen months after the adoption of the Recommendation;

3. Recommends that Member States should inform the Secretary General, as soon as possible after the action referred to in paragraph 2 above, of the measures taken under the present Recommendation to bring it before the competent authority or authorities, with particulars regarding the authority or authorities considered as competent;

4. Recommends further that Member States should report to the Secretary General at the end of three years, and thereafter at intervals of five years, on their law and practice with regard to the matters dealt within the present Recommendation, showing the extent to which effect has been given or is proposed to be given to the provisions of the Recommendation and such modifications as have been found or may be found necessary in adapting or applying it;

5. Requests the Secretary General to prepare for the Commission on the Status of Women a document containing the reports received from Governments concerning methods of implementing the three basic principles of the present Recommendation;

6. Invites the Commission on the Status of Women to examine the reports received from Member States pursuant to the present Recommendation and to report thereon to the Economic and Social Council with such recommendations as it may deem fitting.

TWO

Exposure to Threat

There are a variety of social, economic, legal, and psychological forms of victimization against women. We live in a society in which men are in hold of the majority of institutions. Economically, women are discriminated against in the job market. Sex role stereotyping has victimized and "imprisoned" a number of women, often women have been victimized by the institution of marriage, in which, although they are no longer identified as property, they are still repressed by implied and covert socio-cultural practices. In some cases in the course of a marital relationship, women have been exploited physically, emotionally, and sexually by their husbands. Mental as well as physical "injury" has been inflicted on women by the health profession. Until recently women did not have the right to decide whether they could continue a pregnancy or terminate it. Number of women have suffered through months and years of psychotherapy by therapists whose attempts are being objective all too often fall short of that goal, resulting in the perpetuation of a value system that feeds the sexist social structure. The fact that the Equal Rights Amendment remains unratified is perhaps the most apparent indicator of the victimization of women.

Criminology and Victimology

The study of victims has emerged as a recent development in the field of criminology, criminology itself a discipline not more than a century old. Victimology as a branch of criminology developed first in the United Kingdom, West Germany, France, the Scandinavian countries, Canada, Australia, New Zealand, and the United States. Indian scholars are also focusing their attention on the victimology to understand the importance of victim in criminal justice system.

The dynamics of victimology could be useful tools within the criminal system for administration and policy makers.

Categories of Victims

The term "Victimology" and its parameters of the subject, are not yet well defined. The concept "Victimology" was coined by a French jurist named Benjamin Mendelsohn, who is now a citizen of Israel. He states that victims are of five types:

(a) Completely innocent victims such as children and people who are victims of crime when unconscious;

(b) Victims with minor guilt and victims of ignorance, such as pregnant women who got to quacks for miscarriage;

(c) Voluntary victims, such as the ones who commit suicide or are killed by euthansia;

(d) Victims who are more guilty than the offenders, such as persons who provoke others to commit crime; and

(e) The most guilty type of victims who commit offences against others and get killed by the victim in self-defence (Mendelsohn: 1963).

A more popular categorisation is the triple alliterative pattern, which describes victims as provocative, precipitative and participating. Another recent and fairly authoritative view, as provided by the classification of Abdel Fattah of Canada as follows:

(a) the non-participating,

(b) the latent,

(c) the provocative,

(d) the participating, and

(e) the defiant.

Victimology is basically a study of crime from the point of view of the victim, of persons suffering from injury or destruction by the action of another single person or group of persons. Dadrian (1976:42) has broadly described this field as "the study of the social processes through which individuals and groups are maltreated in such a way that social problems are created." This encompasses two areas of concern: "the social context in which victimization occurs, and the social consequences of such victimization." In this study we will look at the social context of female victimization, its social consequences though organizing a discussion of the social context of female victimization is difficult as the problem has historical, cross-cultural, and inter-disciplinary dimensions. The fact that most men are physically stronger than most women, so that when it comes to fight, women are more often losers is the simplest explanation of male-female maladjustment. To add to this is their vulnerability by their child-bearing function (Chapman and Gates, 1978:10-11).

Two Type of Behaviour

Aggression and victimization are correlated, be it physical or verbal. Men are socialized to be aggressive and women to be victims. Support for the theory that aggressive behaviour is instinctual comes from:

(1) ethologists such as Desmond Morris, Conrad Lorens and Robert Ardrey;

(2) research on electrical and chemical brain stimulation;

(3) psychoanalytic theory.

The ethologists propose that our animal ancestors were instinctively violent beings and that our violent behaviours are products of these inherited instinctual drives. However, this is not always the case—some research (Binford, 1972) confirms that certain animals are not aggressive at all, and humans do not always pattern themselves on other primates' behaviour because of their more complex nervous system. An intriguing theory is that violence is not an instinctual behaviour but a learned one, resulting from the same matrix whereby we learn to speak, dress, and socialize. The expression of such learned aggression may be varied as the environments in which it is learned. Freud and his contemporaries held that aggression is instinctive. Coldstein (1975:19) viewing aggression as a learned behaviour, proposes that there are long-term and situational factors that facilitate either aggressive or non-aggressive behaviour. Long-term factors include the process of socialization, we undergo as children; for example, the values, norms, attitudes, beliefs and expectations that our parents, teachers, and peers instill the selectively reinforce, situational factors facilitating aggression include familiar environments, the presence of a alcohol, or the presence of relatives or peers with whom aggression is associated.

Situations place even the most violent people as non-aggressive and vice versa. Therefore, the factors that facilitate non-aggression are notable. Goldstein (1975) believes that there are certain environments and individuals that do not elicit or facilitate aggression. Inappropriate locations for aggression include churches or theatres, and inappropriate targets are hypothesized to include children and the aged. Psychological experiments demonstrate that aggressive behaviour is learned or acquired (Kagan and Moss, 1962; Loew, 1967). Interestingly, several of these studies find that males are more prone to aggression than females. Kegan and Moss (1962) found that aggressive behaviour learned in childhood persist through adulthood, especially for males. Loew (1967) and Green and Pigg (1970) found this if parents positively reinforce verbal or nonverbal aggressive responses in their children's behaviour.

Theoretical Explanations

Erich Fromm's (1973) analysis of human aggression clearly defines the errors and limitations of both the instinctive and behavioural schools of psychology in explaining the causes and origins of human violence and destruction. Extensive studies of violence as innate and instinctive in origin, as opposed to being learned through the socialization process (nature versus nurture), have ignored the question of observable difference between the levels of male/female human aggression. Regardless of which theory predominates at a given time, it would be logical that the theory hold true for all members of the species, regardless of sex. Fromm specifically includes women in his definition of mankind as it relates to human destructiveness. It will be wrong to assume that the male is innately more violent than the female. There are certain prevailing cultural and psychological conditions which encourage male aggression as its own reward and encourage acceptance of female passivity as its own reward.

There is a little evidence to explain female victimization beyond the shadow of culturally conditioned gender-biases. The major explanations which seem to evidence certain degree of objectivity in their treatment of the subject put the problem of female victimization in a socio-economic, legal and cultural context. Srivastav (1989: 33-

37) views female victimization as a product of socio-economic factors including the status, role, right of women in general. The explanations discover the genesis of female victimization in the institutions of marriage and family, in the different sex-role socialization, etc.

Classifications of Theories

Various scholars namely, Gelles and Strauss (1979), Steinmetz (1974), Strauss (1974), Wolfgang and Weiner (1982) etc. have given different explanations to violence. After a detailed study of these writings Ahuja (1987: 166-185) identifies fourteen theories for understanding violence committed by an individual. Theories range from intrapsychic theories to macro-sociological theories. He divides these theories on the basis of three (theoretical) levels of analysis:

(1) psychiatric or psycho-pathological analysis;
(2) socio-psychological analysis; and
(3) sociological or socio-cultural analysis.

The psycho-pathological model

This focuses on the offender personality characteristics as the chief determinants of criminal violence. This model includes analysis that links mental analysis (i.e., a very small portion of mentally ill persons are violent), alcohol (i.e., what one does under the influence of alcohol and violence).

The socio-psychological model

This assumes that criminal violence can best be understood by a careful examination of the external environmental factors that exercise an impact on the individual offender. This model also examines the types of every-day interactions, patterns, etc., which are precursors to violence. Theories such as the Frustration-Aggression Theory, the Perversion Theory, the Self-Attitude Theory and the Motive Attribution Theory approach criminal violence from a socio-psychological level of analysis.

The sociological or socio-cultural model

This provides a macro-level analysis of criminal violence. This model examines criminal violence in terms of socially structured inequality and social and cultural attitudes and norms regarding anti-social behaviour and interpersonal relations.

Besides the two well-known theories, viz., the structural-functional theory and the theory of sub-culture of violence, the learning theory, the exchange theory, the anomic theory, and the resource theory, etc., also come under a socio-cultural analysis (Ahuja, 1987: 166-167).

Ahuja (1987) examines his own Social Bond Theory to explain crime against women. In view of these theoretical approaches, he calls this a "middle range theoretical proposition" based on the phenomenological approach. This has been borrowed by certain concepts from sociologists and criminologists like Hirschi (1976), Schutz (1964), etc. Social Bond Theory based on adjustment, commitment and attachment and the relative feeling of deprivation is different from the Frustration Aggression Theory in the sense that status frustration as the consequences of interpersonal relations and the functioning of sub-system in the society. Hence, Ahuja (1987) claims his theory has a sociological orientation.

Various explanations have thus been advanced to account for crimes against women discovering the genesis of female victimization in the history, literature and culture of different societies. The dominant view holds that female victimization is a complex phenomenon having deep roots in the male dominated socio-economic, legal and political order. It is an expression of imbalance in the power structure that relegates women to a secondary social position, thereby making them vulnerable to various forms of oppression, exploitation and abuse.

Victimization, Categorised

Ill-treatment of women takes several forms. Singh (1990:104) categories the oppression of Indian women into three manolateralistic forms. All these three take the form of victimization, namely:

(i) ***Patriarchal victimization*** (inter-gender: man *v* woman)

Here men are responsible for crimes like sexual harassment, wife beating, rape, dowry murders, and setting in processes like patriarchisation, genderisation (a process of social differentiation based on gender) (Singh, 1989:1)

(ii) ***Patriarchally propelled self-victimisation*** (extra-intra person)

Here the present suicide committed by four girls of Kanpur (three sisters and the other drawing cue from the former) and the suicides committed by brides figure. In the former case it is the patriarchal forces which compelled the three sisters to commit suicide notwithstanding their being educated.

(iii) ***Victim-propelled victimization*** (intra-gender; women and women)

Here the publicly celebrated rift between mother-in-law / sister-in-law versus daughter-in-law to discredit women as oppressor of her own sex figures.

Ashish Nandy notes that "...even man's cruelty toward women is not match for the cruelty of women toward women." "Indeed", observes A.R. Wadia that "the greatest enemy and the only one that ultimately counts-of women's 'Emancipation' is women herself'. To Renuka Singh "the worse deprivation of the 'deprived class' takes place when the women vs woman battle begins resulting in the loss of support of women for the cause of their own liberation." K.L. Sharma observes, "it has been observed that it is women who obstruct the path of other women even more than men do; as is the case with mothers-in-l;aw and colleagues at work." And a more shocking aspect is that "women are murdered by women themselves" (Taneja: 1987:4). However, it is unjust to say that behind every crime or injustice against a woman there is a woman.

Categories of Crime

Atray (1988:33-34) classifies crime, into three categories. The first category consists of individual acts which stop short of death of the victims like eve-teasing, wife beating, etc. The second category of crimes which is the most common and the least appreciated is the consequences which visit women as a result of enforcement by the society of its own rules and regulations. In the third category would fall cases of outright homicide whether it is intentional murder or forcing a woman to take her own life by committing suicide. In these categories of crimes, the first category of cases are to be treated more as social failing bordering on crime while the second category is out and out criminal. The third category raises certain basic issues concerning the society's own code of conduct and the blame is squarely on the society as a whole.

Mishra and Arora (1982: 5) classify crimes into three broad categories viz., (i) sexual offences, (ii) offences for gain, and (iii) customary laws and customs. Offences of sexual character may be further divided into those which have predatory element, and those which are non-predatory. Predatory element means the element of violence. In an offence is the first category that is a deliberate injury to the victim such as rape or other physical molestation. In an offence in the second category such as prostitution, the 'victim' is a participant who is willing.

Rajan (1981: 84) identifies the following categories of offences against women:

(i) Wolf-whistling, ogling, winking, passing lewd remarks, sometimes openly, and at other times behind the anonymity of the telephone.
(ii) Bottom-pinching and forcing physical intimacy on board public transport, in bus queues, on festivals or on other occasions when large concourses of people together.
(iii) Molestation and rape.
(iv) Harassment at home leading to suicide and murder of young brides.
(v) Immoral trafficking, exploitation of women, and commercialization of sex.

The IPC classifies women related crimes in six categories as follows: Offences against women's bodily interest; offences against women's proprietory interest; offences relating to marriage; offences relating to criminal intimidation, insult and annoyance; suppression of Immoral Traffic in Women and Girls Act; and Dowry Act.

Deshpande (1984:71) classifies crimes against women into three categories which are as follows:

(i) Crime against personal liberty which may be sub-divided into kidnapping and abduction of minors and majors who are mostly women;

(ii) Crime against marriage which includes bigamy, attacks on monogamy, fraud, decoit etc.;

(iii) Crime against persons which includes harm to both body and mind. The two interact on each other and harm done to one affects the other also.

Verma (1990) enumerates crimes against women into categories, namely physical torture and mental cruelties. These are further divided as follows:

Physical Torture

Medical termination of pregnancy, abortion of female foetus (if it found that it is a female child, the pregnancy is terminated), malnutrition of female child, female infanticide, eve-teasing, molestation, abduction and kidnapping, wife beating, wrongful confinement, fraudulent marriage, adultry-enticement of married women, cruelties on married women, rape, outraging the modesty of women, defaming young girls, prostitution, indescent representation of women, etc.

Mental Cruelties

Discrimination in male and female child, married women debarred of employment in several organizations, female generally having no say in her marriage, no equal remunerations, wife having no title in her husband's or in-laws property or home, the dowry menace, discrimination under law etc.

Two significant conclusions emerge from the above classifications: the *first* is biological. This reflects that violence against women occurs only because women are on average weaker. The implication of this statement is clear that the position of women has been historically structured as hierarchy in which men possessed and controlled women. This become the cause of physical violence against women and is one of the most brutal and explicit expressions of patriarchical domination. The *second* is to consider violence in its social-cultural context. A greater understanding of violence against women will be achieved through a consideration of the social environment in which it occurs.

Statistics on Crime Against Women

With the constant rise in dowry deaths, bride burning, rape, molestation, kidnapping and other crimes against women in the country, it has become difficult to determine the extent and nature of crimes against women accurately on the basis of cases reported to the police.

Reasons for Under Reporting of Cases

Firstly, due to the social stigma attached to the victim of sexual offences (i.e., rape, molestation, uttering word, making gesture etc.). Secondly, in dowry cases, parents do not want to stress the issue to the extreme for the future of the victim. Thirdly, to shun publicity being given by the media. Fourthly, in certain societies (Tribal) such crimes are not viewed with concern. Another reason may be the inadequate strength of the women police (Misra and Arora: 1982:7).

Crimes against women may not be reported due to the social stigma attached to the crime. A victim of sexual offences like rape, molestation, etc., may have to suffer the severity of social stigma, if it is made public. Besides, the social situations, there have been increasing reports regarding the rate of crime against women, which gives us an impression that such activities are on the rise. Although statistics regarding criminality against women are compiled officially in accordance with the provision of existing status of our country and collected, codified and classified at the national level in crime in India reports, yet there are no officially recognized figures available except their depiction under broad categories in the publication of significance. Taking IPC crime as an index of the situation of crime, the rise in the rate of crime against women has been reported in all types of crimes ranging from eve-teasing to abductions and killings for the period 1977-1979.

Data which reveal an average percentage of crime against women committed during 1977-79 which represent that a little more than 80 per cent crime against women has been reported: for molestation (28.94 per cent); offences under SITA Act (24.67 per cent); Kidnapping and abduction (20.96 per cent); and rape (10.70 per cent). Moreover, these four crimes have gone up further during the 1983 to 1985. Besides these crimes, there is also an increase in eve-teasing and dowry deaths as reflected by the percentage change in 1985 over 1983. It was pointed out that against 2487 cases of rape in 1971, 4300 cases were reported in 1979 averaging 12 rapes a day or about one every two hours. The All India figures of dowry deaths is about 4000 per year. Similarly, 619 cases of bride burning were registered by the police in Delhi in 1982 against a total of 421 cases in 1980. Registered cases have also been going up alarmingly in the past few years though the number of cases reported is much more than the recorded ones.

Reported figures in Delhi for crimes against women reveal that dowry deaths rose from 43 in 1985 to 64 in 1986 and 59 in 1987 to 71 in 1988. The number of such deaths had risen to 132 between January 1989 and February 1990 as disclosed by the then Union Home Minister in Parliament. This apart, Delhi led all union territories in 1987 with 103 registered cases of rape; worse still innocent minors were the victims in more than of these cases.

The total incidence of such crimes are estimated to be in the country with a population of about 700 million are estimated to be 50 times higher because of the inherent hesitation on the part of victims to complain about such matters. These figures do not represent the whole picture except in the case of murder and suicide. This is particularly so in the case of the offences of eve-teasing where the victim, as a rule, tries not to report the matter as they feel that in the absence of any strong provision in the law to deal with this crime, the only consequences of reporting would be necessary harassment to the victim and her witness. The crime of wife-beating goes almost cent per cent unreported for the same reason of the law and also the fact that reporting of such incidents to the police would put an end to all hopes of future reconciliation (Atray: 1988).

Special Study

Misra and Arora (1982) conducted a study of six districts, namely, Hissar, Sirsa, Jaunsar Bewar (Tehsil Chakrota in Dehradun), Kanpur, Delhi and Bombay representing respectively the agrarian/ smaller towns; tribal areas; and urban/metropolitan cities. Crime against women constitute only a small proportion of the total crime reported to the police. On an average for every 100 cases of crime reported to the police during 1977-79, there were only 0.43 cases of crime against women. In tribal area this ratio was 2.27, in agrarian area the same was 1.68 and in urban area it was 0.42. It also reveals that the ratio of crime against women to the total crime increased in the urban/metropolitan cities and the tribal belt while it declined in the agrarian sector.

The overall ratio of crime against women to total crime has increased from 0.40 in 1977 to 0.43 in 1978 and to 0.47 in 1979. In the urban areas it increased from 0.38 in 1977 to 0.41 in 1978 and further to 0.45 in 1979. In tribal belt, it increased erratically from 0.69 in 1977 to 4.59 in 1978 and declined to 2.04 in 1979. In agrarian area the ratio had declined in 1979 over the year 1977. The ratio in 1977 was 1.63, 1.91 in 1978 and 1.54 in 1979 (*Ibid:* 79-80). The volume of crime against women rose from 12.64 per lakh population in 1977 to 14.18 per lakh population in 1979. In the agrarian areas during the same period, the increase was 10 per cent in 1978 and 11.1 per cent in 1979 over the year 1977. In the tribal area, the percentage increase in 1978 was 400.0 and 100.0 in 1979 over the year 1977. The urban area registered an increase of 0.8 per cent in 1978 and in 1979 by 20.2 per cent over the year 1977. Thus, we see that the crime against women had increased at a much higher rate than the other crimes. Moreover, the ratio of crime against women to the total crime increased in the urban/metropolitan cities and the tribal belt while it declined in the agricultural sector. Out of the total of 6483 cases of crime against women reported, the maximum (37.2 per cent) cases were of Suppression of Immoral Traffic Act, followed by kidnapping/ adduction (21.7 per cent), molestation (14.2 per cent), rape (8.6 per cent), chain-snatching (7.2 per cent), murder (5.1 per cent) and enticing or taking away or detaining with criminal intent a married women (3.9 per cent). These offences together constitute above 98 per cent of the total cases of crime against women.

The other offences committed against women were very less in number. These offences in order of reporting were: Eve-teasing (0.8 per cent), dacoity (0.4 per cent), abetment to suicide (0.3 per cent), Dowry Prohibition Act, unnatural offences, importation and selling of minor for prostitution 0.1 per cent each, procuration of minor (0.04 per cent). In the agricultural sector the highest number of cases were of molestation being 46.8 per cent followed by kidnapping/ abduction (23.2 per cent), rape (14.9 per cent), abetment to suicide (3.1 per cent). A solitary case of eve-teasing was also reported. In the urban areas the order of reporting was SITA Act (38.9 per cent), followed by kidnapping/abduction (21.7 per cent), molestation (12.7 per cent), rape (8.2 per cent), chain-snatching (7.5 per cent), enticing or taking away with criminal intent a married women (4.1 per cent). The other offences committed against women are very less in number and the trend of these offences were similar to the total cases of crime against women as mentioned above. In the tribal areas, the highest cases (75.0 per cent) were of rape/kidnapping/abduction followed by molestation (25.0 per cent). Thus, the nature and extent of crime against women differ from area to area.

Rape Statistics

The victimization of the fair sex has been showing an upward inclination and incidence of these crimes is on the rise. Eventhough the available statistics are very high, they don't represent even 25 per cent of the total because it is well-known that in actual practice hardly one fourth of the cases are reported. The reasons for non-reporting are obvious. A critical perusal of statistical data on crimes against women reveals that rape is increasing throughout India. According to ***Crime in India Report 1986,*** a total of 7,952 cases in rape were registered in 1986 against 7,289 cases in 1985 thereby registering an increase of 9.1 per cent in 1986 over 1985. The highest number of cases among the States was registered by Madhya Pradesh (1,506) followed by Uttar Pradesh (1,292), Maharashtra (804), Bihar (794), West Bengal (612), Rajasthan (598), etc. Thus, about 50 per cent of the total cases in the country are reported in four States of Madhya Pradesh, Uttar Pradesh, Maharashtra, and Bihar together. However, the highest volume of rape cases was reported from the State of Jammu and Kashmir being 2.8, followed by Madhya Pradesh (2.6), and lowest from the State of Punjab (0.3) and Karnataka (0.3) respectively. The volume of rape cases for each population was 1.0 in all the States taken together, in all the union territories taken together as well as in the country as a whole.

Overall the volume of rape cases to per lakh of population had increased critically during the period 1974-86. It increased from 0.5 in 1974 to 1.0 in 1986 exceptionally in 1979, it had declined to 0.66 as compared to the year 1078, which was 0.71. However, in the last one decade, rape cases have just doubled and it would be seen that the percentage victims of rape was the highest in the age-group between 16 to 30 years in all the seven years between 1971 to 1977, the average being 62.5 per cent followed by the age group below 30 years accounted for 14.6 per cent.

Kidnapping and Abduction Statistics

The incidence of kidnapping and abduction has also been increasing in our country. The total number of cases recorded in 1971 was 9,647. In 1973, the incidence under this head increased by 8.7 per cent over 1972; in 1976 the incidence increased by 10.0 per cent over 1977; and in 1978 the incidence increased by 11.2 per cent over 1977. The rate of this crime, per one lakh of population is 2.0 in our country. Manipur topped the list among the States with the average per annum volume per lakh of population being 13.33, followed by Jammu and Kashmir (6.85), Rajasthan (4.09), Uttar Pradesh (3.07) and so on. Delhi topped the list among Union territories with the average per annum volume of 5.0. No case was reported from Dadra and Nagar Haveli and Lakshadweep during the period 1977-79.

Molestation Statistics

The average annual volume per lakh of population of reported cases of molestation of women and girls were the highest in the State of Madhya Pradesh being 5.56 followed by Jammu and Kashmir (5.36), Manipur (4.72), Tripura (3.48) and so on. The average per annum volume in these States was higher than the average volume (1.82) of all States taken together. No cases of molestation of women and girls were reported from the State of Sikkim and the Union Territory of Lakshadweep Islands.

Among the union territories the average per year volume of this crime was the highest in Andaman and Nicobar Islands, bring 12.27 per lakh of population, followed by Mizoram (6.04), Pondicherry (2.33).The average volume per annum in these Union territories was higher than the all Union territories average 7.87. Statistics reveal that the volume of molestation of women and girls per lakh of population on all-India basis had increased from 1.77 in 1977 to 1.92 in 1978.

SITA Statistics

Of the major crimes against women, the volume per lakh of population of cases of SITA taken together were the highest after cases of molestation of women and girls. The highest volume of SITA cases were reported from the State of Tamil Nadu being 10.57 per lakh of population, followed by Karnataka (6.55), Andhra Pradesh (2.37), Maharashtra (1.37) and Uttar Pradesh (0.50). In other States insignificant or negligible cases of SITA were reported. No case was reported during the year 1977-79 in the States of Gujarat, Meghalaya, Nagaland, Sikkim, West Bengal.

Amongst the Union territories, the maximum number of cases of SITA were reported from Delhi with the average volume of (0.77) followed by Pondicherry (0.36). No case of this offence was reported from the other Union territories during 1977-79. In the Union Territory of Delhi, the volume per lakh of population had shown a continuously arising trend.

Dowry Deaths Statistics

The number of dowry deaths is on the rise despite the various legislative and other measures taken from time to time to tackle the problem. This has threatened our way of life (Mir, 1982). There were 162 cases of burning of women reported in the capital only between April 1, 1983 and June 30, 1983. Figures reveal that in many States, the reported cases of dowry deaths or deaths by burning or suicide more than doubled within two years. Andhra Pradesh reported 14 cases of dowry deaths in 1983, 27 cases in 1984 and 38 cases in 1985. In Uttar Pradesh the death figures of bride burning or suicide, were 323 in 1985 and 110 in the first four months of 1986. Madhya Pradesh reported 42 cases of dowry deaths in just five months June-October in 1985. In Maharashtra, there were 129 cases of dowry deaths in 1984, the number of such deaths recorded in 1985 was at 211 and it had reached to 247 in the first ten months of 1986. Maharashtra recorded 411 cases of suicide by young married women in 1983, 652 in 1985 and 662 for the first ten months of 1986 (***Indian Express***, 24.5.1987).

Statistics provided by the Home Ministry regarding dowry deaths also helps us to some extent in assessing the prevalence of this phenomenon in our country. The figures show a sharp increase in the incidence, year after year, which could partly be due to the increased awareness about the problem.

Official figures between January 1980-March 1981 show that there were 139 dowry death cases registered with police in various parts of the country. Of these Punjab and Haryana accounted for

231 cases each and 17 cases were from Uttar Pradesh. Whereas by latest figures, the number of dowry deaths for the year 1987 stands at 1649, and Uttar Pradesh on the whole is found to be the leading State in dowry deaths.

According to statistics, the figures of dowry deaths by burning or suicide are only a part of the actual number of deaths caused in this respect, therefore, the reported figures are usually misleading. Sources of information include the special cell in the Delhi Police Headquarters and numerous non-governmental organization which clearly prove the point of gross variability in information in this regard, the figures supplied in the Rajya Sabha could probably be treated as the third source of information. The number of cases of married women in the age-group 16-30 years with third degree burns admitted in the various hospitals of Delhi is yet another source of information. In the capital 736 cases of death due to burns, suicide and poisoning were reported in the year of 1985. The number of such deaths increased to 775 in 1986 and 426 in the first six months of 1987 (Bhatia, 1988). There is no doubt about the fact that crimes against women are increasing in every country, but in India, like other developing countries the proportion of such trend is on higher level.

To sum up, on an all-India basis taking the 3 years (1977-79) average of all the selected offences against women, the highest number of cases were reported under the head 'Molestation' being 11642 (28.94) per cent of the total cases reported. This was followed by the cases under SITA and Girls 9926 (24.67 per cent) cases; kidnapping/abduction 8432 (20.96 per cent), rape 4305 (10.70 per cent); Enticing or taking away with criminal intent a married women 2736 (6.80 per cent), chain snatching 1298 (3.23 per cent) procuring minor girl 908 (2.26 per cent). Interestingly some of the offences like abetment to suicide and penalty for demanding dowry which are reported in the mass media were comparatively less. The average per year cases reported under abetment to suicide were only 169 (0.42 per cent), demanding dowry-Section 4 were 103 (0.26 per cent).

The vulnerability of women to various forms of oppression, exploitation and abuse should be given its due share while framing of policies and laws so that they can be given their share of respect and status long due to them.

THREE

Better Half under Assault

Women in India through the ages have been victimised, humiliated, tortured and exploited as long as history can tell. There have been incidents of murder, rape, abduction and torture from time immemorial. In spite of such a dark past, violence against has not been given much attention, more so, no attempt was made on the issue of why such a socially relevant theme has been left neglected and ignored.

Living in a country which is the world's largest democracy, a sovereign, socialist republic with a comprehensive charter of right written into its constitution, a signatory to most treaties for struggle against colonialism, imperialism and racism is a matter of great pride for all of us. However, underneath this impressive veneer and national pride about our three thousand-years-old civilization lies a history of systematic violation of basic civil, democratic, and human rights of large sections of our population, such as women. Ironically in a country where womenhood has been put on a pedestal for worship, incidents of wife battering, molestation of women in various forms like rape, eve-teasing, abduction and bride burning keep on increasing year after year. Women find no security be it home, where they are ill-treated by husbands and in-laws, or the streets and work place where they are vulnerable and fall prey antisocials, moneylenders and men-colleagues, bosses and are subjected to innumerable indignities, perhaps in higher frequency than in most of the civilized societies world over. The general perception today is that the crime against women has increased to such a great extent that women cannot move freely and participate in the community. There is no safe territory left for women not even in their *"mohallas"*. Apart from being widely harassed but women are also being assaulted and raped before the eyes of their family members be— they single or married. Significantly, female victims of violence have not been given due attention in the literature on social problems or in that of criminal violence. Nor any attempt was made to explain why both the public and the scientific communities ignored for so long the varied instances where women were being greatly exploited in our society.

This attitude of constant indifference and negligence can be attributed to three factors: (1) a lack of awareness of the seriousness of the problem, (2) the general acceptance of man's superiority over woman because of which violent acts against women were not viewed as violent or deviant, and (3) the denial of violence by women themselves due to their religious values and social attitudes which leaves no recourse.

Minor Girls

Victimization of women in India starts from the time of their birth. Boys are preferred to girls. In most of the cases the birth of a girl child does not make happy even the parents of the child, not to speak about other members of the family. On the contrary, the birth of a son is enthusiastically celebrated with blessings showered on the couple by all the members of the family, friends and neighbours alike. If a woman accidentally gives birth to two or three daughters, she is made to hang her head in shame. She is subjected to abuses and all sort of ill-treatment specially by in-laws. Many women have committed suicide being fed up with torture by mother-in-laws and husbands for being unable to give birth to a son for the family.

There are innumerable instances where the parents leave the female babies at the door-steps of some orphanage or hospital or in parks and say goodbye to the child for ever. A couple from village Tatigharia under Bishungarh police station of Hazaribagh fled the hospital after throwing the baby in the bushes closer to the hospital compound wall. In the meantime a sweeper of the hospital found the baby while cleaning the campus. She brought the baby to her house and started looking after her. Later the police arrested the couple and released them only after executing a bond that both the husband and wife would look after the baby properly.

Dowry Issue

There are cases where the parents kill their young daughters because of their inability to fulfil the demands of dowry and sometimes young girls commit suicide due to their fathers' meagre income sources to fulfil the demands of dowry.

Leading newspapers of India almost daily publish as banner news, crimes against women in various manifestations, i.e., bride burning, rape, abduction, eve-teasing, wife battering both in rural and urban areas of India. This is a news item which is generally noticed, keenly read, and attracts our attention. The issue of crimes committed against women has been a topic of discussion in various forums of public opinion. Press reports reveal that crime against women has increased manifold. The problem of crime against women is not new. Women in Indian society have been victims of humiliation, torture and exploitation for as long as we have had written records of social organisation and family life. There are many records of episodes like rape, abduction, battering, and so forth of women.

Violence is present everywhere though the incidence of violence by men towards women is not identical in all groups and communities, the type, frequency, intensity and control of crime against women may vary from time to time, community to community, or place to place.

No woman who has escaped at one time or another the harassment, humiliation, exploitation and violence that shadows her sex. A woman's life swings between pleasure at one end and danger at other end. Daily women are being defined by sex and even if not all men are potential rapists, kidnappers, eve-teasers and wife batterers, all women are potential victims.

Social Legislations for Protection

There have been scores of amendments and inclusion of various laws in the statute book to check the victimization of women. The Dowry Prohibition Act 1961 was amended twice to make its provisions more punitive. The Indian Penal Code, the Criminal Procedure Code and the Indian Evidence Act have also been amended simultaneously to deal effectively not only with dowry deaths but also cases of cruelty to married women. Similarly, the law against rape was also modified to remove some of its drawbacks. But all these changes cannot reduce the volume of the crime at all. One reason why crime against women continues to increase being that the laws are not deterrent enough. So, the culprits feel that they can easily get away with anything.

Their Implementation

Women in India are way ahead of from women of elsewhere in the matter of social legislation. But the implementation of laws granting rights to women are inversely related being slow, lopsided and haphazard that socially, economically and politically women are kept far behind the men. Even today, many decades after independence, women are suffering from various kinds of discrimination, exploitation and torture, mental and physical in society and within the four walls of the family. In a male-dominated patriarchal society, women are protected by the family from other men, but may be unsafe in their own families.

Incidents may occur in the family, offices, agricultural fields, industries, and even public places for which women have to pay the price. Indian women thus can be described as the underdogs of a society where theoretically, the law of equality is supposed to practise and women are considered to be on a par with their male counterparts, but in practice the men remain powerful and thrive at the expense of the women.

The issue of crime against women has been graduated from a private issue to public issue. The large scale reporting on incidents of crime against women by the mass media has brought the ugliness of such crime right inside our homes and makes us realize that the existing efforts have been hardly able to create even a dent in the structure responsible for such crimes.

Lately, Indian women have started rising against their victimisation and there is a growing understanding of the pathetic condition of woman in our society. However, something substantial is yet to be done. Crime against women is one such problem that now offers a challenge. The problems faced by Indian women and specially the crime committed against them need to be realized and checkmated at the earliest, so that no more time may be lost before the situation deteriorates. This study is meant to contribute something concretely to this understanding.

Norms of behaviour exist in every society and any deviation attracts censure from those who are authorised to enforce these norms. Where the behaviour is intentional and harms another person or property, it amounts to punishable by law. There are numerous acts which have been declared offences under the various laws by the Central and State Governments from time to time which are applicable both to men and women. In this study we confine ourselves to a discussion of crimes against women.

Definition of Crime against Women

The phrase "crime against women" refers to those the crimes involving violence against female. Defining the term in parts: (i) "Crime", (ii) "against women". The latter terms refers only to those crimes in which the victim is a female. The former term refers to those acts which are legally forbidden, intentionally committed, and punishable by courts.

Human violence includes any aggressive behaviour of a person or persons hurting body or positive regard or both of another person or persons. Further analysis reveals:

(a) Aggressive behaviour means vigorous behaviour or action.

(b) A person means victimiser either a male or a female.

(c) Hurting body means inflicting physical injury.

(d) 'Positive regard' means need to be level or accepted.

(e) Another person means the victim. Keeping in view this definition, certain misconceptions regarding crime against women may be removed.

Misconceptions

1. Men alone are involved in crime against women and it is a battle of sexes in the general belief. But crime against women is both an inter-sex and intra-sex problem as the victimiser may be a male or a female or both. In bride burning, the husband alone or with the in-laws, male or female, may be the victimiser. The mother herself discriminates between a male and a female child in rearing practices. In sexual crimes, males are the victimisers. Mostly men are the

victimisers. But in many cases of domestic violence, females also play their roles in victimising women.

2. Violent behaviour is misconceived to be only on physical level. It is not so. Crime may be expressed in physical torture like wife battering, killing, it is also expressed on verbal level in the form of abuse, rebuke, threat or teasing and also in its talent or indirect forms like all sorts of deprivations, discriminations and obstructions imposed upon women in achieving their goals. These latent forms of crime psychologically hurt women.
3. Crime always results in physical injury. This is not so, criminal behaviour of the victimiser may results in physical or psychological injury but both to the victim. When a woman is raped or abducted or battered or burnt, she is not only physically injured, but also psychologically hurt.

Categories

Crime against women may be classified into three broad categories viz., (i) Sexual offences, (ii) Offences for gain, and (iii) Customary laws and customs.

Offences of sexual character may be divided further into those which have a predatory element and those which are non-predatory. Predatory element is violence. In an offence in the first category there is a deliberate injury to the victim such as rape or molestation.

The second category includes prostitution, here the victim is a willing participant. The case of rape constituted by sexual intercourse with a girl below the statutory minimum age, stands on a special footing and may not strictly fit in with the above classification. Reverting to the two broad categories contemplated by the dichotomy, it may be mentioned that crimes in the nature of obscenity and bigamy stand midway between them. There is no coercion here and no physical injury and the 'victim' may or may not be a consenting party. The real damage is to the morale of society and such damage is present even though the parties involved in the act give their implied consent. Bigamy where there is full knowledge of both the parties, involve no fraud in contrast to bigamy, where one of the parties may not be aware of the existence of the previous marriage. Crimes indicated by the impersonal desire for gain do not themselves constitute 'crimes against women'. Robbery, burglary, theft (and even some cases of assault), may occur between persons of two sexes but they cut across several lines. Such crimes are intended to enrich the thief and not to express personal hatred or passion towards the victim. Offences under customary laws and customs are generally peculiar to a particular society. As the customary laws and values are intricately woven in our society through which violence is perpetrated against women, there is need for fundamental changes in the patriarchal values. Else such violence is bound to continue in its familiar forms and newer guises.

FOUR

Causes of Violence

People have always been deeply disturbed about violence against women, but they have never quite understood what makes the sense of pain conveyed by the term violence more painful than any other pain, the sense of fear more awesome and the terror more terrifying than any other. Women suffer and are made to suffer in many ways. In behavioural terms, violence against women ranges from simple suppression to abuse, aggression, exploitation and severe oppression. We know it as female infanticide, the abortion of the female foetus, the neglect and undernourishment of the girl child, denial of education to girls, rape, pre-puberty marriage, wife beating, the harassment of a bride leading to her suicide or murder. Each of these is more awesome than comparable or even greater pain or fear experienced in other contexts. For instance childbirth can be extremely painful, but one never refers to the pain of childbirth as violence, no matter how severe it is. The fear of death in a situation of terminal illness, can be extremely terrifying but one does not refer to it as violence.

In an effort to try and identify the element that makes violence different an attempt has been made here to define violence. A recent Indian report of a study on Women and Violence sponsored in India and in Korea by UNESCO, Bangkok, looked promising in terms of providing a lead. This report, edited by Dr. Krishnaraj, has been prepared by the SNDT University's Research Centre for Women's Studies. It is based on an analysis of violence against women reported in Gujarati, Marathi and English language journals and newspapers and on findings from some case studies specially undertaken for the purpose. It also offers a review of Enactments on Violence against Women made in the decade of the eighties (1980-1990) and discuss women's action groups and the State machinery against women.

Concept and Meaning

According to the report,

> Violence, in general, is a coercive mechanism to impose one's will over another, in order to prove or feel a sense of power. It can be perpetuated by those in power against the powerless, or by the powerless in retaliation against coercion by others, to deny their powerlessness. Any hierarchical system of social organization, where there are categories of dominant groups and subordinate groups, is inevitably accompanied by the victimization of the latter through various means — subtle pressure through the power of ideology, through mechanisms of socialization that reward compliance and punish noncompliance and also through open force. Usually, the last form is resorted to when other methods fail. In fact, it is often not even necessary to actually use physical force or inflict severe injury, for the mere threat to do so is enough to subdue the subordinate person or group. Any individual or group facing the threat of coercion or being disciplined to act in a manner serving the interests of another individual or group, is subject to violence. This is not necessarily confined to physical violence but the creation of an atmosphere of terror, a situation of threat and reprisal..... A hierarchical social structure has violence built into it.

Impressive as it is this statement on violence leaves one feeling more inadequate about the understanding of the concept. To start with the very first line, describing "Violence as a coercive mechanism to assert one's will over another to prove a sense of power" leaves one wondering about where one would place punitive action considered socially legitimate. For instance, the State legitimately uses coercive mechanisms to assert its power over deviants. Whether it does so to "prove" its power or to "assert" the power legitimately given to it is a matter of semantics. What matters here is that this coercion and exercise of power are socially accepted as a legitimate means of resolving a problematic situation. One of the core elements of violence seems to be that the coercion involved is neither legitimate nor socially acceptable. The statement does not make this point. On the contrary, by saying that "any individual or group facing the threat of coercion or being disciplined to act in a manner serving the interests of another individual or group is subject to violence", it reduces all coercion, legitimate or otherwise, to violence.

There are other problems with the definition. For instance, the third line talks of "Any hierarchical system of social organization where there are categories of dominant groups and subordinate groups, etc." The "Any" in this sentence suggests that hierarchy is not a universal feature of social systems and that there may be some social systems without hierarchy. This is not true. All societies, even those that are supposed to be egalitarian, have distinctive hierarchies. Not surprisingly the author of the introduction to the report, who makes this statement on violence, seems, herself, to find it too broad to be of any use. She says, "If we accept this very wide definition of violence, it is difficult to know where to draw the line" and decides to go on with her project with a relatively limited definition of violence against women as sexual harassment and sexual violation.

Among other definitions of the term, Collins dictionary defines violence as :

(i) "Behaviour which is meant to hurt or kill people";

(ii) "a great deal of energy used in doing something — usually because you are very angry";

(iii) "words, actions or other forms of expression which are critical or destructive".

The Oxford dictionary defines violence as :

(1) "the quality of being violent";

(2) "violent conduct or treatment, outrage, injury";

(3) "the unlawful exercise of physical force; (3b) "intimidation by the exhibition of this".

The Thesaurus adds a few additional dimensions to the concept offered by the two dictionaries. It indicates that the noun violence connotes vehemence, impetuosity, vigorousness, excess, destructiveness, vandalism, turbulence, turmoil, roughness, severity, brute force, brutality, savagery, mercilessness, exacerbation, explosion. The adjective 'violent' is explained among other terms by the terms aggressive, charging, disorderly, turbulent, stormy, anarchistic, nihilistic, intemperate, immoderate. Thus, at the end of the exercise of consulting the dictionaries and the Thesaurus, the connotation of the term violence comes across as coercive, destructive behaviour, with a great deal of powerful, aggressive energy and force, destroying in a merciless manner what it is directed at and disorderly, anarchist, turbulent, outrageous and unlawful in its functioning.

Coverage of Violence

This concept is further elucidated in a television series entitled *Maharashtratil Stree Muktichya Paulkhuna* (Footprints of the Movement for Liberation of Women in Maharashtra). Depicting the emergence of new values, a new self-image, self concept and consciousness among the women of Maharashtra during the course of the nineteenth and early twentieth centuries, it depicts how values pertaining to the rights, the status and the situation of women, steadily changed in this part of the country under the influence of Christianity and European Liberalism. History indicates that the change first occurred among Western educated men, who, inspired by these values, were stimulated to social reform. It occurred somewhat later among women. The series also conveys the fact of the gradual change in values very cleverly. It picks characters, events and scenes from novels, plays, biographies and autobiographies from during a century between 1840 and 1940 and uses the dialogues, soliloquies and events from these literary sources to illustrate how awareness perceptions, and values steadily changed in those times. The core element of this change was a gradual transformation in notions of right and wrong. Practices like child marriage and the denial of the right of re-marriage to widows which, were the social norm of yesteryears, came to be considered oppressive. Shaving the heads of widows in particular, a routine practice among Brahmins and other upper caste Maharashtrians, came to be seen as an outrageous violation of the helpless widow. There was something terribly wrong about a situation wherein both the parental family of the woman as well as the family of her husband, responsible for protecting her in her widowed state inflicted such torture on one who was an important member of the family, loved and cared by all. She was disfigured as soon as her husband was gone with no consideration that widows subjected to this practice were often no more that ten or twelve years old did not seem to matter. As change occurred, this fact made the practice seem even more cruel and heinous bringing about protests and movements against such an oppressive custom.

With the unfolding of episodes to reveal how the reactions of the women to some of the traditional practices steadily changed, it was obvious that not only did these practices gradually come to be seen as wrong but the sentiments that they evoked also changed. What was once accepted and respected as religious customs and generated sentiments of pity, sadness and even horror accompanied by a feeling of the inevitability of destiny, a deep sense of awe, and a commitment to surrender to the authority of religion transformed into sense of outrage and injustice, a feeling that what was being done was enormously inhuman and wrong and must be stopped. Initially this was only felt by the reformers. The reaction of the others, including the women subjected to the practices, was that the practices were extremely painful, but virtuous. Steadily this changed. The women themselves started to question these practices and began defying them. In essence, reform thus consisted of a transformation wherein what was earlier acknowledged to be painful but accepted with reverence as something required by religion, now came to be seen as aggressive and inhuman. The religious norms and beliefs that legitimized this aggression were seriously questioned.

Values to Change

Significantly the forces that led to this change came from outside the Hinduism. The change occurred because Christian values and European Liberalism had established their hold, first on the consciousness of the Western educated reformers and then on women. Hindu men and women had acquired a new sense of humanism influenced by these new values. A new notion of the dignity of the self, of the sanctity of personhood and of the obligation to protect the helpless was introduced. Seen from the vantage point of these new values, the earlier practices were a transgression and violation of humanism. What was earlier only seen as painful and sad, now appear to be inhuman and therefore violent. This then seems to be the essence of violence — a feeling of violation, of the transgression of what is considered to be human.

Corollaries of 'Violence'

Thus conceived, the concept of violence has several important corollaries. For instance transgression implies a transgressor. Thus violence is something that a transgressor inflicts upon a victim. Violence in a manner is socially unacceptable. This corollary to the concept of violence fits in very well with the definition of the verb "violate" defined in the Oxford dictionary as: (A) "to disregard, fail to comply with (an oath, treaty, law, etc.)" (B) "to treat profanely or with disrespect" (C) "to break in upon: disturb (privacy etc.)" (D) "to assault sexually, rape etc."

Behaviour viewed as violence in one society may not be so in another is another interesting corollary to the concept of violence, defined as violation, transgression or socially unacceptable infliction of pain. This is so because what is unacceptable in one society may be acceptable in another. There are many examples of this. For instance, female circumcision, routinely practised in some African countries, is viewed as violence by those of us who do not belong to the African culture. A related corollary is that practices that are not perceived as violence in a society at one point of time may be considered to be so in the same society due to transformation of values. For example, the fact that practices such as child marriage or the denial of the right of remarriage to widows, which were acceptable within our society only three or four generations ago, are now considered to be violent by all of us is by far the best example. The change in values that occurred with respect to traditional practices governing the lives of women in our society has been highly uneven, thus generating serious turmoil and unrest, this turmoil has often been channelized into constructive movements for social reform and change. Finally, practices and behaviour that may not be considered to be violent by a person at one point of time may be considered violent by the same person as his/her values or awareness change. This can lead to deep personal conflict, anomie and even complete breakdown if the person experiencing the change is unable to contain or manage the fluctuating values.

An example of the last two corollaries is the transformation in the awareness of Black Americans after the Second World War. Discrimination on the basis of colour resented by the Black population of the United States of America had been broadly accepted until the Second World War where the Black soldiers fought shoulder to shoulder with White, with equal courage and patriotism. On their return from the War these soldiers resented the racial discrimination they had earlier subjected to. They saw it as a serious violation of the equality promised by the Constitution of their country. So did many White Americans. Those who had acquired a new awareness of equality suffered deep resentment and personal conflict when they faced racial discrimination. But this new awareness of equality was not evenly shared in our country. And this led to the strong movements against racial discrimination that rocked American society in the decades of the fifties, sixties and seventies. As the change continues to be uneven, the feeling of violation persists. This is a source of continuing personal and social conflict in the USA. There is no denying the fact that the people may undergo deep personal conflicts and upheavals due to this.

Women all over the world have started to resent the discrimination they suffer in different spheres of life. This has been channelled into constructive activism towards the empowerment of women, and towards legal measures and structural reforms aimed at improving their status and situation in life. However, some of it has given way for angry feminism, and resulted in deep personal conflict, even breakdown, among women who have been unable to cope with their resentment against gender discrimination.

In keeping with the trend of Women Empowerment, SNDT University launched a foundation course entitled Women in a Changing India. The objective of this course is to make the students aware of their situation as women, to help them to look critically and analytically at their status in life, to recognize the restrictions that women face because of gender discrimination. The course also aims at enabling students to recognize their strengths and to inform them about the Constitutional provisions ensuring them equality.

It attempts to introduce them to the range of new provisions and opportunities now available for their advance.

This course has been enormously well received. The feedback from those who teach the course indicates that students are eager, alert, receptive and full of questions. Many of the students at SNDT University come from very orthodox families. As expected, the feedback reveals that exposed to the course, they have started to question the discipline and the traditional values within their families. They have started, questioning traditional role expectations which they had earlier accepted with ease. Many of them now consider some of these expectations to be a violation of their personal dignity and individual freedom. Some of them are able to cope with this sense of violation and advance towards greater autonomy and independence. But many face deep personal conflicts in striking a balance between what they have been raised to believe and what they now determine on their own. This conflict is part of the process of their empowerment. It is part of their advance towards autonomy, freedom, and the new rights and opportunities available to them. But it is difficult to handle. The challenge for the University committed to the empowerment of its students, is to help them to resolve this conflict and to advance without allowing their new awareness and sense of violation to seriously damage their personalities or destroy their relationships within their families. It may not be easy but surely there will be a way out some day.

Society in Transition

Two points are sought to be made here :

First, that India has always been the land of contrasts and that a wide spectrum of value systems, from the extremely "traditional" to the extremely "modern" exist side by side.

Second, that Indian society remains firmly rooted in the patriarchal ideology which is premised upon male supremacy and a legitimization of women's oppression. Because this basic ideology remains largely unchallenged and unchanged, violence against women is also perpetuated, sometimes in the old forms and sometimes in different and newer guises.

The concept of tradition and modernity is debatable as indeed the factors for classification are based on tradition and culture which are largely followed in underdeveloped countries. There is the additional need to distinguish between "modernization" and "Westernization". However, we can bypass these complexities by simply employing the term "tradition" to mean age-old customs and "modernity" to mean partly Westernized social practices thus focusing primarily on the multiple forms of violence against women which remain an oppressive reality.

Patriarchy Prevalent

Patriarchy as prevalent in India a hundred years ago was premised upon the male predominance authority, power and female subordination and subservience, the woman's wife-mother role as her *raison d'être*, and her status as the legal, economic and sexual property of her husband. This was sacralized through the ancient Hindu socio-legal treatises. The most authoritative of these, the *Manusmriti*, stipulated that a woman had to be under the protection and control of her father in childhood, her husband in youth and her sons in her widowed old age, and furthermore that a woman does not deserve independence. This dictate was translated into practice with ease given the practices of universal and early marriage for women (always before puberty in the upper castes and usually so in other castes and also among other religions), immediate post-pubertal consummation of marriage, early and frequent pregnancies and physical and verbal violence in the marital home. Thus, the traditions were legitimized due to sanctions from treatises.

A woman's life revolved around the extended family which was a small community in itself, finely graded along the triple axes of sex, age and degree of relationship with the head of the family. The extended family spanned several generations and comprised the patriarch and his younger brothers with their families, all the married sons with their families, all the unmarried sons and daughters and sometimes widowed or deserted daughters who returned to the parental home. The source of power was the patriarch who designed the chief economic resource of the family, its immoveable property and ancestral wealth, to be held in common by all the males born into the family, as coparceners: so that the daughters were not entitled to a share in this indivisible property and were therefore compensated at marriage with a smaller share of the moveable property, especially jewellery, clothes and household articles. This bridal portion was intended to be treated strictly as her "woman's wealth" solely under her control but was eventually transmuted into "dowry" to which her husband and marital family laid claim. The economic dependence caused by this loss of assets was considerably aggravated in those regions where women were largely economically inactive. Directly or indirectly man controlled all the wealth and made woman a puppet to their whims and fancies.

Male Monopoly

The male monopoly of domestic authority and decision-making powers increased women's dependence on their husbands and grown-up sons through whom alone they could access power. Whereas a son would remain within the family, carry on the family name, care for his parents in their old age, and perform the necessary rituals after their death, a daughter would marry and leave the parental home and was thus in effect "a stranger's wealth" — to be nurtured and trained only to be given away at the great expense of a suitable dowry. The preference for a son and undesirability of daughters stemmed from this situation, as did the mother's possessive love for her son/s as her future protector/s and provider/s. Such values relegated women to a low value premium in the family.

Mother-in-law Syndrome

A bride entered her husband's family after marriage according to the practice of patrilocal residence as the junior-most and most vulnerable member. A strong bond between her and her husband was prevented from developing by his mother who wished to monopolize his affections in the interests of her own survival. Thus the institutionalized harassment of the bride or the "mother-in-law" syndrome came into being. Whereas all the brothers grew up and continued to live together in an atmosphere conducive to male bonding, a parallel female bonding was effectively prevented by the fact that all daughters-in-law were unrelated outsiders in competition with each other for a better share in the common resources for themselves and their children and that the mothers-in-law were in competition with their daughters-in-law. Thus patriarchy effectively pitted the women against one another and revealed the divisive potential of the extended family as far as women were concerned. The pattern thus cultivated was a well calculated move and developed through well-motivated ideals.

Female Undesirability Deprivation

This normative structure has resulted in the traditional institutionalization of violence where violence against women started almost at birth, its most extreme form being the culturally legitimized femicide through female infanticide. Limited to parts of Rajasthan and Gujarat (and was forbidden by British legislation introduced in 1877 specifically in these areas), a girl was usually made to feel unwelcome and undesirable as well as inferior to her brothers and to all men in general. Physical chastisement, sometimes in quite severe forms, was meted out to her by her mother who was solely entrusted with the task of socializing and disciplining her for her future wifely role — thus sometimes obstructing a warm mother-daughter relationship from developing. Given her burden some share in the household duties, a girl experienced only daughterhood and was deprived of a carefree childhood which was reserved for boys. The denial of education to girls even among the traditionally literate upper castes which provided mandatory education for boys was another discrimination largely aimed at keeping females submissive and ill informed about their rights.

Systems of Values

Early Marriage

Marriage well before the age of puberty, the girl was sent to her husband's house as soon as she came of age, and the marriage was consummated immediately usually with appropriate ceremonies. The early start of married life followed by early motherhood — sometimes in the early teens and always by the midteens — was physically traumatic, debilitating and injurious upto the point of death. Failure on the wife's part to produce a child — and sometimes failure to produce a son — could jeopardize her position in the marital family and could lead to her being deserted by her husband making it even worse for the women.

Widowhood

Widowhood in some parts of India (notably Bengal and

Rajasthan) lead to the widow's immolation on the funeral pyre of her husband until stopped by British legislation in 1829. In other regions of India and in the castes which did not practise widow immolation, a widow still suffered a social death. Having outlived her main sexual and reproductive function in life, she was made to live a life of sufferance by renouncing all forms of enjoyment and wear drab clothes. She was sometimes physically disfigured (for example, by shaving off her head as in Maharashtra) considered inauspicious and treated as a household drudge. Upper caste widows were forbidden by religion to remarry, even though they were widowed in childhood and even after the Widow Remarriage Act of 1856 made it legally valid, while widowers were encouraged to remarry at once.

Various Types of Violence

The large bulk of the population living in rural areas has not changed much during the last hundred years and still follows some of the customs outlined above. There are occasional female infanticides in small rural pockets in Tamil Nadu and Rajasthan, frequent early marriages (sometimes below the minimum legal limit), early motherhood, inadequate information about the access to family planning methods. Dowry demands and related harassment, as well as wife-battering are rampant. A few incidents of widow immolation have also been reported in the recent past from rural Rajasthan.

Other forms of violence which are passive include inadequate nutrition and health care for girls and women. Many demographers claim that the unbalanced sex ratio in India, showing a female deficit is due to higher mortality among women caused by health neglect. It is alarming that the general proportion of women in the total population is not only unbalanced but also declining consistently, at the Census of 1901 there were 972 females per 1000 males, while in 1991 there was a further drop to 929 females per 1000 males.

Today's Society

At the other extreme is a very small progressive segment in urban upper class Westernized areas where the situation has changed radically and where women enjoy the benefits of education, careers, economic independence and occasionally of political power, although true gender equality still remains an elusive dream.

Somewhere in the middle lies the urban, educated, relatively well-off and partly conventional section of society where the value system is less harshly patriarchal than before, but where gender discrimination and oppression still continue. The undesirability of daughters still remains deeply entrenched in the Indian psyche, and a new form of eliminating girl babies through female foeticide is becoming prevalent through the diagnostic technique of amniocentesis — basically designed for detecting foetal abnormalities — to determine the sex of the foetus, followed by the selective abortion of female foetuses. The practice continues despite the recent legislation to prevent sex-determination and sex-preselection — a telling example of misuse of science. Having enjoyed a childhood relatively free from cares or household duties, the girls are psychologically always being made aware that marriage is their primary career and educational achievements or job-oriented careers are of secondary importance. Marriage takes place after (usually soon after) the age of 18, the minimum legal age at marriage for women, and still tends to be universal. Though now with education and awareness, girls do not want to join the bandwagon of lifelong drudgery. They would rather settle for an identity of their own through entering into an occupation of their choice and stand on their own feet.

Dowry demands are on the rise whether due to increase in registration or in reality is a matter to be studied. Torture of the bride for extorting more money and consumer goods resulting sometimes in death (either through suicide or outright murder by burning camouflaged as an accident while cooking), continue on a large scale in spite of relataively stringent legal provisions. The culprits are rarely arrested more so, rarely convicted.

The chief attribute which earns a woman true respect is motherhood. The pressure to produce sons remains unabated. The wife/mother has to submit to the decisions of her husband or mother-in-law rarely having any say. Even when families are planned and limited, the chief responsibility for contraception rests with the woman, and usually takes the form of sterilization through surgical procedure.

The man takes the back seat — not ready to face any inconvenience — all at the woman's expense. A widow can rarely claim her rightful share in her marital property and continues to be economically dependent.

Sexual Factor

The ever-present threat of sexual violence, by far the most common type of violence against women, similar in all societies covers a wide range. The least serious is "sexual harassment" or Eve-teasing in India (and the offenders labelled indulgently as "roadside Romeos" and glamorized in Hindi movies) though it remains a very humiliating experience for women. It is encountered in public places and on the streets, in the form of wolf whistles, touching, pushing or pawing. In the workplace it may lead to sexual demands from superiors, in rural areas it is village headmen or other powerful men who exert such pressure. More serious is sexual assault which does not technically amount to rape and does not carry a severe penalty. Rape is legally defined in India as involving penetration of the vagina by the penis, thereby revealing the underlying patriarchal assumption that the offence consists in the violation not of the woman's body and personhood but of another man's sexual property. Another way of holding the man on the helm. A male chauvenistic viewpoint.

Other than the physical trauma, there are several frightening aspects related to sexual assault and rape. The stigma attached to the victim rather than the culprit, even when the cultprit is apprehended (which is well-nigh impossible because of the private nature of the offence and the difficulty of proving lack of consent on the woman's part when her own testimony is not considered sufficient) being one aspect. The second aspect is that the victims are not necessarily adult women of a sexually active age group, but can be small babies or old women, a proof that the crime is directed against the entire sex and stems from a view of women *per se* as sex objects.

If a woman is viewed primarily as her husband's property, an effective way of penalizing him is to snatch away or violate his property, that is, his wife. An increasingly common phenomenon in India today is the large-scale violation of women, with rape used as an instrument of revenge upon men, this has been widely experienced in situations of ethnic violence.

Indian society is a mixture of traditional and modern values. On the one hand, we have the belief that women must get education, employment, better health care and more freedom of choice; we also accept their entry into the professions and positions of power (including the prime ministership, the highest office in the country). On the other hand, the basic view of women as inferior and subordinate remains unchanged. Again, the improvement in their status is usually, though not always, more apparent than real and modern technological knowledge and health facilities are sometimes used to the detriment of women. This is the nature of society — a strange blend of tradition and modernity.

Media's Role

Without changing the basic view of women as inferior, servile, self-sacrificing and as essentially instruments of sexual gratification and reproduction, the problem of violence cannot be resolved. The mass media of entertainment is largely responsible for this image. One powerful influence on public opinion is exerted through movies. In a country which is largely poor and illiterate, movies are inevitably an important source of entertainment; and they provide a skillful combination of the woman's traditional role model as the submissive, self-sacrificing, all-forgiving, nurturing wife-mother and the liberated girl who flaunts her bodily attractions to satisfy the common male fantasies. An additional obnoxious feature of popular movies is the depiction of rape as entertainment.

To resolve the problem of women therefore needs a revolutionary change in values, else the problem will continue in their usual and even newer forms.

FIVE

Targets of Violence

The fact that violence against women should have attracted so much attention in recent years may speak for a greater sensitivity to human suffering, a keener sense of the demands of justice in our society. But that such violence should persist, even increase as a backlash as the women's movement gains strength, would indicate that matters are much more complicated. To combat this violence one must first understand it. Here the breakthrough has come with the feminist movement which has been able to conceptualize violence in terms of an inevitable manifestation of the patriarchal system, a system resting on and vesting in the subordination and exploitation of women, a system that is age-old, worldwide and is only beginning to be challenged. One reason why violence against women is so difficult to eradicate is precisely because it is socially sanctioned to some degree. Even today the wife and mother roles are seen as women's primary roles. Thus patriarchy legitimizes women's oppression.

Kinds of Violence

How pervasive and how brutal the violence is proves by the fact that 50 per cent of Canadian women have experienced at least one instance of violence since the age of 16. Around three quarters of the women killed annually in Canada are by the very men they are living with. Many of these killings are of an exceptionally brutal nature and are accompanied by sexual assault, also brutal. Six women are burnt every day on an average in Gujarat. Studies of the violence that is prostitution indicate that it has taken on the dimensions of an industry. It is estimated, for instance, that 2 lakh Nepali women are working in Indian brothels, the largest number of them belonging to the age group of 10 to 14 years. There are numerous instances of the extreme brutality to which young wives are routinely subjected, such as being locked up without food, light or air, being made to stand on one foot, being made to stand with a grind-stone on the head.

The vulnerability of children to sexual abuse and violence also co-exists in society. No place is safe, not the home, the campus, the work-place or the street. No age is safe: infants, old women, paraplegics can all be victims of rape. Several of the victims of rape are children. There are instances of child brides who develop a horror of sex, leading to their abandonment by their much older husbands. It is devastating to note that vulnerability of children in flesh trade. Exposed to infection and violence at the pre-natal stage, forced to sleep at night under the cot of the mother who is presented herself with a chain of clients, they are, if girls, soon forced into the trade and are constantly exposed to the danger of rape. Lori Haskell cites figures demonstrating the revictimization of women abused in childhood, while Julie Lee stress the utter isolation of such a girl child, whom no one believes and whom her own mother will not protect. Jaya Sagade points to some of the factors such as superstition that prompt men to rape a child.

Mass violence against the weaker sections of society, whether on the basis of class, caste, race, religion or gender, frequently takes the form of mass rapes and gang rapes of the women of the targeted group. This amply bears out our contention that violence is a means of asserting power. The dishonouring of the women of the other group is a blow directed at the men, a violation of their property and it is noteworthy how the upper castes, the upper classes and the state machinery act in collusion in the mass rapes of lower class and caste women whenever their community struggles for its rights, whether it be the right to own the lands they till, or the state's decision in favour of positive discrimination in their favour in matters of education and employment. Police harassment of the poor is a routine, which in time of stress, leads to the targeting of one particular community. It is important to draw attention to a recent tendency that is particularly dangerous to the women's movement, the tendency of women themselves to become polarized in terms of community, setting up a dichotomy between 'our' women who are sacred and 'their' women who are fit targets for attack.

World Scenario

Another issue which is of concern is the violence in the form of racial discrimination that is directed against women of colour in Canada along with their men. These women are assigned ill-paid jobs in the unorganized sector which are not commensurate with their qualifications. Women's organizations working with women of colour are reluctant to recommend mandatory arrest for male offenders, since they are keenly aware that the justice system will deal with them much more harshly than with white offenders.

The machinery of the State — the law, the police, the judiciary — has an important role to play in the eradication of violence. There was a mandate given to the Women's Commission recently set up in Maharashtra State to ensure that the Fundamental Rights and Directive Principles of the Indian Constitution which stipulate equality before the law and prohibit discrimination are effectively implemented. The Commission recommends legislation monitors the implementation of existing laws and frames schemes for more effective implementation. It is privileged the authority to investigate complaints and to inspect detention and custodial centres. The Committee has recommended the setting up of vigilance committees and of police cells among other measures.

The Government of Canada has become increasingly conscious of the demands of gender justice, while recent reports revealing the magnitude of violence against women have spurred the consideration of a national action plan aimed at its eradication. Equal opportunity guidelines and policies on affirmative action have already been formulated. The Provincial Government of Ontario has set up the Ontario Women's Directorate under a minister responsible for women's issues. The Directorate has been able to provide funds for support services such as Rape Crisis Centres and a criminalization strategy has been enforced whereby the laying of charges for wife assault becomes mandatory. One goal of the Directorate is the creation of public awareness along with a programme of sensitization of those responsible for law enforcement for which seminars are being organized for crown attorneys and for the judiciary.

The situation in Alberta where a minister for women's issues who totally lacked a feminist perspective went so far as to say that there are no women's issues left and where appointments to commissions are patronage appointments shows clearly the importance of a feminist perspective. Institutionalized power generally perpetuates violence against women, even services such as health and education. And within this general scenario there is marked discrimination against non-whites and lower classes. There have been instances of bitter experience of the reluctance of the government machinery to fund support services.

Disillusionment with regard to the law, the police and the judiciary is widespread among victims and activists. Studies and statistics show how few cases are reported to the police, an activist who studied law in order to be of greater use to women victims, now advises them to avoid going to court. The reasons for this failure of the machinery of redressal are several. In the first place there are lacunae in the law itself. A glaring instance is the rape law in India. In the law, as it stands, a woman has to prove that consent was withheld and the criteria for this are so framed that it becomes virtually impossible for her to prove that her passive submission was not consent. Then again women are ignorant of legal provisions. Hence they do not know that the law offers them protection. Thus, majority of women do not avail themselves of the law regarding maintenance. Nor do they know that certain necessary measures must be taken in time. The medical report required in cases of rape is an instance.

It is reported that the legal system in the case of women represents further victimization, sentences being light and discriminatory, depending on the race of the perpetrator. The system apparently views crimes against property as more serious than crimes against persons, particularly female persons. The humiliation of rape victims in court and the social stigma that is attached to the victim are reasons for the reluctance of girls and women to appeal for justice. There is evidence corroborating the fact that child victims are disbelieved and are humiliated on interrogation. The poor are subjected to persecution by the police which is why they distrust the machinery of the law. The pressure by local bureaucrats and politicians is particularly unchecked in rural areas and small towns and bribes are freely given so that the woman victim ends by finding herself put in the wrong. Similar discriminatory treatment, in this case of non-whites, is observed in Canada.

Several case studies reveal, the reluctance of victims of domestic violence in their dying declarations to implicate their husbands reasons being: The woman often fears retaliation against her children and her parental family in the event of her accusing her husband or in-laws. She also pathetically clings to the notion of a family honour that must be protected. In the absence of such clear evidence it is often difficult to establish that a death by burning is a case of homicide and not a suicide or accident as claimed by the culprits.

The police and judiciary are all the products of the same patriarchal system that subordinates women. Their attitudes to the victims as well as the perpetrators of violence are shaped by patriarchal beliefs. It is small wonder that there is delay in bringing cases to trial and that the accused get away with light sentences. Activists have therefore come to see the need to liaise with the police, while at the same time striving to bring about a change in their attitudes. An attempt in this direction is being made by the cell run by the Tata Institute of Social Sciences at the police headquarters in Mumbai. Since members of the cell are available to assist victims in registering complaints and obtaining legal aid, victims feel assured of competent advice and a following up of the case. As it is backed with the support of police, the cell in its turn carries more weight. The police have collaborated in rushing emergency aid in crises, in recovering *stridhan* (the wealth given by the parental family to the bride, which is to be treated as her property, not that of her husband) and in obtaining custody of children. Training for police personnel has also been organized in which they are given information regarding the law as well as trained in sympathetic interviewing and investigation. Ultimately it is only a strong women's movement that can galvanize the state machinery into action, change deeply-entrenched social attitudes and provides a safe space and redressal for individual victims. Such a movement gathers strength through organizing study circles to create feminist awareness among women, pressing for changes in legislation, banding women together in mass campaigns imparting awareness in society through pamphlets, posters, songs, street plays and films. The play "A Girl Child is Born", produced by Sharada Sathe's organization, was enacted before large audiences of women all over Maharashtra and sharply brought home to them that the many instances of denial and oppression they had lived through were part of the lot of the girl child in patriarchy.

Research has proved that small determined groups can, in the face of the discouragement and hostility, step by step, build up their services so as to provide a centre for counselling and redressal, a crisis line, access to a safe space. During the worst communal riots in Ahmedabad, it was a women's organization which protested arrests, registered cases, set up night vigilance committees, nursed the injured. In a rare demonstration of courage, a group of women could intervene in a case of rape by accosting the perpetrator. Demonstrations in support of individual victims have been able at least in some cases to press for justice for victims of rape and domestic violence in rural Gujarat and this gives them encouragement. The home for prostitute's children in Pune run by Vijaya Lavate's organization has given these most vulnerable children a chance to have a normal childhood.

Counselling services also provide a great support to victims of violence. All of them stress that a sympathetic hearing brings immense relief to a woman who has hitherto been disbelieved and belittled. Even centres which lack trained workers, such as the student centre at McGill University in Montreal can offer this service, while directing the women to other centres which are staffed by experienced professional counsellors. The stages through which counselling must proceed if it is to lead to resocialization are: in the beginning women learn to identify controlling behaviour and to understand at the impact of violence on themselves and their children. Later they are led to question the patriarchal system itself, which represents a challenge to deeply-embedded cultural and social beliefs. They also undertake the counselling of perpetrators of violence. The object is to make them realize that an act of violence is a conscious choice made by themselves, that they cannot push away the responsibility.

The counselling of children is again skilled task, whether they are themselves victims or are witnesses to violence directed against their mothers.

Activists are acutely aware that without a shelter where women are safe from their persecutors, what they can achieve for these women will always be limited. For want of a shelter there is often no alternative but to work for a compromise and run the risk of sending the woman to her death. There are two major drawbacks of the existing shelters run by government or by charitable organizations lacking a feminist perspective. These will generally not accept children above a certain age and they also confine the women to the premises. Hence many women who can make no alternative arrangement for the children and who must work to support themselves cannot avail themselves of their facilities.

Women in India, however, can draw encouragement from the fact that it was only after a long struggle and much disappointment that these shelters could be established and similarly their own efforts too will, in time, bear fruit. One notes also to what extent can be done even in the absence of a full-time shelter. When the shelter in Kenora (Canada) had to close down for a length of time for lack of funds, members sheltered women in their own homes, accompanied them to the police, the courts and hospitals and operated a crisis line.

Dilemmas and differences of approach do exist even among feminist workers struggling to combat violence. There is a tendency among some to avoid involvement with the police and courts, whereas others take the view that these too serve a purpose. Sharp differences of opinion exist on whether an organization should clearly declare that it is feminist in aims and outlook or should refrain from doing so to avoid alienating some sections of women. For instance, there are several diametrically opposed attitudes to prostitution. Among feminists there are those who see it as a choice of profession by the individual woman which must be respected, while others stress the fact that large numbers of women are not only forced through poverty to turn to prostitution but are literally forced into it, having been sold or abducted. They are then faced with a dilemma: how can they reconcile their support for these women in their struggle for better treatment without condoning prostitution as an institution?

In spite of such differences, their commitment to the cause of women has led women's organizations to network and to fight shoulder to shoulder on issues of common concern. But not all these organizations have a specifically feminist commitment. It is only such a commitment that can take them beyond individual issues and lead them to challenge patriarchy as a system for reaching the desired results.

SIX

Facing Violence

Women are victimized in many ways through overwork, undernourishment and ill treatment, having no say in any matter. It is for us to investigate into the attitude of indifference prevailing in our society and ensure justice and equitable status for them.

Factors which attribute this indifference are: Lack of awareness of seriousness of the problem, general acceptance of man's superiority over woman being the reason why violence against women was not viewed as violent or deviant, and the denial of violence by women themselves owing to their religious values and socio-cultural attitudes. As the cases of wife-battering, rapes, kidnappings and abductions, intra-familial murders, dowry-deaths, eve-teasing, molestation, etc., have been more frequently reported since the late 1960s and early 1970s, the issue of violence against women has been transformed from a private issue into a public problem.

Fundamental Problem

We should focus our study on interpersonal relations and the social context in which violence is committed or atrocities are inflicted on women and in which the victim recovers and adjusts. All these issues have to be examined and assessed with a sociological perspective. The present study presents not only the conceptual perspectives with which to understand the problem but also analyses the socio-cultural and interpersonal determinants of violence, shock, and recovery.

It may be true that the incidence of violence by men towards women is not identical in all groups and communities, and that moral and social beliefs and family arrangements differ from group to group, yet instead of looking into these group differences and analyzing the subcultural and socio-ethical beliefs of these groups, we should concentrate on violence against women as perceived in general terms. There is no woman who has not suffered at one time or another the harassment, humiliation, exploitation and violence that shadows her sex. A woman's life swings between pleasure at one end and danger at the other end. In daily life, women are routinely defined by sex, and even if not all men are potential kidnappers, rapists, batterers, molesters and torturers of women, all women are potential victims.

Position of Women

Women in India are way ahead of their counterparts elsewhere in the matter of social legislation. However, in matters of implementation of laws granting rights to women we have been lagging far behind. Women are discriminated against at work and are denied their due in every field. At home, they are ever worse off, being reduced to slavish drudges and maltreated in a hundred different ways. Constantly rebuked and mocked at, frequently bullied, sometimes assaulted, and occasionally burnt to death, they remain victims in every role. Indian women, thus, have been described as the underdogs of society where, in theory the law of equality exists, and women are considered to be on a par with their male counterparts, but in reality, men remain all powerful and thrive at the expense of women. While in the West, women's problem/issue is mostly one of identity, job equality, and sexual roles, in India, the question is simply one of stark survival.

The Constitution of India guarantees equality, freedom, opportunity and protection to women, and various social legislations give them several exclusive rights. Yet, they enjoy an unequal status. This may be due to the social conditions in our society like illiteracy, poverty, social customs, ignorance, and lack of awareness of rights, while others relate it with their personality characteristics like feeling of helplessness, inferiority complex, poor self-image, lack of self-confidence, self-reliance, and resourcefulness. Added to these is their unrecognized output in domestic chores and help to male family members in their economic pursuits.

Recently, incidents of aggressive violence against women are reported to be escalating alarmingly in our country, and this in itself is a sufficient cause for growing concern, and on the other hand, awareness of rights among women has increased, leading to the rise of feminist movement, resulting in a new sensitivity to all forms of subjugation of women by men. Rise in the rate of crimes against women have been reported in all types of crimes—ranging from eve-teasing to abduction and killing. Such trend has been seen in other crimes too. The number of registered cases having spiralled alarmingly in the past few years, the actual number of cases reported is estimated to be many times more than the number registered. In cases like rape, it may be even 15 to 20 times more—large number of rape, assault, and battering cases being marginalized due to social pressures.

Crime Staistics

Let us first have a glance at the background material for general issues in some important categories of violence against women.

Strangely, no statistics on crimes against women were collected separately by the Ministry of Home Affairs or the Police Research Bureau till 1988. It was only in 1989 that data relating to crimes against women began to be collected. These data relate to: (a) incidence of crimes committed, (b) number of persons arrested, (c) cases disposed of by the police/courts, and (d) social background of victims.

Categories of Offences

Crimes against women are broadly classified under two categories:

(A) crimes identified under the Indian Penal Code (IPC) and
(B) crimes identified under the special laws (SL).

The crimes under the former category include eight types:

(i) rape (section 376 IPC),
(ii) kidnapping and abduction (section 363 and 373),
(iii) dowry homicides (section 302 and 304B),
(iv) torture—physical and mental (section 498A),
(v) molestation (section 354),
(vi) eve-teasing or sexual harassment (section 509),
(vii) importation of girls (section 366B), and
(viii) murder (other than dowry homicides) (section 302).

The crimes under the last category includes four types:

(a) immoral trafficking (1956 Act),

(b) demanding dowry (1961 Act),

(c) commission of *sati* (1987 Act), and

(d) indecent representation of women (1986 Act).

Statistics of Women's Crimes under Law

On the total crimes committed in India under the IPC every year, about 6 per cent are crimes against women. In 1995, of the total crimes committed under the IPC (16.95 lakhs), 6.3 per cent were crimes against women (*Crime in India*, 1995: 223). Taking the total crimes against women recorded under the IPC and the SL, 8 per cent were Local and Special Laws cases and 92 per cent were IPC cases.

The statistics collected point out that the total number of crimes against women (under the IPC and the SL) (excluding murders) increased from 68,000 in 1990 to 74,000 in 1991, 79,000 in 1992, 84,000 in 1993, 99,000 in 1994 and 106,000 in 1995 (*Crime in India*, 1995: 223). Thus, in five years (between 1991 and 1995), crimes against women increased by 45 per cent.

Break-up

Of the crimes against women committed in 1995 under the IPC and the SL (1,06,471), about 29 per cent are torture cases, 27 per cent are molestation cases, 13 per cent are kidnapping and abduction cases, 13 per cent are rape cases, 4.5 per cent are sexual harassment cases, 8 per cent are immoral traffic cases, 5 per cent are dowry-homicide cases, and 0.5 per cent are other cases (*Ibid:* 222). Broadly speaking, every year, under the IPC, there are about 31,000 torture cases (cruelty by husband and other relatives), 28,000 molestation cases, 14,000 kidnapping and abduction cases, 14,000 rape cases, 5,000 eve-teasing cases, and 5,000 dowry-homicide cases (*Ibid:* 222). Likewise under the SL, there are about 7,500 cases of woman trafficking, 2,800 cases of dowry harassment, 400 cases of indecent representation of women, and 170 cases of importing of girls, and one or two *sati* cases.

All India Ranking of Crime

The highest recorded cases of crime are from Maharashtra

(15.3%) followed by Madhya Pradesh (14.4%), Uttar Pradesh (11.2%), Rajasthan (8.8%), Andhra Pradesh (8.5%), Tamil Nadu (8.2%) and West Bengal (6%). Of the 1,06,471 recorded cases in 1995 (under IPC and SL) in the country.

Rajasthan: In Rajasthan, the incidence of crimes against women has sharply increased since 1994. Many committed by influential and moneyed people who could manipulate things in their favour namely — the Shalini Sharma sex scandal of Alwar; the throwing of acid on Shivani Jadeja in Jaipur; the J.C. Bose (Rajasthan University) Hostel gang rape of a girl by seven persons (including the nephew of a minister, an advocate and a police officer); the alleged rape of a woman in Jalore district by a Jain monk who later committed suicide; and the Chomu firing case over the issue of a woman's rape are some of the more serious examples of increasing crime. A point worth noting is that in all these cases, the women involved were blamed and held responsible through manipulation. Rajasthan thus being designated as Rapisthan.

Orissa: In Orissa also, atrocities on women have been similarly on the rise since 1991. Rape cases have registered an alarming increase of about 33 per cent every year. While in 1991, 309 rape cases were registered, their number had gone up to 372 in 1995 and 617 in 1996. Dowry-homicides in the state rose from 98 in 1991 to 169 in 1995 and 354 in 1996, and dowry torture cases from 214 in 1991 to 710 in 1996. The torture of women (not for dowry) was also on the rise with such cases increasing from 183 in 1991 to 361 in 1995 and 405 in 1996. The kidnapping of women increased from 209 in 1991 to 221 in 1995 (*The Hindustan Times*, March 11, 1997).

Delhi: The Delhi figures of crimes against women, as revealed in the latest data issued by the Delhi State Commission for Women are simply shocking wherein *Situation of Girls and Women in Delhi*, Delhi's record in rape cases was twice as bad as that of all the three metropolitan cities (Mumbai, Chennai and Kolkata) put together. That the rate of crimes against women in the capital was far higher than that of the national average (34.1 per lakh of population against 9.5) represented one part of the problem. The alarming aspect was that minor girls were particularly targeted as victims. The incidence of rape cases involving girls below 10 years of age in Delhi was four times higher than that of the rest of the country. What was even more shocking, was the fact that crime in 88 per cent of the cases was committed by relatives or acquaintances, and in 89 per cent of the cases, it was committed at home. The problem thus goes out of the control of police or law and order. It underlines a psychopathic condition (*The Hindustan Times*, March 5, 1997).

Violence, Categorised

There are six categories of violence: sexual violence, kidnapping and abduction, dowry deaths, murder, wife-battering, and a few other specific categories of violence like torture, molestation, etc. These have been discussed in the following pages:

(i) Sexual Violence

Rape

Virginity is valued by man, yet it is man who violates it and commits rape. The important factors in rape are: age, consent (including implied consent and obtaining consent under fraudulent pretext of marriage), duress, state of mind and resistance. Section 376 of the Indian Penal Code describes rape as sex with a woman against her will, or without her consent, or with her consent when the man knows that he is not her husband but she believes him as her husband, or with or without her consent when she is under sixteen years of age. Statistics on rape worldwide show that in the United States, the annual rate of rape offences is about 26, in Canada 8, and in the UK 5.4 per one lakh of total population against 1.38 in India, 3.62 in China and 1.29 in Japan.

There are fewer cases of rape in India as compared to the West. The number of rape cases per one lakh population in 1993 was only 0.5. However, in the last decade, rape cases were more than doubled. Of the 13,754 rape victims reported in 1995, 5.4 per cent were below 10 years, 24.1 per cent between 10 and 16 years, 56.3 per cent between 16 and 30 years, and 14.2 per cent were 30 years and above (*Ibid:* 226). The highest number of rape cases in 1995 was reported from Madhya Pradesh (22.7%), followed by Uttar Pradesh (13.1%), Maharashtra (9.9%), Bihar (9.5%), Rajasthan (7.5%), Andhra Pradesh (6.2%), West Bengal (5.7%), Assam (4.3%) and 21.1 per cent from other states and union territories (*Ibid:* 237).

Causes of Escalation

Though it is difficult to indicate the causes of increase in the incidence of this crime, some factors which appear to have an impact on the conservative social morals and on the increasing rate of rape could be identified as :

(i) urbanization and urbanism;

(ii) industrialization and the growth of slums;

(iii) better reporting by the police;

(iv) co-education and co-work;

(v) movies, obscene and pornographic literature;

(vi) changing attitudes towards women;

(vii) decreasing religious restrictions;

(viii) fall in moral values; and

(ix) emergence of the neo-rich people.

It should be clear that these figures do not reveal the true picture. A high percentage of rape cases go unreported either because the victim does not dare to face the shame and humiliation being heaped on her by society, or because of the disgrace it will bring to her family, or because of the police harassment, or threats and consequences by the rapist. Many cases are put behind the action. It is not only the illiterate and the poor but also the educated and the socially advanced victims of rape who are rejected by their own families, and at times forced to take up the oldest profession. Some victims even commit suicide. Social values turn them into outcastes, a disgrace to their family, and unfit to marry. No wonder, therefore, most victims choose to conceal the fact of having been victims of forcible criminal assault.

Instances

Shamim (real name concealed), a Muslim girl of seven years, was brutally assaulted in Jandhera village near Meerut in 1994 by a 20-year-old truck-driver, a Dalit from the same village. Shamim's mother, accompanied by two policemen, took the traumatized girl to a hospital in Meerut. The little girl had to be operated upon because of which the doctors said, she would never be able to conceive. The case was brought to the notice of a women's organization—Disha—which got her admitted to a hospital in Saharanpur. The rapist was arrested but soon released on bail. He has since been boasting that "in a state where the Dalits reign supreme (Mayawati at that time was the Chief Minister), no one can touch him". He even went to the extent of taunting Shamim's mother: "Shamim is like the *ber* fruit that can be eaten when it is unripe or when it has ripened." The district magistrate had assured a home to Shamim's homeless family but the assurance remained only on paper. For obvious reasons, the villagers dared not throw the rapist out of the village.

Another instance is, a five-year-old girl who was raped in Pehalwan village in Rajasthan by a shop-owner and his servant. The mother was so traumatized by the incident that she became insane and the father committed suicide. The little girl, who was the butt of cruel jokes and taunts in the village, was moved to an *ashram* in Jaipur.

There is a case of two school teachers, 57 and 52 years old, were suspended and arrested for rape/molestation of three school girls of 12, 13 and 14 years in May 1997 in Uttar Pradesh. They were released on bail by the sessions court which maintained that the medical records did not show rape. It so happened that the teachers had taken the girls to school for coaching in view of the forthcoming school examination. They stayed overnight in the school building. Each child was given five tablets in the night. As fate would have it one child did not take any tablet but the other two took two to three tablets. Two girls were found unconscious in the morning and one was bleeding. They were rushed to a doctor, the husband of an 'anganwadi' worker informed the incident to the parents. The villagers beat up the teachers and rushed the children to a hospital in Saharanpur. After the intervention of the National Commission for Women, the teachers were arrested and suspended. The teachers brought to bear tremendous pressure on the parents to take back the cases. Are these girls to become 'Phoolans' to take revenge?

The Vulnerable Sections

The girls belonging to socially deprived classes are not only inclined to be raped, the women employees belonging to socially advanced classes are sexually humiliated and exploited by their employers and thus are equally under the category of possible victims. Similar treatment is meted out to the inmates by the superintendents of hostels, to patients by hospital personnel, to maid-servants by their masters, and to wage-earners by contractors and middlemen. Even the deaf and dumb, lunatics, blind women and beggars are not spared. Women who come from the lower-middle class and who are the main supporters of their families bear sexual abuse silently as a part of life. The reason makes the incidents of rape increase. As culprits are not punished.

At times it is felt that the stories of rape are exaggerated. Women have to deal with these opinions and attitudes as well as with the age-old myths, such as, "a woman cannot be raped unless she wants it". These myths have been coined and propagated by men, for every woman knows that none of these are true, as in India rape is tantamount to death.

The victims are socially ostracized facing disgrace and suffer serious guilt-pangs and personality disorders as a consequence. When pregnancies result from forced rape, all the outraged sentiments of the community are vented on the women. Children are also stigmatized unless their parents marry them, or they are fortunate enough to be adopted into homes sanctified by marriage.

What is the character of rapists? Are they abnormal sexual perverts or ordinary normal men found in all walks of life? Social scientists' contend that by and large they are normal men. A large number of rapes are situational rapes. Criminal assault is instrumental for men either to exploit women or to take revenge. In villages, it is a tool in the hands of the landlords to terrorize their agricultural labourers. One survey on prostitution has revealed that 80 per cent of the prostitutes took up the profession after becoming victims of rape.

Protection by Law for Women at Work

Sexual harassment of women at the workplace is also becoming a serious problem day by day. Public interest petitions were filed in the Supreme Court in 1997 by social activists and NGOs to ensure that women be allowed to work freely and with dignity. The Supreme Court directed the centre and the state governments to enforce twelve guidelines to protect women from harassment at the workplace under which it shall be the duty of the employer or other responsible persons in workplaces to prevent the commission of acts of sexual harassment and provide procedures for the resolution, settlement or prosecution of acts of sexual harassment by taking all relevant steps.

Sexual harassment in workplaces, according to the Supreme Court, includes (*Sunday*, September 28-October 4, 1997):

(i) physical intimacy and advances;

(ii) a demand or request for sexual favours;

(iii) sexually tainted remarks;

(iv) showing porn material to women employees; and

(v) any verbal or non-verbal conduct of sexual nature.

Complaints and Redressals

There has been a great increase in harassment incidence with more women coming out to work. Between 1992 and 1997, of the total complaints (1817) received by the National Commission for Women, as many as 49 were of sexual harassment at the workplace. A sample survey done by the Delhi-based NGO—Sakshi—among women in the private sector has revealed that 60 per cent of the respondents had at some time or other been victims of sexual harassment and that in almost half the cases, a superior was responsible for the harassment (*The Hindustan Times*, September 21, 1997). Most working women have come to regard sexual harassment as an 'occupational hazard' and society in general believes it is 'normal male behaviour'. In its milder form, sexual harassment is generally abstract and therefore hard to prove. There is no evidence, for instance, of a whispered remark, an obscene sound, or just plain ogling can be provided unless it is persistent and repeated and witnesses are available. The humiliation can be as intimidating, embarassing and annoying as being pinched, shoved or solicited by a stranger. In a survey conducted by Sakshi, 46per cent of the victims chose to do nothing about it because they feared they would not be believed or because of the worry that by complaining they would invite allegations of "taking revenge on male colleagues for relationships besmirched".

Myra Dias who was secretary to the Regional Manager (Western region) of Vayudoot Ltd. was subjected to sexual harassment by the Regional Manager and when she did not yield to his advances, he ensured that she was superseded by her juniors. Myra refused to be cowed down. She appealed to the National Commission for Women who took up the issue and after a six-month battle she was upgraded. Myra's case was an exception. She was brave enough to take up the issue and what is more important is that she won. Less fortunate was Ela Chaudhary, a commercial artist in the Government Directorate of Employment and Training: Ela was molested by her immediate boss. Her complaints to the Director General were of no avail. Counter allegations were made against her like having tampered with the attendance register, etc. Ela took the case to the courts and after an eight-year battle, the remarks in her confidential file were expunged. But it was only after her boss retired that she got justice and her stand was vindicated. Somehow the department delayed the procedure because they wanted him to retire with a clean record (*The Hindustan Times*, September 2, 1997).

The Unorganized Sector

Providing protection against sexual harassment may be possible in the organized sector, both in private and government offices, but what about women in unorganized sectors and in rural areas? For example, take the case of domestic female workers or maid-servants or female labourers tilling the land. These women are extremely vulnerable to advances and, having little power to fight such attempts, end up being sexually abused. Caste factor poses another threat. When employees belonging to lower castes are harassed more than those belonging to other castes. In villages, the power structure is controlled by the dominant class. The nexus between the political head of a village and the moneyed gentry is impregnable. Any attempt to quash its stranglehold over the villagers finds with strong resistance.

The court directives to create awareness among women may be used by NGOs. But what about the harassment which female volunteers with NGOs themselves face carrying out their work? Bhanwari Devi, a Sathin in Rajasthan, displeased many upper caste people for trying to prevent child marriage in her village. She was raped as a punishment. And, of course, her rapists were acquitted by the court.

Eventhough the Supreme Court directives on sexual harassment of women in their workplaces may be well intentioned, they do not appear to be practical. Unless the socio-economic ethos undergoes change, unless women themselves show courage, social legislation is likely to fail to make a difference to the life of those who face the danger of sexual harassment. Trade unions can play a significant role by encouraging women to report cases of sexual harassment and then standing by them. Men should also be sensitized and re-educated. Most of men appreciate and recognize the need for laws and change. Men must be subjected to introspection and to look at the problem in their own context as husbands, employers and colleagues. There is also the tendency to dismiss it as a Western input even though it is very much a part of our own male dominated system.The whole matter should be looked at in the Indian context.

(ii) Kidnapping and Abduction

Definitions (under IPC)

Kidnapping (under section 363 of IPC) is taking away or enticing a minor—a female of less than 18 years and a male of less than 16 years of age—without the consent of the lawful guardian.

Abduction (under section 363 of IPC) is forcibly, fraudulently or deceitfully taking away a woman with the intent of seducing her to illicit sex or compelling her to marry a person against her will. Thus 'abduction' differs from 'kidnapping' whereas the latter is committed only in respect of a minor, the former is committed in respect of any person. In kidnapping, the victim's consent is immaterial but in abduction, the victim's free and voluntary consent condones the crime. In kidnapping, the offenders' intent is irrelevant but in abduction, it is an all-important factor. Thus, a girl of 18 and above could only be abducted and not kidnapped; but if she is under 18, she could be kidnapped as well as abducted.

Statistics

The incidents of kidnapping and abduction like rape have been increasing in our country by leaps and bounds. The total number of cases recorded in 1990 was 11,699 which increased to 14,063 in 1995 (*Crime in India*, 1995:237). The highest number of kidnapping and abduction cases in 1995 was found in Rajasthan

(2,579 out of 14,063 or 18.3%) followed by Uttar Pradesh (16.6%), Assam (7.9%), Madhya Pradesh (7.3%), Gujarat (6.9%), West Bengal (5.8%), Maharashtra (5.6%), Andhra Pradesh (4.8%), and Tamil Nadu (4.7%) (*Ibid:* 237). The rate of this crime per one lakh of population is 2 in our country.

Reports of poor girls being abducted and sold either as wives to rich Arabs or as potential prostitutes to pimps are not unknown. A broker is reported to get from Rs. 5,000 to Rs. 10,000 per girl/woman, and sometimes even more if he caters to every whim and fancy of the prospective customer depending on his economic status. A large number of liaison men and agents are reported operating in big cities. Significantly, the Report of the UN Human Rights Panel has pointed out that the phenomenon—child/girl/woman prostitution—has taken an uglier form in India. The sale of unsuspecting innocent children/girls/women brought from remote tribal areas and villages feeding the big metropolises and other towns and cities has increased.

The number of abducted girls and women rescued is woefully small. Some rescued ones are siphoned into the Protection and Correctional Homes. The conditions at Delhi and Agra Nari Niketans which were pursuing flesh trade within their compounds were exposed by the Supreme Court.

(iii) Dowry Deaths

The Dowry Prohibition Act, 1961 has banned the practice of dowry, but in reality all that the law has done is to recognize that the problem exists. It is not often that we hear of a husband or his family being sued for insisting on taking a dowry. If anything, the demands for dowry have escalated over the years along with dowry-deaths.

All India Statistics

At a modest estimate, the figure for deaths in India that occur due to non-payment or partial payment of dowry could be placed around 5,000 for one year. The total number of deaths was 4,836 in 1990, 5,817 in 1993, 4,935 in 1994, and 5,092 in 1995 (Ibid: 222). The highest number of cases in 1995 was found in Uttar Pradesh (36.3 per cent), followed by Maharashtra (9.2 per cent), Bihar (7.5 per cent), Rajasthan (7.2 per cent), Andhra Pradesh (7.1 per cent),

Haryana (4.3 per cent), Karnataka (4 per cent) and West Bengal (1.7 per cent) (*Ibid:* 237). Under the Dowry Prohibition Act (SL), the number of cases registered in 1990 was 2,155 which increased to 2,679 in 1993 and 2,814 in 1995. Bulk of cases in 1995 were reported from Bihar (982), Uttar Pradesh (653) and Karnataka (337) (*Ibid:* 230).

The Dowry Act, 1961 states that dowry is a bailable and non-cognizable offence and ceases to be recognized if demands are made or met one year after marriage. Most dowry-homicides occur in the privacy of the husband's house and with the collusion of the family members. The inability to convict anyone for lack of proof is therefore a natural concomitant. Sometimes, the police are so callous in conducting investigations that even the courts cast a serious reflection on the efficiency and integrity of the police authorities.

The figures of dowry deaths assuming a large number of unreported deaths are as it is unnerving — leave alone if all figures were included. Having their origins in social, economic and psychological factors, too deep-rooted to be tackled by amending the law their genesis lies in the tension created by persistent demands, accompanied by torture, for dowry. The greed for money, the aggressiveness increased by resistance and the ease with which the weaker sex can be exploited, all combine to encourage family members to take the bride's life.

(iv) Murders of Women

Though all-India figures pertaining to murders and their victims on the basis of sex are unavailable, it is well known that the number of female victims of homicides in comparison to male victims is low. Whereas in the United States, female victims comprise between 20 per cent and 25 per cent of the total victims of homicides (about 25,000 to 30,000 every year), in India of about 38,000 murders committed every year, women constitute about 10 per cent to 15 per cent of the total victims.

Reasons

Being inspired by many factors, such as illicit relations, petty quarrels, feeling of revenge, the desire to get rid of a person who is to get a share in the property, and so forth, many murders may be disguised as suicides and some are even called 'accidents', as if they are natural deaths in some epidemic.

At times, the victim is believed to be a major contributor to the criminal act. She perpetrates the murder either by her habit of constant nagging, or her illict relations with some other male, or by completely ignoring her husband's or her in-laws' advice, and so forth. The victim may provoke a person into attack, and though the provocation may be slight, if perceived by an egoistic attacker, it may be sufficient to result in homicide. The analysis of the victim-offender relationship in such homicides is, therefore, considered necessary in criminological literature.

Redressals

The inability of the kith and kin of the victim to get redressal through courts is a common occurrence. This is due to notoriously long-winded legal procedures and the offender's social and economic status prevents it.

Women's organizations have been galvanized with the rising curve of murders and other crimes against women. The realization has come amongst women that the individual protests are not strong enough to enable them to fight against their collective oppression. They have started forming forums and associations. Moreover the government also keeps on amending the social laws pertaining to marriage and family from time to time. But will the women's voluntary organizations and the government's legislative measures reduce women's oppression. Solving the problem of violence against women is a matter of introspection. What social measures need to be adopted to tackle this problem? These are some of the issues that need our immediate attention.

Torturing Women

There can be nothing more shattering for a woman than being battered by a husband who is supposed to love her and look after her and whom she trusted the most. Ranging from slaps, kick to breaking of bones this includes violence torture, attempted murder, and even murder itself. The violence may be related to drunkenesss sometimes but not always. It may also be related to demands for sex, a refusal to obey the husband's commands, extravagance, habit of using vile and disgusting language, and so forth. Battering being occasional or frequent. It may be as frequent as once or twice a week, once or twice a month, or three to four times in a year. In some marital relationships, battering may begin soon after the marriage while, in others it may begin one or two years after marriage. Some wives are held captive by the husbands who insist on controlling their every movement, and knowing every detail of their lives.

Redressals

The Indian cultural system rarely gives examples of a wife reporting to the police of having been battered by her husband. Preferring to suffer humiliation in silence, she takes it as her destiny and does not revolt, due to the fear that her own parents would refuse to accept her in their house permanently after the marriage. It is not always the poor and the illiterate who are battered but even the rich and highly educated are similarly undergone to these sort of ordeal by their husbands. Likewise, even those women who earn and are economically independent also face violence.

Male violence crosses class boundaries and has no association with poverty or lack of education. The common public image of the battering husband is of a working-class male. As wife battering is concealed from the public eye, it is difficult to estimate its extent in society. Since divorce cases in the courts are not always related to marital violence, the extent of divorce also does not reveal the nature and extent of wife battering in society. The battered victims and the indignation they face pose a serious problem for society. There is great need to create an awareness for the scientific study of the problem of domestic violence for ascertaining its intensity.

Other Categories

Torture

Torture of women includes cruelty by husband, in-laws, parents, siblings and relatives. Among crimes reported against women in India, incidence of torture is the highest. Of the total crimes against women (1,06,471) reported in 1995, 29.2 per cent were cases of torture (*Crime in India*, 1995: 222). In a survey, Maharashtra had the highest number of torture cases (28.1 per cent), followed by West Bengal (10.7 per cent), Rajasthan (10.3 per cent), Uttar Pradesh (10.2 per cent), Andhra Pradesh (9.1 per cent), Madhya Pradesh (8.5 per cent) and Gujarat (6.2 per cent) (*Ibid:* 237). Generally, husbands and in-laws are more accused of torture cases, but an exceptional case from Rajasthan in October 1997 shows that brothers and fathers also torture their sisters and daughters. Here, a girl of 22 years was locked in a dark room by her brother for more than two years for her refusal to live with her husband after the marriage. When ultimately the case was reported by a neighbour to the police, she was rescued and admitted to a hospital in Jaipur. The brother and the father of the victim were not arrested till two months after detecting the case.

Molestation

Molestation after torture, is another major crime against women. This constitutes 25 per cent of the total crimes committed against women in our country. While the total number of molestation cases in 1990, 1991, 1992 and 1993 ranged between 20,000 and 21,000, the number increased to 24,117 in 1994 and 28,475 in 1995. The rate of this crime in 1995 was the highest in Madhya Pradesh (25.8 per cent), followed by Maharashtra (12.2 per cent), Andhra Pradesh (9.4 per cent), Uttar Pradesh (9.2 per cent), Rajasthan (7.4 per cent), and West Bengal (4.6 per cent) (*Ibid:* 238) thus accounting for about 70 per cent of the reported cases.

Eve teasing

Eve teasing or sexual harassment is widely prevalent in India. While the total number of these cases was 8,620 in 1990, their number increased to 12,009 in 1993 but decreased to 10,496 in 1994 and 4,756 in 1995. The highest crime rate in 1995 was reported from Tamil Nadu (22.7 per cent), followed by Maharashtra (17 per cent), Andhra Pradesh (16.2 per cent) and Madhya Pradesh (16.1 per cent) (*Ibid:* 238).

Importation of girls

Importation of girls is an insignificant crime in our country. Only 167 cases were reported in 1994 and 191 in 1995. Still the police has to be concerned about this crime. About 80 per cent of the total cases of this crime occurred in the following six states—Andhra Pradesh (33.5 per cent), Punjab (14.1 per cent), Gujarat (11 per cent),

Madhya Pradesh (8.9 per cent), Maharashtra (6.8 per cent), and West Bengal (6.3 per cent).

Violence: Concept and Definition

An aspect of power dynamics of social situations 'violence' is not simply aggression or injury committed by one individual (man) against another (woman); it is more precisely the abuse of power; it is a behaviour in which a more powerful person takes advantage of and abuses a less powerful one. This relationship of power differential is clear in sexual violence against women (rape), in their kidnapping and abduction, in physical battering of wives, as well as in dowry deaths and murder of women. In rape, either a man in authority position victimizes a girl in a subordinate position or a male takes advantage of his physical power and assaults a female. In wife battering, a similar principle of the stronger victimizing the weaker operates. High risk category include women who have less power by virtue of not being an earning member, by virtue of being excluded from participation in decision-making because of being considered socially immature, and by virtue of having no education or less education than her husband. This underlies the need for research in the dynamics of power and how it operates in and outside family.

Violence: Consequences

Violence has been defined as "injurious and destructive behaviour which damages the victim physically, mentally and/or financially". The three consequences of 'violent behaviour' are: (a) pain to victim, (b) social disapproval and public concern, and (c) realising the need for enacting legislation. That violence against women generally occurs in the privacy of the home or in the privacy of the working places or in the institutions away from the public eye sharply reduces the likelihood of a complaint.

Crime Against Women

'Crime against women' refers to crimes in which a woman becomes victim. The phrase contains two terms, viz., 'crime' and 'against women'. While the latter term refers only to those crimes in which the victim is female, the former term is meant by the acts which are legally forbidden, intentionally committed and punishable by courts. If we use the definition of crime as "conduct which incurs the formal punitive pronouncements of the courts", or that crime is "the violation of conduct norms of the normative groups", the scope (of crime) becomes broader and more meaningful vis-a-vis violence against women.

Aggression

'Aggression' refers to injurious behaviour. BUSS (*The Psychology of Aggression*, 1961) defines it as "a response that delivers noxious stimuli to another person". Berkowitz used the term to denote "behaviour aimed at the injury of some object". Many issues cloud the definition of aggression.

Intention

Is injury to the victim the goal of the perpetrator, or is such injury a by-product of some other goal-seeking behaviour? This issue of intention centres on two things:

(a) whether the perpetrator had a reasonable expectation that his behaviour would injure the victim, and

(b) whether such injury was in fact desired by the offender.

Kaufmann (*Aggression and Altruism*, 1970) opine that unless the person performing, he/she had some expectation that the behaviour would deliver noxious stimulation to the recipient the act would not be considered aggressive. Berkowitz maintained that for an act to be considered aggressive, the injury to the victim had to be reinforcing.

Injury

Another issue is, whether the injury need be only physical or whether there can be psychological injury too. Those definitions which limit aggression to acts that physically injure the victims have the advantage of being precise and operational. Psychological injury refers to disparagement, scolding, coercion, harassment, and a variety of other non-physical agonistic behaviour.

Buss distinguished 'angry aggression' behaviour that is reinforced by pain or injury to the victim, from 'instrumental aggression' in which aggression is a means to an end. Delivery of electric shock or verbal criticism are two milder forms of instrumental aggression.

Aggression Vs. Violence

The term 'violence' may be used for more extreme forms of aggressive behaviour that are likely to cause significant injuries to the victim. Although violence refers to physical aggression, it is also applied to psychological stress that causes suffering or trauma. Broadly, the term 'violence' has been applied to the narrow issue of physically striking an individual (Kempe, 1982) and causing injury (Gil, 1970), to the act of striking a person with the intent of causing harm or injury but not actually causing it (Gelles and Strauss, 1979), to the act where there is the high potential of causing injury, and to the act where there is no actual hitting at all, such as verbal abuse or psychological and emotional violence.

Megargee (1982) has defined violence as the "overtly threatened or overtly accomplished application of force which results in the injury or destruction of persons or property or reputation".

Where does one draw the line between aggression and violence? The rapist, for example, uses coercion to obtain sexual advantage over a non-consenting victim. When that coercion involves the overt or threatened use of physical force, it clearly constitutes violence. But what of psychological coercion? A husband may pressurize his wife to submit to sexual relations. This constitutes sexual harassment. Some writers, however, feel that sexual harassment by husband is not an act of violence whereas some others attempt to resolve the issue by making a distinction between 'force' and 'violence'. Hofstadter (1970) defined acts of force as "those which inhibit the normal free action of movement of other persons, or which inhibit them through the threat of violence". Luckenbill and Sanders (1977) have maintained that some actions, for instance rape, are considered violent yet may involve only force. This would exclude acts like kidnapping from the roster of violent crimes, unless the victim is injured.

Thus, if we wish to use the term 'violence' to denote an observable reality, it (violence) must be recognized as a specifically human phenomenon in as much as it consists of the freedom of one person to encroach upon the freedom of another.

SEVEN

Teasing the Innocent

Eve-teasing has been a serious menace in our society The commission of this crime is an indicator of extent to which the women folk are insecure in our society. Eve-teasing which involves the verbal and physical harassment of women is the scourge of the urban society. A woman cannot go out in the street without the fear of being harassed by strange men. In busy crowded areas the women get pawed and pressed, jostled, rubbed and squeezed, the miscreants taking advantage of the press of the crowd and indulging in whatever physical intimacy the situation permits. The miscreants hurl indecent remarks. There is no woman who has not suffered this menace of society. In daily life if not all men are potential eve-teasers, all women are potential victims. All women suffer from the fear of being teased, irrespective of her age, health, appearance, mental state etc.

Having largely affected the peace of mind of women and they are not able to move freely and participate in the social life of the community. This is a challenge to our constitution which ensures all citizens the right "to move freely throughout the territory of India". There is no safe territory left for women, not even in their "mohallas". In a cross-section interview, a girl of Patna women's college says "Eve-teasers are everywhere outside our campus, in the markets, in parks and in buses, you have to face their hooliganism". Do we not understand why girls avoided attending classes on the day Saraswati idols were to be immersed? The girl students avoid attending classes much before the closure of the colleges during Holi festival. The boy students of St. Columba's College, Hazaribagh have started celebrating Holi festivals before fifteen days, creating panic among the girl students. Even the girls' common room which was locked to avoid any ugly scene was also attacked. As a result the police already was posted there owing to an earlier incident of damaging a car, escorted the girl students to their houses. Now the girl students are missing their classes and practicals because college authorities are unable to control the hooliganism in the college. Great resentments is prevailing among girls and their guardians. Eve-teasing hinders healthy academic atmosphere and damages the career of girl students. It is an irony that we talk of the 21st century and don't allow girls to enjoy freedom in society.

The culprits are not only those who belong to goonda class but they belong to the so-called educated and cultured and affluent families. Young men include sons of senior government officers have been named in an eve-teasing case off and on. In case of anti-social elements, eve-teasing is a group activity and often assumes violent proportions. On several occasions eve-teasing led to communal disturbances. Three persons including a woman of Bhabhua were injured when members of the two families clashed over the issue of eve-teasing. A man of village Chhata of Siwan district was killed by an angry mob for teasing a girl of the same village. In the case of boys belonging to educated, cultured and affluent families, eve-teasing is individual and a concealed phenomenon.

Being no longer confined to students, unemployed and unmarried youth only, this evil has no boundaries. Some recent news report eve-teasing committed by professionals like lawyers, teachers, and civil servants. Of course, the elite class is a bit sophisticated in nature. They play with their subordinate working women in lighter form and watch the response of the opposite sex in this regard.

Eve-teasing : Many a Shades

Eve-teasers are in the age bracket of 15 to 40 and some of them are married too. In a cross section interview a girl student has given an interesting twist to the story more than the young boys, middle aged men with receding hairlines and broken teeth, indulge in eve-teasing.

Their despicable deeds cover the following:

1. Indulging in cat-calls, waving wolf whistling, winking and uttering indecent remarks about female anatomy or singing obscene songs in such a way so as to be heard by women. Songs are deliberately chosen from popular film so that these could appear innocuous if it came to an argument.
2. Brushing past hurriedly, pressing against women, trying to pinch the bottoms or the breasts and disappearing in the crowd is very common for such perverts. If caught they pretend that rubbing was all accidental. They get a free hand during the breakdown of power. In the process sometimes the aged women are not spared from this kind of menace.
3. Eve-teasers board crowded buses and trains, prefer to stand or sit next to ladies and depending on the situation, the teaser sometimes gets himself sandwiched with her in the crowd and leans on her.
4. In recent years, in some universities these forms of eve-teasing have replaced with brazen acts as *dupatta* snatching, back patting and in some cases even forced kissing.
5. Eve-teasing has also taken the form of telephone a girl and uttering obscene and suggestive words.
6. Mailing anonymous love letters in the most filthy languages.
7. Exhibiting male genitals in front of women and thereby deriving strange perverted sexual pleasure out of it.

Such vulgar acts occur in educational institutions mostly around women's college and girls' schools. The very act gets intensified particularly during festivals when pre-festivals shopping is on or in the puja pandals, which remain crowded with women folk in the evening.

Social and Legal Aspects

Eve-teasing by itself is not an offence under any law at present. But a close reading of Sections 294 and 354 of the Indian

Penal Code would clearly indicate that the substance of the act of eve-teasing would be covered by them. Section 294 states that "whoever to the annoyance of others (a) does any obscene act in any public place, or (b) sings, recites or utters any obscene song, ballads or words in or near any public place is liable to be punished with imprisonment or with fine." The section is very wide in nature and a person can be hauled up even if the acts forming part of the substance of the offence are addressed to the public at large, provided these cause annoyance. Clearly, a girl or a woman who feels annoyed by any obscene song or words can take recourse to the provision of the section and put up a complaint before a police station. The offence is cognizable, i.e., a police officer can arrest the offender without a warrant but it is bailable. A graver form of eve-teasing is accompanied by the use of gesture indicating threat or use of force. In such a case also, action can be taken against the person using it. It would be covered by section 352 of the Indian Penal Code, which provides the punishment in such a case. The substance of the offence is given in section 351 and is known as assault. The making of gesture should be accompanied with preparation so that the person against whom it is directed has the apprehension that criminal force will be used against her. Apart from this, there is a special provision which recognises the gravity of the offence when it is directed against a woman, and has been given in section 354 of the Indian Penal Code. The punishment in such cases is imprisonment for two years or fine or both. The offence is cognizable. The only condition is that the person should have the intention or knowledge that such an action would outrage her modesty. Small cases of eve-teasing, social disgrace and other inconveniences are rarely fought to the notice of courts, fewer still are challenged in the courts and negligible number end in minor convictions and that also after a long lapse when the offenders and his likes continue committing many more such acts.

The provocation coming from the opposite sex like the style of dressing, talking, walking etc. should not be overlooked while condemning eve-teasing. It is not that all women behave in identical provocative manner. Sometimes women consciously or unconsciously invite such hazards. In a cross-section interview eve-teasing was viewed as reaction and not an action. According to some of the male interviews "Eve-teasing took place only when girls provoke. They incite others by their action, dress and manner. It is a form of admiration. Girls dress not for girls but for boys". Then why not let them be aware that they are looked great. But this is a partial statement. Interview to girls gave another point of view. They said they dress themselves in modern way only to show that they have equal status and not to attract boys. Thus it can be said that eve-teasing may result due to wrong impression of girls' image by the boys.

The social malaise of harassing the women is assuming such proportions that one shudders at the shape of things to come. The exercises of passing annoying and embarassing comments from a distance, if unchecked, are found to lead to more serious forms and proportions. Eve-teasing, if not properly checked will end up in entering a house and committing criminal assault or homicide. Every eve-teaser is a potential murderer.

Effective Measures

1. The need for creating an awareness in society has always been there and as a result the attitude of common people in general and the police may be more sympathetic towards the victims themselves in particular.
2. Girls should be bold and give back to the ruffians in the same coin. They should be taught a lesson. If he gets even a slap from an opponent, he takes to his heels. Training in 'Judo' and 'Karate' to girls is very helpful and for this the government must open training centres.
3. At times fact can be of great help until she is able to sight others who can come to her rescue or get hold of any lethal substance with which she can strike at.
4. It is a must for the case to be reported to police. There should be no leniency exercised on this account.
5. The Parliament should pass stringent laws for the police to enforcing them vigorously. This can be expedited through public pressure.

6. The public have also to help damsels in distress and not behave in an unconcerned and impersonal way. It must encourage the victims to report the incidents to police and help the police and the courts in punishing the offenders by deposing truthfully and by being not won over by the threats or lures of the culprits.
7. There should be a massive boycott by public of eve-teasers and they should make it a point that they do not prevail. The names of eve-teasers may be written on big hoarding to be kept at a public place for days together in every 'Mohalla'. Voluntary women welfare organisations that we have in the country like the All India Women's Conference, Nari Raksha Samiti, Mahila Dakshta Samiti, etc. could well bring awakening and alertness among eves in this regard.
8. The parents must ensure that their children dress properly without an effort to expose the anatomy unncessarily which invites the attention of the evil minded.
9. Parents should be initiated to talk about basic sexual matters with their children. Failing this they gather dangerous knowledge from footpath publications which are worse than anything else. Talk about sex is taboo in Indian society. Society need to change its attitude towards sex education. In fact, eve-teasing is only a superficial manifestation of the imbalance in the relationship between man and women.

What we need is public consciousness and a serious rethinking about our morals and values and public action can go a long way in acting as a deterrent to eve-teasing.

Responsible Factors

Greater degeneration of the male vis-a-vis eve teasing is a symptom of social, economic and moral disorder. It is a symptomatic of a combination of varied and complicated disorder. First and the foremost is the abandonment of the traditional moral values, the lack of religious education and the absence of the sobering effect of the family and the teacher. Secondly no body is born an eve-teaser.

If he is neglected at home, he grows rowdy. Thirdly, there is the pernicious influence of the cinema and the cheap literature in which sex permeates. The current advertisements trying to promote sale of under-garments, towels and bedsheets by incidently exposing the female anatomy also lead to degradation of woman as a commercialised commodity in the mind of man. Fourthly, there is the rush to the urban in search of adventure and employment. Away from the restraining influence of the families, the youngsters look for kicks, excitement and thrills which they seem to get in acts of eve-teasing. Infliction of pain on the eve acts as a stimulant to their sexual desires. Fifthly, there is the lack of fear of punishment or adverse publicity or social disgrace. The police with its insufficient strength and preoccupation with other problems of law and order and the courts with their proverbial delays and intricate legal procedures fail to bring most of the vagrants to book.

EIGHT

Torturing Physically

Physical Harms

Women who are married at a younger age are at higher risk of physical violence. The women who got married at younger age were more victims of physical violence by their husbands in contrast to those who got married at later age. Further, it was noted that there was a progressive decrease in the percentages of victims of physical violence from lower age at marriage category to higher age group. Out of 60 respondents who got married below the age of 18 years, 45 per cent were the victims. In contrast to this, who were married after the age of 21 years, only 24.71 per cent were the victims of physical violence.

It is also interesting to note that median age at marriage of victims of physical violence was lower than those of non-victims. It can, thus, be concluded that those women who married at lower age were at high risk of physical violence in comparison with those who got married at later age in the Indian society, although the age at marriage is increasing yet in the rural areas it still remains quite low that is, 17.81 years. Therefore, class and situational factors may play an important role in determining the age at marriage, which in turn may be associated with violence because young couples are under lot of stress to adjust to new role responsibilities.

A few studies indicate that wives of younger age group are at higher risk of abuse as compared with those of older age group because older women are not prone to file assault charges either because of traditional attitudes or because of the possibility of divorce. The results of National Family Violence Survey conducted in America indicate that all forms of marital violence occur most frequently among those under 30 years of age. The rate of marital violence among those under 30 years of age was found to be more than double the rate for the age for 31 to 50 years.

The data for the present study were tabulated to find out association between the age of the wife and her being victim of physical violence. The respondents were distributed into four age categories. There was a progressive decrease in the percentages of victims of physical violence from lower age category to higher age category. Among the victims of physical violence 45.45 per cent were below the age of 30 years. In contrast to this those who were in the age group of 50 years above, only 18.18 per cent were the victims.

Similarly, if the median age of the victims of physical violence is compared with non-victims, it was noticed that median age of victims was 35 years in contrast to 39.24 years median age of the non-victims. In short, an inverse relationship was found between the age of wives and their physical abuse. In other words, physical violence against wives of younger age group was more frequent as against those of higher age groups. The data of the present study support the findings of studies cited above.

Family Conflicts

Wife abuse can occur at any age but the data on age indicate that wives of younger age are at higher risk of being abused. It may be due to the fact that younger couples are still learning to make adjustment with each other and addition of children in the family puts enormous demands and stresses on the younger people.

Presence or absence of children in the family is likely to affect the quality of relationship between husband and wife. Further, presence of more children in the family would create problem of management and proper training of the younger ones. Researches on the impact of children on marriages consistently show that the level of marital satisfaction and marital adjustment goes down after the birth of the first child.

An additional child would imply a decrease in time for parents to pursue their own interests. Further, each additional child increases the work load and conflicts. In the traditional societies like India, child care still remains under the domain of mothers and for any deviance on the part of child, it is the mother who is blamed. Further, more children put a lot of stress on the limited resources of the family.

Among the victims of physical violence it was found that the rate of violence against mothers who had five or more children or no child was more than double the rate for those who had one or two children. Keeping in view the number of children it was noted that there was a progressive increase in the percentages of victims of physical violence from one to two children category to women having five or more children or with no child. In short, it can be concluded that a large number of children in the family become a source of conflict resulting into violence against wife or mother.

The highest percentages of physical violence was found in those house-holds which had no child. It may be attributed to their younger age as well as wives' inability to have children because children are valued in the Indian society and those women who are unable to bear a child are ridiculed.

In the patriarchal society like India, greater importance is given to the male child. The female child is not only considered a liability because of associated dowry problems, but mothers who give birth to female children only do not get much respect in the family as compared with those who give birth to male children. Lately with the help of amniocentesis the couples would like to know the sex of the child. In case the foetus is of the female sex, they go for abortion. A study of 8000 cases of abortion showed that 7999 of them involved a female foetus. The high female foeticide reinforces the sex preferences prevalent in our society. The victims of physical violence were almost equally divided in the categories of those who had only male or female children of both the sexes. In the present study sex of the children in the family was not found to be associated with wife abuse.

Wives living in extended and joint households are required to make adjustments with a large number of kin in contrast to those who are living in nuclear households. Further, patrilocal residence and patriarchal structure of the family places women into subservient position. The men are more likely to act as sons rather than husbands. The parents-in-law and other kinsmen continue to have greater affiliation with the sons as compared with daughters-in-law.

A number of cases have been reported where because of backbiting, the husbands have maltreated their wives. Hence presence of a large number of members in the family not only creates the problem of adjustment but they also act as instigators for wife abuse. Although there was no marked difference in the percentage of victims living in nuclear and extended households, yet among the victims a relatively higher percentage (36.67) were found to be living in joint and extended households in contrast to those living in nuclear households (32.94). Similarly, among the non-victims no marked difference was found with regard to their pattern of living arrangement. Hence, the composition of household was not found to be associated with wife abuse.

From the foregoing discussion on the demographic correlates of wife abuse, it was found that the younger age at marriage, young wives and those having no child or a large number of children were at higher risk of being victims of physical violence. However, no association was found between the sex of the children as well as living arrangement and wife abuse. Based on the results of this exploratory research, the following hypotheses can be formulated for verification in future researches.

1. The younger the age at marriage of the women, the greater is the possibility of their being battered.
2. The younger the age of wife, the greater are the chances of her being victim of physical violence.
3. The greater the number of children, a woman has the greater is the possibility of her being victim of physical violence of her husband.
4. The absence of child is likely to result in wife battering.

An individual's social milieu not only influences his social position, network of relationships and contents of learning but also his social behaviour pattern. Social behaviour is a function of the life situations which may be physical, economic, social or cultural or an interplay of these elements. It is assumed that persons having differential life situations would react differently to the same stimuli. It is, therefore, essential to explicate the role of these social variables for understanding the quality of conjugal relationship. The social variables considered for the present study are educational and occupational status of the respondents, their social class background, their caste and religious background, their attitudes regarding traditional gender roles in the family and their value orientation in favour of use of violence for the resolution of conflict. Formal education helps an individual to know what is happening outside one's immediate surroundings. It also facilitates him to develop rational outlook towards life. Education widens the horizon and makes the individual more knowledgeable. Education also helps an individual to get jobs of high prestige and with high economic returns. Further, higher education enhances one's social prestige. Efforts have been made to find out association between the level of education one has and the quality of interpersonal relations.

A few studies indicate that the less education a person has, the more likely he or she is to approve of and support violence. Some other studies, however, contradict their findings and on the other hand, they are of opinion that couples with the lowest educational levels are less prone to violence than those who had attained higher education. It is argued that low education level does not cause violence but it aggravates the frustration.

The reason for more violence among those who have higher education, may be that women with high education may not endorse the traditional role relationship and this may be considered as threat to the dominant position by their husbands. However, education can provide people with alternatives for resolving family disagreements. It is, therefore, expected that with the help of education, individual learns different mechanisms to resolve the conflict in the conjugal relationships.

The educational background of the victim wives indicates that those who have low educational attainment or higher educational attainment had over representation as compared with those who had moderate level of education. There is a progressive decrease in the percentage of the victims from illiterate educational category up to graduation with the exception of those who had higher education. This curvilinear distribution of victims of violence indicates that women who have no education or have higher educational attainment are more prone to physical violence by their husbands.

The women with low education designate their complete dependency because with low educational background they will not be able to have economic independence or would be engaged in occupations with low economic returns and low prestige. In the case of those who have higher education they may be in better position to gain economic independence and with the higher education they may start questioning the dominant position of their husbands. Such a threat is not tolerated by the husbands and they use physical violence as their ultimate resource to maintain their dominant position in the family.

Occupation is an important indicator of a person's position in society. It is believed that the higher the education one has, the higher the occupation one holds and the higher the prestige he gets in society. Conversely, the lower the occupation, the lower will be the economic returns and as a consequence thereof, there are likely to be higher frustrations and greater marital conflicts.

Many studies indicate that persons engaged in occupations of lower prestige are more likely to resort to physical violence against their wives to give vent to their economic stresses. It is also argued that women who stay at home and are not engaged in paid work outside their homes are at somewhat greater risk of being physically abused than those engaged in paid work. This is probably because housewives are perceived to contribute less to family subsistence and are consequently valued less than women who are engaged in paid work outside the home. Wife beating is far less common in societies in which women have independent economic and social resources, perhaps because these resources are valuable enough to make a husband think twice before acting in ways that might force his wife to terminate the marriage.

In the sample there are only 65 women respondents who were found to be engaged in paid work. Out of these, 47.69 per cent were victims of physical violence of their husbands. On the other hand, out of those not engaged in paid work outside their homes, only 26.67 per cent were physically abused by their husbands. The results of the present study support the findings of Homung et al.

who, in one representative sample, found housewives had a lower risk of violence than working wives.

The reason housewives are abused less than working wives is because keeping in view their economic dependency they may have "Learned helplessness" with the result they have developed tolerance of such violence and do not share with outsiders that they are being abused or they would endorse the traditional gender roles and would not question the authority of their husbands. Hence, they do not provoke their husbands to use physical violence to maintain their dominant position in the conjugal relationship.

On the other hand, the working wives may not accept the dominant position of the husband in family decision-making and raise questions about asymmetrical conjugal relations. Such a situation may prompt the husband to use physical force to retain his dominant position. The general contention that working gives economic independence to women, hence, they would be relatively free dependence to be correct in the present from abuse is also not found to study. On the other hand, it is the working women who are than the non-working women. The association abused more, status and her physical abuse will between wives' working which these become more clear if the type of occupation in which women are engaged in is taken into consideration.

As the number of respondents under the working category were limited to 65 cases only, their occupations were grouped under three categories, i.e., occupations with low prestige, medium prestige and high prestige. The data reveal that the percentage of the victims goes on decreasing from low occupational prestige category to higher prestige category. In short, there was inverse relationship between occupational prestige and physical violence, i.e., the lower the prestige of paid work, the greater was the violence against wives. The results indicate that it is not the working status per se which provides women freedom from physical violence of their husbands but it is the nature of the occupation and associated prestige and economic returns which facilitate women to be free from physical abuse.

Perception of Class

The concept of social class has been defined by several

sociologists. They have, however, given emphasis to different attributes. One salient feature of different definitions is that members of a class group have common style of living and value orientation. Wolfgang and Ferracuti in their study of subculture of violence have even divided a class into subclasses depending upon value orientation of the members. Similarly, a number of scholars have tried to find out association between class background and family violence. One set of studies maintains a positive association between lower class and wife battering. Whereas some researchers do not endorse their findings and they have contended that wife battering transgresses the boundaries of class.

An attempt has been made to find out association between class background and wife beating. The class background of the respondents has been worked out based on education, occupation and income of the husbands of the respondents because a majority of the women respondents were not found to be working and hence, had no independent income of their own. While selecting the sample their living arrangement was taken into consideration and 50 cases from each house type were included in the sample, which were redistributed into different social classes. The class background of the respondent was also divided into lower, working, middle and high for the purpose of finding out differential behaviour pattern, i.e., wife abuse in different classes.

The data indicate that in contrast to 19.23 per cent victims of physical violence in the upper class, there were 51 .85 per cent victims in the lower class. There is a progressive decrease in the percentages of victims of physical violence from the lower through the middle to the upper class. Similarly, among the non-victims the higher per cent (80.77) belong to the upper class. In short, women belonging to the lower class were at a higher risk of being physically abused by their husbands. The results of the study indicate inverse relationship between class background and wife battering.

These findings support the contention of those researchers who found that women belonging to the lower class were at a higher risk of physical violence which was attributed to their way of life. The use and approval of physical violence in the lower class has been attributed to what Lewis calls, the culture of poverty. The concept implies that the poor people have a distinct subculture.

Due to common experiences they have developed certain attitudes and behaviour pattern which have been transmitted from parents to children. These include the casual resort to physical violence, an inability to plan for the future, seeking of immediate gratification, weak impulse control and fatalistic attitude towards the future. Davis while describing the class linked, violence contends that physical violence in the lower class families is normal, socially approved and socially, inculcated type of behaviour. Similarly, Whitehurst while making a distinction between the middle and the lower class families with regard to control over violence, maintained that violence-responses were much more built into lower class subculture as a means to achieve some goals to assert independence and masculinity.

The members of the lower class are subject to a lot of economic pressures and strains and they cannot show their resentment and frustration, against those who are highly placed and hence they give vent to their frustrations at the slightest provocation by beating their wives on whom they can exert their power. On the other hand, members of the middle and upper classes have more resources and can keep their violence private and additionally, because of the sensitivity of the issue and embarrassment, the victims are not likely to admit its existence in their conjugal' relationship.

Individual's social status is determined by his ascriptive and acquired attributes. In the Indian society ascriptive attributes, like caste, determine not only his social milieu, as castes are hierarchically placed but also his opportunities to acquire new attributes. Although an individual is now theoretically permitted to achieve any position and support any ideology. Yet caste plays an important role in influencing his behaviour pattern. Keeping in view the importance of caste in the Indian society, it will be worthwhile to find out an association between caste and wife battering.

The distribution of the victims of physical violence according to their caste background indicates that respondents belonging to the lower castes group and those who have not specified their caste were more victims in contrast to the respondents belonging to the higher castes. Among the twice-born, the respondents belonging to trading castes were at a higher risk in contrast to Khatris and

Aroras. Similarly, among the non-victims the higher percentages of respondents were found among the twice-born.

The higher frequency of physical violence present among the members of the lower castes may be attributed to their lower class background. Similarly, among those cases who have not specified their caste, most of them belonged to Muslim and Christian religion and these respondents were having lower socio-economic status. The association between caste background and physical violence would remain incomplete unless their economic status is also considered. Preceding analysis has indicated that members belonging to the lower class were more likely to resort to physical violence for the resolution of conjugal conflicts.

Religion is an important institution which instills a particular philosophy of life in an individual. His outlook towards himself and others as well as his behaviour pattern are likely to be influenced by his religious belief system. Is wife abuse a characteristic of a particular religious group? To find out an answer to the question, religious background of the respondents was considered. No clear-cut association was found between religious background and physical violence against wives. Among the two main religious groups present in Chandigarh, there was no marked difference in the percentage of victims.

In case of Muslims and Christians 50 per cent of the respondents belonging to these religious groups were the victims of husband's violence. This again may be attributed to the low economic status of the respondents. The results of the present study do not establish any association between religion and wife battering.

The family as a social institution lays down norms and values to regulate the behaviour of the members of the social group. Family as a social group is structured in such a manner that one member, usually the husband, assumes the dominant position and the other members take up subordinate positions.

The family provides a social setting where husband and wife play complementary roles. One of the conditions which maximises the cooperative elements in the family is the similarity of social values and ideologies which promotes not only cohesiveness and harmony but also helps in the proper functioning of the group. In the patriarchal traditional societies, like India, sex role expectations favour male dominance in the family. Traditional ideology promotes and serves to justify male dominance as well as helps in cultivating a belief system among the husbands and wives as to how they should behave in the marital relationship.

Motivated by traditional ideology, division of labour in the family was worked out into a male provider and a female to focus more narrowly on the domestic realm. Such a task specialization and differential evaluation helped men not only to have greater control over economic resources, but also a greater access to power in the family. The power structure in the family is maintained through the actions of the members involved in the relationships. Those at the top of the power structure behave in dominant ways and they do not hesitate to use coercive methods to retain their dominant position.

Attempts have been made to find out association between traditionality and wife abuse. A number of studies have concluded that men who were more traditional in their attitudes towards women were more likely to become wife abusers. Some importance is also given to sex role orientation of the victims. Walker is of opinion that non-traditional wives if paired with traditional husbands are at higher risk of being abused. An attempt has been made in the present study to find out correlation between wives' traditional orientation and their being victims of abuse.

Traditional sex role orientation of the respondents was worked out based on the responses to eight statements. The level of traditionality was further divided into three: High, Medium and Low, to find out association between level of traditionality and wife battering. It is assumed that respondents who have low level of traditional role orientation are at higher risk of physical violence than those at high level of traditionality because wives with low level of traditional orientation are more likely to question asymmetrical power relations in the family.

In contrast to 22.86 per cent of the wives showing high level of traditional sex role orientation, 40.32 per cent wives indicating low level of traditionality were the victims of physical violence by their husbands. Similarly, among the non-victims, their percentages go on increasing from low level of traditionality to high level of traditionality. In short, it can be concluded that wives with non-traditional sex role orientation are at higher risk of being physically abused- The reason for wives showing less traditional sex role orientation being victims of physical violence may be attributed to their attempt in questioning the traditional power structure in the family. The husbands in such situation are likely to use physical force as the last resort to maintain their dominant position.

The norms and values relating to intra-family violence indicate cultural contradiction. On the one hand, there is a myth of family non-violence which reflects cultural norms for the family as a group characterised by love and harmony. On the other hand, there seems to be social norms which imply right of the family members to strike each other. The legitimation of violence in the family is explicit and mandatory as in the case of rights and obligations of the parent to use a necessary and appropriate level of physical force to adequately train and control a child.

Violent wives as well as violent husbands express more approval of violence than do non-violent husbands and wives. Levinson in his cross cultural study on family violence came to the conclusion that wife beating was more common and frequent in societies in which adults solved conflicts by resorting to physical, violence, indicating attitude in favour of violence.

The cultural norms and values permitting and sometimes encouraging husband to beat wife actually reflect hierarchical and male dominant type of society like India. The right to use force exists, to provide the ultimate support for the existing power structure of the family in which the wife assumes a subordinate position.

Respondents' values in favour or against use of violence in the family were obtained from their reactions to 12 statements. Their scores were divided into three categories depicting low, medium and high scores. This exercise was done with an assumption that the respondents with high score on values in favour of violence in the family would be at a higher risk of being victims than those with low score. The data did not depict any clear-cut association.

On the other hand, it was noted that those respondents who had medium score on values favouring use of violence to resolve family conflict were more victims in contrast to those who had high or low score. The reason for lack of association may be attributed to the fact that there is a lot of gap between values and actual behaviour pattern. Secondly, the values were taken of the wives rather than the husbands who were the perpetrators of physical violence against their wives.

The respondents might be holding values against the use of violence but had no control over the values and behaviour pattern of their husbands.

The above discussion on social variables highlights certain salient features which contribute to husbands' physical violence against wives. Lower caste background, low and high educational attainment, lower working status, lower social class background and low level of traditionality were found to be contributing factors for husbands' physical violence against wives. However, no association was found between religious background and value system of the respondents and their being victims and non-victims of physical violence.

Dependency is a state, both physical and mental, depicting assistance from a person or persons for continuing living in the community. The human child has to depend upon his parents for his growth, development and social recognition. The Indian society has placed women in a state of dependency as a daughter on her father, as a sister on her brother, as a wife on her husband and lastly as a mother on her son. Further, sexual division of labour and gender roles accentuate these differences.

Additionally, patriarchal social norms not only grant control of family resources and property to men but also provide dominant position to them. To maintain their dominant position, the husbands are likely to use coercive methods including physical violence against their wives. Sometimes physical violence is used as a means to an end and at other times as an end in itself. Dependency is also treated as a cause of physical violence in the conjugal relationships. Researches have utilized this explanation in two ways. In case, a wife is completely dependent, both physically and socially, her husband exploits her dependency and uses violence at whim to reinforce his dominant position in the conjugal relationship. A few scholars are also of opinion that when a husband is dependent upon his wife he resorts to physical violence as a last resort against his wife as he is afraid of losing his spouse or a person on whom he can exert his dominant position. Hence, dependency of husband over his wife is also treated as a cause of wife abuse.

As the present study is limited to wife abuse, the analysis is limited to wife's perception regarding the conditions which make her dependent upon her husband and how this state of dependency results into her being abused. To find out association between wife's dependency and her abuse, dependency has been divided into objective and subjective. It does not, however, mean that we can draw watertight compartments between the two. In certain cases objective dependency may lead to subjective dependency, whereas in other cases even though there is no objective dependency yet the individual remains subjectively dependent upon her spouse. It can, however, be assumed that a wife who experiences both objective and subjective dependency is at higher risk of being abused in contrast to those who have only objective or only subjective dependency.

For the purpose of analysis, wife's objective dependency stands for conditions like not working, i.e., being economically dependent upon husband; not having any property in her name; not receiving any financial assistance from her family of orientation; inability to live alone; inability to do shopping alone, and inability to go outside the city alone.

Further, level of objective dependency may vary from case to case. Hence, objective dependency is further divided into three levels: low, medium and high. The wives who are objectively dependent upon their husbands are at higher risk of being abused. Because it would be difficult for these women to come out of the abusive relationship as they do not have the resources to live alone. Their objective dependency is also known to their spouses who may fully exploit the situation knowing fully well that their wives would not be able to leave them. It is further envisaged that wives who have high level of objective dependency are at greater risk of being abused.

Wives with high level of objective dependency are physically abused more in contrast to those who have low level of objective dependency. This is evident in the percentages of the victims at different levels of dependency. Similarly, the percentage of non-victims goes on decreasing to high level. There were 33 respondents who had high level of objective dependency, out of which 60.61 per cent were not the victims of physical violence.

Results

The results of the study support the contention of a few scholars who are of opinion that high level of women's marital dependency is not associated with wife abuse, because husbands of dependent wives can maintain their dominant positions without resorting to violence as their wives are in no position to question their dominance. Although no cause and effect relationship can be established between dependency and wife abuse yet the data show an indicative trend that wives who have high level of objective dependency are abused more as compared to those who have low level of objective dependency.

A few scholars contend that objective dependency, of the wife per se does not result into her abuse but is mediated by her tolerance. One may, however, raise the question why she develops this tolerance to abuse? One reason may be that she remains subjectively dependent upon her husband because her social reality has not been constructed outside the marital relationship. In Indian society marriage is a must for every woman, unless she adopts a life of celibacy. Remaining unmarried or living a life of a divorcee is looked down upon. Hence, whether a wife is objectively dependent upon her husband or not she remains subjectively dependent. It is not, however, true in the case of husbands.

Remarriage after divorce or separation is easily available to a man than a woman. Such a discriminatory practice perpetuate subjective dependency in the wives.

Subjective dependency in the present study stands for, not leaving the husband even under adverse circumstances; divorce not considered good; perception that married women even if abused enjoy higher status than divorced; lack of support from kin; greater commitment and more devotion to marital relationship. It is also expected that wives are likely to have different levels of subjective dependency. Depending upon their scores they are divided into three categories: low, medium and high. It is expected that wives having higher level of subjective dependency will be at higher risk of being physically abused in contrast to those having lower level of subjective dependency.

In contrast to 23-94 per cent wives having low subjective dependency, more than 42 percent of the wives with high level of dependency are the victims of physical violence of their husbands. There was a steady increase in the percentage of abused wives from low level of subjective dependency through medium level to high level of subjective dependency. Taking into account 38 cases having high level of subjective dependency it was noted that more than 42 per cent were the victims of husbands' physical violence and approximately 58 per cent were free from being physically abused.

Although, no positive correlation could be established between subjective dependency of wife and her being victim of physical abuse yet the high percentage of victims having high level of subjective dependency designate a partial association between subjective dependency and her being battered. The reason for high percentage of such victims can be attributed to wife's commitment to marriage and her inability to use alternative mechanisms to get out of the abusive relationships. Such a situation forces her to cultivate tolerance and continue living in the abusive relationship.

Similarly, the husband uses coercive methods to assert his dominant position in the familial network of relationship because he is confident that his violent behaviour would not be challenged and he can attain the desired goal, that is, subduing his wife. The results of the present study on subjective dependency and wife abuse partially support the findings of other researchers.

Subjective dependency in certain cases may be treated as a consequence of objective dependency. In other cases subjective dependency may not be the outcome of objective dependency. It was for this reason that these two facets of dependency were treated separately, however, to find out the impact of dependency on wife abuse, both objective and subjective dependencies have to be combined. In other words, to find out the validity of dependency framework to explicate wife abuse, both the facets of dependency are combined to find out their combined effect on physical violence.

The total dependency scores of the respondents have been arranged into three categories—low, medium and high. The data indicate that wives with higher level of dependency are at higher risk of being abused in contrast to those with lower level of dependency. In contrast to 27.42 per cent of wives with low level of dependency more were the victims of husbands' physical violence. The percentage of non-victims goes on decreasing from lower level of dependency to higher level.

NINE

Kidnapping and Abduction

Kidnapping and abduction is a heinous crime. It affects adversely the career of a large number of girls and women every year. Normally it has been noticed that the abductors and abducted victims are acquainted, rather not strangers to each other. The initial contact between the abductor and his victim frequently occurs in their own homes and neighbourhood rather than in public places. On the other hand, father is too busy with his own world. The mother too has developed a circle outside the home. Thus, the parents do not know or even ask their sons and daughters where they spend the evenings. There is lack of parental control. The bond of love, affection and respect seems to be vanishing from Indian families.

As discussed earlier on the taking or enticing away of a girl less than 18 years of age or of a male less than 16 years of age without the consent of the lawful guardian constitutes kidnapping. Abduction is the forcible, fraudulent or deceitful taking away of a woman with an intension of seducing her to illicit sex or compelling her to marry a person against her will. Thus, "abduction" differs from "kidnapping". The latter is committed only in respect of a minor, while the former in respect to any person. In kidnapping, the victim's consent is immaterial but in abduction, the victim's free and voluntary consent condones the crimes. In kidnapping, the offender's intention is irrelevant but in abduction, it is the all important factor. Thus, a girl of 18 or over, could only be abducted and not kidnapped; but if she is under 18 she could be kidnapped as well as abducted if the taking is by force or the taking or enticing was by deceitful means.

Different Circumstances

There are different circumstances and motivations leading to kidnapping or abduction. Sometimes it is politically motivated, sometimes economically and sometimes it occurs due to some personal reasons. The political kidnapping of famous filmstar Rajkumar, Veerapan attracted much attention. Economically motivated kidnapping is mainly for ransom and sale for prostitution. In this study we are chiefly concerned with the kidnapping of woman for marriage, sex satisfaction or for sale for prostitution.

Kidnapping/abduction may occur with or without the consent of the girls. Sometimes the victims "run away" from their homes willingly to marry persons of their choice and when caught their parents describe the act as an "abduction". Sometimes the victims "run away" from their homes willingly to marry boys of their own choice as they fail to get the consent of their parents and their parents knowingly report to the police, the act as an "abduction". Sometimes even married men "run away" with married girls as even after marriage their affair did not end finally. Sometimes the abduction is done by a man not getting a marriage proposal which drives him to this madness. Sometimes abduction is done by an ascetic. Sometimes abduction of Harijan girls is done by their landlords to demoralise their men in their struggle for an improved existence. Sometimes mishap victims are kidnapped by criminals. A married woman of Mara village under Khagaria Police Station, a victim of the Mansi train disaster of June 6 was kidnapped by a notorious criminal and compelled to live a life of shame. Sometimes abduction is done due to old enemity. A 34-year-old woman of Chandpura village under Begusarai was raped and murdered after being abducted from her house. Old enemity with a fellow villager was said to be the cause of this crime. Sometimes women play major role in abduction for sale and immoral purpose and the women involved in this trade are themselves abducted women.

Kidnapping and Abduction Cases

Consequences of Kidnapping and Abduction

In the majority of cases abductor and the victim are known to each other. Sometimes they kidnap the girls as an adult, sometimes as a minor. Sometimes the consequences of kidnapping is rape and murder. A young unmarried girl of Manpur in Gaya was enticed away by her lover and after the rape murdered her for fear of being detected, and later her body was found in the dry bed of the river Falgu. Sometimes it ends in marriage. A young girl of Shastrinagar Police Station of Patna filed a petition in the Court of Chief Judicial Magistrate, Patna, stating that she was a major (19 years) and nobody has kidnapped her. She also stated that she had married with her own consent and free will at Muzaffarpur and since then she was living with him as his wife. Sometimes kidnapping leads to communal tension. A former student of the T.P. College, Madhepura who had kidnapped a daughter of a noted businessman of Madhepura surrendered in the court. Both told the court that they were married to each other and demanded protection in view of the communal tension mounting in the area due to their marriage. Sometimes parents accept the marriage and choice of their wards. The Chief Judicial Magistrate of Patna ordered the release of the couple after the girl's father had filed an affidavit before the court stating that the case of kidnapping of her daughter filed by him was done under misinformation. He said his daughter was a major and had married on her own. Another affidavit was filed by the boy's father that he had no objection to the marriage. Sometimes, the parents of the victims even after marriage do not accept the choice of the girls and lodge a kidnapping case against their husbands. A school-going girl of Shastrinagar area at Patna returned after marrying a young man in a temple at Muzaffarpur. However, the parents of the girl did not accept the choice of the girl and lodge a kidnapping case against her husband.

The Culprit

A kidnapper may be any person irrespective of his age, education, religion, caste, creed, and culture. He may be a priest. More than 30 young girls were liberated from the Ashram of a Yogi at Gopalganj. According to the police the fake Yogi trapped innocent young girls, women and gents at the gun point. The wife of the temple's pujari near Sataquat Ashram was kidnapped by a frequent visitor of the temple and she was recovered from Vaishali, the kidnapper was holding a respectable position of society. A doctor of Patna Medical College Hospital was arrested by the Kadamkuan police on the charge of kidnapping, wrongful confinement and attempt of criminal assault on a minor girl. Some armed men raided a house in Mehadia village under Arwal police station of Jehanabad, lifted a young girl after taking some household articles at the gun point and escaped. A school clerk of Madhupur was taken into custody by the local police with the co-operation of the Darbhanga police for kidnapping the minor daughter of his landlord. A young girl of Rajendra Nagar near the Station of Patna stated before the Magistrate that she had been kidnapped and criminally assaulted by a person living in the ground floor of the house. An umarried girl of Chausa police station of Madhepura was kidnapped by a co-villager who was arrested by the Delhi police. A student of R.N. College, Hajipur kidnapped a 15- year- old girl student in collusion with some anti-social elements. A girl of 16 years of Mandi village of Begusarai ran away with her servant and was arrested at Lakhminia railway station. A school girl of Giridh was allegedly kidnapped by her tutor about seven years ago, was recovered from a farm at Ludhi in Punjab. A teenage school- going girl of village Jeetpur of Madhepur was kidnapped by her servant. While preparations were being made to sell the girl, the police could find her and arrested two persons in this connection. A young daughter of Munger has accused her father of trafficking in women.

Abduction is definitely related to the absence of parents' control over the victim and non-harmonious relation in the family.

But in the eyes of law kidnapping is proved on three grounds. First involves the age of the victim, second the absence of the consent of the victim and the third is the use of force and physical resistance.

Kidnapping and abduction are very common offences unleashed against minor girls or women. Minor girls are enticed away by unscrupulous persons while young women irrespective of age, fall prey to any sort of deceit or force. What is important is that one should clearly understand the offence that is made out, which would depend upon the nature of allurement or force and the age of person.

Sections of Law

A person who kidnaps or abducts a woman with the intention that she may be compelled to marry another person against her will, commits an offence under Section 366 of the IPC. Even the knowledge that she may be compelled to marry or have illicit intercourse against her will, even if there is no intention, would add to the gravity of the offence and would be punishable under this section. Abuse of authority, or criminal intimidation as defined in the code, or any form of compulsion used for inducing a woman to go from one place to another with the knowledge or intention that she may be forced or seduced for illicit intercourse is also similarly punishable. This section provides a deferrent punishment to persons who resort to the use of force or fraud, for the purpose of marriage or illicit intercourse. However, in all such cases, the intention or the knowledge has to be proved apart from the main ingredients of the offence of kidnapping or abduction as the case may be.

Minor girls have been the victims of various types of nefarious activities by anti-social elements. Sections 366A, 372 and 373 of the IPC take care of such cases where minor girls are subjected to illicit intercourse, sale or purchase. Thus, inducement of a minor girl under the age of eighteen years to go from any place or to do any act with the knowledge or intention that she will be seduced or forced to an illicit intercourse has been made punishable with 10 years imprisonment. The means used for inducement are irrelevant. The basic ingredients of the offence are that she:

(i) should be a minor girl below the age of 18 years;

(ii) she should be induced by whatever means;

(iii) inducement should be to go to any place or do any act;

(iv) there should be knowledge or intention on the part of the person that she will be seduced or forced to an illicit intercourse by another person.

This section would, therefore, help those cases where innocent girls are allured with promises of a good life and are then exploited by anti-social elements for sexual offences, prostitution, etc.

Selling or buying minor girls for the purposes of prostitution is an offence under section 372 and 373 of the IPC. The selling, buying, hiring and disposing of or obtaining possession of a minor person with the intention or the knowledge that the person will be used for prostitution, illicit intercourse, or any unlawful or immoral purpose are the essential ingredients of the offence. It is not necessary that the person should be immediately put to such an abuse. The knowledge that such a person would be used in future for such a person would also constitute the offence. If a minor girl is sold, bought, lent or hired or disposed of to a prostitution or the brothel keeper or is so obtained, there is presumption that she will be used for prostitution. In other words, it is not necessary to prove the intention, as the circumstances amply point out that the girls would be used for illicit intercourse. Illicit intercourse has been given a very wide definition and would include any sexual intercourse between persons not "united by marriage" or any union which is not recognised as marriage by the personal law of the persons.

The provision made in the Indian Penal Code on kidnapping and abduction, particularly where the intention is to seduce a minor girl or force her to an illicit intercourse, provides ample safeguard against the exploitation of innocent girls and women of tender age by anti-social elements.

In spite of the various sections of IPC. that take care of such notorious activities as kidnapping and abduction, the trend of this crime is rising. According to official police records, around two out of every one lakh women are the victims of abduction and kidnapping annually in our country. But the true rate of victimization is far greater than this. Estimates have placed the figures at 2 to 10 times the official rate. This difference can mainly be explained by the reluctance of the victims' parents to report the incidents to police.

Kidnapper Gangs

Trafficking of women and girls has become a highly organised and inter-state business. A gang engaged in kidnapping girls from Bihar and Assam and selling in many districts of UP has brought to light. A gang of kidnappers engaged supplying the girls to middle east has been noticed. A gang of kidnappers usually consists of both males and females, who operate everywhere, in rural as well as in urban area. Female kidnappers have been found to work as domestic servants who facilitate kidnapping of girls. They have been found to be very active in places of public entertainment, educational institutions, hostels, hospitals and in folk festivals, busy railway stations, bus stands etc. and entice away girls.

The gangs of kidnappers and abductors have their own secret methods of transporting girls and shuttle them to and fro, from city to city, to minimise the risk of their being rescued. The kidnapped or abducted girls are escorted by respectable looking men and women so that they cannot be checked or interrogated by the police. They have their agents at the bars, in courts, and in newspaper offices, they have friends in every political organisation and plenty of funds is given to those who can protect from the law. The police have in many cases extorted money from these unspeakable scoundrels. It cannot be denied that corrupt policemen with the help of dishonest politicians in power have made systematic collections from this source. Sometimes male members of the victim's family are killed or injured in a bid to save them from abduction.

Kinds of Abduction

We can classify the victims into four groups by taking all cases "willing" and "unwilling" victim:

1. ***Forced abduction:*** This group of victims who clearly do not consent to accompany their kidnappers are forcibly abducted by the offenders.
2. ***Willing abduction:*** This group of victims willingly agree to live with offenders because they (victims) intend to marry them against the wishes of their parents.
3. ***Accessary abduction:*** This group of victims neither give their consent nor oppose it, thus, aiding or contributing a secondary manner to the abduction activity. The abduction stands in a relationship "power" over the victim because of being older, being an authority figure or some other reason. The abductor then gains access to the victim and pressurizes her to leave her house with him.

4. *Stress abduction:* This group of victims initially agree to leave the house with "offenders" but are stopped when "something goes wrong". Usually what goes wrong is that the offender "exploits" the agreement and rapes the victim, or he brings his friends to have sexual relation with her, or sells her ornaments, or leaves her in the hotel, or at a railway station or bus stand and so forth.

Dubious Motives

The following motives may be identified for kidnapping the unmarried girls or abducting the married women:

The unmarried girls and married women may be kidnapped and abducted in the following circumstances:

1. The abduction of girls who lead an unhappy life in their parent's home. A beautiful girl kidnapped from Jharia in her statement refused to go to her parent's house for fear of being killed. Moreover, she expressed her desire to get herself married with a man of position and means. She refused to accept a constable as her husband saying he would better serve as her servant.
2. The abduction of girls whose parents refuse to marry them to the "abductors". A girl research scholar of Patna University left the hostel without any information with a boy of her own choice as she failed to get the consent of her parents.
3. The abduction of young girls with the object of selling them: A gang engaged in selling of kidnapped girls from Assam and Bihar has come to light.
4. The abduction for sexual purposes: A kidnapped girl of Kolkata alleged before the police that she was brought to Patna for working in the house. But she was raped and was asked to entertain VIPs.

Kinds of Abductors

We may classify abductors in four groups on the basis of the news reported in newspapers.

1. *Accesory Abductor:* He "abducts" victim with her consent to marry him.

2. ***Opportunist Abductor:*** He abducts the victims only for sexual purposes on the enticement for a better life.
3. ***Lover Abductor:*** He is in love with the victim to the extent that he even abducts her to marry her against her own and her parents wishes.
4. ***Fraud abductor:*** He abducts the victim to sell her and earn money.

Categories of Abducted Victims

We may classify the abducted victim in five groups:

1. ***Co-operative Victim:*** She is a woman who willingly agrees to leave her house with the accused, being very unhappy in father's house.
2. ***Accidental Victim:*** She is a woman who by chance falls in the hands of a wrong person who abducts her on false pretexts.
3. ***Misled Victim:*** She is a female who takes the advances of a male seriously.
4. ***Corrupt Victim:*** She is a female who is in search of pleasure.
5. ***Forced Victim:*** She is a female who is forcibly abducted against her wishes.

Steps Advised

Some of the suggestions which need proper attention are as follows:

1. It is desirable that the parents have to be watchful about their wards, both male and female. They must see to it that they keep good company and remain useful engaged.
2. As for the girls, they should be escorted properly in late hours or in desolate areas, they are not to be left to the care of the servants, drivers or even tutors who take liberties with them.
3. Girls and women must enjoy a status of freedom in marriage and position of respect in family and society.

4. Parental control over the children and harmonious relation in the family is necessary for a healthy society. The children both male and female should be equally given due love, affection and respect in the family.

5. Police should be informed about the missing of their wards at the earliest.

Handling the problems of kidnapping/abduction is a difficult task. It can be and ought to be solved through appropriate collective action, the victim, the parents and the police. It is not good blaming the police all the time.

TEN

Rape on Rise

The Oxford Dictionary defines the word rape as "forcible or fradulent sexual intercourse imposed on women". In the words of Susan Brown Miller, "Rape is the only crime for which the victim cannot have a revenge." It represents as "act of violence and humiliation in which the victim experiences not only overwhelming fear for her very existence, but an equally overwhelming sense of powerlessness and helplessness that hardly a few others events in ones life can parallel" (Hilberman, 1976).

What is Rape?

The word rape in many Indian languages, is *balaatkar* derived from the root *bal* meaning strength, basically in a physical sense. But it is also a beastly crime because the time and place where the rape is committed, finds the victim defenceless, weak, alone, or vulnerable. In other words, at that particular moment she is in no position to defend herself against physical assault. Rape for a woman should simply mean a criminal invasion into personal integrity. Seen from the angle of the patriarchal society, it has primarily meant an assault on the legally recognised male rights of possession where he has the right of possession of an unblemished woman. The Hindi phrase for rape is *Izzat lootna* which literally translates as "the robbing of honour".

Legal Definition

According to Section 375 of the Indian Penal Code, rape is committed when a man has sexual intercourse with a woman:

(i) against her will, or

(ii) without her consent, or

(iii) with her consent, when her consent has been obtained by putting her or any person in whom she is interested, in fear of death, or of hurt, or

(iv) with her consent, when he by deception, makes her believe that he is her lawful husband, or

(v) with her consent, given an account of her unsoundness of mind, or intoxication, when she is incapable of understanding the consequences of her consent, or

(vi) with or without consent, when she is under 16 years of age.

'Against her will' means an act is done against a woman's will when she is fully conscious and capable of consenting and a decision-making power and is aware of what is being done and resists or objects to it. 'Without her consent' means that she is insensible and incapable of rational consent, due to fear, shock or intoxication or any other cause.

Rape is the most calculated, cold blooded, deliberate and heinous of crimes committed by one human being on another by virtue of the simple and biological fact that the one who commits rape is physically stronger than this victim. Being by no means accidental or committed in the heat of the moment on a passionate impulse, there is no anger or vengeance involved either.

In a rape, the aggressor is a man, the rapist and the aggrieved party is also a man, the father or the husband and the woman being the damaged property. The woman is the victim and it is she who has to carry the stigma for the rest of her life. The social and religious values make her an outcaste, an untouchable and a disgrace to her family. It is an exceptional crime where harassment, guilt, shame and social disapproval are attached to the victim, not to the offender. Society at large looks down on a victim with suspicion. The woman is made to feel guilty as myths about rape such as "no woman can be raped unless she wants", dressed like that she was asking for it, or "women like being raped", etc. are current in society. This makes it even more difficult for the victim to reveal her tragedy. Often men consider women tempting in any dress good or bad. When she is alone, she can be taken as inviting man and she can be considered flirting when she is socialising.

All women perpetually suffer from the fear of being raped irrespective of her age, health, appearance, mental state, shelter and relations. No woman is immune from being the victim of rape.

The scourage of rape continues to wreak havoc on the nation's thousand of innocent women. Various examples have been gathered, the rape case reported in newspapers that high class men or men in power rape Harijan women.

- Two Harijan girls were allegedly raped, their huts were demolished and a well was polluted by landlords in separate incidents in the interior of Nawada district.
- Teachers rape their students, three minor girls were raped by their teacher in mohalla Machharhatta of Barh Bazar.
- Sometimes the colleagues residents of Myar village under Noorsarai P.S. witnessed the rape of a female teacher at the Myar Middle School by her male colleagues in the school building.
- Students rape their fellows. A young girl, victim of an attempt of rape in the hostel of a local college of Patna, was handed over to her parents by the Pirbahore police after medical examination.
- Doctors rape their patients in hospital and nursing home. Two doctors of Nalanda Medical College Hospital were arrested by Sultanganj police on the charge of criminally assaulting a female patient; Employees rape their co-workers. A nurse of Sadar Hospital, Giridih was criminally assaulted by two employees of the hospital.
- Prison staff rape their undertrials. A Harijan woman undertrial prisoner was allegedly raped to death by the jail staff in Giridih.
- Landlords rape their tenants. A twelve-year-old girl in Barmasia locality of Giridih district was assaulted and raped by her landlord as the parents of the victim were out of the town.

- Tenants rape their landlords. A middle-aged woman of Tekari road, Sultanganj area of Patna was raped by one of her tenant.
- Masters rape their maid servants. A 15-year-old girl working as a maid servant in the lodge in Dhaneshwar Ghat Mohalla under Bihar Sharif Police Station was raped by some students.
- Domestic servants rape the housewives. A domestic servant was arrested by the Bankmore Police of Dhanbad on the charge of criminally assaulting a housewife when the other family members of the house were out.
- Old men and young men alike enjoy the pleasure of sex out of wedlock and even women suffering from T.B. and other ailments undergoing treatment become victims. A poor, sick woman was gangraped by some identified people in village Berhna under Police Station of Patna while she was relaxing under the shade of a tree. A girl of 17 years, living with her sick mother in the hospital of Chaibasa was raped by unknown persons, after disconnecting electric line. A pregnant woman of Sinhpur village under Kasmar Police Station of Bokaro was brutally beaten by three miscreants when the victim resisted their attempt to rape her. An adivasi minor blind girl of Lakha village under Mofussil Police Station was gangraped by three identified persons. An Adivasi woman under treatment for leprosy at Nav Kusth Ashram of Bhagalpur was gang raped by four criminals. Their physical appearance need not be always attractive.
- Sometimes the rape victims are reported to be baby girls. A man was arrested at Jamshedpur on the charge of raping a three-year-old girl.
- Old women have also been raped.
- An old woman of Agrer village under Sasaram block of Rohtas district was raped in her house by some goondas in a drunken state when his husband was out of station. Later on she was strangulated to death.

- Women may not be safe even in their families. A 20-year-old woman was raped and murdered by her father-in-law at Sheonar village of Mokameh.

Rape of women cuts across barriers of caste, class, education, looks, age and status. The rapist may be any person—a holyman, a doctor, a teacher, a servant, a landlord or a farmer, a student, a neighbour or a co-villager, a relative or a criminal. Therefore, the rapist is one among ourselves. He has no distinct identity. There are an umpteen numbers of instances and a plenty of evidence to show that rapist may be no stranger to the victim and the offence could just as easily occur in family setting—offices, educational institutions, hospitals and even homes. The aggressor could even be a boy friend or acquaintance. He could be an employer, or landlord who wields power, a neighbour or a member of the family.

Sexual harassment is unknown in the dingy corridor and cubicles of office and factories in metropolitan and industrial towns. Working women are harassed by their bosses and colleagues. Those who come from cultured families and also have some financial means give up their job as a protest. But women who come from the lower middle-class and are sole supporters of a family or their income is an indispensable supplement to their husband, beat their bosses sexual overtones silently. It is a mistake to assume that all rapists are perverts, normal men do rape. There are the cases male members of the victim's family have even lost their lives in a bid to save the female members from being raped.

It would be more precise to state rape is mostly used to express or to assert class power or as an instrument of class oppression. Rape an assertion of male power as a terrorising instrument of punishment, is indulged in by the elite, by the guardians of the law and order on woman from the rural areas, woman from the scheduled castes and tribes. Why is it that educated women are raped less frequently than illiterate and ignorant women? Why is it that high caste women are raped very rarely. A 19-year-old girl was gang raped by a number of Harijans in village Neura of Barh subdivision in broad day light and the rapists prevented the victim's family from going to the police station and in their bid to do so they opened several rounds of fire. While low caste tribal woman and women from minority communities who are also poor raped quite often? And finally, women from the upper, middle and affluent classes are hardly raped while women from the economically poor classes are subjected to rape every other day. Rape among the middle and upper classes is another taboo subject. Even among middle class women, the general attitude towards rape is that it is something which happens to lower class women, something the rest of society is protected from by virtue of caste or class. In parts of the country even today, landlords demand 'first night' privileges. It is the common allegation in rape case where the authority is the offender and helpless, poor women are the victims that these women are of loose moral character.

The question is: how can the investigating authorities make any positive conclusions about the moral character of any woman, whether she is raped or not, without having any knowledge about her lifestyle except the fact that she is poor, illiterate and belongs to a backward and oppressed community? Even if the women who have been victimised are women of loose morals, what has character got to do with a man's right to rape her? These questions remain unanswered in this male dominated society. It may be known that — a woman is a woman just as man is a man. One human being's moral or immoral or a moral stand does not in any way justify another person's humiliation of her or him, sex notwithstanding. If one were to reverse the theory, then what would women do with men who have loose morals? But women cannot do anything specially if they are poor, illiterate and belong to the backward classes as long as it is the men who man the law and judicial machinery of the country.

Rape is one language often used by two groups of warring men to get even with each other, not considering that the people who are used for this, are flesh-and-blood thinking and living beings because they are women. Rape is not always necessarily for the perverted sense of sexual pleasure of man as was commonly believed for ages together. Brownmiller states that populations have been terrorised by rape : (i) in the two World Wars, (ii) in the wars of Bangladesh and Vietnam, (iii) during partition riots in India in 1947, when there was mass rape of both Hindu and Muslim women. Rape, therefore, has been systematically and calculatedly used as an instrument of intimidation in India, not only for women, but also to humiliate and demoralise the men. After the assassination of Indira Gandhi, about 2000 women were raped in Delhi in the riots following her death.

Rural-urban difference in the incidence of rape in Bihar revealed the following trends.

Rape Incidents

(i) Percentages of rape in rural areas were slightly higher compared to urban areas in all the years except 1981 and 1988.

(ii) In urban areas higher rate of incidence was in 1981 and 1988 when the percentage of incidence was 50.61 and 51.05 respectively.

(iii) Both rural and urban areas demonstrated decreasing as well as increasing tendencies in the rate of rape cases.

The data were further analysed to examine the difference between rural and urban areas within each region.

Studies in Bihar indicate that the incidence of rape was always higher in urban compared to rural areas except in Adivasi region where the incidence was double in number in rural areas compared to the urban areas during the same years in the four regions. When the rape cases were analysed region-wise, the rural-urban differences became more vivid as well as region-specific. In Magahi, Maithili, and Bhojpuri region urban areas contributed more towards the incidence than the rural one. On the other hand, in the Adivasi region it was rural side which reported higher rate of rape cases.

Kinds of Rape

Rape of Dalit and Tribal Women

It is an all-pervasive fact that Dalit and tribal women are oppressed by society at large; rape is simply being used an instrument to oppress women. Dalit and tribal women are raped for a variety of reasons not least of which is the fact that they are vulnerable women and raping them is not likely to result in any punishment. They are also raped as a way of demoralising them in their struggle for an improved existence. For the last two decades Bihar has seen many gruesome violence taking place in different parts of the state. The incidents at Belchi, Pipra, Parashbigha, Arwal, Kansara, and Gua are some of the most prominent ones, where women had been targets of rape and molestation. A big demonstration by about 5000 tribal including women was held in front of the office of the Deputy Commissioner demanding immediate action against the policemen who had allegedly misbehaved with tribal women while they were on their traditional 'Janishikar'.

Rape on the Job

The rape of working women is a national scandal which is at least as widespread as custodial rape, yet it does not receive as much attention. They are harassed by their bosses and male workers. Domestic servants are molested by employer or the relatives or friends of employers. The headmaster of an English medium school at Bhurkunda, 30 km from Ramgarh Cantt was taken into police custody for raping a lady teacher of his school. A nurse of Sadar Hospital, Giridih was criminally assaulted by two young employees of the hospital.

Rape by Strangers

Women are not safe anywhere, may it be the street or the fields or even her own home.

A married woman of Chandi mohalla of Barh was brutally assaulted by six youths at her residence as the other members of the family were out. A Harijan girl of village Musapur under Sarairanjan police station of Dalsingsarai was raped and murdered by identified persons in her house while she was sleeping with her mother.

Rape of Minor

Rape of minor is particularly horrifying and now it has become a common crime. Newspapers regularly print accounts of the rape of minor girls. One person of Jamshedpur was taken into custody on the charge of raping a three-year-old girl. A five-year-old girl was lured away from a Ganesh Puja pandal and raped by an unidentified man and she was taken to the intensive care unit of the Tata Main Hospital in an unconscious state.

Rape in Journey

Women are not safe even while travelling. A minor girl waiting for a particular bus at the Harding Park bus stand of Patna was taken to a lonely place by a worker of a transport agency on the pretext of guiding her to the said bus and was raped. Two women train passengers were kidnapped from North Eastern Railway Dighwara station and allegedly gangraped.

A young woman passenger was criminally assaulted in a compartment of the Munger-Jamalpur local train after locking the gates and her husband who tried to resist them was thrown out of the running train.

Rape of Sick

Even women suffering from T.B. or other ailments undergoing treatment, pregnant, blind women and women suffering from leprosy are the victims of rape.

A sick women of Patna who went to a hospital for her treatment was allegedly raped by three persons.

A pregnant women was brutally beaten by three miscreants when she resisted their attempt to rape her.

A Adivasi minor blind girl was gangraped by three youngsters.

An Adivasi woman under treatment for leprosy was gangraped by four criminals.

Rape within family

Women are not safe even in their own family. A 20-year-old woman was raped and murdered by her father-in-law of Sheonar village in Mokameh. A young married woman deposed before the Judicial Magistrate that her father-in-law entered her room and committed rape on her and it was why she stabbed him.

Thus, it is observed that women are raped at work, on the street, in the fields, at bus or railway platform, in train, in school, in their homes by men who are their employers or employees, their acquaintance, their neighbours, their relatives, and their in-laws. It is not only Dalit women who are victims and not only landlords who are rapists.

Types of Rapists

There may be at least three categories of rapists. There is one whose assault is the explosive expression of a pent-up sexual impulse; he is motivated by sex desire only. In such cases the rapists has no respect of age or looks. The second group is motivated by an impulse to punish and hurt the victim, rather than sex desire. Gang rapes by dacoits after committing a dacoity, rapes on Harijan women, rapes on women during communal riots, rapes due to family dispute and gang rape by policemen all come under this group. And there is a third group of rapist, the aggressive criminals, who is out of pillage and rob, like the soldiery of a conquering army.

Gebhard in a psychological study of rapists found the following five categories of rapists:

(i) ***Sadists:*** who have a past history of violence, a strong hostility to females, and who obtain sexual satisfaction only when it is accompanied by physical violence.

(ii) ***Moral delinquents:*** who are not hostile to females, use force to get what they want and commit rape to satisfy sexual desire without taking interest in victim.

(iii) ***Explosives:*** who are normally "upright" citizens. A disturbed family background usually underlies the behaviour of these offenders.

(iv) ***Drunken variety:*** who after drinking delude themselves into thinking that a female is trying to seduce them.

(v) ***Double standard:*** who divide females into "good" and "bad" and rationalize the use of force, if necessary, on "bad" girls.

Identification of a Rapist

The sex, instinct, indeed had been a very powerful motivation since the time immemorial. In a way, every man in this world is a sexual criminal at the unconscious level. But what matters is the action. People who translate their latent feelings into action give way to the doctrine that pleasure is the chief god. Through psychoanalytic studies, it has been revealed that the rapists are persons with poor judgement and inadequate impulse control.

They lack the power of reasoning which leads them to sexual perversion. A man with a well developed personality and a strong moral standard would never indulge in such activities.

Rape is also attributed to unhappy family life which may be due to various incapabilities such as potency, temperament, habit and economic conditions, as a result of which marital life turns annoying and frustrating. Broken homes and constant friction in family turns children into sex delinquents.

Pornographic literature and the modern movies depicting crude rape and bathing scenes are also contributing to the desire to rape among adolescents and youth. Disregard of moral values and lack of religious sanctions also give rise to urge of rape.

Sex crimes also occur due to psychological factors like desire to rape, exhibition of potency, experience of pleasure in the pain of others (Sadism), taking revenge on a woman and like. A major study of forcible rape (Amir, 1971) has shown that in 85 per cent of all reported rapes there was some form of overt violence such as beating or choking. It may be stated that rape is an act of aggression and violence and it is committed by persons who are not motivated by sexuality; rather they are motivated primarily by power, hostility and the urge to brutalise, humiliate and debase their victims.

According to Mackellar (1975), "The man who rapes does so because he lacks a better means for making the point, 'I am a man,' while Bart (1975) has stressed the anger in rape: "Psychiatrists say a gun is a substitute phallus. Rape is a power trip, not a passion trip. The rapist is more likely to rape in cold blood, with contempt and righteousness, than with passion".

Thus, rape is a universal phenomenon. Its etiology is complex and the manifestations are extremely varied according to time, place and person. It also varies with historical periods, modes of life, economic conditions and social attitudes.

Ways and Consequences of Victimisation

The victims of rape are victimized in sundry ways and rape is pregnant with momentous consequences for its victim. We may distinguish three ways of victimization of, and three types of consequences for, the victim of the rape: psychological, physical and social.

Psychological Victimization

Psychological victimization of the victim and its consequences can be understood in three phases of rape: before, during and after rape.

The fear of rape troubles all women, it is a source of mental anxiety to the victim. Research on the fear of crime and on public opinion, about crime shows that the very possibility of being victimised troubles many people. Freedom from criminal victimisation is a social good, much like any other social good of a just society.

Rape affects all women whether or not they are actually victimized. According to Griffin (1970) who verbalizes as follows, the experience of many women: 'I have never been free of the fear of rape. From a very early age I, like most women, have thought of rape as part of my natural environment something to be feared and prayed against like fire or lightning". Women are under perpetual fear of being raped which induces a continuing state of psychological stress in women due to which they resort to several safety precautions which, in turn, seriously restrict their freedom, such as not moving alone, or avoiding to go to certain places, or going out with certain men. Several studies attest to these consequences of the fear of rape on all women, all the time, everywhere, who may not have been victimized but who, nonetheless, are subjected to the threat of rape and to the concomitant forces of social control.

The actual commission of rape is a "crisis situation" full of stress and strain for a victim thus far leading a normal life. And it is a strange sudden crisis—a crisis with which the victim must deal herself. If she surrenders sexually, then her life is spoilt personally and socially, and if she resists, then she runs the risk of being destroyed physically at the hands of the rapist.

The post-rape period poses a more lingering as the ordeal for the rape victim. The terror of the criminal justice system, social stigma, and the physical injury, combine together to cause psychological malaise beyond description. In her post-rape life, she begins to nurture distrust in men and society, confronts difficulties in her sexual adjustment, and suffers from a host of psychological disturbances, including fear, insomnia, anxiety, dreams, hallucinations and others. Many a time, the victim reconciles with the mental trauma caused by her by taking refuge in suicide.

Physical Victimization

In the process of preventing the rapist from raping the victim incurs a wide variety of physical injuries, depending upon the location and the extent of resistance put up. The injuries from the physical attacks of the rapist are on various parts of the body, throat, neck, cheeks, thighs, legs, arms and genitalia. And injuries themselves are varied 'scratches, bruises, at times being knifed or shot at.

Varieties of physical complaints and complications begin to appear in post-rape period: physical pain in different parts of the body, skeletal muscle tension, gastro-intestinal irritability and genito-urinary disturbances, to cite a few.

The victim's large number of complicated physiological problems warrant immediate medicare. For instance, there is a possibility of contracting venereal diseases and conceiving, besides other physical injuries in course of her struggle to resist the occurrence of rape. It is the victim alone who has to bear the cost of the medicine, besides bearing the physical pain and mental agony. Needless to say, the hospitals lack physicians with special training in handling physical and emotional complications which rape victims are exposed to. Furthermore, the hospitals are not adequately equipped to treat even the physiological damages, what to speak of psychological treatment, facilities which are practically non-existent throughout the length and breadth of the country.

Social Victimization

The Victim's Plane

Rape has several far-reaching social implications both for the victim and for the society. Although it involves a limited number of men and women on the face of it, rape is basically a social problem (Rose, 1977) of great magnitude. On the victim's plane, the implications of rape depend upon whether she is married or unmarried, child or adult, having first sexual experience or not. In case the victim is unmarried, it creates problems in the settlement of her marriage if it becomes public. And, if she is married, there is a possibility of a breakdown of the marriage. Even if the marital life continues, or marriage of the unmarried happens to be solemnized, the sword of the fear of rape being divulged, and consequently being disturbed when it becomes known it always hang will over the head of the rape victim. And, if per chance the rape remains concealed throughout, the psychological stress caused by sexual assault remains for ever.

The volume of physiological pain due to sexual assault differs to different age groups of the victims but psychological complications also vary. The severity of the impact of rape felt by the victims varies depending upon whether the victim is a child or a younger or older or an adult.

In all these, and many other ways rape has a chain of negative consequences in the life of the victim as a wife, a daughter, betrothed, a beloved, a child, parent, working women, and so on. In this manner, rape threatens the very existence of the victim in society.

The Social Plane

Rape is one instance where the atrocities of men against women become naked. Rape is in fact, not the rape of women but the rape of morality and the noble ideals of the society as a whole. The rapist remains a man and, at times, he is honoured in society, whereas, the victim of the same rapist is treated as a 'bad' women. In a male-dominated society, females are subjected to all sorts of subjection—physical, social and psychological. On the social plane, the threat of rape serves as a weapon in the hands of men and the society. They dominate to maintain social control of women by keeping them in a state of perpetual anxiety and by encouraging the self imposition of behaviour restriction in quest for safety (Riger and Gordon, 1981: 71-92). Rape is a crisis for the victim's family members and friends who also need emotional support (Krishna, 1988). If the rape is her first sexual experience, she may find herself quite confused about the relationship between sexuality, violence and humiliation. On attempting to leave her house and have an independent identity, her sense of adequacy is challenged by her feeling that she really cannot take care of herself. The women who have an ongoing sexual relationship may prefer not to disclose it to their man/men for fear of disrupting the relationship.

Rape of women is simultaneously a crisis for the victim's family. The very feeling that a woman of the family has been raped is a kind of shock, difficult for a family to bear. In such a crisis situation, the family members become emotionally disturbed. The prestige of the family in society is lowered, if such cases become public through the court or otherwise. In many cases, raped wives and daughters are not accepted by their husband or parents as the case may be. Many a time they are thrown in the lap of prostitution. Even if the victim survives the shock and remains in the family, social stigma labels her as a 'bad' woman throughout her lifetime.

Rape cannot be consummated until after force and prolonged resistance have been overcome. So if there is no outward evidence of resistance such as a black eye, bruise or scratch, there evidently was no resistance. Right from the beginning the victim is subjected to embarrassing queries which hinge on whether she had resisted sufficiently, and generally the accused gets the benefit of doubt. Rape is a personal crisis in the sense that the victim must deal with the impact and meaning of the event for herself. The stereotype that a woman should always attempt to prevent the rape through struggle leaves women in a double mind. If they do not struggle, they have a very hard time in court. If they do struggle, they run the risk of incurring even more injuries at the hands of the rapist.

Rape involves at least two major crisis for the women. The first is the rape itself. The second is her experience of going through the medical examination and the criminal justice system, with her appearance in court being the most painful part. While it is difficult to provide all the long-term psychological problems of the victim, some of the issues which seems to re-emerge at a later date are mistrust and avoidance of men, sexual disturbances, phobic hallucination, delusions, insomnia, terrifying dreams, anxiety and depression often precipitated by seemingly trivial events which symbolise the original trauma. Due to sexual repulsion and fear there is a decline of interest as well as withdrawal from one's partner. Post-rape adjustment is one of the most important psychological problems, which must be tackled properly in time by counselling. Psychologically problems are more severe when the rapist is a near relative. There is no law that can obliterate the trauma with which she must live.

Change in Attitude Required

The evidence of resistance required in case of rape victim is not required for dacoity, etc. The rape victim is subjected to embarassing questions. The social stigma attached to such cases is deterrent enough to reporting such cases. Under Rule 228(A) of the Act, the identity of the victim and all details of the rape itself will be kept in the strict confidence of the trying court. The entire legal proceedings will be held in camera.

Values and attitudes regarding rape should be changed. When a woman is raped, why should she be held guilty. The man has committed the rape on her person should be held responsible for the shameful act. Why should her identity remain secret? Why should she feel ashamed or guilt or both? Because she is the subordinate and less important sex? Because if she is unmarried, her chances of a good marriage may be lost for ever? Because she has lost her virginity if she is unmarried, and her chastity if she is married and these two things are held at the premium in a society where social values are decided by the males?

Thus, social attitudes towards the victims need to be changed. Thousand of girls and women are victims by society for no fault of their own. Taking unfair advantages of the social stigma, the rapist lead the victim to prostitution. Forms and values of the society should not be misinterpreted for the cause of women. If a sexually active man is perceived as a sexually active man; a sexually active woman should also be perceived as a sexually active woman, not as a bad woman. The objective 'promiscuous' should not be applied only to her. The problems cannot be solved adequately unless we change the Victorian attitude of male dominated society.

Steps Advised

Some of the suggestions which need proper attention are as follows:

1. The accused should not be permitted to question the victim regarding her character or previous sexual relations with any other person.
2. Rape victims should not be maltreated at the hands of the police whose assistance has been sought during the crisis. They should not be submitted to the countless questions about her own sexual mores and behaviour by the police investigator.
3. The victims should be thoroughly examined by an expert doctor and immediate cure of physical injuries, prevention of veneral disease, and prevention of pregnancy should be taken.
4. It is advisable that the burden of proof be shifted from the victim to the offender. Let him prove that he did not rape her. Let it not be the woman's burden to prove that she was criminally assaulted.
5. In recent years, cases of false accusation have come to notice for the purpose of blackmailing the accused to extort money or women offenders, during arrests and search, to level false charges of rape against policemen. Therefore, when women are involved in a crime she must be arrested and searched by a woman police officer. Report of rape victims should be recorded by women police officers and women investigators are to be appointed to investigate such cases.
6. The burden of stigma should not be attached within the victim and his family rather it should be shifted from the victim to the offender.
7. Victims of the rape deserve emotional support and sympathy by family members for post-rape adjustment rather than being disowned by them.
8. No woman should be arrested between sunset and sun rise.
9. Sex education should be imparted to adolescents and youths in order to prevent the crime against women. Parents should not feel ashamed in discussing sex with their children.

Our study of rape shows that the status of women continues to be low, and crime continues to be directed against them. Changes must be brought in the mind, heart and behaviour of men and women in the various compartments of our culture and in our social institutions so that the age-old sex anarchy of rape of women is removed.

ELEVEN

Torture after Marriage

The very foundation of a happy family lies in cordial husband-wife relationships. It affects all — the children, the home and the family. A cordial relationship makes the children feel more secure in their home and relate to everything more effectively, whereas an uncordial relationship makes them dull and inefficient. The suffering of the wife is not to be forgotten. Thus, marital conflict only leads to familial disorganisation and has negative consequences on the children's upbringing. Thus, the quality of interaction between a husband and wife has repercussions on the whole family. Keeping in view the importance of the husband-wife relationship in the family as well as the distinctive nature of quality of the interaction between them, it would be most appropriate to investigate the causes of violence in conjugal relations.

Different studies around the world have shown that wife-beating is the most popular form of violence. Husbands use violence against wives to reinforce their dominant position, because use of coercive methods by husbands against wives have societal approval. Women being women, they tolerate the torture silently keeping it all within themselves sometimes to keep the family fabric intact.

Because of the gender relationships down the ages, women are used as instruments of reproduction with no independent status outside family thus maintaining systemic inequality over time. Further male authority exposes them to swift retributions and confirm their vulnerability. Ganley (1981) suggests that men who batter their wives have learned certain cultural and social values about masculinity and their roles in families that support their aggression and violence. Males are socialized into roles that encourage aggression towards females. Socialization and sex role conditioning appear to be instrumental in defining the attitudes that males have toward violence and are major factors in determining the power relationship between men and women that allows violent behaviour to take place. Unless women raise their voices this process will continue in times to come.

Husband Dominant

With male values superseding female values and emphasis on submission and timidity for women and strength for men as cherished values, it becomes clear that man is born to rule. The first and indeed the life-long recipient of male violence is the female (Krishnan, 1988). Thus within the family the husband enjoys higher status than the wife, who is considered inferior and subordinate. Social pressures force women to maintain the status quo. A woman who does not accept the traditional role of submissiveness and subordination needs to be tamed into accepting this position and any means specially, violence is justified in achieving this goal (Agnes, 1988).

Background

Being a historical phenomena, wife beating has been studied by many historians who have documented the informal and formal sanctions by society that have encouraged wife battering (Davidson 1978; Martin, 1976; Pleck, 1987). Scottish and English laws permitted a husband to discipline his wife physically without prosecution for assault and battery. As a few Scottish sociologists observed about both the United States and Great Britain: "Prior to the late 19th century it was considered a necessary aspect of a husband's marital obligation to control and chastise his wife through the use of physical force." (Shupe *et al.*, 1987). This view can be traced back to the Roman Empire and medieval times in "Laws of Chastisement" found in many countries as well as in selected passages of the Old and New Testaments in the Bible endorsing male authority over women.

For many centuries, during the Dark and Middle ages as well as the Renaissance, women were routinely subjected to physical punishment that accompanied their accepted inferior status and justified by the so-called "laws of chatisement" which went unquestioned. Such violence was simply taken for granted as part of the divinely ordained order of things.

Wife beating was condoned in American culture via the English law. The infamous rule of the thumb which permitted a husband legally to beat his wife with a rod not thicker than his thumb was a formal sanction of British Common Law. Ironically, it was originally intended as an example of compassionate reform to limit how harshly men abused their mates. Thus, man's right to use violence in managing their homes was very much an accepted pattern.

It was only in the 20th century, that the law finally condemned wife abuse and considered it to be a criminal offence. It was not until the women's liberation movement in the 1970s that identified and responded to wife abuse recognising it as a "social problem" (Tierney, 1982). Prior to this time its existence was overlooked and even denied, although it continued to exist. Various historical circumstances led several social scientists to explain that men abused women basically because they are permitted and encouraged to do so (Gelles, 1983).

The patriarchal system of society relegated women to a subordinate position always obeying orders of men. For them, the husbands were *Pati Parmeshwar* (God). They meekly suffered discrimination in shape of female infanticide, Sati Pratha, dowry, denial of widow remarriage, denial of education, denial of share in family property, etc. because of their dependency and lack of alternative support system.

During the nineteenth century, educated Indian elites namely, Raja Ram Mohun Roy, Ishwar Chandra Vidyasagar, Mahatma Phule, Karsandas Mulji and many other social reformists attacked the social practices of child marriage, *Sati* and harsh treatment of widows. They advocated women's education, widow remarriage and such other social reforms. They engaged in advancing the status of women by requiring that the law to take cognizance of their rights by providing them some basic rights such as the right to live.

Pre Independence Legislations Protecting Women's Rights

Lord William Bentick outlawed the practice of *Sati* in 1820. Sati had always been an exaggeration of the Hindu ideal, never practised by the majority, and was therefore successfully eradicated. In 1856, Widow Remarriage Act was passed. It was, however, less successful. The Britishers also passed Infanticide Act in 1870 to abolish this practice to female infanticide. In 1860, following much agitation, the age of consent was raised to ten years and in 1891 it was raised to twelve years. The Sarda Act of 1929 raised the age still further to fifteen. In spite of such legislations there was no visible change in women's status. The British were unwilling to interfere with Indian customs as per the populous measures to keep their government stable. The dogged persistence of their Western-educated Indians compelled them to move, if at all.

Post-Independence Legislations Protecting Women's Rights

There were serious attempts made to elevate the status of women only after Independence. Only in 1955, by passing the Hindu Marriage Act the law forbade polygamy for Hindus, allowed divorce by either husband or wife on the same grounds and specified the marriage age for girls as 15 and for boys as 18. Secular and mixed marriages were legalised by the Special Marriage Act of 1954. These acts were followed by the Hindu Succession Act of 1956, poviding that a son, daughter and widow/mother could inherit equally. The Hindu Adoption and Maintenance Bill of 1956 provided separate maintenance for women under certain conditions, where legal separation or divorce was not sought. The Dowry Prohibition Act was passed in 1961 as an effort to end the practice of demanding dowry. The Act was modified by the Dowry Prohibition (Amendment) Act of 1984, which has again been modified by the Dowry Prohibition (Amendment) Bill, 1986. Other major legislative measures to improve the position of women have been the passage of the State Maternity Benefit Acts and the Termination of Pregnancy Act in 1972.

Literacy among Women

Another force for improvement in the status of women apart from legal reform of social customs is education. After more than four decades, the literacy figure for women is 39.42 per cent as opposed to that of men, which is 63.86 per cent (1991 census). Though education for women, was restricted to a very small upper-class elite, yet it played an important role in opening up avenues for women in gainful employment outside their homes.

Whereas urban upper and middle income group women have changed the rural women and urban poor women still suffer like before. Thus, neglect and exploitation of women continue in its characteristic fashion. According to Desai (1982) the conditions of women in general do not show much improvement and the social economic measures of women's upliftment have not significantly affected their economic status practices, such as the denial of remarriage of upper caste Hindu widows, polygamy and dowry continue in our society despite being illegal. Thus, there is no let up in the suffering of women in spite of legal measures. The widespread incidence of bride burning and dowry deaths still continues. What was known as female infanticide has come in newer form of amniocentesis after sex determination tests in urban areas.

Defending the Victim

A small percentage of women who have gained economic independence are facing the challenge of an exploitative social order. They no longer accept male dictates and are now claimed an egalitarian way of living, which implies change in the traditional relationships between husband and wife. Men being what they are not likely to accept the new position of the wives and may use violence to retain their traditional position. To highlight the plight of women victims, some women organisations, which are however, mostly urban-based, have emerged. These women organisations are engaged not only in militant activism to assert women's right but also have made serious attempts to articulate their thoughts on the root causes of oppression of women. Their main purpose being to create public awareness against the existing exploitative system in society. In the beginning these women organisations took up the issue of dowry, wife beating and subsequently they took up different types of exploitation of women which were not confined to intra-familial relations, for example, sexual harassment at the work place. Women organisations are thus playing an important role to highlight the problem of wife abuse not only in the West but also in India and seek public cooperation for this.

Prevalence of Wife Abuse

Having been given little attention, wife abuse is perhaps the most prevalent form of family violence. It was during the mid-seventees that social scientists in the West started conducting studies to find out the nature and the extent of violence against wives while trying to identify the precipitating factors which led to violent relationship between the marital partners. The research of almost two decades led them to work out not only the coping mechanisms adopted by the victims but also different treatment programmes for the batterer and the battered. Comparatively India, has very few studies which have been conducted in this area. A few isolated attempts have been made after the late 1980's to find out the nature of the problem as well as the precipitating factors which lead to violence against women.

In David Levinson (1989) study of 90 pre-literate and peasant societies of the world it was concluded that beating is the most common and frequent form of family violence.

According to a 1976 national survey in America, violent against wives had reached "epidemic" proportions with nearly 2 million women battered every year. At least one act of violence occurs per year in 16 per cent of all married couples. Nearly one-third of all married couples experience physical abuse at some point (Straus et al., 1980). It was estimated that actually over one-half of all wives will be assaulted sometime during their marriage (Walker, 1979). Other studies in the United States have suggested that incidence is as high as fifty per cent (Straus, 1978). Data from the Second National Family Violence Survey conducted in the United States (Straus and Gelles, 1986) reveals that incidence of battering has decreased as much as 20 per cent since the mid-1970s. Some scholars are of the opinion that wife battering is quite widespread in all the cultures though the problem is hidden away in some cultures as a "private matter" (Seager and Olson, 1986).

There has been no nationally representative sample survey conducted to find out the extent of the problem. Besides a few isolated studies conducted to find out the frequency of wife abuse in India.

A study of dowry victims shows that one in every four were murdered or driven to commit suicide and more than a half (61.3 per cent) were thrown out of their husband's house after putting up with harassment and torture for long. (Ranjana Kumari, 1989). According to the Anti-Dowry Cell set up by the Police Commissioner, New Delhi, in 1983, 690 young women died in Delhi alone of whom 23 were burnt alive (Jain, 1992).

Mahajan, M. (1992) in a study of 200 cases at Chandigarh found that with the exception of 13 families, all the other cases reported presence of one or another form of violence in the relationship thus observed that violence in conjugal relation is common. In 33.5 per cent cases, there was a presence of physical violence against the wives.

Bhatti (1989), while taking into account various forms of violence concluded that 88 per cent of women in lower class were the victims of physical and verbal violence in contrast to 43 per cent from the middle class and 35 per cent from the high income class. With regard to emotional and intellectual violence, he found that representation of the upper and middle classes was more as compared to the lower class.

Devasahayam *et al.* (1991) in a sample of 153 cases of K.V. Kuppan Block (a village in Gujarat) found that approximately 21 per cent admitted the existence of marital violence. Alcoholism was the major cause of violence in their families. Singh (1985) in a study conducted in a village of Punjab found that violence in different forms existed in 50 per cent of the cases and physical violence was present in 9 per cent of the cases out of the sample of 114 cases belonging to different caste groups.

Different studies thus establish that wife abuse is a widespread phenomena around the world.

Offender and the Victim

The precipitating factors leading to wife abuse have been studied by various scholars and some have attributed abuse to the personality factors of either the battered or the batterer or both.

It is assumed that either one or both the spouses possess certain characteristics that make them prone to wife battering. A few sociologists have tried to identify the social variables which are responsible for differential behaviour pattern attributing it to socialization, normative pattern, value system, etc. They attempt to explain the legitimization of intra-familial violence and the victimization of women through social approval.

It is often assumed that batterers suffer from various personality disorders. Men who assault their wives have low self-esteem and use violence to compensate the feelings of inadequacy (Boyd, 1978: Coleman, 1980; Gayford, 1975; Gelles and Cornell, 1990; Rosenbaum & O'Leary, 1981a; Walker, 1979). Violent and abusive men have also been described as feeling helpless, powerless and inadequate (Aggarwal and Thatte, 1988; Ball, 1977; Bhatti, 1989; Weitzman and Dreen, 1982). Wife beaters have been described as sadistic, passive-aggressive, addiction-prone, pathologically jealous, dependent and pathologically passive (Faulk, 1974; Margolin *et. al.*, 1988; Shainess, 1977; Snell *et al.*, 1964) or suffering from neurological or biochemical disorders (Elliott, 1977; Schauss, 1982). These researchers are of the opinion that these personality disorders directly involve abusive behaviour. But comparison studies fail to substantiate that these features are distinctive. Although the negative traits identified by descriptive studies are linked to battered males, they share these traits with non-violent males in distress (Browning, 1983; Dvoskin, 1981; Rosenbaum and O'Leary, 1981; Stark and Flitcraft, 1988; Telch and Lindquist, 1984).

According to Douglas and DerOvanesian, 1983; Hughes and Rau, 1984; Rosewater 1984; Telch and Lindquist, 1984; Walker, 1984) women who have been battered tend to suffer from depression, anxiety and have elevated MMPI profiles. They have often been described as dependent, having low self-esteem and feeling of inadequacy and helplessness (Ball, 1977; Hilberman and Munson, 1977; Mahajan, 1989; Shainess, 1977; Walker, 1979). According to Adams and McCormick, 1982; Bhatti, 1985, 1989; Dobash and Dobash, 1979; Lata, 1989; Mahajan, 1989; Shah, 1989; Straus *et al.*, 1989; Weitzman and Dreen, 1981). Battered women are picturised as shy and reserved and have a tendency to blame themselves for the violence.

As per (Ball, 1977; Graff, 1980; Scott, 1974; Snell *et al.*, 1964) battered women are aggressive, masculine, frigid and masochistic being a totally opposite personality profile. Star (1978) reported that battered women exhibit more independence and ego strength. In a study of issues provoking violence Finn (1985) emphasized the importance of power balances in the relationship and suggested that the abused victim has a better sense of reality than her assailants, particularly with respect to sexual relations.

It is however argued by Gelles and Cornell (1990), that it is not possible to present personality profile of the battered women, as one never really knows whether the personality factors found in battered wives were present before they were battered or are the result of the victimization. As with other studies of family violence, personality studies of battered women frequently use small samples or clinical samples and often fail to have comparison groups. Thus, generalizing from these studies is difficult and demonstrating that battered women are actually different from non-victimized women is nearly impossible using these data.

Responsible Factors

Other than personality factors, researchers have shown that various other factors are also responsible for wife abuse. Due to lack of longitudinal research and failure to differentiate samples according to dimensions, it is difficult to predict factors responsible for violent outcomes, alone or in combination.

Violent Homes of Origin

Violence in the family of origin accentuates both a woman's vulnerability and a man's propensity to abuse his wife and/or children. It is said that men who have experienced violent childhoods are more likely to grow up and assault their wives than are individuals who have not experienced childhood violence. Researchers have found that both offenders and victims had violence-ridden childhoods (Fagan *et al.*, 1983; Roy, 1977; Schulman, 1979; Straus *et al.*, 1980). Studies also find that observing parental violence is related to spousal aggression (Pagelow, 1981; Rosenbaum and O'Leary, 1981). However, two-designed studies using multiple comparison groups and collecting data from men and women found no significant effect of childhood violence on later victimization (Rosenbaum and O'Leary, 1981; Telch and Lindquist, 1984). Although, the chances of being an offender and victim are increased if one grows up in a violent home, there are many violent people who had limited exposure to violence as children and some people who experienced extremely violent childhoods and grew up to be non-violent. (Gelles and Cornell, 1990; Stark and Flitcraft, 1988).

Income and Domestic Violence

There has been an inverse relationship between income and domestic violence reported in various studies. Researchers have highlighted that wife beating is more common in lower classes (Ahuja, 1987; Bhatti, 1985; Gaguin, 1978; Gelles and Cornell, 1983, 1990; Grewal, 1982; Jain, 1992; Mahajan, 1992; Prescott and Letko, 1977; Saunders, 1982; Stark, 1984; Steinmetz, 1974; Straus *et al.*, 1980; Young, 1963). On the other hand, (Berk *et al.*, 1983; Dobash and Dobash, 1979; Giles-Sims, 1983; Hilberman, 1980; Mahajan, 1989; Martin, 1979; Walker, 1979, 1984) show that wife battering cuts across the class boundaries.

Employment Status

Wife battering is found to be more in families where the husband is unemployed (Fitch and Papantonio, 1983; Gaguin, 1978; Gayford, 1975; Lewis, 1987; Prescott and Letko, 1977; Pathy, 1987; Rounsaville, 1987; Straus *et al.*, 1980). Men who are employed part-time have even higher rates of violence, probably because they cannot avail of unemployment benefits (Straus *et al.*, 1980).

Wife abuse is inversely related to wives contribution to the household income. Women who stayed at home and were fully dependant on their husbands income had a greater risk of being abused (Iwarimie Jaja, 1989; Levinson, 1989; Mitchell and Hodson, 1983; Schwartz, 1992). Hornung *et al.*, (1981) held a totally opposite view that housewives had a lower risk of violence than employed women.

There are proofs showing that women's risk of victimization increases if their occupational and educational status are inconsistent with that of their husbands. When some inconsistency develops in the status of either husband or wife, wife abuse results (Bhatti, 1989; Dobash and Dobash, 1979; Jain, 1992; Martin, 1979; Mohan, 1989; Parihar, 1989; Yllo, 1983).

For the victims of abuse, pregnancy is a high risk period when they experience violence at unusually high rates (Dobash and Dobash, 1979; Gelles, 1972, 1988; Helton, 1985; Kaplan, 1972; Pagelow, 1981a; Strak *et al.*, 1981; Teske and Parker, 1983; Walker, 1979). Factors react unfavourably at the prospect of a new entrant in the family regarding the child as an intruder — thus they indulge in violent behaviour.

Alcohol Use and Abuse

Studies of marital violence typically find a relationship between alcohol use and abuse (Ahuja, 1987; Bhatti, 1989; Bordin, 1981; Brekke and Saunders, 1982; Coleman *et al.*, 1980; Grewal, 1982; Mahajan, 1989; Mohan, 1989; Parihar, 1989; Shah, 1989; Snell *et al.*, 1964). Coleman and Straus (1983) reported that men who drink often are likely to abuse their wives 15 times more than non-drinkers.

Some cross-cultural studies of alcohol use and studies of marital violence points that men drink to have a socially acceptable excuse for violent behaviour (Gelles, 1974). Alcohol is not an immediate antecedent of violence in the majority of families in which violence occurs (Kantor and Straus, 1987). Still, Byles (1979) and Orne and Rimmer (1980) in a comprehensive literature review concluded that a casual role for alcohol cannot be supported. Alcohol is a factor in fewer than eight per cent of the domestic abuse cases, where police were called (McClintock, 1978). In sum, although alcohol probably increases the risk of abusive violence, yet in absence of conclusive evidence it should be considered a contextual factor to be treated separately.

Power-imbalanced Relationships

Power-imbalanced relationships are associated with spousal abuse, especially when the males power is threatened (Harris and associates, 1979). Wife beating occurs more often when all the decisions are made either by the wife or the husband (Adler, 1981; Bower, 1983; Coleman and Straus, 1986). It is believed that wife beating tends to decrease in frequency when decision-making becomes more egalitarian (Bowker, 1983; Coleman and Straus, 1986; Straus *et al.*, 1980). Hauser (1982) however argues equal power is seen as a lower position for the husband and as a higher position for the wife, as a consequence, husbands refuse to accept egalitarian way of living and violence continues. The above noted studies on the precipitating factors leading to wife battering highlight one or the other factor. Studies which highlight the characteristics of the battered couples; however, fail to explain adequately why some spouses resort to violence whereas others remain non-violent in spite of being unhappy.

Coping Mechanisms

Coping mechanisms and different treatment programmes for the batterer and the battered have been worked out by scholar in the West on the basis of experience of more than two decades of experience (Andersen *et al.*, 1991; Brockner and Rubin, 1985; Gondolf and Fisher, 1988, 1991; Rieker and Carmen, 1986; Sonkin *et al.*, 1985 and Turner and Shapiro, 1986).

The battered women specifically resist the notion that they should leave their battering husbands (Walker, 1979) and seek outside help only as a last resort when violence becomes intolerable due to long- drawn-out rehabilitation procedures (Kaushik, 1988; Pandhye, 1988; Sriram and Bakshi, 1988) as well as lack of alternative support system, self-image, social stigma, dependency, presence of small children and fear of living alone and embarrassment to admit that she has stayed in such a bad situation for so long etc. which force a woman to hide violence against her in the family and to remain in the violent relationship (Bhatti, 1989; Bergman *et al.*, 1988; Chapman and Gates, 1978; Edgell, 1980; Finch, 1983; Kalmuss and Straus, 1982; Kertzman, 1980; Mahajan, 1992; Martin, 1979; Parihar, 1989; Roy 1977; Russell and Von, 1976; Shah, 1989; Strube and Barbour, 1983; Walker, 1979).

Some researchers say that many abused women opt for leaving such a relationship. This category includes women who are employed, who get support from their family of orientation, friends or those who do not have children. (Gelles, 1976; Moore, 1979; Okun, 1988; Strube, 1988).

Different treatment programmes for the batterers, such as individual therapy, marital and family therapy, psycho-educational or psycho-therapeutic group approach, community intervention and anger control techniques have been suggested by researchers.

(Adams, 1988; Adams and McCormick, 1982; Gondolf, 1985; Roberts, 1984; Rosenbaum, 1986; Sonkin *et al.*, 1985). A variety of counselling approaches have been proposed for battered women (Gondolf and Fisher, 1988, 1991; Rieker and Carmen, 1986; Turner and Shapiro, 1986). It is believed that such programmes are not very successful in checking the abusive behaviour of the batterers (Gondolf and Fisher, 1991; Gondolf and Russell, 1986). Most of the researchers feel that the root cause of wife abuse can be traced to societal values. Unless social definitions are changed and women are allowed to have egalitarian way of life, wife abuse in one form or the other would persist.

Literature available on violence against woman helps in research. A theoretical and holistic approach is absent in literature available and the empirical studies conducted so far.

Explanation and Interpretation

A theoretical framework is needed to explain the phenomena of wife beating in greater detail. Various scholars have propounded different theories in order to explain wife abuse such as: resource theory, symbolic interaction, social control/exchange theory, sub-culture of violence theory, conflict perspective, patriarchal perspective and general systems theory. Dependency framework has been used for this study to explain the nature of wife abuse in the Indian context. As it can be used both at micro and macro levels to understand the victimization of women at socio-cultural level.

Dependencys Framework

Dependency factor in a woman is a need for which the victim has no control. These conditions may be her economic dependency or social definitions which force women to trace out her identity through her husband which makes her more committed to marriage. Dependency framework has been used in three ways to explain wife abuse. Firstly, dependency is treated as a cause of wife abuse. Secondly, it is treated as a condition forcing a woman to assume the role of the victim and thirdly, partial non-dependency also results into wife abuse.

In the first approach, there is a positive association between marital dependency and wife abuse (Dobash and Dobash, 1979; Marsden, 1978; Straus, 1976; Truninger, 1971; Walker, 1978).

Women, enter into marital relationship as subordinates to their husbands. Moreover, they are brought up to be submissive and trace identity through their husbands. Such a situation provides a dominant position to the husband and he uses violence against his wife to maintain his dominant position in the marital relationship. Those who suggest a positive relationship between wife abuse and dependency do not argue that women's marital dependency directly causes wife abuse. They, however, suggest that violence is instigated through women's tolerance of physical violence inflicted by their husbands.

In the second approach, dependency has been considered as a condition of wife abuse. Women who are unemployed, have a low educational level, have children and rely on their husbands for financial support, find themselves it is impossible to leave the abusive partners as they do not possess sufficient alternative resources to negotiate changes in their husband's behaviour (Gelles, 1976; Martin, 1979; Roy, 1977, 1982; Strube and Barbour, 1983; Strube, 1988). According to Roy (1977) and Mahajan (1986) women's explanations for putting up with abusive marriages included economic dependency, young children, fear of living alone, perceived stigma of divorce and lack of alternative support systems.

The third approach is that with partial non-dependency, wife starts questioning asymmetrical power relations which results into her abuse. Economic independence gives a better position to wives challenge their husbands' right to dominate. Since men benefit from the current system of sex stratification, it is unlikely that they will voluntarily give up their prerogative. Husbands, on the other hand, may resort to violence if the struggle for sexual equality increases. Further, violence may be used as the ultimate resort by husbands to keep wives in their place (Allen and Straus, 1980; Brown, 1980; Goode, 1971; Mahajan, 1989). A new type of role relationship will develop between husband and wife based on the ideology of egalitarianism (Kalmuss and Straus, 1982).

Objective Dependency

Dependency has been divided at two levels: objective and subjective. Objective dependency is characterized by conditions that tie a woman to marriage. Objective dependency has been operationalized as :

(a) lack of independent financial resources.

(b) low level of education.

(c) physical insecurity.

(d) presence of young children.

(e) fear of living alone.

(f) fear of physical assault, harassment, etc.

It does not, however, mean that women who are free from objective dependency are not abused by their husbands. They may be economically independent or have no children but are still the victims of violence by their husbands as they remain subjectively dependent.

Subjective Dependency

Women's subjective dependency on marriage refers to how a woman perceives herself to be tied to the marital relationship. This dimension of dependency is a psychological state that may or may not reflect objective conditions. Their social reality has not been constructed outside their marriage. The alternative social identity as a "worker" is not available to them. Their social identity is traced through men. Further, it is the wife and mother's role which gives her a respected position in the society. Subjective dependency has been operationalized as :

(a) differential sex role socialization,

(b) emotional investment in marriage and children,

(c) stigma attached to divorce,

(d) fear of rejection by parents, and

(e) lack of social support system etc.

While for some women, subjective dependency may be a direct function of objective dependency, for others it may not be so in spite of situational and objective factors do not make them particularly dependent. Some women may feel strongly dependent on their marriages. Others who are structurally bound to the relationship because of economic ties may not perceive subjective dependency. Further, the degree of dependency may differ from one segment to another.

Case Study

In order to verify the dependency framework, an empirical study has been carried to find out:

(i) The nature, extent and frequency of wife abuse.

(ii) The frequency with which physical, psychological and verbal violence is used.

(iii) Whether dependency objective or subjective or both is the cause or condition or instigating factor for wife abuse.

(iv) The reasons why abused women continue to stay in the abusive relationship.

As it becomes really difficult for the researcher to probe the personal lives of the respondents because it is treated as a "private affair", only a few studies have been conducted.

The study has been conducted in a village (Dadu Majra) on the outskirts of Union Territory of Chandigarh. 115 households belonging to lower class were selected for the sample. It was decided to limit the study to those households where conjugal unit lived together.

Out of 115 cases 87 wives, i.e., 75.65 per cent confided that their husbands have acted violently against them. Out of 87, 58 per cent admitted that it was a regular and patterned behaviour. Others, however, confessed that it was not a routine with their husbands. Out of 87 cases of violence 65.80 per cent admitted that violence against them is verbal only, 60.38 per cent labelled it as psychological violence whereas 39.16 per cent, that is 45 cases admitted to the existence of physical violence along with other forms of violence.

Statistics clearly indicate that wives with high level of objective and subjective dependency are abused more in contrast to those who have low level of objective and subjective dependency. Similarly, the percentages of non-victim goes on decreasing at high level. The results of the study, thus do not support the contention of those scholars who are of the opinion that high level of women's marital dependency is not associated with wife abuse because husbands of dependent wives can maintain their dominant positions without resorting to violence as their wives are in no position to question their dominance (Allen & Straus, 1980, Brown, 1980; Goode, 1971; Whitehurst, 1974).

Marriage holds an important position in Indian society where remaining unmarried or living a life of a divorcee is looked down upon. Whether a wife is objectively dependent upon her husband or not, she remains subjectively dependent. It is for this reason that subjective dependency is positively associated with the wife being a victim of her husband's violence. The reason for high percentage of such victims can be attributed to the wife's commitment to marriage and her inability to use alternative mechanisms to get out of the abusive relationship. Similarly, the husband uses coercive methods to assert his dominant position in the familial network of relationship, because he is confident that his violent behaviour would not be challenged and he can attain the desired goal, that is, subduing his wife. The results of the present study on subjective dependency and wife abuse partially support the findings of Kalmuss and Straus (1982).

Most of the women victims reported the fact that their husbands abused them in order to subdue them. They admitted that they behaved according to the wishes of their husbands after abused. When the wives were asked, 'why don't you have the abusive relationship?' they confessed that they had no place to go, after of being humiliated. The study reveals that violence in the family occurs when neither the family nor other support systems meet the needs and demands of the individual. When a violent mode of expression is readily available and when it is endorsed and rewarded. The results of the study show that violence in one or the other form persists in the conjugal relations, because it is associated with positive consequences for the abusers. Finally, it shows that wives continue to suffer and stay in abusive marital relationship because of their dependency.

Some Instances

Case One

Ms. Harjit is a 48-year-old matriculate belonging to a Jat Sikh family. Her father was a small shopkeeper. She has two brothers and a sister. She is the youngest of them all. At a very young age, she lost both her parents. When she was 16 years old, she was married to a small shopkeeper of the neighbouring village who was an alcoholic. Her husband is under matriculate, but the only son of his parents. She tried her best to dissuade her husband from indulging in heavy drinking but he did not like her interference and started ill-treating her. Initially such incidents were very few but subsequently it became routine. She tried to seek help of her in-laws but they did not pay any heed to her requests.

During her married span she gave birth to three daughters. Her first daughter, however, died within three months of her birth due to insufficient medical attention and negligence on the part of her husband. Her husband and mother-in-law always blamed Harjit for giving birth to female children only.

Often the husband did not come home for two to three days at a stretch. Whenever Harjit tried to enquire from him of his absence, she was admonished. Very often, on the slightest pretext he would beat her very badly. His attitude towards his daughters was also very rude. She put up with all the sufferings. Her brothers consoled her and advised her to remain submissive and to look forward to a happy future. Left with no alternative she reconciled to her fate and accepted her husband's drunken behaviour and waywardness.

Her sufferings increased. Her husband became all the more rude and harsh towards her when her parents-in-law shifted to Delhi. She was not given money even for household expenses. Her husband started bringing his friends home for drinks and forced her to sit with them. Whenever she refused to oblige him, she would be severely beaten up by him in front of his friends. She realized that her husband could go to any extent only when he asked her to have illicit relations with his friends. She refused to oblige him and locked herself in a room. Finally she fled away from the home along with her daughters and went to stay with her parents-in-laws. She informed them about her husband's behaviour. However, her husband did not come to meet her. This continued for ten years till her daughters passed their matric exams and they wanted to study further, but Harjit's in-laws denied them permission for higher studies. On the other hand, they started looking for matches for them. Harjit realized that if she did not act promptly, her daughters lives would be ruined. She resented her father-in-law's decision. They became very annoyed at Harjit's interference and she was asked to leave their place. Left with no alternative she came back to her husband only to find that he had ruined his life due to his drinking habit. He had sold his shop and household articles. She pleaded with her husband to change his ways and to realize the fact that he is a father of two grown-up daughters. Her pleadings, however, had no impact on him. On the other hand, he would become angry at her. He would call her names and beat up. Her daughters, however, tried to protect her but they too were abused. In spite of constant arguments and ill treatment, she stayed with him for the sake of her daughters. But when Harjit's husband attempted to sell his daughters to clear off his previous loans, she could not control herself and abused her husband. All limits were crossed when her husband pushed her and broke his empty liquor bottle on her head and fled away. She was badly hurt and her clothes were stained with blood. Her daughters called the neighbours for help.

Harjit was forced to make up her mind to leave her husband for ever. Thus, constant threat of physical insecurity of her daughters and herself forced Harjit to take this step. She went to her elder sister in Chandigarh who was full sympathies for her but could not provide her shelter because of her poor economic condition. She, however, made Harjit's living arrangement in a Short Stay Home for Destitute Women. Women Organizations in Chandigarh tried to resolve her marital conflict. Her husband was invited to Chandigarh but he did not come.

Presently Harjit is staying in a Short Stay Home for Destitute Women in Chandigarh. Her elder daughter is working as a storekeeper in a private company, whereas her younger daughter is undergoing vocational training in typing and shorthand. Harjit wants to make her daughters economically independent, so that they can face hard realities of life in a better way. Although Harjit has left her husband for the sake of her daughters, she would like to go back to her husband, once her daughters are settled because she does not want to be stigmatized for the rest of her life.

Case Two

Ms. Kiran Khullar is a 30-year-old graduate, who works as a clerk in a private company. She belongs to a Hindu Khatri family. Her father is a Superintendent in a Government Office at Chandigarh and her mother is a housewife. She has two younger sisters and an younger brother. She got married at the age of 23 to a science graduate of her own caste. Her husband is four years elder to her. He is working as an Assistant in a private firm at Chandigarh. He has two elder brothers and two sisters. All of them are married and well settled. Her father-in-law had died before her marriage. Before settling the marriage, Kiran's parents had expressed their inability to provide any dowry. Her husband and his brothers had also expressed negative views regarding dowry. Kiran's parents thus readily agreed to their proposal and accordingly performed a simple marriage. They did not give her anything in dowry.

Kiran started facing the hostility on her husband's side and his relatives for not bringing any dowry immediately after marriage. Her parents expressed their shock at the changed attitude of her husband regarding dowry. Moreover, they bluntly refused to oblige him. Her husband felt insulted and he humiliated her parents, who did not say anything and tolerated everything silently. He became rude to her. He adopted hostile attitude towards her and would abuse her on flimsy grounds.

Her parents consoled her and advised her to patch up and tolerate. As she was working, her salary was taken away every month after giving a paltry sum as pocket money.

Her husband never took her out with him and would her to go out of his sight as he disliked her. He warned her that she could stay with him, provided she maintained no contact with her family of orientation. Further, when her younger sisters visited Kiran, her husband also insulted them. As a consequence they too stopped visiting her. Thus, she was made socially isolated. Her husband not only denied physical and economic freedom but also made Kiran victim of his jealous and suspicious nature. In case she came late from the office, he would accuse her of immoral character.

Instead of arguing with him, she would prefer to keep mum in order to stop the quarrel because she was in the family way.

Throughout her pregnancy, her husband harassed and humiliated her. Her mother-in-law, who had come to stay with them was also instigated by her son against her. She had to work throughout her pregnancy and her husband did not show any concern for her. She suffered malnutrition and mental agony. Her husband even threatened to kill her if she gave birth to a female child. It was only after the birth of her first son that she felt relieved. She thought that things might improve for her. But her hopes were shattered when her husband did not accept sweets from her parents and abused them. When they left, she was humiliated and she accepted taunts helplessly.

After a gap of two years, she gave birth to another son, but no change was found in the behaviour of her husband. Her husband always looked for an opportunity to humiliate her. He would even try to find fault with her dress, make-up and other personality configurations. She felt very annoyed and sometimes lost her temper. Whenever she resented his remarks, her husband would become furious and beat her. Kiran's husband would not even spare his children. On simple mistakes he would beat them up very badly. She was beaten up also whenever she tried to protect them.

The final and ultimate blow was when Kiran went to see her ailing father in the hospital without taking permission from her husband, she realized that she was a slave in her own home. As she had to stay in the hospital a little longer. On her return her husband refused to open the door and she had to seek the intervention of the neighbours. When the neighbours left, he locked her in the bedroom and started beating her. He refused to listen to her and made insulting remarks about her father. The beating continued till he himself got exhausted. As a consequence of severe beating, she had a black eye and a broken tooth and was also denied any medical aid. She cried and cursed her fate and developed a feeling of insecurity to her life. She even thought of committing suicide, but her love for her children stopped her from taking such an extreme step. She however, decided to seek help from some outside agency. With the assistance of her friends, she contacted a woman organization and sought its intervention. On her request, the members of that organization went to her husband's office and tried to plead her case. In their presence, Kiran's husband did not utter single word but on returning home, she was again beaten by him. She was kicked, slapped and strangled. He even beat both his sons. He threatened to kill them if she even tried to lodge complaints against him.

After this incidence, Kiran become so depressed that she lost the will to fight. She became so pessimistic that she felt that only some miracle can change her husband. Kiran has lost all the hope for her future and continues to suffer. She feels herself that she would either die herself or her husband would kill her one day.

Analysis of the Cases

The above case studies help us analyse the problem of wife abuse. Ms. Harjit belongs to working class became the victim of excessive drinking nature of her husband. It was when her husband tried to force her and her daughters into prostitution that she was compelled to leave her home. Ms. Kiran who represents the middle class is a dowry victim, being educated and working she tried to raise objections to asymmetrical marital relations. Her efforts to have egalitarian conjugal relationship seems to have resulted in her abuse. In both the cases, it was found that these women were objectively dependent because it was difficult for them to live alone. Further, they did not have any support from their family of orientation. Their objective dependency encouraged their husbands to fully exploit the situation knowing fully well that their wives would not be able to leave them and stand alone on their own.

In spite of her economic dependency, presence of female children and no support from informal group. Ms. Harjit separated from her husband when violence became unbearable and her husband tried to force her daughters into prostitution. She still nurtures hopes of living with her husband because of her subjective dependency and hopes that things will improve one day, she does not want to be stigmatized as a separated woman. Kiran, on the other hand, continues to stay in the abusive marital relationship in spite of the fact that she is educated and working. She is unable to feel accepted in society without her husband. Further, social pressures from her family of orientation forces her to continue staying in the abusive marital relationship. Formal agency has also failed to put any end to the wife battering. Additionally, their intervention further deteriorated marital relationship. Thus, we can say that both objective and subjective dependency is related with wife abuse. The women continue to suffer in the marital relationship because of their upbringing and socialization. Dependency thus is a prime condition forcing women to continue living in the abusive marital relationship as they lack alternative support system.

In sum, in India, marriage institution is considered as a religious obligation. More relevant in case of Indian women, whose destiny in life has been marriage and motherhood. The Indian women, values from their childhood are to be submissive, expected to develop patience and courage to face different odds in life but not to seek separation from their spouses. Although legally, she is allowed to seek divorce because of the atrocities of her husband, yet social definitions, values and norms have not undergone appropriate changes to create congenial situation for her to go for divorce, even if circumstances demand so. Divorce for women being stigmatized, it is not easy for her to terminate the marital relationship even though it is abusive. Additionally, she may be economically, psychologically and socially dependent upon her husband or have so much emotional investment in her marital relationship and children that she prefers to suffer rather than to go for separation or divorce and keep the social fabric intact.

TWELVE

Domestic Violence

Living in a society which is largely patriarchal though centered around the wife, the family has its share of marital violence in which the woman bears the brunt in spite of being the pillar of the home.

To maintain their dominant position in the home, men inflict some or the other kind of violence on women and harass her throughout her life. A common name given to wife battering is silent crime. Others are considered as domestic violence like spouse abuse and similar ones. If we examine the variety of names it is known by, besides wife battering, two points emerge at once: that the violence is located at home and the attacker is the husband. The side of violence being the home and the attacker being the 'husband' has distorted, confused and is responsible for the gross trivailisation of the crime.

Wife battering is a crime that is 'victim precipitated'. This has been largely proven by three aspects—social, legal and psychological—with large help from recent cases, at home or abroad and through the numerous myths or sayings. It is a widely prevalent crime that is under cover for being 'too private' to be spoken of. Being an old problem; it is assumed by some to have begun with the first monogamous pairing. What is new, however, is that the fact that the public admission of violence against women occurs in a civilised society and the insistance by the government and responsible citizens that such violence is no longer acceptable, that we are therefore compelled to discuss the problem of such a form of violence and search for solutions to alleviate it.

In the context of marriage, violence towards women becomes more significant when a husband who is supposed to love and protect his wife, batters her. It becomes a big setback for a woman, being battered by a man whom she trusted most.

Misuse of Culture

Wife battering has been largely supported by various cultures down the ages. It was part of the Napoleanic code until a decade back. The very code says: "Women like walnut trees must be beaten every day". In North Africa, the expression "women and camels need to be beaten" is still common. In Europe, they used to say that a man had the right to beat his wife with a stick not thicker than his thumb. In Indian culture we have the quotation of Tulsidas such as "Drums, donkeys and women need to be beaten". So religion has played more or less a crucial role in reinforcing brutal attitudes to women which include "mortification of the flesh" deemed religious and more appropriate to the female. In fact over the ages, religions have constantly admonished woman to stay with her husband, no matter how cruelly he treated her".

General Causes of Violence

Wife battering is the most prevalent form of violence against women which is commonly caused due to maladjustments between husband and wife. Also prevalent among working women as most mothers-in-law, who are non-working and under complete dominance of their husbands feel jealous of and frustrated at the sudden independence and freedom of their daughter-in-law. She counters by poisoning the ears of her son antagonising him against his wife.

The batterer rationalises his battering saying that it happened as he was not satisfied by the conduct of his wife. So she is made to feel guilty of her performance at home — be it cooking or general upkeep of the home. A housewife of Rajouli was beaten to death by her husband as she was not cooking good food and the house being untidy, for which she alone, often at times, is not responsible. Implicit in this viewpoint is that the husband has a right to beat his wife if she does not behave according to what he desires. A young woman of village Taaddih under Amarpur police station of Banka was battered to death by her husband and in-laws as she refused to go out in rain to bring *ganja* for her husband. While attempting to amend her husband a pregnant woman of Samastipur was mercilessly beaten and sent to her parents' house by her husband. The battering resulted in abortion. Her husband along with his two brothers used to commit dacoity. When the wife protested against this, the dacoit started battering her mercilessly. Consequently, an abortion took place and she objected to the illicit relation of her husband. A young housewife of Dalsingsarai was mercilessly beaten to death by her husband when she objected to his having illicit relations with his elder brother's wife.

Surrender and Tolerance

To tame a woman who does not accept the traditional role of submissiveness and subordination, any means including violence is justified. Ironically counsellers and social workers also contribute towards this ideology when they question a woman who gets beaten: 'what did you do to provoke him? Due to this she often begins to have serious doubts about herself, to the extent that she starts questioning her identity as one who is responsible, intelligent or knowledgeable. The women continue to live in a state of fear and uncertainty as it is unpredictable when, where and under what circumstances the violence may suddenly erupt. The consequence of this is that she develops an inferiority complex, so much that she begins to look down upon herself and underestimates her value and potentialities loosing confidence in all her moves.

It is undeniable that some women are so arrogant, haughty, uncompromising and intolerant and make the husband's life so miserable through calculated and well planned acts of social misconduct that even the most reasonable man would lose control of himself beyond a certain limitation and beat up the erring woman. Cases of women suspected of adultery come under this category. A man of village Janui under Nargar Police Station of Garhwa hacked to death his 28-year-old wife as she had illict relations with a man of the same village, in spite of being told to mend her ways, she paid no heed. In a fit of rage he hacked her to death.

Until the mid-1970s and the re-emergent women's movement wife battering was almost completely ignored. In USA many researchers in this field agree with Justice Stewart Oneglias' estimate that 50 per cent of all marriages involve some degree of physical abuse of women. Such statistics are not available in India, but there is no doubt that they would far exceed the American statistics. Being the most frequently referred to "crime in India" reports do not provide information on wife battering. So widely and pervasively is wife battering accepted and tolerated that very rarely it is publicly talked about and still much less written about in the media.

Males Supreme

Wife battering is seriously under-reported crime and the data hard to obtain because of its location, the home... "Gelles Straus and Steinmetz reported that physical assault occurs in one-third of all homes. "In Mumbai, HELP, a voluntary group received over 300 calls in less than a year in which more than 80 per cent were calls for marital violence.

No one dares to interfere or question the man even if he is seen battering his wife because it is considered purely something their family affair. The society also implicitly supports this attitude by leaving the husband and wife to themselves to settle their affairs. On the other hand, if two neighbours get into a fight, the people around immediately intervene to see justice prevails. But in the case of a husband battering his wife, the neighbours tend to be mute spectators. Wife battering is commonly accepted by society and not many people take much notice to it. If the wife happens to retaliate, she is considered a woman of low morals. It is ingrained in the mind of people that no decent woman would beat her husband. Whereas battering one's husband is considered shameful for the husband as well as for the wife, there is no shame attached to wife battering, society being what it is.

Wife Battering, a Crime

Wife battering falls under the general category of assault, under sections 319-326 of Indian Penal Code. Sections 319 and 321 are non-cognizable offences, i.e., the cases in which the police can take no action against the assaulter. Thus, there is no legislation against wife battering.

Grievous Offences

Under Section 320 of the I.P.C. the following kind of offences have been described as grievous:

(a) Emasculation;

(b) Permanent deprivation of the sight of either eye;

(c) Permanent deprivation of hearing of either ear;

(d) Deprivation of any organ or joint;

(e) Destruction or permanent impairing of the power of any organ or any joint;

(f) Permanent disfiguring of the head or face;

(g) Fracture or dislocation of a bone or both;

(h) Any hurt which endangers life or which causes the suffer to remain for twenty days in severe bodi'y pain or unable to follow his ordinary pursuits. Section 324/326 of I.P.C. cover those cases where the assaulter uses dangerous weapons or means.

Thus, unless the wife is grievously beaten up resulting in one or more of the above injuries, the offence is non-cognizable, i.e., not punishable by law.

Line of Action

Wife battering is the most under-reported crime in India. No woman wants to bring her agony and personal life to courtroom and throw herself open to having her *bonafides* questioned and her character maligned. She would rather prefer to cling on to a broken marriage that break up her family reputation.

The first point to be noted is that these laws are ineffective for protection of a woman under the general law of assault. Very often, because a woman's lack of interest in a separation with her husband, people say that she enjoys the batterings. But there are currently very few alternatives to help women to live an independent life. The alternative for her is to go to her parents, only if they are in a position to maintain her with children which is often a rarity. Another option for her is to go to a women's rescue home run by the government which in the Indian context are very few and ill-maintained. Moreover, if she has children over the age of eight, then the children would be sent to a children's remand home. Both these centres are largely, centres of exploitation. A woman can leave her husband for cruelty but it is a ground only for a judicial separation and not for a divorce. It is essential that laws be changed to make wife battering a ground for immediate divorce. Custody of children of such women who are compelled to take divorce is another problem. A woman can get custody of children only after undergoing a lot of legal problems involving time, knowledge, money and of course judicial patronage. These hardships come in the way of making a decision of divorce for the woman and often she is forced to look back and face her destiny and torture.

Women belonging to the poorer groups are more easily swayed by emotions, can leave their husbands and start living alone. Being used to the hardships of life, they can rough it out even living alone. Their society gives them shelter and helps them start a new. Women belonging to the middle class, however, are more guided by social taboos and bindings. Right from the time of maturity, they are taught to be loyal to their husbands, to mould themselves to the whims and caprices of their husbands, bearing stoically the brunt of all hardships and all the abuses their husbands put them to. Under such conditions; they prefer not to leave their husbands in spite of extreme hardships and torture.

Causes of wife battering are high level family conflict, stress and violence in society, family socialisation in an environment marked by violence, cultural norms and sexual inequalities. (Straus, 1983). Wife abuse is seen as a reaffirmation of male self image as an aggressor which has been internalised and encouraged during childhood (Cotlin, 1974). According to (George, 1977) child abuse in own families or parental violence, alcoholism and the husband experience of childhood battering are some of the factors leading to wife battering. Moore (1979) looks into the social, legal, psychological and personal factors to explain the causes of wife battering. Newman hypothesised that the intake of alcohol, hostile dependency, extensive brooding on the part of the husband, husband's frustration in his work and other activities, and the husband having been battered by his parents in childhood, contribute to wife battering.

Factors behind Wife Battering

There are two levels of frustration in a man's life, individual and societal.

Individual

Man's expectations of himself and his inability to face problem and failures which lead to a sense of insecurity lead to individual frustration. If frustrations in a man's life lead to violence, why is it that the wife is always an inevitable target of his violence? Frustrations build up in a woman's life as well, but why is it that this does not lead to spouse abuse? Some cases have been put forward to answer these questions:

1. The unquestioned authority of man in his home/ marriage.
2. The consequent subservient role of the wife.
3. The wife's total dependency on her husband.
4. The social status which the husband provides to his wife.
5. Male confidence that he can make a woman forget and forgive the worst with a show of love and gifts.
6. The fact that a wife is least likely to show resistance to her husband's batterings.
7. If a man has witnessed wife battering during childhood or has been physically abused as a child, he is likely to adopt it as an acceptable way of resolving problems in his marital life.

Societal

The most fundamental factor which leads to wife battering is linked with the sex structure of the society as well as the family. The fundamental rights grant a man and woman equality but as long as the authority of man remains rooted in our culture and in the eyes of the law, wife battering will be perpetuated in society.

It has been seen that while economically dependent and independent women are equally likely to be battered, an economically dependent woman is more likely to stay on in a violent home. Lack of education and poor job opportunities force the middle class women to remain married to men who constantly batter them. This, along with the burden of child care and parental responsibility forces women to remain in violent homes. Knowing this, men continue abusing their wives with relative impunity. They can be relatively confident that she will not leave him because:

(i) She is not economically independent;

(ii) She has no place to go and;

(iii) She has the burden of bringing up the children because society feels that child care is exclusively a mother's job and women who leave children behind became social outcastes.

Immediate Causes

However immediate causes of wife battering may be noted as:

1. Monetary causes
2. Jealousy and suspicion
3. Instigation by in-laws
4. House work
5. Impact of alcohol
6. Economic independence of wife or wife's high self-esteem (she thinks too much of herself)
7. Dispute over children
8. Extra-marital affairs of husband.

Degrading the Battered

There are some myths common to all culture about the "kind of women" who get beaten.

1. The first myth is that middle class women do not undergo wife battering. In reality women come from all sections of the society, belonging to different religions, educational levels and from all socio-economic classes. If we hear more about wife battering in slums or in chawls, it is because these women have less privacy. The middle and upper class women are battered behind closed doors. They live in total isolation and keep up the pretence of a successful marriage. Working class women talk, quite

openly about the violence that they experience in their homes, and generally it seems to affect them less psychologically as they do not see it as being something unrelated to them as individuals whereas middle class women begin to question and doubt themselves.

2. The second myth is that the victim of violence is a small, fragile, helpless woman belonging to the working class. In reality, women holding responsible jobs as doctors, lecturers, journalists and models get beaten by their husbands. Many of them are quite capable of managing their lives. So there is no stereotype of a battered woman.

3. The third myth is that of provocation. This myth conveys the message that women who get beaten are masochistic and they want to get beaten. It further victimizes the women. The burden of guilt falls on her, increasing her shame and degradation.

4. The fourth myth is that the women who don't leave their husbands do not mind the batterings or that they actually like it. It is often asked: why women continue to live in a situation where they are eventually murdered or are driven to suicide. Why don't they seek a way out? The theory of learned helplessness gives an insight into the mental stage of passive resignation experienced by women. According to this approach, some events occur in the battered women's life during childhood and onwards with sufficient regularity due to which they acquire feelings of helplessness and poor self-image and resigning themselves to fate or accepting blame. Some important events in women's early lives which suggest a susceptibility factor include a high level of violence by members of their families in childhood (e.g. being battered by the mother, battered by the father, the father battering the mother, the father-mother battering other children) perception of critical or uncontrollable events in childhood, and experiencing such conditions which place them at high risk for depression in future. The fear of losing the husband's affection and the fear of

disruption of their home life status quo also prompts them to tolerate the husband's battering. The battered wives are thus afraid to stay and at the same time terrified to leave for fear of inescapable reprisals. They prefer to choose the devil than foray into the deep sea.

Knowing the Batterer

As there are myths about the type of women who get beaten, there are myths about the type of husbands, who beat their wives.

1. We generally tend to take it for granted that if a man beats his wife, he must be from the lower strata of society, being frustrated in his job, an alcoholic, or a paranoid person, aggressive in his relationship with the world at large and his wife being one of the victims. The act of wife battering is found elsewhere too, where the males are either professionals like lawyers, teachers, doctors, etc. or the well off economically like businessmen, politicians, etc. In some cases, the males are not alcoholic but they too are not free from this very act towards their wives.
2. The myth that loving husband does not indulge in wife battering is also false. Sometimes some males are quite sober, gentle and lovable to their wives but they too involve in wife battering in case of some frustration.

Hence, more or less from what is found, the wife battering is a general phenomena among all sections of male community of the society throughout the world.

Effective Steps Advised

1. A preventive rather than a curative approach to the problem should be taken by the institution which tries to deal with the problem of wife battering. Unless the structure of the family changes, the help given to battered wife will prove to be only superficial. This does not mean that we should ignore the desperate and immediate situation in which millions of women find themselves, and live their lives in constant fear of violence and death. Despite occasional successes to expect lone women to

fight individually against institutionalised family violence is both cruel and unrealistic. There is not only a desperate need for more homes for battered women, where such women can take refuge when their lives are threatened, we also need homes which will look at the problem of wife battering from a pro-women point of view, and which will help the women rebuild their shattered lives and induce faith and confidence in themselves. These can serve as important educational institutions and consciousness raising places. The time spent here can be utilized in teaching the women useful skills which can eventually make them self-sufficient. In case a woman chooses to go back to the husband, the home should lay down rules that the husband allows her to continue her job training and should not send the women back on their husband's terms. In most cases the husband is more anxious to get the wife back once she leaves, and this is the only time, terms and conditions can be laid for the man. This can be very useful in maintaining contact with the woman, so that when the batterings recur, prompt action can be taken against the husband.

2. There is a need to create an awareness in society so that the attitude of society — doctors, counsellors, institutions, social workers and the police is more sympathetic towards victims of marital violence.
3. Community action like having a *morcha* or a *dharna* outside a wife-battered house goes a long way in acting as a deterrent to marital violence. Men and society at large should recognize once and for all that women are no longer going to take batterings lying down.
4. Support structures for women who decide to break away like legal aid, a place to stay and a job go a long way in bringing a feeling of security to the tortured and oppressed woman. The homes for battered women should be linked up with organisations which help women take up self-employment ventures. We need more committed lawyers who are sympathetic and

understanding and would help to provide legal protection and relief to the women who are battered.

5. In cases where the marriages are resolved and reconciled, full precautions should be exercised so that any future attack on her is frustrated. This can be done by getting help from her neighbours, locking herself in a room, running away from the house, throwing objects or chilli powder at the husband can at times, deter a husband from being violent. There may be several hurdles to a religious mind which is conditioned to accept the husband as lord and master, but unless women can stand upto the batterings and fight back; the power relationship within the family will not change.
6. The situation of assaults by a husband on a wife being quite specific where the wife is economically dependent on the husband, and that the assault occurs in the house of common residence, it is essential that the police operate under different laws than those which cover general assault. A law such as Domestic Violence Act should be passed.

The point that women are often their worst enemies should not be forgotten. Mother-in-laws and sisters-in-law often instigate men to violence. Do they not poison the ears of their sons and brothers respectively and antagonise them against their wives? Voluntary social workers uphold women's dignity through glittering sessions and often have double standards as they subject their own maidservants to cruel humiliations.

Unless women are able to organise themselves, they cannot fight male domination. There is a need, therefore, to set up women's organizations in every area to fight this aspect of women's oppression. Forming into groups will help them raise their voices louder against the men and get them the desired results one day.

THIRTEEN

Curse of Dowry

Dowry is generally believed to be given by the girls parents to the groom to ensure her a happy married life by fulfilling the basic necessities to give a comfortable living. But the greed of the groom's family is growing day by day. Starting from basic needs, the custom has become rigid enough to become an evil associated with social status and family prestige. Monetary considerations receive priority over the merits of the bride. Never before have the demands for dowry been so exorbitant and so widespread as today. It has taken the form of bridegroom price and has developed into a great social evil. There is hardly a day when the cries of dowry victims are not echoed by the media. One day we read that the bride was burnt to death, as she could not bring the expected dowry. The next day, we come across a case where the bride was taken out on the pretext of sightseeing, and pushed from the hill top or into the swelling river. And these are just those cases which are reported in the media. There still remain countless other cases which do not come to the notice of the media or the police or the women's organisation.

Meaning

Dowry normally means gifts given during the marriage to the son-in-law or his parents in cash or kind. From the point of view of women's status, however, dowry has to be looked at as constituting:

(a) what is given to the bride, and often settled before and announced openly or directly; the gift though given to the bride may not be regarded as exclusively her property;

(b) what is given to the bridegroom before and at marriage; and

(c) what is presented to the in-laws of the girl.

The settlement often includes the enormous expenses incurred on travel and entertainment of the bridegroom's party. The gift-giving ritual continues throughout early married life, during festivals and celebrations.

The Justification

Indirectly it is assumed that it is a way of providing a girl with a share of the family property. The Hindu laws on property and ownership do not, in their present form, grant women their due share of family income and property. The Hindu Succession Act gives women the right to a share of the family property. But tradition dies hard, and in most cases the property of the family is given to sons. Daughters usually do not contend this, and hence inadvertently strengthen the argument that the dowry system alone ensures them fair share of her father's property, which will help them tide over any crisis. The latter also explains the importance attached to gold and jewellery and other constituents of dowry. For, unlike land and other immoveable property, they are both easily transportable and readily converted to cash. Demand for dowry is justified on many grounds. Firstly, since they have to pay dowry for their daughters, why not take it for their sons? Secondly, fathers of educated boys want to get back the money spent for their sons' education.

Non-fulfilment of Demand: Consequences

Dowry today is being demanded and paid without any relation to the bride's father's income and wealth: One Ganaur Mahto of Keshopur village under Sakra police station of Muzaffarpur self-immolated as he failed to meet the dowry demand of his son-in-law even after five years of his marriage. With the increased desire for quick money and the luxuries of life, these demands are not confined to the middle class alone. Dowry is being demanded by all levels of people, be they high, middle or low, items of dowry may differ ranging from flats, cars, electricals, furniture, clothes, cash and jewellery. Failure to meet these demands results in ill-treatment to young wives, often driving them to commit suicide. A 22-year-old bride of Banka committed suicide by throwing herself into a well after constant nagging by her in-laws over inadequate dowry. In many instances they have been murdered. These deaths are generally represented as accidents to save the future of the children and the parents from social stigma.

Growing keenness among Girls

Surprisingly now-a-days girls themselves are keen to collect their own dowry without any consideration of the plight of parents and the future of younger brothers and sisters. It is surely their socialization and the influence of the social milieu which have shaped their attitudes and expectations. If they have no rights of membership in the natal family, they also have no obligation to contribute towards its maintenance. Their main concern is to establish themselves in the new family and acquire status there. They look upon dowry as a necessary contribution towards this process and a compensation for their share in the family property.

The Concept

Social scientists differ widely in their interpretations of the concept of dowry reflecting the particularistic features of the societies which they have studied. It is very difficult to arrive at a universal definition from these varied explanations. The sociologists who have analysed the dowry system in South Indian societies define dowry as "female inheritance" because dowry is often termed as 'streedhanam' in South India. On the other hand, those who have studied dowry system in north India emphasise the *daan* or the gift aspect of dowry as it is variously called *daan dahej* (in Bihar) and *Dayaj* (in the Awadh region). They also view it as a compensation related to the institution of hypergamy.

The problem of protecting young married women against harassment on account of dowry has been engaging the attention of social workers and women's organisations for quite sometimes. Unnatural deaths of newly married young women beat headlines in the newspapers. Hardly a day passes without a news item on a tragic event like this. Some social organisations have been urging the government to make suitable provisions both, legal and administrative, to give protection to young married women against cruelty at the hands of their husbands and in-laws.

Women as Perpetrators

Women being the enemy of a woman in cases of bride burning is an interesting feature of this crime. It has been usually found that attitude of a woman as a mother is different from that as a mother-in-law. As a mother she gives all what she has to the daughter but as the in-law she attempts to extract the maximum possible dowry and can go to the extent of causing death of the bride, if the demands are not met to her satisfaction. In other words, in bride burning cases, crime is normally abetted and even committed by the women themselves. It is ironical that in many cases where one woman is killed for dowry another woman with a more handsome dowry is prepared to "console" the bereaved husband.

The government of Bihar set up "anti-dowry cell" in 1976 headed by a Superintendent of Police to give protection to women and Harijans against atrocities against them and the name of this cell was subsequently changed to "Offences against Women Cell". What is interesting is the fact that during the wedding season in 1983, IAS and IPS officers, engineers and doctors fetched more dowry; as IAS officer was paid Rs. 10 lakh as dowry and his marriage ceremony was attended by high officials (*The Statesman*, 18 August, 1983). Thus, if government servants are the perpetrators what more can be said and done is a matter to ponder.

The Prohibition Act

The first attempt by the Government of India to recognise dowry as a social evil and to curb its practice is the Dowry Prohibition Act of 1961. The Act was modified with the Dowry Prohibition (Amendment) Act of 1984 and 1986. Women's organisations have played a key role in this process of change.

The 1961 Act defines dowry and makes the practice of both giving and taking dowry, a punishable offence. Any agreement on dowry is void. If it is given at all, it will be the women's property. With increased awareness of dowry deaths and consequent public condemnation, women's organization made a thorough analysis of the implication of 1961 Dowry Act and criticised it for being theoretical and lacking in clarity.

Amendment 1984

The Dowry Prohibition (Amendment) Act, 1984 makes the offence cognizable by enlarging the meaning of the term "Dowry".

The main features of the Amendment Act are as follows:

Any property given or agreed to be given in connection with a marriage to the bride or bridegroom or any other person is considered as dowry. It is not necessary to show that the same has been given as consideration for the marriage. It also provides for the preparation of list of presents which are given at the time of marriage to the bride or bridegroom in accordance with the rules made under this Act.

Any person giving or taking dowry or abetting the giving or taking of dowry is also punishable with imprisonment which is not less than six months, but which may extend to two years and with a fine which can extend to Rs. 10,000 or the amount of the value of the dowry whichever is higher.

Neither the bride nor the persons giving presents to her at the time of marriage is liable for punishment if the presents have been given to her without any demand on that behalf and the presents are entered in the list maintained in accordance with the rules.

Demands of dowry continue in spite of this significant new amendment of the Dowry Prohibition Act 1961, failing which the bridegroom or his parents take to violence against the bride and sometimes such violence results in her death. Further there is a need for legal registration of gifts to be made compulsory, so that women may not be cheated of her dowry. The 1984 Amendment however makes it a cognizable offence and empowers recognised welfare institutions or organisations to take cognizance of the offence.

Amendment 1986

The Dowry Prohibition (Amendment) Bill 1986 was introduced in the Rajya Sabha. It attempts to tighten the provisions of the Act and includes dowry deaths in the list of offence in the Indian Penal Code. The Bill provides that if a woman dies within seven years of her marriage due to causes other than natural, her property would be transferred to her children and if she has no children to her parents. The burden of proving that no dowry demand was made will be on those who took or abetted in the taking of the dowry, the aggrieved person will be subjected to prosecution. This amendment bill has made the offence non-bailable and raised the minimum punishment to five years and fine upto Rs. 15,000. Provisions for appointment of dowry prohibition officers and their advisory board with two women members had been made. According to this new amendment in the Indian Penal Code whoever, being husband or related to the husband of a woman, subjects such woman to cruelty shall be punishable with imprisonment which may extend to three years and shall also be liable to fine. The cruelty for the purpose of this provision means any wilful conduct which is of such a nature as is likely to drive the woman to commit suicide or cause grave injury and danger to life, or health (whether mental or physical) of the woman. The cruelty also includes harassment of the woman where such harassment is with a view to coercing her or any person related to her to meet unlawful demands for any property or valuable security or on account of failure by her or any person related to her to meet such demand. Under this amendment the police have been empowered to investigate and report cases of unnatural or suspicious deaths of women.

Factors Initiating Investigation

Further, they have been empowered to investigate in the following cases: when

(i) The case involves suicide by a woman within seven years of her marriage, or

(ii) The case relates to the death of women within seven years of her marriage in any circumstances raising a reasonable suspicion that some other person committed an offence in relation to such woman; or

(iii) There is any doubt regarding the cause of death.

More Laws

A new Section 198A has been inserted in the Cr. P.C. 1973, providing that "No court shall take cognizance of an offence punishable under Section 498-A of the I.P.C. except upon a police report of facts which constitute such offence or upon a complaint made by the person aggrieved by the offence or by her father, mother, brother, sister or by her father's or mother's brother or sister or with the leave of the court, by any other person related to her blood, marriage or adoption".

The Section takes into account the various circumstances under which a court can take cognizance of an offence registered under Section 498-A of the IPC.

A new Section 113-A has been added in the Indian Evidence Act, 1972, to the following effect, in relation to the burden of proof:

> "When the question is whether the Commission of suicide by a woman had been abetted by her husband or any relative of her husband and it is shown that she had committed suicide within a period of seven years from the date of her marriage and that her husband or such relatives of her husband had subjected her to cruelty, the court may presume, having regard to all the other circumstances of the case, that such suicide has been abetted by her husband or by such relatives of her husband".

This Section empowers the court to assume that the suicide has been abetted by the husband or a relative of the husband, unless otherwise established. Under this provision, the burden of proof is shifted from the prosecution to the accused. Thus, there is a total departure from the fundamental rules of evidence. The guilt of the accused is assumed if the death of the woman is caused within seven years of marriage and if cruelty against such woman at the hands of the accused is established. However, the accused is at liberty to prove his innocence. He will not be entitled to any benefit of doubt, provided under the law of Evidence.

In spite of this amendment, dowry deaths in the country have not undergone any decline.

New Trends

The names vary. The circumstances differ. The amounts in question are vastly dissimilar. But the victims of dowry death all share one thing in common—an untimely, unnatural, grisly end. Shorn of superficial differences, each story reads the same: the demand for goods and/or money by the boys' side, the inability or the unwillingness, of the girls' parents to pay up: the lack of support structures available to the girl and, therefore, her incapability to walk out of the marriage; the mental, and often physical torture that follows. The barbaric bestial act turned on by the flick of a match stick on kerosene drenched victims marks the end to a helpless being. The demand for dowry and the victimization is carefully planned and plotted by the culprits so as to leave minimum evidence of the crime which they term as accident. The culprits allow some time to pass to give the impression that the couple had good relations. Demands for dowry are conveyed to the bride's father and others in a variety of direct and indirect ways. When demands were made after marriage, it is perceived either as an exercise of the rightful prerogative of the groom and his family, or to express discontent at what was given at the time of marriage or in social comparison with neighbours, at a later date, the dowry was perceived as inadequate.

The list of dowry demands are numerous and diverse and stretch beyond imagination ranging from cash for starting business to TV, tape recorder, motor cycle, refrigerator, car, even wrist watch, cycle or few *tolas* of gold. There are even demands for buffalo or a fan or a job for the groom or transfer of name of husband in fixed deposit. Demands of a grand wedding, share in property of bride's father are also few other demands which may precipitate into serious consequences.

No correlation exists between the level of the education of the bride and her murder on dowry issue is a matter of great surprise. Parent's belief that proper education of their daughter will diminish the margin of dowry is proving wrong . The more a girl an educated, the greater is the demand of dowry. A sixth year Chemistry student of Bihar University was burnt to death by her in-laws and husband for a car. Her parents are said to have given Rs. 4 lakh a few days before she was married. Her father said that a week back his son-in-law had sent a letter threatening him with dire consequences if he was not given a car. In the meanwhile due to constant pressure her father sent two ceiling fans, one cooking range, one table fan and four electric irons. Even working women are not spared for dowry.

Victimization starts immediately after the marriage in most of the cases. But sometimes victimization starts even after several years of marriage. In Gaya town even after eight years of marriage, a mother of two children narrated a woeful tale before the police after regaining consciousness that her husband and mother-in-law with the help of other members of the family inflicted hot iron injuries from her waist to chest till she became unconscious as father of the victim had expressed his inability to comply with the demand of her husband and this led to inhuman treatment with her.

Case Study

A total of 1635 cases of bride burning have been reported during the period 1981-88. This was analysed to examine the rural-urban differences and then regional variation across four regions, namely, Magahi, Maithili, Bhojpuri and Adivasi.

The per cent of distribution of dowry deaths shows increasing trend in Magahi region. When the figure is compared with other regions it is found that all other regions showed a decreasing trend. This result showed that dowry system is more rampant in Magahi areas than in Maithili and Bhojpuri areas, while Adivasi people did not have concept of dowry.

Statistics reveal that incidence of dowry death was always double in urban areas compared to the rural areas during the same years in the four regions. The gap between rural-urban cases was the biggest in Magahi region (39.71) followed by Maithili (35.42), Bhojpuri (29.60) and Adivasi regions (26.21) in that order.

Harassing brides in the name of dowry is not caste or community specific. The dowry deaths are not confined to the Hindu community alone, they are now noticeable among the Muslims. A Muslim girl of Siwan was murdered by her husband. First of all, the boy refused to take his wife to his house. Soon he took her to a place and after a month he sent a message of burning in an accident of her parents. A young Sikh housewife was allegedly murdered by her husband and in-laws for dowry in Punjabi Colony, Chitkohra in Patna.

Dowry among Muslims

Though dowry has been widely prevalent among Muslims

in Bihar "dowry deaths were relatively unknown. It is only in recent times that such incidents have been coming to light. A glance at media reports over the years make it amply evident that no longer are Hindu women alone victim of dowry-related violence, it is taking place among Muslims as well although data available on the topic is inadequate. It is beyond doubt that the incidents of dowry deaths among Muslim is much lower in absolute number, yet their occurrence can no longer be described as a "stray incident" or "an isolated case". Wife battering and torture have always been indulged in by men in a male dominated society. Even Muslims come from the same kind of society and so the problem exists among them too and they are no exceptions to the nature of men all over. But burning of women has been rare occurrence in comparison to Hindus reason being that Muslims have recourse to divorce, a provision in Islam much misused by Indian Muslim men. There are also cases of Muslim brides who are constantly harassed physically or mentally for failure to bring sufficient dowry. Approximately thousand applications of women are pending before the Imarat Sharia, Phulwari Sharif, seeking to get their marriage dissolved as Muslim women have as such right as men to get out of an unhappy marriage through *Khula*. Many of these applicants have complained to the religious heads of the constant torture by their husbands for dowry and gifts. Maulana Mujahidul Islam, Head Qazi, of the Imarat Sharia told that increasing number of applications seeking divorce in the last two years, have forced the religious leaders and Muslim intellectuals of Bihar to sound a warning to Muslims to distant themselves from such practices in future and not to fall prey to the evils that have gripped the Hindu community of late. If this is not done, the dowry death and burning of brides among Muslims would become common. (Muslims asked not to take dowry, *Times of India*, Patna, April 2, 1992).

Various Victims of Dowry

Domestic violence related to dowry takes a particular form of reporting. A dowry victim would be one who is harassed, beaten up, mentally tortured by her in-laws or her husband for failure to bring in the demanded dowry or more dowry; or would be one who has been harassed or deserted; or one who has been burnt to death; or who has committed suicide due to excessive harassment.

Though the dowry death is generally perceived to be the murder of a woman on the dowry issue but before the act of killing, several forms of harassment and humiliation take place against the victim. An innocent bride of Hazaribagh was kept confined in a room without food for days together before being murdered.

Dowry Killings : Modus Operandi

It has been gathered from the newspapers that five different methods were alleged to have been adopted in killing the victims.

Sometimes the victims are first strangulated and then hanged from the roof to make it look like suicide. We shall not attempt to define what exactly is meant by harassment and cruelty, since they are largely subjective terms. At best, some of their physical manifestations on death or injury to body are cognisable. What is more important is that it must be recognised.

Harassment and Torture in Practice

The most common form of harassment of a woman in her in-laws family unfolds in the forms of taunts, abuses, threats, which generally escalate to battering, even abettement to suicide or murder in some cases. However, what remains hidden from us are experiences of woman battered by their husband — for various reasons including inadequacy of dowry. This is viewed by the police as a simple case of domestic assault and by the society as "normal interaction among intimate couples". Women will be women, always striving to keep the family fabric intact. Blinded by the patriarchal notions about the privacy of family matters and because of their assumed weakness, woman seldom choose to get out of these relationships or even complain about it. Putting up with violence becomes the order of the day for an indefinite period until it becomes unbearable when they have to take hard decisions and escape torture by suicide or walking out. Keeping relationships together, despite violence, is also important for practical reasons such as financial support and shelter. Setting out is almost as bad as staying in the relationship. The threat of male violence outside the home is an acutely intimidating reality of women who endure violence within their won homes. Living among constant threats of killing and desertion become a daily ordeal for them, they have to take it or leave it, in most cases they keep taking it.

The mother-in-law, sister-in-law nexus along with an unsympathetic husband make life a living hell for them. Indian conjugal relationships are typically much less closer than those between mother and son: frequently the mother-in-law instigates the harassment against the young bride using her son as her agent. The actual or supposed inadequacy of dowry becomes an excuse for the mother-in-law.

On the slightest pretext the bride is sent back to her parental home—usually to refurbish her "inadequate dowry". To make matters worse and continued harassment, the quality and quantity or whatever she gets from her parents are made the excuse.

On the other extreme the girl is discouraged from frequently visiting her parents. Her isolation from her earlier natal source of support being complete, her natal family is kept in the dark under the impression that all is going well not having an inkling of idea what their daughter is going through. That torture and harassment could reach such limits can be seen in cases where clothes for daily wear were given to the woman by mother-in-law each day; where for a pair of slippers and handkerchiefs she was not given money but was asked to get these from her parents; where every time, she went to her parents, she was not given the rickshaw fare, but was asked to make her parents pay it where the battering has permanently disfigured her finger, where a newly married bride tried to commit suicide because of the hopeless situation she was in and had a miscarriage; where she was not allowed to sleep with her husband or communicate with him for one whole year after marriage; where a woman was tied with a rope, beaten, after which she was burnt, where a woman was burnt within a week after her marriage, and where a girl had been accused of being insane and cast out. These are few of the many instances of harassment the women may have to undergo each day of their lives.

Difficult Options

Reasons

The question that confronts us now is why do so many girls come back even after they have undergone such torture beyond endurance? The first reason being the wish of the girl herself who really sees no respectable position outside her husband's house. Women often feel inadequate to cope with self-sufficiency and consequently the lack of self-confidence often acts as a trap to keep a woman within a violent home. Putting up with physical abuse is the very reason that there is no decline in domestic violence against women.

A daughter's change of status and her transfer from one family to another have a strong cultural sanction. It is said that at marriage the girl dies and is reborn as a new person. The formal advice given to her is that as long as she is alive she is not to leave the house she is entering. The parents themselves ignore the case of the daughter who is being harassed and wishes to come back. They advise her, pressurise her or even force her to stick to the "real" home and try to adjust. They are afraid of the stigma of a married daughter leaving her home and returning to her parents. Their constant advice to her is to "adjust" to maltreatment, the common saying being. "It is nothing unusual or so unbearable—so many women are coping with it". In most cases of wife murder, suicide, maltreatment, the women feels so burdened by the expenditure undertaken by her parents, that she feels duty bound to present a brave picture of "silent courage".

Parents justify their succumbing to these demands, saying that it was done for the daughter's well-being ... the well-being of continued torture, within the four walls rather than independent survival for their daughter. Most women would also undoubtedly opt for the former precisely because they have been conditioned to think along similar lines. Both society and religion sanctify the patient and suffering women.

Women see their recognition in society through matrimony and for this she has to sometimes pay a heavy price. A home for a woman is synonymous with the home her husband would provide her. This is the general understanding of the man, of the parents, of the women, and indeed of Indian society in general. In our culture divorce or widowhood for a woman is worse than death. However, this is in many cases not true for the women of lower castes, as there is greater autonomy to women among them.

Deaths due to Adjustment Problems

It is not always dowry which can lead to woman's burning there are other problems related to adjustment which confront her after her marriage and precipitate into serious consequences. After marriage an young bride joins a new family and she is expected to "adjust" her needs, her behaviour, her personality and her entire self - according to her husbands and his family needs as soon as possible. This adjustment problem creates conflicts between husband and wife and daughter-in-law, and father/mother-in-law and brother/sister-in-law. In this situation of conflict the husband does not always know when and where to side with his wife. Over small conflicts, therefore the girls go to their parents home to get their (parents) sympathy. The parents generally advise them to go back and adjust. The girls, therefore remain frustrated; unable to cope with the harsh realities of married life and getting no emotional support from their husband or their own parents, they seek the easy way "ending it all" by committing suicide. Some of the cases thus reported as dowry-deaths are in fact cases of impulsive suicides. Earlier, it was held that women in the autumn of their life had suicidal tendencies. But nowadays psychologists are of this view that teenagers form the highest risk group, because in this age, rapid hormonal changes in her body which make them more excitable, depressive and vulnerable. When they experience tensions after marriage instead of love and affection from the husband and the family, they take their own lives, often on filmsy pretexts. The young girls with dreams in their eyes fall victim to tension on experiencing small disappointments making them big issues. This amkes them excitable and prone to suicide.

A lady Commissioner of Police in charge of the Anti Dowry Cell of Delhi corroborates the view that 90 per cent of the cases that have been registered with Anti Dowry Cell have no link with dowry and many of them are directly related with the problem of non-adjustment between husband and wife due to variety of factors like physical or mental incompatibility, the wife resenting her mother-in-laws domination and wanting to live separately etc.

Earlier also there were suicides and murders due to conflicts, but now they are reported in the newspapers, due to the awakening of womens rights and the pro-bridal wave. Many women's organisations take up the issue of the so-called "silent sufferers". Thus, it is not that all of a sudden in-laws and husbands have been savages, but that the mass media gives these cases prominence, at the same time not declaring mother-in-law as completely innocent in case of dowry death.

Circumstances Leading to Killings of Wife

It is gathered from newspapers that there are many circumstances in which, ill treatment of young wives, often driving them to commit suicide and many times they have been murdered, take place which are not linked with the dowry death in any way.

It is, however, desirable to be remembered that all broken and problematic marriages do not have dowry as the roots. There are cases where a girl who had been married by the parents against her will, may be because she did not like the proposal or intended to marry some one else with whom she was in love before, cannot adjust with her husband or in-laws and concocts a story of cruelty against her, returns to parents and sends a legal notice levelling dowry and torture charges and uses blackmail to demand a handsome life time maintenance. If this is not met, she might involve the husband and his parents in a criminal case under the Dowry Prohibition Act. Such cases are coming to light in which ultra-modern working women are involved. They do not re-marry but live in adultery with men of their choice.

The laws and bouts of propaganda have created panic, trauma and suspicion all round, without helping to do with the dowry menace. To a great extent, the matrimonial relations in general and the rapport between the parents and in-laws, in particular have deteriorated under the stress of suspicion. It would, however, not be forgotten that the dowry deaths and ill treatment of married women are not as common as they are made out to be, by the recent publicity. In comparison with number of happily married couples and contented families, they are a microscopic minority. So, the generalisation of plights of some particular brides and rampant in-laws baiting will cause immense harm to the social fabric. Every case has to be dealt with individually as all aberration and not as a part of the general state of affairs. After all, marriage is still the cementing factor of the social edifice and nothing should be done to weaken it.

Potential Victims

In some rare cases parents are also equally responsible for the plight of their daughters. Why do they select such boys for their girls for whom they even have to borrow money or spend all their life savings? Why do they marry their daughters in dowry—greedy families? Why do they not bring back their daughters from their in-law's home when they come to know of their harassment? Why are they so concerned about the social stigma and send back their daughters to their in-laws when they are tortured by their husbands and parents-in-laws? Why do they acquisce in the demands of their daughter's in-law? Why do they sacrifice their daughters for the sake of the legality of a tag marriage? Why do they spend thousands of rupees on dowry as demanded rather than spending a little less amount on their daughters to make them economically independent? We may therefore come to a conclusion that the parents of the girls and the girls themselves cannot be absolved of the responsibility. In several instances, the girl has been known to have written to her parents or visited them, just before she died and told them about the cruelty.

The girls as victims to oppression are equally questionable as to — why do they submit to oppression? Why do they not realize that a divorce is better than a marriage where money is the all and end-all of all relations? Why do they not walk out of their marriages and try to stand on their own legs? Why do they not realize that by committing suicide, they are creating problems for their children and an emotional trauma for their younger sisters and parents. Marriage is not the ultimate end in life but happiness certainly is.

Ideally the parents of the girls should take a firm decision to report the matter to the police and to the court, as well. At the same time the girl must also take a decision as to her future course of action. She must decide whether she would continue to live in a state of growing tension, or whether she would prefer to secure release from that tension once and for all.

There have been suggestions for special or separate courts may be established to deal with cases of dowry and bride burning. These courts would contribute to the speedy and efficient disposal of dowry death cases.

Moreover, court proceedings should be made time bound laws amended to make it more effective, particularly by giving recognition not only to written but oral dying declarations made in the presence of a doctor, or a police officer or a magistrate or any respectable citizen. Neighbours who can really be vital witnesses should come forward more often and be involved in a dying declaration.

There is no let up in the rate of crime despite the law. What can be done to prevent dowry violence and crimes related to dowry? People should stop exhibiting dowry items. They must socially boycott dowry seekers. The young girls must fight dowry and take a pledge not to marry those who demand dowry.

Along with amendments and changes in the present law and providing more teeth to police force, the girls, their parents, their husbands and the people at large who matter, can only prevent the bride burning. There is also need for structural changes like assuming easy and less costly education, taking effective measure to reduce unemployment among educated youth devising a system to eliminate bribery in the process of getting employment, providing housing facilities to the employed and simplifying the procedure for lodging complaint to the police, may definitely go a long way in minimizing the rate of bride burning.

Moreover, mutual respect for each other and a degree of tolerance of opposing viewpoints will, in a great measure, contribute to harmonious solution. Men have to be taught to respect women and not treat her as an object of exploitation. Further on, only if women respect themselves can command respect from others.

FOURTEEN

Killing the Innocent

Infanticide is motivated by the necessity of getting rid of an illegitimate child as well as unwelcome offsprings whom the parents cannot afford. Infanticide means murder of an infant or a newly born baby. Infanticide as such has not been defined in the I.P.C. but since it amounts to the killing of a living person, the sections dealing with murder under the penal code is applicable to the offence of infanticide. Those who kill infants or newly born babies cannot claim the benefit of the right of private defence.

Infanticide

Infanticide of the female children in India is usually done out of the undermentioned necessity:

(i) Family vanity among the groups of warrior class.

(ii) Inflated dowy demand.

(iii) Heavy expenses required to be incurred by the bride's party during marriages.

(iv) Craze for a male child drives a family to sacrifice a daughter's life on account of superstitions at times under the influence of the miracleman of the community.

In Practice

The infanticide of girl babies is widely prevalent in Thar desert area of Rajasthan, particularly among the Bhil Rajput family. The infant is subjected to asphyxial deaths through manual strangulation or through administration of opium. The male-female ratio in this area is 750 females per one thousand males, against All India figure of 929 and Rajasthan figure of 913 females per one thousand males. The figure of Jaisalmer district is 800 female per thousand males and among the Bhatti Rajput family, it is 550 females per one thousand males being the lowest among the Rajputs.

In October 1986, the Central Government ordered an inquiry into the alleged killing of a baby girl in the family of an MLA. A CID enquiry was conducted by two officers, an Additional Superintendent of Police and an Assistant Superintendent of Police. The common thing in both the enquires was that there is truth in the matter but since the Gujjar family in Rajasthan are well-off and carry on money-lending business and, therefore, no one was coming forward to give evidence. In the meantime a Public Interest Litigation (P.I.L.) case was filed before the Rajasthan High Court by Ms Summita Satyarthi, a Human Rights Activist, who pleaded for a direction to be issued for holding a C.B.I. enquiry. Great interest having been shown by the people, a case of murder was registered against the Legislature.

The Kellar community of landless farmers having a strength of about two lakh, the economic condition of the people are so deplorable that it is difficult for any family to foot the bill of marriages of their daughters. However, the people somehow manage the marriage of one daughter but the marriage of two daughters is an impossible task. Therefore, a second daughter on being born, becomes an unwelcome child and is quickly done to death by administering a paste made from poisonous oleander berries. The menfolk dig a pit outside the house, watch the cries of baby and when it is stopped, the dead body is slipped into the pit and buried. There are hardly any families where some or other child is not buried.

According to a *Times of India* news report, from Madurai, a 26 years old woman of Chokknathpuram, who had vowed to carry "Agni Chatti" (firepot) to a nearby temple during the "Panguni Uthiram" festival could not fulfil her vow as her husband declined to give her money for that and in frustration, she doused her three daughters with kerosene and set them on fire. Thereafter she herself attempted to commit suicide. On hearing the cries, the neighbours rushed and retrieved the children and hospitalised them. Only one could survive. It is pertinent to mention that she had a male child as well who was spared.

Death before Birth

In contrast to infanticide, foeticide is the unlawful expulsion of foetus. It is also called "criminal abortion" or "causing miscarriage". When used in the legal sense, it includes both abortion and premature labour. As per medical sense, premature labour means expulsion of a child that has attained viability. The term "abortion" or "miscarriage" signify the expulsion of foetus or ovum at an earlier period. Modern methods of detecting the sex of the foetus through amniocentesis are used nowadays.

A Sort of Murder

Abortion may be classified into:

(a) natural and

(b) artificial.

Natural Abortion

Natural abortions occur due to such reasons as mother's ill-health, local disease, or diseases of the generative organs, shocks, fear, excessive joy, accidental falls, etc. Hence, appropriate care is required in respect of the health of the pregnant woman.

Artificial Abortion

Premature evacuation of foetus, whether medically, surgically or through indigenous method is known as artificial abortion. Artificial abortion is a criminal offence punishable under Sections 312-316 of the Indian Penal Code. The Sections run as under:

Sections 312-316 IPC

Sec. 312 Causing Miscarriage

> Whoever voluntarily causes a woman with a child to miscarry, shall, if such miscarriage be not caused in good faith for the purpose of saving the life of the woman, be punished with imprisonment of either description for a term which may extend to three years, or with fine, or with both; and, if the woman be quick with child, shall be punished with imprisonment of either description for a term which may extend to seven years, and shall also be liable to fine.
>
> *Explanation:* A woman who causes herself to miscarry, is within the meaning of this section.

Sec. 313. Causing Miscarriage without Woman's Consent

Whoever, commits the offence defined in the last preceding section without the consent of the woman, whether the woman is quick with child or not, shall be punished with imprisonment for life, or with imprisonment of either description for a term which may extend to ten years, and shall be liable to fine.

Sec. 314. Death caused by act done with intent to cause miscarriage

Whoever with intent to cause the miscarriage of a woman with child, does any act which caused the death of such woman, shall be punished with imprisonment of either description for a term which may extend to ten years, and shall also be liable to fine.

If Act done without woman's consent, the offender shall be punished either with imprisonment for life, or with punishment mentioned above.

Explanation: It is not essential to this offence that the offender should know that the act is likely to cause death.

Sec. 315. Act done with intent to prevent child being born alive or to cause it to die after birth

Whoever, before the birth of any child does any act with the intention of thereby preventing that child from being born alive or causing it to die after its birth, shall, if such act not caused in good faith for the purpose of saving the life of the mother be punished with imprisonment of either description for a term which may extend to ten years, or with fine, or with both.

Sec. 316. Causing death of quick unborn child by act amounting to culpable homicide

Whoever, does any act under such circumstances, that if he thereby causes death he would be guilty of culpable homicide, and does by such act cause the death of a quick unborn child, shall be punished with imprisonment of either description for a term which may extend to ten years, and shall also be liable to fine.

Illustration

A, knowing that he is likely to cause the death of a pregnant woman, does an act which, may cause the death of the woman, this would result in culpable homicide if the woman is, injured but does not die; but the death of an unborn quick child with which she is pregnant is thereby caused, A is guilty of the offence defined in this Section.

Termination of Pregnancy

Legislation

Except for saving the life of the pregnant woman, termination of pregnancy (Bhrun Hatya) was a penal offence in accordance with the provisions of the aforesaid sections of the I.P.C.

After India's independence and with the passage of time, population started growing rapidly with such an alarming speed that it began to be seen that available resources would not be adequate to meet the necessities of the people in the country. Thus, several family planning programmes were evolved and propagated among the people of the country through mass media. It was further thought that a legislation to legalise termination of pregnancy was another means by which the growing population could be checkmated. Thus, Medical Termination of Pregnancy Act (1971) was enacted as a means of population control. According to it (Sec. 3), the objectives of termination of pregnancy are two fold:

Objectives

(a) ***Therapeutic:*** When the continuance of pregnancy is likely to endanger the life of the pregnant woman and could cause grave injuries to her physical and mental health.

(b) ***Eugenic:*** When there is the risk of the child being born with serious physical or mental handicap. This may occur, if the pregnant woman in the first three months of her pregnancy suffers from:

   (a) German measles; chicken pox or small pox, viral infection including viral heptitis, toxoplasmonia or any other disease which would have affected the health of the woman.

(b) The pregnant woman takes certain medicines, whether under medical advice or otherwise which affect the foetus;

(c) The pregnant woman receives radio or any invisible ray therapy; and

(d) Insanity of the either of the two or both spouse.

(c) ***Humanitarian:*** When the pregnancy is in consequence of sexual assault.

(d) ***Social:*** When the pregnancy has occurred on account of failure of contraceptive device.

Abortion having become legalized, this act is a blessing for large number of nursing homes who are thriving through such operations.

New Revolution in Reproduction

Contraceptive means to ensure sex without reproduction. Surrogate motherhood, in vitro fertilisation and artificial insemination are advancements in genetic technology in which reproduction is possible without sex. New techniques have enabled the determination of the abnormalities as well as the sex of the child in advance much before the birth of the child. The prenatal sex-determination is done through amniocentesis, wherein amniotic fluid is drawn through the uterus of a pregnant woman to determine any defect or physical deformity in the child.

Amniocentesis is risky as it constitutes the drawing of amniotic fluid from the uterus. This is the fluid on which the foetus lives until birth. This test is conducted after sixteen weeks pregnancy and if conducted earlier may prove harmful or fatal for the child in which case there can be legal proceedings against the wrong doers.

The determination of sex is also possible through Chorionic Villi Sampling (CVS) by vaginal extraction from eight to sixteen weeks of pregnancy. This method is also dangerous as it causes the pregnant woman to infect and in effect, spontaneous abortions can take place. It may as well result in fatality of the pregnant woman.

The other method of sex determination is through ultrasound scanning which though non-invasive, is unreliable, even at the advanced stage of pregnancy.

Misuse of Technology

Scientists have developed the genetic technology in order to ascertain in advance if the child in the mother's womb has any deformity. Unscrupulous people in the society are using the know-how to reduce the female population in an organised and systematic manner.

The dangerous form of genetic engineering by selectively aborting the newborn child has been flourishing in the capital city of India as well as in several big and small cities of the state on account of no value being attached to a female child in comparison to the male counterpart. Sex clinics have multiplied and mushroomed throughout the cities and towns. According to a rough estimate around 78,000 female foeticides were aborted after prenatal sex determination test through amniocentesis. In 1983, Bombay had only three sex clinics and over a period of next five years, it had multiplied to 258 private clinics in addition to the sixteen recognised Government clinics. No permit or licence is required to set up a clinic of this type. On account of the coming up of a large number of clinics, there is a competition in the market and the fees charged (which had become between Rs. 150 to Rs. 500) is within the reach of a common man. The popularity of the method has spread to small places in far-flung areas. The samples now can be carried to Mumbai or Delhi or Kolkata or any big city of the country from the nearby places. A survey made by Women's Centre has revealed that out of 8000 abortions checked, 7999 were in respect of females.

One clinic in Mumbai is reported to have advertised that the cost of abortion is cheaper than the amount required for the marriage and payment of dowry. Such statement provoking abortion openly advocate murder of the foetus. What more can be said of such a system. There is a battle being fought between doctors and feminist groups on the availability of medical technology which could assist pre-selection of sex. These organisations have demanded a total ban while the lobby of doctors who perform these tests, on the other hand, oppose the demand on the ground that if the ban is enforced, abortions would be performed by quaks. There is some force in the demand of the doctors also. The whole issue is dependent upon the attitude of the people towards the female child. The rate, the pre-natal sex determination tests are gaining popularity and being used in aborting female foetus, the day is not far when the woman may become an endangered species.

Act in Application

The Medical Termination of Pregnancy Act, 1971 only ensures a legal sanction to a Medical Practitioner to abort a female foetus. Thus, the two together, that is MTPA and Sex-determination Technology have put India on its way to technological and legal femicide. Unregulated technology and the legal Act have created a new problem in bringing a decline in female population.

According to the Provision of Section 3 of the Act, a Registered Medical Practitioner is entitled to abort a foetus within twelve weeks of pregnancy and two of them can abort a pregnancy having a length of 12 to 20 weeks. In either case they will have to take a stand that abortion was necessary in the interest of the health of the woman.

The anguish of a pregnancy by sexual assault is presumed to constitute a grave injury to a woman's mental health. However, the failure of a contraceptive device cannot cause any such damage to the mental health. Assessment of the anticipated risk is rather vague and gives a licence to abort female child with the aid of pre-natal sex determination test. Directly or indirectly the MTP is a licence to kill the foetus as some of its statements lack logic.

Business in abortion became possible and flourishing on account of provisions of Section 5 of the MTP Act, 1971, which is an enabling provision for an emergent situation and permits non-application of provisions of Section 3 and Section 4 of the Act. The Section enables a doctor without any experience in gynaecology and obstetrics to operate after having formed an opinion with due care and attention that termination of pregnancy is immediately necessary to save the life of the pregnant woman. It may be pertinent to mention that while making a provision of the Section, care to provide any safeguard has not been introduced to prevent its misuse. A doctor can now be prosecuted under the I.P.C. only. The Act suffers from the following flaws:

Flaws in MTP Act

(i) The Act does not provide any guidelines for calculating the commencement of pregnancy and to assess the period of twelve weeks or twenty weeks. The matter has been left entirely to the wisdom of the doctor.

(ii) The Act does not require that the pregnant woman counter-signs or affixes her signature/thumb impression on the key column of the register containing details regarding the duration of pregnancy. Thus, any evidence, which, otherwise could have been provided, is always missing.

(iii) The evidence is further weakened by the type of consent Form C prescribed under the Central Rules. There is no column that the doctor makes a declaration that he has explained to the pregnant woman the reasons for the termination of her pregnancy.

(iv) As usual, the Act further ensures a cover for the doctor as per Section 8 of the Act which lays down that no suit or proceedings shall lie against the doctor if he has acted in good faith. It is very difficult to prove that the doctor did not exercise reasonable care and lacked good faith.

Initially nearly one dozen doctors in seven states of the country offered to perform these tests which, for the first time was introduced in All India Institute of Medical Sciences, Delhi, primarily to discover genetic disorders in foetus in those cases where the parents had the history of abnormality. Since in course of the determination of the genetic disorder, it was found that the method reveals the sex of the unborn child, it became popular as a method for determination of pre-natal sex of the child. The Medical Termination of Pregnancy Act, 1971, made it a convenient tool for selective abortion.

Consequent upon a widespread resentment against this test, the Maharashtra has taken a lead and the Legislature of

Maharashtra Assembly passed the Regulation; "Use of Pre-natal Diagnostic Techniques Act, 1988".

Related Law

Features

(a) Section 3 of the Act prohibits carrying of the pre-natal diagnostic tests by an unregistered genetic centre laboratory or clinic.

(b) Section 4 of the Act lays down the fulfilment of five conditions for the performance of diagnostic tests. The important conditions are that woman should be near about the age of 35 years and she has a history of at least a couple of abortions, family history of mental retardation and/or physical abnormalities.

FIFTEEN

Violence and Homicide

In law, culpable homicide is differentiated from justifiable and excusable homicide (see Gibbons, *Society, Crime and Criminal Careers*, 3rd ed., 1978: 350).

Justifiable homicide is intentional killing sanctioned by law. It is committed on some legal demands, or discharging one's legal responsibility, such as the execution of a legal sentence of death, or the killing of a person in legitimate self-defence, or a police officer's shooting a fleeing dacoit, or a prison officer's killing a prisoner attempting to escape from the jail.

Excusable homicide is one which results accidentally from lawful acts performed by lawful means. It is unintentional killing where no blame is attached; for example, the death of a patient that results accidentally from a surgery by a doctor. *Culpable homicide* is one for which a person is held criminally responsible and is subjected to prosecution and punishment.

Culpable homicide is further divided into three sub-categories: (a) first-degree murder, (b) second-degree murder, and (c) manslaughter. These distinctions rest on the degrees of premeditation and malice aforethought. Premeditation designates 'intent' (to violate the law) formulated prior to the activity, i.e., a decision to commit crime and planning its execution, etc. Malice aforethought does not involve planning, though it involves 'intent to kill' at the time of the act. Thus, for a person to be convicted of murder in the first-degree, both premeditation and malice aforethought have to be established. In second degree murder, only malice aforethought has to be proved. In manslaughter, neither premeditation nor malice aforethought are present. It (manslaughter) is, thus, unintended homicide.

All types of homicides in this chapter are used as a generic term as 'murders'. Although not all homicides are murders, yet if an act is a homicide it states a reason for regarding it as murder and hence as wrong. Calling an act 'murder' presupposes that the act is homicide; that is the reason why the act is wrong. We could thus say that homicide is morally neutral but not murder.

Official statistics reveal that murder has been on the rise in India during recent years. The figures had gone up from 25,786 in 1984 to 38,577 in 1994, i.e., by 50 per cent (*Crime in India,* 1994:8). Rates also vary by region and by the size of a city, though we cannot say that murder is primarily a city phenomenon. The rates for the rural areas have been higher than the rates for the urban areas. It is rare that murders go unreported and it is also rare that a suspect is not apprehended and charged with murder.

All-India figures of murders in which female victims may be classified on gender basis are not available. No official records are maintained on the incidence of spouse murder. But it is estimated that spousal murders in intra-familial homicides may account for 20 per cent to 30 per cent of all murders and wives killed by their husbands (in comparison to husbands being killed by their wives) make up 68 per cent to 70 per cent of all spousal murders.

Any meaningful study of spousal murder requires to concentrate on four major aspects: the kinds of persons who commit murders, the situations in which murders are committed, the categories of murder, and motivations in murder. We also focused our attention on these and a few other issues. The main concerns of the study of the murder of females were:

* to gain insight into motivations in murder;
* to examine patterns in murders;
* to assess the kinds of men who commit murders;
* to find out the types of women who are usually murdered;
* to study homogeneity-heterogeneity in the offender-victim relationship in murder; and
* to analyze the role of victim in murder.

The data for the present study was collected from prisoners in a jail (all 'lifers' having served one to eight years in jail) and court and police records. In all, 52 cases were studied.

Relation between Offender and Victim

The offender and the victim were closely related to each other as members of the same family in 92 per cent cases and knew each other as acquaintance in 8 per cent cases. Of the 48 cases in the first category (members of the same family), the victim was related to the murderer as wife in 90 per cent cases, as illegal wife in 4 per cent cases, as daughter-in-law in 4% cases, and as sister-in-law in 2 per cent cases. Thus, a large number of murders by men were murders of their wives. Of the four cases in which the victim was not a member of the murderer's family, one was the landlady (the killer being her servant), one was the offender's old co-tenant (a girl of 19 years of age) and two were colleagues (a teacher in school and a clerk in office).

It could, be said that familial maladjustment in general and marital relations in particular are very crucial in female homicides. Or, what needs to be understood in female murders is adjustment and role performance in family relations. Von Hentig's (*The Criminal and his Victim,* 1948: 392) investigation of murders in Germany in 1930 also brought into light a startling that 62 per cent of the women murdered were killed by their husbands. A similar finding was earlier given by McDonald ("Death Penalty and Homicide" in *American Journal of Sociology,* 1911:16) in his perusal of criminal statistics covering the late 19th and early 20th centuries in several countries. Similar conclusion was made by a study in England and Wales for the years 1885-1905. Out of 487 murders committed by men, 124 were women murdered by their husbands and 115 were mistresses or sweethearts of their assailants. Wolfgang's (*Patterns in Criminal Homicide,* 1958:11) Philadelphia (United States) study during the 1950s also revealed the relationship between gender and murder. He emphasized that homicide is directly related to "relatively close, intimate, personal and direct relationships or primary contacts". His research indicated that primary group relationships, accounted for 65 per cent, of all victim-offender relationships, and that the number of wives, homicidally assaulted by their husbands constituted 41 per cent of all women who were killed. Gibson and Klein's study of homicides occurring between 1957 and 1968 in England (Statistical Report on Murder in England and Wales, 1969) also revealed that wives were usually the most frequent victims.

Background of Victim and Offender

As regards age, out of 52 victims, 14 per cent were 20 years of age or below at the time of murder, 44 per cent were between 21 and 30 years of age, 27 per cent between 31 and 40 years, and 15 per cent between 41 and 50 years of age. The mean age of the victims was 29.4. Against this, 7 per cent of the murderers were 20 years or below, 52 per cent were between 21 and 30 years, 25 per cent between 31 and 40 years, 10 per cent between 41 and 50 years, 4 per cent between 51 and 60 years and 2 per cent above 60 years of age. The mean age of the murderers was 30.5 years. This indicates that:

(i) three-fifths of the victims (58%) and three-fifths of the murderers (59%) were young, i.e., below 30 years of age, and

(ii) the ratio of middle-aged offenders to middle-aged victims was 1:1.2.

It may be hypothesized that most victims of murders as well as their murderers are young persons (of 18 to 30 years of age) or that young husbands are more likely to kill their wives than older husbands. This does not support Wolfgang's finding that murderers are generally younger than the victims; though it supports Bensing and Schroeder's contention that relatively young persons carrying out most homicides.

The age difference between the murderer and his victim was less than one year in 11 per cent cases, between 1-3 years in 33 per cent cases, between 4-6 years in 31 per cent cases, between 7-9 years in 17 per cent cases and 10 and above years in 8 per cent cases. Thus, the age difference between offenders and victims was very less. On an average, the killers were about 4.5 years older than the victims. A significant fact to remember here is that the murderer in our study was the victim's husband and in Indian society the age difference between husband and wife varies from

2-5 years. The above figures also support Richard Block's (*Homicide in Chicago*, 1973) finding that the homicide offender is young.

Marital Life

As regards the marital life, of the 48 victims who were married and members of the offender's family, 9 per cent had enjoyed a married life for less than 1 year, 44 per cent between 1-5 years, 26 per cent between 5-10 years, 14 per cent between 10-15 years, and 7 per cent for more than 15 years. The mean period which the victims had spent with their husbands/in-laws was 6.2 years. About 33 per cent of the victims were married before the age of 18 years, 46 per cent in the age group of 19-22 years and 21 per cent after the age of 23 or more years.

Children

Further, 65 per cent of the victims had children and 35 per cent had no children. Of those 31 victims who had children, 31 per cent had one child, 35 per cent had 2 children, 23 per cent had 3 children, and 16 per cent had 4 or more children. The mean number of children was 2.4. The age of the children varied from 1 year to 38 years. Of the total (71) children, the age of 31 per cent of the children was 5 years or less, while 24 per cent of the children belonged to the 6-10 years age-group, 17 per cent to the 11-15 years age-group, 14 per cent to the 16-20 years age-group, 10 per cent to the 21-25 years age-group, and 4 per cent were more than 25 years of age. The mean age of the children was 11 years. Thus, since a little more than half of the victims (53%) had spent one to five years with their husbands/in-laws and a little less than two-fifths (38%) hd one to two children, it may be concluded that—

(i) the rates of murder among women with a marital span of less than 5 years are greater than the rates among women with a marital span of 5-10 years or more than 10 years.

(ii) as the marital span increases, the rate of murder decreases, and

(iii) problems of adjustment of a girl arise not soon after her marriage but after spending several years in the family of procreation.

Education

Regarding education, 29 per cent of the murderers were illiterate or had no formal education, 35 per cent were educated up to the primary/middle level, 19 per cent up to the secondary level, 8 per cent up to the higher secondary level, and 9 per cent were graduates/post-graduates or had a technical degree/diploma. Amongst the victims, 40 per cent were illiterate or had no formal education, 31 per cent were educated up to the primary/middle level, 21 per cent up to the high school level and 8 per cent were graduates and/or postgraduates. Thus 7 out of every 10 victims and 6 out of every 10 murderers were either illiterate or less educated. This indicates that educational achievement or level of education is significantly related to murder.

Caste

In terms of caste, of the 47 Hindus (five were non-Hindus) 55 per cent belonged to the upper castes, 30 per cent to the intermediate castes, and 15 per cent to the lower castes. The ratio of upper caste to lower caste victims was 3.6:1. It may thus be averred that among lower castes there is no high rates of murder as against the common belief. Further, 60 per cent victims hailed from rural areas and 40 per cent from urban areas, showing thereby that female murder largely tends to be a rural phenomenon.

Occupation

In terms of occupation, 39 per cent offenders were cultivators, 17 per cent businessmen (including shopkeepers) 21 per cent service-men (including teachers), and 13 per cent were self-employed (tailor/*sari*-printer/nagina-maker/rickshaw-puller/mason/advocate/black-smith). Of the remaining 10 per cent offenders, two were unemployed and one each was a student, a beggar, and a salesman. Thus, 62 per cent offenders were engaged in occupations of low status. Or, it may be said that homicides of females are more common among low status occupational groups.

Economic Status

Finally, analyzing the economic status, it was found that 88 per cent of the murderers were working and earning while 12 per cent were non-earners. Of the 46 earners, 26 per cent were earning up to Rs. 1,000 per month, 48 per cent between Rs. 1,000 and Rs.

2,000, 20 per cent between Rs. 2,000 and Rs. 5,000, and 6 per cent above Rs. 5,000 per month. Nearly 27 per cent of the murderers were the sole bread winners of their families while 73 per cent had co-earners also in their families. Thus, taking the income of all the earning members in the family, 25 per cent were found belonging to lower class (with an income of less than Rs. 1,000 per month), 29 per cent to lower middle class (with an income of Rs. 1,000-2,000), and 46 per cent to middle and upper-middle classes (with an income of Rs. 2,000 and Rs. 6,000 per month). Amongst the victims, only seven women were earning.

These figures reveal that the rates of homicides of women from the lower and lower-middle classes exceed those from women of middle and upper middle economic status. In other words, economic factor is inextricably related to female murder. Our study, thus confirms Bensing and Schroeder's (*Homicide in an Urban Community*, 1972) thesis that low-income families have high rates of murder. It also supports Wolfgang's contention that murderers are largely located in the low stratum of society. Further, it supports our own earlier study on female murderers in India (*Female offenders in India*, 1969) that female murderers generally come from the lower income groups. This makes it necessary to critically examine the link between homicide and lower and lower-middle class adjustment. Scholars like Miller and Bullock (*Urban Homicide in Theory and Fact*, 1952) Wolfgang and Cohen (*Delinquent Boys: The Culture of the Gang*, 1956) have attempted to trace the root of the violence behaviour pattern in what they call 'lower-class sub-culture'. We will examine this theory later on.

Taking all variables together, it may be concluded that:

(1) murderers of females by and large are members of their own families;

(2) they are not-so-young, but are generally illiterate or less educated and moderately poor persons; and

(3) a positive correlation exists between the incidence of homicide and the level of familial adjustment.

Since the last feature makes an analysis of offenders' families essential, we will now attempt to examine the family structure and family relations vis-a-vis murders.

Family Structure

The family structure pointed out that 37 per cent of the murderers were living in nuclear families, and 63 per cent in joint families. The high incidence of murderers from joint families is probably attributable to the predominance of joint families in the social structure of our society, particularly in rural areas.

It was further found that out of the 48 cases in which victims were members of the killers' families, in 65 per cent cases the murderers were heads of families and in 35 per cent cases they were ordinary members (non-heads). Since the number of murders by heads of families was about two times more than that of non-heads, one must ask if this indicates any relation between murder and the role which the head of the family has to play as leader of the family group.

On the other hand, as far as the status of 48 victims is concerned, 33 per cent of the victims had no young children to bring up in the families, but 67 per cent had small children to look after. Does this not indicate a difficult problem of adjustment in families?

How were relations among members in the families studied? The persistent belief is that if a family is normal, members must love one another and violence must be totally absent. Were then the families of murderers studied abnormal? The respondents did not agree to this contention. Conflicts while common in many families were certainly not abnormally frequent in the homes analyzed. By and large, the families functioned nonviolently. The threat of murder or even physical violence never hung heavy in the air. The murderers interviewed revealed that the victims of their murder had broadly speaking strong feelings for them. That love and threat of murder can coexist in a family is perhaps the most insidious aspect of murderers' family life. Men do hit the people they love. Then what went wrong in the family that led the respondents to commit murders. This is discussed in the following paras on murder motives.

Purpose of Murder

The most common homicide situation starts when the parties to the fatal interaction are involved in arguments and altercations, often over matters that might appear relatively trivial to many people. In our study too, quarrels over behaviour with the in-laws, money, children and sundry situational disputes were found to be the precipitating circumstances in many homicides. Petty quarrels resulting from illicit relations, a dislike for the wife, the wife's chronic illness or property conflicts were also found to be the motivating factors in murders.

An in-depth study showed that the main causes of murders were as follows: petty quarrels — 27 per cent, victim's chronic illness 15 per cent, irritating behaviour of wife — 11 per cent, offender's illicit relations — 10 per cent, victim's illicit relations — 5 per cent, fear of victim's revealing offender's secrets — 6 per cent, property conflict — 6 per cent, feeling of revenge — 6 per cent, wife's insistence on visiting parents — 4 per cent and wife's constant demand for money — 10 per cent. Thus, marital maladjustment (58%) because of domestic altercations or wife's chronic illness and sexual infidelity (15%) were the two most important factors in the murder of females.

It was further found that there was no significant relationship between motivation and planning. The planning was associated only with murders committed for revenge. Murders because of petty quarrels or wife's chronic illness or wife's irritating behaviour or irrational demands or illicit relations, etc., were not always planned.

On the basis of this analysis, we can identify the following four types of murders:

(i) Non-malicious emotional murders.

(ii) Non-malicious accidental murders.

(iii) Malicious murders without explicit intention to kill (say, beating with a view to teaching a lesson).

(iv) Malicious murders with premeditated intention to kill.

Of the 52 murders in our study, 27 per cent fall in the first category, 19 per cent in the second category, 31 per cent in the third category, and 23 per cent in the fourth category. This indicates that a large number of murders are committed in the heat of passion or in a state of high emotionalism or in a situation of negligence. Only a small number of offenders kill females in a cool and calculated manner with malice aforethought. Thus, since the real intent to kill is absent in a large number of the cases, it may be pointed out that homicide is the product of a situation characterized by lack of social control.

Different Patterns

Murders vary not only in terms of causes and relationships between the murderer and the victim but also in terms of operational dimensions like the place and the time of murder, modes of murder, planning in murder, weapon used, help sought, and alcoholic state of mind. We will examine these important dimensions separately.

Place of Murder

In 88 per cent of the cases, murders were committed in the homes and in 12 per cent cases outside the homes. The data further showed that there was a direct relationship between the locale and the type of person killed. Primary (43) and secondary (3) kin were mostly killed in their own homes and acquaintances (4) were killed outside their homes. Thus, our finding that a very large number of murders of females are usually committed in home supports Gibson and Klein's thesis (*Murder*: 1957-1968) in their study of homicides occurred between 1957 and 1968 in England that most murders of women occur in their homes. However, our finding is different from that of Wolfgang, Bullock and Pokorny.

Mode of Killing

In analyzing the modes of killing, it was found that women were killed by stabbing in 23 per cent cases, by strangulation in 19 per cent cases, by hacking (cutting body in pieces) in 25 per cent cases, by poisoning in 15 per cent cases, by slashing (making cuts with sweeping strokes) in 12 per cent cases, and by shooting, electric shock and burning in 6 per cent cases. Of the 21 cases in which weapons were used in killing, a knife was used in 26 per cent cases, an iron-rod in 23 per cent cases, an axe in 35 per cent cases, and a pistol, gun or sword in 5 per cent cases. Thus, the availability of a licensed weapon has no bearing on murder. It was further found that there was some relationship between the mode of killing and the planned and unplanned nature of murder.

Planned Murders

Of the 28 planned murders, 18 per cent were committed by stabbing, 29 per cent by poisoning, 14 per cent by strangulation, 21 per cent by hacking, 7 per cent by shooting and 11 per cent by slashing.

Unplanned Murders

Against this, of the 24 per cent unplanned murders, 29 per cent were committed by stabbing, 25 per cent by strangulation, 29 per cent by hacking, and 17 per cent by strangulation and then burning, by electric wire, and by slashing. Thus, there was no great difference in the methods of both planned and unplanned killing.

Influence of Alcohol

Only five murders were committed in a state of intoxication and 47 in a sober state of mind. This does not mean that all murderers in the second category were non-alcoholics or all murderers in the first category were necessarily alcoholics. If alcoholism is defined as 'habitual drinking' and is operationalized in terms of physical and psychological dependence of individual on alcohol, it was found that murderers by and large were not alcoholics, although 37 per cent did take alcohol occasionally or once in a while. Thus, we cannot demonstrate any positive correlationship between murder and alcoholism.

Presence of Accomplices

Three-fourths of the murders (73%) were committed by the murderers alone while in one-fourth of the cases (27%) someone's help was sought. Of the 14 cases in the latter category (in which the offenders had accomplices), in 12 cases they had only one accomplice and only in two cases did the murderer have two accomplices. Amongst the accomplices, in two cases the accomplice was a member of the murderer's family, in four cases a friend and in one case a brother and his friend. Further, the accomplices were found only in planned murders. The help sought was in terms of killing the victim (9 cases) and in disposing of the body of the victim after the murder (5 cases).

Element of Planning

Nearly 54 per cent of the murders were planned and 46 per

cent were situational. That is, the latter type of murders were committed in a state of momentary outrage, in a situation of tense interaction with the victims, while the former type of murders were committed in a cool and calculated manner.

Murders, Inducing Victims

Several researchers have hold the view that many victims of murder precipitate their own deaths. This mostly occurs when offenders and victims know each other and their tensions and mutual aggravations reach a point where both indulge in violence. Our study, however, indicated that the number of cases in which victims induced their death through their own menacing actions, was not very high. Only in 15 per cent of the cases, was the first initiative for violence taken by the victim, i.e., a large number of homicides involving women were not victim-precipitated. While more husbands have been found to have provoked their wives, the number of wives provoking their husbands is not large. When our earlier study of female murderers (*Female Offenders in India*, 1969) had shown that in quite a large number of cases, husbands had provoked their wives, our present study of women being murdered by males showed that only 15 per cent wives provoked their husbands. Boudouris's work in Detroit (*Homicide and the Family*, 1971) has also revealed a similar pattern.

A few victim-precipitated cases show the pattern of victim-precipitated murders are described below. The use of scurrilous language by the victim, supplemented by outrageous behaviour, characterizes the most common victim-precipitated homicides. Though these cases exist they are not very large.

Cases

In one case, the husband accused his wife of having illicit relations. Once when he was beating her for this, she taunted him that he should kill her if he did not want her in the house. Thus challenged, the husband stabbed her. In the second case, a man (the accused) had married for the second time after paying Rs. 5,000 to have a woman to look after his young children from the first wife. Soon he found that his wife was neglecting the children as well as him (the accused) as well. He tried to argue with her but she always abused him. On one occasion when she started abusing him, he struck with an iron rod and killed her. In the third case, the victim wanted to visit her parents, but the husband (the accused) refused to let her go. On her insistance, he attacked her with an axe. The blow was so fatal that the victim died within a few hours. In the fourth case, the second wife of a husband (the accused) took away ornaments and a lot of cash and gave these to her brother. When the accused went to her house and asked for the money, his brother-in-law started beating him. His wife also started abusing him with a fit of rage, he gave his wife several blows and then struck her with an iron rod. In the fifth case, a husband used to beat his wife regularly; generally the beating was preceded as well as followed by a violent quarrel. One day the wife attacked her husband with a knife. The husband snatched the knife from her hands and stabbed her. In another case, the daughter-in-law and her mother-in-law very frequently quarrelled on petty issues. Both sought the husband's/son's sympathy. The husband tried to pacify both but the quarrels persisted. One night when both started quarrelling in his presence, he physically attacked his wife to calm her down, but the injury was so severe that the wife died in hospital.

Explanation of the Acts

A number of theories have been advanced to explain violence in general and homicide in particular. Four important theories which have absorbed the attention of scholars in this connection are:

1. the Instinctive Aggression Theory (bio-psychological view),
2. the Frustration-Aggression Theory (psychological view),
3. the Learing Theory (sociological view) and
4. the Theory of Sub-culture of Violence (sociological view).

We do not consider these theoretical explanations (including the Theory of Sub-culture) adequate explanations for explaining the murders of females in one's own family, particularly of wives.

Identification of Murderer

Abrahamsen (*The Murdering Mind*, 1973), a psychoanalyst psychologist, has given the following characteristics of a murderer:

1. hateful impulses,
2. feelings of distrust, helplessness, fear, insignificance, and loss of self-esteem,
3. emotional disturbances,
4. inability to withstand frustration and find sufficient gratification by expressing hostile aggressive feelings,
5. suggestibility,
6. a tendency toward transforming identification,
7. an inability to change persistent egocentricity or self-centredness into a healthy conscience resulting in contempt for authority,
8. suicidal tendencies with depression, and
9. a history of a previous antisocial or criminal acts.

An umpteen number of the respondents confessed having the first four attributes, but they denied having the last five characteristics. It is, therefore, difficult to accept the 'personality-type' explanation of Abrahamsen and other psychiatrists of the dynamics of murder. A murderer, in most cases, is a normal individual who acts in an extreme way due to anxiety, fear, anger, or confusion caused by a specific situation. Having said this, it cannot be maintained that we accept the 'emotional-type personality' explanation of a murderer. People who cry at the slightest provocation or who smash things when annoyed are often characterized as 'emotional' people (Newman, G., *Understanding Violence*, 1979). Some studies have referred to the relationship between emotions and aggression, which includes murder. Emotions like fear or rage, etc., erupt as a result of external stimuli though environmental conditions which can lead to a woman's murder cannot be ruled out. However, we do concede that these fear or anxiety or aggression complexes might have developed due to extreme deprivation (of love, sustenance, etc.) at an early age (Kuo, Z.Y., *The Dynamics of Behaviour Development*, 1967).

Reasons behind Murder

A theoretical perspective is needed to explain why a man murders a woman belonging to his own family, particularly his wife. For this, we have to understand the following:

(i) What are the broad expectations from a woman in a specific family setting?

(ii) Why does a woman fail to adjust herself or fail to perform roles according to familial expectations?

(iii) Why does a man (i.e., husband or father-in-law or brother-in-law etc.) react to this failure in a specific way?

(iv) When does the (reacting) man use "murder" as a reaction to woman's failure to familial or individual expectations?

Context-specific Approach

To answer these questions, we have to use a 'Context-specific Approach' as proposed by Wegner (*Pacific Sociological Review*, 1975) and used by Dobash and Dobash (*Violence Against Wives*, 1972) in their researches. In this approach, instead of viewing situations, personalities, feelings, etc., in general terms, we view them in specific contexts and specific domains.

With this approach in the background and drawing on contributions from psychology and sociology, our answers to the questions raised above are:

1. The roles and behaviour expectations from a woman vary according to sub-cultural patterns existing in a specific community and a specific family.
2. The failure of a woman to adopt herself to these expectations is circumstancial and partly her personality traits. Thus failure affects her inter-personal relations in the family.
3. A man's reaction to woman's failure and her specific behaviour is the result of his learning, through the process of socialization, a set of beliefs regarding relationship between man and woman and man's authority over woman, and the demonstration of this authority in certain situations.
4. A man's own personality type determines his aggressive ways in enforcing his authority and domination.

5. A passive man with a submissive personality will tolerate woman's failure, but an aggressive man with a domineering personality will react and use violent techniques in enforcing control.
6. The nature of the precipitation in the specific situation determines a man's violent reaction leading to murder.

Thus, in our theoretical explanation, we do not give importance to unfulfilled childhood experiences, or to pathological personalities, or a sub-culture of violence. Our focus is on the social situation (including family structure, family norms, and intra-family relations, man's status in the family), personality characteristics (like impulsiveness, depression, immaturity, etc.) and socio-cultural interpretations given by man to woman's roles, that is, response learned in the process of inter-personal relations.

Cultural attitudes about women and about violence as a means of self-expression and solving problems are at the root of private violence. There is urgent need to bring about a change on this account. Various social factors may be related to different patterns of murder but we need to consider that people have choices as to how they will respond to immediate crisis and stress. Cultural legacy of violence may, in many ways, influence what choices people consider appropriate.

Since our finding is that most of the murders of women are within the family, particularly of wives by husbands, and these murders are not planned and premeditated but are crimes of violence and passion which occur in the heat of inter-personal conflicts and tensions, it may be said that if women adjust in certain situations while dealing with domineering, aggressive and authoritarian males, and if in certain other situations instead of acting as submissive and passive females, they act as efficient and active females, most of the murders would not occur. The level of violence in family (including murder) is the greatest when wife is either too submissive or too dominant in decisions.

SIXTEEN

Legal Position

There has been a growing trend towards violence against women, more so with development and liberalization and the hunger and greed for material things. The global campaign for elimination of violence against women in the recent years indicates the enormity as well as the seriousness of the atrocities committed against women that are being witnessed the world over. Development along with its progressive changes in personal lifestyle, living standards, varied economic growth caused by urbanisation and changes in social ethos contribute to a violent attitude and tendencies towards women which resulted in an increase in crimes against women. The containment of such incidents is a necessity so that the Indian women attain their rightful share and live in dignity, freedom, peace and free from crimes and aspersions. The battle against crime against women has to be waged by the various sections of society through campaigns and various programmes with social support alongwith legal protection, safeguards and reforms in the Criminal Justice System. In spite of all these safeguards, the women in our country continue to suffer due to unawareness of their rights, illiteracy and oppressive practices and customs. The resultant consequences are many viz. a constant fall in the sex ratio, high infant mortality rate, low literacy rate, high dropout rate of girls from education, low wage rates, etc.

The State has enacted various legislative measures to uphold the Constitutional mandate. This intended to ensure equal rights, to counter social discrimination and various forms of violence and atrocities and to provide support services especially to the working women.

Crimes Classified

Women may be victims of any crime such as murder, robbery, cheating, etc. which are not specifically directed at them, there are crimes identified which are designated as Crime Against Women which are directed specifically against them.

Criminal Acts under IPC

(i) Rape (Sec. 376 IPC)

(ii) Kidnapping and abduction for different purposes (Sec. 363-373 IPC)

(iii) Homicide for Dowry, Dowry deaths or their attempts (Sec. 302/304-B IPC)

(iv) Torture, both mental and physical (Sec. 498-A IPC)

(v) Molestation (Sec. 354 IPC)

(vi) Sexual Harassment (Eve-Teasing) (Sec. 509 IPC).

(vii) Importation of girls (upto 21 years of age) (Sec. 366-B IPC).

Special Laws for Crime Identification

Although all laws are not gender specific, the provisions of law affecting women significantly have been reviewed periodically and amendments carried out to keep pace with the emerging requirements. Some acts which have special provisions to safeguard women and their interests are:

(i) The Employees State Insurance Act, 1948

(ii) The Plantation Labour Act, 1951

(iii) The Family Courts Act, 1954

(iv) The Special Marriage Act, 1954

(v) The Hindu Marriage Act, 1955

(vi) The Hindu Succession Act, 1956

(vii) Immoral Traffic (Prevention) Act, 1956

(viii) The Maternity Benefit Act, 1961 (Amended in 1995)

(ix) Dowry Prohibition Act, 1961

(x) The Medical Termination of Pregnancy Act, 1971

(xi) The Contract Labour (Regulation and Abolition) Act, 1976

(xii) The Equal Remuneration Act, 1976

(xiii) The Child Marriage Restraint (Amendment) Act, 1979

(xiv) The Criminal Law (Amendment) Act, 1983

(xv) The Factories (Amendment) Act, 1986

(xvi) Indecent Representation of Women (Prohibition) Act, 1986

(xvii) Commission of Sati (Prevention) Act, 1987.

Particular Crimes

The Crime head-wise incidence of reported crimes during 1996 to 1998 along with percentage variation is presented in Table. It is observed that Crimes Against Women in 1998 reported an increase of 8.3 per cent and 4.8 per cent over previous years, 1997 and 1996 respectively. In absolute numbers, an increase of 10,073 cases were reported at all-India level in 1998 over 1997.

INCIDENCE OF REPORTED CRIMES AND PERCENTAGE VARIATIONS (1996-1998)

Sl. No.	*Crime Head*	*Year*			*Percentage variation in*
		1996	*1997*	*1998*	*1998 over 1997*
1.	Rape	14846	15330	15031	–2.0
2.	Kidnapping and Abduction	14877	15617	16381	4.9
3.	Dowry Death	5513	6006	6917	15.2
4.	Torture	35246	36592	41318	12.9
5.	Molestation	28939	30764	31046	0.9
6.	Sexual Harassment	5671	5796	8123	40.1
7.	Importation of Girls	182	78	146	87.2
8.	Sati Prevention Act	0	1	0	-100.0
9.	Immoral Traffic (P) Act	7706	8323	8695	4.5
10.	Indecent Rep. of Women (P) Act	96	73	192	163.0
11.	Dowry Prohibition Act	2647	2685	3489	29.9
	Total	1,15,723	1,21,265	1,31,338	8.3

The proportion of IPC crimes committed against women towards total IPC crimes remained around 6.0 per cent during 1996-1998 as shown in Table.

PROPORTION OF CRIME AGAINST WOMEN (IPC) TOWARD TOTAL IPC CRIMES

Sl. No.	*Year*	*Total IPC Crime*	*Crime Against women (IPC cases)*	*Percentage to total IPC crime*
1.	1996	1709576	115723	6.8
2.	1997	1719820	110183	6.4
3.	1998	1779111	118962	6.7

The available data indicates an increasing trend during the last three years in all the IPC crime against women except 'Rape', 'Sati (Prevention) Act' and 'Importation of Girls' which reported a declining trend during this period. All crimes against wcmen reported under Special and Local Laws also resulted increasing trends during last three years except 'Incedent Representation of Women (P) Act' which reported a declining trend.

Statistics of Crime

(Refer to Annexures 7.1 and 7.2 for Statistics under this head)

All India Crime rate i.e. no. of crimes per lakh population for crimes against women reported to the police worked out to be 13.5 during 1998. However, when estimated with reference to female population this rate almost doubles to 28.1 per lakh female population. This rate of crime which does not appear alarming at first sight may be viewed with caution, as a sizable number of crimes against women go unreported due to social stigma attached to them.

Uttar Pradesh State reported highest incidence (13.3%) of these crimes followed by Madhya Pradesh (12.1%) and Maharashtra (10.9%). In contrast, Delhi, which accounted for only 1.9 per cent of total crimes and shared only 1.3% of the population in the country reported third highest rate of such crimes at 19.6 after Madhya Pradesh (20.5).

Rape Cases

Incidence of rape cases (15,031) reported a decline of 2 per cent during 1998 over 1997. Madhya Pradesh alone reported 22.3 per cent of total rape cases in the country. Delhi, which represented only

2.9 per cent cases reported fourth highest rate at 3.4 after Mizoram (9.3), Madhya Pradesh (4.3) and D & N Haveli (3.9).

Rape Victims

According to Table at national level there were 15,033 rape victims compared to 15,336 in the previous year representing a decrease of nearly 2 per cent. Of these 8,414 (56%) were in the age group of 16-30 years, 3,433 (22.8%) in the age group of 10-16 years and 626 (4.2%) of age 10 years and below. Similar to decrease (2%) in the number of rape victims over previous year, the child victims (below 10 years) of age also reported decrease of 18.7 per cent and the victims above 30 years of age reported an increase of 10.8 per cent, signifying decrease of incidents relating to rape of Children.

VICTIMS OF RAPE BY AGE-GROUPS DURING 1996-1998 AND PERCENTAGE CHANGES DURING 1998 OVER 1997

Sl. No.	*Year*	*Below years*	*10-16 years*	*16-30 years*	*30 years & above*	*Total of all age-groups*
1.	1996	608	3475	8281	2485	14849
2.	1997	770	3644	8612	2310	15336
3.	1998	626	3433	8414	2560	15033
4.	Percentage change in 1998 over 1997	–18.7	05.8	–2.3	10.8	–2.0

Custodial Rapes

During the year 1998 only four cases of custodial rape (one each from Andhra Pradesh, Gujarat, Maharashtra, and Uttar Pradesh) were reported in the country.

Kidnapping and Abduction

Incidence of kidnapping and abduction reported an increase of 4.9 per cent in 1998 over 1997. The States of Uttar Pradesh and Rajasthan each reported more than 15 per cent of these cases at national level while Delhi with share of 6.0% cases reported highest rate at 7.5.

Dowry Deaths

Incidence of dowry deaths reported to have a rise of 15.2 per cent over the previous year. 32.2 per cent of these cases at national level were reported by Uttar Pradesh alone followed by Bihar 15.0 per cent.

Torture (Cruelty by Husband and Relatives)

Incidence of torture cases in the country increased by 12.9 per cent in 1998 over the previous year. 18.7 per cent of these were reported by Maharashtra while the highest rate in the country at 9.5 reported from Rajasthan compared to 4.3 national average rate.

Molestation

Incidence of molestation in the country reported an increase of 0.9 per cent over the previous year. Nearly 23.5 per cent of total such cases were reported from Madhya Pradesh which was also significantly higher rate (9.4) than national average rate (3.2). (Annexure).

Sexual Harassment (Eve-Teasing)

The number of sexual harassment cases reported in the country significantly rose by 40.1 per cent over the previous year. More than half (59.7%) of these cases were reported from Andhra Pradesh, Uttar Pradesh and Tamil Nadu. Jammu & Kashmir reported the highest rate at 3.8 compared to 0.8, the national average rate.

Importation of Girls

A total of 146 such cases were registered in 1998 compared to 78 cases in the previous year, a sharp increase of 87.2 per cent over 1997. Gujarat, Madhya Pradesh and Haryana reported 57, 26 and 25 cases respectively.

Trends in Incidence of Crime

Sati Prevention Act

Though the practice of Sati is something unheard of in modern times, there have been few cases now and then. No such case from any of State/UT was reported in the country during 1998.

Immoral Traffic (Prevention) Act

Cases under this Act registered an increase of 4.5 per cent

during 1998 as compared to 1997. More than half (68.3 %) cases were reported from the State of Tamil Nadu only. This should be construed as an indicator of improved policing efforts by Tamil Nadu police in this area.

Indecent Representation of Women (Prohibition) Act (Torture)

A remarkable increase of 163.0 per cent was noticed for cases under this Act as compared to cases reported in the previous year (1997). Nearly 45 per cent cases were collectively reported from Andhra Pradesh and Bihar put together.

Dowry Prohibition Act cases

These cases reported an increase of 29.9 per cent in 1998 as compared to 1997. Of these, a sizable proportion (42.6 %) were reported from Bihar.

Disposal of Crimes Against Women cases

The collection of detailed information on disposal of all the identified crimes committed against women has commenced from the year 1995. The comparative national level status of disposal of these cases by police and courts is presented in the succeeding paragraphs. However State/UT-wise details are presented in the main chapter on Disposal of crime cases.

Disposal by Police

According to Table during 1998, at national level, the disposal of IPC cases by police accounted for 76.5 per cent (including 0.4 per cent cases where investigation was refused). The crime-head-wise analysis of crimes against women cases revealed a fairly high disposal* percentage for 'Sexual Harassment' cases (92.2%), 'Molestation' (85.1%), and 'Cruelty by Husband & Relatives' cases (79.3%). On the other hand, while at national level 87.5 per cent cases reported under SLL were disposed of by police (including 0.6 per cent where investigation was refused), the quantum of cases disposed under 'Dowry Prohibition Act' was comparatively low at 75.4 per cent.

The position of cases charge-sheeted to total cases for investigation was quite satisfactory for all the crimes committed against women when compared to national average of 55.2% for total IPC crimes. Only in case of 'Kidnapping & Abduction of

Women & Girls' the percentage was lower (35.9%) than the national average.

The percentage of charge-sheeted cases under SLL at national level stood at 84.4. Comparatively, the charge-sheet percentage in cases of Dowry Prohibition Act and Indecent Representation of Women (Prohibition) Act was lower than the national average being 62.4 per cent and 62.1 per cent respectively.

Disposal by Courts

The crimes headwise, comparative details of cases of disposal of crimes tried, convicted or pending trial against women (IPC & SLL) by courts during the last two year (1997 and 1998) are presented.

As compared to 76.5 per cent disposal* by police in case of IPC crimes at national level and 87.5 per cent in case of SLL crimes, the disposal** of these cases by courts was reported to be very low at 19.0 per cent and 52.1 per cent respectively.

The disposal by courts of heinous crime cases such as 'Rape' and 'Kidnapping and Abduction of Women & Girls' was reported to be nearly17 per cent and 15.3 per cent respectively during 1998. At the end of the year 48,685 'Rape' cases, 39,103 'Kidnapping and Abduction' cases, 18,523 'Dowry Death' cases and 1,07,192 'Torture' cases were pending for trial in different courts of the country. Amongst SLL cases 42.9 per cent cases under 'Immoral Traffic (P) Act' remained pending for trial while pendency percentage was as high as 80.5 per cent and 86.1 per cent for cases registered under 'Dowry Prohibition Act' and 'Indecent Representation of Women (P) Act' respectively. The only case for trial under 'Sati Prevention Act' during 1998, resulted in acquittal. No case remained pending for trial at the end of the year.

Note: * Disposal of Police is taken as cases investigated by Police + cases where investigation was refused.

** Disposal by Courts is taken as cases tried + cases compounded & withdrawn.

SEVENTEEN

Defended by Law

Fundamental rights which every man or woman should be entitled to by virtue of having been born as a human being constitute what are called Human Rights. Human Rights propagate the concept of non-discrimination and equality. Whereas women represent more than half of the world's population and are engaged in work that contributes immensely to the life and wealth of nations, they are subjected to gender discrimination at work, in their homes, and in every sphere of human activity. This situation will have to change one day, else this exploitation and subjugation will continue thus adversely effecting the social fabric in time to come.

In the recent Dravidian and Aryan cultures, women had free access to educational opportunities and discrimination on the basis of sex was unknown. Women rose to high positions during Dravidian and Aryan culture in different disciplines and *brahmaradinis* like Gargi challenged great men and scholars in learned discourses on equal grounds. This was the status of women in the ancient times. Woman was the *sahadharmi* equal partner in the performance of *dharm*, the righteous duties in life.

It has been said by various scholars that only when women are educated and respected will the world emerge prosperous. This world may be as small as the family or as large as the nation — it implies for all. The subjugation of women started in the Smriti period. Manu and Yagna Valkya subscribed a subordinate social role to women. The degradation of women's position was reflected in customs relating to marriage, religion and property where socio-economic freedom was denied to them. They were expected to be under the "protective control" of the father, husband and son. This deterioration continued during the medieval and British periods.

Apart from the Dravidian and Aryan civilization where women were respected, the past of Indian women is the story of subjugation. During India's 5000 years of civilization, its history has to a great extent been "his" story. Women by and large led circumscribed lives. The nineteenth century was one of social reformers who highlighted the problems faced by women — the horrors of *devdasis*, child marriage, child widows and female exclusion, they included Raja Ram Mohun Roy, Ishwar Chandra Vidya Sagar and enlightened Westerners such as Macaulay, William Bentinck and Marcus Puller. A few Indian women writers in the latter part of the nineteenth century and beginning of twentieth century wrote about women and their experiences. But these have been largely about educated women, the elite, the Brahmins, or about women who participated in the political struggle.

The freedom movement brought in a new dimension to this struggle. Gandhiji with his foresight comprehended that only with the active participation of women, could every Indian home be turned into a bastion of the freedom struggle. The manner in which hundreds and thousands of women shed their veils and left their sheltered homes to come into the street to fight side by side in the struggle with their brothers and often put to shame their menfolk was a landmark in the political and social history of India.

The twentieth century, particularly after Independence saw the Indian women bring in a number of achievements to their credit. In all fields of higher learning — engineering, nuclear physics, computer sciences, administration, management, the arts and humanities — women have proved equal to men and have won laurels. It may be a reason to be proud but we cannot ignore the fact that even now 75 per cent of India's over 400 million women are illiterate, invisible and unaware of the going on in the universe. So immersed are they in their daily chores that they have no time to think of what is happening in the world. They are voiceless and subjected to myriad forms of class, caste and gender oppression. Responsible for the pathetic situation of women are the deep-rooted societal and religious traditions. The arbitrary division of male and female roles in society initiate sex-based discrimination and deprivation. Women, by and large have little access to productive resources and control over family income. Ranging from the exclusion of women from development programmes, sex discrimination is seen in wage discrimination and also perpetrates violence against women. A number of laws have been enacted to protect and promote the rights/interests of women, some of which are:

British Laws

In the pre-Independence colonial era, the few laws relating to crimes against women were mainly those relating to rape, causing miscarriage, assault on women's modesty, kidnapping/abduction, etc. and offences relating to marriage (all non cognisable). Social legislation for protection of women was even less and was limited to — Sati prohibition, maintenance laws or some laws enabling widow remarriage, etc. Laws relating to property, adoption, divorce, etc. were heavily subscribed by males keeping their interests in mind furthering the inferior or subordinate position of women in society and confirming their superiority over them in all respects.

Laws after Independence

The post-Independence period witnessed a spate of enactments — criminal, civil and social — besides amendments to some old laws to protect and improve the status of women which came about as a result of the provision in our Constitution on equality in all respects and spheres and non-discrimination on any ground, and even special protection to women and children as part of state policy. The new-found political and social awakening and agitations and movements for women's causes, to which both men and women contributed, gave further impetus to this process of legislation aimed at implementing the philosophy behind the Constitution. (The only exception to this policy would appear to be the Muslim Womens' Protection of Rights on Divorce Act, 1986, apparently an instance of misconceived and miscalculated political opportunism).

These enactments can be divided into two broad categories— those directly relating to checking of violence against women and preventing their exploitation and those aimed at improving their legal and social status.

The first category included the laws relating to domestic violence, which for the first time took cognisance of the concept of mental cruelty besides physical violence, changes in rape laws, laws relating to dowry prohibition and prevention of immoral traffic, 'Sati' indecent representation of women, etc., with some changes in evidence and procedural laws to facilitate their implementation.

The second category included laws relating to woman's/ daughter's share in property, adoption laws, changes in divorce laws, etc. In the criminal laws, the emphasis was mainly on stringent punishments and more helpful procedures. The second category of laws were pursued through institutions of family courts, legal aid bureaus, etc.

Lacunae and Loopholes in Laws

Expected to remove various legal lacunae and hurdles, criminal laws were made to provide effective deterrence to violence against women, while those falling in the category of social legislation were meant to work as catalysts for social change. In practice, however, none of the two expectations have been fulfilled. Deterrence in law remains confined to the status book with symbolic convictions and a large majority of cases remaining undisposed of in courts for years together while crimes against women have been showing a continuously increasing trend. Social legislation being relegated to paper only, without any proper awareness about their provisions, either amongst the people or the police. The laws themselves are to be blamed for this ineffective trend in their implementation despite intentions of their framers to the contrary. Often badly conceived and poorly drafted these legislations have many lacunae and loopholes thus exposing inadequacies of the criminal justice system and procedures and lack of public awareness. Generally found missing is the acceptability or support sometimes even positive antipathy — due to the absence of any efforts for public education, either about their provisions or their purpose.

Act for Prohibiting Dowry

With the noble objective of putting a stop to the practice of dowry which had degenerated into one of the worst instruments of exploitation and even extortion, particularly in Hindu society, the Act was brought about in 1961 and was amended twice in 1984 and 1986 to streamline its provisions and make the penalties more deterrent, but continues to be one of the most ineffective laws. Despite the efforts through amendments to remove some of the earlier lacunae several major anomalies still remain. Most of the cases registered fall under the category of Sections (u/s) 4 or 6 of the Act (usually along with Sec. 498-A, IPC) for demand of dowry and harassment or non-return of Dowry/Istridhan by the husband/in-laws reported after the marriage has run aground. A few cases included belong to u/s 3 of the Act for dowry giving and taking before or at the time of marriage even though the Section was specifically amended in 1984 to provide for a stringent minimum punishment of 5 years' imprisonment and Rs. 15,000 or amount of value of dowry (whichever is more) as fine.

Objectives of the Act

The basic objective behind this enactment and subsequent amendments which followed the alarming increase in reported cases of bride burning for dowry in the late seventies and early eighties, was to prevent extortion of dowry.

Lacunae of the Act

Even the definition of dowry "any property or valuable security given or agreed to be given" (Sec. 2) emphasizes on 'giving' rather than on the 'demand' or 'extortion' aspect. Demand of dowry is specifically punishable u/s 4 but the validity of this section is under a question mark in view of judgements of two High Courts, Calcutta (*Shankar Pd. Shaw and ors. vs State & ors* - 1991 Cr. : L.J. 639 Calcutta H.C.) and Allahabad (Ramesh Chand vs. State of U.P. - 1992 (3) RCR 511), both holding that in view of the very definition of 'dowry' which has 'giving' or agreement to give as its basic ingredients, mere demand cannot be termed as an offence unless there was 'giving' or 'agreement to give'. The Calcutta High Court had, accordingly even suggested a change in the definition of "dowry u/s 2 of the Act in the light of sub clause

(6) u/s 498-A of the Penal Code" if demand for dowry or extortion was proposed to be brought under its ambit. Even otherwise, u/s 3 which makes giving or taking of dowry an offence, both the 'giver' and the 'taker' are placed on a par although the giver, in most of the cases, is a helpless victim of extortion under the evil social custom rather than a willful or conscious offender. Despite all the enactments it is not surprising that only a few cases are reported under this section before or at the time of marriage, even while dowry continues to be given and taken extensively and even openly and spread through the fabric of society.

Difficulties also arise because of other provisions. The term "in connection with marriage" and "in consideration for marriage" used earlier need further clarification. That the demand or payment was "in connection with the marriage", particularly in cases of 'extended' dowry demands/payments after the marriage for example, in the garb of customary gifts/presents on occasions of marriages in the natal or marital families, child births, birthdays and other religious or social festivals/occasions, or on grounds of financing foreign education trips, purchase of house or setting up or expanding of business by the husband, etc. is often difficult to prove especially when they are not 'agreed to be given' at the time of marriage. Section 3(3) while exempting the presents given or taken at the time of marriage to the bride/bridegroom if they are: (i) given without any demand with entry in lists as per rules, (ii) of customary nature and not excessive to the financial status of the giver, provide further loopholes for enforcement because of the impracticability and vagueness of these conditions.

Having been obviously made to save customary gifts given voluntarily and within their means by the parents and other persons of the bride's party out of love and consideration for the daughter from coming under its ambit, this provision excludes from its scope any gifts given before or after the marriage (e.g. on the occasion of *Tika, Sagai* or other ceremonies or child birth etc.) even though they may also be given voluntarily as part of tradition/custom. Even this limited provision is exploited to cover forcible demand or extortion of dowry since the desire of parents of girls, keen to somehow or the other fulfil their filial and social obligation of marrying off their daughter ovrrules the complain of demand of dowry. They do not, in any way, wish to jeopardize the marriage itself or prevent the likelihood of future proposals coming their way, thus putting the girls in worse trouble. Regarding the condition of preparation of lists of dowry gifts, there is a provision framed in this connection by the Central Government (Dowry Prohibition Maintenance of Lists of Presents to the Bride and Bridegroom Rules, 1985) which requires these lists to be prepared and signed by the bride and the bridegroom. As the lists are required to be prepared at the time of or soon after the marriage with full details about the presents and the givers this provision is impractical. Most of the giving and taking of presents at the time of the marriage is done by the parents of the bride and not by the bridegroom who should be the proper persons to be fixed with this responsibility.

Unless made mandatory the inhibitions and apprehensions on the part of parents of the bride in asking for such lists to be prepared or signed by the bridegroom will hamper the very objective of this provision. Under the present social ethos in the Hindu society, no such system has generally prevailed so far (unlike the Muslim community where preparation of such lists, particularly for jewellery and other costly presents, is considered to be a normal and acceptable convention). By making it mandatory with specific rsponsibility, particularly of the receiver (parents of the bridegroom even for gifts received on behalf of the bride) this new practice will be effective in its objective. Provision for mandatory filing of a copy of the lists with the area 'Dowry Prohibition Officer' or 'Marriage Registration Officer' could even be considered.

Due to the aforesaid lacunae, this Act does not curb the practice of giving, taking or demand of dowry before or at the time of marriage or even afterwards. It is not taken recourse to as long as the marriage works or the girl is prepared to suffer quietly. Recourse to this Act is sought in case of breakdown of marriaged or death of the girl by violence, with a large majority of cases being registered u/s 6 of the Act often along with sections 498-A/406, IPC) for return of dowry/Istridhan.

The 'matrimonial home' after the marriage concept poses difficulties in seeking redressal after breakdown of marriage. Under this Section (Sec. 6) for non/return of dowry/Istridhan articles since the proceedings can be initiated only at the place where the dowry/Istridhan was given or was due to be transferred to the wife, normally the matrimonial home after the marriage. Since the wife, after the breakdown of the marriage (when only such complaints are normally filed) is generally not staying in the matrimonial home and usually shifts to another place either to stay with her parents or take up a job, etc. she is hardly in a position to pursue the case in the court at the place of her matrimonial home.

Similar lacunae exist in provision (b) under sec. 6(3) of the Act which provides for the property to "be held in trust" for the children of the woman who dies from unnatural causes within seven years of her marriage, pending its transfer to the children (normally when they attain the age of majority). Due to this provision the aggressor husband or in-laws merrily continue to hold the property and enjoy the fruits of their crime on the pretext of keeping the property "in trust" and indulge in other malpractices, thus further perpetrating such crimes.

Therefore, in spite of the protection provided to "the person aggrieved by the offence" (which would include the "giver") u/s 7(3) of the Act, saving such a person from prosecution on the basis of his statement and shifting the onus of proof on the accused u/s 8-A in case of offence u/s 3 or 4, there has been no case under the Act, which has ended in conviction in Delhi, Mumbai and Bangalore up to the time of the study and the all-India rate of conviction had also been only about 5 per cent (between 28 per cent and 36 per cent of decided cases) from 1988-1991, according to *Crime in India* published by NCRB (cases under this Act were not published separately before 1988).

Provisions of Dowry Prohibition Act

Section 8-B(1) of the Act provides for appointment of Dowry Prohibition Officers and Section 8-B(4) for constitution of Advisory Boards comprising social workers of the area for advising and assisting such officers. The Dowry Prohibition Officers are to be responsible (u/s 8-B(2)) for compliance with provisions of the Act, preventing demand or taking of dowry and collecting evidence for prosecution of the offenders. They may, for this purpose, be conferred with requisite police powers (Sec. 8-B(3)). Rules for functioning of such officers are to be framed by the State

Government u/s 10(2) of the Act. These provisions introduced under 1984 amendments, were deliberately meant to involve the social workers of the area in enforcement of the Act rather than depending on the police alone for curbing the evil of dowry. The few officers who have been appointed do not generally perform any duties with regard to prevention of demand or giving or taking of dowry in the absence of rules which should have been framed by the Central or State Governments for their functioning. Similarly there is absence of Advisory Committees and no area social workers have been appointed at most places nor have any rules been framed for their constitution.

It appears that while the Act was framed and later modified twice with a lot of fanfare under pressure from women's groups and other social workers, not much effort has gone into ensuring its proper enforcement therafter, as is evident from this lack of even basic follow up action in these matters.

Due to the Acts being masterminded by men who form the majority of law makers, there are many places which have been deliberately left untouched so as to give vent to their plans and furtherance of social norms whilst ignoring their misgivings.

Suggestions for Effective Implementation

(a) An amendment in definition of dowry so as to bring about a clear-cut picture of demand and giving aspect of dowry. In fact, subjecting the daughter-in-law to threats, harassment or cruelty to coerce her if she does not get 'extended' dowry after the marriage, amounts to 'extortion' which should be treated as an aggravated form of 'dowry demand' carrying a higher punishment. Section 498-A IPC, which covers such cases at present is hardly adequate to deal with this type of crime. A lot of cases where the daughter-in-law is threatened with grievious hurt or death by burning etc. if she does not get further dowry or property, would squarely make out offences u/s 386 or 387 of IPC, punishable with imprisonment up to ten years or seven years respectively, besides fine as against a punishment of up to two years only (with a minimum punishment of 6 months) u/s 4 of Dowry Prohibition Act and three years only u/s 498-A IPC.

(b) Clarification is needed on the term "in connection with the marriage". It should either be deleted entirely or an 'explanation' added to the section. The demand from or giving of any property or valuable security by the party of the bride to the party of the bridegroom 'without any consideration' other than consideration of marriage itself, should be considered as being "in connection with the marriage". The onus for proving any such other consideration being on the receiver/the person demanding such consideration.

(c) Unless and until active initiative or connivance on the part of the given in the transaction is proved, culpability of the "giver" should be limited.

(d) It should be made mandatory for the bridegrooms party to prepare a list of presents to the bride or the bridegroom covered under Section 3 of Dowry Prohibition Act failing which they should be held fully responsible. Incomplete or false lists being made offences. Such lists should be prepared at the time of or within one month of the marriage, signed by both the parties (bride's/bridegroom's) and a copy thereof given to the bride's parents/guardians.

(e) The value of gifts should commensurate with the economic standing of the bride's parents. A maximum limit should be prescribed for such gifts. They should be limited to a prescribed proportion of the gross annual income/wealth in case of those assessed for Income or Wealth Tax and a maximum prescribed sum in case of others. Demand or acceptance of dowry above the prescribed maximum should be deemed to be "Dowry extortion" and punishable as such under law.

(f) There should be in-built incentives for proper listing of such gifts or presents wherein:

(i) Such presents up to the prescribed maximum limit should be free of any Gift Tax.

(ii) Source of payment in case of such gifts/presents should not be accountable. A provision for Income Tax rebate u/s 88 of Income Tax Act for such gifts may be made. This suggestion may be opposed on the ground that it will encourage 'black money' as parents could settle for maximum dowry to lighten their tax accruals and also encourage dowry. To fight the tax evaders the government has however, already, been periodically launching schemes for unearthing 'black' or 'tainted' money by allowing declaration or investment in specified schemes without any penal consequences. Relating voluntary gifts to the bride as permissible under the law to a similar scheme would have the merit of making such gifts, which are being given and taken in any case, at least properly accountable and for the benefit and interest of the daughter, not only in affluent but even amongst middle class families, and help in improving social acceptability of the provision, thus making it easier for law to intervene in case of marriage breakups and reclaim for the woman her *streedhan* or any matter connected to it.

(g) As a reimbursement for her share in parental property the gifts should be deductible from her share. Similarly, to put the sons and daughters on a par in this regard, gifts of jewellery or other costly items to the daughter-in-law should be deductible from the share of the son. For this a proper planning of property has to be done so as to prevent problems in the future.

(h) Cognisance of a complaint u/s 6 of the Act should be registered at a place where the wife has been residing continuously for six months or more as it is not possible in case of marriage breakdown for the women to reside in her matrimonial home any more and therefore make her unable to get the case registered there.

(i) To arrest the spirit of unhealthy competition which has entered society regarding dowry gifts, display of dowry should be totally banned.

(j) A curb should be placed on the ostentatious and wasteful expenditure on marriage which is another source of trouble to the not-so-well-off parents of girls. A limit on such expenditure as well as on the size of marriage party/number of guests and entertainment etc. should be strictly enforced.

To implement the Dowry Prohibition Act effectively a team of Dowry Prohibition Officers and Advisory Boards comprising local social workers already provided under the Act should be appointed with proper rules and powers to regulate the functioning of such officers and constitution of the Advisory Boards. The responsibility for preventing any demand or giving or taking of dowry in violation of the provisions of the Act should basically be fixed on such officers. Police should stay out of enforcement in this regard. This is suggested in order to avoid complaints of malpractices even though they should remain fully responsible for handling cases of dowry-related violence or deaths. Requisite powers of a police officer should be conferred on Dowry Prohibition Officers in terms of section 8-B(3) of the Act. Under Section 7, cognisance of offences under the Act can be taken, inter alia, on a complaint from any 'recognised' Welfare Institution or Organisation. The recognition for the purpose should be accorded by the Central or the State Governments. Proper rules for grant of such recognition should be framed to ensure effective and responsible functioning of such organisations/institutions and provide motivation and incentive to the more active and responsible ones among them.

In sum, 'dowry' as discussed elsewhere in the study, is a complex social problem closely related to the matter of the daughter's share in the parental property. The practice can as such be checked basically through cooperation from society and public education after taking steps to effectively ensure that the daughter actually gets her share. The thrust of criminal law needs to be on curbing 'dowry extortion' through exploitation, harassment and cruelty which is totally indefensible. The above suggestions have been made to facilitate the achieving of this objective. The amendments to the law should be accompanied by an extensive campaign to educate the public, both about the objectives of the law as well as the substance of provisions and punishments provided under the Act, and strict enforcement thereof as part of a well-defined and unambiguous clear public policy. The important role which the media — print and electronic can play in safeguarding and promoting the interests of women is no doubt worth mentioning laws relating to 'Dowry Deaths' and dowry related 'cruelty' by Husband/his Relatives, are discussed below under head 'Domestic Violence'.

Violence in the Household

Domestic violence against married women — wife beating and harassment, sometimes even wife murders — arises from various causes. Legislative measures were introduced as late as 1983 and 1986 to bring domestic violence against married women specifically within the ambit of criminal law. Earlier there were no specific legal provisions for dealing with such gender-related violence within the home which was covered only under the general laws relating to murder, homicide, abetment to suicide, hurt, assault, wrongful confinement, etc. In cases of wife harassment or battering, cognisance and action by the police depended on the nature of physical injury caused or the weapon used. Cases not involving grievious injury as defined under Section 320 IPC or use of dangerous weapon or means or poison in terms of Section 324 IPC fell in the category of non-cognisable offences in which no cognisance or action could be taken by the police except with the magistrate's permission.

The main provisions/amendments are discussed below:

1. Murders of married women by husband/in-laws or suicides as a result of cruelty or harassment by them

Such cases were earlier dealt with u/s 302 IPC (murder) or 306 IPC (abetment to suicide). The evidence of the standard as required under criminal law (proof beyond doubt) in such crimes which normally occurs within the privacy of the matrimonial home with no witnesses other than the perpetrators of the crime or their associates present is hard to get. It is sometimes difficult even to establish whether it is a case of 'murder' or 'suicide'. Convictions accordingly u/s 302 or 306 IPC in such cases were an exception, if at all. The basic strategy followed in legal amendments to get over this problem and facilitate successful prosecutions in such cases has been to shift the burden of proof on to the accused. The amendments made were as follows:

(i) Section 304-B, IPC (Dowry Deaths)

(enacted under Act No. 43 of 1986)

The Section, unique to the Indian penal law to deal with a crime typical to Indian society, introduced a new offence in the penal code viz. 'dowry death'. The term covers any death of a married woman which satisfies three basic criteria:

(a) under unnatural circumstances;

(b) within seven years of marriage; and

(c) preceded by cruelty or harassment by the husband or any of his relatives in connection with demand for 'dowry' (as defined under Dowry Prohibition Act).

The Section provides for a presumption of 'guilt' against the husband/his relatives in case of death of a woman in such circumstances and lays down a minimum punishment of seven years, extendable to life imprisonment. The provision for presumption under this Section was further reinforced u/s 113/B introduced in the Evidence Act in 1986 providing specifically for a statutory presumption of 'causing dowry death' against a person subjecting a woman to cruelty or harassment in connection with dowry demand soon before her death. This Section is in addition to the earlier provisions u/s 302 and 306, IPC, covering both homicidal and suicidal deaths and can be invoked where no direct evidence is available to substantiate a charge of murder against the offenders but 'unnatural' death follows dowry — demand — related harassment/cruelty, evidence basically required being about such cruelty. Cases where specific evidence is available are still to be dealt u/s 302 or 306 IPC, depending on the nature and circumstances of death.

(ii) Section 306 IPC (Abetment to Suicide)/113-A Evidence Act

While no amendment was made to Section 306 IPC itself which is taken recourse to for prosecuting the offenders for abetment in case of suicide by a married woman as a result of cruelty or harassment by the husband or in-laws, etc., to get over the difficulty in getting evidence to satisfy the essential ingredients of willful, 'instigation', 'conspiracy' or 'intentional aiding' for constituting 'abetment' in terms of Sec. 107 IPC, and to facilitate successful prosecution under the section, a new section (113-A) was introduced in the Evidence Act in 1983 (Act No. 46) providing for presumption of abetment to suicide against the husband/his relatives where the wife commits suicide within seven years of marriage following cruelty by them. Unlike Sec. 304-B IPC, this section is applicable only to cases of suicide but is not confined to dowry related cases and covers suicides by married women following 'cruelty' or 'harassment' for reasons other than dowry demand.

(iii) Section 174(3) and 176 Cr. P.C. (Inquest Reports)

These amendments to the existing provisions were made basically to streamline and further tighten the procedure for enquiries into suicides/unnatural deaths of women within seven years of marriage by making examination of the dead body by a doctor (sub-section (3) of Sec. 174 Cr. P.C.) and magisterial enquiry, either instead of or in addition to police investigation (Sec. 176, Cr. P.C.) mandatory. Amendment to Sec. 176, Cr. P.C. also provided for the relatives of the deceased in such cases to be informed and being allowed to remain present at such enquiries by a Magistrate.

The facilitating provisions and shifting of the burden of proof on the accused and streamlining of procedures for investigations/ enquiries in such cases have not had any positive results. Due to lack of public support and ooperation and loopholes present, there has been no hange in statistics related to dowry.

Convictions and Aquittals

In Delhi, only 4 (0.7%) cases of dowry deaths had ended in conviction with acquittals 20 (4%) and in Mumbai, only in one case (0.3%) there was conviction with 6 (2%) acquittals till the time of collection of information for the study. Bangalore was better with 23 (5%) convictions with 57 (12%) acquittals. In respect of cases under Dowry (Prohibition) Act, and in dowry deaths also, there was heavy pendency — 91 per cent in Delhi, 88 per cent in Mumbai and 76 per cent in Bangalore.

Causes of Failures

The reasons for these failures, however, are not caused by the laws themselves but mostly elsewhere. Even though the amended laws presume guilt against the accused in cases of unnatural deaths within seven years of marriage, the basic requirement for raising this presumption, namely, dowry demand and cruelty or harassment in that connection (or for any other reason u/s 306 IPC) soon before the death has itself been difficult to prove. The reason being the extreme reluctance on the part of the women and their parents to report such earlier demands or cruelty/harassment often till the very end (after the death), and gross lack of awareness of legal requirements of such cases among the public. Besides a substantial number of cases where the main witnesses, mostly the parents and other close relatives of the deceased turn hostile during trials under various pressures, as is evident from case studies of acquitted cases. Indifferent, even shoddy, investigation of cases and inconsistent attitude of the courts sometimes further compound the situation, thus the law is not only to be blamed.

These amended and liberalised laws themselves have come under some criticism from the more radical among women activists. The restriction on the period for drawing the statutory presumption against the accused may by far be fair but it should not be forgotten that eventhough majority of such deaths take place within the period of seven years their occurrence afterwards is not unknown, where the violence starts much earlier. These provisions may not, in fact, be of much help if the woman/her parents have continued to bear the violence/harassment without any resistance or action for seven years. Any further relaxation regarding requirements of evidence can only make a mockery of the judicial system and throw the flood-gates open for exploitation and misuse of these provisions. The remedy would lie not in doing away with all evidence but educating women and their parents to recognise the storm signals of violence and be on their toes in time and take timely action, including reports to the police, the National Commission State Commissions for Women, voluntary organisations, panchayats, etc. before it gets too late. Such action may if not save the victim at least help to provide the required evidence for successful action against the guilty.

Improvement in Laws Suggested

Some suggestions for improvements in laws did, however, emerge during the study which might help in making them more purposeful:

1. To make the provision more rational and avoid any pitfalls arising from the definition of 'dowry' as discussed

earlier. It is suggested to substitute the term "any demand for dowry" u/s 304 B(1) IPC by the term "any unlawful demand for any property or valuable security" (b) for "cruelty u/s 498-A IPC and deletion of explanation of the term dowry under the sub-section.

2. A suggestion for representative of the Social Welfare Department or any recognised non-governmental organization of the area, in addition to other respectables of the neighbourhood, in enquiries both u/s 174 and 176, Cr. P.C. was met with resistance from a majority of police officers during the study but is expected to help in improving the credibility of such enquiries and will improve coordination between NGOs and police. Every care should be taken in associating NGOs with a proven track record and enjoying the trust of the community. They should have transparency and full accountability in their functioning.

3. Regarding post-mortem examinations there were statutory provision under sub-section (3) (v) of section 174, Cr.P.C.; or rules made by the state governments under this sub-section, for the examination of the body in such cases to be conducted by a team of at least two doctors, to replace the executive instructions of the Home Ministry on 22 July 1980 addressed to all State Governments and Union Territory Administrations which are not often complied with. The date of marriage should be given in all requests for post-mortem examination or even a separate colour-coding given to forms in such cases to enable the doctors conducting post mortem examination to know about the applicability of this provision.

4. Specific provision under Cr. P.C. or Dowry Prohibition Act on the lines of Section 5A of Prevention of Corruption Act. The Act provides for Investigation of cases of 'dowry deaths' or suicides (u/s 304-B or 302 or 306 IPC) in case of unnatural death or suicide of a married woman within seven years of marriage, to be conducted by an officer not below the rank of Inspector. This should replace the

earlier executive instructions of the Ministry of Home Affairs for investigation of such cases by officers not below the rank of Dy. S.P. issued on 22 July 1980 referred to above.

Wife beating and harassment u/s 498 — A I.P.C. (cruelty by husband or his relatives)

This Section, introduced in 1983 (Act No. 46), makes such 'cruelty' a specific cognisable offence punishable with imprisonment up to three years and fine. The offence is 'non bailable' under the entry in the First Schedule of Cr. P.C. for this section and 'non compoundable' because of non-inclusion of this section in the list of 'compoundable offences' u/s 320 of the Cr.P.C. Even 'mental cruelty' under specified circumstances has become actionable under this provision.

The definition of 'cruelty' in the 'Explanation' under this section is in two parts, part (i) to cover conduct unconnected with dowry demand but depending on its consequences or likely consequences; and part (ii) to specifically deal with harassment relating to 'any unlawful demand for property or valuable security' — 'dowry demand' in common parlance though the use of the term has been wisely avoided.

Cognisance of Offences

Cognisance of offences under this Section by the Court is, however, restricted u/s 198-A Cr.P.C., also introduced by amendments under Act No. 46 of 1983, only upon a police report or a complaint by the aggrieved person or specified relatives (father, mother, brother, sister, father's or mother's brother or sister) or with the leave of the court, any other person related by blood, marriage or adoption. Cognisance by police has also been restricted under Col. 4 of the entry under this section in the First Schedule of Cr.P.C. (amended in 1983) on the basis of report by the aggrieved person or a person related by blood, marriage or adoption, or, in the absence of any such relative by a public servant of the class or category notified by the State Government for the purpose (No such notification had been issued by the concerned State Governments till the time of the study). Neither the Magistrate nor the police can take cognisance of an offence under this section on their own information or report or information from any other source.

Main Thrust of the Provision

While the provision would appear to cover all types of domestic violence, dowry-related or from other causes, with the background of public and media concern over increasing incidence of 'bride burnings' and suicides by girls and married women, the main thrust of this provision too is on combating property (dowry) demand related harassment and violence.

Attitude of Society

The attitude of ambivalence, both in society and in law towards domestic violence, excepting when it is related to 'dowry demand' or results in serious consequences — death or grievous injury, etc., is the basic reason for efforts and measures to curb such violence remaining ineffective in spite of all the legal amendments. What is required is a clear and unambiguous message that such violence in marital relationship, whatever its nature, extent or causation, is unacceptable. Unless the prevailing social notion of the wife being the husband's property, which can be ill-treated or abused as he likes is removed, there is no chance of ending marital violence against women. The women should ensure proper, timely action and provide ample scope for proof that the crime is being perpetrated only then can be the offender to be punished and discouraged from initiating such violence in future.

Rape

The offence of rape is the ultimate violation of the self and the most humiliating event in a woman's life. This is particularly so when the victim happens to be a young girl raped, within or outside her home, molested and beaten she has no option but to cope in silence. The social dimensions of rape have a special relevance and significance in harbouring such crimes in future. The girl is slienced due to social stigma which makes the offender have no fear whatsoever in repeating such an act. It is not only the victim, but her entire family which suffers in one way or the other deprived of any formal support whether financial, social or psychological; police investigations merely add to the trauma. The end result is that whereas the victim cannot conceal her shame a man can successfully hide his sin.

Mere statistics or laws do not explain the dimensions of this problem. There have been various case studies and interviews with police officers, lawyers and women's groups which have helped in understanding and analysing the various dimensions of the problem. On the persistent demand of women's groups and social activists, the Indian Penal Code was amended in 1983, providing for more stringent punishment for rape. However, according to government statistics, incidents of rape have over the years reached menacing proportions thereby demonstrating not just the inefficacy of the partly, changed law but also the warped nature of the machinery designed to implement it. While the social stigma attached to rape is deterrence enough to reporting such crimes, the callous attitude of the police which puts the victim through most gruelling and embarrassing interrogation, also prevents women from seeking the help of the law. Men as law makers and in positions of power have been lenient to such crimes and have further helped in perpetrating the crime. The rape victims hopes of getting any kind of justice have further been stifled. It is because of these circumstances that rape is the most under reported crime, "out of every case that comes to light 20 go unrecorded" says Ms. Pramila Dandavate, of Mahila Dakshata Samiti a well known Delhi based NGO.

The Special Cell to deal with crimes against women set up by the Delhi Police at Nanak Pura has no comprehensive data on rape. If this is the story of New Delhi, then where is the hope for smaller towns and villages. This is because rape cases are dealt with by different police stations and not necessarily referred to them. In Mumbai too the number of rape cases has been rising over the years. The police officers believe it is largely the result of love affairs where the young couple indulge in sex on the sly. Some social workers feel that in a majority of cases the rapist is known to the victims. However, it would be wrong to take a simplistic view and evade such gruesome acts.

The Indian Evidence Act, still permits the character of the victim to be used as a defence, and thereby undercuts the positive amendments to the Indian Penal Code. In any case Section 376 of the IPC, which lays down a minimum punishment of ten years' rigorous punishment and even a life term applies only to custodial rape, of a girl under twelve and gang rape.

Punishment, Arrests and Convictions

Shri L.K. Advani, present Union Minister of Home Affairs has suggested capital punishment for rapists. While the National Commission for Women has supported the Minister, several women's organisations and individual activists hold a different view. According to them, if the death penalty is made mandatory, trials will continue for a long time and judges will be reluctant to award the sentence. According to Ms. Indira Jai Singh, a well known lawyer "It is not the severity of the punishment but its certainty that deters a crime. And also the most important view is not how the guilty is punished but to what extent the crimes of rape and other violence against women can be prevented". She is highly critical of the Indian system of administration of justice which is heavily loaded against the victim. Accordingly, to rough estimates, out of an averge of 3,50,000 sexual assault cases filed in courts all over the country the number of accused arrested was less than 2,00,000 and those convicted a mere 33,000.

A review of laws dealing with women has been taken up by the Law Commission and the National Commission for Women with the assistance of lawyers and women's organizations.

A draft is being prepared by the National Commission for Women on the amendments to the obsolete rape laws. The proposals under consideration include public shaming/ ostracization of the accused, enhancement of punishment where the accused is also HIV positive and has passed on the infection to the victim. Other suggestions proposed by NCW are insertion of a statutory provision in the rape laws to allow adequate compensation, and provision for counselling for the victims. The exercise is an outcome of years of concerted effort of women activists across the country who have been advocating a complete overhaul of the rape laws. Such suggestions hold weight and have been made after years of research on laws dealing with women. Only if they are kept in mind in future will we have any hope for a change for the better in future.

As many as 20 offences under the Indian Penal Code and Local and special laws are considered broadly to be crimes against women:

A. Offences Affecting the Human Body

1. Abetting the commission of suicide (Sec. 306 IPC).
2. Molestation (Sec. 354 IPC).
3. Kidnapping, abduction or inducing a woman to compel her marriage etc. (Sec. 364/366 IPC).
4. Procuration of minor girl (Sec. 366-A IPC).
5. Importation of girls (Sec. 366-B IPC).
6. Selling minor for purposes of prostitution (Sec. 372 IPC).
7. Buying minor for purposes of prostitution (Sec. 373 IPC).
8. Rape (Sec. 376 IPC).
9. Unnatural offence, involving women (Sec. 377 IPC).

B. Offences Against Property

10. Chain snatching (Sec. 356 and Sec. 392 IPC).

C Offences Relating to Marriage

11. Marrying again during the life time of wife (Sec. 494 IPC).
12. Adultery (Sec. 497 IPC).
13. Enticing or taking away or detaining with criminal intent a married women (Sec. 498 IPC).

D. Offences Relating to Criminal Intimidation, Insult and Annoyance

14. Uttering any word, making any gesture or act intended to insult the modesty of women (Sec. 509 IPC).

E. Suppression of Immoral Traffic of Women and Girls Act

15. Punishment for keeping a brothel or allowing premises to be used as a brothel (Sec. 3 of Suppression of Immoral Traffic in Women and Girls Act—SITA).
16. Procuring, inducing or taking a woman or girl for the sake of prostitution (Sec. 5 of SIT Act).

17. Detaining woman or girl in premises where prostitution is carried on (Sec. 6 of SIT Act).
18. Seducing a girl for purpose of prostitution (Sec. 8 of SIT Act).
19. Seduction of a woman or girl in custody (Sec. 9 of SIT Act).

F. ***Dowry Act***

20. Penalty for demanding dowry (Sec. 4 of Dowry Prohibition Act 1961).

In all, we selected only five important crimes for our study, viz. (i) Rape or Seduction, (ii) Kidnapping and abduction, (iii) Dowry deaths, (iv) Wife battering, and (v) Eve-teasing which take prominent place in media.

EIGHTEEN

Protection under the Statute

Our Constitution makers could foresee the social problems associated with the emancipation of women. They had seen prevailing gender inequality during their time and had visualised that the sex-equality was crucial for the development of the country. In order to do away with the inequality and to provide reasonable opportunities and create awareness for the exercise of human rights and claim, it was necessary to promote with special care, educational and economic interests not only of men but women too and to provide necessary protection from social injustice and exploitation. The Constitution of India provides the following:

(i) Right to equality (Article 14, 15 and 16).

(ii) Right against exploitation (Article 23).

(iii) Directive Principles of State Policy (Articles 38, 39(a) & (d), 42 and 44)

(iv) Fundamental Duties (Article 51A Q (e))

(v) Elections (Article 325)

Besides the above, the Preamble, which incorporates the chief goal enshrined in the Constitution reflects the spirit of equality. A look into the Preamble will enable us to locate the ideal incorporated into the Constitution.

The Constitution Preamble

The Preamble of the Constitution of India, has been expressed in the following words:

"We the people of India having solemnly resolved to constitute India into a Sovereign Socialist Secular Democratic Republic and to secure to all citizens:

Justice, social, economic and political;

Liberty of thought, expression, belief, faith and worship;

Equality of status and of opportunity; and to promote among them all,

Fraternity, assuring the dignity of the individual, (unity and integrity of the nation);

In our Constituent Assembly, this twenty-sixth day of November, 1949 do hereby adopt, enact and give to ourselves this Constitution."

The expression appearing in the Preamble of our Constitution was then described by Pandit Jawaharlal Nehru in the Objective Resolution which he moved in the Constituent Assembly in its first session and the Assembly adopted the same unanimously. But Nehru's Resolution itself had taken shape out of what had already been said by Mahatma Gandhi in 1931 when Mahatmaji was standing on the deck of a ship taking him to London in the capacity of the spokesman and representative of Nationalist India to the Second Round Table Conference. When asked by a correspondent at that time as to what Constitution he would bring back if he could help it, Mahatma Gandhi offered the following reply:

"I shall strive for a Constitution which will release India from all that dom and patronage and give her, if need be, the right to sin. I shall work for an India, in which the poorest shall feel that it is their country in whose making they have an effective voice; an India where there shall not be high class and low class of people; an India in which all communities shall live in perfect harmony; there can be no room in such an India for the curse of untouchability or the curse of intoxicating drinks or drugs. Women shall enjoy the same right as men. Since we shall be at the pace with all the rest of the world neither exploiting nor being exploited by any of them. We shall have the smallest army imaginable. All interests not to be in conflict with the interests of the millions of dumb that will be respected, whether foreign or indigenous. This is the India of my dream."

The opening words of the Preamble emphasise on the ultimate authority of the people from whom the Constitution emerges. There is no sex discrimination. The words "We the People of India" includes both males and females.

Explanation

The Preamble outlines four objectives of the Indian Republic, viz. justice, liberty, equality and faternity. Justice implies a harmonious reconcilement of individual conduct with the general welfare of the society. The essence of justice lies in the attainment of the common good. It embraces as the preamble proclaims the entire social, economic and political spheres of human activity.

It is in the interest of the society to ensure the maximum liberty of thought and action of the individual consistent with the circumstances and social conditions. 'Liberty' in the Preamble, signifies not only the absence of any arbitrary restraint on the freedom of individual's action but also for the creation of conditions which would provide for the necessary ingredient required for the proper development of the personality of the individual. Since society consists of individuals, social progress depends on the progress of individuals.

The two words 'liberty' and 'equality' are complimentary. Equality does not mean that all human beings are mentally and physically equal. It signifies equality of status and equal opportunity.

It is the spirit of brotherhood that is emphasised by the expression 'fraternity'. In a country like ours with diverse religion, language, culture and social system, unity can be achieved through the spirit of faternity. Fraternity ensures two things, viz. the dignity of the individual and unity and integrity of the country.

Fundamental Rights

Fundamental Rights, receives its treatment under Articles 12 to 35 of the Constitution and includes such principles as right to equality, right to freedom, right against exploitation, right to religion, right to culture and education, saving of certain laws and right to constitutional remedies.

1. Right to Equality

Art 14. Equality Before Law

"The State shall not deny to any person equality before law or equal protection of laws within the territory of India."

Notes: The Constitution of India guarantees equality before law or equal protection of law to every person irrespective of the fact that he is, or he is not the citizen of India. Both the phrases aim to establish what is called the equality of status and of opportunities as envisaged in the Preamble. Article 14 of the Constitution prevents any arbitrary discrimination.

Interpreting the scope of this Article, the Supreme Court of India held as under:

1. In considering the fundamental right of equality of opportunity, a technical pendantic or doctrinaire approach should not be made and the doctrine should not be involved even if different scales of pay, service conditions, leave, etc. are introduced in different or dissimilar posts.
2. Article 14 forbids hostile discrimination but not reasonable classification. Thus, where persons belonging to a particular class in view of their special attributes, qualities, mode of recruitment and the like are differently treated in public interests to advance and boost members belonging to backward classes, such a classification shall be outside the scope of discrimination having a close nexus with the object sought to be achieved so that in such a case, Article 14 will be completely out of the way.
3. Article 14 certainly applies where equals are treated differently without any reasonable basis.
4. Where equals and unequals are treated differently, Article 14 would have no application.
5. Even if there be one class of service having several categories with different attributes and incidents, such a category becomes a separate class by itself and no difference or discrimination between such category and the general members of the other class would amount to any discrimination or to denial of equality of opportunity.
6. In order to judge whether a separate category has been carved out of a class of service, the following circumstances have generally to be examined:

(i) the nature, the mode and the manner of recruitment of a particular category from the very start;

(ii) the classification of the particular category;

(iii) the terms and conditions of service of the members of the category;

(iv) the nature and character of the posts and promotional avenues;

(v) the specific attributes that the particular category possesses which are not to be found in other classes and the like."

It is rather difficult to lay down a rule of universal application but the circumstances mentioned above may be taken as illustrative guidelines for determining the question.

In its struggle for social and political freedom, mankind has always tried to move forward to the idea of equality for all. The urge for equality and liberty has been the moving force of many resolutions. The Charter of the United Nations records the determination of the member Nations to reaffirm their faith in the equal rights of men and women.

However, fulfilment of complete equality between men and women in all spheres of life has always been proved to be a distant dream. The laws of a country can at best assure to its citizens only a limited measure of equality. The Constitution makers gave only political and legal equality and the status of a fundamental right. Aspects like economic and social equality were included within the scope of Directive Principles of the State Policy.

Article 15

Article 15 of the Constitution ensures prohibition of discrimination on grounds of religion, race, caste, sex or place of birth. Stated in words, it stands as follows:

1. The State shall not discriminate against any citizen on grounds only of religion, race, caste, sex, place of birth or any of them.
2. No citizen shall, on grounds only of religion, race, caste, sex, place of birth or any of them be subject to any

disability, liability, restriction or conditions with regard to—

(a) access to shops, public restaurants, hotels and places of public entertainment; or

(b) the use of wells, tanks, bathing ghats, roads and places of public resort maintained wholly or partly out of state funds or dedicated to the use of general public.

3. Nothing in this Article shall prevent the State from making any provision for women.

3[(4)Nothing in this Article or in Clause (2) of Article 29 shall prevent the State from making any special provision for the advancement of any socially and economically backward classes of citizen or for the Scheduled Castes and Scheduled Tribes.]

Article 15 guarantees non-discrimination on special grounds, that is religion, race, caste, sex, place of birth or any of them. But, this right is available to citizens only.

Article 15(1) is conferred on a citizen as an individual and is a guarantee against his being subjected to discrimination in the matters of rights, privileges and immunities pertaining to him by virtue of his status as a citizen.

The significance of Article 15 is that it is a guarantee against every form of discrimination by the state on the basis of religion, race, caste or sex. Article 15 strikes at the root of provincialism by prohibiting discrimination based upon one's place of birth. It is also in conformity with the ideal of a single citizenship which the Constitution establishes for the whole of the country.

Article 15, however, has provided a couple of exceptions in its application. Article 15(3) allows the state to make any special provision for women and children. Article 15(4) permits the state to make any special provision for the advancement of socially and educationally backward classes or for the Scheduled Caste or Scheduled Tribes. The treatment meted out to women and children is in the larger and longer range interest of the community. Article 15(e) was included in the Constitution as a result of the First Consitutional Amendment in 1951.

Article 16

This Article guarantees equality of opportunity in matters of public employment. It is stated in the following words:

1. There shall be equality of opportunity for all citizens in matters relating to employment or appointment to any office under the state.
2. No citizen shall, on grounds only of religion, race, caste, sex, descent, place of birth, residence or any of them be ineligible for, or discriminated against in respect of any employment or office under the state.
3. Nothing in this Article shall prevent Parliament from making any law prescribing, in regard to a class or classes of employment to an office (under the Government of, or any local or other authority within a state or Union Territory, any requirement as to residence within that State or Union Territory) prior to such employment or appointment.
4. Nothing in this Article shall prevent the state from making provision for the reservation of posts in favour of any backward class of citizen which, in the opinion of the state is not adequately represented in the services under the state.
5. Nothing in this Article shall affect the operation of any law which provides that the incumbent of any office in connection with the affairs of any religious or denominational institution or any member of the Governing body thereof shall be a person professing a peculiar religion or belonging to a particular denomination.

Notes: Under Article 16(1), the general rule laid down is that there shall be equal opportunity for all citizens in matters of public appointment under the State, thereby the universality of Indian citizenship is emphasised.

Article 16(2) prohibits discrimination to any citizen in respect of appointment on grounds of religion, caste, race, sex, descent, place of birth or residence, should that appointment be under the State.

Articles 16(3) to 16(5) are in the nature of exceptions. According to Article 16(3), residence, qualifications may be made necessary in case of appointments under the State for particular positions. The discretion, however, does not rest with the state but within the powers of the Parliament. Article 16(4) empowers the state Government to make reservation of positions in public employment for any backward class. The state is empowered to declare a class of people as backward class. The exceptions embodied in Article 16(5) seek to take out of the scope of the general principle, the management of the affairs of any religious or denominational institutions under any special law providing for the same.

What Article 15(1) and 16(2) prohibit is that discrimination should not be made only on the ground of sex. However, these Articles do not prohibit the state from making discrimination on the ground of sex coupled with other considerations. In case titled *"Yusuf Aziz* Vs. *State of Bombay* and *Hussainbhoy Laljea,"* sex was held to be a permissible classification. While dealing with this aspect of the matter, the Supreme Court remarked as under:

"Article 14 is general and must be read with the other provisions which set out the ambit of fundamental rights. Sex is a sound classification and although there can be no discrimination in general on that ground, the Constitution itself makes special provisions in respect of women and children. The two Articles when read together validate the impugned chance in Sec. 497 I.P.C."

Justice Krishna Iyer in the case titled *Ms. C.B. Muthamma* Vs. *Union of India* expressed somewhat similar views in the following words:

"We do not mean to universalise or dogmatise that men and women are equal in all occupations and all situations and do not exclude the need programatise where the requirement of particular employment, the sensitivities of sex or the peculiarities of social sectors or the handicaps of either sex may compel sensitivity. But save, where the differentiation is demonstrable, the rule of equality must govern."

An example of violation of Article 14 is the case *Air India* Vs. *Nargesh Mirza,* where the Supreme Court observed that having taken the air hostess in service and after having utilised her services for four years, to terminate her services by the management in the event of her becoming pregnant amounts to compelling the poor air hostess not to have any children and thus interfere with and divert the ordinary course of human nature. The termination of the services of an air hostess under such circumstances is not only a callous and cruel act but an open insult to Indian womanhood, the most sacrosant and cherished institution. Such a course of action is extremely detestable and abhorant to the notion of a civilised society. Apart from being grossly unethical, it smacks of a deep rooted sense of an utter selfishness at the cost of all human values. Such a provision, therefore is not only manifestly unreasonable and arbitrary but contains the quality of unfairness and is, therefore, clearly violative of Article 14.

The Supreme Court while dealing with a rule barring married women from working in a particular firm criticised validity of the rule in the following words:

"We are not impressed by these reasons for retaining a rule of this type ... Nor do we think that because the work has to be done as a team, it cannot be done by married women. We also feel that there is nothing to show that married women would be more likely to be absent than unmarried women or widows. If it is the presence of children which would account for greater absentation of married women, that would be so with the widows having children. The fact that the work has to be carried out by the workers as a team and presence of all these workmen, is in our opinion no disqualification. So far as married women or widows are entitled to such leave as the rule of the Respondent's Firm provide and they would be availing themselves of these facilities."

2. Right Against Exploitation

The following expression constitute the relevant portion in Article 23 of the Constitution.

"Prohibition of traffic in human beings and forced labour"

1. Traffic in human beings and 'begar' and other similar forms of forced labour are prohibited and any contravention of this provision shall be an offence punishable in accordance with law.

2. Nothing in this Article shall prevent the State from imposing compulsory service for public purposes and in imposing such service, the State shall not make any discrimination on grounds only of religion, race, caste or class or any of them."

While comparing Article 23 to the 13th Amendment of the Constitution of America which abolished slavery, it may be seen that in our country, at the time of adoption of the Constitution, there was no such practice like slavery in India but there existed large scale exploitation of forced bonded labour practiced by upper caste people upon the unprivileged section of the society. There existed a practice under which people mortgaged their labour to the upper caste masters in lieu of the interest that would accrue on the principal amount taken as loan and this bondage could continue from generations to generations. The labour working under this situation had no right to seek employment without his master's approval and consent. His dependence on his master or landlord was so severe that it virtually amounted to slavery.

According to the practice of devdasi women or girls were either sold or dedicated to temples in the name of gods, where they could become an object of lust and instrument of sexual exploitation so long as their youth lasted. The practice of *devdasi, jogan* and other similar practices in Southern, Western part of the country and some of the temples in Orissa particularly bordering Andhra Pradesh were rampant and are still existing.

The ideal of human dignity pervades the entire Constitution and has been expressed in explicit terms in the form of this Article. The expression 'Traffic in Human Beings' means disposal by way of sale or hire or otherwise of human beings more or less in the same manner as man does with the disposable articles.

The trafficking in women and girls in the male dominated society has been treated as the evil practice since old times. Medieval feudalism brought down the position of women to a very low mark. Prostitution became rampant and flesh trade established itself with agents and pimps and the dignity of women had gone down to the lowest ebb. To counter this, the Parliament enacted "The Suppression of Immoral Traffic in Women and Girls Act, 1956." This Act was renamed as "Immoral Traffic (Prevention)

Act, 1956" and was substituted by Act No. 44 of 1986 with effect from Jan 26, 1987. The Act was enacted by the Parliament in persuance of the ratification by India of the International Convention of the Suppression of Traffic in persons and of the prostitution by others, signed in New York in 1950 on May 9. (Detailed study of this problem is being dealt with in the Chapter on Prostitution.)

3. *Cultural and Educational Rights*

Under Articles 29 and 30, certain cultural and educational rights are guaranteed.

Article 29: Protection of interests of minorities

1. Any section of the citizen residing in the territory of India or any part thereof having a distinct language, script or culture of its own, shall have the right to conserve the same.
2. No citizen shall be denied admission into any educational institution maintained by the State or receiving aid out of State funds on grounds only of religion, race, caste, language or any of them.

Thus sex is a prohibited ground of discrimination under Article 15 and Article 16, but not under Article 29. Courts, however, have come to settle down with an interpretation which means that sex as a basis of classification may be a suspect but cannot altogether be prohibited. Special laws for women can be made in different kinds of cases notwithstanding the fact whether they are favourable or unfavourable to women. It has only to be seen in such a situation that such orders may not only be reasonable but also seem to be reasonable. The following cases are cited by way of example:

1. In the case titled *Anjali Roy* Vs. *The State*, the fact involved was that after opening of a college exclusively for women, girl students were denied admission into another college which was a co-educational institution. Accordingly one Anjali Roy was denied admission in the co-educational college under the orders of the Director of Public Instruction of the Government of West Bengal. The petitioner challenged the orders of

the D.P.I. as arbitrary malafide and unreasonable. The Hon'ble High Court of Kolkata dismissed the Writ Petition holding that the order prohibiting the admission of the girl students to the former co-educational institution was with the intention to make the girl students to take admission in women's college so that the same could be popular and well established and thus, become a self-sufficient. This was thus, a special provision as contemplated by Article 15(3) for the benefit of women and in consequence the provisions of Article 15(1) was not available for this. It was further held that Article 15(1) was of wider implications as compared to Article 29(2) and prohibited discrimination on the ground of sex on all matters and so it included discrimination in matters of admission into educational institutions with the result that Article 15(1) should control Article 29(2).

2. In the case titled *"University of Madras* Vs. *Santhabai and another*. The High Court of Madras took a different view to deny admission to *Santhabai* in a newly opened college. The Court held the view that the University of Madras is not a 'State' as defined in Article 12 of the Constitution and thus its regulation will not be subject to prohibition of Article 15(1) of the Constitution of India. Another point is that admissions are regulated within the ambit of Article 29(2) and the regulation of the University required that colleges should have the necessary infrastructure to provide essential facilities for women before they could be admitted. This fact is not discriminatory on ground of sex.

So far as the scope of Article 15(3) is concerned, the High Court expressed that notwithstanding Article 15(1), it was lawful for the state to establish educational institutions solely for women and the exclusion of men students from such institutions does not contravene Article 15(1). The cumulative effect of Article 15(3) and 29(2) is that while male students have no right to get admission in women's college, the women's right to admission to other colleges is a matter within the regulation of authorities. Article 29(2) contains the controlling provisions where the question relating to admission to colleges involves.

The scope of Article 29(2) came up for detailed interpretation before the Apex Court in two cases, both of which were appeals against the judgement and order of Madras High Court relating to admission to Educational Institutions maintained by the state. The Supreme Court, after a threadbare discussion, observed as follows:

"It will be noticed that while Cl. (1) protects the language, script or culture of a section of the citizen, Cl. (2) guarantees the fundamental right of an individual, who is citizen. The right to get admission into any educational institution of the type appearing in Cl. (2) is a right which an individual has as a citizen and not by virtue of belonging to any community or class of citizen. The right of the citizen is not to be denied to him on grounds only of sex, religion, race, caste, or language or any of them. If a citizen, who seeks admission into any such educational institution but does not possess the requisite academic qualifications and on this account is denied admission on that ground only, certainly he cannot be held to complain of any infraction of his fundamental rights under the Constitution within the framework of this Article. In the event of his having the required academic qualifications if he is refused admission only on grounds of religion, race, caste, language or any of them, then it amounts to clear violation of his fundamental rights."

The State, contended that Article 46, charged the state with promoting with special care, the educational and special interests of the weaker section of the people and in particular of the SC/ST and with protecting them from social justice and all forms of exploitation. But, the court rejected this argument holding that this was a Directive Principle—a non-justiciable right—and it could not over-ride a Fundamental Right which was justiciable. It was the duty of the court to enforce a Fundamental Right.

The passing of the 42nd Amendment of the Constitution of India in 1976, Sec. 3, w.e.f. January 1, 1977 ensured the Supremacy of the Parliament and gave primacy to Directive Principles over the Fundamental rights. In view of the passing away of this Amendment, the aforesaid argument of the Court has little force.

4. The Right to Constitutional Remedy

The declaration of Fundamental Rights becomes infructuous unless there is an effective instrument for enforcement of the right. Article 32 of the Constitution provides a remedy for the enforcement of the fundamental rights. The remedy is in the forms of specific writs mentioned in the Article. Hence, if there is an aggrieved person who seeks a remedy from the court through a particular writ, the nature of the remedy itself is clear both to the aggrieved person and to the court.

The writs mentioned in the Constitution are:

(1) Habeas Corpus

This is a Latin term which literally means "You May Have The Body". The Writ was regarded in English as a foundation of the human freedom and the British citizen insisted upon this privilege wherever he wanted whether for business or for colonisation. This is how it found a place in the Constitution of the United States when the British colonies in America won their independence and established a new State under the Constitution.

In India, the power to issue a writ vests only in Supreme Court and the High Court. The Writ is a direction of the court to a person who is detaining another, commanding him to bring the body of the person in his custody at a specified time to a specified place for a specified purpose.

The writ has only one purpose, that is, to set at liberty a person who is confined without legal jurisdiction; to secure release from confinement of a person detained unlawfully. The writ, in accordance with circumstances can be issued against the State and its authorities as well as private individual or organisation.

(2) Mandamus

This is a Latin expression and means "We Order". The Writ of Mandamus is an order of the Supreme Court or the High Court commanding a person or a body to do that which is his or its duty to do so. For instance an appointing authority is obliged to issue a letter of appointment to a candidate if all the formalities of selection is over and the candidate is declared fit for appointment to the post. But despite the fulfilment of such condition, if the officer or the authority concerned refuses or fails to issue the appointment letter, the aggrieved person has a right to seek the remedy through a Writ of Mandamus.

(3) Prohibition

A Writ of Prohibition is issued primarily to prevent a lower court from exceeding its jurisdiction, or acting contrary to the rules of natural justice. For instance, a judge may be restrained from adjudication upon a case wherein he is personally interested. The Writ of Prohibition is a counterpart of the Writ of Certiorari and an aggrieved person may make an application to the issue of both the Writs, that is 'Prohibition' and 'Certiorari'.

(4) Certiorari

It is a Writ which orders the removal of a suit from any court to another which is superior to the first. It may be used before a trial commences to prevent an excess or abuse of jurisdiction and to transfer the case for trial before a higher court. It may be invoked after trial as well in order to quash an order which has been made without jurisdiction or in defiance of the Rules of Natural Justice.

(5) Quo Warranto

An application for Writ of Quo Warranto seeks an order from the Supreme Court or High Court to restrain a person from acting in an office to which he is not entitled. It may also seek the office to be declared as vacant. What the court has to do is to determine where there has been unsurpation of an office of a public nature. For instance, a member of a Municipal Corporation may, through an application of Writ of Quo Warranto, challenge the authority of the Mayor, if he is of opinion that the Mayor was not properly elected.

The High Court can issue Writ under provisions of Articles 226 and 227 of the Constitution.

Article 226. Powers of High courts to issue Writs

1. Notwithstanding anything in Article 32, every High Court shall have power, throughout the territories in relation to which it exercises jurisdiction to issue to any person or authority, including in appropriate cases, any Government, within those territories, directions,

orders or Writs, including Writs in the nature of habeas corpus, mandamus, prohibition, quo warranto and certiorari, or any of them, for the enforcement of any of the rights conferred in Part III and for any other purpose.

2. The power conferred by Clause (1) to issue directions, orders or Writs to any Government authority or person may also be exercised by any High Court exercising jurisdiction in relation to the territories within which the cause of action, wholly or in part, arises for the exercise of such power, notwithstanding that the seat of such Government or authority or the residence is not within those territories.

3. Where any party against whom an interim order, whether by way of injunction or stay or in any other manner, is made on, or in any proceeding relating to, a petition under Clause (1), without

   (a) furnishing to such party copies of such petition and all documents in support of the plea for such interim order; and

   (b) giving such party an opportunity of being heard, makes an application to the High Court for the vacation of such order and furnishes a copy of such application to the party in whose favour such order has been made or to the counsel of such party, the High Court shall dispose of the application within a period of four weeks from the date on which the copy of such application is so furnished, whichever is later, or where the High Court is closed, on the last day of that period, before the expiry of the next day afterwards on which the High Court is open, and if the application is not so disposed of, the interim order, shall on the expiry of that period, or as the case may be, the expiry of the said next day, stand vacated.

4. The power conferred on a High Court by this Article shall not be in derogation of the power conferred on the Supreme Court by Clause (2) of Article 32.

Article 227. Power of Superintendence over all courts by the High Court

1. Every High Court shall have superintendence over all courts and tribunals throughout the territories in relation to which it exercises jurisdiction.
2. Without prejudice to the generality of the foregoing provisions, the High Court may:
   (a) call for returns from such courts;
   (b) make and issue general rules and prescribe forms for regulating the practice and proceedings of such courts; and
   (c) prescribe forms in which books, entries and accounts shall be kept by the officers of any such courts.
3. The High Court may also settle tables of fees to be allowed to the sheriff and all clerks and officers of such courts and to attorneys, advocates and pleaders practising therein.

   Providing that any rules made, forms prescribed or tables settled under Clause (2) or Clause (3) shall not be inconsistent with the provision of any law for the time being in force, and shall require the previous approval of the Governor.
4. Nothing in this Article shall be deemed to confer on a High Court powers to superintendence over any court or tribunal constituted by or under any law relating to the Armed Forces.

Directive Principles of the State Policy

The Directive Principles of State Policy constitute the third part of the Constitution and are unique and novel in so far as they depict the ambitions and aspirations of the fathers of the Constitution. It was laid down that these provisions are not enforceable in any court but they are fundamental in the governance of the country and it was the duty of the State to apply these principles in making laws.

Article 39. Certain Principles of Policy to be followed by the State

The State shall, in particular, direct the policy towards securing:

(a) that the citizens, men and women, equally have the right to an adequate means of livelihood;

(b) that the ownership and control of the material resources of the community are so distributed as best to subserve the common good;

(c) that the operation of the economic system does not result in the concentration of wealth and means of production to the common detriment;

(d) that there is equal pay for equal work for both men and women;

(e) that the health and strength of workers, men and women, and the tender age of children are not abused and the citizens are not forced by economic necessity to enter a vocation unsuited to their age of strength;

(f) that the children are given opportunities and facilities to develop in a healthy manner and in conditions of freedom and dignity and that childhood and youth are protected against exploitation and against moral and material abandonment.

The picture, so far as it relates to the Constitutional Provision of equal pay for equal work for both, men and women is concerned is very grim. According to the "Report of the Committee on the Status of Women", wage discrimination is very much practised in the form of fixing lower wage rate for women as compared to their male counterparts. The minimum wages fixed for non-skilled male workers is Rs. 7 to 9 per day for 8 hours a day whereas the wages for women for the same type of work and for the same period is Rs. 4 to 7 per day.

A case came up for consideration before the Supreme Court which involved the question of equal pay for equal work for both men and women. The facts of the case was that Andrey D'Costa, a confidential lady stenographer of the company was being paid remuneration at the rate less favourable than her male colleague doing the same work. The company opposed it by saying that she was not doing the same work. The Supreme Court held that the discrimination between the male and female stenographer of the company was only on the ground of sex and the act does not permit the management to pay to a section of its employees doing the same work or a work of similar nature lesser pay contrary to the provisions of Section 4(1) of Equal Remuneration Act, 1976 (No. 25 of 1976).

Article 42. Provision for just and humane conditions of work and maternity relief.

The State shall make a provision for securing just and humane conditions of work and for maternity relief.

Article 44. Uniform Civil Code for the Citizen

The State shall endeavour to secure for the citizens a uniform Civil Code throughout the territory of India.

The passing of a Uniform Civil Code is not an easy proposition in a country where the population is composed of diverse religious and ethnic groups and different customs and rituals are being practised by each of them. The passing of the Hindu Marriage Act (1955) and the Hindu Succession Act (1956) are examples of such efforts. However, on the question of giving maintenance to Shah Bano by the Supreme Court in accordance with Sec. 125 of Cr. P.C. (Act 2 of 1974) generated sufficient opposition from a section of the society and the Government of India was pressurised to make a separate Act for Muslim women. Nevertheless, the courts in our country are granting maintenance applying Sec. 125 Cr. P.C. to Muslim women in appropriate cases.

Misuse of Acts of Conversion

The absence of a Uniform Civil Code in India puts Muslim women to disadvantage as according to Shariat, a Muslim male can marry and keep up to four wives as against the Hindus, Parsis, and Christian, etc. Thus, converting to Islam to gain a new spouse is being practised by a few Hindus. The following cases are being cited by way of example.

1. JM, a businessman married to N are having three children out of this wedlock, over a period of fifteen years, changed his religion and embraced Islam. He took a Muslim alias and married a girl friend S and when confronted by N ended the matter saying that his relationship with S was perfectly justified and legitimate as both had embraced Islam. And after three months of his conversion, JM declared through an oath his decision to become a Hindu.
2. The case of RK, whose marriage to VK dates back to the year 1978 was equally expedient. From the very beginning of the marriage VK alleged harassment by her in-laws over the question of dowry. One day RK brought home another woman 'A' and legitimised their relationship through conversion to Islam and weeks later reconverted to Hinduism in a temple.

Thus, the convenience afforded by the Islamic personal law to opportunistic Hindu men with bigamy in their mind is misused to gain a new spouse as well as to escape payment of maintenance. The thing becomes all the more difficult for the discarded wife as the onus to prove bigamy is on the complainant and where can she get evidence to prove this. Thus, such misuse of religion and conversions should be stopped. Having a Uniform Civil Code can go a long way in propagating this.

NINETEEN

Basic Rights

As the universality and pervasiveness of violence against women cuts across geographical, cultural and ethnic boundaries, it also persists despite social changes. Difference being of cultural and temporally specific manifestations, and rarely of presence or absence of this violence.

A telling illustration of pervasiveness of violence against women through the ages is of the Indian society and its transition from traditional to modern Indian women have done us proud and have also been revered down the ages.

India probably is the only nation in the world which exclusively enshrines female deities in artistically built temples. The Meenakshi temple at Madurai, Ambabai temple at Kolhapur and the Shantadurga and Mahalaxmi temples at Goa are ample proof of the Hindu reverence for female deities. India has also been proud of women's extraordinary ventures in the field of welfare, politics, art, literature and of late, sports. However, these women who forged themselves undauntedly in a male dominated milieu are exceptions. These women established their identity due to their special upbringing, push of circumstances, familial factors and the motivation of freedom fighters and reformers. India boasted of a woman prime minister. Currently too, we have women who have made a mark for themselves in fields hitherto reserved exclusively for men, for example P.T. Usha the sportswoman and Kiran Bedi, the Deputy Commissioner of Police.

The truth, however, which stares us in the face, indicates clearly the pitiable condition of Indian womanhood trapped in the web of socio-cultural factors such as superstitions and blind faith perpetuated by a male dominated society. The saga of the Indian woman is riddled with cruel, inhuman and pathetic attacks on her physical, emotional, social, political, and even spiritual growth. Her struggle for survival continues from the womb to the tomb without respite.

Rights for Women

In order to state and analyse the various types of violence tampling her human rights beginning with the female foetus and going on till old age, the following rights have been discussed — the right to life, liberty and security of the person, right to education, right to work, the right to be free from torture and the right to knowledge.

(i) Right to Life

Female Abortion and Infanticide

The struggle for survival continues throughout the woman's life from womb to tomb. The advent of amniocentesis in India has given yet another sound blow to this struggle. Prior to the Maharashtra Regulation of Use of Prenatal Diagnostic Techniques Act of 1988, both the municipal and governmental hospitals as well as private practitioners were conducting abortions of female foetuses. Although the Act is a deterrent, private practitioners have continued to conduct abortions with a sex bias. They are safeguarded by the Medical Termination of Pregnancy Act of 1971 which has legalised abortion under specific conditions such as the danger of the health of the mother and/or the child. The Government of India has implicitly sanctioned female foeticide because, apart from Maharashtra and Goa, no other state has passed legislation against female foeticide following amniocentesis. The dire need of such a law at a national level has often been discussed at various fora but, as yet, there is no universal law banning sex specific abortion. In fact, amniocentesis is propagated through advertisements which influence the psychology of parents. There are advertisements in Delhi such as "Pay Rs. 500 now or Rs. 5 lakhs later (dowry)." It is estimated that between 1978 and 1983 as many as 78,000 female foetuses in India have been aborted.

In certain states, such as Gujarat, Rajasthan, U.P. and Tamil Nadu, female infants in some communities are murdered as soon as they are born. They are drowned in a basin of milk, poisoned by opium applied to the breasts of mothers, strangled to death or sacrificed at an altar to a god. Four out of ten of those killed are murdered with a wet towel. It is pitiable that the mother herself is asked to do these things. No questions are asked.

In the Bhatti community in Jaisalmer, Rajasthan, the sex ratio is 550 women to 1000 men, the all-India ratio being 929 women to 1000 men. There has been no *barat* for decades in this community. Rajendra Singh, a Congressman of Bharatpur, Rajasthan had made a statement that 34 girls in his community had been reportedly murdered soon after birth (*India Today* — October 1988).

(ii) Right to Education and Knowledge

Girls' education is generally neglected despite the constitutional provision for compulsory education for all upto the age of 14 years. The percentage of girls attending school varies from state to state, being sometimes ranging between 20-50 per cent.

Female literacy in India is 24.8 per cent as compared to the male literacy of 46.9 per cent. The right to education is indirectly related to violence against women, as it has been observed that education contributes to women's assertion of other rights such as decision-making. There is a direct relation between education of women and adoption of small family norm according to researchers in family planning.

(iii) Right to be Free from Torture

The Indian woman is a slave to the so-called institutionalised cultural shackles where she is relegated to right from birth. Her mobility is restricted within the four walls of the kitchen, her self expression is monitored and her thoughts influenced by others in her milieu. She is the victim of suspicion by her brothers, parents, husband and in-laws. The following illustration will suffice to prove the point. In Dharavi, a large slum in Mumbai, a young man bashed the head of his sister because he suspected her of having an affair with a young man in the neighbourhood. The brother intended to kill his sister but she survived and now is a severely handicapped person totally dependent on him. In marital conflict cases, suspicion of the wife is a common reason. Some wives are brutally beaten, tortured and thrown out of their homes due to the husband's suspicion.

Exploitation and Gender Bias

Women take on additional responsibility of supplementary family income due to economic constraints and demands of improved lifestyles. Lower class women have, of course, always been working. In this area too, women do not have the freedom to regulate their lives. Research by Dr. Pramila Kapur indicates that earning women from the middle and upper middle classes have no control over their income. They are expected to hand over their salary to their in-laws and forfeit all their rights over it. Coping with the homefront and office the alcoholic husbands squandering away their wives, earnings and the suspicions about the woman's character further aggravate the situation. There was a case of a lady doctor who was given only Rs. 2 daily for her expenses by her in-laws. The male dominance is all-pervading and there are implicit assumptions that the wife should have a lesser designation at the work place and earn a lower salary than her husband. Gender bias at work expects a woman executive to "look like a woman, behave like a lady, think like a man and work like a dog" ("Gender Bias" *Times of India*, 2.8.1993). Junior women lawyers report molestation by male lawyers. Molestations at the work place are reported by a few bold women while others suffer in silence.

Countless cases both in rural as well as urban areas are recorded. Dalit women fall a prey to the lust of the land owners and the other affluent individuals in the rural areas. There are cases of the anganwadi workers being abused sexually or otherwise by the male senior officers. In Mumbai, recently there were two reported cases of women lecturers being harassed by their seniors because of their refusal to satisfy the sexual demands of higher-ups. The case of the air-hostess molested by a senior minister is still fresh in our minds. Discrimination is still prevalent in the matter of wages paid to male and female casual labourers. In the earthquake-affected region of Latur, women were paid Rs. 8 per day for casual labour while men were paid Rs. 20.

Most women have no freedom to select their careers. Elders in the family, neighbours and friends influence young women to take up stereotyped jobs hitherto reserved for women such as nursing and teaching. In the cities the scenario is different. We do observe women gradually coming out of homes. And yet, they have to work doubly hard to prove their efficiency to keep their status.

At an interview of women executives on TV it was stated that in order to keep their positions and climb the career ladder, they needed to be consistent, persevering, professional, confident, analytical, objective in interpersonal relationships, patient and continuously strive for knowledge and efficiency. The demands on male executives are not so numerous nor strong.

Childhood Marriage and Motherhood

In the matter of marriage too, women have no choice. Most marriages are arranged by the families of the groom and bride. In the cities parents of a few communities in the upper middle and upper classes give the freedom to their daughters to select their marriage partners. Even though there are restrictions based on religion, caste and community.

In spite of the Child Marriage Restraint Act passed in the early part of this century, infants are being married in their cradles, in Rajasthan. Early marriage, frequent pregnancies and deliveries take their toll and 13 per cent of deaths before the woman reaches her 25th year are due to complications in child birth. Maternal mortality is the main cause of death among women in the reproductive stage. It is estimated that maternal mortality in India is 500 per 100,000 live births. The danger of death is the greatest when the mother is below 20 years and above 35 years. The average Indian woman becomes pregnant 8 times, produces 6-7 children out of which 4 survive. It seems as if 8 per cent of her reproductive life is gone for pregnancy and lactation (Dr. Shanti Ghosh. *The Girl Child in India*, 1993).

The process of arranging the marriage and the ceremony itself is a humiliatory experience for the prospective bride. In Maharashtra the groom and his family are invited to tea party by the bride's parents. The bride is to be asked to prepare snacks and tea and serve them to their guests. Her culinary and other skills are praised by her parents in order to impress the parents of the potential groom. The girl is asked questions about her education, hobbies, friends and other matters and thus the party ends. The boy is rarely asked any questions. The matter of dowry is finalised at such meetings. The humiliation for a girl is worsened when she is rejected.

Killing for Dowry

Among the cases of violence against women, the problem of dowry is the most brutal and oft-repeated. It is estimated that a bride is burnt every two days in India, thus giving India the unenviable reputation of being the country with an unbeaten record of bride burning.

The Statistics

The Dowry Prohibition Act of 1961, amended in 1986, was meant to be a deterrent to this evil custom. The reality, however, was different. The number of dowry deaths increased from 1912 in 1987 to 5157 in 1991. It is estimated that one woman is burnt to death every five days in India for not bringing 'adequate' dowry.

Reasons for Non-Redressal by Parents

It is difficult to estimate the exact figures in relation to dowry harassment and death because many cases are not reported. Women suffer in silence as they are conditioned to do so from childhood. Parents of the bride who is burnt to death, at times, do not pursue the matter in the court. Some of the reasons for such behaviour are as follows:

1. When the girls reach marriageable age the parents in their desire to fulfil their duties and also to lighten their burdens marry their daughters accepting all conditions of the grooms party. They are forced to borrow money from the moneylender, sell their property such as land in order to 'marry off ' their daughter. As a consequence, they are steeped in debt. They, therefore, are financially too weak to legally pursue the matter of their daughter's death and thus do not seek any redressal.
2. Parents thus resign themselves to fate feeling that it is futile to aggravate the matter as their daughter will not come

back to life. They are also worried about the marriage of their other daughters, if any.

3. Being emotionally and physically exhausted in the nexus formed, at times, between the bridegroom's family, lawyers and the police, parents surrender.
4. In case of dying declarations taken in suspicious circumstances generally in cases of deaths due to burns, most women tend to state that their burns are due to an accident or that they have attempted suicide. This is due to the following reasons:
   (i) The victim's husband's family threatens her that if she tells the truth, her parents' family will be murdered.
   (ii) The dying woman is worried about her children's upbringing and future, in case, her husband is convicted.
   (iii) She is weary of the stigma which her children may have to suffer if their father is convicted.
   (iv) She is also apprehensive that if she survives, her husband and in-laws may again try to murder her.
   (v) She is afraid that if she lives, her life would be hell as she accused her in-laws of murder. Generally parents also disown their daughters in such cases.

A girl in India is brought up to be obedient, docile, patient and tolerant and self-sacrificing. In the urban areas girls from the middle and upper middle classes are educated and, at times, given occupational training. Some of them take up jobs before marriage. All this freedom ends with the marriage, which symbolically represents the *lakshman rekha*.

Justifications for Claiming Dowry

1. Most men assume obtaining dowry is their 'birth right'. The groom's parents justify dowry by stating that they have made tremendous financial sacrifices in order to educate their son. Therefore, they expect to recover the expenses by obtaining dowry from the bride.

2. The groom and his parents believe that the bride will be an eternal economic burden on them. They therefore demand dowry to make up for her lifetime expenses.
3. The myth that dowry is considered a monopoly of the affluent classes is not true because the lower classes in the process of identifying with the rich have imbibed some of the unethical customs.
4. There is an impression that only the Hindus demand dowry, in reality except for Zoroastrians, all other religious groups have the custom of dowry. However, there are some sections in each religious group which do not believe in dowry this differs from family and individual beliefs.
5. It is the mother-in-law who demands dowry. We have often heard that woman is her own enemy. In our experiences and observations we find that this is not true. In the 54 cases of dowry harassment studied by the students placed in Sakhya, the Anti-Dowry Guidance Cell, only in 8 cases was the mother-in-law exclusively responsible for demanding dowry and harassing the daughter-in-law. Mothers-in-law are made to do the dirty job representing the wishes of the family, unlike common impression of their villainous role in perpetrating the crime. Their acts are rationalized due to the following reasons:
   (i) Her family coaxes her to demand dowry, stating that since she is elderly and a woman, the bride's family will not reject her demands. This is true in most cases as elderly women are still respected in most homes.
   (ii) The mother-in-law demands dowry so that she, in turn, can give it to her daughter. Who then is the cause of dowry? Only the mother-in-law?
   (iii) The mother-in-law, in most cases, has herself been exploited, suppressed and victimised as a young daughter-in-law. She, therefore, nurtures hostility against those who harassed her and displaces these feelings onto her daughter-in-law. The dynamics can be understood in the theory postulated by Paulo Freire, namely, that the oppressed internalise the qualities and behaviour of the oppressor.

6. Girls in their desire to take maximum assets and riches at their marriage time which would result in their happiness also welcome taking dowry to their new homes. We cannot generalise because most girls are so conditioned as to adjust to any type of life.
7. Giving large sums of money and expensive presents need not be a ticket to a happy married life. Girls have been harassed regardless of the quantum of dowry.

The Virtual Reality of Dowry

1. Dowry is not a one shot affair. It is an unending ritual taking its toll at every festival and celebration throughout married life.
2. Most people are vaguely aware of the law against dowry. They are, therefore, doubly careful in camouflaging their demands. They suggest that the bride's parents present a 'Honda' or a 'Maruti' car to the groom so that he can return home from work early enough to take his wife out in the evening!
3. Most brides suffer harassment in silence for many years. They do so as they are conditioned to believe that after a girl's marriage her permanent place is with her husband and in-laws. Moreover they fear that their parents would have to suffer social ostracism. There have been incidents of young unmarried girls committing suicide to protect their parents from the burden of dowry.
4. Men who do not take dowry are not thought much of their community. It is felt that they might have some shortcoming in them which could be the reason for their no dowry marriage.
5. In dowry death cases (mostly due to burns) most women give a false dying declaration stating that the burns are due to an accident or that they have attempted suicide. Appreciations of the future for their children and parents make them prevent their in-laws and husband from being punished by giving false declaration.

Abusing Wife

Wife beating is generally accepted as a cultural phenomenon. Most men take it upon themselves to beat their wives to 'improve them'. Women too tolerate it as a part of life. It is perceived as a token of the husband's affection. The police too, especially of the lower ranks, all view it as a societal norm. The legislation against physical and mental torture (Sec. 498 A) is of recent origin. Unfortunately, there are lapses in its implementation.

Mental torture of the wife is equally injurious. It may be even more devasting than the physical assaults. It is manifested in the following forms — taunting the wife, insulting her in the presence of the children, guests and domestic help, ignoring her completely and cutting off communication with her. In a case of harassing daugher-in-law, a home visit was paid to conduct a family interview. The wife was not permitted to participate in the interview saying that she was stupid and that he was the spokesman of the family. Insistence to interview was thoroughly criticized saying that 'Women libbers wreck families'. In another case a marital conflict the working wife stated that her husband locked up all the kitchen gadgets such as the mixer, peeler and pressure cooker so that she had to spend more time in the kitchen and consequently report late for work. This case has now been solved.

Why the wives suffer?

The harassed wives suffer in silence because of the following reasons:

(a) They have been conditioned to obey their husbands.

(b) Culturally it is assumed that the wife will silently bear the assaults.

(c) They have no support as such. Their parental family and other relatives refuse to accept them back and bear the burden of supporting them and the children (if any) for the rest of their lives.

(d) They are ignorant of the provision in the law to safeguard their rights, as well as of shelter homes run by welfare organisations and the government.

(e) Even if they are aware of seeking redressal through law, they are brainwashed to keep the *Khandan ki Izzat* unblemished.

Rape by the husband is not as yet a cognisable offence in India. Women are conditioned to play a submissive role especially in the matter of sexual relations. Most husbands feel a sense of exclusive possession over their wives. Hence in sexual relations, the wife's consent is rarely taken. Cases have been reported to deviant sexual behaviour of the husband, for example, beating the wife prior to the sexual intercourse, burning her with cigarette butts or thrusting hard objects in her vagina. Refusal to give in to the insatiable sexual desire of the husband is interpreted as the result of her extramarital relations. She is therefore, 'duly punished'.

There was a case of murder of a young housewife in Mumbai. She had been married for eight months. Her husband was impotent but this was not revealed to her prior to their marriage. In his efforts to cure his impotency, the husband forced her to have sexual relations with his friends in his presence. She was also victimized by her brother-in-law and father-in-law. On one occasion when she strongly resisted her father-in-law's advances, he strangled her and then threw her out of their sixteenth floor apartment. But for the intervention of a passerby nurse, this case would have been registered as suicide because the in-laws made a statement to the police that the woman was mentally deranged. Cases of cruelty by the husband and his relatives have increased from 11603 in 1989 to 15949 in 1991 (*Social Welfare,* Vol. XXXIX, no. 11-12 Feb.-Mar. 1993).

Consumption of liquor is one of the prime causes of domestic violence and misery in the family. Liquor, foreign and indigenous is freely available in most Indian states. The hard-earned money of both the husband and wife is devoured by alcohol. Consequently, the wives resort to taking up extra jobs and hiding their income. Deaths' due to the consumption of alcohol are increasing but there is no statistical data available. It is estimated that the number of deaths due to spurious liquor exceeds the deaths due to communal riots. Many cases, however go unreported. The death of the husband due to liquor consumption places heavy burdens on the wife. She has to shoulder the entire responsibility of supporting her family if she has no grown-up children. At times, men have been blinded as a result of spurious liquor thus leaving the family in unending miseries.

Practice of Family Planning

Passive Role of Women

The average Indian woman has no choice in relation to important events in her life such as marriage, parenthood, family planning, participation in community activities and divorce. "We have mouths but we use them only for crying", a young woman said in a camp conducted for rural women. The family, community and society in general, assume that women have to be told, nay ordered, to behave in accordance with the norms of the family community and society. The in-laws, especially the mother-in-law, play a strong part in the matter of the number of children that the couple has. The wife is often blamed, ostracised and even divorced for her inability to produce sons or in case of sterility. The small family norm has not been effective. Despite India's acceptance of family planning in 1952 as a national issue. There are, of course, regional differences. In the family planning programme it is the woman who is at the receiving end. Men are still reluctant to undergo vasectomy or to use condoms. Women are forced to undergo sterilization despite their ill health and protests. They are not involved neither in the selection of family planning methods nor in the matter of family size. On the other hand they have to suffer all the pain.

Women, especially from the low and middle income groups suffer from ill-health and malnutrition and are the worst suffers from contraceptive services. Women with loops inserted complain of heavy bleeding and backache. Lack of adequate follow-up services is a deterrent to the acceptance of loops and other contraceptive devices or methods. The Indian Council of Medical Research (ICMR) intended to recruit 20,000 women for experimenting with NORPLANT through the medical college hospital even though a case registered against NORPLANT was still pending in the court (Karkal, July 1992). Men do not want to face any inconvenience and leave that for the woman 'a traditional beast of burden'.

Inadequate medical information supplied to patients, both men and women causes the break up of the family. To illustrate when a man undergoes vasectomy he has to be advised to get his semen tested periodically to ensure that it is free of sperms. In the interim period the couple has to be advised to utilise other contraceptive methods or devices. In some cases that is not done. When pregnancy occurs, the husband accuses his wife of infidelity and throws her out of the house thus causing family break-ups.

Voluntary efforts in the medical field have been geared mostly to women. While one appreciates the concern of the voluntary sector in relation to women and family planning, one wonders why similar efforts are not directed towards the males. Women from the low income groups have no privacy in their homes which prevents them from utilising devices such as the diaphram and jelly. Dr. Billing's ovulation method, though very sound, feasible and scientifically tested also cannot be utilised by all women. This method also requires that women have some privacy to test the vaginal mucous.

By and large, women in slums find it very difficult to stick to the schedule of oral pills. There have been cases when women have forgotten to take the pill for a few days and then have swallowed a whole lot of pills to make up the deficit. Most women do not know that a thorough medical examination is essential prior to the acceptance of this method nor are they aware of the positive and negative effects of the pills.

It is stated that one-fifth of 132 sterilisation camps surveyed by the ICMR had no life-saving drugs, as a result of which there were 180 deaths in Maharashtra, 92 in U.P., 86 in Gujarat, 82 in Kerala, 76 in Orissa and 66 in Andhra Pradesh from 1985 to 1987 (*Times of India,* 27th July, 1989).

In amniocentesis too women are not the ones to take a decision. Most of them are harassed for producing daughters and the choice of amniocentesis is imposed on them. Some are brainwashed to such an extent that they opt for an abortion. In a survey of 100 women at a Delhi clinic who underwent abortion following amniocentesis, most women said that they were taunted continuously by their in-laws for having given birth to a daughter ("Licence to Kill" *Grassroot Action,* 3rd Issue, April 1990).

The eldest male in the family is still the decision-maker in relation to familial issues with a few exceptions. It is only in minor matters such as those relating to the kitchen that the women can have their say.

Lack of Awareness of Methods of Family Planning

Eventhough T.V. has invaded all homes in the length and breadth of the country breaking all information barriers, how many utilise this opportunity? Interests of the rural women are limited to film songs and films. This leaves them ignorant about the functioning of their bodies, especially the reproductive system. Lack of sex education and the consequent faculty attitude towards sex and sexuality increases morbidity in women. Most women are ignorant of the types of contraceptives available, their advantages and disadvantages. An incident related by an institution working in the area of family planning in Tamil Nadu illustrates how women were taken for granted in this programme. The institution spread the word regarding the loop, motivated women in rural areas and inserted loops in a large number of women. It soon observed that the number of women coming for loop insertion decreased day by day. Exploration of this phenomenon revealed the rumour taking rounds that one or two women had large worms due to the loop. Investigations revealed that the loop inserted in these women had fallen out and was viewed as a large worm. One of the reasons for such miscommunication is the fact that the doctors had not explained the process of loop insertion to the women concerned. In the survey mentioned earlier, most women who underwent amniocentesis did not know the names of these tests nor their harmful effects.

Laws for Protection

Women are not aware of their legal rights nor are they aware of the political situation and its effects on the masses. In a study in Bihar it was found that most women knew about the right of inheritance to paternal property. The least known rights were the (MTP) Medical Termination of Pregnancy Act (among the rural and urban women of Gaya). Minimum Wages Act and Child Marriage Restraint Act (among Women of Bhojpur) and Widow Remarriage Act (among urban women of Madhubani)

(Sachidananda Sinha, 1984). There is no question of assertion of their rights in respect of these laws. If women are ignorant of the laws passed in their interest.

Gram Panchayats

The Government of India has recently passed legislation reserving 30 per cent of the seats for women in the gram panchayat (GP) and Zilla Parishad (ZP). Orientation programmes for these women at the ZP level are organised by voluntary organisations. In one such programme many of the participants lacked knowledge of the philosophy of reservations for women, the procedures of GP and ZP and their role therein. Some admitted that their husbands represent them at the meetings of GP or ZP. Those who were not educated said that when resolutions are passed at the meetings of GP, papers are sent to the homes of these women members for their thumb impression. Most women representatives do not take an active role in decision-making. They are merely 'nodders' at these meetings. One representative of a GP was beaten up for taking an active role in one of the meetings. She expressed her opinion on an issue very effectively and was applauded by all including her husband who was present at this meeting. When the couple returned home, the husband beat her mercilessly and asked her not to open her mouth henceforth. Some of these women are being monitored by their husbands and are forced to stand for the election of GP and ZP.

Women's Organisations

The following chart depicts a picture of some women's organisations in Bombay and their main area of work.

Name of the Organisation	*Focal Point/Objectives*
1. Majlis	Legislation for women and its implications.
2. Stree Hitakarni	Health and its implications for women.
3. Prerana	Problems of prostitutes and their children.
4. Sakhya	Eradication of dowry and management of marital conflicts.

5.	Stree Mukti Sanghatana	Women's problems in general.
6.	Maitrini	Status of women in terms of employment, rights, violence against women, services available, etc.
7.	Mahila Dakshata Samiti	
8.	Women's Forum	
9.	Swadhar	

There are numerous other women's organizations spread all over India. SEWA of Ahmedabad concentrated on forming trade unions of women handcart-pullers has now expanded its field to women's self-employment as a whole. Similarly, Saheli in Delhi, Sathin in Rajasthan, Stree Adhar Kendra in Pune are some other organisations working towards the improvement of women's status. All these organisations have shifted from a welfare approach to a development one. The improvement of women being their major thrust.

National Commission for Women

Functions covered by the Commission

The NCW was set up on 31st January 1992 as per the National Commission for Women Act 1990. The mandate of the commission covers a wide range of functions which are summarised as under:

(i) Investigate and examine the legal safeguards provided for women under the Constitution and other laws and recommend to government measures for their effective implementation.

(ii) Review the existing provisions of the Constitution and other laws affecting women and recommend amendments to meet any lacunae, inadequacies or shortcomings in such laws.

(iii) Look into complaints and take suo moto notice of matters relating to deprivation of women's rights and take up the issue with appropriate authorities.

(iv) Take up studies/research on socio-economic issues.

(v) Participate and advise on the planning process of socio-economic development of women and evaluate the progress made.

(vi) Inspect jails, remand homes where women are kept under custody and seek remedial action where necessary.

While investigating cases of violation of safeguards for women and complaints relating to deprivation of women's rights the Commission has the powers of a civil court trying a suit. The Commission can summon any person and examine the person under oath.

In order to carry out the functions effectively, eleven expert committees have been set up on women- related issues to tender advice and suggest appropriate measures, for corrective action. A complaints and pre-litigation cell to resolve conflicts outside the legal proceedings is functioning with the active collaboration of counsellors deputed by NGOs.

As an autonomous statutory body, the Commission is working relentlessly towards its goal and has adopted a holistic multipronged approach towards empowerment of women, taking up cudgels against legal, social, cultural as well as political barriers to their advancement. A number of bills have been proposed, which include the Marriage Bill, 1994 Compulsory Regulations of Marriage, Domestic Violence, etc.

Effective Measures

A number of important recommendations have been made by the National Commission for Women which include inter alia the following:

(i) GPC be amended to provide that women should normally not be remanded to police custody;

(ii) Bail be relaxed in three cases — where the accused is a woman, is ill, or is a juvenile;

(iii) Speedy investigations and speedy trials should take place in respect of women undertrials;

(iv) More women should be appointed in the police departments;

(v) The investigating officers should not be authorized to publish the name of the victim;

(vi) Mandatory training programmes on gender sensitization of the police and all those responsible for administration of justice should be organized regularly;

(vii) The Legal Services Authority Act should be amended to incorporate provision for holding Parivarik Mahila Lok Adalats to ensure speedy justice to women;

(viii) Sex education be included in the school curricula for adolescent girls and boys;

(ix) A fund (statutory or otherwise) should be created for rehabilitation of rape victims. The sources of fund could be fine/penalty imposed on the accused, donations from charitable trusts and contributions from government and local bodies. Further vocational training/skill development centres-cum-production units should be set up by NGOs and local bodies for the benefit of victims of abuse and violence;

(x) Community awareness and advocacy campaigns should be conducted for parents and local community members on the importance of girls' education and related needs; and

(xi) Support forums should be set up to analyse policies and develop strategies for amending laws related to women and to promote an agenda for the betterment of women.

Central Social Welfare Board

Programmes and Schemes

The Central Social Welfare Board established in 1953 and subsequently registered as a charitable company in the mid-sixties, has been serving the cause of women, children and other underprivileged groups through NGOs. In keeping with its objectives, the Central Social Welfare Board provides financial support and assistance for several need-based programmes which facilitate the socio-economic empowerment of women. These include Condensed Course of Education, Vocational Training Courses, Awareness Generation Camps, Voluntary Action Bureaus and Family Counselling Centres. The latter two schemes offer preventive and rehabilitative services to women who are victims of family violence and atrocities. These programmes are providing focal points for evolving social consciousness in respect of violence against women, and are helping them by adopting a "conciliatory approach".

The Voluntary Actions Bureau and Family Counselling Centres run by NGOs with financial support from Central Social Welfare Board follow a policy which leads to better integration of women within the family, rather than a policy which would lead to disintegration of the family as an institution. The family continues to be the basic social unit, with common interests and enjoys the advantage of a common front and can be a catalyst of change for the betterment of all its members.

Achievements of Women's Organisations

The chart above depicts the area(s) of work selected by different women's organisations. However, all of them adopt different strategies in relation to their objectives. The main ones are as follows:

(i) Micro Level Intervention

This involves dealing with individual cases in the setting of their families and immediate environment. It includes dealing with various types of groups, for example, groups of dowry-affected women.

The micro level is linked with the meso, exo and macro levels. The women's issues (or any other for that matter) are linked with other sub-systems of society, for example, education and health. It is important that the organisations working towards the empowerment of women study the impact of the micro-level system on women's issues and devise strategies to handle it. Issues such as the ineffective educational systems which is not geared to the consistent involvement of the girl child. The atrocious onslaught of contraceptives on women in the family welfare planning programme are raised.

(ii) Macro Level Intervention

Unless our efforts are not geared towards changes at the macro level they will go waste. The policy-makers have to be galvanised into action. Changes in the age-old laws, machinery for their implementation, projects for women and their functioning have to be scrutinised and geared to women's overall development. On the whole, most of the women's organisations have been working on the above mentioned lines. The establishment of the National Women's Commission followed by the state level commission is a big step towards the establishment of separate identities for women. These commissions operate at macro level but do take up individual cases if they involve a larger issue, for example rape. The National Commission in its attempt to review the law against rape and to effect changes in it has consulted women's organizations in various parts of India on this issue before final submission of its recommendations to the Central Government.

The problem of alcoholism has driven the village women of Tamil Nadu and Maharashtra to wage a war against this evil. There are distilleries galore in slums and villages. For ages together women have suffered the demonic attacks of alcohol on their families' health, economy and happiness in general. These women have organised themselves and forced the closure of distilleries in their vicinity. They have approached the state government to enact legislation accordingly. Thus, their power lies informing groups of like-minded women fighting for their causes.

(iii) International Linkages

Collaboration with international women's organisations is indispensable to effect global change in the status of women. They are one of the most powerful means to effective change in women's status. The Nairobi conference had set the ball rolling, here women all over the world unite once in two years to share their experiences and interventional strategies. The India-Canada conference on violence against women held in December 1993 was also an attempt in the same direction.

(iv) Seeking Implementation through Collaboration with Government Machinery

The Government on its part, makes efforts to stem violence against women. The Judiciary and the police system do make all the possible efforts towards this goal. The setting up of family courts and the enactment of Sec. 498A are the concrete forms of these efforts. The role of a women's organisation is that of a vigilant group to see to the proper implementation of these legal provisions.

A few years ago, women's organisations in Mumbai observed that cases of mental cruelty against women were not registered by the Police under Sec. 498A. A recent development in the process of women's improvement is the collaboration with the police. The College of Social Work, Nirmala Niketan, initiated students, placement in police stations in 1983, so as to sensitize the police to the social issues and to their role therein so as to effect good police-public relations. The common issues highlighted are those related to the status of women, prostitution, drugs, AIDS, street children and dowry. Accordingly, we give these inputs in the training of the police at various levels at different training centres. Similarly social work intervention in the area of women police constables (WPC) has also been initiated. Regular workshops are conducted for male police constables and officers and for WPCs. Small surveys are also conducted on the functioning of the police and reports are regularly submitted to the Commissioner of Police. The Tata Institute of Social Sciences has instituted a special cell for women and children in the office of the Commissioner of Police as well as in one police station in Mumbai. Sakhya, a voluntary organisation has been granted permission to work in three police stations in Mumbai.

The widespread and rampant atrocities against women prompted the State Women's Commission to plan women's security cells in each of the 72 police stations in Mumbai. The Commission called a meeting of all women's organisations and explained the rationale for the Mahila Suraksha Samiti (Women's Security Cells) inviting volunteers to work through the police stations. The members of this Samiti will act as vigilant groups to ensure that the police deal justly in relation to women's issues, for example, dying declarations. The law states that a police officer and a Special Executive Magistrate be present to note the dying declarations of women dying under suspicious circumstances, the presence of relatives being prohibited. However, we find that this is not adhered to and the woman's in-laws force her to tell lies, thus rendering all laws ineffective.

Creating Public Awareness

The status and self esteem of women needs to be drastically uplifted and given their due share in all spheres.

There is a dire need to create awareness among different groups regarding the status of women, gender bias and injustice against women generally. The perceptions of youth regarding marriage, women's status and roles in the family need to be revised and changed. Young boys and girls need to develop skills to strengthen the bond of marriage and family life. Young women should learn to assert themselves in their families of origin and matrimony. They should be empowered to take firm decisions in relation to the selection of marriage partners, type of wedding, refusal to give dowry, number of children, type of contraceptives and other familial and non-familial matters. Men, too, need to realise the dignity of women and to appreciate their contribution in various fields.

In a workshop with a group of young girls and boys between the ages of 16 to 22 years belonging to the lower middle class with the above mentioned objectives, there was a question related to their reasons for marriage. The answers of all the boys indicated that they needed a wife to work at home. Their responses were as follows:

"My mother is too old to do housework and hence I need a wife."

"My parents can't work on our farm any more. Therefore, I want to marry so that my wife can take over from them." "I am the only earning member in my family, and my income is insufficient to support six family members. I, therefore, want to marry a working woman."

It was indeed sad to note that none of them said that they need a companion for life to share their joys and sorrows, to enjoy life's bounty together and to jointly achieve their goals in life. The girls had a more positive bent of mind and were emphatic in their decision to marry someone to share their joys and sorrows. In the subsequent session there was a mutual confrontation and the boys later stated that no one had earlier explained to them the significance of marriage.

Family life including sex education should be introduced in schools beginning with the nursery. The objective of such an education should be to impart scientific facts about sex and sexuality, roles and responsibilities in the family and to shape attitudes conducive to a happy family life without a gender bias.

Women's organisations are also becoming vigilant about the portrayals of women in the audio-visual media. Except for a few art serials, the woman in most commercial movies is portrayed as a sex bomb, a cantankerous wife/mother-in-law or an obedient and dutiful wife. Remarks about violence against women need to be scrutinized. A film named *Damini* portrays the courage of a woman who raises her voice against rape and the unjust judicial system. However, there are two sentences uttered by the barrister in the movie which are shocking. Regarding a gang rape of a married domestic worker by the employer's son and his friends, he says: *Ladkon ne jo kuch kiya utni badi baat nahi hai. Jawani me to yeh sub kuch hota hi raheta hai."* (There is nothing objectionable in what the boys have done. Such things keep happening in youth). Unfortunately this has gone unnoticed except for the letter to the Editors of Newspapers written by the author. One would have expected the PTAs of schools, women's organizations and the union of domestic workers to raise a hue and cry. Education of the masses in relation to violence against women could be imparted in the context of human rights.

The focus on women as an exploited, victimised and marginalised group is a recent development in the world. It has been now recognised that despite all their rights being violated, women have been suffering in silence. In India, the concept of Seeta/Savitri (dutiful wives) is imbibed in a girl's mind from the early stages of her life. A vigorous multi-pronged and multi-professional effort is needed to establish the woman as a human being in her own right. It is time to dispel myths, superstitions and misconceptions about woman and her duties and adopt a rational attitude towards the woman as a human being and not a beast of burden.

TWENTY

Females behind Bars

Accordingly, custodial justice to women has been one of the thrust areas of the activities of the Commission since its inception. The visits to the jails revealed extremely unsatisfactory conditions under which women prisoners live. While the visiting members conveyed to the concerned authorities their general observations about the living condition of women and made specific suggestions about certain hard cases, it was felt that a study should be undertaken to assess the existing conditions in the jails throughout the country.

Observations and Suggestions made by Members Inspecting the Jails

(i) Adequate arrangements for vocational training should be made for women inmates in jail and a programme prepared for rehabilitation of released prisoners. To take an example the visiting Members came across the case of life convict in Assam who was to be released shortly but was very apprehensive of her future since the thought that her husband and society might not accept her. She wanted to acquire some professional skill to be economically independent. She had aptitude for nursing. At the suggestion of the member she was given training in midwifery and was ultimately able to make her by into the profession.

(ii) Courts should ensure that female prisoners are handed over to bona fide guardians after release, so that they may not fall into the hands of imposter guardians who may force them into immoral trafficking the some happens in many cases.

(iii) Mentally ill women should be kept separate from the other women prisoners.

(iv) Certain women prisoners had been kept in custody on the ground of being lunatic despite the fact that they were not actually lunatics. There should therefore, be an objective medical examination of such cases.

(v) The women's wing of Tihar jail was found to be overcrowded by more than four times its capacity. Construction of additional accommodation was suggested to ameliorate the condition of women inmates. It was noted that the women inmates were encouraged to engage themselves in the training of various vocations. Also, a de-addition centre had been set up by the jail authorities. However, revamping of the training programme was suggested so that the inmates were enabled to produce marketable goods and make an earning for themselves for future security.

(vi) In the Jail, Delhi there was a case of a smart girl who had secured the job of a police A.S.I. by impersonation but she was a Karate expert. It was suggested to the Jail authorities to engage her in some fruitful activity like imparting physical training to other prisoners. A similar approach is necessary in like cases.

(vii) In certain prisons, some women inmates were found to suffer from T.B. It was suggested that they should be separated from the others and also given proper medical treatment.

(viii) In the Central Jail in Mumbai the Tata Institute of Social Science was conducting some useful services for the jail inmates in collaboration with the Mumbai Police such as literacy classes, creches for children vocational training counselling, legal guidance, placement on release, etc. This was considered as a good example to be followed.

(ix) The authorities at Sabarmati Central Jail, Ahmedabad expressed the view that the vocational training facilities for male prisoners could not be extended to female inmates as their number was too small. It was suggested that in such cases women inmates could be congregated in one or two suitable jails for making such facilities available or, alternatively provided with such other work as gardening, cooking, etc. and wages paid for the same.

(x) In several jails, regular visits by doctors are not made but they are called only when needed. Also no facilities for lady doctors or nurses exist for women prisoners. It was suggested to the concerned jail authorities that it is desirable that women prisoners are treated only by women doctors, unless the prisoners opt otherwise. However, medical examination should be provided as a matter of routine.

(xi) In the jails visited in Madhya Pradesh, it was found that most of the prisoners were tribal and had their own cultural tradition. The crimes committed by them were not pre-planned and had altogether different background. Therefore, instead of convicting them straightaway under the provisions of Criminal Procedure Code, a lenient view should be taken in the context of their socio-economic environment. It was as suggested that suitable training should be given to Adivasi women prisoners in bidi making sericultre and other related industries to which they are traditionally accustomed.

(xii) Women prisoners convicted under TADA were generally found to be young school and college-going girls. It was suggested that they should be provided with facilities to continue their studies and persistently motivated to return to the mainstream of life.

Conditions in Prisons

The personal visits of Members to the jails convinced the Commission that there was a serious shortfall in the delivery of services to women who are in custody in jails. The Commission therefore decided to issue a questionnaire to all the States and Union Territories calling for data/information in respect of facilities available to women inmates with regard to diet accommodation medical aid sanitation, education vocational training, legal aid, recreational opportunities, provisions for children accompanying prisoners, visitorial facilities ventilation of grievances, etc.

The information received from all over the country is being processed in the Commission and an analysis thereof will be presented before the Export Committee with a view to formulating recommendations bearing on the conditions of women in custody and norms therefore.

The Commission also thought it fit that some immediate suggestions should be preferred it the Ministry of Home affairs, Government of India, for adoption in order to secure custodial justice for women behind the bar. While drawing up these suggestions, consideration was given also to the aspect of gender justice in the realm of criminal law a administration after taking a stock of the recommendations made by various commissions and committees on the subject, notable among which is the Report of the National Expert Committee on Women prisoners headed by justice Krishna Iyer as well as that of All India Committee for Jail Reforms and also various findings of the Supreme Court of India on the subject.

The suggestions were want for immediate implementation as these are supposed not to entail any substantial strain on the governmental exchequer and are implementable as a short-term measure. These are given below.

1. Women shall not be arrested between sunset and sunrise and shall not be arrested expect in the presence of women. This will necessitate amendment of section 46 Cr. P.C. 1973.
2. In all cases of bailable offences, bail on her bond shall be granted forthwith by the police themselves. As far as possible in non-bailable cases also, bail should be granted unless special circumstances warrant a different course, in which case, the arrested woman

shall be remanded to judicial custody with utmost expedition.

3. On arrest, the police should immediately obtain from the arrestee the name a relative or friend to whom the intimation of her arrest should be promptly given.
4. If consideration of arrestee's own safety and freedom from ensnarement by anti-social elements demand detention in public institutions, bail shall be refused to the women in her own interest unless she is specifically states her willingness to be thus released even after being altered to the above consideration.
5. The person of a women shall not be searched except by a women authorised by law, and in a manner strictly in accordance with the requirement of decency. Whether in custody or in transit, the arrested woman must always be guarded by a woman police or female surrogate. A relative may be permitted to accompany the female arrestee.
6. Whenever a woman is to be examined by the police or other investigative agency as a witness it should be done only at her residence; nor should she be summoned to the police or investigative station unless she expresses her preference to be examined at the station.
7. No female prisoner shall be subjected to any form of corporal punishment or use of handcuffs fetters or isolation as a form of disciplining.
8. When women are examined in court as accused or as witnesses, due courtesy and decency shall be shown. If circumstances so demand in the interest of modesty and privacy of a woman, the trial may be held in camera or the woman may be examined on commission through women advocates.

Exclusive Custody for Women:

1. There should be police stations exclusive for women and exclusive lockups under the control of women police. This will necessitate amendment of prison Act

and police Act. Separated space for female arrestees in every police lockup and complete segregation of women prisoners in jail and other custody should be maintained.

2. Where such facility is not available, a female arrestee may be lodged in a special home or institution designated under any law for the time being in force to receive women. At no, time shall a woman arrestee be left unguarded by a woman guard or surrogate.

   In all places of police custody, basic amenities such as living space, water, toilet, food medical examination and care, and provisions to meet the special needs of women shall be provided.

3. As far as possible each state should have at least one or more separate jail for women.

4. There should be separate custodial facilities for convicts and under trial women. Separate institutions or reception centres where undertrial and remanded women may be kept, should be set up in larger cities, district headquarters, and in female-crime-endemic areas. Where convicts and undertrials are currently housed in one institution they must be kept apart in separate wings until independent facilities are set up.

Visitorial Provision in Custody:

1. Additional provision should be made in the existing legislation conferring visitorial rights on recognised institutions or individuals, institutional and individual accountability for lapses and excesses should also be provided for.

2. Information on women in custody should be made available to recognised social organisations and individuals on request. Persons and institutions accredited as visitors should be allowed as of right free access to police stations and records.

3. Visiting Committees to jails should be constituted in consultation with professional bodies and university

department of laws, criminologists, social workers and social scientists from the neighbouring area. Visitors should be nominated on the bases of merit, public spiritedness activist record and actual time likely to be made available to the visitorial function.

A woman DIG should be appointed at state headquarters preferably from the prison service to specifically look after the work relating to women prisoners and women prison staff.

Autonomous Jails

Women superintendents of separate prisons for women (currently six in number) should be made fully autonomous in functioning.

Counselling Prisoners

Prisoners Councils or Bandi Sabhas should be set up in all prisons to help airing prisoners grievances and difficulties.

Counselling at Social Level

1. Socio-legal counselling cells should be set up in every prison for women inmates.
2. In exceptional circumstances when a woman arrestee is taken to a police lock-up the police should immediately give intimation to the nearest Legal Aid Committee or recognized legal service or body which must render all necessary legal services at State expense.
3. Magistrates shall inform women when first produced of their right to legal aid at state expense and direct the provision of necessary services. They shall also explain the nature and scope of the proceedings against her and her rights in it.
4. Legal aid and counselling through professional bodies assisted by para-legal and social workers should be institutionalised in respect of every prison and custodial institution.

   Law schools and schools of social work should be encouraged and permitted to render socio-legal counselling service to the inmates.

5. In the disposition of women offenders courts should mandatorally call for and give due regard to the probation officers report and to the report of medical/ psychiatric examination. Where probation officers are not available, probation investigation should be entrusted to recognized and accredited institutions and individuals.

Assistance Outside Jail

1. Released Prisoners' Aid Societies should operate in every district to provide a single-window assistance towards rehabilitation and mainstreaming of the released women prisoners.
2. Before a female prisoner is released, her relatives should be informed and where no relative exists or shows up the released prisoner should be sent to her destination with a female escort.
3. Appropriate assistance should be rendered to every female prisoner on release whether during or after completion of sentence. For this purpose a centre for assisting released prisoners should be set up to serve a cluster of prisons and custodial institutions on an area-wise basis. Even without the centre the prison authorities should take necessary steps to arrange the rehabilitation of the released prisoner either through the family, the relief centre or a voluntary organisation.

4) Aftercare and short-stay homes for women prisoners may be established in every state to serve those prisoners who are homeless or rejected by their families.

Children Accompanying Women in Police Custody/Jail Custody:

1. When arresting a women, proper arrangements for the protection and care of her accompanying children should be the responsibility of the state. Children who need to be custodialized jointly with their mothers should enjoy rights justly needed, while in custody in

terms of food, living space, health, clothing and visitation.

2. In the disposition of women to custody or otherwise, the magistrate must enquire and direct that suitable for the welfare of their children be made in a manner that protects the rights of children. While sentencing women to imprisonment or any form of custodialisation suitable orders should be made for the custody and welfare of their children.
3. Expectant mothers in custody should be shown special consideration by way of medical and nutritional care, education in child rearing and mother craft.

Police Unit for Help

1. Women's Assistance Police Unit contacting cadre of men and women police with specific task of crime prevention work and assistance to women should be set up in each district.
2. In endemic female crime areas, or wherever otherwise desirable exclusive police station or booths and counters within police stations, shall be set up to deal with women needing protection of or coming in conflict with law. Such booths and police stations should be managed by an integrated cadre of men and women police specially trained and sensitized to deal with women.

On 3rd February, 1993, the Commission organised in New Delhi a conference of Inspectors General of Prisons from all over the country with a view to obtaining their views on the diverse issues relating to custodial justice as well as gender justice in the realm of criminal law administration.

The Conference discussed at length a host of issues arising out of the topic of custodial justice to women as well as gender justice in the realm of criminal law administration. It was felt that the issues deserve a more thorough probe in the light of desirability as well as implement ability of the various suggestions emerging out of the Conference.

Moreover, the suggestions were also desired to be screened and reviewed by the Expert Committee on Custodial Justice in order that light may be shed from all angles of views and a consensus arrived at. Accordingly a sub-committee of eight persons out of the participants of the Conference was appointed to interact with the Expert Committee on Custodial Justice to women on all the significant suggestions and in particular about the suggested amendments to the laws in force in the realm. This culminated in formulation of recommendations by the Commission for amendment of the code of Criminal Procedure.

TWENTY ONE

Scene in Countryside

Before the advent of the Aryans, women had a high status in the family and in society under the matriarchal system that was then practised. Then came the patriarchal system, taking the men to a superior status and leading to men the subordination of women and the beginning of domestic violence.

Life in Villages

In order to understand the nature of domestic violence in rural areas, we must study the lifestyle of the rural population. The Indian rural economy is based on agriculture. Most of the farmers are marginal farmers, owning even less than ten acres of land. Most of them cultivate only one crop. They cannot look after their land properly. When they face economic problems like a daughter's marriage or a death in the family, they are forced to sell their land.

Marginal farmers, landless labourers, scheduled caste communities, self-employed workers whose occupation is connected with agriculture, form more than 90 per cent of the population in rural areas. Every member of the family, whether old or young, male or female has to work hard for his/her living. Although some superficial changes have occurred in their work habits like the use of fertilisers, chemicals, machines and modern communication systems, they do not commensurate with their economic conditions. The society continues to be a traditional one, characterized by relatively slow rate of social change. Child marriages are common. People are aware of the law against polygamy, but they find the loopholes in it. They do not consider women to be humans but beasts of burden.This reduces their self-image and esteem.

They are brought up since childhood to cherish values like patience and tolerance supposed to be inherent qualities of women. This encourages the men to suppress and torture them knowing fully well that they won't retaliate.

Dowry System

The dowry system is prevalent among the higher castes and rich families in rural areas, now the middle and lower middle class also tend to taking dowry to establish their status in society. In the poor class, the dowry amounts to a few hundred rupees, wedding clothes for the bridegroom and some utensils. However, this amount is also too much for the bride's father who earns his bread on daily wages. If the bride's father cannot keep the promises made to the bridegroom's father before the ceremony, this creates problems for the daughter with her husband's family. She faces domestic violence. She cannot disclose her problems to her parents. The parents also believe that a married daughter should not complain against her in-laws or her husband. Moving cases like the ones described below raise a pertinent question in our mind — who to blame and how to put an end to this slaughter.

In one case a newly-married pregnant daughter sent a letter to her father requesting him to send the promised dowry amount of Rs. 15,000 which had not been given and gifts for her first pregnancy. Her father could not manage the amount and one day the girl was found dead in the garbage tank behind the house. Her elder sister who is married, came to register the case in our centre. She told us that her sister's husband and other members of his family had tied her hands, legs and mouth, had given her electric shocks and had thrown her body into the tank. Her father registered a complaint with the police, saying that their daughter had been murdered by her husband for money.

Who is responsible for the death of a young, innocent and pregnant girl? Her parents? Her in-laws? Or she herself? Or Society? We have observed many cases of women facing violence, being driven away from home with their children, or committing suicide, simply because their parents could not fulfil the promises given to the bridegroom's parents.

In many cases, girls are punished either by the husband or his family. The nature of these punishments is beyond human imagination. One husband forced his wife to stand on one leg. When she could not, he beat her brutally. Locking up of girls in a room without food or water is very common. In one case, a father-in-law said his daughter-in-law was dead, when she had actually been locked up in a dark lumber room at the top of the house. At midnight, her mother-in-law would give her a small piece of bread and a cup of water. One day, a cricket ball fell into the room and the children trying to retrieve it saw the dreadful figure of the woman. They told their parents that they had seen a female goblin. Their parents complained about it at the police station. A young police officer raided the house suddenly and released the young girl. She stayed at Manaswini shelter home for a year. She earns her living now, but is very weak and has very poor eyesight due to continuous weeping. Punishments like thrusting hands into boiling water or oil, forcing women to stand for hours together with a mill-stone on the head, are very common.

Marriage

The average age at which girls are married in rural areas is 13-14 years. According to tradition, a daughter must be married before puberty. Usually, a newly-married girl knows nothing of sexual relations and when she cannot co-operate with her husbands' advances and naturally she is harassed by him. A repulse towards sexual relations develops in her at times leading to her husband's second marriage. In many cases, the newly-married girls escape to their parents' home where they receive no sympathy and are forced to return. Being of a tender and excitable age and unable to cope with constant nagging and violence, many girls commit suicide.

In rural areas, a man does not go by personal factors in his choice of a wife. He is attracted to easy money which he can get with his bride's dowry having availed of all benefits, he no longer likes his wife. He beats her and harasses her. She is not given enough food, or is given left overs. Finally, she is driven out of the house with her girl child. In many cases, the husband takes written permission from his wife for a second marriage — through violent methods. Legally, it has no value.

Women in rural areas accept polygamy as a natural phenomenon of man's personality and do not object to a second marriage. But both wives cannot live together peacefully. One of them suffers all her life. Very few women file suits in the court against their husbands.

Addiction to liquor is one of the main causes of domestic violence. Women in villages say that liquor is their rival. Intoxication makes a man brutal and savage, and he behaves inhumanly towards his wife. Some men behave badly only under intoxication, which

Commission of Violence

Now let us look at the various types of violence.

1. Physical harassment, beating with the hand or a stick, kicking.
2. Dragging the woman by the hair.
3. Scorching her on various parts of the body.
4. Sometimes she is not given food and is imprisoned in an isolated room.
5. Abusing her and using foul language. Actually to insult a woman and demean her by foul language is very common in this area.
6. Taunting for dowry makes her conscious of her secondary status. "Your father is a beggar," "You are a fool," "Your relatives are like animals" — this type of language is very common and if a woman expresses resentment, she'll be definitely a victim of violence. The perpetrators of verbal violence hardly consider it as violence. The taunting of a woman on her lack of looks or household skills may drive the woman to commit suicide many a time.

The perpetrators of violence:

1. In most of the cases the married woman is harassed by her husband, then her in-laws.
2. In case of unmarried girls her own father, brother and mother also make her a victim of violence.

General Attitude and Response

The woman prefers to be silent during the early stage of violence. She generally reacts through speech and rarely by resorting to violence. Rarely does she decide to take help from the police or the court. Immediate relief is what she looks for in the situation of violence, so that she can be somewhat at ease. She always looks for help from her parental family. When she gets moral support, she feels that she is empowered and then she struggles against domestic violence. This attitude is mostly seen in labour class women, whereas middle or upper class women expect somebody else to fight for them. The women of all classes endure violence for the sake of their children.

Structures for Assistance

In resorting to counselling the woman finds the much needed relief and gains confidence by seeing a way out of her desperate situation. Counselling of both parties also plays a good role in the process of her struggle for existence. At times when a woman takes help from the some organization, Panch, the police or the court, one has to take into account the expense, time and energy involved. And if they fail to understand her problem from her angle she gets frustrated. Women's issues from a feminist perspective. It is a bitter truth that even her paternal relatives also do not understand her reality and help her half-heartedly.

It is our general experience that nobody is sincerely interested in helping the woman, not even her own paternal relatives. Once in a while, even if they want to teach a lesson to the cruel in-laws, after some time they do not pursue the matter or they make a compromise. Nowadays it is often maintained that I.P.C. Section 498-A provides help to women victims and if this section is applied properly by the police, court and lawyers it can be useful. But bitter reality faced by the organisation is corruption at all levels of the state machinery. The case takes such a peculiar turn that the woman is placed in a position where she becomes the accused and she has to defend herself from false allegations. And in such circumstances all our efforts are in vain and even one experience of failure affects the image of an organisation whereas when the work is done in the right way, accompanies a feeling of victory.

Believing that an organisation would prove more effective than an individual 'Astitva' organization was founded. Soon it was realized that the state machinery does not help positively. When they feel that a strong group is supporting the woman, that time they have to take an interest in her case but their interest is not genuine. Actually, without the help of police and court the organisational efforts can sometimes get hopeful results also. The District Level Committee against Violence Against Women, Free Legal Aid Centres or the Lok Adalats are also some support structures set up to help the women against violence. They too have not succeeded because of limited resources, lack of time, proper knowledge of the root causes and of co-ordination. No one tends to understand the problem from a feminist perspective. Even the language of the law, the procedure of the case in the court, the police and the persons who are handling the case all come from the patriarchal value-based society. This is the reality which is very disappointing. Yet we feel that if we can respond to the problems of the woman properly and give her moral support in her struggle, that itself is an achievement. And this optimistic attitude encourages us to continue our work in the field.

To create an environment against violence in the society, awareness generation programmes are employed. They include leaflet distribution, camps, seminars, street plays and songs. The Nari Mukti Din is also celebrated on the 8th March and 25th November every year, this is the International Day against Violence against Women. These programmes have difficulties of funds, time and commitment and other resources.

Even though no support structure gets 100 per cent success they should not be ignored, may they be the police or the court they are needed in many a case. Media too has its importance as it can play a good role in educating society even though at times the messages may create confusion and contradiction resulting in an adverse effect.

Appendices

INCIDENCE AND RATE OF CRIME COMMITTED AGAINST WOMEN IN STATES AND UTs DURING 1998

Sl. No.	*State/UT*	*Incidence of Total COG. Crimes*	*Percentage Contribution To All-India Total*	*Estimated Mid-Year Population (In Lakhs)*	*Rate of Total COG. Crimes*	*Rank**	*Rank***
(1)	*(2)*	*(3)*	*(4)*	*(5)*	*(6)*	*(7)*	*(8)*
States							
1.	Andhra Pradesh	11201	8.5	741.7	15.1	9	6
2.	Arunachal Pradesh	125	0.1	11.3	11.1	16	21
3.	Assam	3388	2.6	256.5	13.2	12	13
4.	Bihar	7105	5.4	969.6	7.3	22	7
5.	Goa	109	0.1	15.1	7.2	23	22
6.	Gujarat	6658	5.1	471.0	14.1	11	9
7.	Haryana	3002	2.3	193.4	15.5	8	14
8.	Himachal Pradesh	778	0.6	64.2	12.1	14	18
9.	Jammu & Kashmir	1715	1.3	95.4	18.0	5	16
10.	Karnataka	5516	4.2	509.8	10.8	17	10
11.	Kerala	4799	3.7	317.8	15.1	10	11
12.	Madhya Pradesh	15865	12.1	774.0	20.5	2	2

(Contd.)

(Annexure Contd.)

(1)	(2)	(3)	(4)	(5)	(6)	(7)	(8)
13.	Maharashtra	14266	10.9	894.1	16.0	6	3
14.	Manipur	86	0.1	23.9	3.6	28	24
15.	Meghalaya	71	0.1	23.1	3.1	29	25
16.	Mizoram	141	0.1	9.0	15.6	7	20
17.	Nagaland	32	0.0	15.9	2.0	31	28
18.	Orissa	4450	3.4	353.0	12.6	13	12
19.	Punjab	1238	0.9	231.0	5.4	27	17
20.	Rajasthan	12159	9.3	520.1	23.4	1	4
21.	Sikkim	37	0.0	5.3	7.0	25	27
22.	Tamil Nadu	11201	8.5	608.8	18.4	4	6
23.	Tripura	319	0.2	35.8	8.9	20	19
24.	Uttar Pradesh	17497	13.3	1640.4	10.7	18	1
25.	West Bengal	6811	5.2	772.5	8.8	21	8
	Total (States)	**128569**	**97.9**	**9552.6**	**13.5**		
Union Territories							
26.	A & N Islands	26	0.0	3.7	7.1	24	29
27.	Chandigarh	97	0.1	8.4	11.5	15	23
28.	D & N Haveli	17	0.0	1.8	9.4	19	30
29.	Daman & Diu	2	0.0	1.3	1.5	32	32
30.	Delhi	2556	1.9	130.4	19.6	3	15
31.	Lakshadweep	2	0.0	0.7	3.0	30	32
32.	Pondicherry	69	0.1	10.5	6.6	26	26
	Total (UTs)	**2769**	**2.1**	**156.8**	**17.7**		
	Total (All-India)	**131338**	**100.0**	**9709.3**	**13.5**		

Note: 1. *Rank on the basis of Rate of total cognizable crimes (Col. 6).
2. **Rank on the basis of Percentage share (Col. 4).

INCIDENCE OF CRIMES COMMITTED AGAINST WOMEN DURING 1998

Sl. No.	State/UT	Est.Mid Year Popula-tion	Rape			Kidnapping & Abduction			Dowry Deaths			Cruelty by Husband and Relatives		
			I	R	P	I	R	P	I	R	P	I	R	P
(1)	(2)	(3)	(4)	(5)	(6)	(7)	(8)	(9)	(10)	(11)	(12)	(13)	(14)	(15)
States														
1.	Andhra Pradesh	741.7	869	1.2	5.8	738	1.0	4.5	500	0.7	7.2	4310	5.8	10.4
2.	Arunachal Pradesh	11.3	32	2.8	0.2	38	3.4	0.2	0	0.0	0.0	8	0.7	0.0
3.	Assam	256.5	744	2.9	4.9	1117	4.4	6.8	32	0.1	0.5	739	2.9	1.8
4.	Bihar	969.6	1421	1.5	9.5	1043	1.1	6.4	1039	1.1	15.0	1507	1.6	3.6
5.	Goa	15.1	16	1.1	0.1	14	0.9	0.1	3	0.2	0.0	16	1.1	0.0
6.	Gujarat	471.0	368	0.8	2.4	1182	2.5	7.2	90	0.2	1.3	3602	7.6	8.7
7.	Haryana	193.4	364	1.9	2.4	318	1.6	1.9	309	1.6	4.5	977	5.1	2.4
8.	Himachal Pradesh	64.2	128	2.0	0.9	115	1.8	0.7	7	0.1	0.1	228	3.5	0.6
9.	Jammu & Kashmir	95.4	178	1.9	1.2	629	6.6	3.8	9	0.1	0.1	18	0.2	0.0
10.	Karnataka	509.8	233	0.5	1.6	312	0.6	1.9	200	0.4	2.9	1501	2.9	3.6
11.	Kerala	317.8	589	1.9	3.9	130	0.4	0.8	21	0.1	0.3	2125	6.7	5.1
12.	Madhya Pradesh	774.0	3354	4.3	22.3	925	1.2	5.6	598	0.8	8.6	2765	3.6	6.7
13.	Maharashtra	894.1	1154	1.3	7.7	772	0.9	4.7	420	0.5	6.1	7728	8.6	18.7
14.	Manipur	23.9	13	0.5	0.1	60	2.5	0.4	0	0.0	0.0	0	0.0	0.0
15.	Meghalaya	23.1	42	1.8	0.3	16	0.7	0.1	1	0.0	0.0	0	0.0	0.0

(Contd.)

(Annexure Contd.)

(1)	(2)	(3)	(4)	(5)	(6)	(7)	(8)	(9)	(10)	(11)	(12)	(13)	(14)	(15)
16.	Mizoram	9.0	84	9.3	0.6	4	0.4	0.0	0	0.0	0.0	0	0.0	0.0
17.	Nagaland	15.9	13	0.8	0.1	14	0.9	0.1	0	0.0	0.0	0	0.0	0.0
18.	Orissa	353.0	679	1.9	4.5	514	1.5	3.1	240	0.7	3.5	935	2.6	2.3
19.	Punjab	231.0	219	0.9	1.5	222	1.0	1.4	219	0.9	3.2	397	1.7	1.0
20.	Rajasthan	520.1	1266	2.4	8.4	2499	4.8	15.3	433	0.8	6.3	4947	9.5	12.0
21.	Sikkim	5.3	7	1.3	0.0	4	0.8	0.0	0	0.0	0.0	2	0.4	0.0
22.	Tamil Nadu	608.8	362	0.6	2.4	993	1.6	6.1	176	0.3	2.5	440	0.7	1.1
23.	Tripura	35.8	73	2.0	0.5	39	1.1	0.2	10	0.3	0.1	115	3.2	0.3
24.	Uttar Pradesh	1640.4	1605	1.0	10.7	2882	1.8	17.6	2229	1.4	32.2	5113	3.1	12.4
25.	West Bengal	772.5	757	1.0	5.0	783	1.0	4.8	249	0.3	3.6	3704	4.8	9.0
	Total States	**9552.6**	**14570**	**1.5**	**96.9**	**15363**	**1.6**	**93.8**	**6785**	**0.7**	**98.1**	**41177**	**4.3**	**99.7**
Union Territories														
26.	A & N Islands	3.7	4	1.1	0.0	2	0.5	0.0	0	0.0	0.0	3	0.8	0.0
27.	Chandigarh	8.4	11	1.3	0.1	31	3.7	0.2	5	0.6	0.1	25	3.0	0.1
28.	D & N Haveli	1.8	7	3.9	0.0	2	1.1	0.0	0	0.0	0.0	7	3.9	0.0
29.	Daman & Diu	1.3	0	0.0	0.0	0	0.0	0.0	0	0.0	0.0	1	0.8	0.0
30.	Delhi	130.4	438	3.4	2.9	978	7.5	6.0	126	1.0	1.8	103	0.8	0.2
31.	Lakshadweep	0.7	0	0.0	0.0	0	0.0	0.0	0	0.0	0.0	1	1.5	0.0
32.	Pondicherry	10.5	1	0.1	0.0	5	0.5	0.0	1	0.1	0.0	1	0.1	0.0
	Total (UTs)	**156.8**	**461**	**2.9**	**3.1**	**1018**	**6.5**	**6.2**	**132**	**0.8**	**1.9**	**141**	**0.9**	**0.3**
	Total (All-India)	**9709.3**	**15031**	**1.5**	**100.0**	**16381**	**1.7**	**100.0**	**6917**	**0.7**	**100.0**	**41318**	**4.3**	**100.0**

(Contd.)

(Annexure Contd.)

Sl. No.	State/UT	Molestation			Eve-Teasing			Importing of Girls			Sati Pre. Act		
		I	R	P	I	R	P	I	R	P	I	R	P
(1)	(2)	(16)	(17)	(18)	(19)	(20)	(21)	(22)	(23)	(24)	(25)	(26)	(27)
States													
1.	Andhra Pradesh	2967	4.0	9.6	1050	1.4	12.9	8	0.0	5.5	0	0.0	-
2.	Arunachal Pradesh	46	4.1	0.1	1	0.1	0.0	0	0.0	0.0	0	0.0	-
3.	Assam	648	2.5	2.1	12	0.0	0.1	0	0.0	0.0	0	0.0	-
4.	Bihar	432	0.4	1.4	89	0.1	1.1	1	0.0	0.7	0	0.0	-
5.	Goa	22	1.5	0.1	8	0.5	0.1	0	0.0	0.0	0	0.0	-
6.	Gujarat	1210	2.6	3.9	139	0.3	1.7	57	0.1	39.0	0	0.0	-
7.	Haryana	611	3.2	2.0	385	2.0	4.7	25	0.1	17.1	0	0.0	-
8.	Himachal Pradesh	283	4.4	0.9	15	0.2	0.2	0	0.0	0.0	0	0.0	-
9.	Jammu & Kashmir	516	5.4	1.7	361	3.8	4.4	0	0.0	0.0	0	0.0	-
10.	Karnataka	1340	2.6	4.3	139	0.3	1.7	0	0.0	0.0	0	0.0	-
11.	Kerala	1773	5.6	5.7	96	0.3	1.2	0	0.0	0.0	0	0.0	-
12.	Madhya Pradesh	7310	9.4	23.5	741	1.0	9.1	26	0.0	17.8	0	0.0	-
13.	Maharashtra	2923	3.3	9.4	765	0.9	9.4	0	0.0	0.0	0	0.0	-
14.	Manipur	13	0.5	0.0	0	0.0	0.0	0	0.0	0.0	0	0.0	-
15.	Meghalaya	12	0.5	0.0	0	0.0	0.0	0	0.0	0.0	0	0.0	-
16.	Mizoram	53	5.9	0.2	0	0.0	0.0	0	0.0	0.0	0	0.0	-

(Contd.)

(Annexure Contd.)

(1)	(2)	(16)	(17)	(18)	(19)	(20)	(21)	(22)	(23)	(24)	(25)	(26)	(27)
17.	Nagaland	4	0.3	0.0	0	0.0	0.0	0	0.0	0.0	0	0.0	-
18.	Orissa	1586	4.5	5.1	234	0.7	2.9	0	0.0	0.0	0	0.0	-
19.	Punjab	150	0.6	0.5	10	0.0	0.1	7	0.0	4.8	0	0.0	-
20.	Rajasthan	2908	5.6	9.4	54	0.1	0.7	3	0.0	2.1	0	0.0	-
21.	Sikkim	22	4.3	0.1	2	0.4	0.0	0	0.0	0.0	0	0.0	-
22.	Tamil Nadu	1779	2.9	5.7	1230	2.0	15.1	5	0.0	3.4	0	0.0	-
23.	Tripura	73	2.0	0.2	0	0.0	0.0	9	0.3	6.2	0	0.0	-
24.	Uttar Pradesh	2423	1.5	7.8	2571	1.6	31.7	3	0.0	2.1	0	0.0	-
25.	West Bengal	1243	1.6	4.0	27	0.0	0.3	2	0.0	1.4	0	0.0	-
	Total States	**30347**	**3.2**	**97.7**	**7929**	**0.8**	**97.6**	**146**	**0.0**	**100.0**	**0**	**0.0**	**-**
Union Territories													
26.	A & N Islands	15	4.1	0.0	2	0.5	0.0	0	0.0	0.0	0	0.0	-
27.	Chandigarh	10	1.2	0.0	10	1.2	0.1	0	0.0	0.0	0	0.0	-
28.	D & N Haveli	1	0.6	0.0	0	0.0	0.0	0	0.0	0.0	0	0.0	-
29.	Daman & Diu	0	0.0	0.0	1	0.8	0.0	0	0.0	0.0	0	0.0	-
30.	Delhi	653	5.0	2.1	172	1.3	2.1	0	0.0	0.0	0	0.0	-
31.	Lakshadweep	1	1.5	0.0	0	0.0	0.0	0	0.0	0.0	0	0.0	-
32.	Pondicherry	19	1.8	0.1	9	0.9	0.1	0	0.0	0.0	0	0.0	-
	Total (UTs)	**699**	**4.5**	**2.3**	**194**	**1.2**	**2.4**	**0**	**0.0**	**0.0**	**0**	**0.0**	**-**
	Total (All-India)	**31046**	**3.2**	**100.0**	**8123**	**0.8**	**100.0**	**146**	**0.0**	**100.0**	**0**	**0.0**	**-**

(Contd.)

(Annexure Contd.)

Sl. No.	State/UT	ITP Act			Ind. Rep. of Women (P) Act			Dowry Proh. Act			Total		
		I	R	P	I	R	P	I	R	P	I	R	P
(1)	(2)	(28)	(29)	(30)	(31)	(32)	(33)	(34)	(35)	(36)	(37)	(38)	(39)
States													
1.	Andhra Pradesh	507	0.7	5.8	40	0.1	20.8	212	0.3	6.1	11201	15.1	8.5
2.	Arunachal Pradesh	0	0.0	0.0	0	0.0	0.0	0	0.0	0.0	125	11.1	0.1
3.	Assam	34	0.1	0.4	0	0.0	0.0	62	0.2	1.8	3388	13.2	2.6
4.	Bihar	37	0.0	0.4	48	0.0	25.0	1488	1.5	42.6	7105	7.3	5.4
5.	Goa	30	2.0	0.3	0	0.0	0.0	0	0.0	0.0	109	7.2	0.1
6.	Gujarat	8	0.0	0.1	2	0.0	1.0	0	0.0	0.0	6658	14.1	5.1
7.	Haryana	4	0.0	0.0	1	0.0	0.5	8	0.0	0.2	3002	15.5	2.3
8.	Himachal Pradesh	1	0.0	0.0	0	0.0	0.0	1	0.0	0.0	778	12.1	0.6
9.	Jammu & Kashmir	1	0.0	0.0	0	0.0	0.0	3	0.0	0.1	1715	18.0	1.3
10.	Karnataka	1403	2.8	16.1	4	0.0	2.1	384	0.8	11.0	5516	10.8	4.2
11.	Kerala	27	0.1	0.3	30	0.1	15.6	8	0.0	0.2	4799	15.1	3.7
12.	Madhya Pradesh	16	0.0	0.2	2	0.0	1.0	128	0.2	3.7	15865	20.5	12.1
13.	Maharashtra	444	0.5	5.1	36	0.0	18.8	24	0.0	0.7	14266	16.0	10.9
14.	Manipur	0	0.0	0.0	0	0.0	0.0	0	0.0	0.0	86	3.6	0.1
15.	Meghalaya	0	0.0	0.0	0	0.0	0.0	0	0.0	0.0	71	3.1	0.1
16.	Mizoram	0	0.0	0.0	0	0.0	0.0	0	0.0	0.0	141	15.6	0.1

(Contd.)

(Annexure Contd.)

(1)	(2)	(28)	(29)	(30)	(31)	(32)	(33)	(34)	(35)	(36)	(37)	(38)	(39)
17.	Nagaland	0	0.0	0.0	1	0.1	0.5	0	0.0	0.0	32	2.0	0.0
18.	Orissa	11	0.0	0.1	2	0.0	1.0	249	0.7	7.1	4450	12.6	3.4
19.	Punjab	5	0.0	0.1	7	0.0	3.6	2	0.0	0.1	1238	5.4	0.9
20.	Rajasthan	47	0.1	0.5	1	0.0	0.5	1	0.0	0.0	12159	23.4	9.3
21.	Sikkim	0	0.0	0.0	0	0.0	0.0	0	0.0	0.0	37	7.0	0.0
22.	Tamil Nadu	5937	9.8	68.3	10	0.0	5.2	269	0.4	7.7	11201	18.4	8.5
23.	Tripura	0	0.0	0.0	0	0.0	0.0	0	0.0	0.0	319	8.9	0.2
24.	Uttar Pradesh	31	0.0	0.4	7	0..0	3.6	633	0.4	18.1	17497	10.7	13.3
25.	West Bengal	43	0.1	0.5	0	0.0	0.0	3	0.0	0.1	6811	8.8	5.2
	Total (States)	**8586**	**0.9**	**98.7**	**191**	**0.0**	**99.5**	**3475**	**0.4**	**99.6**	**128569**	**13.5**	**97.9**
Union Territories													
26.	A & N Islands	0	0.0	0.0	0	0.0	0.0	0	0.0	0.0	26	7.1	0.0
27.	Chandigarh	5	0.6	0.1	0	0.0	0.0	0	0.0	0.0	97	11.5	0.1
28.	D & N Haveli	0	0.0	0.0	0	0.0	0.0	0	0.0	0.0	17	9.4	0.0
29.	Daman & Diu	0	0.0	0.0	0	0.0	0.0	0	0.0	0.0	2	1.5	0.0
30.	Delhi	75	0.6	0.9	1	0.0	0.5	10	0.1	0.3	2556	19.6	1.9
31.	Lakshadweep	0	0.0	0.0	0	0.0	0.0	0	0.0	0.0	2	3.0	0.0
32.	Pondicherry	29	2.8	0.3	0	0.0	0.0	4	0.4	0.1	69	6.6	0.1
	Total (UTs)	**109**	**0.7**	**1.3**	**1**	**0.0**	**0.5**	**14**	**0.1**	**0.4**	**2769**	**17.7**	**2.1**
	Total (All-India)	**8695**	**0.9**	**100.0**	**192**	**0.0**	**100.0**	**3489**	**0.4**	**100.0**	**131338**	**13.5**	**100.0**

* In absence of data for newly created crime heads in crime in india data.
Figures of monthly crime statistics have been used against Daman & Diu UT.

Source: Crime in India data except col. 21 which is based on Monthly crime statistics.
I: Incidence; R: Rate; P: Percentage.

DISPOSAL OF CRIMES AGAINST WOMEN CASES BY POLICE DURING 1997 AND 1998

Sl. No.	Crime Head	Total No. of cases for investigation including pending cases		Percentage of cases investigated		Percentage of cases charge-sheeted		No. of cases pending investigation		Percentage of cases pending investigation	
		1997	1998	1997	1998	1997	1998	1997	1998	1997	1998
1.	Rape	20736	20864	71.7	72.1	62.4	62.1	5828	5793	28.1	27.8
2.	Kidnapping and Abduction	23448	24966	62.8	61.3	36.1	35.9	8586	9565	36.6	38.3
3.	Dowry Deaths	7543	8938	72.3	72.7	63.5	63.8	2048	2393	21.2	26.8
4.	Molestation	34937	35594	86.8	85.0	79.1	77.0	4528	5306	13.0	14.9
5.	Sexual Harassment	6131	8578	92.4	92.1	89.3	88.3	461	668	7.5	7.8
6.	Cruelty by Husband and Relatives	43130	49532	80.5	79.1	67.9	65.9	8268	10248	19.2	20.7
7.	Immoral Traffic (Prevention) Act	9076	9895	86.8	89.3	86.5	89.1	1198	1062	13.2	10.7
8.	Dowry Prohibition Act	3853	4649	70.8	75.3	59.3	62.4	1100	1142	28.6	24.6
9.	Indecent Rep. of Women (P) Act	96	206	85.4	80.1	81.3	62.1	14	41	14.6	19.9
10.	Sati Prevention Act	1	0	100.0		100.0		0	0	0.0	-

Note: Similar details for importation of girls (upto 21 years of age) are not available.

DISPOSAL OF CRIME AGAINST WOMEN CASES BY COURTS DURING 1997 AND 1998

Sl. No.	Crime Head	Total No. of Cases for Trial Including Pending Cases		Percentage of Cases Tried		Percentage of of Cases Convicted		No. of Cases Pending Trial		Percentage of Cases PendingTrial	
		1997	1998	1997	1998	1997	1998	1997	1998	1997	1998
1.	Rape	55863	58655	17.4	16.6	4.9	4.4	45955	48685	82.3	83.0
2.	Kidnapping and Abduction	44262	46165	14.7	14.5	3.9	4.0	37254	39103	84.2	84.7
3.	Dowry Deaths	19435	22055	14.8	15.2	5.2	4.9	16455	18523	84.7	84.0
4.	Molestation	100654	105204	17.1	14.1	6.3	4.3	78200	84869	77.7	80.7
5.	Sexual Harassment	14130	16945	29.5	23.9	18.0	14.4	9437	12407	66.8	73.2
6.	Cruelty by Husband and Relatives	13181	127691	13.0	13.2	3.1	2.6	95409	107192	84.3	84.0
7.	Immoral Traffic (Prevention) Act	12660	14302	54.1	56.8	49.4	53.1	5505	6134	43.5	42.9
8.	Dowry Prohibition Act	8295	8974	22.7	17.8	8.3	5.7	6186	7223	74.6	80.5
9.	Indecent Rep of Women (P) Act	578	625	13.3	13.4	6.2	7.4	499	538	86.3	86.1
10.	Sati Prevention Act	4	1	0.0	100.0	0.0	0.0	1	0	25.0	0.0

VICTIMS OF RAPE UNDER DIFFERENT AGE GROUPS DURING 1998

Sl. No.	State/UT/City	No. of Cases Reported	Number of Victims: Below 10 Years	10-16 Years	16-30 Years	30 Years & Above
(1)	(2)	(3)	(4)	(5)	(6)	(7)
States						
1.	Andhra Pradesh	869	57	231	427	154
2.	Arunachal Pradesh	32	3	7	20	2
3.	Assam	744	25	184	460	75
4.	Bihar	1421	4	193	919	305
5.	Goa	16	1	5	9	1
6.	Gujarat	368	27	108	193	40
7.	Haryana	364	25	106	177	56
8.	Himachal Pradesh	128	5	28	81	14
9.	Jammu & Kashmir	178	0	15	135	28
10.	Karnataka	233	15	64	119	35
11.	Kerala	589	25	146	352	66
12.	Madhya Pradesh	3354	81	725	1882	666
13.	Maharashtra	1154	79	373	522	180
14.	Manipur	13	2	5	4	2
15.	Meghalaya	42	4	7	29	2
16.	Mizoram	84	20	29	28	7
17.	Nagaland	13	1	3	9	0
18.	Orissa	679	11	111	437	120
19.	Punjab	219	13	78	104	24
20.	Rajasthan	1266	25	132	755	354
21.	Sikkim	7	2	0	3	2
22.	Tamil Nadu	362	16	75	233	38
23.	Tripura	73	2	14	57	0
24.	Uttar Pradesh	1605	98	418	845	244
25.	West Bengal	757	15	199	455	88
	Total States	**14570**	**556**	**3256**	**8255**	**2503**

(Contd.)

(Contd.)

(1)	(2)	(3)	(4)	(5)	(6)	(7)
Union Territories						
26.	A & N Islands	4	0	2	2	0
27.	Chandigarh	11	2	2	4	3
28.	D & N Haveli	7	1	1	5	0
29.	Daman & Diu	0	0	0	0	0
30.	Delhi	438	67	172	147	54
31.	Lakshadweep	0	0	0	0	0
32.	Pondicherry	1	0	0	1	0
	Total UTs	**461**	**70**	**177**	**159**	**57**
	Total (ALL-INDIA)	**15031**	**626**	**3433**	**8414**	**2560**
Cities						
33.		20	3	9	7	1
34.	Bangalore	41	4	13	20	4
35.	Bhopal	39	0	8	17	14
36.	Calcutta	27	7	4	15	1
37.	Chennai	24	0	6	18	0
38.	Coimbatore	2	1	1	0	0
39.	Delhi*	365	56	143	122	46
40.	Hyderabad	36	7	16	7	6
41.	Indore	30	1	2	25	2
42.	Jaipur	38	1	7	23	7
43.	Kanpur	41	4	5	25	7
44.	Kochi	10	0	5	3	2
45.	Lucknow	23	0	4	17	2
46.	Ludhiana	17	3	12	2	0
47.	Madurai	3	0	3	0	0
48.	Mumbai	118	9	56	48	5
49.	Nagpur	53	8	15	28	2
50.	Patna	16	0	0	13	3
51.	Pune	56	4	21	27	4
52.	Surat	31	2	10	15	4
53.	Vadodara	9	0	3	6	0
54.	Varanasi	8	0	3	5	0
55.	Vishakhapatnam	11	0	3	8	0

Note: *Victims were more than the cases reported.

Bibliography

Alghazi, M.H., *Torture against Women*, Surya Publication, Mumbai, 2003.

Albari, K.M., *Women, a Vulnerable Lot*, Mumbai, 1985.

Altekar, A.S., *The Position of Women in Hindu Civilization*, Motilal Banarsidas, Varanasi, 1962.

Anshen, R.N., (ed.), *The Family: Its Functions and Destiny*, Harper & Row, New York, 1959.

Asthana, P., *Women's Movement in India*, Vikas Publishing House, New Delhi, 1974.

Baig, T.A., *India's Women Power*, S. Chand & Co., New Delhi, 1976.

Bhasin, K. (ed.), *The Position of Women in India*, Leslie Sawny, Bombay, 1971.

Blalock, H.M. and Blalock, A.B., *Methodology in Social Research*, McGraw-Hill, New York, 1969.

Caplow, T., *Sociology of Work*, Mc-Graw-Hill, New York, 1954.

Chaturvedi, Geeta., *Women Administration in India: A study of the socio-economic background*, RBSA Publication, Jaipur, 1985.

Deckard, B.S, *The Women's Movement*, Harper and Row, New York, 1979.

Drucker, P.F., *An Introductory View of Management*, Harper College Press, New York, 1977.

Evan, M. William, *Organizational Theory Structure, Systems and Environments*, Wiley Interscience Publications, John Wiley and Sons Inc, London, 1976.

Giri Mohini, *Kanya*, Gyan Publishing House, New Delhi, 1998.

Good, W.J., *World Revolution and Family Patterns*, CollierMacMillan, London, 1963.

Gorwaney, N., *Self Image and Social Change: A Study of Female Students*, Sterling Publishers, Delhi, 1977.

Hate, C.A., *Changing Status of Women in Post-Independence India*, Allied Publications, Bombay, 1969.

Inkeles, A. and Smith, D., *Becoming Modern*, Heinmann Educational Books Ltd., London, 1974.

Kuppuswamy, B., *Social Change in India*, Vikas Publishing House, Delhi, 1972.

Mies, M., *Indian Women and Patriarchy: Conflicts and Dilemmas of Students and Working Women*. Concept Publishers, New Delhi, 1980.

Myrdal, A. and Klien, V., *Woman's Two Roles*, Routledge & K. Paul, London, 1968.

Prakash, G., *After Colonialism: Imperial Histories and Post Colonial Displacements*, Princeton University Press, Princeton, 1995.

Rajawat, Mamta, *Human Rights: Burning Issues*, Gyan Publishing House, New Delhi, 2002.

Rani, K., *Role Conflict in Working Wives*, Chetana Publications, New Delhi, 1976.

Roby, Pamela, *Women in the Work Place*, MA. Schenkrnan, Cambridge, UK, 1981.

Vitels, M.S., *Motivation and Morale in Industry*. Morton, New York, 1953.

Watson, T., *Management Organization and Employment Strategy*, Routledge and Kegan Paul, London, 1986.

Whyte, F.W., *Money and Motivation*, Harper and Row. Inc., New York, 1955.

Zaheer, M., *The Myth of Protection*,Nile Publications, Cairo, 2001.

Zeni, A.H., *Exposure of the Weaker Sex*, Pacific Publications, Singapore, 2002.

References

Blau, P. (ed.), *Focus on Social Structure*, an Introduction to the Programme of the ASA meeting in Montreal, 1974.

Blau, P.M., 'A Macrosociological Theory of Social Structure', *American Journal of Sociology*, 1977.

Brayfield, A.H. and Crockatt, W.H., 'Employee attitude and employee performance', *Psychological Bulletin*, 1955.

Burke, P.J. and Reitzes, D.C., 'An Identity Theory Approach to Commitment', *Social Psychological Quarterly*, 1991.

Cofer, C.N. and Appley, M.N., *Motivation Theory and Research*, A Wiley International Edition, John Wiley and Sons Inc., 1964.

Fleishman, E.A., A Relationship Between Incentive, Motivation and Ability Level in Psychomotor, *J. Exp. Psychol.*

French, Elizabeth, G., Effects of Interaction of Achievement Motivation and Intelligence on Problem Solving Success, *American Psychologist*, 1951.

Gender Indicators of Developing Asian and Pacific Countries, 1993, Asian Development Bank.

Human Development Report, UNDP, New York: Oxford University Press, 1996.

Marshall, Katherine, Employed Parents and Division of Housework, *Perspectives*, Autumn, 1993.

Mead, M., Adolescence Issue, *UNICEF News*, 1974.

Noditch, Murray, P. and Demaw, T., 'Locus of Control and Competence', *Journal of Personality*. Dec. 1975.

Report of the Committee on Status of Women in India (1974), *Towards Equality*. Department of Social Welfare, Government of India, New Delhi.

Rotter, J.B., 'Generalized expectancies for internal versus external control or reinforcement'. *Psychological Monographs.* General Applied, 1966.

Safilios-Rothschild, C., The Influence of the Wife's Degree of Work Commitment upon Some Aspects of Family Organization and Dynamics, *Journal of Marriage and the Family*, 1970.

Taylor, Ronald, N., Age and experience as determinants of managerial information processing and decision making performance. *Academy of Management Journal*, 1975.

Index

□□□

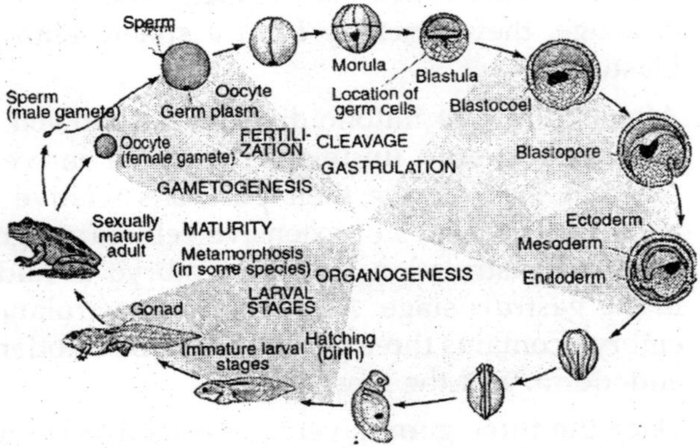

Fig. Developmental history of a frog. The stages from fertilization through hatching (birth) are known collectively as embryogenesis. The region set aside for producing germ cells is shown in bright purple. Gametogenesis, which is completed in the sexually mature adult, begins at different times during development, depending on the species.

One of the major triumphs of descriptive embryology was the idea of a generalizable life cycle. Each animal, whether an earthworm, an eagle, or a beagle, passes through similar stages of development. The major stages of animal development are illustrated in Figure. The life of a new individual is initiated by the fusion of genetic material from the two gametes—the sperm and the egg. This fusion, called fertilization, stimulates the egg to begin development. The stages of development between fertilization and hatching are collectively called embryogenesis.

THE CIRCLE OF LIFE: THE STAGES OF ANIMAL DEVELOPMENT

Throughout the animal kingdom, an incredible variety of embryonic types exist, but most patterns of embryogenesis are variations on five themes:

1. Immediately following fertilization, cleavage occurs. Cleavage is a series of extremely rapid mitotic divisions wherein the enormous volume of zygote cytoplasm is divided into numerous smaller cells.

These cells are called blastomeres, and by the end of cleavage, they generally form a sphere known as a blastula.

2. After the rate of mitotic division has slowed down, the blastomeres undergo dramatic movements wherein they change their positions relative to one another. This series of extensive cell rearrangements is called gastrulation, and the embryo is said to be in the gastrula stage. As a result of gastrulation, the embryo contains three germ layers: the ectoderm, the endoderm, and the mesoderm.

3. Once the three germ layers are established, the cells interact with one another and rearrange themselves to produce tissues and organs. This process is called organogenesis. Many organs contain cells from more than one germ layer, and it is not unusual for the outside of an organ to be derived from one layer and the inside from another. For example, the outer layer of skin comes from the ectoderm, while the inner layer (the dermis) comes from the mesoderm. Also during organogenesis, certain cells undergo long migrations from their place of origin to their final location. These migrating cells include the precursors of blood cells, lymph cells, pigment cells, and gametes. Most of the bones of our face are derived from cells that have migrated ventrally from the dorsal region of the head.

4. Many species a specialized portion of egg cytoplasm gives rise to cells that are the precursors of the gametes (the sperm and egg). The gametes and their precursor cells are collectively called germ cells, and they are set aside for reproductive function. All the other cells of the body are called somatic cells. This separation of somatic cells (which give rise to the individual body) and germ cells (which contribute to the formation of a new generation) is often one of the first differentiations to occur during animal development. The germ cells eventually migrate to

the gonads, where they differentiate into gametes. The development of gametes, called gametogenesis, is usually not completed until the organism has become physically mature. At maturity, the gametes may be released and participate in fertilization to begin a new embryo. The adult organism eventually undergoes senescence and dies.

5. In many species, the organism that hatches from the egg or is born into the world is not sexually mature. Indeed, in most animals, the young organism is a larva that may look significantly different from the adult. Larvae often constitute the stage of life that is used for feeding or dispersal. In many species, the larval stage is the one that lasts the longest, and the adult is a brief stage solely for reproduction. In the silkworm moths, for instance, the adults do not have mouthparts and cannot feed. The larvae must eat enough for the adult to survive and mate. Indeed, most female moths mate as soon as they eclose from their pupa, and they fly only once—to lay their eggs. Then they die.

THE FROG LIFE CYCLE

The development of a frog to show a representative life cycle. Let us look at this life cycle in a bit more detail. First, in most frogs, gametogenesis and fertilization are seasonal events for this animal, because its life depends upon the plants and insects in the pond where it lives and on the temperature of the air and water. A combination of photoperiod (hours of daylight) and temperature tells the pituitary gland of the female frog that it is spring. If the frog is mature, the pituitary gland secretes hormones that stimulate the ovary to make estrogen. Estrogen is a hormone that can instruct the liver to make and secrete the yolk proteins, which are then transported through the blood into the enlarging eggs in the ovary. The yolk is transported into the bottom portion of the egg.

Another ovarian hormone, progesterone, signals the egg to resume its meiotic division. This is necessary because the egg had been "frozen" in the metaphase of its first meiosis. When it has completed this first meiotic division, the egg is released from the ovary and can be fertilized. In many species, the eggs are enclosed in a jelly coat that acts to enhance their size (so they won't be as easily eaten), to protect them against bacteria, and to attract and activate sperm.

Sperm also occur on a seasonal basis. The male leopard frogs make their sperm in the summer, and by the time they begin hibernation in autumn, they have all the sperm that are to be available for the following spring's breeding season. In most species of frogs, fertilization is external. The male frog grabs the female's back and fertilizes the eggs as the female frog releases them. *Rana pipiens* usually lays around 2500 eggs, while the bullfrog, *Rana catesbiana,* can lay as many as 20,000. Some species lay their eggs in pond vegetation, and the jelly adheres to the plants and anchors the eggs. Other species float their eggs into the centre of the pond without any support.

Fertilization accomplishes several things. First, it allows the egg to complete its second meiotic division, which provides the egg with a haploid pronucleus. The egg pronucleus and the sperm pronucleus will meet in the egg cytoplasm to form the diploid zygotic nucleus. Second, fertilization causes the cytoplasm of the egg to move such that different parts of the cytoplasm find themselves in new locations. Third, fertilization activates those molecules necessary to begin cell cleavage and development. The sperm and egg die quickly unless fertilization occurs.

During cleavage, the volume of the frog egg stays the same, but it is divided into tens of thousands of cells. The animal hemisphere of the egg divides faster than the vegetal hemisphere does, and the cells of the vegetal hemisphere become progressively larger the more vegetal the cytoplasm. A fluid-filled cavity, the blastocoel, forms in the animal hemisphere. This cavity will be important for allowing cell movements to occur during gastrulation.

Gastrulation in the frog begins at a point on the embryo surface roughly 180 degrees opposite the point of sperm entry with the formation of a dimple, called the blastopore. Cells migrate through the blastopore and toward the animal pole. These cells become the dorsal mesoderm. The blastopore expands into a circle, and cells migrating through this circle become the lateral and ventral mesoderm. The cells remaining on the outside become the ectoderm, and this outer layer expands vegetally to enclose the entire embryo. The large yolky cells that remain at the vegetal hemisphere (until they are encircled by the ectoderm) become the endoderm. Thus, at the end of gastrulation, the ectoderm (the precursor of the epidermis and nerves) is on the outside of the embryo, the endoderm (the precursor of the gut lining) is on the inside of the embryo, and the mesoderm (the precursor of connective tissue, blood, skeleton, gonads, and kidneys) is between them.

Organogenesis begins when the notochord—a rod of mesodermal cells in the most dorsal portion of the embryo—tells the ectodermal cells above it that they are not going to become skin. Rather, these dorsal ectoderm cells are to form a tube and become the nervous system. At this stage, the embryo is called a neurula. The neural precursor cells elongate, stretch, and fold into the embryo, forming the neural tube. The future back epidermal cells cover them. The cells that had connected the neural tube to the epidermis become the neural crest cells. The neural crest cells are almost like a fourth germ layer. They give rise to the pigment cells of the body (the melanocytes), the peripheral neurons, and the cartilage of the face. Once the neural tube has formed, it induces changes in its neighbours, and organogenesis continues. The mesodermal tissue adjacent to the notochord becomes segmented into somites, the precursors of the frog's back muscles, spinal cord, and dermis (the inner portion of the skin). These somites appear as blocks of mesodermal tissue. The embryo develops a mouth and an anus, and it elongates into the typical tadpole structure. The neurons make their connections to the muscles and to other neurons, the gills form, and the larva is ready to hatch from its egg jelly. The hatched tadpole will soon feed for itself once the yolk supply given it by its mother is exhausted.

Metamorphosis of the tadpole larva into an adult frog is one of the most striking transformations in all of biology. In amphibians, metamorphosis is initiated by hormones from the tadpole's thyroid gland, and these changes prepare an aquatic organism for a terrestrial existence. In anurans (frogs and toads), the metamorphic changes are most striking, and almost every organ is subject to modification. The changes in form are very obvious. For locomotion, the hindlimbs and forelimbs differentiate as the paddle tail recedes. The cartilaginous skull of the tadpole is replaced by the predominantly bony skull of the young frog. The horny teeth the tadpole uses to tear up pond plants disappear as the mouth and jaw take a new shape, and the fly-catching tongue muscle of the frog develops. Meanwhile the large intestine characteristic of herbivores shortens to suit the more carnivorous diet of the adult frog. The gills regress, and the lungs enlarge.

As metamorphosis ends, the development of the first germ cells begins. In *Rana pipiens,* egg development lasts 3 years. At that time, the frog is sexually mature and can produce offspring of her own. The speed of metamorphosis is carefully keyed to environmental pressures. In temperate regions, for instance, metamorphosis must occur before the pond becomes frozen. A *Rana pipiens* frog can burrow into the mud and survive the winter; its tadpole cannot. Since the bottom half of the egg usually contains the yolk, it divides more slowly (because the large yolk deposits interfere with cleavage). This portion is the vegetal hemisphere of the egg. Conversely, the upper half of the egg usually has less yolk and divides faster. This upper portion is called the animal hemisphere of the egg.

THE EVOLUTION OF DEVELOPMENTAL PATTERNS IN UNICELLULAR PROTISTS

Every living organism develops. Development can be seen even among the unicellular organisms. Moreover, by studying the development of unicellular protists.

Control of Developmental Morphogenesis: The Role of the Nucleus

A century ago, it had not yet been proved that the nucleus contained hereditary or developmental information. Some of the best evidence for this theory came from studies in which unicellular organisms were fragmented into nucleate and anucleate pieces. When various protists were cut into fragments, nearly all the pieces died. However, the fragments containing nuclei were able to live and to regenerate entire complex cellular structures.

Nuclear control of cell morphogenesis and the interaction of nucleus and cytoplasm are beautifully demonstrated in studies of *Acetabularia*. This enormous single cell (2–4 cm long) consists of three parts: a cap, a stalk, and a rhizoid. The rhizoid is located at the base of the cell and holds it to the substrate. The single nucleus of the cell resides within the rhizoid. The size of *Acetabularia* and the location of its nucleus allow investigators to remove the nucleus from one cell and replace it with a nucleus from another cell. J. Hämmerling took advantage of these unique features and exchanged nuclei between two morphologically distinct species, these two species have very different cap structures. Hämmerling found that when he transferred the nucleus from one species into the stalk of another species, the newly formed cap eventually assumed the form associated with the *donor* nucleus. Thus, the nucleus was seen to control *Acetabularia* development.

The formation of a cap is a complex morphogenic event involving the synthesis of numerous proteins, which must be accumulated in a certain portion of the cell and then assembled into complex, species-specific structures. The transplanted nucleus does indeed direct the synthesis of its species-specific cap, but it takes several weeks to do so. Moreover, if the nucleus is removed from an *Acetabularia* cell early in development, before it first forms a cap, a normal cap is formed weeks later, even though the organism will eventually die. These studies suggest that:

1. The nucleus contains information specifying the type of cap produced (i.e., it contains the genetic information that specifies the proteins required for the production of a certain type of cap), and
2. Material containing this information enters the cytoplasm long before cap production occurs. This information in the cytoplasm is not used for several weeks.

One current hypothesis proposed to explain these observations is that the nucleus synthesizes a stable mRNA that lies dormant in the cytoplasm until the time of cap formation. This hypothesis is supported by an observation that Hämmerling published in 1934. Hämmerling fractionated young *Acetabularia* into several parts. The portion with the nucleus eventually formed a new cap, as expected; so did the apical tip of the stalk. However, the intermediate portion of the stalk did not form a cap. Thus, Hämmerling postulated (nearly 30 years before the existence of mRNA was known) that the instructions for cap formation originated in the nucleus and were somehow stored in a dormant form near the tip of the stalk. Many years later, researchers established that nucleus-derived mRNA does accumulate in the tip of the stalk, and that the destruction of this mRNA or the inhibition of protein synthesis in this region prevents cap formation.

It is clear from the preceding discussion that nuclear transcription plays an important role in the formation of the *Acetabularia* cap. But note that the cytoplasm also plays an essential role in cap formation. The mRNAs are not translated for weeks, even though they are in the cytoplasm. Something in the cytoplasm controls when the message is utilized. Hence, the expression of the cap is controlled not only by nuclear transcription, but also by the translation of the cytoplasmic RNA. In this unicellular organism, "development" is controlled at both the transcriptional and translational levels.

Unicellular Protists and the Origins of Sexual Reproduction

Sexual reproduction is another invention of the protists that has had a profound effect on more complex organisms. It should be noted that sex and reproduction are two distinct and separable processes. Reproduction involves the creation of new individuals. Sex involves the combining of genes from two different individuals into new arrangements. Reproduction in the absence of sex is characteristic of organisms that reproduce by fission (i.e., splitting into two); there is no sorting of genes when an amoeba divides or when a hydra buds off cells to form a new colony.

Sex without reproduction is also common among unicellular organisms. Bacteria are able to transmit genes from one individual to another by means of sex pili. This transmission is separate from reproduction. Protists are also able to reassort genes without reproduction. Paramecia, for instance, reproduce by fission, but sex is accomplished by conjugation. When two paramecia join together, they link their oral apparatuses and form a cytoplasmic connection through which they can exchange genetic material. Each macronucleus (which controls the metabolism of the organism) degenerates, while each micronucleus undergoes meiosis to produce eight haploid micronuclei, of which all but one degenerate. The remaining micronucleus divides once more to form a stationary micronucleus and a migratory micronucleus. Each migratory micronucleus crosses the cytoplasmic bridge and fuses with ("fertilizes") the stationary micronucleus, thereby creating a new diploid nucleus in each cell. This diploid nucleus then divides mitotically to give rise to a new micronucleus and a new macronucleus as the two partners disengage. Therefore, no reproduction has occurred, only sex.

The union of these two distinct processes, sex and reproduction, into sexual reproduction is seen in unicellular eukaryotes. This organism is usually haploid, having just one copy of each chromosome (like a mammalian gamete). The individuals of each species, however, are divided into two mating types: plus and minus. When a plus and a minus meet, they join their cytoplasms, and their nuclei fuse to form a diploid zygote. This zygote is the only diploid cell in the life cycle, and it eventually undergoes meiosis to form four new *Chlamydomonas* cells. This is true sexual reproduction, for chromosomes are reassorted during the meiotic divisions and more individuals are formed. Note that in this protist type of sexual reproduction, the gametes are morphologically identical; the distinction between sperm and egg has not yet been made.

In evolving sexual reproduction, two important advances had to be achieved. The first was the mechanism of meiosis, whereby the diploid complement of chromosomes is reduced to the haploid state. The second was a mechanism whereby the two different mating types could recognize each other. In *Chlamydomonas*, recognition occurs first on the flagellar membranes. The flagella of two individuals twist around each other, enabling specific regions of the cell membranes to come together. These specialized regions contain mating type-specific components that enable the cytoplasms to fuse. Following flagellar agglutination, the plus individuals initiate fusion by extending a fertilization tube. This tube contacts and fuses with a specific site on the minus individual. Interestingly, the mechanism used to extend this tube—the polymerization of the protein actin—is also used to extend processes of sea urchin eggs and sperm. In later Chapter, we will see that the recognition and fusion of sperm and egg occur in an amazingly similar manner.

Unicellular eukaryotes appear to possess the basic elements of the developmental processes that characterize the more complex organisms: protein synthesis is controlled such that certain proteins are made only at certain times and in certain places; the structures of individual genes and chromosomes are as they will be throughout eukaryotic evolution; mitosis and meiosis have been perfected; and sexual reproduction exists, involving cooperation between individual cells. Such intercellular cooperation becomes even more important with the evolution of multicellular organisms.

MULTICELLULARITY: THE EVOLUTION OF DIFFERENTIATION

One of evolution's most important experiments was the creation of multicellular organisms. There appear to be several paths by which single cells evolved multicellular arrangements; we will discuss only two of them here. The first path involves the orderly division of the reproductive cell and the subsequent differentiation of its progeny into different cell types. This path to multicellularity can be seen in a remarkable series of multicellular organisms collectively referred to as the family Volvocaceae, or the volvocaceans.

The Volvocaceans

The simpler organisms among the volvocaceans are ordered assemblies of numerous cells, each resembling the unicellular protist *Chlamydomonas*, to which they are related. A single organism of the volvocacean genus *Gonium*, for example, consists of a flat plate of 4 to 16 cells, each with its own flagellum. In a related genus, *Pandorina*, the 16 cells form a sphere; and in *Eudorina*, the sphere contains 32 or 64 cells arranged in a regular pattern. In these organisms, then, a very important developmental principle has been worked out: the ordered division of one cell to generate a number of cells that are organized in a predictable fashion. As occurs during cleavage in most animal embryos, the cell divisions by which a single volvocacean cell produces an organism of 4 to 64 cells occur in very rapid sequence and in the absence of cell growth.

The next two genera of the volvocacean series exhibit another important principle of development: the differentiation of cell types within an individual organism. The reproductive cells become differentiated from the somatic cells. In all the genera mentioned earlier, every cell can, and normally does, produce a complete new organism by mitosis. In the genera *Pleodorina* and *Volvox*, however, relatively few cells can reproduce. In *Pleodorina californica*, the cells in the anterior region are restricted to a somatic function; only those cells on the posterior side can reproduce. In *P. californica*, a colony usually has 128 or 64 cells, and the ratio of the number of somatic cells to the number of reproductive cells is usually 3:5. Thus, a 128-cell colony typically has 48 somatic cells, and a 64-cell colony has 24.

In *Volvox*, almost all the cells are somatic, and very few of the cells are able to produce new individuals. In some species of *Volvox,* reproductive cells, as in *Pleodorina,* are derived from cells that originally look and function like somatic cells before they enlarge and divide to form new progeny. However, in other members of the genus, such as *V. carteri,* there is a complete division of labour: the reproductive cells that will create the next generation are set aside during the division of the original cell that is forming a new individual. The reproductive cells never develop functional flagella and never contribute to motility or other somatic functions of the individual; they are entirely specialized for reproduction. Thus, although the simpler volvocaceans may be thought of as colonial organisms (because each cell is capable of independent existence and of perpetuating the species), in *V. carteri* we have a truly multicellular organism with two distinct and interdependent cell types (somatic and reproductive), both of which are required for perpetuation of the species. Although not all animals set aside the reproductive cells from the somatic cells (and plants hardly ever do), this separation of germ cells from somatic cells early in development is characteristic of many animal phyla and will be discussed in more detail in later Chapter.

Although all the volvocaceans, like their unicellular relative *Chlamydomonas,* reproduce predominantly by asexual means, they are also capable of sexual reproduction, which involves the production and fusion of haploid gametes. Sexual reproduction is isogamous ("the same gametes"), since the haploid gametes that meet are similar in size, structure, and motility. However, in other species of *Chlamydomonas*—as well as many species of colonial volvocaceans—swimming gametes of very different sizes are produced by the different mating types. This pattern is called heterogamy ("different gametes"). But the larger volvocaceans have evolved a specialized form of heterogamy, called oogamy, which involves the production of large, relatively immotile eggs by one mating type and small, motile sperm by the other. Here we see one type of gamete specialized for the retention of nutritional and developmental resources and the other type of gamete specialized for the transport of nuclei. Thus, the volvocaceans include the simplest organisms that have distinguishable male and female members of the species and that have distinct developmental pathways for the production of eggs or sperm. In all the volvocaceans, the fertilization reaction resembles that of *Chlamydomonas* in that it results in the production of a dormant diploid zygote, which is capable of surviving harsh environmental conditions. When conditions allow the zygote to germinate, it first undergoes meiosis to produce haploid offspring of the two different mating types in equal numbers.

DIFFERENTIATION AND MORPHOGENESIS IN DICTYOSTELIUM: CELL ADHESION

The Life Cycle of Dictyostelium

Another type of multicellular organization derived from unicellular organisms is found in *Dictyostelium discoideum.* In its asexual cycle, solitary haploid amoebae (called myxamoebae or "social amoebae" to distinguish them from amoeba species that always remain solitary) live on decaying logs, eating bacteria and reproducing by binary fission. When they have exhausted their food supply, tens of thousands of these myxamoebae join together to form moving streams of cells that converge at a central point. Here they pile atop one another to produce a conical mound called a tight aggregate. Subsequently, a tip arises at the top of this mound, and the tight aggregate bends over to produce the migrating slug (with the tip at the front). The slug (often given the more dignified title of pseudoplasmodium or grex) is usually 2–4 mm long and is encased in a slimy sheath. The grex begins to migrate (if the environment is dark and moist) with its anterior tip slightly raised. When it reaches an illuminated area, migration ceases, and the grex differentiates into a fruiting body composed of spore cells and a stalk. The anterior cells, representing 15–20% of the entire cellular population, form the tubed stalk. This process begins as some of the central anterior cells, the prestalk cells, begin secreting an extracellular coat and extending a tube through the grex. As the prestalk cells differentiate, they form vacuoles and enlarge, lifting up the mass of prespore cells that had made up the posterior four-fifths of the grex. The stalk cells die, but the prespore cells, elevated above the stalk, become spore cells. These spore cells disperse, each one becoming a new myxamoeba.

In addition to this asexual cycle, there is a possibility for sex in *Dictyostelium.* Two myxamoebae can fuse to create a giant cell, which digests all the other cells of the aggregate. When it has eaten all its neighbours, it encysts itself in a thick wall and undergoes meiotic and mitotic divisions; eventually, new myxamoebae are liberated.

Dictyostelium has been a wonderful experimental organism for developmental biologists because initially identical cells are differentiated into one of two alternative cell types, spore and stalk. It is also an organism wherein individual cells come together to form a cohesive structure composed of differentiated cell types, akin to tissue formation in more complex organisms. The aggregation of thousands of myxamoebae into a single organism is an incredible feat of organization that invites experimentation to answer questions about the mechanisms involved.

Aggregation of Dictyostelium Cells

The first question is, What causes the myxamoebae to aggregate? Time-lapse microcinematography has shown that no directed movement occurs during the first 4–5 hours following nutrient starvation. During the next 5 hours, however, the cells move at about 20 ìm/min for 100 seconds. This movement ceases for about 4 minutes, then resumes. Although the movement is directed toward a central point, it is not a simple radial movement. Rather, cells join with one another to form streams; the streams converge into larger streams, and eventually all streams merge at the centre. Bonner and Shaffer showed that this movement is due to chemotaxis: the cells are guided to aggregation centres by a soluble substance. This substance was later identified as cyclic adenosine 3′,5′-monophosphate (cAMP), the chemical structure.

Aggregation is initiated as each of the cells begins to synthesize cAMP. There are no dominant cells that begin the secretion or control the others. Rather, the sites of aggregation are determined by the distribution of myxamoebae. Neighbouring cells respond to cAMP in two ways: they initiate a movement toward the cAMP pulse, and they release cAMP of their own. After this, the cell is unresponsive to further cAMP pulses for several minutes. The result is a rotating spiral wave of cAMP that is propagated throughout the population of cells. As each wave arrives, the cells take another step toward the centre.

The differentiation of individual myxamoebae into either stalk (somatic) or spore (reproductive) cells is a complex matter. Raper and Bonner demonstrated that the anterior cells normally become stalk, while the remaining, posterior cells are usually destined to form spores. However, surgically removing the anterior part of the slug does not abolish its ability to form a stalk. Rather, the cells that now find themselves at the anterior end (and which originally had been destined to produce spores) now form the stalk. Somehow a decision is made so that whichever cells are anterior become stalk cells and whichever are posterior become spores. This ability of cells to change their developmental fates according to their location within the whole organism and thereby compensate for missing parts is called regulation.

Cell Adhesion Molecules in Dictyostelium

How do individual cells stick together to form a cohesive organism? This problem is the same one that embryonic cells face, and the solution that evolved in the protists is the same one used by embryos: developmentally regulated cell adhesion molecules.

While growing mitotically on bacteria, *Dictyostelium* cells do not adhere to one another. However, once cell division stops, the cells become increasingly adhesive, reaching a plateau of maximum cohesiveness around 8 hours after starvation. The initial cell-cell adhesion is mediated by a 24,000-Da (24-kDa) glycoprotein that is absent in myxamoebae but appears shortly after division ceases. This protein is synthesized from newly transcribed mRNA and becomes localized in the cell membranes of the myxamoebae. If myxamoebae are treated with antibodies that bind to and mask this protein, they will not stick to one another, and all subsequent development ceases.

Once this initial aggregation has occurred, it is stabilized by a second cell adhesion molecule. This 80-kDa glycoprotein is also synthesized during the aggregation phase. If it is defective or absent in the cells, small slugs will form, and their fruiting bodies will be only about one-third the normal size. Thus, the second cell adhesion system seems to be needed for retaining a large enough number of cells to form large fruiting bodies. In addition, a third cell adhesion system is activated late in development, while the slug is migrating. This protein appears to be important in the movement of the prestalk cells to the apex of the mound. Thus, *Dictyostelium* has evolved three developmentally regulated systems of cell-cell adhesion that are necessary for the morphogenesis of individual cells into a coherent organism. As we will see in subsequent chapters, metazoan cells also use cell adhesion molecules to form the tissues and organs of the embryo.

Dictyostelium is a "part-time multicellular organism" that does not form many cell types, and the more complex multicellular organisms do not form by the aggregation of formerly independent cells. Nevertheless, many of the principles of development demonstrated by this "simple" organism also appear in embryos of more complex phyla. The ability of individual cells to sense a chemical gradient (as in the myxamoeba's response to cAMP) is very important for cell migration and morphogenesis during animal development. Moreover, the role of cell surface proteins in cell cohesiveness is seen throughout the animal kingdom, and differentiation-inducing molecules are beginning to be isolated in metazoan organisms.

Differentiation in Dictyostelium

Differentiation into stalk cell or spore cell reflects another major phenomenon of embryogenesis: the cell's selection of a developmental pathway. Cells often select a particular developmental fate when alternatives are available. A particular cell in a vertebrate embryo, for instance, can become either an epidermal skin cell or a neuron. In *Dictyostelium,* a simple dichotomous decision, because only two cell types are possible. How is it that a given cell becomes a stalk cell or a spore cell? Although the details are not fully known, a cell's fate appears to be regulated by certain diffusible molecules. The two major candidates are differentiation-inducing factor (DIF) and cAMP. DIF appears to be necessary for stalk cell differentiation. This factor, like the sex-inducing factor of *Volvox,* is effective at very low concentrations ($10^{-10}M$); and, like the *Volvox* protein, it appears to induce differentiation into a particular type of cell. When added to isolated myxamoebae or even to prespore (posterior) cells, it causes them to form stalk cells. The synthesis of this low molecular weight lipid is genetically regulated, for there are mutant strains of *Dictyostelium* that form only spore precursors and no stalk cells. When DIF is added to these mutant cultures, stalk cells are able to differentiate, and new prestalk-specific mRNAs are seen in the cell cytoplasm. While the mechanisms by which DIF induces 20% of the grex cells to become stalk tissue are still controversial, DIF may act by releasing calcium ions from intracellular compartments within the cell.

Although DIF stimulates myxamoebae to become prestalk cells, the differentiation of prespore cells is most likely controlled by the continuing pulses of cAMP. High concentrations of cAMP initiate the expression of prespore-specific mRNAs in aggregated myxamoebae. Moreover, when slugs are placed in a medium containing an enzyme that destroys extracellular cAMP, the prespore cells lose their differentiated characteristics

DEVELOPMENTAL PATTERNS AMONG THE METAZOA

Since the remainder of this book concerns the development of metazoans—multicellular animals that pass through embryonic stages of development—we will present an overview of their developmental patterns here. The most striking pattern is that life has not evolved in a straight line; rather, there are several branching evolutionary paths. We can see that metazoans belong to one of three major branches: Diploblasts, protostomes, and deuterostomes.

Sponges develop in a manner so different from that of any other animal group that some taxonomists do not consider them metazoans at all, and call them "parazoans." A sponge has three major types of somatic cells, but one of these, the archeocyte, can differentiate into all the other cell types in the body. Individual cells of a sponge passed through a sieve can reaggregate to form new sponges. Moreover, in some instances, such reaggregation is species-specific: if individual sponge cells from two different species are mixed together, each of the sponges that re-forms contains cells from only one species. In these cases, it is thought that the motile archeocytes collect cells from their own species and not from others. Sponges contain no mesoderm, so the Porifera have no true organ systems; nor do they have a digestive tube or circulatory system, nerves, or muscles. Thus, even though they pass through an embryonic and a larval stage, sponges are very unlike most metazoans. However, sponges do share many features of development (including gene regulatory proteins and signaling cascades) with all the other animal phyla, suggesting that they share a common origin.

Diploblasts

Diploblastic animals are those who have ectoderm and endoderm, but no true mesoderm. These include the cnidarians (jellyfish and hydras) and the ctenophores (comb jellies).

Cnidrians and ctenophores constitute the Radiata, so called because they have radial symmetry, like that of a tube or a wheel. In these animals, the mesoderm is rudimentary, consisting of sparsely scattered cells in a gelatinous matrix.

Protostomes and Deuterostomes

Most metazoans have bilateral symmetry and three germ layers. The animals of these phyla, known collectively as the

Bilatera, are classified as either protostomes or deuterostomes. All Bilateria are thought to have descended from a primitive type of flatworm. These flatworms were the first to have a true mesoderm (although it was not hollowed out to form a body cavity), and they may have resembled the larvae of certain contemporary coelenterates.

There are two divisions of bilaterian phyla, the protostomes and the deuterostomes. Protostomes (Greek, "mouth first"), which include the mollusc, arthropod, and worm phyla, are so called because the mouth is formed first, at or near the opening to the gut, which is produced during gastrulation. The anus forms later at another location. The coelom, or body cavity, of these animals forms from the hollowing out of a previously solid cord of mesodermal cells.

There are two major branches of the protostomes. The ecdysozoa includes those animals that molt. Its major constituent is Arthropoda, a phylum containing insects, arachnids, mites, crustaceans, and millipedes. The second major group of protostomes are the lophotrochozoa. They are characterized by a common type of cleavage (spiral), a common larval form, and a distinctive feeding apparatus. These phyla include annelids, molluscs, and flatworms.

Phyla in the deuterostome lineage include the chordates and echinoderms. Although it may seem strange to classify humans, fish, and frogs in the same group as starfish and sea urchins, certain embryological features stress this kinship. First, in deuterostomes ("mouth second"), the mouth opening is formed after the anal opening. Also, whereas protostomes generally form their body cavities by hollowing out a solid mesodermal block (schizocoelous formation of the body cavity), most deuterostomes form their body cavities from mesodermal pouches extending from the gut (enterocoelous formation of the body cavity). It should be mentioned that there are many exceptions to these generalizations.

The evolution of organisms depends on inherited changes in their development. One of the greatest evolutionary advances—the amniote egg—occurred among the deuterostomes. This type of egg, exemplified by that of a chicken, is thought to have originated in the amphibian ancestors of reptiles about 255 million years ago. The amniote egg allowed vertebrates to roam on land, far from existing ponds. Whereas most amphibians must return to water to lay their eggs, the amniote egg carries its own water and food supplies. It is fertilized internally and contains yolk to nourish the developing embryo. Moreover, the amniote egg contains four sacs: the yolk sac, which stores nutritive proteins; the amnion, which contains the fluid bathing the embryo; the allantois, in which waste materials from embryonic metabolism collect; and the chorion, which interacts with the outside environment, selectively allowing materials to reach the embryo. The entire structure is encased in a shell that allows the diffusion of oxygen but is hard enough to protect the embryo from environmental assaults and dehydration. A similar development of egg casings enabled arthropods to be the first terrestrial invertebrates. Thus, the final crossing of the boundary between water and land occurred with the modification of the earliest stage in development: the egg.

Embryology provides an endless assortment of fascinating animals and problems to study. In this text, we will use but a small sample of them to illustrate the major principles of animal development. This sample is an incredibly small collection. We are merely observing a small tidepool within our reach, while the whole ocean of developmental phenomena lies before us.

After a brief outline of the experimental and genetic approaches to developmental biology, we will investigate the early stages of animal embryogenesis: fertilization, cleavage, gastrulation, and the establishment of the body axes. Later chapters will concentrate on the genetic and cellular mechanisms by which animal bodies are constructed. Although an attempt has been made to survey the important variations throughout the animal kingdom, a certain deuterostome chauvinism may be apparent.

Chapter 3

Principles of Experimental Embryology

Descriptive embryology and evolutionary embryology both had their roots in anatomy. At the end of the nineteenth century, however, the new biological science of physiology made inroads into embryological research. The questions of "what?" became questions of "how?" A new generation of embryologists felt that embryology should not merely be a guide to the study of anatomy and evolution, but should answer the question, "How does an egg become an adult?" Embryologists were to study the mechanisms of organ formation (morphogenesis) and differentiation. This new programme was called *Entwicklungsmechanik,* often translated as "causal embryology," "physiological embryology," or "developmental mechanics." Its goals were to find the molecules and processes that caused the visible changes in embryos. Experimentation was to supplement observation in the study of embryos, and embryologists were expected to discover the properties of the embryo by seeing how the embryonic cells responded to perturbations and disruptions. Wilhelm Roux, one of the founders of this branch of embryology, saw it as a grand undertaking:

We must not hide from ourselves the fact that the causal investigation of organisms is one of the most difficult, if not the most difficult, problem which the human intellect has attempted to solve ... since every new cause ascertained only gives rise to fresh questions regarding the cause of this cause.

In this chapter, we will discuss three of the major research programmes in experimental embryology. The first concerns how forces outside the embryo influence its development. The second concerns how forces within the embryo cause the differentiation of its cells. The third looks at how the cells order themselves into tissues and organs.

ENVIRONMENTAL DEVELOPMENTAL BIOLOGY

The developing embryo is not isolated from its environment. In numerous instances, environmental cues are a fundamental part of the organism's life cycle. Moreover, removing or altering these environmental parameters can alter development.

Environmental Sex Determination

When developmental mechanics was first formulated, some of the obvious variables to manipulate were the temperature and media in which embryos were developing. These early studies initiated several experimental programmes on the effects of the environment on development. For instance, Baltzer showed that the sex of the echiuroid worm *Bonellia viridis* depended on where the *Bonellia* larva settled. The female *Bonellia* worm is a marine, rock-dwelling animal, with a body about 10 cm long. She has a proboscis that can extend over a meter in length. The male *Bonellia,* however, is only 1–3 mm long and resides within the uterus of the female, fertilizing her eggs. Baltzer showed that if a *Bonellia* larva settles on the seafloor, it becomes a female. However, should a larva land on a female's proboscis (which apparently emits chemical signals that attract the larva), it enters the female's mouth, migrates into her uterus, and differentiates into a male. Thus, if a larva lands on the seafloor, it becomes female; if it settles on a proboscis, it becomes male. Baltzer and Leutert were able to duplicate this phenomenon in the labouratory, incubating larvae in either the absence or presence of adult females.

Sex Determination in a Vertebrate: Alligator

Recent research has shown that the effects of the environment on development can have important consequences. Such research has shown that the sex of the alligators, crocodiles, and many other reptiles depends not on chromosomes, but on temperature. After studying the sex determination of the Mississippi alligator both in the labouratory and in the field, Ferguson and Joanen concluded that sex is determined by the temperature of the egg during the second and third weeks of incubation. Eggs incubated at 30°C or below during this time period produce female alligators, whereas those eggs incubated at 34°C or above produce males. (At 32°C, 87% of the hatchlings were female.) Moreover, nests constructed on levees (close to 34°C) give rise to males, whereas nests built in wet marshes (close to 30°C) produce females. These findings are obviously important to wildlife managers and farmers who wish to breed this species; but they also raise questions of environmental policy. The shade of buildings or the heat of thermal effluents can have dramatic effects on the sex ratios of reptiles. We will discuss the mechanisms of temperature-dependent sex determination further in later Chapter.

ADAPTATION OF EMBRYOS AND LARVAE TO THEIR ENVIRONMENTS

Norms of Reaction

Another programme of environmental developmental biology concerns how the embryo adapts to its particular environment. August Weismann pioneered the study of larval adaptations, and recent research in this area has provided some fascinating insights into how an organism's development is keyed to its environment. Weismann noted that butterflies that hatched during different seasons were coloured differently, and that this season-dependent colouration could be mimicked by incubating larvae at different temperatures.

Phenotypic variations caused by environmental differences are often called morphs. One example of such seasonal variation is the European map butterfly, *Araschnia lèvana,* which has two seasonal phenotypes so different that Linnaeus classified them as two different species. The spring morph is bright orange with black spots, while the summer form is mostly black with a white band. The change from spring to summer morph is controlled by changes in both day length and temperature during the larval period. When researchers experimentally mimic spring conditions, summer caterpillars can give rise to "spring" butterflies.

Another dramatic example of seasonal change in development occurs in the moth *Nemoria arizonaria*. This moth has a fairly typical insect life cycle. Eggs hatch in the spring, and the caterpillars feed on young oak flowers (catkins). These larvae metamorphose in the late spring, mate in the summer, and produce another brood of caterpillars on the oak trees. These caterpillars eat the oak leaves, metamorphose, and mate. Their eggs overwinter to start the cycle over again next spring. What is remarkable is that the caterpillars that hatch in the spring look nothing like their progeny that hatch in the summer. The caterpillars that hatch in the spring and eat oak catkins (flowers) are yellow-brown, rugose, and beaded, resembling nothing else but an oak catkin. They are magnificently camouflaged against predation. But what of the caterpillars that hatch in the summer, after all the catkins are gone? They, too, are well camouflaged, resembling year-old oak twigs. What controls this difference? By doing reciprocal feeding experiments, Greene was able to convert spring caterpillars into summer morphs by feeding them oak leaves. The reciprocal experiment did not turn the summer morphs into catkin-like caterpillars. Thus, it appears that the catkin form is the "default state" and that something induces the twiglike morphology. That something is probably a tannin that is concentrated in oak leaves as they mature.

Embryologists have emphasized that what gets inherited is not a deterministic genotype, but rather a genotype that encodes a potential range of phenotypes. The environment is often able to select the phenotype that is adaptive for that season or habitat. This continuous range of phenotypes expressed by a single genotype across a range of environmental conditions is called the reaction norm. The reaction norm is thus a property of the genome and is also subject to selection. Different genotypes will be expected to differ in the direction and amount of plasticity that they are able to express.

PROTECTION OF THE EGG BY SUNSCREENS AND REPAIR ENZYMES

The survival of embryos in their environments poses major problems. Indeed, as Darwin clearly noted, most eggs and embryos fail to survive. A sea urchin may broadcast tens of thousands of eggs into the seawater, but only one or two of the resulting embryos will become adult urchins. Most become food for other organisms. Moreover, if the environment changes, embryonic survival may be increased or decreased dramatically. For instance, many eggs and early embryos lie in direct sunlight for long periods. If we lie in the sun for hours without sunscreen, we get sunburn from the ultraviolet rays of the sun; this radiation is harmful to our DNA. How can eggs survive all those hours of constant exposure to the sun (often on the same beaches where we sun ourselves)? First, it seems that many eggs have evolved natural sunscreens. The eggs of many marine organisms possess high concentrations of mycosporine amino acid pigments, which absorb ultraviolet radiation (UV-B). Moreover, just like our melanin pigment, these pigments can be induced by exposure to UV-B radiation. The eggs of tunicates are very resistant to UV-B radiation, and much of this resistance comes from extracellular coats that are enriched with mycosporine compounds. Similarly, Adams and Shick experimentally modulated the amount of mycosporine amino acids in sea urchin eggs and found that embryos from eggs with more of these compounds were better protected from UV damage than embryos with less. So some of the beautiful pigments found in marine eggs have a very practical function.

The possibility exists that the recent global decline of amphibian populations may be caused by increasing amounts of UV-B reaching the Earth's surface. Populations of amphibians in widely scattered locations have been drastically reduced in the past decade, and some of these species (such as the golden toad of Costa Rica) have recently become extinct. While no single cause for these declines has been identified (and the extinctions may be due to the convergence of more than one cause), the fact that they have occurred in undisturbed areas and throughout the world has prompted considerations of global phenomena.

Blaustein and his colleagues have looked at levels of photolyase, an enzyme that repairs UV damage to DNA by excising and replacing damaged thymidine residues, in amphibian eggs and oocytes. Levels of photolyase varied 80-fold among the tested species and correlates with the site of egg laying. Those eggs more exposed to the sun had higher levels of photolyase. These levels also correlated with whether or not the species was suffering population decline. The highest photolyase levels were in those species (such as the Pacific tree frog, *Hyla regilla*) whose populations were not seen to be in decline. The lowest levels were seen in those species (such as the Western toad, *Bufo boreas,* and the Cascades frog, *Rana cascadae*) whose populations had declined dramatically.

Blaustein and his colleagues tested whether or not UV-B could be a factor in lowering the hatching rate of amphibian eggs. At two field sites, they divided the eggs of each of three amphibian species into three groups. The first group developed without any sun filter. The second group developed under a filter that allowed UV-B to pass through. The third group developed under a filter that blocked UV-B from reaching the eggs. For *Hyla regilla,* the filters had no effect, and hatching success was excellent under all three conditions. For *Rana cascadea* and *Bufo boreas,* however, the UV-B blocking filter raised the percentage of eggs hatched from about 60% to close to 80%.

The environmental programmes of experimental embryology were a major part of the discipline when *Entwicklungsmechanik* was first established. However, it soon became obvious that experimental variables could be better controlled in the labouratory than in the field, and that a scientist could do many more experiments in the labouratory. Thus, field experimentation in embryology dwindled in the first decades of the twentieth century. However, with our increasing concern about the environment, this area of developmental biology has become increasingly important. Other recent work in this field will be detailed in later Chapter.

THE DEVELOPMENTAL MECHANICS OF CELL SPECIFICATION

An embryo's environment may be a tide pool, a pond, or a uterus. As we saw above, the embryo interacts with its environment, and its developmental trajectory can be guided by information from its surroundings. On a smaller scale, the environment of an embryonic cell consists of the surrounding tissues within the embryo, and the fate of that cell (for instance, whether it becomes part of the skin or part of the lens) often depends upon its interactions with other components of its immediate "ecosystem."

Thus, a second research programme of experimental embryology studies how interactions between embryonic cells generate the embryo. The development of specialized cell types is called differentiation. These overt changes in cellular biochemistry and function are preceded by a process involving the commitment of the cell to a certain fate. At this point, even though the cell or tissue does not appear phenotypically different from its uncommitted state, its developmental fate has become restricted. The process of commitment can be divided into two stages. The first stage is a labile phase called specification. The fate of a cell or a tissue is said to be *specified* when it is capable of differentiating autonomously when placed in a neutral environment such as a petri dish or test tube. (The environment is neutral with respect to the developmental pathway.) At this stage, the commitment is still capable of being reversed. The second stage of commitment is determination. A cell or tissue is said to be *determined* when it is capable of differentiating autonomously even when placed into another region of the embryo. If it is able to differentiate according to its original fate even under these circumstances, it is assumed that the commitment is irreversible.

Autonomous Specification

Three basic modes of commitment have been described. The first is called autonomous specification. In this case, if a particular blastomere is removed from an embryo early in its development, that isolated blastomere will produce the same cells that it would have made if it were still part of the embryo. Moreover, the embryo from which that cell is taken will lack those cells (and only those cells) that would have been produced by the missing blastomere. Autonomous specification gives rise to a pattern of development referred to as mosaic development, since the embryo appears to be constructed like a tile mosaic of independent self-differentiating parts. Invertebrate embryos, especially those of molluscs, annelids, and tunicates, often use autonomous specification to determine the fate of their cells. In these embryos, morphogenetic determinants (certain proteins or messenger RNAs) are placed in different regions of the egg cytoplasm and are apportioned to the different cells as the embryo divides. These morphogenetic determinants specify the cell type.

Autonomous specification was first demonstrated in 1887 by a French medical student, Laurent Chabry. Chabry desired to know the causes of birth defects, and he reasoned that such malformations might be caused by the lack of certain cells. He decided to perform experiments on tunicate embryos, since they have relatively large cells and were abundant in a nearby bay. This was a fortunate choice, because tunicate embryos develop rapidly into larvae with relatively few cells and cell types. Chabry set out to produce specific malformations by isolating or lancing specific blastomeres of the cleaving tunicate embryo. He discovered that each blastomere was responsible for producing a particular set of larval tissues. In the absence of particular blastomeres, the larva lacked just those structures normally formed by those cells. Moreover, he observed that when particular cells were isolated from the rest of the embryo, they formed their characteristic structure apart from the context of the other cells. Thus, each of the tunicate cells appeared to be developing autonomously.

Recent studies have confirmed that when particular cells of the 8-cell tunicate embryo are removed, the embryo lacks those structures normally produced by the missing cells, and the isolated cells produce these structures away from the embryo. J. R. Whittaker provided dramatic biochemical confirmation of the cytoplasmic segregation of the morphogenetic determinants responsible for this pattern. Whittaker stained blastomeres for the presence of the enzyme acetylcholinesterase. This enzyme is found only in muscle tissue and is involved in enabling larval muscles to respond to repeated nerve impulses. From the cell lineage studies of Conklin and others, it was known that only one pair of blastomeres (the posterior vegetal pair, B4.1) in the 8-cell tunicate embryo is capable of producing tail muscle tissue. When Whittaker removed these two cells and placed them in isolation, they produced muscle tissue that stained positively for the presence of acetylcholinesterase. When he transferred some of the yellow crescent cytoplasm of the B4.1 (muscle-forming) blastomere into the b4.2 (ectoderm-forming) blastomere of an 8-cell tunicate embryo, the ectoderm-forming blastomere generated muscle cells as well as its normal ectodermal progeny.

Conditional Specification

A second mode of commitment involves interactions with neighbouring cells. In this type of specification, each cell originally has the ability to become many different cell types. However, the interactions of the cell with other cells restricts the fate of one or both of the participants. This mode of commitment is sometimes called conditional specification, because the fate of a cell depends upon the conditions in which the cell finds itself. If a blastomere is removed from an early embryo that uses conditional specification, the remaining embryonic cells alter their fates so that the roles of the missing cells can be taken over. This ability of the embryonic cells to change their fates to compensate for the missing parts is called regulation. The isolated blastomere can also give rise to a wide variety of cell types (and sometimes generates cell types that the cell would normally not have made if it were part of the embryo). Thus, conditional specification gives rise to a pattern of embryogenesis called regulative development. Regulative development is seen in most vertebrate embryos, and it is obviously critical in the development of identical twins. In the formation of such twins, the cleavage-stage cells of a single embryo divide into two groups, and each group of cells produces a fully developed individual.

The research leading to the discovery of conditional specification began with the testing of a hypothesis claiming that there was no such thing. In 1883, August Weismann proposed the first testable model of cell specification, the germ plasm theory. Based on the scant knowledge of fertilization available at that time, Weismann boldly proposed that the sperm and egg provided equal chromosomal contributions, both quantitatively and qualitatively, to the new organism. Moreover, he postulated that the chromosomes carried the inherited potentials of this new organism. However, not all the determinants on the chromosomes were thought to enter every cell of the embryo. Instead of dividing equally, the chromosomes were hypothesized to divide in such a way that different chromosomal determinants entered different cells. Whereas the fertilized egg would carry the full complement of determinants, certain somatic cells would retain the "blood-forming" determinants while others would retain the "muscle-forming" determinants. Only in the nuclei of those cells destined to become gametes (the germ cells) were all types of determinants thought to be retained. The nuclei of all other cells would have only a subset of the original determinant types.

In postulating this model, Weismann had proposed a hypothesis of development that could be tested immediately. Based on the fate map of the frog embryo, Weismann claimed that when the first cleavage division separated the future right half of the embryo from the future left half, there would be a separation of "right" determinants from "left" determinants in the resulting blastomeres. The testing of this hypothesis pioneered three of the four major techniques involved in experimental embryology:

- The defect experiment, wherein one destroys a portion of the embryo and then observes the development of the impaired embryo.
- The isolation experiment, wherein one removes a portion of the embryo and then observes the development of the partial embryo and the isolated part.
- The recombination experiment, wherein one observes the development of the embryo after replacing an original part with a part from a different region of the embryo.
- The transplantation experiment, wherein one portion of the embryo is replaced by a portion from a different embryo. This fourth technique was used by some of the same scientists when they first constructed fate maps of early embryos.

One of the first scientists to test Weismann's hypothesis was Wilhelm Roux, a young German embryologist. In 1888, Roux published the results of a series of defect experiments in which he took 2- and 4-cell frog embryos and destroyed some of the cells of each embryo with a hot needle. Weismann's hypothesis predicted the formation of right or left half-embryos. Roux obtained half-blastulae, just as Weismann had predicted. These developed into half-neurulae having a complete right or left side, with one neural fold, one ear pit, and so on. He therefore concluded that the frog embryo was a mosaic of self-differentiating parts and that it was likely that each cell received a specific set of determinants and differentiated accordingly.

Nobody appreciated Roux's work and the experimental approach to embryology more than Hans Driesch. Driesch's goal was to explain development in terms of the laws of physics and mathematics. His initial investigations were similar to those of Roux. However, while Roux's studies were *defect* experiments that answered the question of how the remaining blastomeres of an embryo would develop when a subset of them was destroyed, Driesch sought to extend this research by performing *isolation* experiments. He separated sea urchin blastomeres from each other by vigourous shaking (or, later, by placing them in calcium-free seawater). To Driesch's surprise, each of the blastomeres from a 2-cell embryo developed into a complete larva. Similarly, when Driesch separated the blastomeres from 4- and 8-cell embryos, some of the isolated cells produced entire pluteus larvae. Here was a result drastically different from the predictions of Weismann or Roux. Rather than self-differentiating into its future embryonic part, each isolated blastomere regulated its development so as to produce a complete organism. Moreover, these experiments provided the first experimentally observable instance of regulative development.

Driesch confirmed regulative development in sea urchin embryos by performing an intricate *recombination* experiment. In sea urchin eggs, the first two cleavage planes are meridional, passing through both the animal and vegetal poles, whereas the third division is equatorial, dividing the embryo into four upper and four lower cells. Driesch changed the direction of the third cleavage by gently compressing early embryos between two glass plates, thus causing the third division to be meridional like the preceding two. After he released the pressure, the fourth division was equatorial. This procedure reshuffled the nuclei, causing a nucleus that normally would be in the region destined to form endoderm to now be in the presumptive ectoderm region. Some nuclei that would normally have produced dorsal structures were now found in the ventral cells. If segregation of nuclear determinants had occurred (as had been proposed by Weismann and Roux), the resulting embryo should have been strangely disordered. However, Driesch obtained normal larvae from these embryos. He concluded, "The relative position of a blastomere within the whole will probably in a general way determine what shall come from it."

The consequences of these experiments were momentous, both for embryology and for Driesch personally. First, Driesch had demonstrated that the prospective potency of an isolated blastomere (those cell types it was possible for it to form) is greater than its prospective fate (those cell types it would normally give rise to over the unaltered course of its development). According to Weismann and Roux, the prospective potency and the prospective fate of a blastomere should be identical. Second, Driesch concluded that the sea urchin embryo is a "harmonious equipotential system" because all of its potentially independent parts functioned together to form a single organism. Third, he concluded that the fate of a nucleus depended solely on its location in the embryo. Driesch hypothesized a series of events wherein development proceeded by the interactions of the nucleus and cytoplasm:

> Insofar as it contains a nucleus, every cell, during development, carries the totality of all primordia; insofar as it contains a specific cytoplasmic cell body, it is specifically enabled by this to respond to specific effects only. ...When nuclear material is activated, then, under its guidance, the cytoplasm of its cell that had first influenced the nucleus is in turn changed, and thus the basis is established for a new elementary process, which itself is not only the result but also a cause.

This strikingly modern concept of nuclear-cytoplasmic interaction and nuclear equivalence eventually caused Driesch to abandon science. Because the embryo could be subdivided into parts that were each capable of re-forming the entire organism, he could no longer envision it as a physical machine. In other words, Driesch had come to believe that development could not be explained by physical forces. Harking back to Aristotle, he invoked a vital force, *entelechy* ("internal goal-directed force"), to explain how development proceeds. Essentially, he believed that the embryo was imbued with an internal psyche and wisdom to accomplish its goals despite the obstacles embryologists placed in its path. Unable to explain his results in terms of the physics of his day, Driesch renounced the study of developmental physiology and became a philosophy professor, proclaiming vitalism (the doctrine that living things cannot be explained by physical forces alone) until his death in 1941. Others, especially Oscar Hertwig, were able to incorporate Driesch's experiments into a more sophisticated experimental embryology.

The difference between isolation and defect experiments and the importance of the interactions among blastomeres were highlighted in 1910, when J. F. McClendon showed that isolated frog blastomeres behave just like separated sea urchin cells. Therefore, the mosaic-like development of the first two frog blastomeres in Roux's study was an artifact of the defect experiment. Something in or on the dead blastomere still informed the live cells that it existed. Therefore, even though Weismann and Roux pioneered the study of developmental physiology, their proposition that differentiation is caused by the segregation of nuclear determinants was soon shown to be incorrect.

THE INFLUENCE OF NEIGHBOURING CELLS

Driesch referred to the embryo as an "harmonious equipotential system" because each of the composite cells had surrendered most of its potential in order to form part of a single complete organism. Each cell could have become a complete animal on its own, yet didn't. What made the cells cooperate instead of becoming autonomous entities? Recent evidence suggests that the "harmonious equipotential system" is the result of negative induction events that mutually restrict the fates of neighbouring cells. Jon Henry and colleagues in Rudolf Raff's labouratory showed that if one isolates pairs of cells from the animal cap of a 16-cell sea urchin embryo, those cells can give rise to both ectodermal and mesodermal components. However, their capacity to form mesoderm is severely restricted if they are aggregated with other animal cap pairs. Thus, the presence of neighbour cells, even of the same kind, restricts the potencies of both partners. Ettensohn and McClay and Khaner and Wilt showed that potency is also restricted when a cell is combined with its neighbours along the animal-vegetal axis. First, they demonstrated that the number of skeletal mesoderm cells is fixed and can be regulated by changes in the cells that normally produce the gut endoderm. If all the 60 skeletal mesoderm cells of the sea urchin *Lytechinus variegatus* are removed from the early gastrula, an equal number of skeletal cells is produced from cells that would otherwisehave become part of the gut. If one removes 20 skeletal precursor cells, about 20 gut precursor cells become skeletal mesoderm. Thus, the skeletal mesoderm cells have a restrictive influence, preventing the formation of new skeletal mesoderm cells from the gut precursors.

MORPHOGEN GRADIENTS

Cell fates may be specified by neighbouring cells, but cell fates can also be specified by specific amounts of soluble molecules secreted at a distance from the target cells. Such a soluble molecule is called a morphogen, and a morphogen may specify more than one cell type by forming a concentration gradient. The concept of morphogen gradients had been used to model another phenomenon of regulative development: regeneration. It had been known since the 1700s that when hydras and planarian flatworms were cut in half, the head half would regenerate a tail from the wound site, while the tail half would regenerate a head. Allman had called attention to the fact that this phenomenon indicated a polarity in the organization of the hydra. It was not until 1905, however, that Thomas Hunt Morgan realised that such polarity indicated an important principle in development.

He pointed out that if the head and tail were both cut off a flatworm, leaving only the medial segment, this segment would regenerate a head from the former anterior end and a tail from the former posterior end— never the reverse. Moreover, if the medial segment were sufficiently small, the regenerating portions would be abnormal. Morgan postulated a gradient of anterior-producing materials concentrated in the head region. The middle segment would be told what to regenerate at both ends by the concentration gradient of these materials. If the piece were too small, however, the gradient would not be sensed within the segment. (It is possible that there are actually two gradients in the flatworm, one to instruct the formation of a head and one to instruct the production of a tail. Regeneration will be discussed in more detail in later Chapter.

In the 1930s through the 1950s, gradient models were used to explain conditional cell specification in sea urchin and amphibian embryos. In the 1960s, these gradient models were extended to explain how cells might be told their position along an embryonic axis. In such models, a soluble substance—the morphogen—is posited to diffuse from its site of synthesis (source) to its site of degradation (sink). Wolpert illustrated this type of positional information using "the French flag analogy." Imagine a row of "flag cells," each of which is capable of differentiating into a red, white, or blue cell. Then imagine a morphogen whose source is on the left-hand edge of the blue stripe, and whose sink is at the other end of the flag, on the right-hand edge of the red stripe. A concentration gradient is thus formed, being highest at one end of the "flag tissue" and lowest at the other. The specification of what type of cell any of the multipotential cells in this tissue will become is accomplished by the concentration of the morphogen. Cells sensing a high concentration of the morphogen become blue. Then there is a threshold of morphogen concentration below which cells become white. As the declining concentration of morphogen falls below another threshold, the cells become red.

Other tissues may use the same gradient system, but respond to the gradient in a different way. If cells that would normally become the middle segment of a *Drosophila* leg are removed from the leg-forming area of the larva and placed into the region that will become the tip of the fly's antenna, they differentiate into *claws*. These cells retain their committed status as leg cells, but respond to the positional information of their environment. Thereby, they became leg tip cells—claws. This phenomenon, said Wolpert, is analogous to reciprocally transplanting portions of American and French flags into each other. The segments will retain their identity (French or American), but will be positionally specified (develop colours) appropriate to their new positions.

The molecules involved in establishing such gradients are beginning to be identified. For a diffusible molecule to be considered a morphogen, it must be demonstrated that cells respond directly to that molecule and that the differentiation of those cells depends upon the concentration of that molecule. One such system currently being analyzed concerns the ability of different concentrations of the protein activin to specify different fates in the frog *Xenopus*. In the *Xenopus* blastula, the cells in the middle of the embryo become mesodermal by responding to activin (or an activin-like compound) produced in the vegetal hemisphere. Makoto Asashima and his colleagues have shown that the animal cap of the *Xenopus* embryo (which normally becomes ectoderm, but which can be induced to form mesoderm if transplanted into other regions within the embryo) responds differently to different concentrations of activin. If left untreated in saline solution, animal cap blastomeres form an epidermis-like mass of cells. However, if exposed to small amounts of activin, they form ventral mesodermal tissue—blood and connective tissue. Progressively higher concentrations of activin will cause the animal cap cells to develop into other types of mesodermal cells: muscles, notochord cells, and heart cells.

John Gurdon's labouratory has shown that these animal cap cells respond to activin by changing the expression of particular genes. Gurdon and his colleagues placed activin-releasing beads or control beads into "sandwiches" of *Xenopus* animal cap cells. They found that cells exposed to little or no activin failed to express any of the genes associated with mesodermal tissues. These cells differentiated into ectoderm. Higher concentrations of activin turned on genes such as *Brachyury,* which are responsible for instructing cells to become mesoderm. Still higher concentrations of activin caused the cells to express genes such as *goosecoid,* which are associated with the most dorsal mesodermal structure, the notochord. The expression of the *Brachyury* and *goosecoid* genes has been correlated with the number of activin receptors on each cell that are bound by activin. Each cell has about 500 activin receptors. If about 100 of them are bound, this activates *Brachyury* expression, and the tissue becomes ventrolateral mesoderm, such as blood and connective tissue cells. If about 300 of these receptors are occupied, the cell turns on its *goosecoid* gene and differentiates into a more dorsal mesodermal cell type such as notochord.

MORPHOGENETIC FIELDS

One of the most interesting ideas to come from experimental embryology has been that of the morphogenetic field. A morphogenetic field can be described as a group of cells whose position and fate are specified with respect to the same set of boundaries. The general fate of a morphogenetic field is determined; thus, a particular field of cells will give rise to its particular organ (forelimb, eye, heart, etc.) even when transplanted to a different part of the embryo. However, the the individual cells *within* the field are not committed, and the cells of the field can regulate their fates to make up for missing cells in the field. Moreover, as described earlier (i.e., the case of presumptive *Drosophila* leg cells transposed to the tip region of the presumptive antennal field), if cells from one field are placed within another field, they can use the positional cues of their new location, even if they retain their organ-specific commitment.

One of the first morphogenetic fields identified was the limb field. The mesodermal cells that give rise to a vertebrate limb can be identified by:

1. Removing certain groups of cells and observing that a limb does not develop in their absence,
2. Transplanting these cells to new locations and observing that they form a limb in this new place, and

3. Marking groups of cells with dyes or radioactive precursors and observing that their descendants partake in limb development. The prospective forelimb area in the tailbud stage of the salamander *Ambystoma maculatum*. The centre of this disc normally gives rise to the limb itself. Adjacent to it are the cells that will form the peribrachial flank tissue and the shoulder girdle. However, if all these cells are extirpated from the embryo, a limb will still form, albeit somewhat later, from an additional ring of cells that surrounds this area (and which would not normally form a limb). If this last ring of cells is included in the extirpated tissue, no limb will develop. This larger region, representing all the cells in the area capable of forming a limb, is called the limb field.

When it first forms, the limb field has the ability to regulate for lost or added parts. In the tailbud stage of *Ambystoma*, any half of the limb disc is able to regenerate the entire limb when grafted to a new site. This potential can also be shown by splitting the limb disc vertically into two or more segments and placing thin barriers between the segments to prevent their reunion. When this is done, each segment develops into a full limb. The regulative ability of the limb bud has recently been highlighted by a remarkable experiment of nature. In several ponds in the United States, numerous multilegged frogs and salamanders have been found. The presence of these extra appendages has been linked to the infestation of the larval abdomen by parasitic trematode worms. The eggs of these worms apparently split the limb buds in several places while the tadpoles were first forming these structures. Thus, like an early sea urchin embryo, the limb field represents a "harmonious equipotential system" wherein a cell can be instructed to form any part of the limb.

The morphogenetic field has been referred to as a "field of organization" and as a "cellular ecosystem". The ecosystem metaphor is quite appropriate, in that recent studies have shown that there are webs of interactions among the cells in different regions of a morphogenetic field. The molecular connections among the various cells of such fields are now being studied in the limb, eye, and heart fields of several vertebrates, as well as in the imaginal discs that form the eyes, antennae, legs, wings, and balancers of insects.

SYNCYTIAL SPECIFICATION

Many insects also use a third means, known as syncitial specification, to commit cells to their fates. Here, interactions occur not between cells, but between parts of one cell. In early embryos of these insects, cell division is not complete. Rather, the nuclei divide within the egg cytoplasm. This creates many nuclei in the large egg cell. A cytoplasm that contains many nuclei is called a syncytium. The egg cytoplasm, however, is not uniform. Rather, the anterior of the egg cytoplasm is markedly different from the posterior. In *Drosophila*, for instance, the anteriormost portion of the egg contains an mRNA that encodes a protein called Bicoid. The posteriormost portion of the egg contains an mRNA that encodes a protein called Nanos. When the egg is laid and fertilized, these two mRNAs are translated into their respective proteins. The concentration of Bicoid protein is highest in the anterior and declines toward the posterior; that of Nanos protein is highest in the posterior and declines as it diffuses anteriorly. Thus, the long axis of the *Drosophila* egg is spanned by two opposing gradients—one of Bicoid protein coming from the anterior, and one of Nanos protein coming from the posterior. The Bicoid and Nanos proteins form a coordinate system based on their ratios, such that each region of the embryo will be distinguished by a different ratio of the two proteins. As the nuclei divide and enter different regions of the egg cytoplasm, they will be instructed by these ratios as to their position along the anterior-posterior axis.

Those nuclei in regions containing high amounts of icoid and little Nanos will be instructed to activate those genes necessary for producing the head. Those nuclei in regions with slightly less Bicoid but with a small amount of Nanos will be instructed to activate those genes that generate the thorax.

Those nuclei in regions that have little or no Bicoid and plenty of Nanos will be instructed to form the abdominal structures. The mechanisms of syncytial specification will be detailed in later.

No embryo uses only autonomous, conditional, or syncytial mechanisms to specify its cells. One finds autonomous specification even in a "regulative embryo" such as the sea urchin, and the nervous system and some musculature of the "autonomously developing" tunicate have been shown to come from regulative interactions between its cells. Insects such as *Drosophila* use all three modes of specification to commit their cells to particular fates. Later chapters will detail the mechanisms by which cell fates are committed in these species.

MORPHOGENESIS AND CELL ADHESION

A body is more than a collection of randomly distributed cell types. Development involves not only the differentiation of cells, but also their organization into multicellular arrangements such as tissues and organs. When we observe the detailed anatomy of a tissue such as the neural retina of the eye, we see an intricate and precise arrangement of many types of cells. How can matter organize itself so as to create a complex structure such as a limb or an eye?

There are Five Major Questions for Embryologists who Study Morphogenesis:

1. How are tissues formed from populations of cells? For example, how do neural retina cells stick to other neural retina cells and not become integrated into the pigmented retina or iris cells next to them? How are the various cell types within the retina (the three distinct layers of photoreceptors, bipolar neurons, and ganglion cells) arranged so that the retina is functional?
2. How are organs constructed from tissues? The retina of the eye forms at a precise distance behind the cornea and the lens. The retina would be useless if it

developed behind a bone or in the middle of the kidney. Moreover, neurons from the retina must enter the brain to innervate the regions of the brain cortex that analyze visual information. All these connections must be precisely ordered.

3. How do organs form in particular locations, and how do migrating cells reach their destinations? Eyes develop only in the head and nowhere else. What stops an eye from forming in some other area of the body? Some cells—for instance, the precursors of our pigment cells, germ cells, and blood cells—must travel long distances to reach their final destinations. How are cells instructed to travel along certain routes in our embryonic bodies, and how are they told to stop once they have reached their appropriate destinations?
4. How do organs and their cells grow, and how is their growth coordinated throughout development? The cells of all the tissues in the eye must grow in a coordinated fashion if one is to see. Some cells, including most neurons, do not divide after birth. In contrast, the intestine is constantly shedding cells, and new intestinal cells are regenerated each day. The mitotic rate of this tissue must be carefully regulated. If the intestine generated more cells than it sloughed off, it could produce tumorous outgrowths. If it produced fewer cells than it sloughed off, it would soon become nonfunctional. What controls the rate of mitosis in the intestine?
5. How do organs achieve polarity? If one were to look at a cross section of the fingers, one would see a certain organized collection of tissues—bone, cartilage, muscle, fat, dermis, epidermis, blood, and neurons. Looking at a cross section of the forearm, one would find the same collection of tissues. But they are arranged very differently in different parts

of the arm. How is it that the same cell types can be arranged in different ways in different parts of the same structure?

All these questions concern aspects of cell behaviour. There are two major types of cell arrangements in the embryo: epithelial cells, which are tightly connected to one another in sheets or tubes, and mesenchymal cells, which are unconnected to one another and which operate as independent units. Morphogenesis is brought about through a limited repertoire of variations in cellular processes within these two types of arrangements:

1. The direction and number of cell divisions;
2. Cell shape changes;
3. Cell movement;
4. Cell growth;
5. Cell death; and
6. Changes in the composition of the cell membrane or secreted products. We will discuss the last of these considerations here.

DIFFERENTIAL CELL AFFINITY

Many of the answers to our questions about morphogenesis involve the properties of the cell surface. The cell surface looks pretty much the same in all cell types, and many early investigators thought that the cell surface was not even a living part of the cell. We now know that each type of cell has a different set of proteins in its surfaces, and that some of these differences are responsible for forming the structure of the tissues and organs during development. Observations of fertilization and early embryonic development made by E. E. Just suggested that the cell membrane differed among cell types, but the modern analysis of morphogenesis began with the experiments of Townes and Holtfreter in 1955. Taking advantage of the discovery that amphibian tissues become dissociated into single cells when placed in alkaline solutions, they prepared single-cell suspensions from each of the three germ layers of amphibian embryos soon after the neural tube had formed. Two or more of these single-cell suspensions could be combined in various ways, and when the pH was normalized, the cells adhered to one another, forming aggregates on agar-coated petri dishes. By using embryos from species having cells of different sizes and colours, Townes and Holtfreter were able to follow the behaviour of the recombined cells.

The results of their experiments were striking. First, they found that reaggregated cells become spatially segregated. That is, instead of the two cell types remaining mixed, each cell type sorts out into its own region. Thus, when epidermal (ectodermal) and mesodermal cells are brought together to form a mixed aggregate, the epidermal cells move to the periphery of the aggregate and the mesodermal cells move to the inside. In no case do the recombined cells remain randomly mixed, and in most cases, one tissue type completely envelops the other.

Such selective affinities were also noted by Boucaut, who injected individual cells from specific germ layers into the body cavity of amphibian gastrulae. He found that these cells migrated back to their appropriate germ layer. Endodermal cells found positions in the host endoderm, whereas ectodermal cells were found only in host ectoderm. Thus, selective affinity appears to be important for imparting positional information to embryonic cells.

The third conclusion of Holtfreter and his colleagues was that selective affinities change during development. This should be expected, because embryonic cells do not retain a single stable relationship with other cell types. For development to occur, cells must interact differently with other cell populations at specific times. Such changes in cell affinity are extremely important in the processes of morphogenesis.

The reconstruction of aggregates from cells of later embryos of birds and mammals was accomplished by the use of the protease trypsin to dissociate the cells from one another.

When the resulting single cells were mixed together in a flask and swirled so that the shear force would break any nonspecific adhesions, the cells sorted themselves out according to their cell type. In so doing, they reconstructed the organization of the original tissue. The "reconstruction" of skin tissue from a 15-day embryonic mouse. The skin cells are separated by proteolytic enzymes and then aggregated in a rotary culture. The epidermal cells of each aggregate migrate to the periphery, and the dermal cells migrate toward the centre. In 72 hours, the epidermis has been reconstituted, a keratin layer has formed, and interactions between these tissues form hair follicles in the dermal region. Such reconstruction of complex tissues from individual cells is called histotypic aggregation.

THE THERMODYNAMIC MODEL OF CELL INTERACTIONS

Cells, then, do not sort randomly, but can actively move to create tissue organization. What forces direct cell movement during morphogenesis? In 1964, Malcolm Steinberg proposed the differential adhesion hypothesis, a model that explained patterns of cell sorting based on thermodynamic principles. Using cells derived from trypsinized embryonic tissues, Steinberg showed that certain cell types always migrate centrally when combined with some cell types, but migrate peripherally when combined with others.

When single-cell suspensions of these two cell types are mixed together, they form aggregates of randomly arranged cells. However, after several hours, the pigmented retina cells are no longer seen on the periphery of the aggregates, and after 2 days, two distinct layers are seen, with the pigmented retina cells lying internal to the neural retina cells. Moreover, such interactions form a hierarchy. If the final position of one cell type, A, is internal to a second cell type, B, and the final position of B is internal to a third cell type, C, then the final position of A will always be internal to C. For example, pigmented retina cells migrate internally to neural retina cells, and heart cells migrate internally to pigmented retina cells. Therefore, heart cells migrate internally to neural retina cells.

This observation led Steinberg to propose that cells interact so as to form an aggregate with the smallest interfacial free energy. In other words, the cells rearrange themselves into the most thermodynamically stable pattern. If cell types A and B have different strengths of adhesion, and if the strength of A-A connections is greater than the strength of A-B or B-B connections, sorting will occur, with the A cells becoming central. On the other hand, if the strength of A-A connections is less than or equal to the strength of A-B connections, then the aggregate will remain as a random mix of cells. Finally, if the strength of A-A connections is far greater than the strength of A-B connections—in other words, if A and B cells show essentially no adhesivity toward one another—then A cells and B cells will form separate aggregates. According to this hypothesis, the early embryo can be viewed as existing in an equilibrium state until some change in gene activity changes the cell surface molecules. The movements that result seek to restore the cells to a new equilibrium configuration.

All that is needed for sorting to occur is that cell types differ in the strengths of their adhesion. In 1996, Foty and his colleagues in Steinberg's labouratory demonstrated that this was indeed the case: the cell types that had greater surface cohesion sorted within those cells that had less surface tension. In the simplest form of this model, all cells could have the same type of "glue" on the cell surface. The amount of this cell surface product, or the cellular architecture that allows the substance to be differentially distributed across the surface, could cause a difference in the number of stable contacts made between cell types. In a more specific version of this model, the thermodynamic differences could be caused by different types of adhesion molecules. When Holtfreter's studies were revisited using modern techniques, found that the tissue surface tensions of the individual germ layers were precisely those required for the sorting patterns observed both in vitro and in vivo.

CADHERINS AND CELL ADHESION

Recent evidence shows that boundaries between tissues can indeed be created both by:

1. Different cell types having different types of cell adhesion molecules and
2. Different cell types having different amounts of cell adhesion molecules. There are several classes of molecules that can mediate cell adhesion. The major cell adhesion molecules appear to be the cadherins. As their name suggests, they are *ca*lcium-dependent *adh*esion molecules. Cadherins are critical for establishing and maintaining intercellular connections, and they appear to be crucial to the spatial segregation of cell types and to the organization of animal form.

Cadherins interact with other cadherins on adjacent cells, and they are anchored into the cell by a complex of proteins called catenins. The cadherin-catenin complex forms the classic adherens junctions that connect epithelial cells together. Moreover, since the catenins bind to the actin cytoskeleton of the cell, they integrate the epithelial cells together into a mechanical unit.

In Vertebrate Embryos, Several Major Cadherin Classes have been identified:

- E-cadherin (epithelial cadherin, also called uvomorulin and L-CAM) is expressed on all early mammalian embryonic cells, even at the 1-cell stage. Later, this molecule is restricted to epithelial tissues of embryos and adults.
- P-cadherin (placental cadherin) appears to be expressed primarily on the trophoblast cells (those placental cells of the mammalian embryo that contact the uterine wall) and on the uterine wall epithelium. It is possible that P-cadherin facilitates the connection of the embryo to the uterus, since P-cadherin on the uterine cells is seen to contact P-cadherin on the trophoblast cells of mouse embryos.
- N-cadherin (neural cadherin) is first seen on mesodermal cells in the gastrulating embryo as they

lose their E-cadherin expression. It is also highly expressed on the cells of the developing central nervous system.

- EP-cadherin (C-cadherin) has been found to be critical for maintaining adhesion between the blastomeres of the *Xenopus* blastula and is required for the normal movements of gastrulation.
- Protocadherins are calcium-dependent adhesion proteins that differ from the classic cadherins in that they lack connections to the cytoskeleton through catenins. Protocadherins have been found to be very important in separating the notochord from the other mesodermal tissues during *Xenopus* gastrulation.

Cadherins join cells together by binding to the same type of cadherin on another cell. Thus, cells with E-cadherin stick best to other cells with E-cadherin, and they will sort out from cells containing N-cadherin in their membranes. This pattern is called homophilic binding. Cells expressing N-cadherin readily sort out from N-cadherin-negative cells in vitro, and univalent (Fab) antibodies against cadherins will convert a three-dimensional, histotypic aggregate of cells into a single layer of cells. Moreover, when activated E-cadherin genes are added to and expressed in cultured mouse fibroblasts (mesenchymal cells that usually do not express this protein), E-cadherin is seen on their cell surfaces, and the treated fibroblasts become tightly connected to one another. In fact, these cells begin acting like epithelial cells. The sorting out of cells can be explained by the amounts and types of cadherins on their cell surfaces. Fibroblasts made to express E-cadherin adhere to other E-cadherin-bearing fibroblasts, while fibroblasts made to express P-cadherin stick to other fibroblasts expressing P-cadherin.

These adhesion patterns may have important consequences in the embryo. In the gastrula of the frog *Xenopus*, the neural tube expresses N-cadherin, while the epidermis expresses E-cadherin. Normally, these two tissues separate from each other such that the neural tube is inside the body and the epidermis covers the body. If the epidermis is experimentally manipulated to remove its E-cadherin, the epidermal epithelium cannot hold together. If the epidermis is made to express N-cadherin, or if the neural cells are made to lose it, the neural tube will not separate from the epidermis.

The amount of cadherin can also mediate the formation of embryonic structures. This was first shown to be a possibility when Steinberg and Takeichi collabourated on an experiment using two cell lines that were identical except that they synthesized different amounts of P-cadherin. When these two groups of cells were mixed, the cells that expressed more cadherin had a higher surface cohesion and sorted out within the lower-expressing group of cells. Recent studies show that differences in the degree of cell adhesion may be critical in the development of the fruit fly embryo. Within the *Drosophila* ovary, the developing egg, or oocyte, is always found at the most posterior side of the egg chamber, or follicle. The oocyte's nurse cells (which export messenger RNA and ribosomes into the oocyte) are found more anteriorly. This pattern reflects the distribution of E-cadherin in these cells. Although all follicle cells, nurse cells, and the oocyte express E-cadherin, the oocyte and the posterior follicle cells express it at far higher levels than the other cells. Moreover, when E-cadherin was experimentally removed from the oocyte and nurse cells (or from the follicle cells), the position of the oocyte became random.

During development, the cadherins often work with other adhesion systems. For instance, one of the most critical times in a mammal's life is when the embryo is passing through the uterus. If development is to continue, the embryo must adhere to the uterus and embed itself in the uterine wall. That is why the first differentiation event in mammalian development distinguishes the trophoblast cells (the outer cells that bind to the uterus) from the inner cell mass (those cells that will generate the adult organism). This process occurs as the embryo travels down from the upper regions of the oviduct on its way to the uterus. The trophoblast cells are endowed with several adhesion molecules to anchor the embryo to the uterine wall. First, they contain both E-cadherins and P-cadherins, and these cadherins recognize similar cadherins on the uterine cells. Second, they have receptors (the integrin proteins) for the collagen and the heparan sulfate glycoproteins of the uterine wall. Third, the trophoblast cells also have a modified glycosyltransferase enzyme that extends out from the membrane and that can bind to specific carbohydrate residues on uterine glycoproteins. For something as important as the implantation of the mammalian embryo, it is not surprising that several cell adhesion systems appear to be working together.

Chapter 4

Genes and Development: Techniques and Ethical Issues

"Between the characters that furnish the data for the theory, and the postulated genes, to which the characters are referred, lies the whole field of embryonic development." Here Thomas Hunt Morgan noted in 1926 that the only way to get from genotype to phenotype is through developmental processes.

In the early twentieth century, embryology and genetics were not considered separate sciences. They diverged in the 1920s, when Morgan redefined genetics as the science studying the *transmission* of traits, as opposed to embryology, the science studying the *expression* of traits. Within the past decade, however, the techniques of molecular biology have effected a rapprochement of embryology and genetics. In fact, the two fields have become linked to a degree that makes it necessary to discuss molecular genetics early in this text. Problems in animal development that could not be addressed a decade ago are now being solved by a set of techniques involving nucleic acid synthesis and hybridization. This chapter seeks to place these new techniques within the context of the ongoing dialogues between genetics and embryology.

THE EMBRYOLOGICAL ORIGINS OF THE GENE THEORY

Nucleus or cytoplasm: Which controls heredity?

Mendel called them *bildungsfähigen Elemente,* "form-building elements"; we call them genes. It is in Mendel's term, however, that we see how closely intertwined were the concepts of inheritance and development in the nineteenth century. Mendel's observations, however, did not indicate where these hereditary elements existed in the cell, or how they came to be expressed. The gene theory that was to become the cornerstone of modern genetics originated from a controversy within the field of physiological embryology. In the late 1800s, a group of scientists began to study the mechanisms by which fertilized eggs give rise to adult organisms. Two young American embryologists, Edmund Beecher Wilson and Thomas Hunt Morgan, became part of this group of "physiological embryologists," and each became a partisan in the controversy over which of the two compartments of the fertilized egg—the nucleus or the cytoplasm—controls inheritance. Morgan allied himself with those embryologists who thought the control of development lay within the cytoplasm, while Wilson allied himself with Theodor Boveri, one of the biologists who felt that the nucleus contained the instructions for development. In fact, Wilson declared that the processes of meiosis, mitosis, fertilization, and unicellular regeneration (only from the fragment containing the nucleus) "converge to the conclusion that the chromatin is the most essential element in development." He did not shrink from the consequences of this belief. Years before the rediscovery of Mendel or the gene theory, Wilson noted, "Now, chromatin is known to be closely similar, if not identical with, a substance known as nuclein ... which analysis shows to be a tolerably definite chemical composed of a nucleic acid (a complex organic acid rich in phosphorus) and albumin. And thus we reach the remarkable conclusion that inheritance may, perhaps, be effected by the physical transmission of a particular chemical compound from parent to offspring."

Some of the major support for the chromosomal hypothesis of inheritance was coming from the embryological studies of Theodor Boveri, a researcher at the Naples Zoological Station. Boveri fertilized sea urchin eggs with large concentrations of their sperm and obtained eggs that had been fertilized by two sperm. At first cleavage, these eggs formed four mitotic poles and divided into four cells instead of two. Boveri then separated the blastomeres and demonstrated that each cell developed abnormally, and in a different way, as a result of each of the cells having different types of chromosomes. Thus, Boveri claimed that each chromosome had an individual nature and controlled different vital processes.

Adding to Boveri's evidence, E. B. Wilson and demonstrated a critical correlation between nuclear chromosomes and organismal development: XO or XY embryos became male; XX embryos became female. Here was a nuclear property that correlated with development. Eventually, Morgan began to obtain mutations that correlated with sex and with the X chromosome, and he began to view the genes as being physically linked to one another on the chromosomes. The embryologist Morgan had shown that nuclear chromosomes are responsible for the development of inherited characters.

THE SPLIT BETWEEN EMBRYOLOGY AND GENETICS

Morgan's evidence provided a material basis for the concept of the gene. Originally, this type of genetics was seen as being part of embryology, but by the 1930s, genetics became its own discipline, developing its own vocabulary, journals, societies, favoured research organisms, professorships, and rules of evidence. Hostility between embryology and genetics also emerged. Geneticists believed that the embryologists were old-fashioned and that development would be completely explained as the result of gene expression. Conversely, the embryologists regarded the geneticists as uninformed about how organisms actually developed and felt that genetics was irrelevant to embryological questions. Embryologists such as Frank Lillie, Ross Granville Harrison, Hans Spemann, and Ernest E. Just claimed that there could be no genetic theory of development until at least three major challenges had been met by the geneticists:

1. Geneticists had to explain how chromosomes—which were thought to be identical in every cell of the organism—produce different and changing types of cell cytoplasms.
2. Geneticists had to provide evidence that genes control the early stages of embryogenesis. Almost all the genes known at the time affected the final modeling steps in development (eye colour, bristle shape, wing venation in *Drosophila*). As Just said, embryologists were interested in how a fly forms its back, not in the number of bristles on its back.
3. Geneticists had to explain phenomena such as sex determination in certain invertebrates (and vertebrates such as reptiles), in which the environment determines sexual phenotype.

The debate became quite vehement. In rhetoric reflecting the political anxieties of the late 1930s, warned:

> Now that the necessity of relating the data of genetics to embryology is generally recognized and the Wanderlust of geneticists is beginning to urge them in our direction, it may not be inappropriate to point out a danger of this threatened invasion. The prestige of success enjoyed by the gene theory might easily become a hindrance to the understanding of development by directing our attention solely to the genom, whereas cell movements, differentiation, and in fact all of developmental processes are actually effected by cytoplasm. Already we have theories that refer the processes of development to gene action and regard the whole performance as no more than the realization of the potencies of genes. Such theories are altogether too one-sided.

Until geneticists could demonstrate the existence of inherited variants during early development, and until geneticists had a well-documented theory for how the same chromosomes could produce different cell types, embryologists generally felt no need to ground their science in gene action.

EARLY ATTEMPTS AT DEVELOPMENTAL GENETICS

Some scientists, however, felt that neither embryology nor genetics was complete without the other. There were several attempts to synthesize the two disciplines, but the first successful reintegration of genetics and embryology came in the late 1930s from two embryologists, Salome Gluecksohn-Schoenheimer (now S. Gluecksohn Waelsch) and Conrad Hal Waddington. Both were trained in European embryology and had learned genetics in the United States from Morgan's students. Gluecksohn-Schoenheimer and Waddington attempted to find mutations that affected early development and to discover the processes that these genes affected.Gluecksohn-Schoenheimer showed that mutations in the *Brachyury* genes of the mouse caused the aberrant development of the posterior portion of the embryo, and she traced the effects of these mutant genes to the notochord, which would normally have helped induce the dorsal axis.

At the same time, Waddington isolated several genes that caused wing malformations in fruit flies (*Drosophila*). He, too, analyzed these mutations in terms of how the genes might affect the developmental primordia that give rise to these structures. The *Drosophila* wing, he correctly claimed, "appears favourable for investigations on the developmental action of genes." Thus, one of the main objections of embryologists to the genetic model of development—that genes appear to be working only on the final modeling of the embryo and not on its major outlines—was countered.

EVIDENCE FOR GENOMIC EQUIVALENCE

The other major objection to a genetically based embryology still remained: How could nuclear genes direct development when they were the same in every cell type? The existence of this genomic equivalence was not so much proved as assumed (because every cell is the mitotic descendant of the fertilized egg), so one of the first problems of developmental genetics was to determine whether every cell of an organism indeed had the same set of genes, or genome, as every other cell.

Metaplasia

The first evidence for genomic equivalence came from embryologists studying the regeneration of excised tissues. The study of salamander eye regeneration demonstrated that even adult differentiated cells can retain their potential to produce other cell types. Therefore, the genes for these other cell types' products must still be present in the cells, though not normally expressed. In the salamander eye, removal of the neural retina promotes its regeneration from the pigmented retina, and if the lens is removed, a new lens can be formed from the cells of the dorsal iris. The regeneration of lens tissue from the iris (called Wolffian regeneration after the person who first observed it, in 1894) has been intensively studied. Yamada and his colleagues found that a series of events leads to the production of a new lens from the iris. The nuclei of the dorsal side of the iris begin to synthesize enormous numbers of ribosomes, their DNA replicates, and a series of mitotic divisions ensues. The pigmented iris cells then begin to dedifferentiate by throwing out their melanosomes (the pigmented granules that give the eye its colour) These melanosomes are ingested by macrophages that enter the wound site. The dorsal iris cells continue to divide, forming a globe of dedifferentiated tissue in the region of the removed lens. These cells then start synthesizing the products of differentiated lens cells, the crystallin proteins. These crystallins are made in the same order as in normal lens development. Once a new lens has formed, the cells on the dorsal side of the iris cease mitosis.

These events are not the normal route by which the vertebrate lens is formed. As mentioned in earlier Chapter, the lens normally develops from a layer of head epithelial cells induced by the underlying retinal precursor cells. The formation of the lens by the differentiated cells of the iris is an example of metaplasia (or transdifferentiation), the transformation of one differentiated cell type into another. The salamander iris, then, has not lost any of the genes that are used to differentiate the cells of the lens.

AMPHIBIAN CLONING: THE RESTRICTION OF NUCLEAR POTENCY

The ultimate test of whether the nucleus of a differentiated cell has undergone any irreversible functional restriction is to have that nucleus generate every other type of differentiated cell in the body. If each cell's nucleus is identical to the zygote nucleus, then each cell's nucleus should be totipotent (capable of directing the entire development of the organism) when transplanted into an activated enucleated egg. Before such an experiment could be done, however, three techniques for transplanting nuclei into eggs had to be perfected:

1. A method for enucleating host eggs without destroying them;
2. A method for isolating intact donor nuclei; and
3. A method for transferring such nuclei into the host egg without damaging either the nucleus or the oocyte.

All three techniques were developed in the 1950s by Robert Briggs and Thomas King. First, they combined the enucleation of the host egg with its activation. When an oocyte from the leopard frog (*Rana pipiens*) is pricked with a clean glass needle, the egg undergoes all the cytological and biochemical changes associated with fertilization. The internal cytoplasmic rearrangements of fertilization occur, and the completion of meiosis takes place near the animal pole of the cell. The meiotic spindle can easily be located as it pushes away the pigment granules at the animal pole, and puncturing the oocyte at this site causes the spindle and its chromosomes to flow outside the egg. The host egg is now considered both activated (the fertilization reactions necessary to initiate development have been completed) and enucleated. The transfer of a nucleus into the egg is accomplished by disrupting a donor cell and transferring the released nucleus into the oocyte through a micropipette. Some cytoplasm accompanies the nucleus to its new home, but the ratio of donor to recipient cytoplasm is only $1:10^5$, and the donor cytoplasm does not seem to affect the outcome of the experiments. In 1952, Briggs and King, using these techniques, demonstrated that blastula cell nuclei could direct the development of complete tadpoles when transferred into the oocyte cytoplasm.

What happens when nuclei from more advanced developmental stages are transferred into activated enucleated oocytes? King and Briggs found that whereas most blastula nuclei could produce entire tadpoles, there was a dramatic decrease in the ability of nuclei from later stages to direct development to the tadpole stage. When nuclei from the somatic cells of tailbud-stage tadpoles were used as donors, normal development did not occur. However, nuclei from the germ cells of tailbud-stage tadpoles (which could give rise to a complete organism after fertilization) were capable of directing normal development in 40% of the blastulae that developed. Thus, most somatic cells appeared to lose their ability to direct development as they became determined and differentiated.

AMPHIBIAN CLONING: THE PLURIPOTENCY OF SOMATIC CELLS

Is it possible that some differentiatied cell nuclei differ from others in their ability to direct development? John Gurdon and his colleagues, using slightly different methods of nuclear transplantation on the frog *Xenopus,* obtained results suggesting that the nuclei of some differentiated cells can remain totipotent. Gurdon, too, found a progressive loss of potency with increasing developmental age, although *Xenopus* cells retained their potencies for a longer period than did the cells of *Rana.* The exceptions to this rule, however, proved very interesting. Gurdon transferred nuclei from the intestinal endoderm of feeding *Xenopus* tadpoles into activated enucleated eggs. These donor nuclei contained a genetic marker (one nucleolus per cell instead of the usual two) that distinguished them from host nuclei. Out of 726 nuclei transferred, only 10 (1.4%) promoted development to the feeding tadpole stage. Serial transplantation (transplanting an intestinal nucleus into an egg and, when the egg had become a blastula, transferring the nuclei of the blastula cells into several more eggs) increased the yield to 7%.

In some instances, nuclei from tadpole intestinal cells were capable of generating all the cell lineages—neurons, blood cells, nerves, and so forth—of a living tadpole. Moreover, seven of these tadpoles (from two original nuclei) metamorphosed into fertile adult frogs; these two nuclei were totipotent.

King and his colleagues criticized these experiments, pointing out that:

1. Not enough care was taken to make certain that primordial germ cells, which can migrate through to the gut, were not used as sources of nuclei, and
2. The intestinal epithelial cells of such a young tadpole may not qualify as a truly differentiated cell type because such cells of feeding tadpoles still contain yolk platelets. To answer these criticisms, Gurdon and his colleagues cultured epithelial cells from adult frog foot webbing. These cells were shown to be differentiated; each of them contained a specific keratin, the characteristic protein of adult skin cells. When nuclei from these cells were transferred into activated, enucleated *Xenopus* oocytes, none of the first-generation transfers progressed further than the formation of the neural tube shortly after gastrulation. By serial transplantation, however, numerous tadpoles were generated. Although these tadpoles all died prior to feeding, they showed that a single differentiated cell nucleus still retained incredible potencies.

CLONING MAMMALS

In 1997, Ian Wilmut announced that a sheep had been cloned from a somatic cell nucleus from an *adult* female sheep. This was the first time that an adult vertebrate had been successfully cloned from another adult. To do this, Wilmut and his colleagues took cells from the mammary gland of an adult (6-year-old) pregnant ewe and put them into culture. The culture medium was formulated to keep the nuclei in these cells at the resting stage of the cell cycle (G_0). They then obtained oocytes (the maturing egg cell) from a different strain of sheep and removed their nuclei.

The fusion of the donor cell and the enucleated oocyte was accomplished by bringing the two cells together and sending electrical pulses through them. The electric pulses destabilized the cell membranes, allowing the cells to fuse together. Moreover, the same pulses that fused the cells activated the egg to begin development. The resulting embryos were eventually transferred into the uteri of pregnant sheep. Of the 434 sheep oocytes originally used in this experiment, only one survived: Dolly. DNA analysis confirmed that the nuclei of Dolly's cells were derived from the strain of sheep from which the donor nucleus was taken. Thus, it appears that the nuclei of adult somatic cells can be totipotent. No genes necessary for development have been lost or mutated in a way that would make them nonfunctional.

This result has been confirmed in cows and mice. In mice, somatic cell nuclei from the cumulus cells of the ovary were injected directly into enucleated oocytes. These re-nucleated oocytes were able to develop into mice at a frequency of 2.5%. Interestingly, nuclei from other somatic cells (such as neurons or Sertoli cells) that are similarly blocked at the G_0 stage did not generate any live mice. Cumulus cell nuclei from cows have also directed the complete development of oocytes into mature cows.

DIFFERENTIAL GENE EXPRESSION

If the genome is the same in all somatic cells within an organism (with the exception of the above-mentioned lymphocytes), how do the cells become different from one another? If every cell in the body contains the genes for hemoglobin and insulin proteins, how are the hemoglobin proteins made only in the red blood cells, the insulin proteins made only in certain pancreas cells, and neither made in the kidney or nervous system? Based on the embryological evidence for genomic equivalence (and on bacterial models of gene regulation), a consensus emerged in the 1960s that cells differentiate through differential gene expression. The three postulates of differential gene expression are as follows:

1. Every cell nucleus contains the complete genome established in the fertilized egg. In molecular terms, the DNAs of all differentiated cells are identical.
2. The unused genes in differentiated cells are not destroyed or mutated, and they retain the potential for being expressed.
3. Only a small percentage of the genome is expressed in each cell, and a portion of the RNA synthesized in the cell is specific for that cell type.

The first two postulates have already been discussed. The third postulate—that only a small portion of the genome is active in making tissue-specific products—was first tested in insect larvae. Fruit fly larvae have certain cells whose chromosomes become polytene.

These chromosomes, beloved by *Drosophila* geneticists, undergo DNA replication in the absence of mitosis and therefore contain 512 (2^9), 1024 (2^{10}), or even more parallel DNA double helices instead of just one. These cells do not undergo mitosis, and they grow by expanding to about 150 times their original volume. Beermann showed that the banding patterns of polytene chromosomes were identical throughout the larva, and that no loss or addition of any chromosomal region was seen when different cell types were compared. However, he and others showed that in different tissues, different regions of these chromosomes were making organ-specific RNA. In certain cell types, particular regions of the chromosomes would loosen up, "puff" out, and transcribe mRNA. In other cell types, these regions would be "silent," but other regions would puff out and synthesize mRNA.

The idea that the genes of chromosomes were differentially expressed in different cell types was confirmed using DNA-RNA hybridization. This technique involves annealing single-stranded pieces of RNA and DNA to allow complementary strands to form double-stranded hybrids. While some mRNAs from one cell type were also found in other cell types (as expected for mRNAs encoding enzymes concerned with cell metabolism), many mRNAs were found to be specific for a particular type of cell and were not expressed in other cell types, even though the genes encoding them were present. Thus, differential gene expression was shown to be the way a single genome derived from the fertilized egg could generate the hundreds of different cell types in the body. The question then became, How does this differential gene expression occur? The answers to that question will be the topic of the next chapter. To understand the results that will be presented there, however, one must become familiar with some of the techniques of molecular biology that are being applied to the study of development. These include techniques to determine the spatial and temporal location of specific mRNAs, as well as techniques to determine the functions of these messages.

RNA LOCALIZATION TECHNIQUES

Northern blotting

We can determine the temporal and spatial locations where RNAs are expressed by running an RNA blot (often called a Northern blot). First, one extracts the RNA from embryos at different stages of development, or from different organs of the same embryo. The investigator then places the RNA samples side by side at one end of a gel and runs an electrical current through the gel. The smaller the RNA, the faster it moves through the gel. Thus, different RNAs are separated by their sizes.

This technique is called electrophoresis. The investigator then transfers the separated RNAs to a nitrocellulose paper or nylon membrane filter, and incubates the RNA-containing filter in a solution containing a radioactive single-stranded DNA fragment from a particular gene. This radioactively labeled DNA probe binds only to regions of the filter where the complementary RNA is located. If the mRNA for that gene is present in a sample, the labeled DNA will bind to it and can be detected by autoradiography. X-ray film is placed above the filter and incubated in the dark. The localized radioactivity in the probe reduces the silver in the X-ray film, and grains form. The resulting spots, which appear directly above the places where the radioactive DNA has bound, appear black when viewed directly. Autoradiographs of this type, in which RNAs from several stages or tissues are compared simultaneously, are called developmental Northern blots.

A developmental Northern blot used to investigate the expression of *Pax6* expression in the mammalian embryo. Pax6 is a protein that is critical for normal eye development; mutations in this gene give small eyes (in heterozygous mice) or no eyes or nose (in mice or humans homozygous for the loss-of-function mutation). The Northern blot shows that this gene is expressed in the embryo in the brain, eyes, and pancreas, but in no other tissue.

IN SITU HYBRIDIZATION

But where was this gene expressed in the eye? Northern blot analysis (which uses mRNA extracted from pieces of tissue that have been removed from the embryo) can give only an approximate location and time for gene expression. A more detailed map of gene expression patterns can be obtained by using a process called in situ hybridization. Instead of using a DNA probe to seek mRNA on a filter, the probe is hybridized with the mRNA in the organ itself. Embryos or organs are fixed to preserve their structure and to prevent the RNA from being degraded, then sectioned for microscopy and placed on a slide. When the radioactive DNA probe is added, it binds only where the complementary mRNA is present. After any unbound probe is washed off, the slide is covered with a transparent photographic emulsion for autoradiography. By means of computer-mediated bright-field imaging, the reduced silver grains can be shown in a colour that contrasts with the background stain.

THE POLYMERASE CHAIN REACTION

The polymerase chain reaction (PCR) is a method of in vitro gene cloning that can generate enormous quantities of a specific DNA fragment from a small amount of starting material. It can be used for cloning a specific gene or for determining whether a specific gene is actively transcribing RNA in a particular organ or cell type. The standard methods of cloning use living microorganisms to amplify recombinant DNA. PCR, however, can amplify a single region of a DNA molecule several million times in a few hours, and can do it in a test tube. This technique has been extremely useful in cases in which there is very little nucleic acid to study. Preimplantation mouse embryos, for instance, have very little mRNA, and we cannot obtain millions of such embryos to study. If we wanted to know whether the preimplantation mouse embryo contained the mRNA for a particular protein, it would be very difficult to find out using standard methods. We would have to lyse thousands of mouse embryos to get enough mRNA. However, the PCR technique allows us to find this message in a few embryos by specifically amplifying only that message millions of times.

First, the mRNAs from a group of cells are purified and converted into complementary DNA (cDNA) using an enzyme called reverse transcriptase. By using DNA polymerase and S1 nuclease, this population of single-stranded cDNAs is then made into double-stranded cDNAs. Next a specific cDNA is targeted for amplification. In preparation for this step, the cDNA double helices are separated, or denatured, by heating them. Two small oligonucleotide primers that are complementary to a portion of the message being looked for are then added to the denatured cDNA. Oligonucleotides are relatively short stretches of DNA (about 20 bases). If the oligonucleotides recognize sequences in the cDNA, this means that the mRNA being sought was present in the source of the original DNA. The oligonucleotide primers are made so that they hybridize to opposite strands at opposite ends of the targeted sequence. (If we are trying to isolate the gene or mRNA for a specific protein of known sequence, we can synthesize oligonucleotides that are complementary to the amino end and the carboxyl end of the protein.) The 32 ends of these primers face each other, so that replication is through the target DNA. Once the first primer has hybridized with the DNA, DNA polymerase can be used to synthesize a new strand.

The DNA polymerase used in this process is not normal *E. coli* DNA polymerase, however; it is DNA polymerase from bacteria such as *Thermus aquaticus* or *Thermococcus littoralis.* These bacteria live in hot springs (such as those in Yellowstone National Park) or in submarine thermal vents, where the temperature reaches nearly 90°C. These DNA polymerases can withstand temperatures near boiling. PCR takes advantage of this evolutionary adaptation. Once the second strand is made, it is heat-denatured from its complement. (The temperatures used would inactivate the *E. coli* DNA polymerase, but the thermostable polymerases are not damaged.) The second primer is added, and now both strands can synthesize new DNA. Repeated cycles of denaturation and synthesis amplify this region of DNA in geometric fashion. After 20 such rounds, that specific region has been amplified 2^{20} (a little more than a million) times. When the DNA is subjected to electrophoresis, the presence of such an amplified fragment is easily detected. Its presence shows that in the original messenger RNA population there was an mRNA with the sequence of interest.

DETERMINING THE FUNCTION OF GENES DURING DEVELOPMENT

Transgenic Cells and Organisms

While it is important to know the sequence of a gene and its temporal-spatial pattern of expression, what's really crucial is to know the functions of that gene during development. Recently developed techniques have enabled us to study gene function by moving certain genes into and out of embryonic cells.

Inserting New DNA into a Cell

Cloned pieces of DNA can be isolated, modified (if so desired), and placed into cells by several means. One very direct technique is microinjection, in which a solution containing the cloned gene is injected very carefully into the nucleus of a cell.

This is an especially useful technique for injecting genes into newly fertilized eggs, since the haploid nuclei of the sperm and egg are relatively large. In transfection, DNA is incorporated directly into cells by incubating them in a solution that makes them "drink" it in. The chances of a DNA fragment being incorporated into the chromosomes in this way are relatively small, however, so the DNA of interest is usually mixed with another gene, such as a gene encoding resistance to a particular antibiotic, that enables those rare cells that incorporate the DNA to survive under culture conditions that will kill all the other cells. Another technique is electroporation, in which a high-voltage pulse "pushes" the DNA into the cells.

A more "natural" way of getting genes into cells is to put the cloned gene into a transposable element or retroviral vector. These are naturally occurring mobile regions of DNA that can integrate themselves into the genome of an organism. Retroviruses are RNA-containing viruses. Within a host cell, they make a DNA copy of themselves (using their own virally encoded reverse transcriptase); the copy then becomes double-stranded and integrates itself into a host chromosome. The integration is accomplished by two identical sequences (long terminal repeats) at the ends of the retroviral DNA. Retroviral vectors are made by removing the viral packaging genes (needed for the exit of viruses from the cell) from the centre of a mouse retrovirus. This extraction creates a vacant site where other genes can be placed. By using the appropriate restriction enzymes, researchers can insert an isolated gene (such as a gene isolated by PCR) and insert it into a retroviral vector. These retroviral vectors infect mouse cells with an efficiency approaching 100%. Similarly, in *Drosophila,* new genes can be carried into a fly via P elements. These DNA sequences are naturally occurring transposable elements that can integrate like viruses into any region of the *Drosophila* genome. Moreover, they can be isolated, and cloned genes can be inserted into the centre of the P element. When the recombined P element is injected into a *Drosophila* oocyte, it can integrate into the DNA and provide the embryo with the new gene.

CHIMERIC MICE

The techniques described above have been used to transfer genes into every cell of the mouse embryo. During early mouse development, there is a stage when only two cell types are present: the outer trophoblast cells, which will form the fetal portion of the placenta, and the inner cell mass, whose cells will give rise to the embryo itself. These inner cells are the cells whose separation can lead to twins, and if an inner cell mass blastomere of one mouse is transferred into the embryo of a second mouse, that donor cell can contribute to every organ of the host embryo.

Inner cell mass blastomeres can be isolated from the embryo and cultured in vitro; such cultured cells are called embryonic stem cells (ES cells). ES cells retain their totipotency, and each of them can contribute to all organs if injected into a host embryo. Moreover, once in culture, these cells can be treated as described in the preceding section so that they will incorporate new DNA. A treated ES cell (the entire cell, not just the DNA) can then be injected into another early-stage mouse embryo, and will integrate into the host embryo. The result is a chimeric mouse. Some of this mouse's cells will be derived from the host embryonic stem cells, but some portion of its cells will be derived from the treated embryonic stem cell. If the treated cells become part of the germ line of the mouse, some of its gametes will be derived from the donor cell. If such a chimeric mouse is mated with a wild-type mouse, some of its progeny will carry one copy of the inserted gene. When these heterozygous progeny are mated to one another, about 25% of the resulting offspring will carry two copies of the inserted gene in every cell of their bodies. Thus, in three generations—the chimeric mouse, the heterozygous mouse, and the homozygous mouse—a gene that was cloned from some other organism will be present in both copies of the chromosomes within the mouse genome. Strains of such transgenic mice have been particularly useful in determining how genes are regulated during development.

GENE TARGETING ("KNOCKOUT") EXPERIMENTS.

The analysis of early mammalian embryos has long been hindered by our inability to breed and select animals with mutations that affect early embryonic development. This block has been circumvented by the techniques of gene targeting (or, as it is sometimes called, gene knockout). These techniques are similar to those that generate transgenic mice, but instead of *adding* genes, gene targeting *replaces* wild-type alleles with mutant ones. As an example, we will look at the gene knockout of bone morphogenetic protein 7 (BMP7). Bone morphogenetic proteins are involved in numerous developmental interactions whereby one set of cells interacts with other neighbouring cells to alter their properties. BMP7 has been implicated as a protein that prevents cell death and promotes cell division in several developing organs. Dudley and his colleagues used gene targeting to find the function of BMP7 in the development of the mouse.

First, they isolated the *BMP7* gene, cut it at one site with a restriction enzyme, and inserted a bacterial gene for neomycin resistance into that site. In other words, they mutated the *BMP7* gene by inserting into it a large piece of foreign DNA, destroying the ability of the BMP7 protein to function. These mutant *BMP7* genes were electroporated into ES cells that were sensitive to neomycin. Once inside the nucleus of an ES cell, the mutated *BMP7* gene may replace a normal allele of *BMP7* by a process called homologous recombination. In this process, the enzymes involved in DNA repair and replication incorporate the mutant gene in the place of the normal copy. It's a rare event, but such cells can be selected by growing the ES cells in neomycin. Most of the cells are killed by the drug, but the ones that have acquired resistance from the incorporated gene survive. The resulting cells have one normal *BMP7* gene and one mutated *BMP7* gene.

These heterozygous ES cells were then microinjected into mouse blastocysts, where they were integrated into the cells of the embryo. The resulting mice were chimeras composed of wild-type cells from the host embryo and heterozygous *BMP7*-containing cells from the donor ES cells. The chimeras were mated to wild-type mice, producing progeny that were heterozygous for the *BMP7* gene. These heterozygous mice were then bred with each other, and about 25% of their progeny carried two copies of the mutated *BMP7* gene. These homozygous mutant mice lacked eyes and kidneys. In the absence of BMP7, it appears that many of the cells that normally form these two organs stop dividing and die. In this way, gene targeting can be used to analyze the roles of particular genes during mammalian development.

DETERMINING THE FUNCTION OF A MESSAGE: ANTISENSE RNA

Another method for determining the function of a gene is to use "antisense" copies of its message to block the function of that message. Antisense RNA allows developmental biologists to determine the function of genes during development and to analyze the action of genes that would othe.

Antisense messages can be generated by cloning DNA into vectors that have promoters at both ends of the inserted gene.When incubated with a particular RNA polymerase and nucleotide triphosphates, the promoter will initiate transcription of the message "in the wrong direction." In so doing, it synthesizes a transcript that is complementary to the natural one. This complementary transcript is called antisense RNA because it is the complement of the original ("sense") message. When large amounts of antisense RNA are injected or transfected into cells containing the normal mRNA from the same gene, the antisense RNA binds to the normal message, and the resulting double-stranded nucleic acid is degraded. (Cells have enzymes to digest double-stranded nucleic acids in the cytoplasm.) This causes a functional deletion of the message, just as if there were a deletion mutation for that gene.

The similarities between the phenotypes produced by a loss-of-function mutation and by antisense RNA treatment were seen when antisense RNA was made to the *Krüppel* gene of *Drosophila.Krüppel* is critical for forming the thorax and abdomen of the fly. If this gene is absent, fly larvae die because they lack thoracic and anterior abdominal segments. A similar situation is created when large amounts of antisense RNA against the *Krüppel* message are injected into early fly embryos.

IDENTIFYING THE GENES FOR HUMAN DEVELOPMENTAL ANOMALIES

One cannot experiment on human embryos, nor can one selectively breed humans to express a particular mutant phenotype. How, then, can we find the genes that are involved in normal human development and whose mutations cause congenital (inborn) developmental malformations? Two approaches have revolutionized human embryology within the past five years.

The first approach is positional gene cloning. Here, pedigree analysis highlights a region of the genome where a particular mutant gene is thought to reside. By making a DNA map of that area, one can hope to find a region of DNA that differs between people who have the mutation and people who lack it. Then, by sequencing that region of the genome, the gene can be located. As an example, we will look at the discovery of the human Aniridia gene. Ton and his colleagues attempted to find the gene whose absence caused defects in normal eye development.

People heterozygous for this gene, *Aniridia,* lack the irises of their eyes. Fetuses homozygous for this condition are stillborn and have no eyes or nose. Using DNA from individuals with aniridia having chromosomal breaks in this region, Ton and co-workers found a region of chromosome 11 that was present in wild-type individuals but completely or partially absent in individuals with aniridia. Moreover, this region of DNA contained a region that could be a gene (i.e., it had a promoter site, and sequences connoting introns and exons). To determine whether this sequence was a gene that was active in eye development, they did a Northern blot, using this region of DNA as a probe. The probe found complementary mRNA primarily in the brain and eye regions of the body. This fragment of DNA contained a gene that was indeed expressed in the brain and eye. Sequencing this fragment showed that it was the human *PAX6* gene: the human homologue of the *Pax6* gene already known in mice. This was confirmed through in situ hybridization.

The second approach is candidate gene mapping. This approach is similar to positional cloning, but here, one starts with a correlation between the genetic mapping of a particular syndrome and the genetic mapping for a particular gene. As an example, we will take another condition that produces small eyes: Waardenburg syndrome type 2.

This autosomal dominant condition is characterized by deafness, heterochromatic (multicoloured) irises, and a white forelock. By analyzing the pedigrees of several families whose members had this condition, Hughes and her colleagues showed that it is caused by a mutation in a gene on the small arm of chromosome 3, between bands 12.3 and 14.4. A strikingly similar condition is found in mice, in which it is called *microphthalmia*. Mutations of the microphthalmia gene (*mi*) cause a dominant syndrome involving deafness, a white patch of fur, and eye abnormalities. Could Waardenburg syndrome type 2 be caused by mutations in the human equivalent of the microphthalmia gene? The mouse *mi* gene was cloned, and was found (by sequencing and in situ hybridization) to encode a DNA-binding protein that is expressed in the pigment cells of the eyes, ears, and hair follicles of embryonic mice. DNA-binding proteins are important because they often act to regulate the transcription of other genes.

The mouse *mi* gene was used to make a probe to look for similar genes in the human genome. Indeed, the probe found a human homologue of the mouse microphthalmia gene, and this homologous sequence (*MITF*) mapped to the exact same region as Waardenburg syndrome type 2. When Waardenburg syndrome patients were studied, it was found that they each had mutations of the *MITF* gene. Thus, Waardenburg syndrome type 2 was correlated with mutations in a DNA-binding protein encoded by the human *MITF* locus.

Candidate gene and positional gene mapping techniques have brought together medical embryology and medical genetics. This fusion has enabled scientists and physicians to understand normal human development and the causes of many malformations.

Chapter 5

The Genetic Core of Development: Differential Gene Expression

Different cell types make different sets of proteins, even though their genomes are identical. Each human being has roughly 150,000 genes in each nucleus, but each cell uses only a small subset of these genes. Moreover, different cell types use different subsets of these genes. Red blood cells make globins, lens cells make crystallins, melanocytes make melanin, and endocrine glands make their specific hormones. Developmental genetics is the discipline that examines how the genotype is transformed into the phenotype, and the major paradigm of developmental genetics is *differential gene expression from the same nuclear repertoire*. The regulation of gene expression can be accomplished at several levels:

- Differential gene transcription, regulating which of the nuclear genes are transcribed into RNA
- Selective nuclear RNA processing, regulating which of the transcribed RNAs (or which parts of such a nuclear RNA) enter into the cytoplasm to become messenger RNAs
- Selective messenger RNA translation, regulating which of the mRNAs in the cytoplasm become translated into proteins
- Differential protein modification, regulating which proteins are allowed to remain or function in the cell

Some genes (such as those coding for the globin proteins of hemoglobin) are regulated at each of these levels. This chapter will discuss the mechanisms of cell differentiation: how different genes from the same genetic repertoire are activated or repressed at particular times and places to cause cells to become different from one another.

DIFFERENTIAL GENE TRANSCRIPTION

There are two fundamental differences distinguishing most eukaryotic genes from most prokaryotic genes. First, eukaryotic genes are contained within a complex of DNA and protein called chromatin. The protein component constitutes about half the weight of chromatin and is composed largely of nucleosomes. The nucleosome is the basic unit of chromatin structure. It is composed of an octamer of histone proteins (two molecules each of histones H2A-H2B and histones H3-H4) wrapped with two loops containing approximately 140 base pairs of DNA. Chromatin can thus be visualized as a string of nucleosome beads linked by ribbons of DNA. While classic geneticists have likened genes to "beads on a string," molecular geneticists liken genes to "string on the beads." Most of the time, the nucleosomes are themselves wound into tight "solenoids" that are stabilized by histone H1. Histone H1 is found in the 60 or so base pairs of "linker" DNA between the nucleosomes. This H1-dependent conformation of nucleosomes inhibits the transcription of genes in somatic cells by packing adjacent nucleosomes together into tight arrays that prohibit the access of transcription factors and RNA polymerases to the genes. It is generally thought, then, that the "default" condition of chromatin is a repressed state, and that tissue-specific genes become activated by local interruption of this repression.

The second difference is that eukaryotic genes are not colinear with their peptide products. Rather, the single nucleic acid strand of eukaryotic mRNA comes from noncontiguous regions on the chromosome. Between the regions of DNA coding for a protein—exons—are intervening sequences—introns—that have nothing whatsoever to do with the amino acid sequence of the protein. The structure of a typical eukaryotic gene can be represented by the human β-globin gene. This gene consists of the following elements:

1. A promoter region, which is responsible for the binding of RNA polymerase and for the subsequent initiation of transcription. The promoter region of the human β-globin gene has three distinct units and extends from 95 to 26 base pairs before ("upstream from") the transcription initiation site (i.e., from -95 to -26).
2. The transcription initiation site, which for human β-globin is ACATTTG. This site is often called the cap sequence because it represents the 5′ end of the RNA, which will receive a "cap" of modified nucleotides soon after it is transcribed. The specific cap sequence varies among genes.
3. The translation initiation site, ATG. This codon (which becomes AUG in the mRNA) is located 50 base pairs after the transcription initiation site in the human β-globin gene (although this distance differs greatly among different genes). The intervening sequence of 50 base pairs between the initiation points of transcription and translation is the 5′ untranslated region, often called the 5′ UTR or leader sequence. The 5′ UTR can determine the rate at which translation is initiated.
4. The first exon, which contains 90 base pairs coding for amino acids 1–30 of human β-globin.
5. An intron containing 130 base pairs with no coding sequences for the globin protein. The structure of this intron is important in enabling the RNA to be processed into messenger RNA and exit from the nucleus.
6. An exon containing 222 base pairs coding for amino acids 31–104.
7. A large intron—850 base pairs—having nothing to do with the globin protein structure.

8. An exon containing 126 base pairs coding for amino acids 105–146.
9. A translation termination codon, TAA. This codon becomes UAA in the mRNA. The ribosome dissociates at this codon, and the protein is released.
10. A 3′ untranslated region that, (3′ UTR) although transcribed, is not translated into protein. This region includes the sequence AATAAA, which is needed for polyadenylation: the placement of a "tail" of some 200 to 300 adenylate residues on the RNA transcript. This poly(A) tail (1) confers stability on the mRNA, (2) allows the mRNA to exit the nucleus, and (3) permits the mRNA to be translated into protein. The poly(A) tail is inserted into the RNA about 20 bases downstream of the AAUAAA sequence. Transcription continues beyond the AATAAA site for about 1000 nucleotides before being terminated.

The original nuclear RNA transcript for such a gene contains the capping sequence, the 5′ untranslated region, the exons, the introns, and the 3′ untranslated region. In addition, both its ends become modified. A cap consisting of methylated guanosine is placed on the 5′ end of the RNA in opposite polarity to the RNA itself. This means that there is no free 5′ phosphate group on the nuclear RNA. The 5′ cap is necessary for the binding of mRNA to the ribosome and for subsequent translation. The 3′ terminus is usually modified in the nucleus by the addition of a poly(A) tail. These adenylate residues are put together enzymatically and are added to the transcript; they are not part of the gene sequence. Both the 5′ and 3′ modifications may protect the RNA from exonucleases that would otherwise digest the mRNA. The modifications thus stabilize the message and its precursor.

ANATOMY OF THE GENE: PROMOTERS AND ENHANCERS

In addition to the protein-encoding region of the gene, there are regulatory sequences that can be on either end of the gene (or even within it). These sequences—the promoters and enhancers—are necessary for controlling where and when a particular gene is transcribed.

Promoters are the sites where RNA polymerase binds to the DNA to initiate transcription. Promoters of genes that synthesize messenger RNAs are typically located immediately upstream from the site where the RNA polymerase initiates transcription. Most of these promoters contain the sequence TATA, where RNA polymerase will be bound. This site, known as the TATA box, is usually about 30 base pairs upstream from the site where the first base is transcribed. Eukaryotic RNA polymerases, however, will not bind to this naked DNA sequence. Rather, they require additional protein factors to bind efficiently to the promoter. The protein-encoding genes are transcribed by RNA polymerase II, and at least six nuciear proteins have been shown to be necessary for the proper initiation of transcription by RNA polymerase II. These proteins are called basal transcription factors. The first of these, TFIID, recognizes the TATA box through one of its subunits, TATA-binding protein (TBP). TFIID serves as the foundation of the transcription initiation complex, and it also serves to keep nucleosomes from forming in this region. Once TFIID is stabilized by TFIIA, it becomes able to bind TFIIB. Once TFIIB is in place, RNA polymerase can bind to this complex. Other transcription factors (TFIIE, F, and H) are then used to release RNA polymerase from the complex so that it can transcribe the gene, and to unwind the DNA helix so that the RNA polymerase will have a free template from which to transcribe.

In addition to these basal transcription factors, which are found in each nucleus, there is also a set of transcription factors called TBP-associated factors, or TAFs, which can stabilize the TBP. This function is critical for gene transcription, for if the TBP is not stabilized, it can fall off the small TATA sequence. The TAFs are bound by upstream promoter elements on the DNA. These DNA sequences are near the TATA sequence, and usually upstream from it. These TAFs need not be in every cell of the body, however. Cell-specific transcription factors can also activate the gene by stabilizing the transcription initiation complex. They can do so by binding to the TAFs, by binding directly to other factors such as TFIIB, or by destabilizing nucleosomes.

An enhancer is a DNA sequence that can activate the utilization of a promoter, controlling the efficiency and rate of transcription from that particular promoter. Enhancers can activate only *cis*-linked promoters (i.e., promoters on the same chromosome), but they can do so at great distances (some as great as 50 kilobases away from the promoter). Moreover, enhancers do not need to be on the 5′ (upstream) side of the gene. They can also be at the 3′ end, in the introns, or even on the complementary DNA strand. The human β-globin gene has an enhancer in its 3′ UTR, roughly 700 base pairs downstream from the AATAAA site. This sequence is necessary for the temporal- and tissue-specific expression of the β-globin gene in adult red blood cell precursors. Like promoters, enhancers function by binding specific regulatory proteins called transcription factors.

Enhancers can regulate the temporal and tissue-specific expression of any differentially regulated gene, but different types of genes normally have different enhancers. In the pancreas, for instance, the exocrine protein genes (for the digestive proteins chymotrypsin, amylase, and trypsin) have enhancers different from that of the gene for the endocrine protein insulin. These enhancers both lie in the 5′ flanking sequences of their genes. Walker and colleagues created transgenes by placing flanking regions from the genes for chymotrypsin and insulin onto the gene for bacterial chloramphenicol acetyltransferase (CAT), an enzyme that is not found in mammalian cells. CAT activity is easy to assay in mammalian cells, so the bacterial *CAT* gene can be used as a reporter gene to tell investigators whether a particular enhancer is functioning. The researchers then transfected the transgenes into:

1. Ovary cells (which do not secrete either insulin or chymotrypsin),

2. An insulin-secreting cell line, and
3. A chymotrypsin-secreting cell line, and measured the activity of CAT in each of these cells.

Neither enhancer sequence caused the enzyme to be made in the ovarian cells. In the insulin-secreting cell, however, the 5′ flanking region from the insulin gene enabled the *CAT* gene to be expressed, but the 5′ flanking region of the chymotrypsin gene did not. Conversely, when the clones were placed into the exocrine pancreatic cell line, the chymotrypsin 5′ flanking sequence allowed *CAT* expression, while the insulin enhancer did not. The enhancers for 10 different exocrine proteins share a 20-base-pair consensus sequence, suggesting that these similar sequences play a role in activating an entire set of genes specifically expressed in the exocrine cells of the pancreas. Thus, the expression of genes in exocrine and in endocrine cells of the pancreas appears to be controlled by different enhancers.

By taking an enhancer from one gene and fusing it to another gene, it has been shown that enhancers can direct the expression of any gene sequence. For instance, the β-galactosidase gene from *E. coli* (the *lacZ* gene) can be used as a reporter gene and placed onto an enhancer that normally directs a particular mouse gene to become expressed in muscles. If the resulting transgene is injected into a newly fertilized mouse egg and gets incorporated into its DNA, the β-galactosidase gene will be expressed in the muscle cells. By staining for the presence of β-galactosidase, the expression pattern of that muscle-specific gene can be seen. Similarly, if the gene for green fluorescent protein (GFP, a reporter protein that is usually made only in jellyfish) is placed on the enhancer of genes encoding the crystallin proteins of the eye lens, GFP expression is seen solely in the lens.

Enhancers are critical in the regulation of normal development. Over the past decade, six generalizations that emphasize their importance for differential gene expression have been made:

1. Most genes require enhancers for their transcription.
2. Enhancers are the major determinant of differential transcription in space (cell type) and time.
3. The ability of an enhancer to function while far from the promoter means that there can be multiple signals to determine whether a given gene is transcribed. A given gene can have several enhancer sites linked to it, and each enhancer can be bound by more than one transcription factor.
4. The interaction between the proteins bound to the enhancer sites and the transcription initiation complex assembled at the promoter is thought to regulate transcription. The mechanism of this association is not fully known, nor do we comprehend how the promoter integrates all these signals.
5. Enhancers are modular. There are various DNA elements that regulate temporal and spatial gene expression, and these can be mixed and matched. As we will see, the enhancers for endocrine hormones such as insulin and for lens-specific proteins such as crystallins both have sites that bind Pax6 protein. But Pax6 doesn't tell the lens to make insulin or the pancreas to make crystallins, because there are other transcription factor proteins that also must bind. It is the combination of transcription factors that causes particular genes to be transcribed.
6. A gene can have several enhancer elements, each turning it on in a different set of cells.
7. Enhancers can also be used to inhibit transcription. In some cases, the same transcription factors that activate the transcription of one gene can be used to repress the transcription of other genes. These "negative enhancers " are also called silencers.

TRANSCRIPTION FACTORS

Some major transcription factor families and subfamilies

Family	Representative transcription factors	Some functions
Homeodomain:		
Hox	Hoxa-1, Hoxb-2, etc.	Axis formation
POU	Pit-1, Unc-86, Oct-2	Pituitary development; neural fate
LIM	Lim-1, Forkhead	Head development
Pax	Pax1, 2, 3, etc.	Neural specification; eye development
Basic helix-loop-helix (bHLH)	MyoD, achaete, daughterless	Muscle and nerve specification; *Drosophila* sex determination
Basic leucine zipper (bZip)	C/EBP, AP1	Liver differentiation; fat cell specification
Zinc finger:		
Standard	WT1, Krüppel, Engrailed	Kidney,.gonad, and macrophage development; *Drosophila* segmentation
Nuclear hormone receptors	Glucocorticoid receptor, estrogen receptor, testosterone receptor, retinoic acid receptors	Secondary sex determination; craniofacial development; limb development
Sry-Sox	Sry, SoxD, Sox2	Bend DNA; mammalian primary sex determination; ectoderm differentiation

Transcription factors are proteins that bind to enhancer or promoter regions and interact to activate or repress the transcription of a particular gene. Most transcription factors can bind to specific DNA sequences. These proteins can be grouped together in families based on similarities in structure. The transcription factors within such a family share a common framework structure in their DNA-binding sites, and slight differences in the amino acids at the binding site can alter the sequence of the DNA to which the factor binds.

Transcription factors have three major domains. The first is a DNA-binding domain that recognizes a particular DNA sequence. The second is a *trans*-activating domain that activates or suppresses the transcription of the gene whose promoter or enhancer it has bound. Usually, this *trans*-activating domain enables the transcription factor to interact with proteins involved in binding RNA polymerase (such as TFIIB or TFIIE). In addition, there may be a protein-protein interaction domain that allows the transcription factor's activity to be modulated by TAFs or other transcription factors.

Examples of Transcription Factors: MITF and Pax6

As examples of transcription factors, we can look at the Pax6 and microphthalmia proteins mentioned in earlier Chapter. The microphthalmia (MITF) protein is necessary for the production of pigment cells and their pigments.

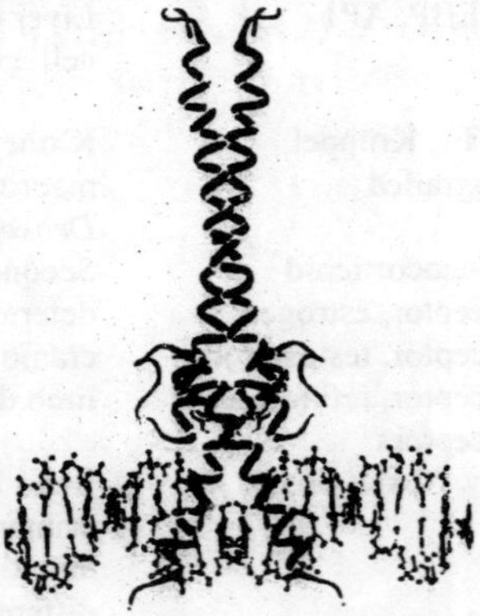

Fig. Three-dimensional model of the MITF dimer binding to its promoter element in DNA. The amino termini are located at the bottom of the figure and form the DNA-binding domain. The protein-protein interaction domain is located immediately above it, and the carboxyl end of the molecule is thought to be the trans-activating domain that binds the p300/CBP co-activator protein.

There are three functionally important domains of the MITF protein. First, MITF has a protein-protein interaction domain that enables it to dimerize with another MITF protein. This homodimer (two microphthalmia proteins bound together) forms the functional protein that can bind to DNA and activate the transcription of certain genes. The second region, the DNA-binding domain, is close to the amino-terminal end of the protein and contains numerous basic amino acids that make contact with the DNA. This assignment was confirmed by the discovery of various human and mouse mutations that map within the DNA-binding site for MITF and prevent the attachment of the MITF protein to the DNA. Sites for MITF binding have been found in the promoter regions for three pigment-cell-specific proteins of the tyrosinase family. Without MITF, these proteins are not synthesized properly and the melanin pigment is not made. These promoters all contain the same 11-base-pair sequence, including the core sequence CATGTG.

The third functional region of MITF is its *trans*-activating domain. This domain includes a long stretch of amino acids in the centre of the protein. When the MITF dimer is bound to its target element in a promoter or enhancer, the *trans*-activating region is able to bind a TAF called p300/CBP. The p300/CPB protein is a histone acetyltransferase enzyme that can transfer acetyl groups to each histone in the nucleosomes. This acetylation of the nucleosomes destabilizes them and allows the genes for pigment-forming enzymes to be expressed. Recent discoveries have shown that numerous transcription factors operate by recruiting histone acetyltransferases. It is thought that once the nucleosomes are destabilized, other transcription factors and RNA polymerase can bind more easily to the DNA in that region.

The Pax6 transcription factor, which is needed for mammalian eye, nervous system, and pancreas development, contains two potential DNA-binding domains. The major DNA-binding site of the Pax6 protein resides at its amino-terminal end, and these amino acids interact with a specific 20–26-base-pair sequence of DNA. Such Pax6-binding sequences have been found in the enhancers of vertebrate lens crystallin genes and in the genes expressed in the endocrine cells of the pancreas (insulin, glucagon, and somatostatin). When Pax6 binds to a particular site in an enhancer or promoter, it can either activate or repress that gene. The *trans*-activating domain of Pax6 is rich in proline, threonine, and serine. Mutations in this region cause severe nervous system, pancreatic, and optic abnormalities in humans.

The use of Pax6 by different organs demonstrates the modular nature of transcriptional regulatory units. The first is that of the chick *δ1* lens crystallin gene. This gene has a promoter containing a site for TBP binding and an upstream site that binds Sp1, a general transcriptional activator found in all cells. The gene also has an enhancer in its third intron that controls the time and place of crystallin gene expression. This enhancer has two Pax6-binding sites. The crystallin gene will not be expressed unless Pax6 is present in the nucleus and bound to these enhancer sites. As mentioned in earlier Chapter, Pax6 is present during early development in the central nervous system and head surface ectoderm of the chick. Moreover, this enhancer has a site for another transcription factor, the Sox2 protein. Sox2 is not usually found in the outer ectoderm, but it appears in those outer ectodermal cells that will become lens by virtue of their being induced by the optic vesicle evaginating from the brain. Thus, only those cells that contain both Sox2 and Pax6 can express the lens crystallin gene. In addition, there is a third site that can bind either an activator (the δEF3 protein) or a repressor (the δEF1 protein) of transcription. It is thought that the repressor may be critical in preventing crystallin expression in the nervous system. Thus, enhancers function in a combinatorial manner, wherein several transcription factors work together to promote or inhibit transcription.

Another set of regulatory regions that use Pax6 are the enhancers regulating the transcription of the insulin, glucagon, and somatostatin genes of the pancreas. Here, Pax6 is essential for gene expression, and it works in cooperation with other transcription factors such as Pdx1 (specific for the pancreatic region of the endoderm) and Pbx1. In the absence of Pax6 (as in the homozygous small eye mutation in mice and rats), the endocrine parts of the pancreas do not develop properly, and the production of these proteins from those cells is deficient. In this way, transcription factors can regulate the timing and place of gene expression.

There are other genes that are activated by Pax6 binding, and one of them is the *Pax6* gene itself. Pax6 protein can bind to the *Pax6* gene promoter. This means that once the *Pax6* gene is turned on, it will be continue to be expressed, even if the signal that originally activated it is no longer given.

Within the past decade, our knowledge of transcription factors has progressed enormously, giving us a new, dynamic view of gene expression. The gene itself is no longer seen as an independent entity controlling the synthesis of proteins. Rather, the gene both directs and is directed by protein synthesis. Natalie Angier has written, "A series of new discoveries suggests that DNA is more like a certain type of politician, surrounded by a flock of protein handlers and advisers that must vigourously massage it, twist it and, on occasion, reinvent it before the grand blueprint of the body can make any sense at all."

CASCADES OF TRANSCRIPTION FACTORS

We now know that the tissue-specific expression of a particular gene, such as the gene encoding the δ1 crystallin of the lens, is the result of the presence of a particular constellation of transcription factors in the nucleus. In the case of this lens crystalline, the Pax6 and Sox2 transcription factors are especially important. It is important to see that this combinatorial mode of operation means that none of these transcription factors has to be cell type-specific.

But how do the transcription factors themselves get to be expressed in a tissue-specific manner? In many cases, the genes for transcription factors are activated by other transcription factors. Let us look again at the *Pax6* gene as an example. Not only does the Pax6 protein regulate other genes (such as the ones for insulin and crystallins); it is itself regulated. The regulatory regions of the mouse *Pax6* gene were discovered by taking regions from its 5′ flanking sequence and introns and fusing them to a β-galactosidase reporter gene. This transgene was then microinjected into newly fertilized mouse pronuclei, and the resulting embryos were stained for β-galactosidase. An enhancer farthest upstream from the promoter contains the regions necessary for *Pax6* expression in the pancreas, while a second enhancer activates *Pax6* expression in surface ectoderm (lens, cornea, and conjunctiva). A third enhancer resides in the leader sequence, and it contained the sequences that direct *Pax6* expression in the neural tube. A fourth enhancer sequence, located in an intron shortly after the translation initiation sequence, determines the expression of *Pax6* in the retina. The search is on now for those transcription factors that activate the gene for the Pax6 transcription factor. Wilhelm Roux described this situation eloquently in his manifesto for experimental embryology when he stated that the causal analysis of development may be the greatest problem the human intellect has attempted to solve, "since every new cause ascertained only gives rise to fresh questions concerning the cause of this cause."

SILENCERS

Some sequences act specifically to block transcription. These silencer domains are useful in restricting the transcription of a particular gene to a particular group of cells or for regulating the timing of the gene's expression. For example, the fetal mouse liver makes serum albumin, but only after a certain stage of gut development. At first, the endodermal cells that will form the liver do not transcribe this albumin gene. However, when the endodermal tube contacts the cardiac mesoderm (which is in the process of forming a heart), the heart precursors are able to instruct the endodermal tube to begin forming the liver and to start transcribing liver-specific genes.

This contact is thought to release a transcription factor bound to a silencer region in the serum albumin gene. This silencer site is occupied prior to the contact of the endoderm with the cardiac mesoderm, but it becomes vacant in the endodermal tube immediately after contact with the heart-forming cells.

Another example of a silencer is found in certain neural genes. There is a sequence found in certain promoters that prevents the promoter's activation in any tissue except neurons. This sequence was given the name neural restrictive silencer element (NRSE), and it has been found in several mouse genes whose expression is limited to the nervous system: those for synapsin I, sodium channel type II, brain-derived neurotrophic factor, Ng-CAM, and L1. The protein that binds to the NRSE is a zinc finger transcription factor called neural restrictive silencer factor (NRSF). NRSF appears to be expressed in every cell that is not a mature neuron. Thus, the down-regulation of NRSF seems to be a key event in allowing the expression of several genes that are critical to neural function.

To test the hypothesis that NRSE was necessary in the normal repression of neural genes in non-neural cells, *lacZ* transgenes were made by fusing a β-galactosidase gene (*lacZ*) with part of the *L1* neural cell adhesion gene. (L1 is a protein whose function is critical for brain development, as we will see in later chapters.) In one case, the *L1* gene, from its promoter through the fourth exon, was fused to the *lacZ* sequences. A second transgene was made just like the first, except that the NRSE had been deleted from the *L1* promoter. The two transgenes were separately inserted into the pronuclei of fertilized oocytes, and the resulting transgenic mice were analyzed for the expression of β-galactosidase. In the embryos receiving the complete transgene (which included the NSRE), expression was seen only in the nervous system. However, in those mice whose transgene lacked the NRSE, expression was seen in the heart, limb mesenchyme and limb ectoderm, kidney mesoderm, ventral body wall, and cephalic mesenchyme.

LOCUS CONTROL REGIONS IN GLOBIN GENES

There are some regions of DNA called locus control regions (LCRs), which function as "super-enhancers." These LCRs establish an "open" chromatin configuration, inhibiting the normal repression of transcription over an area spanning several genes. The mechanism by which the LCR opens up the chromatin is not yet known.

One of the best-studied LCRs is that regulating the tissue-specific expression of the β-globin family of genes in humans, mice, and chicks. In many species, including chicks and humans, the embryonic or fetal hemoglobin differs from that found in adult red blood cells. Human hemoglobin consists largely of four globin chains of two different types and four molecules of heme. Human embryonic hemoglobin has two zeta (ς) globin chains and two epsilon (ε) globin chains (and four molecules of heme). During the second month of human gestation, ς- and ε-globin synthesis abruptly ceases, while alpha (α) and gamma (γ) globin synthesis increases. The association of two γ-globin chains with two α-globin chains produces fetal hemoglobin ($\alpha_2\gamma_2$). (The physiological importance of the γ-globin chain in fetal hemoglobin is examined in earlier Chapter.) At 3 months gestation, the beta (β) globin and delta (δ) globin genes begin to be active, and their products slowly increase, while γ-globin levels gradually decline. This switchover is greatly accelerated after birth, and fetal hemoglobin is replaced by adult hemoglobin ($\alpha_2\beta_2$). The normal adult hemoglobin profile is 97% $\alpha_2\beta_2$, 2–3% $\alpha_2\delta_2$, and 1% $\alpha_2\gamma_2$.

A schematic diagram of human hemoglobin types and the genes that code for them is shown in. In humans, the ς- and α-globin genes are located on chromosome 16, but the ε-, γ-, δ-, and β-globin genes (known as the β-globin gene family) are linked together, in order of appearance, on chromosome 11. It appears, then, that there is a mechanism that directs the sequential switching of the chromosome 11 genes from embryonic, to fetal, to adult globins.

The discovery of the human globin LCR came from studies of the genetic disease *β*-thalassemia. This anemic condition results from a lack of *β*-globin and can be caused in several ways. The usual causes of *β*-thalassemia involve deletions or mutations in either the coding region of the β-globin gene or its promoter. However, in some patients, there is a deletion in a region *upstream* from the β-globin gene family, while the genes themselves are normal. Moreover, without this upstream region, the β-globin family DNA was found to be DNase I-insensitive. DNase I treatment is used to see whether the DNA in chromatin is accessible to transcription factors. If the DNA in chromatin is not digested by DNase I, it means that DNase I cannot reach it, and therefore, transcription factors couldn't reach it either. Promoters are usually DNase I-sensitive in the cells where they function; and they are usually DNase I-insensitive in those cells where they are not active. So it appeared that there was a region of DNA upstream from the β-globin gene cluster that was responsible for "opening up" the chromatin of the genes, making them accessible to transcription factors. This region of DNA was termed the β-globin locus control region.

The locus control region for the β-globin gene complex is located far upstream from its most 5′ member (ε). This LCR contains four sites that are DNase I-hypersensitive only in erythroid precursor cells. Sites are said to be DNase-hypersensitive when the DNA in the chromatin can be digested there with only small amounts of DNase I. In most instances, a site is thought to be DNase I hypersensitive when it lacks nucleosomes. These sites in the LCR are therefore within nucleosome coils in most cells' nuclei, but in the precursors of the red blood cells, this DNA is exposed. The entire LCR is necessary for activating high levels of erythroid cell-specific transcription of the entire β-globin gene family on human chromosome 11. Deletion or mutation of the LCR causes the silencing of all these genes. Conversely, if the LCR is placed adjacent to a gene that is not usually expressed in red blood cells (such as the T cell-specific *thy-1* gene) and then transfected into erythroid precursor cells, the additional gene will be expressed in the red blood cells. This effect is specific for red blood cell precursors, since only they have the appropriate transcription factors to bind to the LCR. If any of the globin genes are separated from the LCR, they are repressed, even in the erythroid cells that would normally be transcribing them. The locus control region is crammed with binding sites for transcription factors. As Gary Felsenfeld observed, "The domains look as though they were put together by an overenthusiastic student determined to construct a powerful *cis*-acting element." He suggested that one of the functions of the LCR is to loop around to one of the globin promoter regions during DNA replication and bind to it in a manner that prevents nucleosomes from forming on that promoter. Indeed, the globin promoters are not DNase I-hypersensitive (i.e., accessible to transcription factors) except in the presence of the LCR.

It is not known why the genes closest to the LCR are transcribed earlier than the genes farther from it. Interestingly, experiments have shown that the distance between the LCR and the globin genes does affect their activation. When linked closely to the LCR, the human β-globin gene becomes expressed in transgenic mouse *embryonic* cells. Its correct activation (in *adult* red cells only) is restored only when it is placed farther away from the LCR. Similarly, the human γ-globin gene is repressed earlier (like the normal β-globin gene) when it is placed farther from the LCR. These findings suggest that the interaction between the LCR and the globin genes is polarized: those globin genes closest to the LCR are turned on earliest, while those genes more distal are turned on later. Presumably, there is physical contact between the LCR and the gene-specific promoters and enhancers.

LCRs have been found for other genes, such as the human growth hormone locus, the macrophage-specific lysozyme gene, and the CD2 and CD4 genes expressed in T lymphocytes

METHYLATION PATTERN AND THE CONTROL OF TRANSCRIPTION

DNA methylation and gene activity

How does a pattern of transcription become stable? How can a lens cell continue to remain a lens cell and not activate muscle-specific genes? How can cells undergo rounds of mitosis and still maintain their differentiated characteristics? The answer appears to be DNA methylation. The promoters of inactive genes become methylated at certain cytosine residues, and the resulting methylcytosine stabilizes nucleosomes and prevents transcription factors from binding.

It is often assumed that a gene contains exactly the same nucleotides whether it is active or inactive; that is, that a β-globin gene in a red blood cell precursor has the same nucleotides as a β-globin gene in a fibroblast or retinal cell of the same animal. There is, however, a subtle difference in the DNA. In 1948, R. D. Hotchkiss discovered a "fifth base" in DNA, 5-methylcytosine. In vertebrates, this base is made enzymatically after DNA is replicated, at which time about 5% of the cytosines in mammalian DNA are converted to 5-methylcytosine. This conversion can occur only when the cytosine residue is followed by a guanosine. Recent studies have shown that the degree to which the cytosines of a gene are methylated can control the level of the gene's transcription. Cytosine methylation appears to be a major mechanism of transcriptional regulation in vertebrates. However, *Drosophila*, nematodes, and perhaps most invertebrates do not methylate their DNA.

In vertebrates, the presence of methylated cytosines in the promoter of a gene correlates with the repression of transcription from that gene. In developing human and chick red blood cells, the DNA of the globin promoters is almost completely unmethylated, whereas the same promoters are highly methylated in cells that do not produce globin. Moreover, the methylation pattern changes during development. The cells that produce hemoglobin in the human embryo have unmethylated promoters for the genes encoding the ε-globins of embryonic hemoglobin. These promoters become methylated in the fetal tissue. Similarly, when the fetal globin gives way to adult globin, the γ-globin gene promoters become methylated. The correlation between methylated cytosines and transcriptional repression has been confirmed experimentally. By adding transgenes to cells and giving them different patterns of methylation, Busslinger and co-workers showed that methylation in the promoter or enhancer of a gene correlates extremely well with the repression of gene transcription. In vertebrate development, the absence of DNA methylation correlates well with the tissue-specific expression of many genes.

POSSIBLE MECHANISMS BY WHICH METHYLATION REPRESSES GENE TRANSCRIPTION

How is methylation involved in repressing genes? One hypothesis is that methylated DNA stabilizes nucleosomes. Here, DNA methylation is linked to histone deacetylation. Whereas acetylated histones are relatively unstable and cause the nucleosomes to disperse, deacetylated histones form a stable nucleosome. The protein MeCP2 selectively binds to methylated regions of DNA; it also binds to histone deacetylases. Thus, when MeCP2 binds to methylated DNA it can stabilize the nucleosomes in that particular region of chromatin. Methylated DNA may also be preferentially bound by histone H1, the histone that associates nucleosomes into higher-order folded complexes. These patterns are maintained through cell division by the enzyme DNA (cytosine-5)-methyltransferase. During replication, one strand of the DNA (the template strand) retains the methylation pattern, while the newly synthesized strand does not. However, the enzyme DNA (cytosine-5)-methyltransferase has a strong preference for DNA that has one methylated strand, and when it sees a methyl-CpG on one side of the DNA, it methylates the new C on the other side.

TRANSCRIPTIONAL REGULATION OF AN ENTIRE CHROMOSOME: DOSAGE COMPENSATION

In *Drosophila* and mammals, females are characterized as having two X chromosomes per cell, while males are characterized as having a single X chromosome per cell. Unlike the Y chromosome, the X chromosome contains thousands of genes that are essential for cell activity. Yet, despite the female's cells having double the number of X chromosomes the male's have, male and female cells contain approximately equal amounts of X chromosome-encoded gene products. This equalization is called dosage compensation. The transcription rates of the X chromosomes are altered so that male and female cells transcribe the same amount of RNAs from their X chromosomes. In *Drosophila,* both X chromosomes in the female are active, but there is increased transcription from the male's

X chromosome, so that the single X chromosome of male cells produces as much product as the two X chromosomes in female cells. This is accomplished by the binding of particular transcription factors to hundreds of sites along the male X chromosome.

In mammals, X chromosome dosage compensation occurs through the inactivation of one X chromosome in each female cell. Thus, each mammalian somatic cell, whether male or female, has only one functioning X chromosome. This phenomenon is called X chromosome inactivation. The chromatin of the inactive X chromosome is converted into heterochromatin—chromatin that remains condensed throughout most of the cell cycle and replicates later than most of the other chromatin (the euchromatin) of the nucleus. The heterochromatic (inactive) X chromosome can often be seen on the nuclear envelope of female cells and is referred to as a Barr body. X chromosome inactivation must occur early in development. Using a mutated X chromosome that would not inactivate, Tagaki and Abe showed that the expression of two X chromosomes per cell in mouse embryos leads to ectodermal cell death and the absence of mesoderm formation, eventually causing embryonic death at day 10 of gestation.

The early inactivation of one X chromosome per cell has important phenotypic consequences. One of the earliest analyses of X chromosome inactivation was performed by Mary Lyon, who observed coat colour patterns in mice. If a mouse is heterozygous for an autosomal gene controlling hair pigmentation, then it resembles one of its two parents, or has a colour intermediate between the two. In either case, the mouse is a single colour. But if a female mouse is heterozygous for a pigmentation gene on the X chromosome, a different result is seen: patches of one parental colour alternate with patches of the other parental colour. Lyon proposed the following hypothesis to account for these results:

1. Very early in the development of female mammals, both X chromosomes are active.
2. As development proceeds, one X chromosome is turned off in each cell.

3. This inactivation is random. In some cells, the paternally derived X chromosome is inactivated; in other cells, the maternally derived X chromosome is shut off.
4. This process is irreversible. Once an X chromosome has been inactivated, the same X chromosome is inactivated in all that cell's progeny. Since X inactivation happens relatively early in development, an entire region of cells derived from a single cell may all have the same X chromosome inactivated. Thus, all tissues in female mammals are mosaics of two cell types.

The Lyon hypothesis of X chromosome inactivation provides an excellent account of differential gene inactivation at the level of transcription. Some interesting exceptions to the general rules further show its importance. First, X chromosome inactivation holds true only for somatic cells, not germ cells. In female germ cells, the inactive X chromosome is reactivated shortly before the cells enter meiosis. Thus, in early oocytes, both X chromosomes are unmethylated (and active). In each generation, X chromosome inactivation has to be established anew.

Second, there are some exceptions to the rule of randomness in the inactivation pattern. For instance, the first X chromosome inactivation in the mouse is seen in the fetal portion of the placenta, where the paternally derived X chromosome is specifically inactivated. Third, X chromosome inactivation does not extend to every gene on the human X chromosome. There are a few genes (such as that encoding steroid sulfatase) on both arms of the X chromosome that "escape" X inactivation.

The fourth exception really ends up proving the rule. There are a few male mammals with coat colour patterns we would not expect to find unless the animals exhibited X chromosome inactivation. Male calico and tortoiseshell cats are among these examples. These orange and black spotted coat patterns are normally seen in females and are thought to result from random X chromosome inactivation. But rare males exhibit these coat patterns as well. How can this be? It turns out that these cats are XXY. The Y chromosome makes them male, but one X chromosome undergoes inactivation, just as in females, so there is only one active X per cell. Thus, these cats have cells with a Barr body and random X chromosome inactivation. It is clear, then, that one mechanism for transcription-level control of gene regulation is to make a large number of genes heterochromatic and thus transcriptionally inert.

DIFFERENTIAL RNA PROCESSING

The regulation of gene expression is not confined to the differential transcription of DNA. Even if a particular RNA transcript is synthesized, there is no guarantee that it will create a functional protein in the cell. To become an active protein, the RNA must be

1. Processed into a messenger RNA by the removal of introns,
2. Translocated from the nucleus to the cytoplasm, and
3. Translated by the protein-synthesizing apparatus. In some cases, the synthesized protein is not in its mature form and
4. Must be posttranslationally modified to become active. Regulation can occur at any of these steps during development.

The essence of differentiation is the production of different sets of proteins in different types of cells. In bacteria, differential gene expression can be effected at the levels of transcription, translation, and protein modification. In eukaryotes, however, another possible level of regulation exists—namely, control at the level of RNA processing and transport. There are two major ways in which differential RNA processing can regulate development. The first involves the "censoring" of which nuclear transcripts are processed into cytoplasmic messages. Here, different cells can select different nuclear transcripts to be processed and sent to the cytoplasm as messenger RNA. The same pool of nuclear transcripts can thereby give rise to different populations of cytoplasmic mRNAs in different cell types. The second mode of differential RNA processing is the splicing of the mRNA precursors into messages for different proteins by using different combinations of potential exons. If an mRNA precursor had five potential exons, one cell might use exons 1, 2, 4, and 5; a different cell might utilize exons 1, 2, and 3; and yet another cell type might use yet another combination. Thus, one gene can create a family of related proteins.

CONTROL OF EARLY DEVELOPMENT BY NUCLEAR RNA SELECTION

In the late 1970s, numerous investigators found that mRNA was not the primary transcript from the genes. Rather, the genes transcribed nuclear RNA (nRNA), sometimes called heterogeneous nuclear RNA (hnRNA) or pre-messenger RNA (pre-mRNA). This nRNA is usually many times longer than the messenger RNA because the nuclear RNA contains introns that get spliced out during the passage from nucleus to cytoplasm. Originally, investigators thought that whatever RNA was transcribed in the nucleus was processed into cytoplasmic mRNA. But studies of sea urchins showed that different cell types could be *transcribing* the *same* type of nuclear RNA, but *processing* different subsets of this population into mRNA in different types of cells. Wold and her colleagues (1978) showed that sequences present in sea urchin blastula *messenger* RNA, but absent in gastrula and adult tissue mRNA, were nonetheless present in the *nuclear* RNA of the gastrula and adult tissues.

More genes are transcribed in the nucleus than are allowed to become mRNAs in the cytoplasm. This censoring of RNA transcripts has been confirmed for specific messages by probing for the introns and exons of specific genes. Gagnon and his colleagues performed such an analysis on the transcripts from the *CyIIIa* genes of the sea urchin *Strongylocentrotus purpuratus*. These genes encode calcium-binding and actin proteins, respectively, that are expressed only in a particular part of the ectoderm of the sea urchin larva. Using probes that bound to an exon (which is included in the mRNA) and to an intron (which is not included in the mRNA), they found that these genes were being transcribed not only in the ectodermal cells, but also in the mesoderm and endoderm. The analysis of the *CyIIIa* gene showed that the concentration of introns was the same in both the gastrula ectoderm and in the mesoderm/endoderm samples, suggesting that this gene was being transcribed at the same rate in the nuclei of all cell types, but was made into cytoplasmic mRNA only in ectodermal cells. The unprocessed nRNA for CyIIIa is degraded while still in the nuclei of the endodermal and mesodermal cells.

CREATING FAMILIES OF PROTEINS THROUGH DIFFERENTIAL NRNA SPLICING

The average vertebrate nRNA consists of relatively short exons (averaging about 140 bases) separated by introns that are usually much longer. Most mammalian nRNAs contain numerous exons. By splicing together different sets of exons, different cells can make different types of mRNAs, and hence, different proteins. Whether a sequence of RNA is recognized as an exon or as an intron is a crucial step in gene regulation. What is an intron in one cell's nucleus may be an exon in another cell's nucleus.

Alternative nRNA splicing is based on determining which sequences can be spliced out as introns. This can occur in several ways. Cells can differ in their ability to recognize the 5′ splice site (at the beginning of the intron) or the 3′ splice site (at the end of the intron). Or some cells could fail to recognize a sequence as an intron at all, retaining it within the message. The splicing of nRNA is mediated through a complex called a spliceosome, made up of small nuclear RNAs (snRNA) and proteins, that assembles at a splice site. Whether a spliceosome recognizes the splice sites depends on certain factors in the nucleus that can interact with those sites and compete or cooperate with the proteins that direct spliceosome formation. The 5′ splice site is normally recognized by small nuclear RNA U1 (U1 snRNA) and splicing factor 2 (SF2; also known as alternative splicing factor). The choice of alternative 3′ splice sites is often controlled by which splice site can best bind a protein called U2AF. The spliceosome forms when the 5′ and 3′ splice sites are brought together and the intervening RNA is cut out.

Differential RNA processing has been found to control the alternative forms of expression of genes encoding over 100 proteins. The deletion of certain potential exons in some cells but not in others enables one gene to create a family of closely related proteins. Instead of one gene-one polypeptide, one can have one gene-one family of proteins. For instance, alternative RNA splicing enables the α-tropomyosin gene to encode brain, liver, skeletal muscle, smooth muscle, and fibroblast forms of this protein. The nuclear RNA for α-tropomyosin contains 11 potential exons, but different sets of exons are used in different cells. Such different proteins encoded by the same gene are called splicing isoforms of the protein.

In some instances, alternatively spliced RNAs yield proteins that play similar, yet distinguishable, roles in the same cell. The nuclear RNA for the Pax6 transcription factor is actually spliced to yield two types of Pax6 proteins. In about half the mRNAs, there is an added exon that interrupts one major DNA-binding site and enables another to be used. The two forms of Pax 6 appear to be made at similar rates in all the cells expressing the *Pax6* gene. If the human gene for *PAX6* is mutated such that the 5′ splicing site becomes more efficient, the Pax6 isoform containing the amino acids encoded by the alternatively spliced exon is made in excess. The eyes of people with this mutation have defects in their lenses, corneas, and pupils.

If you think that differential splicing means that certain genes with dozens of introns can create thousands of different related proteins, you are probably correct. Proteins derived from the neurexin genes, for example, are found on the cell surfaces of developing neurons, and they may be important in specifying the connections that these neurons make. These genes can be alternatively spliced at several different sites, creating hundreds of proteins from the same gene.

CONTROL OF GENE EXPRESSION AT THE LEVEL OF TRANSLATION

Once the RNA has reached the cytoplasm, there is still no guarantee that it will be translated. The control of gene expression at the level of translation can occur by many means; some of the most important of these are described below.

Differential mRNA Longevity

The longer an mRNA persists, the more protein can be translated from it. If a message with a relatively short half-life were selectively stabilized in certain cells at certain times, it would make large amounts of its particular protein only at those times and places. The stability of a message is often dependent upon the length of its poly(A) tail. This, in turn, appears to depend upon sequences in the 3′ untranslated region. Certain 3′ UTR sequences allow longer poly(A) tails than others. If these regions are experimentally traded, the half-lives of the resulting mRNAs will be altered: usually long-lived messages will decay rapidly, while normally short-lived mRNAs will remain around longer. In some instances, messenger RNAs can be selectively stabilized at specific times in specific cells. The mRNA for casein, the major protein of milk, has a half-life of 1.1 hours in rat mammary gland tissue. However, during periods of lactation, the presence of the hormone prolactin increases this half-life to 28.5 hours.

SELECTIVE INHIBITION OF MRNA TRANSLATION

Some of the most remarkable cases of translational regulation of gene expression occur in the oocyte. The oocyte often makes and stores mRNAs that will be used only after fertilization occurs. These messages stay in a dormant state until they are actived by ionic signals that spread through the egg during ovulation or sperm binding.

Some mRNAs stored in oocyte cytoplasm and translated at or near fertilization

mRNAs encoding	Function(s)	Organism(s)
Cyclins	Cell division regulation	Sea urchin, clam, starfish, frog
Actin	Cell movement and contraction	Mouse, starfish
Tubulin	Formation mitotic spindles, cilia, flagella	Clam, mouse
Small subunit of ribonucleotide reductase	DNA synthesis	Sea urchin, clam, starfish
Hypoxanthine phosphoribosyl-transferase	Purine synthesis	Mouse
Vg1	Mesodermal determination(?)	Frog
Histones	Chromatin formation	Sea urchin, frog, clam
Cadherins	Blastomere adhesion	Frog
Metalloproteinases	Implantation in uterus	Mouse
Growth factors	Cell growth; uterine cell growth(?)	Mouse
Sex determination factor FEM-3	Sperm formation	*C. elegans*
PAR gene products	Segregate morphogenetic determinants	*C. elegans*
SKN-1 morphogen	Blastomere fate determination	*C. elegans*
Hunchback morphogen	Anterior fate determination	*Drosophila*
Caudal morphogen	Posterior fate determination	*Drosophila*
Bicoid morphogen	Anterior fate determination	*Drosophila*
Nanos morphogen	Posterior fate determination	*Drosophila*
GLP-1 morphogen	Anterior fate determination	*C. elegans*
Germ cell-less protein	Germ cell determination	*Drosophila*
Oskar protein	Germ cell localization	*Drosophila*
Ornithine transcarbamylase	Urea cycle	Frog
Elongation factor 1α	Protein synthesis	Frog
Ribosomal proteins	Protein synthesis	Frog, *Drosophila*

Table gives a partial list of some of the mRNAs that are stored in the oocyte cytoplasm. Some of these stored mRNAs are for proteins that will be needed during cleavage, when the embryo makes enormous amounts of chromatin, cell membranes, and cytoskeletal components. Some of them encode cyclin proteins that regulate the timing of early cell division. Indeed, in many species (including sea urchins and *Drosophila*), maintenance of the normal rate and pattern of early cell divisions does not require a nucleus; rather, it requires continued protein synthesis from stored maternal mRNAs. Other stored messages encode proteins that determine the fates of cells. These include the *bicoid* and *nanos* messages that provide positional information in the *Drosophila* embryo, as we saw in earlier Chapter, and the *glp-1* mRNA of the nematode *C. elegans*.

In some instances, these messages are prevented from being translated by the binding of some inhibitory protein. For instance, the smaug protein binds to the 3′ UTR of the *Drosophila nanos* message, and this prevents the translation of *nanos* mRNA in the oocyte until fertilization. (At that time, the Nanos protein will become critical for determining which part of the fly will be its abdomen.) In other instances, the translatability of the mRNA is regulated by the length of its poly(A) tail. In oocytes, having a short poly(A) tail does not lead to the degradation of the message; however, such messages are not translated. In the *Drosophila* oocyte, the *bicoid* message remains untranslated until signals at fertilization allow the Cortex and Grauzone proteins to add poly(A) residues to the *bicoid* mRNA. At that point, the *bicoid* message becomes translatable (and its product determines which part of the embryo becomes the head and thorax). Other organisms use ingenious ways of regulating the translatability of their messages. The oocyte of the tobacco hornworm moth makes some of its mRNAs without their methylated 5′ caps. In this state, they cannot be efficiently translated. However, at fertilization, a methyltransferase completes the formation of the caps, and these mRNAs can be translated.

One of the most remarkable ways of regulating the translation of a specific message is seen in *Caenorhabditis elegans*. This nematode lives up to its name, having evolved a particularly elegant solution to the problem of controlling larval gene expression. It makes a naturally occuring antisense mRNA to one of its own messages. High levels of the LIN-14 transcription factor are important in the development of early larval organs. Thereafter, the LIN-14 protein is no longer seen, although *lin-14* messages can be detected throughout development. *C. elegans* is able to inhibit the synthesis of LIN-14 from these messages by activating the *lin-4* gene. The *lin-4* gene does not encode a protein. Rather, it encodes two small RNAs (the most abundant being 25 nucleotides long, the other continuing for 40 more nucleotides) that are complementary to an imperfectly repeated site in the *lin-14* 3′ UTR. It appears that the binding of the *lin-4* transcripts to the *lin-14* mRNA 3′ UTR does not signal the destruction of the message, but rather prevents the message from being translated.

CONTROL OF RNA EXPRESSION BY CYTOPLASMIC LOCALIZATION

Not only is the time of mRNA translation regulated, but so is the place of RNA expression. Just like the selective repression of mRNA translation, the selective localization of messages is also often accomplished through their 3′ UTRs, and it is also often performed in oocytes. Rebagliati and colleagues showed that there are certain mRNAs in *Xenopus* embryos that are selectively transported to the vegetal pole of the frog oocyte. After fertilization, these messages make proteins that are found only in the vegetal blastomeres. In *Drosophila*, the *bicoid* and *nanos* messages are each localized to different ends of the oocyte. The 3′ UTR of the *bicoid* mRNA allows this message to bind to the microtubules through its association with two other proteins (swallow and staufen). If the *bicoid* 3′ UTR is attached to some other message, that mRNA also will be bound to the anterior pole of the oocyte. The 3′ UTR of the *nanos* message similarly allows it to be transported to the posterior pole of the egg, where it will be bound to the cytoskeleton. As we saw in earlier Chapter, this localization allows the Bicoid protein to form a gradient wherein the highest amount of it is at the anterior pole, while the Nanos protein forms a gradient with its peak at the posterior pole. The ratio of these two proteins will eventually determine the anterior-posterior axis of the *Drosophila* embryo and adult.

EPILOGUE: POSTTRANSLATIONAL GENE REGULATION

When a protein is synthesized, the story is still not over. Once a protein is made, it becomes part of a larger level of organization. For instance, it may become part of the structural framework of the cell, or it may become involved in one of the myriad enzymatic pathways for the synthesis or breakdown of cellular metabolites. In any case, the individual protein is now part of a complex "ecosystem" that integrates it into a relationship with numerous other proteins. Thus, several changes can still take place that determine whether or not the protein will be active. Some newly synthesized proteins are inactive without the cleaving away of certain inhibitory sections. This is what happens when insulin is made from its larger protein precursor. Some proteins must be "addressed" to their specific intracellular destinations in order to function. Proteins are often sequestered in certain regions, such as membranes, lysosomes, nuclei, or mitochondria. Some proteins need to assemble with other proteins to form a functional unit. The hemoglobin protein, the microtubule, and the ribosome are all examples of numerous proteins joining together to form a functional unit. And some proteins are not active unless they bind an ion such as calcium, or are modified by the covalent addition of a phosphate or acetate group. This last type of protein modification will become very important in the next chapter, since many important proteins in embryonic cells are just sitting there until some signal activates them. We turn next to how the embryo develops by activating certain proteins in specific cells.

Chapter 6

Cell-cell Communication in Development

The formation of organized bodies has been one of the great sources of wonder for humankind. Indeed, the "miracle of life" seems just that—matter has become organized in such a way that it lives. While each organism starts off as a single cell, the progeny of that cell form complex structures—tissues and organs—that are themselves integrated into larger systems. Probably no one better recognizes how remarkable life actually is than the developmental biologists who get to study how all this complexity arises. In the past decade, developmental biologists have started to answer some of the most important questions of natural science: We have begun to understand how organs form.

INDUCTION AND COMPETENCE

Organs are complex structures composed of numerous types of tissues. In the vertebrate eye, for example, light is transmitted through the transparent corneal tissue and focused by the lens tissue (the diameter of which is controlled by muscle tissue), eventually impinging on the tissue of the neural retina. The precise arrangement of tissues in this organ cannot be disturbed without impairing its function. Such coordination in the construction of organs is accomplished by one group of cells changing the behaviour of an adjacent set of cells, thereby causing them to change their shape, mitotic rate, or fate. This kind of interaction at close range between two or more cells or tissues of different history and properties is called proximate interaction, or induction. There are at least two components to every inductive interaction. The first component is the inducer: the tissue that produces a signal (or signals) that changes the cellular behaviour of the other tissue. The second component, the tissue being induced, is the responder.

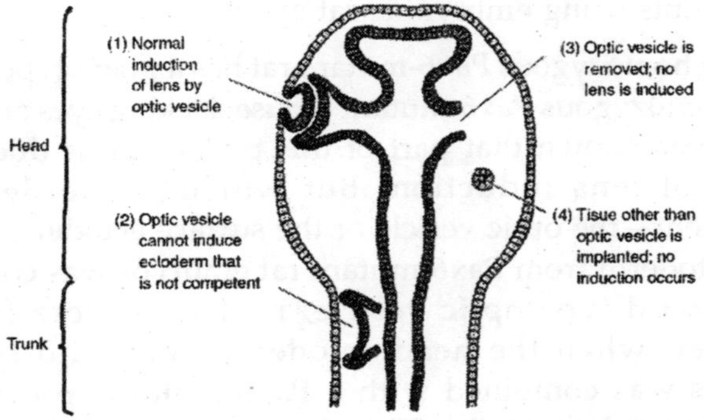

Fig. Ectodermal competence and the ability to respond to the optic vesicle inducer in *Xenopus*. (1) The optic vesicle is able to induce lenses in the anterior portion of the ectoderm, but not in the presumptive trunk and abdomen (2). If the optic vesicle is removed (3), the surface ectoderm forms either an abnormal lens or no lens at all. (4) Most other tissues are not able to substitute for the optic vesicle.

Not all tissues can respond to the signal being produced by the inducer. For instance, if the optic vesicle (presumptive retina) of *Xenopus laevis* is placed in an ectopic location (i.e., in a different place from where it normally forms) underneath the head ectoderm, it will induce that ectoderm to form lens tissue. Only the optic vesicle appears to be able to do this; therefore, it is an inducer. However, if the optic vesicle is placed beneath ectoderm in the flank or abdomen of the same organism, that ectoderm will not be able to respond. Only the head ectoderm is competent to respond to the signals from the optic vesicle by producing a lens.

This ability to respond to a specific inductive signal is called competence. Competence is not a passive state, but an actively acquired condition. For example, in the developing chick and mammalian eye, the Pax6 protein appears to be important in making the ectoderm competent to respond to the inductive signal from the optic vesicle. Pax6 expression is seen in the head ectoderm, which can respond to the optic vesicle by forming lenses, and it is not seen in other regions of the surface ectoderm. Moreover, the importance of Pax6 as a competence factor was demonstrated by recombination experiments using embryonic rat eye tissue.

The homozygous Pax6-mutant rat has a phenotype similar to the homozygous Pax6-mutant mouse, lacking eyes and nose. It has been shown that part of this phenotype is due to the failure of lens induction. But which is the defective component—the optic vesicle or the surface ectoderm? When head ectoderm from Pax6-mutant rat embryos was combined with a wild-type optic vesicle, no lenses were formed. However, when the head ectoderm from wild-type rat embryos was combined with a Pax6-mutant optic vesicle, lenses formed normally. Therefore, Pax6 is needed for the surface ectoderm to respond to the inductive signal from the optic vesicle. The inducing tissue does not need it. It is not known how Pax6 becomes expressed in the anterior ectoderm of the embryo, although it is thought that its expression is induced by the anterior regions of the neural plate. Competence to respond to the optic vesicle inducer can be conferred on ectodermal tissue by incubating it next to anterior neural plate tissue.

Thus, there is no single inducer of the lens. Studies on amphibians suggest that the first inducers may be the pharyngeal endoderm and heart-forming mesoderm that underlie the lens-forming ectoderm during the early- and mid-gastrula stages. The anterior neural plate may produce the next signals, including a signal that promotes the synthesis of Pax6 in the anterior ectoderm. Thus, the optic vesicle appears to be *the* inducer, but the anterior ectoderm has already been induced by at least two other factors. (The situation is like that of the player who kicks *the* "winning goal" of a soccer match.) The optic vesicle appears to secrete two induction factors, one of which is BMP4, a protein that induces the transcription of the Sox2 and Sox3 transcription factors (and another, as yet unidentified, signal that induces the appearance of the l-Maf transcription factor. The combination of Pax6, Sox2, Sox3, and l-Maf ensures the production of the lens.

CASCADES OF INDUCTION: RECIPROCAL AND SEQUENTIAL INDUCTIVE EVENTS

Another feature of induction is the reciprocal nature of many inductive interactions. Once the lens has formed, it can then induce other tissues. One of these responding tissues is the optic vesicle itself. Now the inducer becomes the induced. Under the influence of factors secreted by the lens, the optic vesicle becomes the optic cup, and the wall of the optic cup differentiates into two layers, the pigmented retina and the neural retina. Such interactions are called reciprocal inductions.

At the same time, the lens is also inducing the ectoderm above it to become the cornea. Like the lens-forming ectoderm, the cornea-forming ectoderm has achieved a particular competence to respond to inductive signals, in this case the signals from the lens. Under the influence of the lens, the corneal ectodermal cells become columnar and secrete multiple layers of collagen. Mesenchymal cells from the neural crest use this collagen matrix to enter the area and secrete a set of proteins (including the enzyme hyaluronidase) that further differentiate the cornea. A third signal, the hormone thyroxine, dehydrates the tissue and makes it transparent. Thus, there are sequential inductive events, and multiple causes for each induction.

INSTRUCTIVE AND PERMISSIVE INTERACTIONS

Howard Holtzer distinguished two major modes of inductive interaction. In instructive interaction, a signal from the inducing cell is necessary for initiating new gene expression in the responding cell. Without the inducing cell, the responding cell would not be capable of differentiating in that particular way. For example, when the optic vesicle is experimentally placed under a new region of the head ectoderm and causes that region of the ectoderm to form a lens, that is an instructive interaction. Wessells has proposed three general principles characteristic of most instructive interactions:

1. In the presence of tissue A, responding tissue B develops in a certain way.
2. In the absence of tissue A, responding tissue B does not develop in that way.
3. In the absence of tissue A, but in the presence of tissue C, tissue B does not develop in that way.

The second type of induction is permissive interaction. Here, the responding tissue contains all the potentials that are to be expressed, and needs only an environment that allows the expression of these traits.‡ For instance, many tissues need a solid substrate containing fibronectin or laminin in order to develop. The fibronectin or laminin does not alter the type of cell that is to be produced, but only enables what has been determined to be expressed.

EPITHELIAL-MESENCHYMAL INTERACTIONS

Some epithelial-mesenchymal interactions

Organ	Epithelial component	Mesenchymal component
Cutaneous structures (hair, feathers, sweat glands, mammary glands)	Epidermis (ectoderm)	Dermis (mesoderm)
Limb	Epidermis (ectoderm)	Mesenchyme (mesoderm)
Gut organs (liver, pancreas, salivary glands)	Epithelium (endoderm)	Mesenchyme (mesoderm)
Pharyngeal and respiratory associated organs (lungs, thymus, thyroid)	Epithelium (endoderm)	Mesenchyme (mesoderm)
Kidney	Ureteric bud epithelim (mesoderm)	Mesenchyme (mesoderm)
Tooth	Jaw epithelium (ectoderm)	Mesenchyme (neural crest)

Some of the best-studied cases of induction are those involving the interactions of sheets of epithelial cells with adjacent mesenchymal cells. These interactions are called epithelial-mesenchymal interactions. Epithelia are sheets or tubes of connected cells; they can originate from any germ layer. Mesenchyme refers to loosely packed, unconnected cells. Mesenchymal cells are derived from the mesoderm or neural crest. All organs consist of an epithelium and an associated mesenchyme, so epithelial-mesenchymal interactions are among the most important phenomena in nature. Some examples are listed in Table.

REGIONAL SPECIFICITY OF INDUCTION.

Using the induction of cutaneous structures as our examples, we will look at the properties of epithelial-mesenchymal interactions. The first of these properties is the regional specificity of induction. Skin is composed of two main tissues: an outer epidermis, an epithelial tissue derived from ectoderm, and a dermis, a mesenchymal tissue derived from mesoderm. The chick epidermis signals the underlying dermal cells to form condensations (probably by secreting Sonic hedgehog and TGF-β2 proteins, which will be discussed below), and the condensed dermal mesenchyme responds by secreting factors that cause the epidermis to form regionally specific cutaneous structures. These structures can be the broad feathers of the wing, the narrow feathers of the thigh, or the scales and claws of the feet. Researchers can separate the embryonic epithelium and mesenchyme from each other and recombine them in different ways.

The dermal mesenchyme is responsible for the regional specificity of induction in the competent epidermal epithelium. The same type of epithelium develops cutaneous structures according to the region from which the mesenchyme was taken. Here, the mesenchyme plays an instructive role, calling into play different sets of genes in the responding epithelial cells.

GENETIC SPECIFICITY OF INDUCTION.

The second property of epithelial-mesenchymal interactions is the genetic specificity of induction. Whereas the mesenchyme may instruct the epithelium as to what sets of genes to activate, the responding epithelium can comply with these instructions only so far as its genome permits. This property was discovered through experiments involving the transplantation of tissues from one species to another. In one of the most dramatic examples of interspecific induction, Hans Spemann and Oscar Schotté transplanted flank ectoderm from an early frog gastrula to the region of a newt gastrula destined to become parts of the mouth. Similarly, they placed presumptive flank ectodermal tissue from a newt gastrula into the presumptive oral regions of frog embryos. The structures of the mouth region differ greatly between salamander and frog larvae. The salamander larva has club-shaped balancers beneath its mouth, whereas the frog tadpole produces mucus-secreting glands and suckers. The frog tadpole also has a horny jaw without teeth, whereas the salamander has a set of calcareous teeth in its jaw. The larvae resulting from the transplants were chimeras. The salamander larvae had froglike mouths, and the frog tadpoles had salamander teeth and balancers. In other words, the mesodermal cells instructed the ectoderm to make a mouth, but the ectoderm responded by making the only kind of mouth it "knew" how to make, no matter how inappropriate.

Thus, the instructions sent by the mesenchymal tissue can cross species barriers. Salamanders respond to frog signals, and chick tissue responds to mammalian inducers. The response of the epithelium, however, is species-specific. So, whereas organ type specificity (e.g., feather or claw) is usually controlled by the mesenchyme within a species, species specificity is usually controlled by the responding epithelium. As we will see in later Chapters, large evolutionary changes can be brought about by changing the response to a particular inducer.

PARACRINE FACTORS

How are the signals between inducer and responder transmitted? While studying the mechanisms of induction that produce the kidney tubules and teeth, Grobstein and others found that some inductive events could occur despite a filter separating the epithelial and mesenchymal cells. Other inductions, however, were blocked by the filter. The researchers therefore concluded that some of the inductive molecules were soluble factors that could pass through the small pores of the filter, and that other inductive events required physical contact between the epithelial and mesenchymal cells. When cell membrane proteins on one cell surface interact with receptor proteins on adjacent cell surfaces, these events are called juxtacrine interactions (since the cell membranes are juxtaposed). When proteins synthesized by one cell can diffuse over small distances to induce changes in neighbouring cells, the event is called a paracrine interaction, and the diffusible proteins are called paracrine factors or growth and differentiation factors (GDFs). We will consider paracrine interactions first and then return to juxtacrine interactions later in the chapter.

Whereas *endocrine* factors (hormones) travel through the blood to exert their effects, *paracrine* factors are secreted into the immediate spaces around the cell producing them. These proteins are the "inducing factors" of the classic experimental embryologists. During the past decade, developmental biologists have discovered that the induction of numerous organs is actually effected by a relatively small set of paracrine factors. The embryo inherits a rather compact "tool kit" and uses many of the same proteins to construct the heart, the kidneys, the teeth, the eyes, and other organs. Moreover, the same proteins are utilized throughout the animal kingdom; the factors active in creating the *Drosophila* eye or heart are very similar to those used in generating mammalian organs. Many of these paracrine factors can be grouped into four major families on the basis of their structures. These families are the fibroblast growth factor (FGF) family, the Hedgehog family, the Wingless (Wnt) family, and the TGF-β superfamily.

THE FIBROBLAST GROWTH FACTORS

The fibroblast growth factor (FGF) family currently has over a dozen structurally related members. FGF1 is also known as acidic FGF; FGF2 is sometimes called basic FGF; and FGF7 sometimes goes by the name of keratinocyte growth factor. Over a dozen distinct FGF genes are known in vertebrates, and they can generate hundreds of protein isoforms by varying their RNA splicing or initiation codons in different tissues. FGFs can activate a set of receptor tyrosine kinases called the fibroblast growth factor receptors (FGFRs).

As we will discuss later in this chapter, receptor tyrosine kinases are proteins that extend through the cell membrane. On the extracellular side is the portion of the protein that binds the paracrine factor. On the intracellular side is a dormant tyrosine kinase (i.e., a protein that can phosphorylate another protein by splitting ATP). When the FGF receptor binds an FGF (and only when it binds an FGF), the dormant kinase is activated, and it phosphorylates certain proteins within the responding cell. The proteins are now activated and can perform new functions. FGFs are associated with several developmental functions, including angiogenesis (blood vessel formation), mesoderm formation, and axon extension. While FGFs can often substitute for one another, their expression patterns give them separate functions. FGF2 is especially important in angiogenesis, and FGF8 is important for the development of the midbrain and limbs.

THE HEDGEHOG FAMILY

The Hedgehog proteins constitute a family of paracrine factors that are often used by the embryo to induce particular cell types and to create boundaries between tissues. Vertebrates have at least three homologues of the Drosophila hedgehog gene: sonic hedgehog (shh), desert hedgehog (dhh), and indian hedgehog (ihh). Desert hedgehog is expressed in the Sertoli cells of the testes, and mice homozygous for a null allele of dhh exhibit defective spermatogenesis. Indian hedgehog is expressed in the gut and in cartilage and is important in postnatal bone growth.

Sonic hedgehog is the most widely used of the three vertebrate homologues. Made by the notochord, it is processed so that only the amino-terminal two-thirds of the molecule is secreted. This peptide is responsible for patterning the neural tube such that motor neurons are formed from the ventral neurons and sensory neurons are formed from the dorsal neurons. Sonic hedgehog is also responsible for patterning the somites so that the portion of the somite closest to the notochord becomes the cartilage of the spine. As we will see in later chapters, Sonic hedgehog has been shown to mediate the formation of the left-right axis in chicks, to initiate the anterior-posterior axis in limbs, to induce the regionally specific differentiation of the digestive tube, and to induce feather formation. Sonic hedgehog often works with other paracrine factors, such as Wnt and FGF proteins. In the developing tooth, Sonic hedgehog, FGF4, and other paracrine factors are concentrated in the region where cell interactions are creating the cusps of the teeth.

THE WNT FAMILY

The Wnts constitute a family of cysteine-rich glycoproteins. There are at least 15 members of this family in vertebrates. Their name comes from fusing the name of the *Drosophila* segment polarity gene *wingless* with the name of one of its vertebrate homologues, *integrated*. While Sonic hedgehog is important in patterning the ventral portion of the somites (causing the cells to become cartilage), Wnt1 appears to be active in inducing the dorsal cells of the somites to become muscle. Wnt proteins also are critical in establishing the polarity of insect and vertebrate limbs, and they are used in several steps of urogenital system development.

There are over 30 structurally related members of the TGF-b superfamily, and they regulate some of the most important interactions in development. The proteins encoded by TGF-β superfamily genes are processed such that the carboxy-terminal region contains the mature peptide. These peptides are dimerized into homodimers (with themselves) or heterodimers (with other TGF-β peptides) and are secreted from the cell. The TGF-β superfamily includes the TGF-β family, the activin family, the bone morphogenetic proteins (BMPs), the Vg1 family, and other proteins, including glial-derived neurotrophic factor (necessary for kidney and enteric neuron differentiation) and Müllerian inhibitory factor (which is involved in mammalian sex determination).

TGF-β family members TGF-β1, 2, 3, and 5 are important in regulating the formation of the extracellular matrix between cells and for regulating cell division (both positively and negatively). TGF-β1 increases the amount of extracellular matrix epithelial cells make (both by stimulating collagen and fibronectin synthesis and by inhibiting matrix degradation). TGF-βs may be critical in controlling where and when epithelia can branch to form the ducts of kidneys, lungs, and salivary glands. The effects of the individual TGF-β family members are difficult to sort out, because members of the TGF-β family appear to function similarly and can compensate for losses of the others when expressed together. Moreover, targeted deletions of the *Tgf-β1* gene in mice are difficult to interpret, since the mother can supply this factor through the placenta and milk.

The members of the BMP family were originally discovered by their ability to induce bone formation; hence, they are the *b*one *m*orphogenetic *p*roteins. Bone formation, however, is only one of their many functions, and they have been found to regulate cell division, apoptosis (programmed cell death), cell migration, and differentiation. BMPs can be distinguished from other members of the TGF-β superfamily by their having seven, rather than nine, conserved cysteines in the mature polypeptide. The *Drosophila* Decapentaplegic protein is homologous to the vertebrate BMP4, and human BMP4 can replace the *Drosophila* homologue, rescuing those flies deficient in Dpp.

OTHER PARACRINE FACTORS

Although most of the paracrine factors are members of the above-mentioned four families, some have few or no close relatives. Factors such as epidermal growth factor, hepatocyte growth factor, neurotrophins, and stem cell factor are not in the above-mentioned families, but each plays important roles during development. In addition, there are numerous factors involved almost exclusively with developing blood cells: erythropoietin, the cytokines, and the interleukins. These factors will be discussed when we detail blood cell formation in later Chapter.

CELL SURFACE RECEPTORS AND THEIR SIGNAL TRANSDUCTION PATHWAYS

The paracrine factors are inducer proteins. We now turn to the molecules involved in the *response* to induction. These molecules include the receptors in the membrane of the responding cell, which binds the paracrine factor, and the cascade of interacting proteins that transmit a signal through a pathway from the bound receptor to the nucleus. These pathways between the cell membrane and the genome are called signal transduction pathways. Several types of signal transduction pathways have been discovered, and we will outline some of the major ones here. They appear to be variations on a common and rather elegant theme: Each receptor spans the cell membrane and has an extracellular region, a transmembrane region, and a cytoplasmic region. When a ligand (the paracrine factor) binds its receptor in the extracellular region, the ligand induces a conformational change in the receptor's structure. This shape change is transmitted through the membrane and changes the shape of the cytoplasmic domains. The conformational change in the cytoplasmic domains gives them enzymatic activity—usually a kinase activity that can use ATP to phosphorylate proteins, including the receptor molecule itself. The active receptor can now catalyze reactions that phosphorylate other proteins, and this phosphorylation activates their latent activities in turn. Eventually, the cascade of phosphorylation activates a dormant transcription factor, which activates (or represses) a particular set of genes.

THE RTK PATHWAY

The RTK signal transduction pathway was one of the first pathways to unite various areas of developmental biology. Researchers studying *Drosophila* eyes, nematode vulvae, and human cancers found that they were all studying the same genes. The RTK-Ras pathway begins at the cell surface, where a receptor tyrosine kinase (RTK) binds its specific ligand. Ligands that bind to RTKs include the fibroblast growth factors, epidermal growth factors, platelet-derived growth factors, and stem cell factor. Each RTK can bind only one or a small set of these ligands. (Stem cell factor, for instance, will bind to only one RTK, the Kit protein.) The RTK spans the cell membrane, and when it binds its ligand, it undergoes a conformational change that enables it to dimerize with another RTK. This conformational change activates the latent kinase activity of each RTK, and these receptors phosphorylate each other on particular tyrosine residues. Thus, the binding of the ligand to the receptor causes the autophosphorylation of the cytoplasmic domain of the receptor.

The phosphorylated tyrosine on the receptor is then recognized by an adaptor protein. The adaptor protein serves as a bridge that links the phosphorylated RTK to a powerful intracellular signaling system. While binding to the phosphorylated RTK through one of its cytoplasmic domains, the adaptor protein also activates a G protein. Normally, the G protein is in an inactive, GDP-bound state. The activated receptor stimulates the adaptor protein to activate the guanine nucleotide releasing factor· This protein exchanges a phosphate from a GTP to transform the bound GDP into GTP. The GTP-bound G protein is an active form that transmits the signal. After delivering the signal, the GTP on the G protein is hydrolyzed back into GDP. This catalysis is greatly stimulated by the complexing of the Ras protein with the GTPase-activating protein (GAP). In this way, the G protein is returned to its inactive state, where it can await further signaling. One of the major G proteins is called Ras; mutations in the *RAS* gene account for a large proportion of human tumors, and the mutations of *RAS* that make it oncogenic all inhibit the binding of the GAP protein. Without the GAP protein, Ras protein cannot catalyze GTP well, and so remains in its active configuration.

The active G protein associates with a kinase called Raf. The G protein recruits the inactive Raf protein to the cell membrane, where it becomes active. The Raf protein is a kinase that activates the MEK protein by phosphorylating it. MEK is itself a kinase, which activates ERK by phosphorylation. And ERK is a kinase that can enter the nucleus and phosphorylate certain transcription factors. This pathway is critical in numerous developmental processes.

In the migrating neural crest cells of humans and mice, the RTK pathway is important in activating the microphthalmia transcription factor (Mitf) to produce the pigment cells. We have been following the Mitf transcription factor for the past two chapters. It is transcribed in the pigment-forming melanoblast cells that migrate from the neural crest into the skin and in the melanin-forming cells of the pigmented retina. But we have not yet discussed what proteins signal this transcription factor to become active. The clue lay in two mouse mutants whose phenotypes resemble those of mice homozygous for microphthalmia mutations. Like those mice, homozygous *White* mice and homozygous *Steel* mice are white because their pigment cells have failed to migrate. Perhaps all three genes (*Mitf,Steel,* and *White*) are on the same developmental pathway. In 1990, several labouratories demonstrated that the *Steel* gene encodes a paracrine protein called stem cell factor. Stem cell factor binds to and activates the Kit receptor tyrosine kinase encoded by the *White* gene. The binding of stem cell factor to the Kit RTK dimerizes the Kit protein, causing it to become phosphorylated. The phosphorylated Kit activates the pathway whereby phosphorylated ERK is able to phosphorylate the Mitf transcription factor. Only the phosphorylated form of Mitf is able to bind the p300/CBP coactivator protein that enables it to activate transcription of the genes encoding tyrosinase and other proteins of the melanin-formation pathway.

THE SMAD PATHWAY

Members of the TFG-β superfamily of paracrine factors activate members of the Smad family of transcription factors. The TGF-β ligand binds to a type II TGF-β receptor, which allows that receptor to bind to a type I TGF-β receptor. Once the two receptors are in close contact, the type II receptor phosphorylates a serine or threonine on the type I receptor, thereby activating it. The activated type I receptor can now phosphorylate the Smad proteins. (Researchers named the Smad proteins by eliding the names of the first identified members of this family: the *C. elegans* Sma protein and the *Drosophila* Mad protein.) Smads 1 and 5 are activated by the BMP family of TGF-β factors, while the receptors binding activin and the TGF-β family phosphorylate Smads 2 and 3. These phosphorylated Smads bind to Smad 4 and form the transcription factor complex that will enter the nucleus. In vertebrates, the TGF-β superfamily ligand Nodal appears to activate the Smads pathway in those cells responsible for the formation of the mesoderm and for specifying the left-right axis in vertebrates.

THE JAK-STAT PATHWAY

Another important pathway transducing information on the cell membrane to the nucleus is the JAK-STAT pathway. Here the set of transcription factors consists of the STAT (*s*ignal *t*ransducers and *a*ctivators of *t*ranscription) proteins (Ihle 1995Ihle 1996). STATs are phosphorylated by certain receptor tyrosine kinases, including fibroblast growth factor receptors and the JAK family of tyrosine kinases.

The JAK-STAT pathway is extremely important in the differentiation of blood cells and in the activation of the casein gene during milk production. Here, the endocrine factor prolactin binds to the extracellular regions of prolactin receptors, causing them to dimerize. A JAK protein kinase is bound to each of the receptors (in their respective cytoplasmic regions), and these JAK proteins are now brought together, where they can phosphorylate the receptors at several sites. The receptors are now activated and have their own protein kinase activity. Therefore, the JAK proteins convert a receptor into a receptor tyrosine kinase. The activated receptors can now phosphorylate particular inactive STATs and cause them to dimerize. These dimers are the active form of the STAT transcription factors, and they are translocated into the nucleus, where they bind to specific regions of DNA. In this case, they bind to the upstream promoter elements of the casein gene, causing it to be transcribed.

The STAT pathway is very important in the regulation of human fetal bone growth. Mutations that prematurely activate the STAT pathway have been implicated in some severe forms of dwarfism such as the lethal thanatophoric dysplasia, wherein the growth plates of the rib and limb bones fail to proliferate. The short-limbed newborn dies because its ribs cannot support breathing. The genetic lesion resides in the gene encoding fibroblast growth factor receptor 3 (FGFR3). This protein is expressed in the cartilage precursor cells—known as chondrocytes—in the growth plates of the long bones. Normally, the FGFR3 protein is activated by a fibroblast growth factor, and it signals the chondrocytes to stop dividing and begin differentiating into cartilage. This signal is mediated by the STAT1 protein, which is phosphorylated by the activated FGFR3 and then translocated into the nucleus. Inside the nucleus, this transcription factor activates the genes encoding a cell cycle inhibitor, the p21 protein. The mutations causing thanatophoric dwarfism result in a gain-of-function phenotype, wherein the mutant FGFR3 is active constitutively—that is, without the need to be activated by an FGF. This causes the chondrocytes to stop proliferating shortly after they are formed, and the bones fail to grow. Mutations that activate FGFR3 to a lesser degree produce achondroplasic (short-limbed) dwarfism, the most prevalent human dominant syndrome.

THE WNT PATHWAY

Members of the Wnt family of paracrine factors interact with transmembrane receptors of the Frizzled family. In most instances, the binding of Wnt by the Frizzled protein causes the Frizzled protein to activate the Disheveled protein. Once the Disheveled protein is activated, it inhibits the activity of the glycogen synthase kinase-3 enzyme. GSK-3, if it were active, would prevent the dissociation of the β-catenin protein from the APC protein, which targets β-catenin for degradation. However, when the Wnt signal is given and GSK-3 is inhibited, β-catenin can dissociate from the APC protein and enter the nucleus. Once inside the nucleus, it can form a heterodimer with an LEF or TCF DNA-binding protein, becoming a transcription factor. This complex binds to and activates the Wnt-responsive genes.

This model is undoubtedly an oversimplification, because different cells use this pathway in different ways. Moreover, its components can have more than one function in the cell. In addition to being part of the Wnt signal transduction cascade, GSK-3 is also a metabolic enzyme regulating glycogen metabolism. The β-catenin protein was first recognized as being part of the cell adhesion complex on the cell surface before it was also found to be a transcription factor. The APC protein also functions as a tumor suppressor in adults. The transformation of normal colon cells into colon cancer is thought to occur when the APC gene is mutated and can no longer keep the β-catenin protein out of the nucleus. Once in the nucleus, β-catenin can bind with another transcription factor and activate genes for cell division.

One principle that is readily seen in the Wnt pathway (and which is also evident in the Hedgehog pathway) is that activation is often accomplished by inhibiting an inhibitor. Thus, the GSK-3 protein is an inhibitor that is itself repressed by the Wnt signal.

THE HEDGEHOG PATHWAY

Members of the Hedgehog protein family function by binding to a receptor called Patched. The Patched protein, however, is not a signal transducer. Rather, it is bound to a signal transducer, the Smoothened protein. The Patched protein prevents the Smoothened protein from functioning. In the absence of Hedgehog binding to Patched, the Smoothened protein is inactive, and the Cubitus interruptus (Ci) protein is tethered to the microtubules of the responding cell. While on the microtubules, it is cleaved in such a way that a portion of it enters the nucleus and acts as a transcriptional repressor. This portion of the Ci protein binds to the promoters and enhancers of particular genes and acts as an inhibitor of transcription. When Hedgehog binds to the Patched protein, the Patched protein's shape is altered such that it no longer inhibits Smoothened. The Smoothened protein acts (probably by phosphorylation) to release the Ci protein from the microtubules and to prevent its being cleaved. The intact Ci protein can now enter the nucleus, where it acts as a transcriptional *activator* of the same genes it used to repress.

The Hedgehog pathway is extremely important in limb and neural differentiation in vertebrates. When mice were made homozygous for a mutant allele of Sonic hedgehog, they had major limb abnormalities as well as cyclopia—a single eye in the centre of the forehead. The vertebrate homologues of the Ci protein in *Drosophila* are the Gli proteins. Severe truncations of the human *GLI3* gene produce a nonfunctional protein that gives rise to Grieg cephalopoly-syndactyly, a condition involving a high forehead and extra digits. A less severe truncation retains the DNA binding domain of the GLI3 protein, but deletes the activion region. Thus, this mutant GLI3 protein can act only as a repressor. This protein is found in patients with Pallister-Hall syndrome, a much more severe syndrome (indeed, lethal soon after birth) involving not only extra digits, but also poor development of the pituitary gland, hypothalamus, anus, and kidneys. While mutations that inactivate the Hedgehog pathway can cause malformations, mutations that activate the pathway ectopically can cause cancers. If the Patched protein is mutated in somatic tissues such that it can no longer inhibit Smoothened, it can cause basal cell carcinomas, tumors of the basal cell layer of the epidermis. Heritable mutations of the *patched* gene cause basal cell nevus syndrome, a rare autosomal dominant condition characterized by both developmental anomalies (fused fingers, rib and facial abnormalities) and multiple malignant tumors such as basal cell carcinoma.

One remarkable feature of the Hedgehog signal transduction pathway is the importance of cholesterol. First, cholesterol is critical for the catalytic cleavage of Sonic hedgehog protein. Only the amino-terminal portion of the protein is functional and secreted. Second, the Patched protein that binds the Sonic hedgehog protein also needs cholesterol in order to function. It has recently been found that some human cyclopia syndromes are caused by mutations in genes that encode either Sonic hedgehog or the enzymes that synthesize cholesterol. Moreover, certain chemicals that induce cyclopia do so by interfering with the cholesterol biosynthetic enzymes. Environmental factors that cause developmental anomalies are called teratogens (from the Greek, meaning "monster-former"), and they will discussed in more detail in later Chapter. Two teratogens known to cause cyclopia in vertebrates are jervine and cyclopamine. Both substances are found in the plant *Veratrum californicum*, and both block the synthesis of cholesterol.

THE CELL DEATH PATHWAYS

"To be, or not to be: that is the question." While we all are poised at life-or-death decisions, this existential dichotomy is exceptionally stark for embryonic cells. Programmed cell death, called apoptosis, is a normal part of development. In the nematode *C. elegans*, in which we can count the number of cells, exactly 131 cells die according to the normal developmental pattern. All the cells of this nematode are "programmed" to die unless they are actively told not to undergo apoptosis. In humans, as many as 10^{11} cells die in each adult each day and are replaced by other cells. (Indeed, the mass of cells we lose each year through normal cell death is close to our entire body weight!) Within the uterus, we were constantly making and destroying cells, and we generated about three times as many neurons as we eventually ended up with when we were born. Lewis Thomas has aptly noted,

By the time I was born, more of me had died than survived. It was no wonder I cannot remember; during that time I went through brain after brain for nine months, finally contriving the one model that could be human, equipped for language.

Different tissues use different signals for apoptosis. One of the signals often used in vertebrates is bone morphogenetic protein 4 (BMP4). Some tissues, such as connective tissue, respond to BMP4 by differentiating into bone. Others, such as the frog gastrula ectoderm, respond to BMP4 by differentiating into skin. Still others, such as neural crest cells and tooth primordia, respond by degrading their DNA and dying. In the developing tooth, for instance, numerous growth and differentiation factors are secreted by the enamel knot. After the cusp has grown, the enamel knot synthesizes BMP4 and shuts itself down by apoptosis.

In other tissues, the cells are "programmed" to die, and they will remain alive only if some growth or differentiation factor is present to "rescue" them. This happens during the development of mammalian red blood cells. The red blood cell precursors in the mouse liver need the hormone erythropoietin in order to survive. If they do not receive it, they undergo apoptosis. The erythropoietin receptor works through the JAK-STAT pathway, activating the Stat5 transcription factor. In this way, the amount of erythropoietin present can determine how many red blood cells enter the circulation.

One of the pathways for apoptosis was largely delineated through genetic studies of *C. elegans*. It was found that the proteins encoded by the *ced-3* and *ced-4* genes were essential for apoptosis, but that in the cells that did not undergo apoptosis, those genes were turned off by the product of the *ced-9* gene. The CED-4 protein is a protease activating factor that activates CED-3, a protease that initiates the destruction of the cell. Mutations that inactivate the CED-9 protein cause numerous cells that would normally survive to activate their *ced-3* and *ced-4* genes and die. This leads to the death of the entire embryo. Conversely, gain-of-function mutations of *ced-9* cause CED-9 protein to be made in cells that would otherwise die. Thus, the *ced-9* gene appears to be a binary switch that regulates the choice between life and death on the cellular level. It is possible that every cell in the nematode embryo is poised to die, and those cells that survive are rescued by the activation of the *ced-9* gene.

The CED-3 and CED-4 proteins form the centre of the apoptosis pathway that is common to all animals studied. The trigger for apoptosis can be a developmental cue such as a particular molecule (such as BMP4 or glucocorticoids) or the loss of adhesion to a matrix. Either type of cue can activate the CED-3 or CED-4 proteins or inactivate the CED-9 molecules. In mammals, the homologues of the CED-9 protein are members of the *Bcl-2* family of genes. This family includes *Bcl-2,Bcl-X,* and similar genes. The functional similarities are so strong that if an active human *BCL-2* gene is placed into *C. elegans* embryos, it prevents normally occurring cell deaths in the nematode embryos. In vertebrate red blood cell development (mentioned above), the Stat5 transcription factor activated by erythropoietin functions by binding to the promoter of the *Bcl-X* gene, where it activates the synthesis of that anti-apoptosis protein.

The mammalian homologue of CED-4 is called Apaf-1 (*a*poptotic *p*rotease *a*ctivating *f*actor-1), and it participates in the cytochrome *c*-dependent activation of the mammalian CED-3 homologues, the proteases caspase-9 and caspase-3. The activation of the caspases causes the autodigestion of the cell. Caspases are strong proteases, and they digest the cell from within. The cellular proteins are cleaved and the DNA is fragmented.

While apoptosis-deficient nematodes deficient for CED-4 are viable (despite their having 15% more cells than wild-type worms), mice with loss-of-function mutations for either caspase-3 or caspase-9 die around birth from massive cell overgrowth in the nervous system. Mice homozygous for targeted deletions of *Apaf-1* have severe craniofacial abnormalities, brain overgrowth, and webbing between their toes.

In mammals, there is more than one pathway to apoptosis. The apoptosis of the lymphocytes, for instance, is not affected by the deletion of *Apaf-1* or *caspase-9*, and works by a separate pathway initiated by the CD95 protein Different caspases may be functioning in different cell types to mediate the apoptotic signals.

JUXTACRINE SIGNALING

In juxtacrine interactions, proteins from the inducing cell interact with receptor proteins of adjacent responding cells. The inducer does not diffuse from the cell producing it. There are three types of juxtacrine interactions. In the first type, a protein on one cell binds to its receptor on the adjacent cell. We saw this type of juxtacrine interaction when we discussed the interaction between the Bride of sevenless protein and its receptor, Sevenless. In the second type, a receptor on one cell binds to its ligand on the extracellular matrix secreted by another cell. In the third type, the signal is transmitted directly from the cytoplasm of one cell through small conduits into the cytoplasm of an adjacent cell.

The Notch Pathway: Juxtaposed Ligands and Receptors

While most known regulators of induction are diffusible proteins, some inducing proteins remain bound to the inducing cell surface. In one such pathway, cells expressing the Delta, Jagged, or Serrate proteins in their cell membranes activate neighbouring cells that contain the Notch protein in their cell membranes. Notch extends through the cell membrane, and its external surface contacts Delta, Jagged, or Serrate proteins extending out from an adjacent cell. When complexed to one of these ligands, Notch undergoes a conformational change that enables it to be cut by a protease. The cleaved portion enters the nucleus and binds to a dormant transcription factor of the CSL family. When bound to the Notch protein, the CSL transcription factors activate their target genes.

Notch proteins are extremely important receptors in the nervous system. In both the vertebrate and *Drosophila* nervous system, the binding of Delta to Notch tells the receiving cell not to become neural. In the vertebrate eye, the interactions between Notch and its ligands seem to regulate which cells become optic neurons and which become glial cells.

THE EXTRACELLULAR MATRIX AS A SOURCE OF CRITICAL DEVELOPMENTAL SIGNALS

Proteins and Functions of the Extracellular Matrix

The extracellular matrix consists of macromolecules secreted by cells into their immediate environment. These macromolecules form a region of noncellular material in the interstices between the cells. The extracellular matrix is a critical region for much of animal development. Cell adhesion, cell migration, and the formation of epithelial sheets and tubes all depend on the ability of cells to form attachments to extracellular matrices. In some cases, as in the formation of epithelia, these attachments have to be extremely strong. In other instances, as when cells migrate, attachments have to be made, broken, and made again. In some cases, the extracellular matrix merely serves as a permissive substrate to which cells can adhere, or upon which they can migrate. In other cases, it provides the directions for cell movement or the signal for a developmental event.

Extracellular matrices are made up of collagen, proteoglycans, and a variety of specialized glycoprotein molecules, such as fibronectin and laminin. These large glycoproteins are responsible for organizing the matrix and cells into an ordered structure. Fibronectin is a very large (460-kDa) glycoprotein dimer synthesized by numerous cell types. One function of fibronectin is to serve as a general adhesive molecule, linking cells to one another and to other substrates such as collagen and proteoglycans. Fibronectin has several distinct binding sites, and their interaction with the appropriate molecules results in the proper alignment of cells with their extracellular matrix. As we will see in later chapters, fibronectin also has an important role in cell migration. The "roads" over which certain migrating cells travel are paved with this protein. Fibronectin paths lead germ cells to the gonads and lead heart cells to the midline of the embryo. If chick embryos are injected with antibodies to fibronectin, the heart-forming cells fail to reach the midline, and two separate hearts develop.

Laminin and type IV collagen are major components of a type of extracellular matrix called the basal lamina. This basal lamina is characteristic of the closely knit sheets that surround epithelial tissue. The adhesion of epithelial cells to laminin (upon which they sit) is much greater than the affinity of mesenchymal cells for fibronectin (to which they must bind and release if they are to migrate). Like fibronectin, laminin plays a role in assembling the extracellular matrix, promoting cell adhesion and growth, changing cell shape, and permitting cell migration.

Integrins, the Cell Receptors for Extracellular Matrix Molecules

The ability of a cell to bind to adhesive glycoproteins depends on its expressing a cell membrane receptor for the cell-binding site of these large molecules. The main fibronectin receptors were identified by using antibodies that block the attachment of cells to fibronectin. The fibronectin receptor complex was found not only to bind fibronectin on the outside of the cell, but also to bind cytoskeletal proteins on the inside of the cell. Thus, the fibronectin receptor complex appears to span the cell membrane and unite two types of matrices.

On the outside of the cell, it binds to the fibronectin of the extracellular matrix; on the inside of the cell, it serves as an anchorage site for the actin microfilaments that move the cell. Horwitz and co-workers have called this family of receptor proteins integrins because they integrate the extracellular and intracellular scaffolds, allowing them to work together. On the extracellular side, integrins bind to the sequence arginine-glycine-aspartate (RGD), found in several adhesive proteins in extracellular matrices, including fibronectin, vitronectin (found in the basal lamina of the eye), and laminin. On the cytoplasmic side, integrins bind to talin and α-actinin, two proteins that connect to actin microfilaments. This dual binding enables the cell to move by contracting the actin microfilaments against the fixed extracellular matrix.

Bissell and her colleagues have proposed that the extracellular matrix is capable of inducing specific gene expression in developing tissues, especially those of the liver, testis, and mammary gland, in which the induction of specific transcription factors depends on cell-substrate binding. Often, the presence of bound integrin prevents the activation of genes that specify apoptosis. The chondrocytes that produce the cartilage of our vertebrae and limbs can survive and differentiate only if they are surrounded by an extracellular matrix and are joined to that matrix through their integrins. If chondrocytes from the developing chick sternum are incubated with antibodies that block the binding of integrins to the extracellular matrix, they shrivel up and die. While the mechanisms by which bound integrins inhibit apoptosis remain controversial, the extracellular matrix is obviously an important source of signals that can be transduced into the nucleus to produce specific gene expression.

Some of the genes induced by matrix attachment are being identified. When plated onto tissue culture plastic, mouse mammary gland cells will divide. Indeed, the genes for cell division (c-*myc,cyclinD1*) are expressed, while the genes for the differentiated products of the mammary gland (casein, lactoferrin, whey acidic protein) are not expressed. If the same cells are plated onto plastic coated with a laminin-containing basement membrane, the cells stop dividing and the differentiated genes of the mammary gland are expressed. This happens only after the integrins of the mammary gland cells bind to the laminin of the extracellular basement membrane. Then the gene for lactoferrin is expressed, as is the gene for p21, a cell division inhibitor. The c-*myc* and *cyclinD1* genes become silent. Eventually, all the genes for the developmental products of the mammary gland are expressed and the cell division genes remain turned off. At this time, the mammary cells will have enveloped themselves in the basement membrane, forming a secretory epithelium reminiscent of the mammary gland tissue. The binding of integrins to laminin is essential for the transcription of the casein gene, and the integrins act in concert with prolactin to activate that gene's expression.

Recent studies have shown that the binding of integrins to the extracellular matrix can stimulate the RTK-Ras pathway. When an integrin on the cell membrane of one cell binds to the fibronectin or collagen secreted by a neighbouring cell, the integrin can activate the tyrosine kinase cascade through an adaptor protein-like complex that connects the integrin to the Ras G protein. Cadherins and other cell adhesion molecules can also transmit signals by "hijacking" the FGF receptors. Cadherins, for example, are able to bind to the intramembrane region of FGF receptors and thereby dimerize these receptors just like the normal FGF ligands.

DIRECT TRANSMISSION OF SIGNALS THROUGH GAP JUNCTIONS

Throughout this chapter we have been discussing the reception of signals by cell membrane receptors. In these mechanisms, the receptor is in some manner altered by binding the ligand, so that its cytoplasmic domain transmits the signal into the cell. Another mechanism transmits small, soluble signals directly through the cell membrane, for the membrane is not continuous in all places. There are regions called gap junctions that serve as communication channels between adjacent cells. Cells so linked are said to be "coupled," and small molecules (molecular weight <1500) and ions can freely pass from one cell to the other. In most embryos, at least some of the early blastomeres are connected by gap junctions. The ability of cells to form gap junctions with some cells and not with others creates physiological "compartments" within the developing embryo.

The gap junction channels are made of connexin proteins. In each cell, six identical connexins in the membrane group together to form a transmembrane channel containing a central pore. The channel complex of one cell connects to the channel complex of another cell, enabling the cytoplasms of both cells to be joined. Different types of connexin proteins have separate, but overlapping, roles in normal development. For example, connexin-43 is found throughout the developing mouse embryo, in nearly every tissue. However, if the connexin-43 genes are knocked out by gene targeting, the mouse embryo will still develop. It appears that most of the functions of the connexin-43 protein can be taken over by other related connexin proteins—but not all. Shortly after birth, connexin-43-deficient mice take gasping breaths, turn bluish, and die. Autopsies of these mice show that the right ventricle—the chamber that pumps blood through the pulmonary artery to the lungs—is filled with tissue that occludes the chamber and obstructs blood flow. Although loss of the connexin-43 protein can be compensated for in many tissues, it appears to be critical for normal heart development.

The importance of gap junctions in development has been demonstrated in amphibian and mammalian embryos. When antibodies to connexins were microinjected into one specific cell of an 8-cell *Xenopus* blastula, the progeny of that cell, which are usually coupled through gap junctions, could no longer pass ions or small molecules from cell to cell. Moreover, the tadpoles that resulted from such treated blastulae showed defects specifically relating to the developmental fate of the injected cell. The progeny of the injected cell did not die, but they were unable to develop normally. In the mouse embryo, the first eight blastomeres are also connected to one another by gap junctions. Although loosely associated with one another, these eight cells move together to form a compacted embryo. If compaction is inhibited by antibodies against connexins, the treated blastomeres continue to divide, but further development ceases. If antisense RNA to connexin messages is injected into one of the blastomeres of a normal mouse embryo, that cell will not form gap junctions and will not be included in the embryo.

CROSS-TALK BETWEEN PATHWAYS

We have been representing the major signal transduction pathways as if they were linear chains, through which information flows in a single conduit. However, these pathways are just the major highways of information flow. Between them, avenues and streets connect one pathway with another. (This may be why there are so many steps between the cell surface and the nucleus. Each step is a potential regulatory point as well as a potential intersection.) This cross-talk can be seen in numerous tissues, wherein two signaling pathways reinforce each other. We must remember that a cell has numerous receptors and is constantly receiving many signals simultaneously.

Two signals are needed to effect the differentiation of the T lymphocyte. The first signal comes from the receptors that bind the antigen. The second signal comes from the binding of the CD28 protein to the B7 protein on the surface of the antigen-presenting cell. The first signal directs the synthesis of one subunit of the AP-1 transcription factor. The second signal directs the synthesis of the other subunit. The two subunits, c-Fos and c-Jun, form the AP-1 transcription factor, which can activate T cell-specific enhancers such as that regulating interleukin 2 production.

In some cells, gene transcription requires two signals. This pattern is seen during lymphocyte differentiation, for which two signals are needed, each one producing one of the two peptides of a transcription factor needed for the production of interleukin 2 (IL-2, also known as T cell growth factor). One peptide, c-Fos, is produced by the binding of the T cell receptor to an antigen. This signal activates the Ras pathway, creating a transcription factor, Elk-1, that activates the *c-fos* gene to synthesize c-Fos. The second signal comes from the B7 glycoprotein on the surface of the cell presenting the antigen. This signal activates a second cascade of kinases, eventually producing c-Jun. The two peptides, c-Fos and c-Jun, can join to make the AP-1 protein, a transcription factor that binds to the *IL-2* enhancer and activates its expression.

We also have seen that one receptor can activate several different pathways. The fibroblast growth factors, for instance, can activate the RTK pathway, the STAT pathway, or even a third pathway that involves lipid turnover and increases the levels of calcium ions in the cell.

CODA

In 1782, the French essayist Denis Diderot posed the question of morphogenesis in the fevered dream of a noted physicist. This character could imagine that the body was formed from myriads of "tiny sensitive bodies" that collected together to form an aggregate, but he could not envision how this aggregate could become an animal. A hundred years later, Charles Darwin wrote that the eye must have evolved by small useful variations, but he did not know the mechanisms by which the intricate coordination of eye development occurred.

Recent studies have shown that this coordination of cells to form organs and organisms is due to the molecules on the embryonic cell surfaces. Inducers and their competent responders interact with one another to instruct and coordinate the further development of the component parts. In subsequent chapters, we will look more closely at some of these morphogenetic interactions. As we continue our study of animal development, we will find that induction and competence provide the core of morphogenesis. Moreover, we will find these signal transduction pathways wherever we look, both throughout the animal kingdom and within each developing embryo. We are now at the stage where we can begin our study of early embryogenesis and see the integration of the organismal, genetic, and cellular processes of animal development.

Chapter 7

Fertilization: Beginning a New Organism

Fertilization is the process whereby two sex cells (gametes) fuse together to create a new individual with genetic potentials derived from both parents. Fertilization accomplishes two separate ends: sex (the combining of genes derived from the two parents) and reproduction (the creation of new organisms). Thus, the first function of fertilization is to transmit genes from parent to offspring, and the second is to initiate in the egg cytoplasm those reactions that permit development to proceed.

Although the details of fertilization vary from species to species, conception generally consists of four major events:

1. Contact and recognition between sperm and egg. In most cases, this ensures that the sperm and egg are of the same species.
2. Regulation of sperm entry into the egg. Only one sperm can ultimately fertilize the egg. This is usually accomplished by allowing only one sperm to enter the egg and inhibiting any others from entering.
3. Fusion of the genetic material of sperm and egg.
4. Activation of egg metabolism to start development.

STRUCTURE OF THE GAMETES

A complex dialogue exists between egg and sperm. The egg activates the sperm metabolism that is essential for fertilization, and the sperm reciprocates by activating the egg metabolism needed for the onset of development. But before we investigate these aspects of fertilization, we need to consider the structures of the sperm and egg—the two cell types specialized for fertilization.

Sperm

Fig. The human infant preformed in the sperm, as depicted by Nicolas Hartsoeker.

It is only within the past century that the sperm's role in fertilization has been known. Anton van Leeuwenhoek, the Dutch microscopist who co-discovered sperm in 1678, first believed them to be parasitic animals living within the semen (hence the term *spermatozoa,* meaning "sperm animals"). He originally assumed that they had nothing at all to do with reproducing the organism in which they were found, but he later came to believe that each sperm contained a preformed embryo. Leeuwenhoek wrote that sperm were seeds (both *sperma* and *semen* mean "seed") and that the female merely provided the nutrient soil in which the seeds were planted. In this, he was returning to a notion of procreation promulgated by Aristotle 2000 years earlier. Try as he might, Leeuwenhoek was continually disappointed in his attempts to find the preformed embryo within the spermatozoa. Nicolas Hartsoeker, the other co-discoverer of sperm, drew a picture of what he hoped to find: a preformed human ("homunculus") within the human sperm. This belief that the sperm contained the entire embryonic organism never gained much acceptance, as it implied an enormous waste of potential life. Most investigators regarded the sperm as unimportant.

The first evidence suggesting the importance of sperm in reproduction came from a series of experiments performed by Lazzaro Spallanzani in the late 1700s. Spallanzani demonstrated that filtered toad semen devoid of sperm would not fertilize eggs. He concluded, however, that the viscous fluid retained by the filter paper, and not the sperm, was the agent of fertilization. He, like many others, felt that the spermatic "animals" were parasites.

The combination of better microscopic lenses and the cell theory led to a new appreciation of spermatic function. In 1824, J. L. Prevost and J. B. Dumas claimed that sperm were not parasites, but rather the active agents of fertilization. They noted the universal existence of sperm in sexually mature males and their absence in immature and aged individuals. These observations, coupled with the known absence of spermatozoa in the sterile mule, convinced them that "there exists an intimate relation between their presence in the organs and the fecundating capacity of the animal." They proposed that the sperm entered the egg and contributed materially to the next generation.

These claims were largely disregarded until the 1840s, when A. von Kolliker described the formation of sperm from cells within the adult testes. He ridiculed the idea that the semen could be normal and yet support such an enormous number of parasites. Even so, von Kolliker denied that there was any physical contact between sperm and egg. He believed that the sperm excited the egg to develop, much as a magnet communicates its presence to iron. It was only in 1876 that Oscar Hertwig and Herman Fol independently demonstrated sperm entry into the egg and the union of the two cells' nuclei. Hertwig had sought an organism suitable for detailed microscopic observations, and he found that the Mediterranean sea urchin, *Toxopneustes lividus,* was perfect. Not only was it common throughout the region and sexually mature throughout most of the year, but its eggs were available in large numbers and were transparent even at high magnifications. After mixing sperm and egg suspensions together, Hertwig repeatedly observed a sperm entering an egg and saw the two nuclei unite. He also noted that only one sperm was seen to enter each egg, and that all the nuclei of the embryo were derived from the fused nucleus created at fertilization. Fol made similar observations and detailed the mechanism of sperm entry. Fertilization was at last recognized as the union of sperm and egg, and the union of sea urchin gametes remains one of the best-studied examples of fertilization.

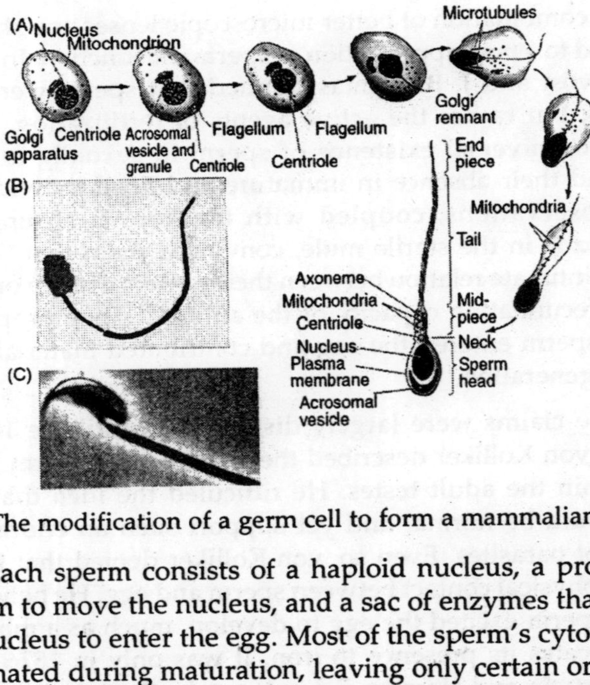

Fig. The modification of a germ cell to form a mammalian sperm.

Each sperm consists of a haploid nucleus, a propulsion system to move the nucleus, and a sac of enzymes that enable the nucleus to enter the egg. Most of the sperm's cytoplasm is eliminated during maturation, leaving only certain organelles that are modified for spermatic function. During the course of sperm maturation, the haploid nucleus becomes very streamlined, and its DNA becomes tightly compressed. In front of this compressed haploid nucleus lies the acrosomal vesicle, or acrosome, which is derived from the Golgi apparatus and contains enzymes that digest proteins and complex sugars; thus, it can be considered a modified secretory vesicle. These stored enzymes are used to lyse the outer coverings of the egg. In many species, such as sea urchins, a region of globular actin molecules lies between the nucleus and the acrosomal vesicle. These proteins are used to extend a fingerlike acrosomal process from the sperm during the early stages of fertilization. In sea urchins and several other species, recognition between sperm and egg involves molecules on the acrosomal process. Together, the acrosome and nucleus constitute the head of the sperm.

The means by which sperm are propelled vary according to how the species has adapted to environmental conditions. In some species (such as the parasitic roundworm *Ascaris*), the sperm travel by the amoeboid motion of lamellipodial extensions of the cell membrane. In most species, however, each sperm is able to travel long distances by whipping its flagellum. Flagella are complex structures. The major motor portion of the flagellum is called the axoneme. It is formed by microtubules emanating from the centriole at the base of the sperm nucleus. The core of the axoneme consists of two central microtubules surrounded by a row of nine doublet microtubules. Actually, only one microtubule of each doublet is complete, having 13 protofilaments; the other is C-shaped and has only 11 protofilaments.

Although tubulin is the basis for the structure of the flagellum, other proteins are also critical for flagellar function. The force for sperm propulsion is provided by dynein, a protein that is attached to the microtubules. Dynein hydrolyzes molecules of ATP and can convert the released chemical energy into the mechanical energy that propels the sperm. This energy allows the active sliding of the outer doublet microtubules, causing the flagellum to bend. The importance of dynein can be seen in individuals with the genetic syndrome called the Kartagener triad. These individuals lack dynein on all their ciliated and flagellated cells, rendering these structures immotile. Males with this disease are sterile (immotile sperm), are susceptible to bronchial infections (immotile respiratory cilia), and have a 50% chance of having the heart on the right side of the body. Another important flagellar protein appears to be histone H1. This protein is usually found inside the nucleus, where it folds the chromatin into tight clusters. However, Multigner and colleagues found that this same protein stabilizes the flagellar microtubules so that they do not disassemble.

The "9 + 2" microtubule arrangement with the dynein arms has been conserved in axonemes throughout the eukaryotic kingdoms, suggesting that this arrangement is extremely well suited for transmitting energy for movement. The ATP needed to whip the flagellum and propel the sperm comes from rings of mitochondria located in the neck region of the sperm. In many species (notably mammals), a layer of dense fibers has interposed itself between the mitochondrial sheath and the axoneme. This fiber layer stiffens the sperm tail. Because the thickness of this layer decreases toward the tip, the fibers probably prevent the sperm head from being whipped around too suddenly. Thus, the sperm has undergone extensive modification for the transport of its nucleus to the egg.

The differentiation of mammalian sperm is not completed in the testes. After being expelled into the lumen of the seminiferous tubules, the sperm are stored in the epididymis, where they acquire the ability to move. Motility is achieved through changes in the ATP-generating system (possibly through modification of dynein) as well as changes in the plasma membrane that make it more fluid. The sperm released during ejaculation are able to move, yet they do not yet have the capacity to bind to and fertilize an egg. These final stages of sperm maturation (called capacitation) do not occur until the sperm has been inside the female reproductive tract for a certain period of time.

The Egg

All the material necessary for the beginning of growth and development must be stored in the mature egg (the ovum). Whereas the sperm has eliminated most of its cytoplasm, the developing egg (called the oocyte before it reaches the stage of meiosis at which it is fertilized) not only conserves its material, but is actively involved in accumulating more. The meiotic divisions that form the oocyte conserve its cytoplasm (rather than giving half of it away), and the oocyte either synthesizes or absorbs proteins, such as yolk, that act as food reservoirs for the developing embryo. Thus, birds' eggs are enormous single cells, swollen with their accumulated yolk. Even eggs with relatively sparse yolk are comparatively large.

The volume of a sea urchin egg is about 200 picoliters (2×10^{-4} mm^3, more than 10,000 times the volume of the sperm). So, while sperm and egg have equal haploid nuclear components, the egg also has a remarkable cytoplasmic storehouse that it has accumulated during its maturation. This cytoplasmic trove includes the following:

- *Proteins:* It will be a long while before the embryo is able to feed itself or obtain food from its mother. The early embryonic cells need a supply of energy and amino acids. In many species, this is accomplished by accumulating yolk proteins in the egg. Many of the yolk proteins are made in other organs (liver, fat body) and travel through the maternal blood to the egg.
- *Ribosomes and tRNA*: The early embryo needs to make many of its own proteins, and in some species, there is a burst of protein synthesis soon after fertilization. Protein synthesis is accomplished by ribosomes and tRNA, which exist in the egg. The developing egg has special mechanisms to synthesize ribosomes, and certain amphibian oöcytes produce as many as 10^{12} ribosomes during their meiotic prophase.
- *Messenger RNA:* In most organisms, the instructions for proteins made during early development are already packaged in the oocyte. It is estimated that the eggs of sea urchins contain 25,000 to 50,000 different types of mRNA. This mRNA, however, remains dormant until after fertilization.

- *Morphogenetic factorsL:* Molecules that direct the differentiation of cells into certain cell types are present in the egg. They appear to be localized in different regions of the egg and become segregated into different cells during cleavage.
- *Protective chemicals*: The embryo cannot run away from predators or move to a safer environment, so it must come equipped to deal with threats. Many eggs contain ultraviolet filters and DNA repair enzymes that protect them from sunlight; some eggs contain molecules that potential predators find distasteful; and the yolk of bird eggs even contains antibodies.

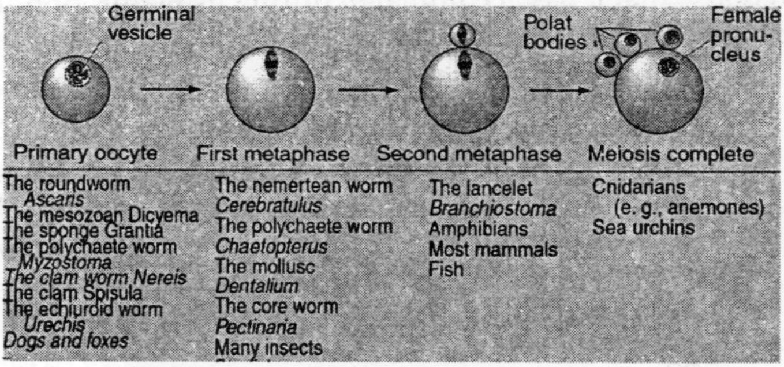

Fig. Stages of egg maturation at the time of sperm entry in different animal species. The germinal vesicle is the name given to the large diploid nucleus of the primary oocyte. The polar bodies are seen as smaller cells.

Within this enormous volume of cytoplasm resides a large nucleus. In some species (e.g., sea urchins), the nucleus is already haploid at the time of fertilization. In other species (including many worms and most mammals), the egg nucleus is still diploid, and the sperm enters before the meiotic divisions are completed. The stage of the egg nucleus at the time of sperm entry in different species is illustrated in Figure.

Enclosing the cytoplasm is the egg plasma membrane. This membrane must regulate the flow of certain ions during fertilization and must be capable of fusing with the sperm plasma membrane. Outside the plasma membrane is the vitelline envelope, which forms a fibrous mat around the egg. This envelope contains at least eight different glycoproteins and is often involved in sperm-egg recognition. It is supplemented by extensions of membrane glycoproteins from the plasma membrane and by proteinaceous vitelline posts that adhere the vitelline envelope to the membrane. The vitelline envelope is essential for the species-specific binding of sperm. In mammals, the vitelline envelope is a separate and thick extracellular matrix called the zona pellucida. The mammalian egg is also surrounded by a layer of cells called the cumulus, which is made up of the ovarian follicular cells that were nurturing the egg at the time of its release from the ovary. Mammalian sperm have to get past these cells to fertilize the egg. The innermost layer of cumulus cells, immediately adjacent to the zona pellucida, is called the corona radiata.

Lying immediately beneath the plasma membrane of the egg is a thin shell (about 5 μm) of gel-like cytoplasm called the cortex. The cytoplasm in this region is stiffer than the internal cytoplasm and contains high concentrations of globular actin molecules. During fertilization, these actin molecules polymerize to form long cables of actin known as microfilaments. Microfilaments are necessary for cell division, and they also are used to extend the egg surface into small projections called microvilli, which may aid sperm entry into the cell. Also within the cortex are the cortical granules. These membrane-bound structures, which are homologous to the acrosomal vesicle of the sperm, are Golgi-derived organelles containing proteolytic enzymes. However, whereas each sperm contains one acrosomal vesicle, each sea urchin egg contains approximately 15,000 cortical granules. Moreover, in addition to digestive enzymes, the cortical granules contain mucopolysaccharides, adhesive glycoproteins, and hyalin protein. The enzymes and mucopolysaccharides are active in preventing other sperm from entering the egg after the first sperm has entered, and the hyalin and adhesive glycoproteins surround the early embryo and provide support for the cleavage-stage blastomeres.

Many types of eggs also have an egg jelly outside the vitelline envelope. This glycoprotein meshwork can have numerous functions, but most commonly is used either to attract or to activate sperm. The egg, then, is a cell specialized for receiving sperm and initiating development.

RECOGNITION OF EGG AND SPERM

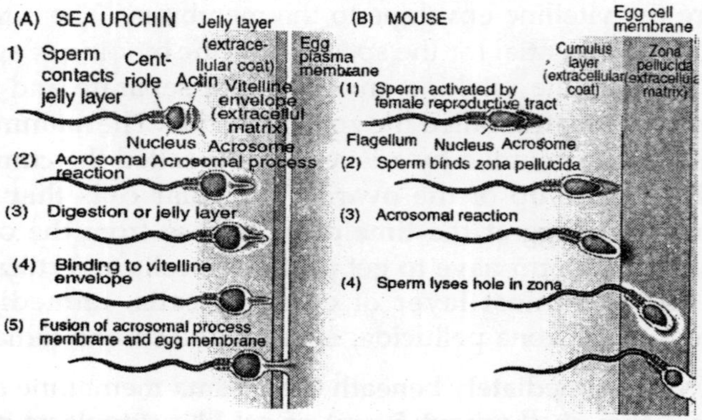

Fig. Summary of events leading to the fusion of egg and sperm plasma membranes in the sea urchin (A) and the mouse (B).

The interaction of sperm and egg generally proceeds according to five basic steps:

1. The chemoattraction of the sperm to the egg by soluble molecules secreted by the egg.
2. The exocytosis of the acrosomal vesicle to release its enzymes.
3. The binding of the sperm to the extracellular envelope (vitelline layer or zona pellucida) of the egg.
4. The passing of the sperm through this extracellular envelope.
5. Fusion of egg and sperm cell plasma membranes

Sometimes steps 2 and 3 are reversed (as in mammalian fertilization) and the sperm binds to the egg before releasing the contents of the acrosome. After these five steps are accomplished, the haploid sperm and egg nuclei can meet, and the reactions that initiate development can begin.

In many species, the meeting of sperm and egg is not a simple matter. Many marine organisms release their gametes into the environment. That environment may be as small as a tide pool or as large as an ocean. Moreover, it is shared with other species that may shed their sex cells at the same time. These organisms are faced with two problems: How can sperm and eggs meet in such a dilute concentration, and how can sperm be prevented from trying to fertilize eggs of another species? Two major mechanisms have evolved to solve these problems: species-specific attraction of sperm and species-specific sperm activation.

SPERM ATTRACTION: ACTION AT A DISTANCE

Species-specific sperm attraction has been documented in numerous species, including cnidarians, molluscs, echinoderms, and urochordates. In many species, sperm are attracted toward eggs of their species by chemotaxis, that is, by following a gradient of a chemical secreted by the egg. In 1978, Miller demonstrated that the eggs of the cnidarian *Orthopyxis caliculata* not only secrete a chemotactic factor but also regulate the timing of its release. Developing oocytes at various stages in their maturation were fixed on microscope slides, and sperm were released at a certain distance from the eggs. Miller found that when sperm were added to oocytes that had not yet completed their second meiotic division, there was no attraction of sperm to eggs. However, after the second meiotic division was finished and the eggs were ready to be fertilized, the sperm migrated toward them. Thus, these oocytes control not only the type of sperm they attract, but also the time at which they attract them.

The mechanisms of chemotaxis differamong species. One chemotactic molecule, a 14-amino acid peptide called resact, has been isolated from the egg jelly of the sea urchin *Arbacia punctulata*. Resact diffuses readily in seawater and has a profound effect at very low concentrations when added to a suspension of *Arbacia* sperm. When a drop of seawater containing *Arbacia* sperm is placed on a microscope slide, the sperm generally swim in circles about 50 ìm in diameter.

Within seconds after a minute amount of resact is injected into the drop, sperm migrate into the region of the injection and congregate there. As resact continues to diffuse from the area of injection, more sperm are recruited into the growing cluster. Resact is specific for *A. punctulata* and does not attract sperm of other species. *A. punctulata* sperm have receptors in their plasma membranes that bind resact and can swim up a concentration gradient of this compound until they reach the egg.

Resact also acts as a sperm-activating peptide. Sperm-activating peptides cause dramatic and immediate increases in mitochondrial respiration and sperm motility. The sperm receptor for resact is a transmembrane protein, and when it binds resact on the extracellular side, a conformational change on the cytoplasmic side activates the receptor's enzymatic activity. This activates the mitochondrial ATP-generating apparatus as well as the dynein ATPase that stimulates flagellar movement in the sperm.

THE ACROSOMAL REACTION IN SEA URCHINS

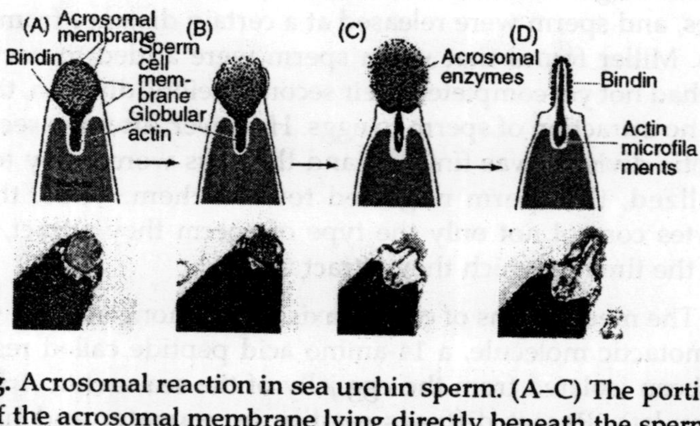

Fig. Acrosomal reaction in sea urchin sperm. (A–C) The portion of the acrosomal membrane lying directly beneath the sperm plasma membrane fuses with the plasma membrane to release the contents of the acrosomal vesicle. (D) The actin molecules assemble to produce microfilaments, extending the acrosomal process outward. Actual photographs of the acrosomal reaction in sea urchin sperm are shown below the diagrams.

A second interaction between sperm and egg is the acrosomal reaction. In most marine invertebrates, the acrosomal reaction has two components: the fusion of the acrosomal vesicle with the sperm plasma membrane (an exocytosis that results in the release of the contents of the acrosomal vesicle) and the extension of the acrosomal process. The acrosomal reaction in sea urchins is initiated by contact of the sperm with the egg jelly. Contact with egg jelly causes the exocytosis of the sperm's acrosomal vesicle and the release of proteolytic enzymes that can digest a path through the jelly coat to the egg surface. The sequence of these events is outlined in Figure.

In sea urchins, the acrosomal reaction is thought to be initiated by a fucose-containing polysaccharide in the egg jelly that binds to the sperm and allows calcium to enter into the sperm head.The exocytosis of the acrosomal vesicle is caused by the calcium-mediated fusion of the acrosomal membrane with the adjacent sperm plasma membrane. The egg jelly factors that initiate the acrosomal reaction in sea urchins are often highly specific to each species.

The second part of the acrosomal reaction involves the extension of the acrosomal process. This protrusion arises through the polymerization of globular actin molecules into actin filaments.

SPECIES-SPECIFIC RECOGNITION IN SEA URCHINS

Once the sea urchin sperm has penetrated the egg jelly, the acrosomal process of the sperm contacts the surface of the egg. A major species-specific recognition step occurs at this point. The acrosomal protein mediating this recognition is called bindin.Vacquier and co-workers isolated this nonsoluble 30,500-Da protein from the acrosome of *Strongylocentrotus purpuratus* and found it to be capable of binding to dejellied eggs of the same species. Further, its interaction with eggs is relatively species-specific: bindin isolated from the acrosomes of *S. purpuratus* binds to its own dejellied eggs, but not to those of *Arbacia punctulata*. Using immunological techniques, demonstrated that bindin is located specifically on the acrosomal process—exactly where it should be for sperm-egg recognition.

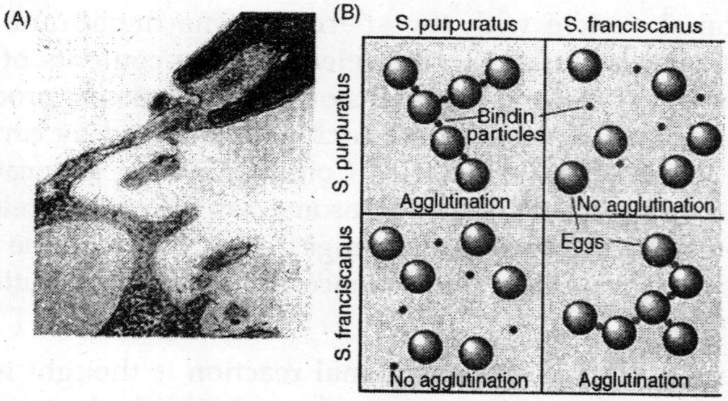

Fig. Species-specific binding of acrosomal process to egg cell surface in sea urchins. (A) Actual contact of a sea urchin sperm acrosomal process with an egg microvillus. (B) In vitro model of species-specific binding. The agglutination of dejellied eggs by bindin was measured by adding bindin aggregates to a plastic well containing a suspension of eggs. After 2–5 minutes of gentle shaking, the wells were photographed. Each bindin bound to and agglutinated only eggs from its own species.

Biochemical studies have shown that the bindins of closely related sea urchin species are indeed different. This finding implies the existence of species-specific bindin receptors on the egg, vitelline envelope, or plasma membrane. Such receptors were also suggested by the experiments of Vacquier and Payne, who saturated sea urchin eggs with sperm. Sperm binding does not occur over the entire egg surface. Even at saturating numbers of sperm (approximately 1500), there appears to be room on the ovum for more sperm heads, implying a limiting number of sperm-binding sites. The bindin receptor on the egg has recently been isolated. This 350-kDa protein may have several regions that interact with bindin. At least one of these sites recognizes only the bindin of the same species. The other site or sites appear to recognize a general bindin structure and can recognize the bindin of many species. The bindin receptors are thought to be aggregated into complexes on the egg cell surface, and hundreds of these complexes may be needed to tether the sperm to the egg. Thus, species-specific recognition of sea urchin gametes occurs at the levels of sperm attraction, sperm activation, and sperm adhesion to the egg surface.

GAMETE BINDING AND RECOGNITION IN MAMMALS

ZP3: the sperm-binding protein of the mouse zona pellucida.

The zona pellucida in mammals plays a role analogous to that of the vitelline envelope in invertebrates. This glycoprotein matrix, which is synthesized and secreted by the growing oocyte, plays two major roles during fertilization: it binds the sperm, and it initiates the acrosomal reaction after the sperm is bound. The binding of sperm to the zona is relatively, but not absolutely, species-specific. (Species-specific gamete recognition is not a major problem when fertilization occurs internally.)

The binding of mouse sperm to the mouse zona pellucida can be inhibited by first incubating the sperm with zona glycoproteins. Bleil and Wassarman isolated an 83-kDa glycoprotein, ZP3, from the mouse zona that was the active competitor for binding in this inhibition assay. The other two zona glycoproteins they found, ZP1 and ZP2, failed to compete for sperm binding. Moreover, they found that radiolabeled ZP3 bound to the heads of mouse sperm with intact acrosomes. Thus, ZP3 is the specific glycoprotein in the mouse zona pellucida to which the sperm bind. ZP3 also initiates the acrosomal reaction after sperm have bound to it. The mouse sperm can thereby concentrate its proteolytic enzymes directly at the point of attachment at the zona pellucida.

The molecular mechanism by which the zona pellucida and the mammalian sperm recognize each other is presently being studied. The current hypothesis of mammalian gamete binding postulates a set of proteins on the sperm capable of recognizing specific carbohydrate regions of ZP3. Removal of these threonine- or serine-linked carbohydrate groups from ZP3 abolishes its ability to bind sperm. Several proteins have been identified on the sperm cell surface that specifically bind to the ZP3 carbohydrates. Moreover, the deletion of these proteins from the sperm can inhibit or eliminate sperm-zona binding.

INDUCTION OF THE MAMMALIAN ACROSOMAL REACTION BY ZP3

Unlike the sea urchin acrosomal reaction, the acrosomal reaction in mammals occurs only after the sperm has bound to the zona pellucida. The mouse sperm acrosomal reaction is induced by the crosslinking of ZP3 with the receptors for it on the sperm membrane. This crosslinking opens calcium channels to increase the concentration of calcium in the sperm. The mechanism by which ZP3 induces the opening of the calcium channels and the subsequent exocytosis of the acrosome remains controversial, but it may involve the receptor's activating a cation channel (for sodium, potassium, or calcium), which would change the resting potential of the sperm plasma membrane. The calcium channels in the membrane would be sensitive to this change in membrane potential, allowing calcium to enter the sperm.

The difference between the acrosomal reaction in sea urchins and mammals may be due to the thickness of the extracellular envelopes surrounding the egg. In the sea urchin, the vitelline envelope is very thin and porous. Once a sperm has bound there, it is very close to the egg plasma membrane, and, indeed, the bindin receptor may extend through the vitelline envelope. In mammals, however, the zona pellucida is a very thick matrix, so the sperm is far removed from the egg. By undergoing the acrosomal reaction directly on the zona, the sperm is able to concentrate its proteolytic enzymes to lyse a hole in this envelope. Indeed, sperm that undergo the acrosomal reaction before they reach the zona pellucida are unable to penetrate it.

SECONDARY BINDING OF SPERM TO THE ZONA PELLUCIDA

During the acrosomal reaction, the anterior portion of the sperm plasma membrane is shed from the sperm. This region is where the ZP3-binding proteins are located, and yet the sperm must still remain bound to the zona in order to lyse a path through it. In mice, it appears that secondary binding to the zona is accomplished by proteins in the inner acrosomal membrane that bind specifically to ZP2. Whereas acrosome-intact sperm will not bind to ZP2, acrosome-reacted sperm will. Moreover, antibodies against the ZP2 glycoprotein will not prevent the binding of acrosome-intact sperm to the zona, but will inhibit the attachment of acrosome-reacted sperm. The structure of the zona consists of repeating units of ZP3 and ZP2, occasionally crosslinked by ZP1. It appears that the acrosome-reacted sperm transfer their binding from ZP3 to the adjacent ZP2 molecules. After a mouse sperm has entered the egg, the egg cortical granules release their contents. One of the proteins released by these granules is a protease that specifically alters ZP2. This inhibits other acrosome-reacted sperm from moving closer toward the egg.

In guinea pigs, secondary binding to the zona is thought to be mediated by the protein PH-20. Moreover, when this inner acrosomal membrane protein was injected into adult male or female guinea pigs, 100% of them became sterile for several months. The blood sera of these sterile guinea pigs had extremely high concentrations of antibodies to PH-20. The antiserum from guinea pigs sterilized in this manner not only bound specifically to PH-20, but also blocked sperm-zona adhesion in vitro. The contraceptive effect lasted several months, after which fertility was restored. These experiments show that the principle of immunological contraception is well founded.

GAMETE FUSION AND THE PREVENTION OF POLYSPERMY

Fusion of the Egg and Sperm Plasma Membranes

Recognition of sperm by the vitelline envelope or zona pellucida is followed by the lysis of that portion of the envelope or zona in the region of the sperm head by the acrosomal enzymes. This lysis is followed by the fusion of the sperm plasma membrane with the plasma membrane of the egg.

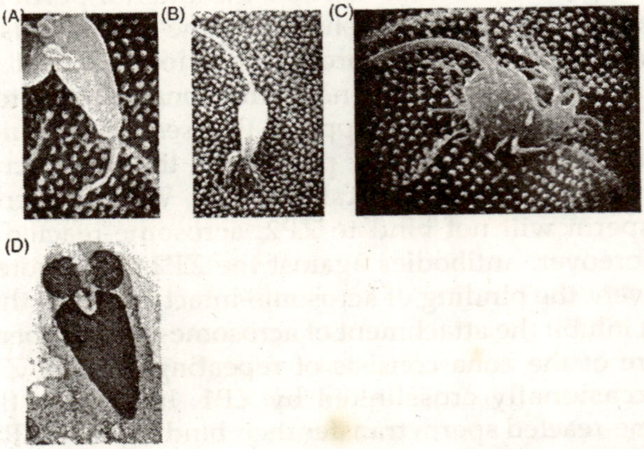

Fig. Scanning electron micrographs of the entry of sperm into sea urchin eggs. (A) Contact of sperm head with egg microvillus through the acrosomal process. (B) Formation of fertilization cone. (C) Internalization of sperm within the egg. (D) Transmission electron micrograph of sperm internalization through the fertilization cone.

The entry of a sperm into a sea urchin egg is illustrated in Figure. Sperm-egg binding appears to cause the extension of several microvilli to form the fertilization cone. Homology between the egg and the sperm is again demonstrated, because the transitory fertilization cone, like the acrosomal process, appears to be extended by the polymerization of actin. The sperm and egg plasma membranes then join together, and material from the sperm membrane can later be found on the egg membrane. The sperm nucleus and tail pass through the resulting cytoplasmic bridge, which is widened by the actin polymerization. A similar process occurs during the fusion of mammalian gametes.

In the sea urchin, all regions of the egg plasma membrane are capable of fusing with sperm. In several other species, certain regions of the membrane are specialized for sperm recognition and fusion. Fusion is an active process, often mediated by specific "fusogenic" proteins. It seems that bindin plays a second role as a fusogenic protein. Glabe has shown that sea urchin bindin will cause phospholipid vesicles to fuse together and that, like viral fusogenic proteins, bindin contains a long stretch of hydrophobic amino acids near its amino terminus. This region is able to fuse phospholipid vesicles.

In mammals, the fertilin proteins in the sperm plasma membrane are essential for sperm membrane-egg membrane fusion. Mouse fertilin is localized to the posterior plasma membrane of the sperm head. It adheres the sperm to the egg by binding to the α6β1 integrin protein on the egg plasma membrane. Moreover, like sea urchin bindin (to which it is not structurally related), fertilin has a hydrophobic region that could potentially mediate the union of the two membranes. Thus, fertilin appears to bind the sperm plasma membrane to the egg plasma membrane and then to fuse the two of them together. Mice homozygous for mutant fertilin have sperm with several defects, one of them being the inability to fuse with the egg plasma membrane. When the membranes are fused, the sperm nucleus, mitochondria, centriole, and flagellum can enter the egg.

THE PREVENTION OF POLYSPERMY

As soon as one sperm has entered the egg, the fusibility of the egg membrane, which was so necessary to get the sperm inside the egg, becomes a dangerous liability. In sea urchins, as in most animals studied, any sperm that enters the egg can provide a haploid nucleus and a centriole to the egg. In normal monospermy, in which only one sperm enters the egg, a haploid sperm nucleus and a haploid egg nucleus combine to form the diploid nucleus of the fertilized egg (zygote), thus restoring the chromosome number appropriate for the species. The centriole, which is provided by the sperm, will divide to form the two poles of the mitotic spindle during cleavage.

The entrance of multiple sperm—polyspermy—leads to disastrous consequences in most organisms. In the sea urchin, fertilization by two sperm results in a triploid nucleus, in which each chromosome is represented three times rather than twice. Worse, since each sperm's centriole divides to form the two poles of a mitotic apparatus, instead of a bipolar mitotic spindle separating the chromosomes into two cells, the triploid chromosomes may be divided into as many as four cells. Because there is no mechanism to ensure that each of the four cells receives the proper number and type of chromosomes, the chromosomes would be apportioned unequally. Some cells receive extra copies of certain chromosomes and other cells lack them. Theodor Boveri demonstrated in 1902 that such cells either die or develop abnormally.

Species have evolved ways to prevent the union of more than two haploid nuclei. The most common way is to prevent the entry of more than one sperm into the egg. The sea urchin egg has two mechanisms to avoid polyspermy: a fast reaction, accomplished by an electric change in the egg plasma membrane, and a slower reaction, caused by the exocytosis of the cortical granules.

THE FAST BLOCK TO POLYSPERMY.

The fast block to poly-spermy is achieved by changing the electric potential of the egg plasma membrane. This membrane provides a selective barrier between the egg cytoplasm and the outside environment, and the ionic concentration of the egg differs greatly from that of its surroundings. This concentration difference is especially significant for sodium and potassium ions. Seawater has a particularly high sodium ion concentration, whereas the egg cytoplasm contains relatively little sodium. The reverse is the case with potassium ions. This condition is maintained by the plasma membrane, which steadfastly inhibits the entry of sodium ions into the oocyte and prevents potassium ions from leaking out into the environment. If we insert an electrode into an egg and place a second electrode outside it, we can measure the constant difference in charge across the egg plasma membrane. This resting membrane potential is generally about

70 mV, usually expressed as –70 mV because the inside of the cell is negatively charged with respect to the exterior.

Within 1–3 seconds after the binding of the first sperm, the membrane potential shifts to a positive level, about +20 mV. This change is caused by a small influx of sodium ions into the egg. Although sperm can fuse with membranes having a resting potential of –70 mV, they cannot fuse with membranes having a positive resting potential, so no more sperm can fuse to the egg. It is not known whether the increased sodium permeability is due to the *binding* of the first sperm or to the *fusion* of the first sperm with the egg.

The importance of sodium ions and the change in resting potential was demonstrated by Laurinda Jaffe and colleagues. They found that polyspermy can be induced if sea urchin eggs are artificially supplied with an electric current that keeps their membrane potential negative. Conversely, fertilization can be prevented entirely by artificially keeping the membrane potential of eggs positive. The fast block to polyspermy can also be circumvented by lowering the concentration of sodium ions in the water. If the supply of sodium ions is not sufficient to cause the positive shift in membrane potential, polyspermy occurs. It is not known how the change in membrane potential acts on the sperm to block secondary fertilization. Most likely, the sperm carry a voltage-sensitive component (possibly a positively charged fusogenic protein), and the insertion of this component into the egg plasma membrane could be regulated by the electric charge across the membrane. An electric block to polyspermy also occurs in frogs, but probably not in most mammals.

THE SLOW BLOCK TO POLYSPERMY.

The eggs of sea urchins (and many other animals) have a second mechanism to ensure that multiple sperm do not enter the egg cytoplasm. The fast block to polyspermy is transient, since the membrane potential of the sea urchin egg remains positive for only about a minute. This brief potential shift is not sufficient to prevent polyspermy, which can still occur if the sperm bound to the vitelline envelope are not somehow removed. This removal is accomplished by the cortical granule reaction, a slower, mechanical block to polyspermy that becomes active about a minute after the first successful sperm-egg attachment.

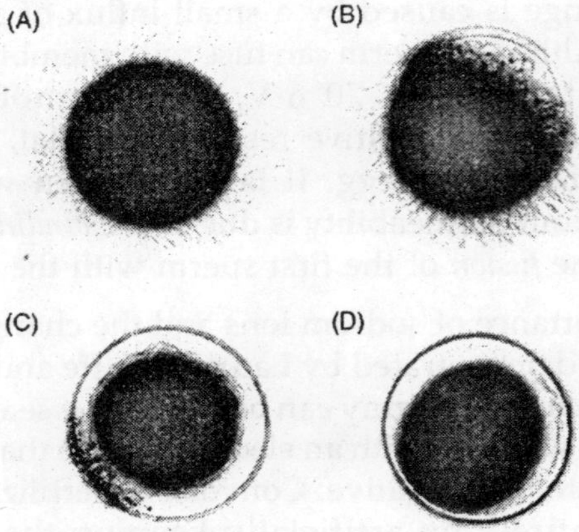

Fig. Formation of the fertilization envelope and removal of excess sperm. To create these photographs, sperm were added to sea urchin eggs, and the suspension was fixed in formaldehyde to prevent further reactions.

Directly beneath the sea urchin egg plasma membrane are about 15,000 cortical granules, each about 1 ìm in diameter. Upon sperm entry, these cortical granules fuse with the egg plasma membrane and release their contents into the space between the plasma membrane and the fibrous mat of vitelline envelope proteins. Several proteins are released by this cortical granule exocytosis. The first are proteases. These enzymes dissolve the protein posts that connect the vitelline envelope proteins to the cell membrane, and they clip off the bindin receptor and any sperm attached to it. Mucopolysaccharides released by the cortical granules produce an osmotic gradient that causes water to rush into the space between the plasma membrane and the vitelline envelope, causing the envelope to expand and become the fertilization envelope. A third protein released by the cortical granules, a peroxidase enzyme, hardens the fertilization envelope by crosslinking tyrosine residues on adjacent proteins. As shown in Figure, the fertilization envelope starts to form at the site of sperm entry and continues its expansion around the egg. As it forms, bound sperm are released from the envelope. This process starts about 20 seconds after sperm attachment and is complete by the end of the first minute of fertilization. Finally, a fourth cortical granule protein, hyalin, forms a coating around the egg. The egg extends elongated microvilli whose tips attach to this hyaline layer. This layer provides support for the blastomeres during cleavage.

In mammals, the cortical granule reaction does not create a fertilization envelope, but its ultimate effect is the same. Released enzymes modify the zona pellucida sperm receptors such that they can no longer bind sperm. During this process, called the zona reaction, both ZP3 and ZP2 are modified. Florman and Wassarman have proposed that the cortical granules of mouse eggs contain an enzyme that clips off the terminal sugar residues of ZP3, thereby releasing bound sperm from the zona and preventing the attachment of other sperm. Cortical granules of mouse eggs have been found to contain N-acetylglucosaminidase enzymes capable of cleaving N-acetylglucosamine from ZP3 carbohydrate chains. N-acetylglucosamine is one of the carbohydrate groups that sperm can bind to, and Miller and co-workers have demonstrated that when the N-acetylglucosamine residues are removed at fertilization, ZP3 will no longer serve as a substrate for the binding of other sperm. ZP2 is clipped by the cortical granule proteases and loses its ability to bind sperm as well. Thus, once a sperm has entered the egg, other sperm can no longer initiate or maintain their binding to the zona pellucida and are rapidly shed.

CALCIUM AS THE INITIATOR OF THE CORTICAL GRANULE REACTION

The mechanism of the cortical granule reaction is similar to that of the acrosomal reaction. Upon fertilization, the intracellular calcium ion concentration of the egg increases greatly. In this high-calcium environment, the cortical granule membranes fuse with the egg plasma membrane, releasing their contents. Once the fusion of the cortical granules begins near the point of sperm entry, a wave of cortical granule exocytosis propagates around the cortex to the opposite side of the egg.

In sea urchins and mammals, the rise in calcium concentration responsible for the cortical granule reaction is not due to an influx of calcium into the egg, but rather comes from within the egg itself. The release of calcium from intracellular storage can be monitored visually using calcium-activated luminescent dyes such as aequorin (isolated from luminescent jellyfish) or fluorescent dyes such as fura-2. These dyes emit light when they bind free calcium ions. When a sea urchin egg is injected with dye and then fertilized, a striking wave of calcium release propagates across the egg. Starting at the point of sperm entry, a band of light traverses the cell. The calcium ions do not merely diffuse across the egg from the point of sperm entry. Rather, the release of calcium ions starts at one end of the cell and proceeds actively to the other end. The entire release of calcium ions is complete in roughly 30 seconds in sea urchin eggs, and the free calcium ions are resequestered shortly after they are released. If two sperm enter the egg cytoplasm, calcium ion release can be seen starting at the two separate points of entry on the cell surface.

Several experiments have demonstrated that calcium ions are directly responsible for propagating the cortical granule reaction, and that these calcium ions are stored within the egg itself. The drug A23187 is a calcium ionophore (a compound that transports free calcium ions across lipid membranes, allowing these cations to traverse otherwise impermeable barriers). Placing unfertilized sea urchin eggs into seawater containing A23187 causes the cortical granule reaction and the elevation of the fertilization envelope. Moreover, this reaction occurs in the absence of any calcium ions in the surrounding water. Therefore, A23187 must be causing the release of calcium ions already sequestered in organelles within the egg.

The calcium ions responsible for the cortical granule reaction are stored in the endoplasmic reticulum of the egg. In sea urchins and frogs, this reticulum is pronounced in the cortex and surrounds the cortical granules. In *Xenopus*, the cortical endoplasmic reticulum becomes ten times more abundant during the maturation of the egg and disappears locally within a minute after the wave of cortical granule exocytosis occurs in any region of the cortex. Once initiated, the release of calcium is self-propagating. Free calcium is able to release sequestered calcium from its storage sites, thus causing a wave of calcium ion release and cortical granule exocytosis.

THE ACTIVATION OF EGG METABOLISM

Although fertilization is often depicted as merely the means to merge two haploid nuclei, it has an equally important role in initiating the processes that begin development. These events happen in the cytoplasm and occur without the involvement of the nuclei.

The mature sea urchin egg is a metabolically sluggish cell that is activated by the sperm. This activation is merely a stimulus, however; it sets into action a preprogrammed set of metabolic events. The responses of the egg to the sperm can be divided into "early" responses, which occur within seconds of the cortical reaction, and "late" responses, which take place several minutes after fertilization begins.

EARLY RESPONSES

As we have seen, contact between sea urchin sperm and egg activates the two major blocks to polyspermy: the fast block, initiated by sodium influx into the cell, and the slow block, initiated by the intracellular release of calcium ions. The activation of all eggs appears to depend on an increase in the concentration of free calcium ions within the egg. Such an increase can occur in two ways: calcium ions can enter the egg from outside, or calcium ions can be released from the endoplasmic reticulum within the egg. Both mechanisms are used to different degrees in different species. In snails and worms, much of the calcium probably enters the egg from outside, while in fishes, frogs, sea urchins, and mammals, most of the calcium ions probably come from the endoplasmic reticulum. In both cases, a wave of calcium ions sweeps across the egg, beginning at the site of sperm-egg fusion.

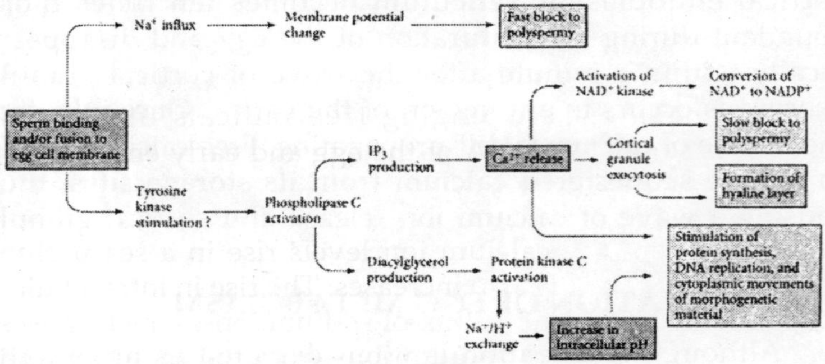

Fig. Model of possible pathway of egg activation in the sea urchin.

The presence of calcium ions is essential for activating the development of the embryo. If the calcium-chelating chemical EGTA is injected into the sea urchin egg, there is no cortical granule reaction, no change in membrane resting potential, and no reinitiation of cell division. Conversely, eggs can be activated artificially in the absence of sperm by procedures that release free calcium into the oocyte. Steinhardt and Epel found that injection of micromolar amounts of the calcium ionophore A23187 into a sea urchin egg elicits most of the responses characteristic of a normally fertilized egg. The elevation of the fertilization envelope, a rise of intracellular pH, a burst of oxygen utilization, and increases in protein and DNA synthesis are all generated in their proper order. In most of these cases, development ceases before the first mitosis because the egg is still haploid and lacks the sperm centriole needed for division. Calcium release activates a series of metabolic reactions. One of these is the activation of the enzyme NAD^+ kinase, which converts NAD^+ to $NADP^+$. This change may have important consequences for lipid metabolism, since $NADP^+$ (but not NAD^+) can be used as a coenzyme for lipid biosynthesis. Thus, the conversion of NAD^+ to $NADP^+$ may be important in the construction of the many new cell membranes required during cleavage. Another effect of calcium release involves oxygen consumption. A burst of oxygen reduction (to hydrogen peroxide) is seen during fertilization, and much of this "respiratory burst" is used to crosslink the fertilization envelope. The enzyme responsible for this reduction of oxygen is also NADPH-dependent. Lastly, NADPH helps regenerate glutathione and ovothiols, which may be crucial for scavenging free radicals that could otherwise damage the DNA of the egg and early embryo.

LATE RESPONSES

Shortly after the calcium ion levels rise in a sea urchin egg, its intracellular pH also increases. The rise in intracellular pH begins with a second influx of sodium ions, which causes a 1:1 exchange between sodium ions from the seawater and hydrogen ions from the egg. This loss of hydrogen ions causes the pH to rise. It is thought that the pH increase and the calcium ion elevation act together to stimulate new protein synthesis and DNA synthesis. If one experimentally elevates the pH of an unfertilized egg to a level similar to that of a fertilized egg, DNA synthesis and nuclear envelope breakdown ensue, just as if the egg were fertilized.

The late responses of fertilization brought about by these ionic changes include the activation of DNA synthesis and protein synthesis. In sea urchins, a burst of protein synthesis usually occurs within several minutes after sperm entry. This protein synthesis does not depend on the synthesis of new messenger RNA; rather, it utilizes mRNAs already present in the oocyte cytoplasm. These messages include mRNAs encoding proteins such as histones, tubulins, actins, and morphogenetic factors that are utilized during early development. Such a burst of protein synthesis can be induced by artificially raising the pH of the cytoplasm using ammonium ions.

FUSION OF THE GENETIC MATERIAL

Fusion of Genetic Material in Sea Urchins

In sea urchins, the sperm nucleus enters the egg perpendicular to the egg surface. After fusion of the sperm and egg plasma membranes, the sperm nucleus and its centriole separate from the mitochondria and the flagellum. The mitochondria and the flagellum disintegrate inside the egg, so very few, if any, sperm-derived mitochondria are found in developing or adult organisms. In mice, it is estimated that only 1 out of every 10,000 mitochondria is sperm-derived. Thus, although each gamete contributes a haploid genome to the zygote, the mitochondrial genome is transmitted primarily by the maternal parent. Conversely, in almost all animals studied (the mouse being the major exception), the centrosome needed to produce the mitotic spindle of the subsequent divisions is derived from the sperm centriole.

The egg nucleus, once it is haploid, is called the female pronucleus. Once inside the egg, the sperm nucleus decondenses to form the male pronucleus. The sperm nucleus undergoes a dramatic transformation. The nuclear envelope vesiculates into small packets, thereby exposing the compact sperm chromatin to the egg cytoplasm. The proteins holding the sperm chromatin in its condensed, inactive state are exchanged for other proteins derived from the egg cytoplasm. This exchange permits the decondensation of the sperm chromatin. In sea urchins, decondensation appears to be initiated by the phosphorylation of two sperm-specific histones that bind tightly to the DNA. This process begins when the sperm comes into contact with a glycoprotein in the egg jelly that elevates the level of cAMP-dependent protein kinase activity. These protein kinases phosphorylate several of the basic residues of the sperm-specific histones and thereby interfere with their binding to DNA. This loosening is thought to facilitate the replacement of the sperm-specific histones with other histones that have been stored in the oocyte cytoplasm. Once decondensed, the DNA can begin transcription and replication.

After the sea urchin sperm enters the egg cytoplasm, the male pronucleus rotates 180° so that the sperm centriole is between the sperm pronucleus and the egg pronucleus. The sperm centriole then acts as a microtubule organizing centre, extending its own microtubules and integrating them with egg microtubules to form an aster.These microtubules extend throughout the egg and contact the female pronucleus, and the two pronuclei migrate toward each other. Their fusion forms the diploid zygote nucleus. The initiation of DNA synthesis can occur either in the pronuclear stage (during migration) or after the formation of the zygote nucleus.

FUSION OF GENETIC MATERIAL IN MAMMALS

In mammals, the process of pronuclear migration takes about 12 hours, compared with less than 1 hour in the sea urchin. The mammalian sperm enters almost tangentially to the surface of the egg rather than approaching it perpendicularly, and it fuses with numerous microvilli. The mammalian sperm nucleus also breaks down as its chromatin decondenses and is then reconstructed by coalescing vesicles.

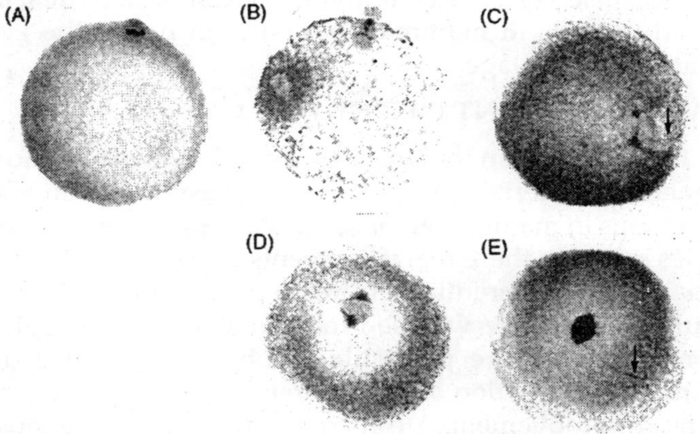

Fig. Pronuclear movements during human fertilization. The microtubules have been stained green, while the DNA is dyed blue. (A) The mature unfertilized oocyte completes the first meiotic division, budding off a polar body. (B) As the sperm enters the oocyte (left side), microtubules condense around it, as the oocyte completes its second meiotic division at the periphery. (C) By 15 hours, the two pronuclei have come together, and the centrosome splits to organize a bipolar microtubule array. (The sperm tail can still be seen.) (D) At first mitotic prophase, the sperm-derived and egg-derived chromosomes condense separately as the mitotic spindle poles form. (E) At prometaphase, chromosomes from the sperm and egg intermix on the metaphase equator and a mitotic spindle initiates the first mitotic division.

The DNA of the sperm nucleus is bound by basic proteins called protamines, and these nuclear proteins are tightly compacted through disulfide bonds. In the egg cytoplasm, glutathione reduces these disulfide bonds and allows the uncoiling of the sperm chromatin. The mammalian male pronucleus enlarges while the oocyte nucleus completes its second meiotic division. The centrosome (new centriole) accompanying the male pronucleus produces its asters (largely from proteins stored in the oocyte) and contacts the female pronucleus. Then each pronucleus migrates toward the other, replicating its DNA as it travels. Upon meeting, the two nuclear envelopes break down. However, instead of producing a common zygote nucleus (as happens in sea urchin fertilization), the chromatin condenses into chromosomes that orient themselves on a common mitotic spindle. Thus, a true diploid nucleus in mammals is first seen not in the zygote, but at the 2-cell stage.

REARRANGEMENT OF THE EGG CYTOPLASM

Fertilization can initiate radical displacements of the egg's cytoplasmic materials. While these cytoplasmic movements are not obvious in mammalian or sea urchin eggs, there are several species in which these rearrangements of oocyte cytoplasm are crucial for cell differentiation later in development. In the eggs of tunicates, as we will see in later Chapter, cytoplasmic rearrangements are particularly obvious because of the differing pigmentation of the different regions of the egg. Such cytoplasmic movements are also easy to see in amphibian eggs. In frogs, a single sperm can enter anywhere on the animal hemisphere of the egg; when it does, it changes the cytoplasmic pattern of the egg. Originally, the egg is radially symmetrical about the animal-vegetal axis. After sperm entry, however, the cortical (outer) cytoplasm shifts about 30° toward the point of sperm entry, relative to the inner cytoplasm. In some frogs (such as *Rana*), a region of the egg that was formerly covered by the dark cortical cytoplasm of the animal hemisphere is now exposed. This underlying cytoplasm, located near the equator on the side opposite the point of sperm entry, contains diffuse pigment granules and therefore appears gray. Thus, this region has been referred to as the gray crescent. As we will see in subsequent chapters, the gray crescent marks the region where gastrulation is initiated in amphibian embryos.

In frogs such as *Xenopus,* in which no gray crescent appears, dye labeling confirms that the cortical cytoplasm rotates 30° relative to the internal, subcortical cytoplasm. The motor for these cytoplasmic movements in amphibian eggs appears to be an array of parallel microtubules that form between the cortical and inner cytoplasm of the vegetal hemisphere parallel to the direction of cytoplasmic rotation. These microtubular tracks are first seen immediately before the rotation commences, and they disappear when rotation ceases. Treating the egg with colchicine or ultraviolet radiation at the beginning of rotation stops the formation of these microtubules, thereby inhibiting the cytoplasmic rotation. Using antibodies that bind to the microtubules, Houliston and Elinson found that these tracks are formed from both sperm- and egg-derived microtubules, and that the sperm centriole directs the polymerization of the microtubules so that they grow into the vegetal region of the egg. Upon reaching the vegetal cortex, the microtubules angle away from the point of sperm entry, toward the vegetal pole. The off-centre position of the sperm centriole as it initiates microtubule polymerization provides the directionality to the rotation. The motive force for the rotation may be provided by the ATPase kinesin. Like dynein and myosin, kinesin is able to attach to fibers and produce energy through ATP hydrolysis. This ATPase is located on the vegetal microtubules and the membranes of the cortical endoplasmic reticulum.

The movement of the cortical cytoplasm with respect to the inner cytoplasm causes profound changes within the inner cytoplasm. Danilchik and Denegre have labeled yolk platelets with Nile blue and watched their movement by fluorescent microscopy (the bound dye fluoresces red). During the middle part of the first cell cycle, a mass of central egg cytoplasm flows from the presumptive ventral (belly) to the future dorsal (back) side of the embryo. By the end of first division, the cytoplasm of the prospective dorsal side of the embryo is distinctly different from that of the prospective ventral side. What had been a radially symmetrical embryo is now a bilaterally symmetrical embryo. As we will see in later Chapter, these cytoplasmic movements initiate a cascade of events that determine the dorsal-ventral axis of the frog. Indeed, the parallel microtubules that allow these rearrangements to stretch along what will become the dorsal-ventral axis of the frog.

PREPARATION FOR CLEAVAGE

The increase in intracellular free calcium ions that activates DNA and protein synthesis also sets in motion the apparatus for cell division. The mechanisms by which cleavage is initiated probably differ among species, depending on the stage of meiosis at which fertilization occurs. However, in all species studied, the rhythm of cell divisions is regulated by the synthesis and degradation of a protein called cyclin. As we will see in later Chapters, cyclin keeps cells in metaphase, and the breakdown of cyclin enables the cells to return to interphase. In addition to their other activities, calcium ions appear to initiate the degradation of cyclin. Once the cyclin is degraded, the cycles of cell division can begin anew.

Cleavage has a special relationship to the egg regions established by the cytoplasmic movements described above. In tunicate embryos, the first cleavage bisects the egg, with its established cytoplasmic pattern, into mirror-image duplicates. From that stage on, every division on one side of the cleavage furrow has a mirror-image division on the opposite side. Similarly, the gray crescent is bisected by the first cleavage furrow in amphibian eggs. Thus, the position of the first cleavage is not random, but tends to be specified by the point of sperm entry and the subsequent rotation of the egg cytoplasm. The coordination of cleavage plane and cytoplasmic rearrangements is probably mediated through the microtubules of the sperm.

Toward the end of the first cell cycle, then, the cytoplasm is rearranged, the pronuclei have met, DNA is replicating, and new proteins are being translated. The stage is set for the development of a multicellular organism.

Chapter 8

Early Development in Selected Invertebrates

Remarkable as it is, fertilization is but the initiating step in development. The zygote, with its new genetic potential and its new arrangement of cytoplasm, now begins the production of a multicellular organism. Between these events of fertilization and the events of organ formation are two critical stages: cleavage and gastrulation. During cleavage, rapid cell divisions divide the cytoplasm of the fertilized egg into numerous cells. These cells then undergo dramatic displacements during gastrulation, a process whereby they move to different parts of the embryo and acquire new neighbours. During cleavage and gastrulation, the major axes of the embryo are determined, and the cells begin to acquire their respective fates.

While cleavage always precedes gastrulation, axis formation can begin as early as oocyte formation. It can be completed during cleavage (as is the case with *Drosophila*) or extend all the way through gastrulation (as it does in *Xenopus*). There are three axes that need to be specified: the anterior-posterior (head-anus) axis, the dorsal-ventral (back-belly) axis, and the left-right axis. Different species specify these axes at different times, using different mechanisms.

AN INTRODUCTION TO EARLY DEVELOPMENTAL PROCESSES

Cleavage

After fertilization, the development of a multicellular organism proceeds by a process called cleavage, a series of mitotic divisions whereby the enormous volume of egg cytoplasm is divided into numerous smaller, nucleated cells. These cleavage-stage cells are called blastomeres. In most species (mammals being the chief exception), the rate of cell division and the placement of the blastomeres with respect to one another is completely under the control of the proteins and mRNAs stored in the oocyte by the mother. The zygotic genome, transmitted by mitosis to all the new cells, does not function in early-cleavage embryos. Few, if any, mRNAs are made until relatively late in cleavage, and the embryo can divide properly even when chemicals are used experimentally to inhibit transcription. During cleavage, however, cytoplasmic volume does not increase. Rather, the enormous volume of zygote cytoplasm is divided into increasingly smaller cells. First the egg is divided in half, then quarters, then eighths, and so forth. This division of egg cytoplasm without increasing its volume is accomplished by abolishing the growth period between cell divisions (that is, the G_1 and G_2 phases of the cell cycle). Meanwhile, the cleavage of nuclei occurs at a rapid rate never seen again (not even in tumor cells). A frog egg, for example, can divide into 37,000 cells in just 43 hours. Mitosis in cleavage-stage *Drosophila* embryos occurs every 10 minutes for over 2 hours and in just 12 hours forms some 50,000 cells. This dramatic increase in cell number can be appreciated by comparing cleavage with other stages of development.

One consequence of this rapid cell division is that the ratio of cytoplasmic to nuclear volume gets increasingly smaller as cleavage progresses. In many types of embryos (such as those of *Xenopus* and *Drosophila,* but not those of *C. elegans* or mammals), this decrease in the cytoplasmic to nuclear volume ratio is crucial in timing the activation of certain genes. For example, in the frog *Xenopus laevis,* transcription of new messages is not activated until after 12 divisions. At that time, the rate of cleavage decreases, the blastomeres become motile, and nuclear genes begin to be transcribed. This stage is called the mid-blastula transition. It is thought that some factor in the egg is being titrated by the newly made chromatin, because the time of this transition can be changed by experimentally altering the ratio of chromatin to cytoplasm in the cell. Thus, cleavage begins soon after fertilization and ends shortly after the stage when the embryo achieves a new balance between nucleus and cytoplasm.

From Fertilization to Cleavage

The transition from fertilization to cleavage is caused by the activation of mitosis promoting factor (MPF). MPF was first discovered as the major factor responsible for the resumption of meiotic cell divisions in the ovulated frog egg. It continues to play a role after fertilization, regulating the biphasic cell cycle of early blastomeres. Blastomeres generally progress through a cell cycle consisting of just two steps: M (mitosis) and S (DNA synthesis). Gerhart and co-workers showed that MPF undergoes cyclical changes in its level of activity in mitotic cells. The MPF activity of early blastomeres is highest during M and undetectable during S. Newport and Kirschner demonstrated that DNA replication (S) and mitosis (M) are driven solely by the gain and loss of MPF activity. Cleaving cells can be experimentally trapped in S phase by incubating them in an inhibitor of protein synthesis. When MPF is microinjected into these cells, they enter M. Their nuclear envelope breaks down and their chromatin condenses into chromosomes. After an hour, MPF is degraded and the chromosomes return to S phase.

What causes this cyclic activity of MPF? Mitosis-promoting factor contains two subunits. The large subunit is called cyclin B. It is this component that shows a periodic behaviour, accumulating during S and then being degraded after the cells have reached M. Cyclin B is often encoded by mRNAs stored in the oocyte cytoplasm, and if the translation of this message is specifically inhibited, the cell will not enter mitosis. The presence of cyclin B depends upon its synthesis and its degradation. Cyclin B regulates the small subunit of MPF, the cyclin-dependent kinase. This kinase activates mitosis by phosphorylating several target proteins, including histones, the nuclear envelope lamin proteins, and the regulatory subunit of cytoplasmic myosin. This brings about chromatin condensation, nuclear envelope depolymerization, and the organization of the mitotic spindle.

Without cyclin, the cyclin-dependent kinase will not function. The presence of cyclin is controlled by several proteins that ensure its periodic synthesis and degradation. In most species studied, the regulators of cyclin (and thus, of MPF) are stored in the egg cytoplasm. Therefore, the cell cycle is independent of the nuclear genome for numerous cell divisions. These early divisions tend to be rapid and synchronous. However, as the cytoplasmic components are used up, the nucleus begins to synthesize them. The embryo now enters the mid-blastula transition, in which several new phenomena are added to the biphasic cell divisions of the embryo. First, the growth stages (G_1 and G_2) are added to the cell cycle, permitting the cells to grow. Before this time, the egg cytoplasm was being divided into smaller and smaller cells, but the total volume of the organism remained unchanged. *Xenopus* embryos add those phases to the cell cycle shortly after the twelfth cleavage. *Drosophila* adds G_2 during cycle 14 and G_1 during cycle 17. Second, the synchronicity of cell division is lost, as different cells synthesize different regulators of MPF. Third, new mRNAs are transcribed. Many of these messages encode proteins that will become necessary for gastrulation. If transcription is blocked, cell division will occur at normal rates and at normal times in many species, but the embryo will not be able to initiate gastrulation.

THE CYTOSKELETAL MECHANISMS OF MITOSIS

Cleavage is actually the result of two coordinated processes. The first of these cyclic processes is karyokinesis—the mitotic division of the nucleus. The mechanical agent of this division is the mitotic spindle, with its microtubules composed of tubulin (the same type of protein that makes up the sperm flagellum). The second process is cytokinesis—the division of the cell. The mechanical agent of cytokinesis is a contractile ring of microfilaments made of actin (the same type of protein that extends the egg microvilli and the sperm acrosomal process).

Karyokinesis and Cytokinesis

Process	Mechanical agent	Major protein composition	Location	Major disruptive drug
Karyokinesis	Mitotic spindle	Tubulin microtubules	Central cytoplasm	Colchicine, nocodazole[a]
Cytokinesis	Contractile ring	Actin microfilaments	Cortical cytoplasm	Cytochalasin B

Table presents a comparison of these agents of cell division. The relationship and coordination between these two systems during cleavage is depicted in Figure, in which a sea urchin egg is shown undergoing first cleavage. The mitotic spindle and contractile ring are perpendicular to each other, and the spindle is internal to the contractile ring. The contractile ring creates a cleavage furrow, which eventually bisects the plane of mitosis, thereby creating two genetically equivalent blastomeres.

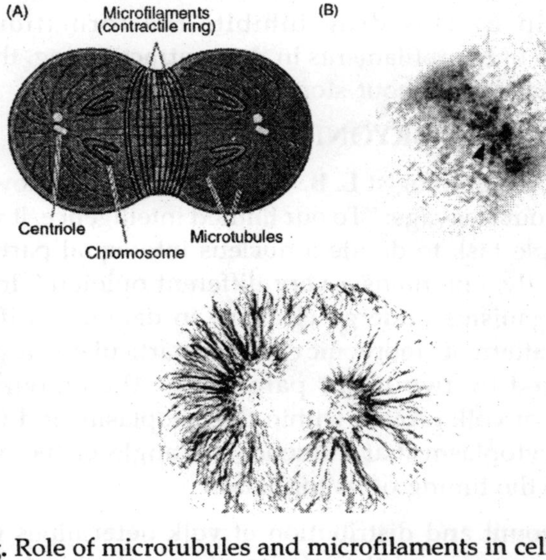

Fig. Role of microtubules and microfilaments in cell division.

The actin microfilaments are found in the cortex of the egg rather than in the central cytoplasm. Under the electron microscope, the ring of microfilaments can be seen forming a distinct cortical band 0.1 μm wide. This contractile ring exists only during cleavage and extends 8–10 μm into the centre of the egg. It is responsible for exerting the force that splits the zygote into blastomeres; for if it is disrupted, cytokinesis stops. Schroeder has proposed a model of cleavage wherein the contractile ring splits the egg like an "intercellular purse-string," tightening about the egg as cleavage continues. This tightening of the microfilamentous ring creates the cleavage furrow. Microtubules are also seen near the cleavage furrow (in addition to their role in creating the mitotic spindles), since they are needed to bring membrane material to the site of membrane addition.

Although karyokinesis and cytokinesis are usually coordinated, they are sometimes separated by natural or experimental conditions. In insect eggs, karyokinesis occurs several times before cytokinesis takes place. Another way to produce this state is to treat embryos with the drug cytochalasin B. This drug inhibits the formation and organization of microfilaments in the contractile ring, thereby stopping cleavage without stopping karyokinesis.

PATTERNS OF EMBRYONIC CLEAVAGE

In 1923, embryologist E. B. Wilson reflected on how little we knew about cleavage: "To our limited intelligence, it would seem a simple task to divide a nucleus into equal parts. The cell, manifestly, entertains a very different opinion." Indeed, different organisms undergo cleavage in distinctly different ways. The pattern of embryonic cleavage particular to a species is determined by two major parameters: the amount and distribution of yolk protein within the cytoplasm, and factors in the egg cytoplasm that influence the angle of the mitotic spindle and the timing of its formation.

The amount and distribution of yolk determines where cleavage can occur and the relative size of the blastomeres. When one pole of the egg is relatively yolk-free, the cellular divisions occur there at a faster rate than at the opposite pole.

The yolk-rich pole is referred to as the vegetal pole; the yolk concentration in the animal pole is relatively low. The zygote nucleus is frequently displaced toward the animal pole. In general, yolk inhibits cleavage. Figure provides a classification of cleavage types and shows the influence of yolk on cleavage symmetry and pattern.

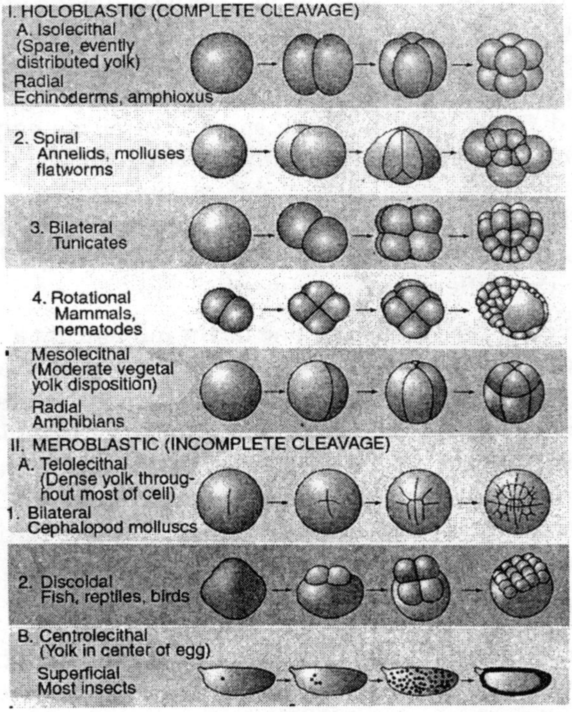

Fig. Summary of the Main Patterns of Cleavage

At one extreme are the eggs of sea urchins, mammals, and snails. These eggs have sparse, equally spaced yolk and are thus isolecithal (Greek, "equal yolk"). In these species, cleavage is holoblastic (Greek *holos*, "complete"). meaning that the cleavage furrow extends through the entire egg. These embryos must have some other way of obtaining food. Most will generate a voracious larval form, while mammals get their nutrition from the placenta.

At the other extreme are the eggs of insects, fishes, reptiles, and birds. Most of their cell volumes are made up of yolk. The yolk must be sufficient to nourish these animals. Zygotes containing large accumulations of yolk undergo meroblastic cleavage, wherein only a portion of the cytoplasm is cleaved. The cleavage furrow does not penetrate into the yolky portion of the cytoplasm. The eggs of insects have their yolk in the centre (i.e., they are centrolecithal), and the divisions of the cytoplasm occur only in the rim of cytoplasm around the periphery of the cell (i.e., superficial cleavage). The eggs of birds and fishes have only one small area of the egg that is free of yolk (telolecithal eggs), and therefore, the cell divisions occur only in this small disc of cytoplasm, giving rise to the discoidal pattern of cleavage. These are general rules, however, and closely related species can evolve different patterns of cleavage in a different environment.

However, the yolk is just one factor influencing a species' pattern of cleavage. There are also inherited patterns of cell division that are superimposed upon the constraints of the yolk. This can readily be seen in isolecithal eggs, in which very little yolk is present. In the absence of a large concentration of yolk, four major cleavage types can be observed: radial holoblastic, spiral holoblastic, bilateral holoblastic, and rotational holoblastic cleavage.

GASTRULATION

Gastrulation is the process of highly coordinated cell and tissue movements whereby the cells of the blastula are dramatically rearranged. The blastula consists of numerous cells, the positions of which were established during cleavage. During gastrulation, these cells are given new positions and new neighbours, and the multilayered body plan of the organism is established. The cells that will form the endodermal and mesodermal organs are brought inside the embryo, while the cells that will form the skin and nervous system are spread over its outside surface. Thus, the three germ layers—outer ectoderm, inner endoderm, and interstitial mesoderm—are first produced during gastrulation. In addition, the stage is set for the interactions of these newly positioned tissues.

The movements of gastrulation involve the entire embryo, and cell migrations in one part of the gastrulating embryo must be intimately coordinated with other movements occurring simultaneously. Although the patterns of gastrulation vary enormously throughout the animal kingdom, there are only a few basic types of cell movements. Gastrulation usually involves some combination of the following types of movements:

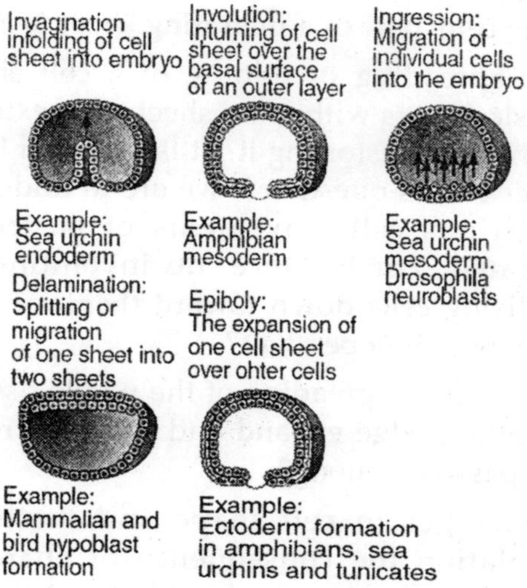

Fig. Types of cell movements during gastrulation. The gastrulation of any particular organism is an ensemble of several of these movements.

- Invagination. The infolding of a region of cells, much like the indenting of a soft rubber ball when it is poked.
- Involution. The inturning or inward movement of an expanding outer layer so that it spreads over the internal surface of the remaining external cells.
- Ingression. The migration of individual cells from the surface layer into the interior of the embryo.

- Delamination. The splitting of one cellular sheet into two more or less parallel sheets.
- Epiboly. The movement of epithelial sheets (usually of ectodermal cells) that spread as a unit, rather than individually, to enclose the deeper layers of the embryo.

As we look at gastrulation in different types of embryos, we should keep in mind the following questions:

- What is the unit of migration? Is migration dependent on the movements of individual cells, or are the cells part of a migrating sheet or region?
- Is the spreading or folding of a cell sheet due to intrinsic factors within the sheet or to extrinsic forces stretching or distorting it? It is essential to know the answer to this question if we are to understand how the various cell movements of gastrulation are integrated. For instance, do involuting cells pull epibolizing cells down toward them, or are the two movements independent?
- Is there active spreading of the whole tissue, or does the leading edge expand and drag the rest of a cell sheet passively along?
- Are changes in cell shape and motility during gastrulation the consequence of changes in cell surface properties, such as adhesiveness to the substrate or to other cells?

Contrary to expectations, some regional migrational properties may be totally controlled by cytoplasmic factors that are independent of cellularization. F. R. Lillie was able to parthenogenetically activate eggs of the annelid *Chaetopterus* and suppress their cleavage. Many of the events of early development occurred even in the absence of cells. The cytoplasm of the zygote separated into defined regions, and cilia differentiated in the appropriate parts of the egg. Moreover, the outermost clear cytoplasm migrated down over the vegetal regions in a manner specifically reminiscent of the epiboly of animal hemisphere cells during normal development. This occurred at precisely the time that epiboly would have taken place during normal gastrulation. Thus, epiboly may be (at least in some respects) independent of the cells that form the migrating region.

AXIS FORMATION

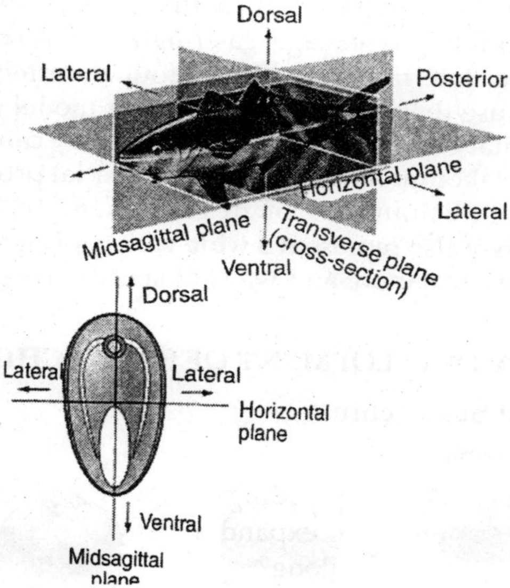

Fig. Axes of a bilaterally symmetric animal. A single plane, the midsagittal plane, divides the animal into left and right halves. Cross sections are taken along the anterior-posterior axis.

Some of the most important phenomena in development concern the formation of embryonic axes. Embryos must develop three very important axes that are the foundations of the body: the anterior-posterior axis, the dorsal-ventral axis, and the right-left axis. The anterior-posterior (or anteroposterior) axis is the line extending from head to tail (or mouth to anus in those organisms that lack heads and tails). The dorsal-ventral (dorsoventral) axis is the line extending from back (dorsum) to belly (ventrum). For instance, in vertebrates, the neural tube is a dorsal structure. In insects, the neural cord is a ventral structure. The right-left axis is a line between the two lateral sides of the body. Although we may look symmetrical, recall that in most of us, the heart and liver are in the left half of the body only. Somehow, the embryo knows that some organs go on one side and other organs go on the other.

In this chapter, we will look at how four selected invertebrates—a sea urchin, a tunicate, a snail, and a nematode—undergo cleavage, gastrulation, axis specification, and cell fate determination. These four invertebrates were chosen because they have been important model systems for developmental biologists. In other words, they can be studied easily in the labouratory, and they have special properties that allow their mechanisms of development to be readily observed. They also represent a wide variety of cleavage types, patterns of gastrulation, and ways of specifying axes and cell fates.

THE EARLY DEVELOPMENT OF SEA URCHINS

Cleavage in Sea Urchins

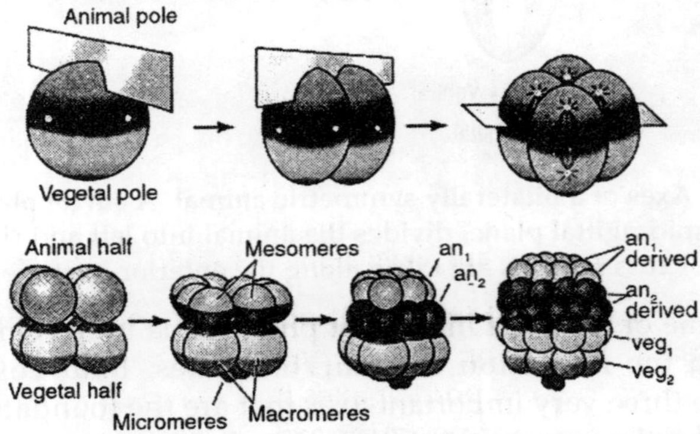

Fig. Cleavage in the sea urchin. Planes of cleavage in the first three divisions and the formation of tiers of cells in divisions 3–6.

Sea urchins exhibit radial holoblastic cleavage. The first and second cleavages are both meridional and are perpendicular to each other. That is to say, the cleavage furrows pass through the animal and vegetal poles. The third cleavage is equatorial, perpendicular to the first two cleavage planes, and separates the animal and vegetal hemispheres from one another. The fourth cleavage, however, is very different from the first three. The four cells of the animal tier divide meridionally into eight blastomeres, each with the same volume. These cells are called mesomeres. The vegetal tier, however, undergoes an *unequal* equatorial cleavage to produce four large cells, the macromeres, and four smaller micromeres at the vegetal pole. As the 16-cell embryo cleaves, the eight mesomeres divide to produce two "animal" tiers, an_1 and an_2, one staggered above the other. The macromeres divide meridionally, forming a tier of eight cells below an_2. The micromeres also divide, albeit somewhat later, producing a small cluster beneath the larger tier. All the cleavage furrows of the sixth division are equatorial, and the seventh division is meridional, producing a 128-cell blastula.

Blastula Formation

The blastula stage of sea urchin development begins at the 128-cell stage. Here the cells form a hollow sphere surrounding a central cavity, or blastocoel. By this time, all the cells are the same size, the micromeres having slowed down their cell division. Every cell is in contact with the proteinaceous fluid of the blastocoel on the inside and with the hyaline layer on the outside. At this time, tight junctions unite the once loosely connected blastomeres into a seamless epithelial sheet that completely encircles the blastocoel. As the cells continue to divide, the blastula remains one cell layer thick, thinning out as it expands. This is accomplished by the adhesion of the blastomeres to the hyaline layer and by an influx of water that expands the blastocoel.

These rapid and invariant cell cleavages last through the ninth or tenth cell division, depending upon the species. After that time, there is a mid-blastula transition, when the synchrony of cell division ends, new genes become expressed, and many of the nondividing cells develop cilia on their outer surfaces. The ciliated blastula begins to rotate within the fertilization envelope. Soon afterward, differences are seen in the cells. The cells at the vegetal pole of the blastula begin to thicken, forming a vegetal plate. The cells of the animal half synthesize and secrete a hatching enzyme that digests the fertilization envelope. The embryo is now a free-swimming hatched blastula.

FATE MAPS AND THE DETERMINATION OF SEA URCHIN BLASTOMERES

Cell Fate Determination

The fate map of the sea urchin embryo was originally created by observing each of the cell layers and what its descendants became. More recent investigations have refined these maps by following the fates of individual cells injected with fluorescent dyes such as diI. These studies have shown that by the 60-cell stage, most of the embryonic cell fates are specified, but that the cells are not irreversibly committed. In other words, particular blastomeres consistently produce the same cell types in each embryo, but these cells remain pluripotent and can give rise to other cell types if experimentally placed in a different part of the embryo.

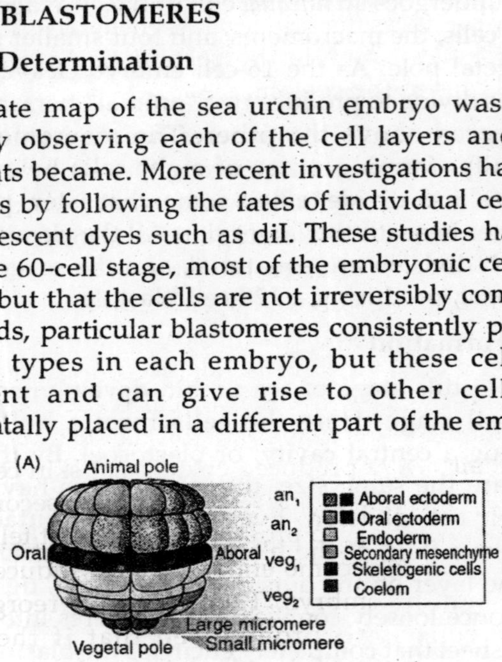

Fig. Fate map and cell lineage of the sea urchin Strongylocentrotus purpuratus.

A fate map of the 60-cell sea urchin embryo is shown in Figure. The animal half of the embryo consistently gives rise to the ectoderm—the larval skin and its neurons. The veg_1 layer produces cells that can enter into either the ectodermal or endodermal organs. The veg_2 layer gives rise to cells that can populate three different structures—the endoderm, the coelom (body wall), and secondary mesenchyme (pigment cells, immunocytes, and muscle cells). The first tier of micromeres produces the primary mesenchyme cells that form the larval skeleton, while the second tier of micromeres contributes cells to the coelom.

Although the early blastomeres have consistent fates in the larva, most of these fates are achieved by conditional specification. The only cells whose fates are determined autonomously are the skeletogenic micromeres. If these micromeres are isolated from the embryo and placed in test tubes, they will still form skeletal spicules. Moreover, if these micromeres are transplanted into the animal region of the blastula, not only will their descendants form skeletal spicules, but the transplanted micromeres will alter the fates of nearby cells by inducing a secondary site for gastrulation. Cells that would normally have produced ectodermal skin cells will be respecified as endoderm and will produce a secondary gut. The micromeres appear to produce a signal that tells the cells adjacent to them to become endoderm and induces them to invaginate into the embryo. Their ability to reorganize the embryonic cells is so pronounced that if the isolated micromeres are recombined with an isolated animal cap (the top two animal tiers), the animal cap cells will generate endoderm, and a more or less normal larva will develop.

In a normal embryo, the veg_2 cells become specified by the micromeres, and they, in turn, help specify the veg_1 layer. Without the veg_2 layer, the veg_1 cells are able to produce endoderm, but the endoderm is not specified as foregut, midgut, or hindgut. Thus, there appears to be a cascade wherein the vegetal pole micromeres induce the cells above them to become the veg_2 cells, and the veg_2 cells induce the cells above them to assume the veg_1 fates.Thus, the micromeres undergo autonomous specification to become skeletogenic mesenchyme, and these micromeres produce the initial signals that specify the other tiers of cells.

The identities of the signaling molecules involved in this process are just now becoming known (Sherwood and McClay 1997). The molecule responsible for specifying the micromeres (and their ability to induce the neighbouring cells) appears to be β-catenin. As we saw in previous Chapter, β-catenin is a transcription factor that is often activated by the Wnt pathway, and several pieces of evidence suggest it for this role. First, during normal sea urchin development, β-catenin accumulates in the nuclei of those cells fated to become endoderm and mesoderm. This accumulation is autonomous and can occur even if the micromere precursors are separated from the rest of the embryo. Second, this accumulation appears to be responsible for specifying the vegetal half of the embryo. Treating sea urchin embryos with lithium chloride causes the accumulation of β-catenin in all their cells, and this treatment transforms the presumptive ectoderm into endoderm. Conversely, experimental procedures that inhibit β-catenin accumulation in the vegetal cell nuclei prevent the formation of endoderm and mesoderm. It is possible that the levels of nuclear β-catenin accumulation help to determine the mesodermal and endodermal fates of the vegetal cells. Third, β-catenin is essential for giving the micromeres their inductive ability. Experiments described above demonstrated that the micromeres were able to induce a second embryonic axis when transplanted to the animal hemisphere. However, micromeres from embryos in which β-catenin was prevented from entering the nucleus were unable to induce the animal hemisphere cells to form endoderm, and a second axis was not formed.

It appears that the specification of cell fates in sea urchins involves a cascade initiated by the micromeres. It has been hypothesized that the signal from the micromeres induces a post-translational modification in some factor in the veg_2 layer. Similarly, the signal from the veg_2 layer probably modifies some protein (possibly a transcription factor) in the veg_1 layer. In this way, the different tiers are assigned different fates.

Axis Specification

In the sea urchin blastula, the cell fates line up along the animal-vegetal axis established in the egg cytoplasm prior to fertilization. The animal-vegetal axis also appears to structure the future anterior-posterior axis, with the vegetal region sequestering those maternal components necessary for posterior development.

In most sea urchins, the dorsal-ventral and left-right axes are specified after fertilization, but the manner of their specification is not well understood. Since the first cleavage plane can be either parallel, perpendicular, or oblique with respect to the eventual dorsal-ventral axis, it is probable that the dorsal-ventral axis is not specified until the 8-cell stage, when there are cell boundaries that correspond to these positions. Interestingly, in those sea urchins that bypass the larval stage to develop directly into juveniles, the dorsal-ventral axis is specified maternally in the egg cytoplasm.

Sea Urchin Gastrulation

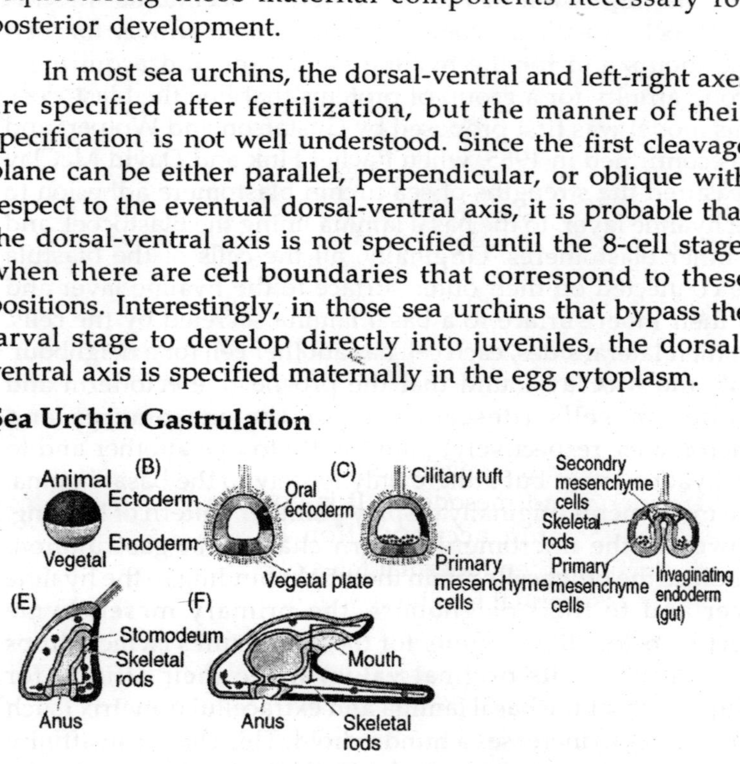

Fig. Normal sea urchin development, following the fate of the cellular layers of the blastula.

The late sea urchin blastula consists of a single layer of about 1000 cells that form a hollow ball, somewhat flattened at the vegetal end. The blastomeres, derived from different regions of the zygote, have different sizes and properties. Figures show the fates of the various regions of the blastula as it develops through gastrulation to the pluteus larva stage characteristic of sea urchins. The fate of each cell layer can be seen through its movements during gastrulation.

INGRESSION OF PRIMARY MESENCHYME

Importance of Extracellular Lamina Inside the Blastocoel

The ingression of the micromere descendants into the blastocoel is caused by these cells losing their affinity for their neighbours and for the hyaline membrane and acquiring a strong affinity for a group of proteins that line the blastocoel. This model was first proposed by Gustafson and Wolpert and was confirmed in 1985, when Rachel Fink and David McClay measured the strengths of sea urchin blastomere adhesion to the hyaline layer, to the basal lamina lining the blastocoel, and to other blastomeres. Originally, all the cells of the blastula are connected on their outer surface to the hyaline layer and on their inner surface to a basal lamina secreted by the cells. On their lateral sides, each cell has another cell for a neighbour. Fink and McClay found that the prospective ectoderm and endoderm cells (descendants of the mesomeres and macromeres, respectively) bind tightly to one another and to the hyaline layer, but adhere only loosely to the basal lamina. The micromeres originally display a similar pattern of binding. However, the micromere pattern changes at gastrulation. Whereas the other cells retain their tight binding to the hyaline layer and to their neighbours, the primary mesenchyme precursors lose their affinity for these structures (which drops to about 2% of its original value) while their affinity for components of the basal lamina and extracellular matrix (such as fibronectin) increases a hundredfold. This change in affinity causes the micromeres to release their attachments to the external hyaline layer and their neighbouring cells and, drawn in by the basal lamina, migrate up into the blastocoel. These changes in affinity have been correlated with changes in cell surface molecules that occur during this time.

As shown in Figure, there is a heavy concentration of extracellular material around the ingressing primary mesenchyme cells. Once inside the blastocoel, the primary mesenchyme cells appear to migrate along the extracellular matrix of the blastocoel wall, extending their filopodia in front of them. Several proteins (including fibronectin and a particular sulfated glycoprotein) are necessary to initiate and maintain this migration.

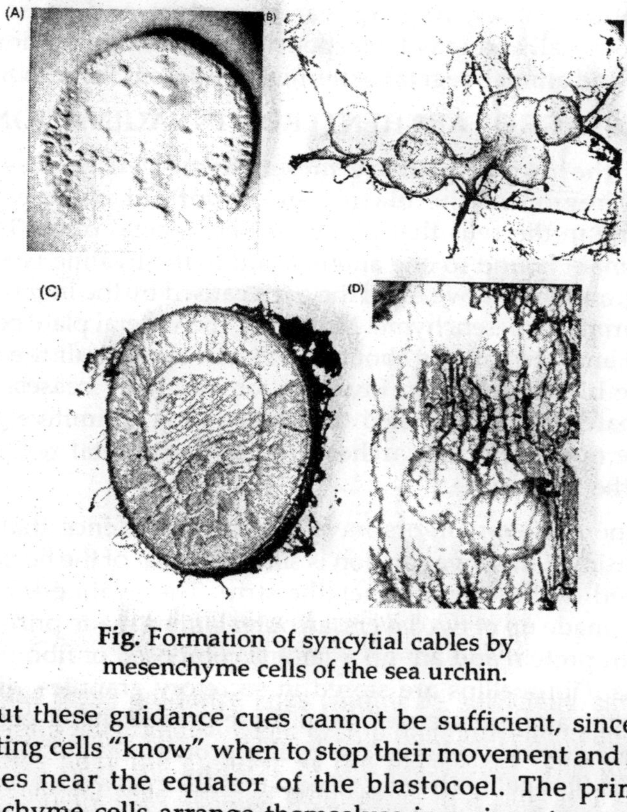

Fig. Formation of syncytial cables by mesenchyme cells of the sea urchin.

But these guidance cues cannot be sufficient, since the migrating cells "know" when to stop their movement and form spicules near the equator of the blastocoel. The primary mesenchyme cells arrange themselves in a ring at a specific position along the animal-vegetal axis. At two sites near the future ventral side of the larva, many of these primary mesenchyme cells cluster together, fuse with each other, and initiate spicule formation. If a labeled micromere from another embryo is injected into the blastocoel of a gastrulating sea urchin embryo, it migrates to the correct location and contributes to the formation of the embryonic spicules. It is thought that this positional information is provided by the prospective ectodermal cells and their basal laminae. Only the primary mesenchyme cells (and not other cell types or latex beads) are capable of responding to these patterning cues. Miller and colleagues have reported the existence of extremely fine (0.3-μm diameter) filopodia on the skeleton-forming mesenchyme. These filopodia are not thought to function in locomotion; rather, they appear to explore and sense the blastocoel wall and may be responsible for picking up dorsal-ventral and animal-vegetal patterning cues from the ectoderm.

FIRST STAGE OF ARCHENTERON INVAGINATION

As the ring of primary mesenchyme cells leaves the vegetal region of the blastocoel, important changes are occurring in the cells that remain at the vegetal plate. These cells remain bound to one another and to the hyaline layer of the egg, and they move to fill the gaps caused by the ingression of the primary mesenchyme. Moreover, the vegetal plate bends inward and invaginates about one-fourth to one-half the way into the blastocoel. Then invagination suddenly ceases. The invaginated region is called the archenteron (primitive gut), and the opening of the archenteron at the vegetal region is called the blastopore.

Lane and co-workers have provided evidence that the mechansim of this invagination is similar to that of the buckling produced by heating a bimetallic strip. The hyaline layer is actually made up of two layers, an outer lamina made primarily of hyalin protein and an inner lamina composed of fibropellin proteins. Fibropellins are stored in secretory granules within the oocyte, and are secreted from those granules after cortical granule exocytosis releases the hyalin protein. By the blastula stage, the fibropellins have formed a meshlike network over the embryo surface. At the time of invagination, the vegetal plate cells (and only those cells) secrete a chondroitin sulfate proteoglycan into the inner lamina of the hyaline layer directly beneath them. This hygroscopic (water-absorbing) molecule swells the inner lamina, but not the outer lamina. This causes the vegetal region of the hyaline layer to buckle. Slightly later, a second force arising from the movements of epithelial cells adjacent to the vegetal plate may facilitate this invagination by drawing the buckled layer inward.

At the stage when the skeletogenic mesenchyme cells begin ingressing into the blastocoel, the fates of the vegetal plate cells have already been specified. The endodermal cells adjacent to the micromere-derived mesenchyme become foregut, migrating the farthest distance into the blastocoel. The next layer of endodermal cells becomes midgut, and the last circumferential row to invaginate forms the hindgut and anus.

SECOND AND THIRD STAGES OF ARCHENTERON INVAGINATION

The invagination of the vegetal cells occurs in three discrete stages. After a brief pause, the second phase of archenteron formation begins. During this time, the archenteron extends dramatically, sometimes tripling its length. In this process of extension, the wide, short gut rudiment is transformed into a long, thin tube. To accomplish this extension, the cells of the archenteron rearrange themselves by migrating over one another and by flattening themselves. This phenomenon, wherein cells intercalate to narrow the tissue and at the same time move it forward, is called convergent extension. Moreover, cell division continues, producing more endodermal and secondary mesenchyme cells as the archenteron extends.

In at least some species of sea urchins, a third stage of archenteron elongation occurs. This last phase is initiated by the tension provided by secondary mesenchyme cells, which form at the tip of the archenteron and remain there. Filopodia are extended from these cells through the blastocoel fluid to contact the inner surface of the blastocoel wall. The filopodia attach to the wall at the junctions between the blastoderm cells and then shorten, pulling up the archenteron. Hardin ablated the secondary mesenchyme cells with a laser, with the result that the archenteron could elongate to only about two-thirds of the normal length. If a few secondary mesenchyme cells were left, elongation continued, although at a slower rate. The secondary mesenchyme cells, then, play an essential role in pulling the archenteron up to the blastocoel wall during the last phase of invagination.

But can the secondary mesenchyme filopodia attach to any part of the blastocoel wall, or is there a specific target in the animal hemisphere that must be present for attachment to occur? Is there a region of the blastocoel wall that is already committed to becoming the ventral side of the larva? Studies by Hardin and McClay show that there is a specific "target" site for the filopodia that differs from other regions of the animal hemisphere. The filopodia extend, touch the blastocoel wall at random sites, and then retract. However, when the filopodia contact a particular region of the wall, they remain attached there, flatten out against this region, and pull the archenteron toward it. When Hardin and McClay poked in the other side of the blastocoel wall so that the contacts were made most readily with that region, the filopodia continued to extend and retract after touching it. Only when the filopodia found their "target" did they cease these movements. If the gastrula was constricted so that filopodia never reached the target area, the secondary mesenchyme cells continued to explore until they eventually moved off the archenteron and found the target tissue as freely migrating cells. There appears, then, to be a target region on what is to become the ventral side of the larva that is recognized by the secondary mesenchyme cells, and which positions the archenteron in the region where the mouth will form.

As the top of the archenteron meets the blastocoel wall in the target region, the secondary mesenchyme cells disperse into the blastocoel, where they proliferate to form the mesodermal organs. Where the archenteron contacts the wall, a mouth is eventually formed. The mouth fuses with the archenteron to create a continuous digestive tube. Thus, as is characteristic of deuterostomes, the blastopore marks the position of the anus.

THE EARLY DEVELOPMENT OF SNAILS

Cleavage in Snail Eggs

Spiral holoblastic cleavage is characteristic of several animal groups, including annelid worms, some flatworms, and most molluscs. It differs from radial cleavage in numerous ways. First, the cleavage planes are not parallel or perpendicular to the animal-vegetal axis of the egg; rather, cleavage is at oblique angles, forming a "spiral" arrangement of daughter blastomeres. Second, the cells touch one another at more places than do those of radially cleaving embryos. In fact, they assume the most thermodynamically stable packing orientation, much like that of adjacent soap bubbles. Third, spirally cleaving embryos usually undergo fewer divisions before they begin gastrulation, making it possible to follow the fate of each cell of the blastula. When the fates of the individual blastomeres from annelid, flatworm, and mollusc embryos were compared, many of the same cells were seen in the same places, and their general fates were identical. Blastulae produced by radial cleavage have no blastocoel and are called stereoblastulae.

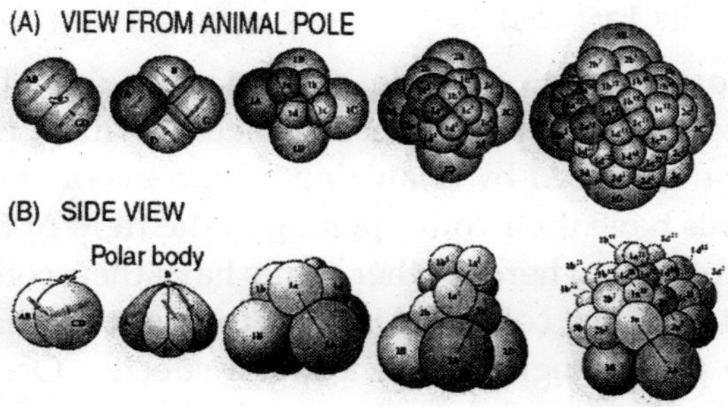

Fig. Spiral cleavage of the mollusc Trochus viewed (A) from the animal pole and (B) from one side. In (B), the cells derived from the A blastomere are shown in colour. The mitotic spindles, sketched in the early stages, divide the cells unequally and at an angle to the vertical and horizontal axes.

Figures depict the cleavage of mollusc embryos. The first two cleavages are nearly meridional, producing four large macromeres (labeled A, B, C, and D). In many species, the blastomeres are different sizes (D being the largest), a characteristic that allows them to be individually identified. In each successive cleavage, each macromere buds off a small micromere at its animal pole. Each successive quartet of micromeres is displaced to the right or to the left of its sister macromere, creating the characteristic spiral pattern. Looking down on the embryo from the animal pole, the upper ends of the mitotic spindles appear to alternate clockwise and counterclockwise. This causes alternate micromeres to form obliquely to the left and to the right of their macromere. At the third cleavage, the A macromere gives rise to two daughter cells, macromere 1A and micromere 1a. The B, C, and D cells behave similarly, producing the first quartet of micromeres. In most species, the micromeres are to the right of their macromeres (looking down on the animal pole). At the fourth cleavage, macromere 1A divides to form macromere 2A and micromere 2a; and micromere 1a divides to form two more micromeres, $1a^1$ and $1a^2$. Further cleavage yields blastomeres 3A and 3a from macromere 2A, and micromere $1a^2$ divides to produce cells $1a^{21}$ and $1a^{22}$.

The orientation of the cleavage plane to the left or to the right is controlled by cytoplasmic factors within the oocyte. This was discovered by analyzing mutations of snail coiling. Some snails have their coils opening to the right of their shells (dextral coiling), whereas other snails have their coils opening to the left (sinistral coiling). Usually, the direction of coiling is the same for all members of a given species. Occasionally, though, mutants are found. For instance, in species in which the coils open on the right, some individuals will be found with coils that open on the left. Crampton analyzed the embryos of such aberrant snails and found that their early cleavage differed from the norm. The orientation of the cells after the second cleavage was different in the sinistrally coiling snails owing to a different orientation of the mitotic apparatus. All subsequent divisions in left-coiling embryos are mirror images of those in dextrally coiling embryos. The position of the 4d blastomere (which is extremely important, as its progeny will form the mesodermal organs) is different in the two types of spiraling embryos. Eventually, two snails are formed, with their bodies on different sides of the coil opening.

The direction of snail shell coiling is controlled by a single pair of genes. In the snail *Limnaea peregra,* most individuals are dextrally coiled. Rare mutants exhibiting sinistral coiling were found and mated with wild-type snails. These matings showed that there is a right-coiling allele *D,* which is dominant to the left-coiling allele *d.* However, the direction of cleavage is determined not by the genotype of the developing snail, but by the genotype of the snail's mother. A *dd* female snail can produce only sinistrally coiling offspring, even if the offspring's genotype is *Dd.* A *Dd* individual will coil either left or right, depending on the genotype of its mother. Such matings produce a chart like this:

		Genotype	Phenotype
DD ♀ X *dd* ♂	→	*Dd*	All right-coiling
DD ♂ X *dd* ♀	→	*Dd*	All left-coiling
Dd X *Dd*	→	*1Dd:2Dd:1dd*	All right-coiling

The genetic factors involved in snail coiling are brought to the embryo by the oocyte cytoplasm. It is the genotype of the ovary in which the oocyte develops that determines which orientation cleavage will take. When Freeman and Lundelius injected a small amount of cytoplasm from dextrally coiling snails into the eggs of *dd* mothers, the resulting embryos coiled to the right. Cytoplasm from sinistrally coiling snails did not affect the right-coiling embryos. These findings confirmed that the wild-type mothers were placing a factor into their eggs that was absent or defective in the *dd* mothers.

THE POLAR LOBE: CELL DETERMINATION AND AXIS FORMATION

Molluscs provide some of the most impressive examples of mosaic development, in which the blastomeres are specified autonomously, and of cytoplasmic localization, wherein morphogenetic determinants are placed in a specific region of the oocyte. Mosaic development is widespread throughout the animal kingdom, especially in protostomal organisms such as annelids, nematodes, and molluscs, all of which initiate gastrulation at the future anterior end after only a few cell divisions. Moreover, the cytoplasmic factors responsible for specification are actively moved to one pole of the cell so that a blastomere containing these factors can restrict their transmission to only one of its two daughter cells. The fate of the two daughter cells is thus changed by which one of them gets the morphogenetic determinant.

E. B. Wilson demonstrated that mosaic development characterizes the early snail embryo. He also was able to demonstrate that such development is predicated on the segregation of specific morphogenetic determinants into specific blastomeres. Certain spirally cleaving embryos (mostly in the mollusc and annelid phyla) extrude a bulb of cytoplasm immediately before first cleavage. This protrusion is called the polar lobe. In certain species of snails, the region uniting the polar lobe to the rest of the egg becomes a fine tube. The first cleavage splits the zygote asymmetrically, so that the polar lobe is connected only to the CD blastomere. In several species, nearly one-third of the total cytoplasmic volume is present in this anucleate lobe, giving it the appearance of another cell. This three-lobed structure is often referred to as the trefoil-stage embryo. The CD blastomere then absorbs the polar lobe material, but extrudes it again prior to second cleavage. After this division, the polar lobe is attached only to the D blastomere, which absorbs its material. Thereafter, no polar lobe is formed.

Wilson showed that if one removes the polar lobe at the trefoil stage, the remaining cells divide normally. However, instead of producing a normal trochophore (snail) larva, they produce an incomplete larva, wholly lacking its mesodermal organs—muscles, mouth, shell gland, and foot. Moreover, Wilson demonstrated that the same type of abnormal embryo can be produced by removing the D blastomere from the 4-cell embryo. Wilson concluded that the polar lobe cytoplasm contains the mesodermal determinants, and that these determinants give the D blastomere its mesoderm-forming capacity. Wilson also showed that the localization of the mesodermal determinants is established shortly after fertilization, thereby demonstrating that a specific cytoplasmic region of the egg, destined for inclusion in the D blastomere, contains whatever factors are necessary for the special cleavage rhythms of the D blastomere and for the differentiation of the mesoderm.

The morphogenetic determinants sequestered within the polar lobe are probably located in the cytoskeleton or cortex, not in the diffusible cytoplasm of the embryo. Evidence for this localization came from the studies of A. C. Clement. When he separated the animal hemisphere of the egg of the snail *Ilyanassa obsoleta* from the vegetal hemisphere, the animal hemisphere formed ectodermal organs that resembled those formed by lobeless embryos. Clement then took embryos that had begun resorbing their second polar lobe and placed them into gelatin slabs. He centrifuged the embedded embryos, forcing the fluid, yolky cytoplasm from the vegetal part of the cell into the animal hemisphere. By centrifuging these embryos in a second, viscous medium, he caused the separation of the animal and vegetal hemispheres. The animal halves from such centrifuged embryos did not develop any more mesodermal or endodermal structures than those of uncentrifuged eggs. Thus, the determinants of the polar lobe were not transferred to the animal hemisphere in the fluid contents of the vegetal hemisphere. Van den Biggelaar obtained similar results when he removed the cytoplasm from the polar lobe with a micropipette. Cytoplasm from other regions of the cell flowed into the polar lobe, replacing the portion that he had removed. The subsequent development of these embryos was normal. In addition, when he added the soluble polar lobe cytoplasm to the B blastomere, duplications of structures were not seen. Therefore, the diffusible part of the cytoplasm does not contain the morphogenetic determinants. They probably reside in the nonfluid cortical cytoplasm or on the cytoskeleton.

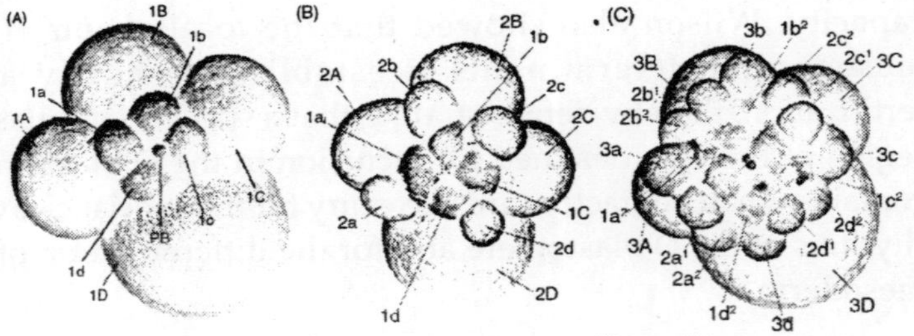

Fig. Spiral cleavage of the snail Ilyanassa. The D blastomere is larger than the others, allowing the identification of each cell. Cleavage is dextral.

Clement also analyzed the further development of the D blastomere in order to observe the further appropriation of these determinants. The development of the D blastomere is illustrated in Figure. This macromere, having received the contents of the polar lobe, is larger than the other three. When one removes the D blastomere or its first or second macromere derivatives (1D or 2D), one obtains an incomplete larva, lacking heart, intestine, velum (the ciliated border of the larva), shell gland, eyes, and foot. When one removes the 3D blastomere (after the division of the 2D cell to form the 3D and 3d blastomeres), one obtains an almost normal embryo, having eyes, foot, velum, and some shell gland, but no heart or intestine. Therefore, some of the morphogenetic determinants originally present in the D blastomere must have been apportioned to the 3d cell. After the 4d cell is given off (by the division of the 3D blastomere), removal of the D derivative (the 4D cell) produces no qualitative difference in development. In fact, all the essential determinants for heart and intestine formation are now in the 4d blastomere, and removal of that cell results in a heartless and gutless larva. The 4d blastomere is responsible for forming (at its next division) the two mesentoblasts, the cells that give rise to both the mesodermal (heart) and endodermal (intestine) organs.

The material in the polar lobe is also responsible for organizing the dorsal-ventral (back-belly) polarity of the embryo. When polar lobe material is forced to pass into the

AB blastomere as well as into the CD blastomere, twin larvae are formed that are joined at their ventral surfaces.

Thus, experiments have demonstrated that the nondiffusible polar lobe cytoplasm is extremely important in normal mollusc development for a number of reasons:

- It contains the determinants for the proper cleavage rhythm and cleavage orientation of the D blastomere.
- It contains certain determinants (those entering the 4d blastomere and hence leading to the mesentoblasts) for mesodermal and intestinal differentiation.
- It is responsible for permitting the inductive interactions (through the material entering the 3d blastomere) leading to the formation of the shell gland and eye.
- It contains determinants needed for specifying the dorsal-ventral axis of the embryo.

Although the polar lobe is clearly important for normal snail development, we still do not know the mechanisms of its effects. There appear to be no major differences in mRNA or protein synthesis between lobed and lobeless embryos. One possible clue has been provided by Atkinson, who has observed differentiated cells of the velum, digestive system, and shell gland within lobeless embryos. Thus, lobeless embryos can produce these cells, but they appear unable to organize them into functional tissues and organs. Tissues of the digestive tract can be found, but they are not connected; muscle cells are scattered around the lobeless larva, but are not organized into a functional muscle tissue. Thus, the developmental functions of the polar lobe may be very complex.

GASTRULATION IN SNAILS

The snail stereoblastula is relatively small, and its cell fates have already been determined by the D series of macromeres. Gastrulation is accomplished primarily by epiboly, wherein the micromeres at the animal cap multiply and "overgrow" the vegetal macromeres. Eventually, the micromeres will cover the entire embryo, leaving a small slit at the vegetal pole.

EARLY DEVELOPMENT IN TUNICATES

Tunicate Cleavage

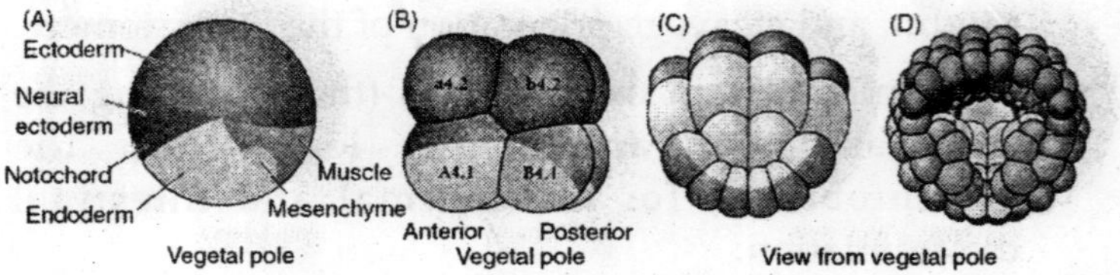

Fig. Bilateral symmetry in the egg of the tunicate Styela partita.

Ascidians, members of the tunicate subphylum, are fascinating animals for several reasons, but the foremost is that they are invertebrate chordates. They have a notochord as larvae (and therefore are chordates), but they lack vertebrae. As larvae, they are free-swimming tadpoles; but when the tadpole undergoes metamorphosis, it sticks to the sea floor, its nerve cord and notochord degenerate, and it secrete a cellulose tunic (which gave the name "tunicates" to these creatures). These animals are characterized by bilateral holoblastic cleavage, a pattern found primarily in tunicates. The most striking phenomenon in this type of cleavage is that the first cleavage plane establishes the earliest axis of symmetry in the embryo, separating the embryo into its future right and left sides. Each successive division orients itself to this plane of symmetry, and the half-embryo formed on one side of the first cleavage plane is the mirror image of the half-embryo on the other side. The second cleavage is meridional, like the first, but unlike the first division, it does not pass through the centre of the egg. Rather, it creates two large anterior cells (the A and D blastomeres) and two smaller posterior cells (blastomeres B and C). Each side now has a large and a small blastomere. During the next three divisions, differences in cell size and shape highlight the bilateral symmetry of these embryos. At the 32-cell stage, a small blastocoel is formed, and gastrulation begins.

The Tunicate Fate Map

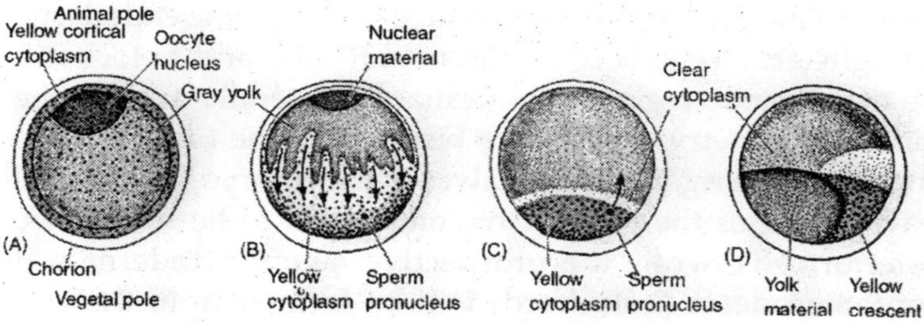

Fig. Cytoplasmic rearrangement in the fertilized egg of *Styela partita*.

As mentioned in earlier Chapter, early tunicate cells are specified autonomously, each cell acquiring a specific type of cytoplasm that will determine its fate. In tunicates such as *Styela partita,* the different regions of cytoplasm have distinct pigmentation, and the cell fates can easily be seen to correspond to the type of cytoplasm taken up by each cell. These cytoplasmic regions are apportioned to the egg during fertilization. In the unfertilized egg of *Styela partita,* a central gray cytoplasm is enveloped by a cortical layer containing yellow lipid inclusions. During meiosis, the breakdown of the nucleus releases a clear substance that accumulates in the animal hemisphere of the egg. Within 5 minutes of sperm entry, the inner clear and cortical yellow cytoplasms migrate into the vegetal (lower) hemisphere of the egg. As the male pronucleus migrates from the vegetal pole to the equator of the cell along the future posterior side of the embryo, the yellow lipid inclusions migrate with it. This migration forms a yellow crescent, extending from the vegetal pole to the equator; this region will produce most of the tail muscles of the tunicate larva. The movement of these cytoplasmic regions depends on microtubules that are generated by the sperm centriole and on the wave of calcium ions that contracts the animal pole cytoplasm.

Edwin Conklin took advantage of the differing colouration of these regions of cytoplasm to follow each of the cells of the tunicate embryo to its fate in the larva. He found that cells receiving clear cytoplasm become ectoderm; those containing yellow cytoplasm give rise to mesodermal cells; those that incorporate slate-gray inclusions become endoderm; and light gray cells become the neural tube and notochord. The cytoplasmic regions are localized bilaterally around the plane of symmetry, so they are bisected by the first cleavage furrow into the right and left halves of the embryo. The second cleavage causes the prospective mesoderm to lie in the two posterior cells, while the prospective neural ectoderm and chordamesoderm (notochord) will be formed from the two anterior cells. The third division further partitions these cytoplasmic regions such that the mesoderm-forming cells are confined to the two vegetal posterior blastomeres, and the chordamesoderm cells are likewise restricted to the two vegetal anterior cells.

AUTONOMOUS AND CONDITIONAL SPECIFICATION OF TUNICATE BLASTOMERES

As mentioned in earlier Chapter, the autonomous specification of tunicate blastomeres was one of the first observations in the field of experimental embryology. Reverberi and Minganti extended this analysis in a series of isolation experiments, and they, too, observed the self-differentiation of each isolated blastomere and of the remaining embryo. When the 8-cell embryo is separated into its four doublets (the right and left sides being equivalent), mosaic determination is the rule. The animal posterior pair of blastomeres gives rise to the ectoderm, and the vegetal posterior pair produces endoderm, mesenchyme, and muscle tissue, just as expected from the fate map.

From the cell lineage studies of Conklin and others, it was known that only one pair of blastomeres (posterior vegetal; B4.1) in the 8-cell embryo is capable of producing tail muscle tissue. These cells contain the yellow crescent cytoplasm. When yellow crescent cytoplasm is transferred from the B4.1 (muscle-forming) blastomere to the b4.2 (ectoderm-forming) blastomere of an 8-cell tunicate embryo, the ectoderm-forming blastomere generates muscle cells as well as its normal ectodermal progeny. Moreover, cytoplasm from the yellow crescent area of the fertilized egg can cause the a4.2 blastomere to express muscle-specific proteins. Conversely, Tung and colleagues showed that when larval cell nuclei are transplanted into enucleated tunicate egg fragments, the newly formed cells show the structures typical of the egg regions providing the cytoplasm, not of those cells providing the nuclei. We can conclude, then, that certain determinants that exist in the cytoplasm cause the formation of certain tissues. These morphogenetic determinants appear to work by selectively activating (or inactivating) specific genes. The determination of the blastomeres and the activation of certain genes are controlled by the spatial localization of the morphogenetic determinants within the egg cytoplasm.

Conditional specification, however, also plays an important role in tunicate development. One example of this process involves the development of neural cells. The nerve-producing cells are generated from both the animal and the vegetal anterior cells, yet neither the anterior or posterior cell of each half can produce them alone. When these anterior pairs are reunited, though, the brain and palp tissues arise. Ortolani has shown that this region of ectoderm is not determined for "neuralness" until the 64-cell stage, right before gastrulation. Similarly, while most muscles form autonomously from the yellow crescent material of the B4.1 blastomere, the most posterior muscle cells form through conditional specification by cell interactions with the descendants of the A4.1 and b4.2 blastomeres. Thus, although most tissues are determined autonomously by segregation of the egg cytoplasm, certain tissues in tunicate embryos have a conditional determination by cell-cell interaction.

SPECIFICATION OF THE EMBRYONIC AXES

The axes of the tunicate larva are among its earliest committments. Indeed, all of its embryonic axes are determined by the cytoplasm of the zygote prior to first cleavage. The first axis to be determined is the dorsal-ventral axis, which is defined by the cap of cytoplasm at the vegetal pole. This cap defines the future dorsal side of the larva and the site where gastrulation is initiated. When small regions of vegetal pole cytoplasm were removed from the zygote (between the first and second waves of zygote cytoplasmicmovement), the eggs neither gastrulated nor formed a dorsal-ventral axis.

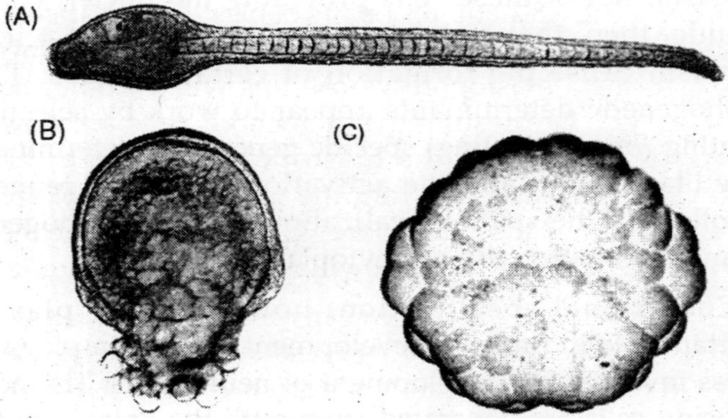

Fig. Comparison of normal tunicate embryos and embryos from which posterior vegetal cytoplasm has been removed.

The second axis to appear is the anterior-posterior axis, which is also determined during the migration of the oocyte cytoplasm. The yellow crescent forms in the region of the egg that will become the posterior side of the larva. When roughly 10% of the cytoplasm from this posterior vegetal region of the egg was removed after the second wave of cytoplasmic movement, most of the embryos failed to form an anterior-posterior axis. Rather, these embryos developed into radially symmetrical larvae with anterior fates. This posterior vegetal cytoplasm (PVC) was "dominant" to other cytoplasms in that when it was transplanted into the anterior vegetal region of zygotes that had had their own PVC removed, the anterior of the cell became the new posterior, and the axis was reversed. The left-right axis is specified as a consequence of these first two axes, and the first cleavage divides the embryo into its future right and left sides.

Gastrulation in Tunicates

Tunicate gastrulation is characterized by the invagination of the endoderm, the involution of the mesoderm, and the epiboly of the ectoderm. About 4–5 hours after fertilization, the vegetal (endoderm) cells assume a wedge shape, expanding their apical margins and contracting near their vegetal margins. The A8.1 and B8.1 pairs of blastomeres appear to lead this invagination into the centre of the embryo. This invagination forms a blastopore whose lips will become the mesodermal cells. The presumptive notochord cells are now on the anterior portion of the blastopore lip, while the presumptive tail muscle cells (from the yellow crescent) are on the posterior lip of the blastopore. The lateral lips of the blastopore comprise those cells that will become mesenchyme.

The second step of gastrulation involves the involution of the mesoderm. The presumptive mesoderm cells involute over the lips of the blastopore, and by migrating upon the basal surfaces of the ectodermal cells, move inside the embryo. The ectodermal cells then flatten and epibolize over the mesoderm and endoderm, eventually covering the embryo. After gastrulation is completed, the embryo elongates along its anterior-posterior axis. The dorsal ectodermal cells that are the precursors of the neural tube invaginate into the embryo and are enclosed by neural folds. This forms the neural tube, which will form a brain anteriorly and a spinal chord posteriorly. Meanwhile, the presumptive notochord cells on the right and left sides of the embryo migrate to the midline and interdigitate to form the notochord, a single row of 40 cells. The muscle cells of the tail differentiate on either side of the neural tube and notochord. Thus, a tadpole is formed and will now search for a substrate on which to settle and metamorphose into an adult tunicate.

EARLY DEVELOPMENT OF THE NEMATODE CAENORHABDITIS ELEGANS

Why C. Elegans?

Our ability to analyze development requires appropriate organisms. Sea urchins have long been a favourite organism of embryologists because their gametes are readily obtainable in large numbers, their eggs and embryos are transparent, and fertilization and development can occur under labouratory conditions. But sea urchins are difficult to rear in the labouratory for more than one generation, making their genetics difficult to study. Geneticists, on the other hand (at least those working with multicellular eukaryotes), favour *Drosophila.* Its rapid life cycle, its readiness to breed, and the polytene chromosomes of the larva (which allow gene localization) make the fruit fly superbly suited for hereditary analysis. But *Drosophila* development is complex and difficult to study.

A research programme spearheaded by Sydney Brenner was set up to identify an organism wherein it might be possible to identify each gene involved in development as well as to trace the lineage of every single cell. The researchers settled upon *Caenorhabditis elegans,* a small (1 mm long), free-living soil nematode. It has a rapid period of embryogenesis (about 16 hours), which it can accomplish in a petri dishe, and relatively few cell types. Moreover, its predominant adult form is hermaphroditic, with each individual producing both eggs and sperm. These roundworms can reproduce either by self-fertilization or by cross-fertilization with the infrequently occurring males. The body of an adult *C. elegans* hermaphrodite contains exactly 959 somatic cells, whose entire lineage has been traced through its transparent cuticle. Furthermore, unlike vertebrate cell lineages, the cell lineage of *C. elegans* is almost entirely invariant from one individual to the next. There is little room for randomness.

ANTERIOR-POSTERIOR AXIS FORMATION

The elongated axis of the *C. elegans* egg defines the future anterior-posterior axis of the nematode's body. The decision as to which end will become the anterior and which the posterior seems to reside with the position of sperm pronucleus. When it enters the oocyte cytoplasm, the centriole associated with the sperm pronucleus initiates cytoplasmic movements that push the male pronucleus to the nearest end of the oblong oocyte. This end becomes the posterior pole.

A second anterior-posterior asymmetry seen shortly after fertilization is the migration of the P-granules. P-granules are ribonucleoprotein complexes that probably function in specifying the germ cells. Using fluorescent antibodies to a component of the P-granules, Strome and Wood discovered that shortly after fertilization, the randomly scattered P-granules move toward the posterior end of the zygote, so that they enter only the blastomere (P1) formed from the posterior cytoplasm. The P-granules of the P1 cell remain in the posterior of the P1 cell and are thereby passed to the P2 cell when P1 divides. During the division of P2 and P3, however, the P-granules become associated with the nucleus that enters the P3 cytoplasm. Eventually, the P-granules will reside in the P4 cell, whose progeny become the sperm and eggs of the adult. The localization of the P-granules requires microfilaments, but can occur in the absence of microtubules. Treating the zygote with cytochalasin D (a microfilament inhibitor) prevents the segregation of these granules to the posterior of the cell, whereas demecolcine (a colchicine-like microtubule inhibitor) fails to stop this movement. The partitioning of the P-granules and the orientation of the mitotic spindles are both deficient in those embryos whose mothers were deficient in any of the *par* (partition-defective) genes. The proteins encoded by these genes are found in the cortex of the embryo and appear to interact with the actin cytoskeleton.

Formation of the Dorsal-Ventral and Right-Left Axes

The dorsal-ventral axis of the nematode is seen in the division of the AB cell. As the AB cell divides, it becomes longer than the eggshell is wide. This causes the cells to slide, resulting in one AB daughter cell being anterior and one being posterior (hence their names, ABa and ABp, respectively). This squeezing also causes the ABp cell to take a position above the EMS cell that results from the division of the P1 blastomere. The ABp cell defines the future dorsal side of the embryo, while the EMS cell, the precursor of the muscle and gut cells, marks to future ventral surface of the embryo. The left-right axis is specified later, at the 12-cell stage, when the MS blastomere (from the division of the EMS cell) contacts half the "granddaughters" of the ABa cell, distinguishing the right side of the body from the left side.

Control of Blastomere Identity

C. elegans demonstrates both the conditional and autonomous modes of cell specification. Both modes can be seen if the first two blastomeres are experimentally separated. The P1 cell develops autonomously without the presence of AB. It makes all the cells that it would normally make, and the result is the posterior half of an embryo. However, the AB cell, in isolation, makes only a fraction of the cell types that it would normally make. For instance, the resulting ABa blastomere fails to make the anterior pharyngeal muscles that it would have made in an intact embryo. Therefore, the specification of the AB blastomere is conditional, and it needs the descendants of the P1 cell to interact with it.

Autonomous Specification

The determination of the P1 lineages appears to be autonomous, with the cell fates determined by internal cytoplasmic factors rather than by interactions with neighbouring cells. It is thought that protein factors might determine cell fate by entering the nuclei of the appropriate blastomeres and activating or repressing specific fate-determining genes. Have any transcription factors been found in autonomously determined cell lineages? While the P-granules of *C. elegans* are localized in a way consistent with a role as a morphogenetic determinant, they do not enter the nucleus, and their role in development is still unknown. However, the SKN-1, PAL-1, and PIE-1 proteins are thought to encode transcription factors that act intrinsically to determine the fates of cells derived from the four P1-derived somatic founder cells, MS, E, C, and D.

The SKN-1 protein is a maternally expressed polypeptide that may control the fate of the EMS blastomere, the cell that generates the posterior pharynx. After first cleavage, only the posterior blastomere, P1, has the ability to autonomously produce pharyngeal cells when isolated. After P1 divides, only EMS is able to generate pharyngeal muscle cells in isolation. Similarly, when the EMS cell divides, only one of its progeny, MS, has the intrinsic ability to generate pharyngeal tissue. These findings suggest that pharyngeal cell fate may be determined autonomously by maternal factors residing in the cytoplasm that are parceled out to these particular cells. Bowerman and his co-workers found maternal effect mutants lacking pharyngeal cells, and isolated a mutation in the *skn-1* gene. Embryos from homozygous *skn-1*-deficient mothers lack both pharyngeal mesoderm and endoderm derivatives of EMS. Instead of making the normal intestinal and pharyngeal structures, these embryos seem to make extra hypodermal (skin) and body wall tissue where their intestine and pharynx should be. In other words, EMS appears to be respecified as C. Only those cells that are destined to form pharynx or intestine are affected by this mutation. Moreover, the protein encoded by the *skn-1* gene has a DNA-binding site motif similar to that seen in the bZip family of transcription factors.

A second possible transcription factor, PAL-1, is also required for the differentiation of the P1 lineage. PAL-1 activity is needed for the normal development of the somatic descendants of the P2 blastomere. Thus, embryos lacking PAL-1 have no somatic cell types derived from the C and D stem cells. PAL-1 is regulated by the MEX-3 protein, an RNA-binding protein that appears to inhibit the translation of the *pal-1* mRNA. Wherever MEX-3 is expressed, PAL-1 is absent. Thus, in *mex-3*-deficient mutants, PAL-1 is seen in every blastomere. SKN-1 also inhibits PAL-1 (thereby preventing it from becoming active in the EMS cell).

A third putative transcription factor, PIE-1, is necessary for germ line fate. PIE-1 appears to inhibit both SKN-1 and PAL-1 function in the P2 and subsequent germ line cells. Mutations of the maternal *pie-1* gene result in germ line blastomeres adopting somatic fates, with the P2 cell behaving similarly to a wild-type EMS blastomere. The localization and the genetic properties of PIE-1 suggest that it represses the establishment of somatic cell fate and preserves the totipotency of the germ cell lineage.

Conditional Specification

The *C. elegans* embryo uses both autonomous and conditional modes of specification. Conditional specification can be seen in the development of the endoderm cell lineage. At the 4-cell stage, the EMS cell requires a signal from its neighbour (and sister), the P2 blastomere. Usually, the EMS cell divides into an MS cell (which produces mesodermal muscles) and an E cell (which produces the intestinal endoderm). If the P2 cell is removed at the early 4-cell stage, the EMS cell will divide into two MS cells, and endoderm will not be produced. If the EMS cell is recombined with the P2 blastomere, however, it will form endoderm; it will not do so, however, when combined with ABa, ABp, or both AB derivatives.

The P2 cell produces a signal that interacts with the EMS cell and instructs the EMS daughter that is next to it to become the E cell. This message is transmitted through the Wnt signaling cascade. The P2 cell produces the *C. elegans* homologue of a Wnt protein, the MOM-2 peptide. The MOM-2 peptide is received in the EMS cell by the MOM-5 protein, the *C. elegans* version of the Wnt receptor protein, Frizzled. The result of this signaling cascade is to down-regulate the expression of the *pop-1* gene in the EMS daughter destined to become the E cell. In *pop-1*-deficient embryos, both EMS daughter cells become E cells.

The P2 cell is also critical in giving the signal that distinguishes ABp from its sister, ABa. ABa gives rise to neurons, hypodermis, and the anterior pharynx cells, while ABp makes only neurons and hypodermal cells. However, if one experimentally reverses their positions, their fates are similarly reversed, and a normal embryo is formed. In other words, ABa and ABp are equivalent cells whose fate is determined by their positions within the embryo. Transplantation and genetic studies have shown that ABp becomes different from ABa through its interaction with the

P2 cell. In an unperturbed embryo, both ABa and ABp contact the EMS blastomere, but only ABp contacts the P2 cell. If the P2 cell is killed at the early 4-cell stage, the ABp cell does not generate its normal complement of cells. Contact between ABp and P2 is essential for the specification of ABp cell fates, and the ABa cell can be made into an ABp-type cell if it is forced into contact with P2.

Moreover, these studies show that this interaction is mediated by the GLP-1 protein on the ABp cell and the APX-1 (anterior pharynx excess) protein on the P2 blastomere. In embryos whose mothers have mutant *glp-1*, ABp is transformed into an ABa cell. The GLP-1 protein is a member of a widely conserved family called the Notch proteins, which serve as cell membrane receptors in many cell-cell interactions, and it is seen on both the ABa and ABp cells. As mentioned in earlier Chapter, one of the most important ligands for Notch proteins such as GLP-1 is another cell surface protein called Delta. In *C. elegans,* the Delta-like protein is APX-1, and it is found on the P2 cell. This APX-1 signal breaks the symmetry between ABa and ABp, since it stimulates the GLP-1 protein solely on the AB descendant that it touches, namely, the ABp blastomere. In doing this, the P2 cell initiates the dorsal-ventral axis of *C. elegans,* and it confers on the ABp blastomere a fate different from that of its sister cell.

Gastrulation in C. Elegans

Gastrulation in *C. elegans* starts extremely early, just after the generation of the P4 cell in the 24-cell embryo. At this time, the two daughters of the E cell (Ea and Ep) migrate from the ventral side into the centre of the embryo. There, they will divide to form a gut consisting of 20 cells. There is a very small and transient blastocoel prior to the movement of the Ea and Ep cells, and their inward migration creates a tiny blastopore. The next cell to migrate through this blastopore is the P4 cell, the precursor of the germ cells. It migrates to a position beneath the gut primordium. The mesodermal cells move in next: the descendants of the MS cell migrate inward from the anterior side of the blastopore, and the C- and D-derived muscle precursors enter from the posterior side. These cells flank the gut tube on the left and right sides. Finally, about 6 hours after fertilization, the AB-derived cells that contribute to the pharynx are brought inside, while the hypoblast (hypodermal precursor) cells move ventrally by epiboly, eventually closing the blastopore. During the next 6 hours, the cells move and organize into organs, and the ball-shaped embryo stretches out to become a worm. This hermaphroditic worm will have 558 somatic cells. An additional 115 cells will have formed, but undergone apoptosis. After four molts, this worm will be a sexually mature adult, containing 959 somatic cells, as well as numerous sperm and eggs.

Chapter 9

The Genetics of Axis Specification in Drosophila

Thanks largely to the studies by Thomas Hunt Morgan's labouratory during the first decade of the twentieth century, we know more about the genetics of *Drosophila* than about any other multicellular organism. The reasons for this have to do with both the flies and the people who first studied them. *Drosophila* is easy to breed, hardy, prolific, tolerant of diverse conditions, and the polytene chromosomes of its larvae are easy to identify. The techniques for breeding and identifying mutants are easy to learn. Moreover, the progress of *Drosophila* genetics was aided by the relatively free access of every scientist to the mutants and the techniques of every other researcher. Mutants were considered the property of the entire scientific community, and Morgan's labouratory established the database and exchange network whereby anyone could obtain them.

Undergraduates (starting with Calvin Bridges and Alfred Sturtevant) played important roles in *Drosophila* research, which achieved its original popularity as a source of undergraduate research projects. As historian Robert Kohler noted (1994), "Departments of biology were cash poor but rich in one resource: cheap, eager, renewable student labour." The *Drosophila* genetics programme was "designed by young persons to be a young person's game," and the students set the rules for *Drosophila* research: "No trade secrets, no monopolies, no poaching, no ambushes."

But *Drosophila* was a difficult organism on which to study embryology. Although Jack Schultz and others attempted to relate the genetics of *Drosophila* to its development, the fly embryos proved too complex and too intractable to study, being neither large enough to manipulate experimentally nor transparent enough to observe. It was not until the techniques of molecular biology allowed researchers to identify and manipulate the genes and RNAs of the insect that its genetics could be related to its development. And when that happened, a revolution occurred in the field of biology. The merging of our knowledge of the molecular aspects of *Drosophila* genetics with our knowledge of its development built the foundations on which are current sciences of developmental genetics and evolutionary developmental biology are based.

EARLY DROSOPHILA DEVELOPMENT

In the last chapter, we discussed the specification of early embryonic cells by their acquisition of different cytoplasmic determinants that had been stored in the oocyte. The cell membranes establish the region of cytoplasm incorporated into each new blastomere, and it is thought that the morphogenetic determinants then direct differential gene expression in these blastomeres. During *Drosophila* development, however, cellular membranes do not form until after the thirteenth nuclear division. Prior to this time, all the nuclei share a common cytoplasm, and material can diffuse throughout the embryo. In these embryos, the specification of cell types along anterior-posterior and dorsal-ventral axes is accomplished by the interactions of cytoplasmic materials *within* the single, multinucleated cell. Moreover, the initiation of the anterior-posterior and dorsal-ventral differences is controlled by the position of the egg within the mother's ovary. Whereas the sperm entry site may fix the axes in ascidians and nematodes, the fly's anterior-posterior and dorsal-ventral axes are specified by interactions between the egg and its surrounding follicle cells.

Cleavage

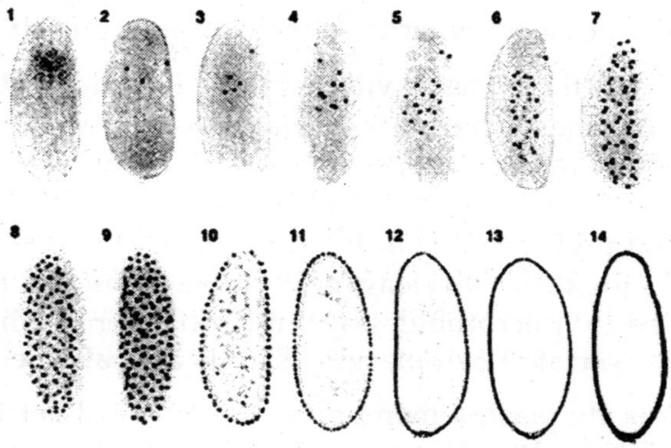

Fig. Superficial cleavage in a Drosophila embryo. The early divisions occur centrally. The numbers refer to the cell cycle. At the tenth cell cycle (512-nucleus stage 2 hours after fertilization), the pole cells form in the posterior, and the nuclei and their cytoplasmic islands ("energids") migrate to the periphery of the cell. This creates the syncytial blastoderm. After cycle 13, the oocyte membranes ingress between the nuclei to form the cellular blastoderm.

Most insect eggs undergo superficial cleavage, wherein a large mass of centrally located yolk confines cleavage to the cytoplasmic rim of the egg. One of the fascinating features of this cleavage type is that cells do not form until after the nuclei have divided. Cleavage in a *Drosophila* egg is shown in Figure. The zygote nucleus undergoes several mitotic divisions within the central portion of the egg. In *Drosophila,* 256 nuclei are produced by a series of eight nuclear divisions averaging 8 minutes each. The nuclei then migrate to the periphery of the egg, where the mitoses continue, albeit at a progressively slower rate. During the ninth division cycle, about five nuclei reach the surface of the posterior pole of the embryo. These nuclei become enclosed by cell membranes and generate the pole cells that give rise to the gametes of the adult. Most of the other nuclei arrive at the periphery of the embryo at cycle 10 and then undergo four more divisions at progressively slower rates. During these stages of nuclear division, the embryo is called a syncytial blastoderm, meaning that all the cleavage nuclei are contained within a common cytoplasm. No cell membranes exist other than that of the egg itself.

Although the nuclei divide within a common cytoplasm, this does not mean that the cytoplasm is itself uniform. Karr and Alberts have shown that each nucleus within the syncytial blastoderm is contained within its own little territory of cytoskeletal proteins. When the nuclei reach the periphery of the egg during the tenth cleavage cycle, each nucleus becomes surrounded by microtubules and microfilaments. The nuclei and their associated cytoplasmic islands are called energids

The oocyte plasma membrane folds inward between the nuclei, eventually partitioning off each somatic nucleus into a single cell. This process creates the cellular blastoderm, in which all the cells are arranged in a single-layered jacket around the yolky core of the egg. Like any other cell formation, the formation of the cellular blastoderm involves a delicate interplay between microtubules and microfilaments. The first phase of blastoderm cellularization is characterized by the invagination of cell membranes and their underlying actin microfilament network into the regions between the nuclei to form furrow canals. This process can be inhibited by drugs that block microtubules. After the furrow canals have passed the level of the nuclei, the second phase of cellularization occurs. Here, the rate of invagination increases, and the actin-membrane complex begins to constrict at what will be the basal end of the cell. In *Drosophila,* the cellular blastoderm consists of approximately 6000 cells and is formed within 4 hours of fertilization.

THE MIDBLASTULA TRANSITION

After the nuclei reach the periphery, the time required to complete each of the next four divisions becomes progressively longer. While cycles 1–10 are each 8 minutes long, cycle 13, the last cycle in the syncytial blastoderm, takes 25 minutes to complete. Cycle 14, in which the *Drosophila* embryo forms cells (i.e., after 13 divisions), is asynchronous. Some groups of cells complete this cycle in 75 minutes, whereas other groups of cells take 175 minutes. Transcription from the nuclei (which begins around the eleventh cycle) is greatly enhanced at this stage. This slowdown of nuclear division and the concomitant increase in RNA transcription is often referred to as the midblastula transition. Such a transition is also seen in the embryos of numerous vertebrate and invertebrate phyla. The control of this mitotic slowdown (in *Xenopus*, sea urchin, starfish, and *Drosophila* embryos) appears to be effected by the ratio of chromatin to cytoplasm. Edgar and his colleagues compared the early development of wild-type *Drosophila* embryos with that of a haploid mutant. These haploid *Drosophila* embryos have half the wild-type quantity of chromatin at each cell division. Hence a haploid embryo at the eighth cell cycle has the same amount of chromatin that a wild-type embryo has at cell cycle 7. The investigators found that whereas wild-type embryos formed their cellular blastoderm immediately after the thirteenth division, the haploid embryos underwent an extra, fourteenth, division before cellularization. Moreover, the lengths of cycles 11–14 in wild-type embryos corresponded to those of cycles 12–15 in the haploid embryos. Thus, the haploid embryos follow a pattern similar to that of the wild-type embryos—only they lag by one cell division.

GASTRULATION

At the time of midblastula transition, gastrulation begins. The first movements of *Drosophila* gastrulation segregate the presumptive mesoderm, endoderm, and ectoderm. The prospective mesoderm—about 1000 cells constituting the ventral midline of the embryo—folds inward to produce the ventral furrow. This furrow eventually pinches off from the surface to become a ventral tube within the embryo. It then flattens to form a layer of mesodermal tissue beneath the ventral ectoderm. The prospective endoderm invaginates as two pockets at the anterior and posterior ends of the ventral furrow. The pole cells are internalized along with the endoderm. At this time, the embryo bends to form the cephalic furrow.

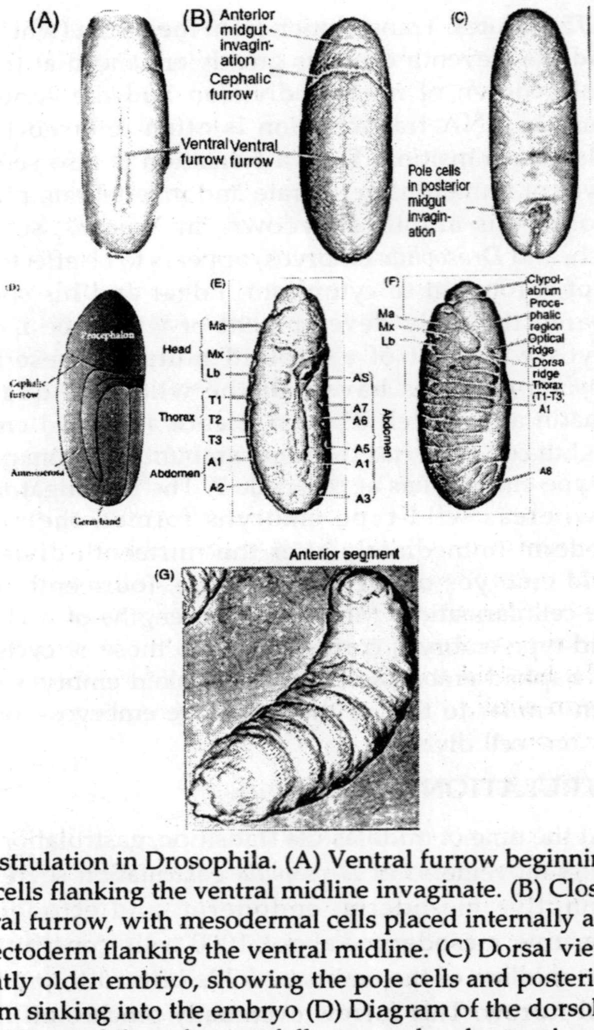

Fig. Gastrulation in Drosophila. (A) Ventral furrow beginning to form as cells flanking the ventral midline invaginate. (B) Closing of ventral furrow, with mesodermal cells placed internally and surface ectoderm flanking the ventral midline. (C) Dorsal view of a slightly older embryo, showing the pole cells and posterior endoderm sinking into the embryo (D) Diagram of the dorsolateral view of Drosophila embryo at fullest germ band extension, just prior to segmentation.(E) Lateral view, showing fullest extension of germ band and the beginnings of segmentation and labial head segments; T1-T3, the thoracic segments; A1-A8, the abdominal segments. (F) Germ band reversing direction. The true segments are now visible, as well as the other territories of the dorsal head, such as the clypolabrum, procephalic region, optic ridge, and dorsal ridge. (G) Newly hatched first-instar larva.

The ectodermal cells on the surface and the mesoderm undergo convergence and extension, migrating toward the ventral midline to form the germ band, a collection of cells along the ventral midline that includes all the cells that will form the trunk of the embryo. The germ band extends posteriorly and, perhaps because of the egg case, wraps around the top (dorsal) surface of the embryo. Thus, at the end of germ band formation, the cells destined to form the most posterior larval structures are located immediately behind the future head region. At this time, the body segments begin to appear, dividing the ectoderm and mesoderm. The germ band then retracts, placing the presumptive posterior segments into the posterior tip of the embryo.

While the germ band is in its extended position, several key morphogenetic processes occur: organogenesis, segmentation, and the segregation of the imaginal discs. In addition, the nervous system forms from two regions of ventral ectoderm. As described in earlier Chapter, neuroblasts differentiate from this neurogenic ectoderm within each segment (and also from the nonsegmented region of the head ectoderm). Therefore, in insects like *Drosophila,* the nervous system is located ventrally, rather than being derived from a dorsal neural tube as in vertebrates.

The general body plan of *Drosophila* is the same in the embryo, the larva, and the adult, each of which has a distinct head end and a distinct tail end, between which are repeating segmental units. Three of these segments form the thorax, while another eight segments form the abdomen. Each segment of the adult fly has its own identity. The first thoracic segment, for example, has only legs; the second thoracic segment has legs and wings; and the third thoracic segment has legs and halteres (balancers). Thoracic and abdominal segments can also be distinguished from each other by differences in the cuticle. How does this pattern arise? During the past decade, the combined approaches of molecular biology, genetics, and embryology have led to a detailed model describing how a segmented pattern is generated along the anterior-posterior axis and how each segment is differentiated from the others.

The anterior-posterior and dorsal-ventral axes of *Drosophila* form at right angles to one another, and they are both determined by the position of the oocyte within the follicle cells of the ovary. The rest of this chapter is divided into three main parts. The first part concerns how the anterior-posterior axis is specified and how it determines the identity of each segment. The second part concerns how the dorsal-ventral axis is specified by the interactions between the oocyte and its surrounding follicle cells. The third part concerns how embryonic tissues are specified to become particular organs by their placement along these two axes.

THE ORIGINS OF ANTERIOR-POSTERIOR POLARITY

The anterior-posterior polarity of the embryo, larva, and adult has its origin in the anterior-posterior polarity of the egg. The maternal effect genes expressed in the mother's ovaries produce messenger RNAs that are placed in different regions of the egg. These messages encode transcriptional and translational regulatory proteins that diffuse through the syncytial blastoderm and activate or repress the expression of certain zygotic genes. Two of these proteins, Bicoid and Hunchback, regulate the production of anterior structures, while another pair of maternally specified proteins, Nanos and Caudal, regulates the formation of the posterior parts of the embryo. Next, the zygotic genes regulated by these maternal factors are expressed in certain broad (about three segments wide), partially overlapping domains. These genes are called gap genes (because mutations in them cause gaps in the segmentation pattern), and they are among the first genes transcribed in the embryo. Differing concentrations of the gap gene proteins cause the transcription of pair-rule genes, which divide the embryo into periodic units. The transcription of the different pair-rule genes results in a striped pattern of seven vertical bands perpendicular to the anterior-posterior axis. The pair-rule gene proteins activate the transcription of the segment polarity genes, whose mRNA and protein products divide the embryo into 14 segment-wide units, establishing the periodicity of the embryo. At the same time, the protein products of the gap, pair-rule, and segment polarity genes interact to regulate another class of genes, the homeotic selector genes, whose transcription determines the developmental fate of each segment.

THE MATERNAL EFFECT GENES

Embryological Evidence of Polarity Regulation by Oocyte Cytoplasm

Classic embryological experiments demonstrated that there are at least two "organizing centres" in the insect egg, one in the anterior of the egg and one in the posterior. For instance, Klaus Sander found that if he ligated the egg early in development, separating the anterior from the posterior region, one half developed into an anterior embryo and one half developed into a posterior embryo, but neither half contained the middle segments of the embryo. The later in development the ligature was made, the fewer middle segments were missing. Thus, it appeared that there were indeed gradients emanating from the two poles during cleavage, and that these gradients interacted to produce the positional information determining the identity of each segment. Moreover, when the RNA of the anterior of insect eggs was destroyed (by either ultraviolet light or RNase), the resulting embryos lacked a head and thorax. Instead, these embryos developed two abdomens and telsons (tails) with mirror-image symmetry: telson-abdomen-abdomen-telson. Thus, Sander's labouratory postulated the existence of a gradient at both ends of the egg, and hypothesized that the egg sequesters an RNA that generates a gradient of anterior-forming material.

The Molecular Model: Protein Gradients in the Early Embryo

In the late 1980s, the gradient hypothesis was united with a genetic approach to the study of *Drosophila* embryogenesis. If there were gradients, what were the morphogens whose concentrations changed over space? What were the genes that shaped these gradients? And did these morphogens act by activating or inhibiting certain genes in the areas where they were concentrated? Christiane Nüsslein-Volhard led a research programme that addressed these questions. The researchers found found that one set of genes encoded gradient morphogens for the anterior part of the embryo, another set of genes encoded morphogens responsible for organizing the posterior region of the embryo, and a third set of genes encoded proteins that produced the terminal regions at both ends of the embryo. This work resulted in a Nobel Prize for Nüsslein-Volhard and her colleague, Eric Wieschaus, in 1995.

The anterior-posterior axis of the *Drosophila* embryo appears to be patterned before the nuclei even begin to function. The nurse cells of the ovary deposit mRNAs in the developing oocyte, and these mRNAs are apportioned to different regions of the cell. In particular, four maternal messenger RNAs are critical to the formation of the anterior-posterior axis:

- *Bicoid* and *hunchback* mRNAs, whose protein products are critical for head and thorax formation
- *Nanos* and *caudal* mRNAs, whose protein products are critical for the formation of the abdominal segments

The *bicoid* mRNAs are located in the anterior portion of the unfertilized egg, and are tethered to the anterior microtubules. The *nanos* messages are bound to the cytoskeleton in the posterior region of the unfertilized egg. The *hunchback* and *caudal* mRNAs are distributed throughout the oocyte. Upon fertilization, these mRNAs can be translated into proteins. At the anterior pole, the *bicoid* RNA is translated into Bicoid protein, which forms a gradient highest at the anterior. At the posterior pole, the *nanos* message is translated into Nanos protein, which forms a gradient highest at the posterior. Bicoid protein inhibits the translation of the *caudal* RNA, allowing Caudal protein to be synthesized only in the posterior of the cell. Conversely, Nanos protein, in conjunction with Pumilio protein, binds to *hunchback* RNA, preventing its translation in the posterior portion of the embryo. Bicoid also elevates the level of Hunchback protein in the anterior of the embryo by binding to the enhancers of the *hunchback* gene and stimulating its transcription. The result of these interactions is the creation of four protein gradients in the early embryo:

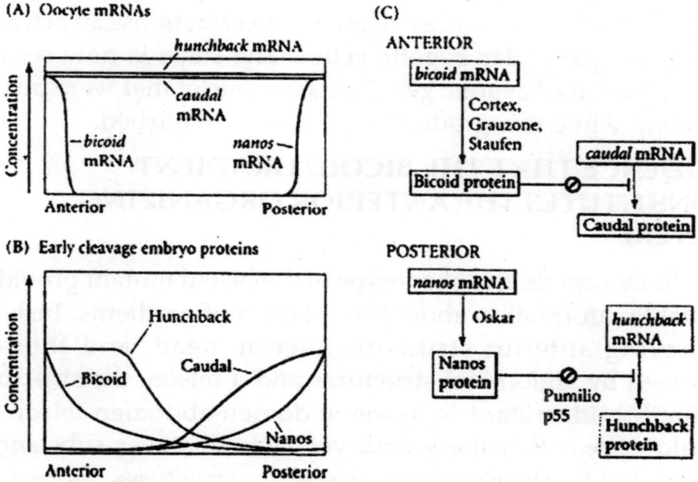

Fig. A model of anterior-posterior pattern generation by the Drosophila maternal effect genes. (A) The bicoid, nanos, hunchback, and caudal messenger RNAs are placed in the oocyte by the ovarian nurse cells. The bicoid message is sequestered anteriorly. The nanos message is sent to the posterior pole. (B) Upon translation, the Bicoid protein gradient extends from anterior to posterior, and the Nanos protein gradient extends from posterior to anterior. Nanos inhibits the translation of the hunchback message (in the posterior), while Bicoid prevents the translation of the caudal message (in the anterior). This inhibition results in opposing Caudal and Hunchback gradients. The Hunchback gradient is secondarily strengthened by the transcription of the hunchback gene in the anterior nuclei (since Bicoid acts as a transcription factor to activate hunchback transcription). (C) Parallel interactions whereby translational gene regulation establishes the anterior-posterior patterning of the Drosophila embryo

- An anterior-to-posterior gradient of Bicoid protein
- An anterior-to-posterior gradient of Hunchback protein

- A posterior-to-anterior gradient of Nanos protein
- A posterior-to-anterior gradient of Caudal protein

The Bicoid, Hunchback, and Caudal proteins are transcription factors whose relative concentrations can activate or repress particular zygotic genes. The stage is now set for the activation of zygotic genes in those nuclei that were busily dividing while this gradient was being established.

EVIDENCE THAT THE BICOID GRADIENT CONSTITUTES THE ANTERIOR ORGANIZING CENTRE

In *Drosophila,* the phenotype of the bicoid mutant provides valuable information about the function of gradients. Instead of having anterior structures (acron, head, and thorax) followed by abdominal structures and a telson, the structure of the bicoid mutant is telson-abdomen-abdomen-telson. It would appear that these embryos lack whatever substances are needed for the formation of anterior structures. Moreover, one could hypothesize that the substance that these mutants lack is the one postulated by Sander and Kalthoff to turn on genes for the anterior structures and turn off genes for the telson structures.

Further studies have strengthened the view that the product of the wild-type *bicoid* gene is the morphogen that controls anterior development. First, *bicoid* is a maternal effect gene. Messenger RNA from the mother's *bicoid* genes is placed in the embryo by the mother's ovarian cells. The *bicoid* RNA is strictly localized in the anterior portion of the oocyte, where the anterior cytoskeleton anchors it through the message's 3′ untranslated region. This mRNA is dormant until fertilization, at which time it receives a longer polyadenylate tail and can be translated. Driever and Nüsslein-Volhard have shown that when Bicoid protein is translated from this RNA during early cleavage, it forms a gradient, with the highest concentration in the anterior of the egg and the lowest in the posterior third of the egg. Moreover, this protein soon becomes concentrated in the embryonic nuclei in the anterior portion of the embryo.

Further evidence that Bicoid protein is the anterior morphogen came from experiments that altered the steepness of the gradient. Two genes, *exuperantia* and *swallow*, are responsible for keeping the *bicoid* message at the anterior pole of the egg. In their absence, the *bicoid* message diffuses farther into the posterior of the egg, and the gradient of Bicoid protein is less steep. The phenotype produced by these two mutants is similar to that of *bicoid*-deficient embryos, but less severe. These embryos lack their most anterior structures and have an extended mouth and thoracic region. Thus, by altering the gradient of Bicoid protein, one correspondingly alters the fate of the embryonic regions.

Confirmation that the Bicoid protein is crucial for initiating head and thorax formation came from experiments in which purified *bicoid* RNA was injected into early-cleavage embryos. When injected into the anterior of *bicoid*-deficient embryos (whose mothers lacked *bicoid* genes), the *bicoid* RNA rescued the embryos and caused them to have normal anterior-posterior polarity. Moreover, any location in an embryo where the *bicoid* message was injected became the head. If *bicoid* RNA was injected into the centre of an embryo, that middle region became the head, and the regions on either side of it became thorax structures. If a large amount of *bicoid* RNA was injected into the posterior end of a wild-type embryo (with its own endogenous *bicoid* message in its anterior pole), two heads emerged, one at either end.

The next question then emerged: How might a gradient in Bicoid protein control the determination of the anterior-posterior axis? Recent evidence suggests that Bicoid acts in two ways to specify the anterior of the *Drosophila* embryo. First, it acts as a repressor of posterior formation. It does this by binding to and suppressing the translation of *caudal* RNA, which is found throughout the egg and early embryo. The Caudal protein is critical in specifying the posterior domains of the embryo, and it activates the genes responsible for the invagination of the hindgut. The Bicoid protein binds to a specific region of the *caudal* message's 3′ untranslated region, thereby preventing the translation of this message in the anterior section of the embryo. This suppression is necessary, for if Caudal protein is made in the anterior, the head and thorax are not properly formed.

Second, the Bicoid protein functions as a transcription factor. Bicoid protein enters the nuclei of early-cleavage embryos, where it activates the *hunchback* gene. The transcription of *hunchback* is seen only in the anterior half of the embryo—the region where Bicoid protein is found. Mutants deficient in maternal and zygotic Hunchback protein lack mouthparts and thorax structures. In the late 1980s, two labouratories independently demonstrated that Bicoid protein binds to and activates the *hunchback* gene. The Hunchback protein derived from the synthesis of new *hunchback* mRNA joins the Hunchback protein synthesized by the translation of maternal messages in the anterior of the embryo. The Hunchback protein, also a transcription factor, represses abdominal-specific genes, thereby allowing the region of *hunchback* expression to form the head and thorax.

The Hunchback protein also works with Bicoid in generating the anterior pattern of the embryo. Based on two pieces of evidence, Driever and co-workers predicted that at least one other anterior gene besides *hunchback* must be activated by Bicoid. First, deletions of *hunchback* produce only some of the defects seen in the bicoid mutant phenotype. Second, as we saw in the *swallow* and *exuperantia* experiments, only moderate levels of Bicoid protein are needed to activate thorax formation (i.e., *hunchback* gene expression), but head formation requires higher concentrations. Driever and co-workers predicted that the promoters of such a head-specific gap gene would have low-affinity binding sites for Bicoid protein. This gene would be activated only at extremely high concentrations of Bicoid protein—that is, near the anterior tip of the embryo. Since then, three gap genes of the head have been discovered that are dependent on very high concentrations of Bicoid protein for their expression. The *buttonhead,empty spiracles,* and *orthodenticle* genes are needed to specify the progressively anterior regions of the head. In addition to needing high Bicoid levels for activation, these genes also require the presence of Hunchback protein to be transcribed. The Bicoid and Hunchback proteins act synergistically at the enhancers of these "head genes" to promote their transcription.

THE POSTERIOR ORGANIZING CENTRE: LOCALIZING AND ACTIVATING NANOS

The posterior organizing centre is defined by the activities of the *nanos* gene. The *nanos* RNA is produced by the ovarian nurse cells and is transported into the posterior region of the egg (farthest away from the nurse cells). The *nanos* message is bound to the cytoskeleton in the posterior region of the egg through its 3′ UTR and its association with the products of several other genes (*oskar, valois, vasa, staufen,* and *tudor*). If *nanos* or any other of these maternal effect genes are absent in the mother, no embryonic abdomen forms.

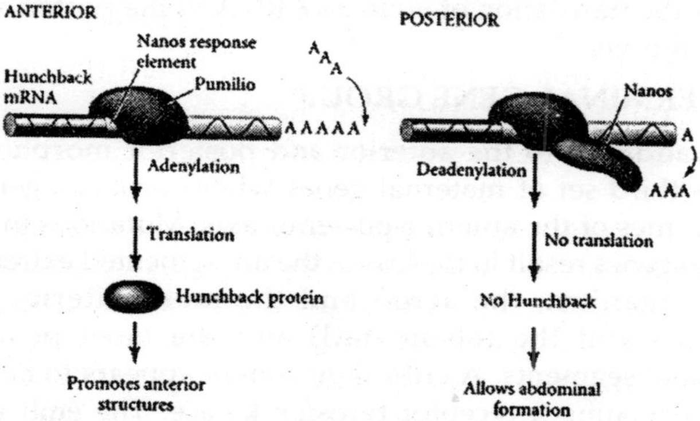

Fig. Control of hunchback mRNA translation by Nanos.

In the anterior of the embryo, Pumilio protein binds to the Nanos Response Element (NRE) in the 3′ UTR of the hunchback message, and the message is polyadenylated normally. This polyadenylated message can be translated into Hunchback protein. In the posterior of the embryo, where Nanos protein is found, Nanos binds to Pumilio to cause the deadenylation of the hunchback message. This prevents the translation of the hunchback message.

The *nanos* message is dormant in the unfertilized egg, as it is repressed by the binding of the Smaug protein to its 3′ UTR. At fertilization, this repression is removed, and Nanos protein can be synthesized. The Nanos protein forms a gradient that is highest at the posterior end. Nanos functions by inactivating *hunchback* mRNA translation. In the anterior of the cleavage-stage embryo, the *hunchback* message is bound in its 3′ UTR by the Pumilio protein, and the message can be translated into Hunchback protein. In the posterior of the early embryo, however, the bound Pumilio can be joined by the Nanos protein. Nanos binds to Pumilio and deadenylates the *hunchback* mRNA, preventing its translation. The *hunchback* RNA is initially present throughout the embryo, although more can be made from zygotic nuclei if they are activated by Bicoid protein. Thus, the combination of Bicoid and Nanos proteins causes a gradient of Hunchback protein across the egg. The Bicoid protein activates *hunchback* gene transcription in the anterior part of the embryo, while the Nanos protein inhibits the translation of *hunchback* RNA in the posterior part of the embryo.

THE TERMINAL GENE GROUP

In addition to the anterior and posterior morphogens, there is third set of maternal genes whose proteins generate the extremes of the anterior-posterior axis. Mutations in these terminal genes result in the loss of the unsegmented extremities of the organism: the acron and the most anterior head segments and the telson (tail) and the most posterior abdominal segments. A critical gene here appears to be *torso*, a gene encoding a receptor tyrosine kinase. The embryos of mothers with mutations of the *torso* gene have neither acron nor telson, suggesting that the two termini of the embryo are formed through the same pathway. The *torso* RNA is synthesized by the ovarian cells, deposited in the oocyte, and translated after fertilization. The transmembrane Torso protein is not spatially restricted to the ends of the egg, but is evenly distributed throughout the plasma membrane. Indeed, a dominant mutation of *torso*, which imparts constitutive activity to the receptor, converts the entire anterior half of the embryo into an acron and the entire posterior half into a telson. Thus, Torso must normally be activated only at the ends of the egg.

Stevens and her colleagues have shown that this is the case. Torso protein is activated by the follicle cells only at the two poles of the oocyte. Two pieces of evidence suggest that the activator of the Torso protein is probably the Torso-like protein: first, loss-of-function mutations in the *torso-like* gene create a phenotype almost identical to that produced by torso mutants, and second, ectopic expression of Torso-like causes the activation of the Torso protein in the new location. The *torso-like* gene is usually expressed only in the anterior and posterior follicle cells, and the secreted Torso-like protein can cross the perivitelline space to activate the Torso protein in the egg membrane. In this manner, the Torso-like protein activates the Torso protein in the anterior and posterior regions of the oocyte membrane. The end products of the RTK-kinase cascade activated by the Torso protein diffuse into the cytoplasm at both ends of the embryo. These kinases are thought to inactivate a transcriptional inhibitor of the *tailless* and *huckebein* gap genes. These two genes then specify the termini of the embryo. The distinction between the anterior and posterior termini depends on the presence of Bicoid. If the terminal genes act alone, the terminal regions differentiate into telsons. However, if Bicoid is also present, the region forms an acron.

The anterior-posterior axis of the embryo is therefore specified by three sets of genes: those that define the anterior organizing centre, those that define the posterior organizing centre, and those that define the terminal boundary region. The anterior organizing centre is located at the anterior end of the embryo and acts through a gradient of Bicoid protein that functions as a transcription factor to activate anterior-specific gap genes and as a translational repressor to suppresses posterior-specific gap genes. The posterior organizing centre is located at the posterior pole and acts translationally through the Nanos protein to inhibit anterior formation and transcriptionally through the Caudal protein to activate those genes that form the abdomen. The boundaries of the acron and telson are defined by the product of the torso gene, which is activated at the tips of the embryo. The activation of those genes responsible for constructing the posterior is performed by Caudal, a protein whose synthesis is inhibited in the anterior portion of the embryo. The next step in development will be to use these gradients of transcription factors to activate specific genes along the anterior-posterior axis.

THE SEGMENTATION GENES

The process of cell fate commitment in *Drosophila* appears to have two steps: specification and determination. Early in development, the fate of a cell depends on environmental cues, such as those provided by the protein gradients mentioned above. This specification of cell fate is flexible and can still be altered in response to signals from other cells. Eventually, the cells undergo a transition from this loose type of commitment to an irreversible determination. At this point, the fate of a cell becomes cell-intrinsic. The transition from specification to determination in *Drosophila* is mediated by the segmentation genes. These genes divide the early embryo into a repeating series of segmental primordia along the anterior-posterior axis. Mutations in segmentation genes cause the embryo to lack certain segments or parts of segments. Often these mutations affect parasegments, regions of the embryo that are separated by mesodermal thickenings and ectodermal grooves. The segmentation genes divide the embryo into 14 parasegments.

The parasegments of the embryo do not become the segments of the larva or adult; rather, they include the posterior part of an anterior segment and the anterior portion of the segment behind it. While the segments are the major anatomical divisions of the larval and adult body plan, they are built according to rules that use the parasegment as the basic unit of construction.

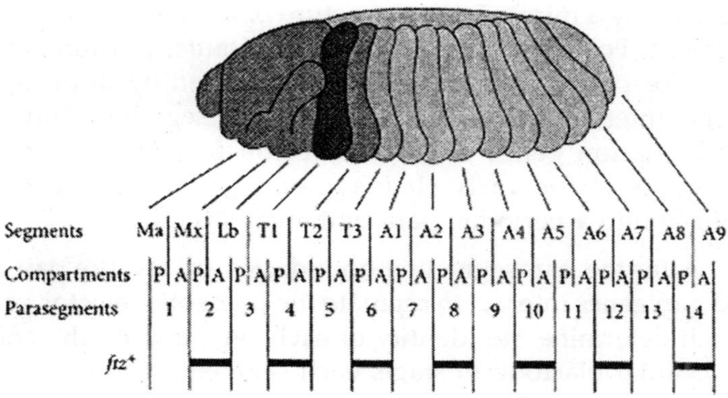

Fig. Segments and parasegments. A and P represent the anterior and posterior compartments of the segments. The parasegments are shifted one compartment forward. Ma, Mx, and Lb represent three of the head segments (mandibular, maxillary, and labial), the T segments are thoracic, and the A segments are abdominal. The parasegments are numbered 1 through 14. The bars below the map show the boundaries of gene expression observed by the in situ hybridization of radioactive cDNA from the pair-rule gene fushi tarazu (ftz).

There are three classes of segmentation genes, which are expressed sequentially. The transition from an embryo characterized by gradients of morphogens to an embryo with distinct units is accomplished by the products of the gap genes. The gap genes are activated or repressed by the maternal effect genes, and they divide the embryo into broad regions, each containing several parasegment primordia. The *Krüppel* gene, for example, is expressed primarily in parasegments 4–6, in the centre of the *Drosophila* embryo; the absence of the Krüppel protein causes the embryo to lack these regions. The protein products of the gap genes interact with neighbouring gap gene proteins to activate the transcription of the pair-rule genes. The products of these genes subdivide the broad gap gene regions into parasegments. Mutations of pair-rule genes, such as *fushi tarazu,* usually delete portions of alternate segments. Finally, the segment polarity genes are responsible for maintaining certain repeated structures within each segment. Mutations in these genes cause a portion of each segment to be deleted and replaced by a mirror-image structure of another portion of the segment. For instance, in *engrailed* mutants, portions of the posterior part of each segment are replaced by duplications of the anterior region of the subsequent segment. Thus, the segmentation genes are transcription factors that use the gradients of the early-cleavage embryo to transform the embryo into a periodic, parasegmental structure.

After the parasegmental boundaries are set, the pair-rule and gap genes interact to regulate the homeotic selector genes, which determine the identity of each segment. By the end of the cellular blastoderm stage, each segment primordium has been given an individual identity by its unique constellation of gap, pair-rule, and homeotic gene products.

THE GAP GENES

The gap genes were originally discovered through a series of mutant embryos that lacked groups of consecutive segments. Deletions caused by mutations of the *hunchback,Krüppel,* and *knirps* genes span the entire segmented region of the *Drosophila* embryo. The *giant* gap gene overlaps with these three, and mutations of the *tailless* and *huckebein* genes delete portions of the unsegmented termini of the embryo.

The expression of the gap genes is dynamic. There is usually a low level of transcriptional activity across the entire embryo that becomes defined into discrete regions of high activity as cleavage continues. The critical element appears to be the expression of the Hunchback protein, which by the end of nuclear division cycle 12 is found at high levels across the anterior part of the embryo, and then forms a steep gradient through about 15 nuclei. The last third of the embryo has undetectable Hunchback levels. The transcription patterns of the anterior gap genes are initiated by the different concentrations of the Hunchback and Bicoid proteins. High levels of Hunchback protein induce the expression of *giant,* while the *Krüppel* transcript appears over the region where Hunchback begins to decline. High levels of Hunchback protein also prevent the transcription of the posterior gap genes (such as *knirps*) in the anterior part of the embryo. It is thought that a gradient of the Caudal protein, highest at the posterior pole, is responsible for activating the abdominal gap genes *knirps* and *giant*. The *giant* gene has two methods for its activation, one for its anterior expression band and one for its posterior expression band (Rivera-Pomar 1995; Schulz and Tautz 1995).

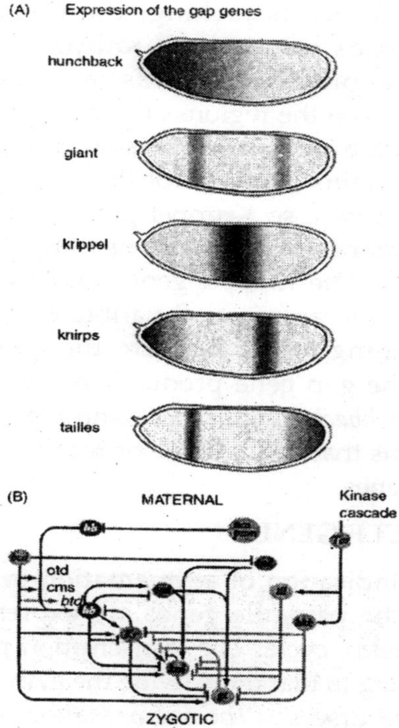

Fig. Conversion of maternal protein gradients into zygotic gap gene expression. (A) Gap gene expression patterns. (B) The gradients of maternal transcription factors Bicoid, Caudal, and Hunchback regulate the transcription of the gap genes. Hunchback and Caudal proteins come from both maternal messages and new zygotic transcription. These gap-gene encoded proteins diffuse, and the interactions between them are critical in activating the transcription of the pair-rule genes. At the two termini of the embryo, the interaction between Torso and Torsolike activates the tailless (tll) and huckebein (hkb) gap genes.

After the establishment of these patterns by the maternal effect genes and Hunchback, the expression of each gap gene becomes stabilized and maintained by interactions between the different gap gene products themselves. For instance, *Krüppel* gene expression is negatively regulated on its anterior boundary by the Hunchback and Giant proteins and on its posterior boundary by the Knirps and Tailless proteins. If Hunchback activity is lacking, the domain of *Krüppel* expression extends anteriorly. If Knirps activity is lacking, *Krüppel* gene expression extends more posteriorly. The boundaries between the regions of gap gene transcription are probably created by mutual repression. Just as the Giant and Hunchback proteins can control the anterior boundary of *Krüppel* transcription, so Krüppel protein can determine the posterior boundaries of *giant* and *hunchback* transcription. If an embryo lacks the *Krüppel* gene, *hunchback* transcription continues into the area usually allotted to *Krüppel*. These boundary-forming inhibitions are thought to be directly mediated by the gap gene products, because all four major gap genes (*hunchback,giant,Krüppel,* and *knirps*) encode DNA-binding proteins that can activate or repress the transcription of other gap genes.

THE PAIR-RULE GENES

The first indication of segmentation in the fly embryo comes when the pair-rule genes are expressed during the thirteenth division cycle. The transcription patterns of these genes are striking in that they divide the embryo into the areas that are the precursors of the segmental body plan.

How are some nuclei of the *Drosophila* embryo told to transcribe a particular gene while their neighbours are told not to transcribe it? The answer appears to come from the distribution of the protein products of the gap genes. Whereas the RNA of each of the gap genes has a very discrete distribution that defines abutting or slightly overlapping regions of expression, the *protein* products of these genes extend more broadly. In fact, they overlap by at least 8–10 nuclei (which at this stage accounts for about two to three segment primordia). This was demonstrated in a striking manner by Štanojevíc and co-workers (1989). They fixed cellularizing blastoderms (i.e., the stage when cells are beginning to form at the rim of the syncytial embryo), stained the Hunchback protein with an antibody carrying a red dye, and simultaneously stained the Krüppel protein with an antibody carrying a green dye. Cellularizing regions that contained both proteins bound both antibodies and were stained bright yellow. Krüppel protein overlaps with Knirps protein in a similar manner in the posterior region of the embryo.

Three genes are known to be the primary pair-rule genes. These genes—*hairy,even-skipped,* and *runt*—are essential for the formation of the periodic pattern, and they are directly controlled by the gap gene proteins. The enhancers of the primary pair-rule genes are recognized by gap gene proteins, and it is thought that the different concentrations of gap gene proteins determine whether a pair-rule gene is transcribed or not. The enhancers of the primary pair-rule genes are often modular: the control over each stripe is located in a discrete region of the DNA. One of the best-studied enhancers is that for the *even-skipped* gene. It is composed of modular units arranged in such a way that each unit regulates a separate stripe. For instance, the second *even-skipped* stripe is repressed by both Giant and Krüppel proteins and is activated by Hunchback protein and low concentrations of Bicoid. DNase I footprinting showed that the enhancer region for this stripe contains six binding sites for Krüppel protein, three for Hunchback protein, three for Giant protein, and five for Bicoid protein. Similarly, *even-skipped* stripe 5 is regulated negatively by Krüppel protein (on its anterior border) and by Giant protein (on its posterior border).

The importance of these enhancers can be shown by both genetic and biochemical means. First, a mutation in a particular enhancer can delete its particular stripe and no other. Second, if a reporter gene such as *lacZ* (encoding β-galactosidase) is fused to one of these enhancer elements, the *lacZ* gene is expressed only in that particular stripe. Third, the placement of the stripes can be altered by deleting the gap genes that regulate them. Thus, the placement of the stripes of pair-rule gene expression is a result of (1) the modular *cis*-regulatory enhancer elements of the pair-rule genes and (2) the *trans*-regulatory gap gene proteins that bind to these enhancer sites.

Once initiated by the gap gene proteins, the transcription pattern of the primary pair-rule genes becomes stabilized by their interactions among themselves. The primary pair-rule genes also form the context that allows or inhibits the expression of the later-acting secondary pair-rule genes. One such secondary pair-rule gene is *fushi tarazu* (*ftz*; Japanese, "too few segments". Early in cycle 14, *ftz* RNA and protein are seen throughout the segmented portion of the embryo. However, as the proteins from the primary pair-rule genes begin to interact with the *ftz* enhancer, the *ftz* gene is repressed in certain bands of nuclei to create interstripe regions. Meanwhile, the Ftz protein interacts with its own promoter to stimulate more transcription of the *ftz* gene.

The expression of the each pair-rule gene in seven stripes divides the embryo into fourteen parasegments, with each pair-rule gene being expressed in alternate parasegments. Moreover, each row of nuclei within each parasegment expresses a particular and unique combination of pair-rule products. These products will activate the next level of segmentation genes, the segment polarity genes.

THE SEGMENT POLARITY GENES

So far, our discussion has described interactions between molecules within the syncytial embryo. But once cells form, interactions take place between the cells. These intercellular interactions are mediated by the segment polarity genes, and they accomplish two important tasks. First, they reinforce the parasegmental periodicity established by the earlier transcription factors. Second, through this cell-to-cell signaling, cell fates are established within each parasegment.

The segment polarity genes encode proteins that are constituents of the Wingless and Hedgehog signal transduction pathways. Mutations in these genes lead to defects in segmentation and in gene expression pattern across each parasegment. The development of the normal pattern relies on the fact only one row of cells in each parasegment is permitted to express the Hedgehog protein, and only one row of cells in each parasegment is permitted to express the Wingless protein. The key to this pattern is the activation of the *engrailed* gene in those cells that are going to express the Hedgehog protein. The *engrailed* gene is activated when cells have high levels of the Even-skipped, Fushi tarazu, or Paired transcription factors. Moreover, it is repressed in those cells that receive high levels of Odd-skipped, Runt, or Sloppy-paired proteins. As a result, Engrailed is expressed in fourteen stripes across the anterior-posterior axis of the embryo. (Indeed, in mutations that cause the embryo to be deficient in Fushi tarazu, only seven bands of Engrailed are expressed.) These stripes of *engrailed* transcription mark the anterior boundary of each parasegment (and the posterior border of each segment). The *wingless* gene is activated in those bands of cells that receive little or no Even-skipped or Fushi tarazu proteins, but which do contain the Sloppy-paired protein. This causes *wingless* to be transcribed solely in the row of cells directly anterior to the cells where *engrailed* is transcribed.

Once *wingless* and *engrailed* expression is established in adjacent cells, this pattern must be maintained to retain the parasegmental periodicity of the body plan established by the pair-rule genes. It should be remembered that the mRNAs and proteins involved in initiating these patterns are short-lived, and that the patterns must be maintained after their initiators are no longer being synthesized. The maintenance of these patterns is regulated by interactions between cells expressing *wingless* and those expressing *engrailed*. The Wingless protein, secreted from the *wingless*-expressing cells, diffuses to adjacent cells. The cells expressing *engrailed* can bind this protein because they contain the *Drosophila* membrane receptor protein for Wingless, D-Frizzled-2. This receptor activates the Wnt signal transduction pathway, resulting in the continued expression of *engrailed*.

Moreover, this activation starts another portion of this reciprocal pathway. The Engrailed protein activates the transcription of the *hedgehog* gene in the *engrailed*-expressing cells. The Hedgehog protein can bind to the Hedgehog receptor (the Patched protein) on neighbouring cells. When it binds to the adjacent posterior cells, it stimulates the expression of the *wingless* gene. The result is a reciprocal loop wherein the Engrailed-synthesizing cells secrete the Hedgehog protein, which maintains the expression of the *wingless* gene in the neighbouring cells, while the Wingless-secreting cells maintain the expression of the *engrailed* and *hedgehog* genes in their neighbours in turn. In this way, the transcription pattern of these two types of cells is stabilized. This interaction creates a stable boundary, as well as a signaling centre from which Hedgehog and Wingless proteins diffuse across the parasegment.

The diffusion of these proteins is thought to provide the gradients by which the cells of the parasegment acquire their identities. This process can be seen in the dorsal epidermis, where the rows of larval cells produce different cuticular structures depending on their position within the segment. The 1° row consists of large, pigmented spikes called denticles. Posterior to these cells, the 2° row produces a smooth epidermal cuticle. The next two cell rows have a 3° fate, making small, thick hairs, and these are followed by several rows of cells that adopt the 4° fate, producing fine hairs.

The *wingless*-expressing cells lie within the region producing the fine hairs, while the *hedgehog*-expressing cells are near the 1° row of cells. The fates of the cells can be altered by experimentally increasing or decreasing the levels of Hedgehog or Wingless protein. For example, if the *hedgehog* gene is fused to a heat shock promoter and the embryos are grown at a temperature that activates the gene, more Hedgehog protein is made, and the cells normally showing 3° fates will become 2° cells. The rows of 4° cells farthest from the Wingless-secreting cells may also become 3° or 2° cells. It seems that the cells closest to the Wingless secreters cannot respond to Hedgehog, and Hedgehog cannot, by itself, specify the 1° fate (which may require the expression of certain pair-rule gene products). Thus, Hedgehog and Wingless appear necessary for elabourating the entire pattern of cell types across the parasegment. However, the mechanism by which they accomplish this specification is not clear. Either these signals act in a graded fashion, as morphogens, or they act locally to initiate a cascade of local signaling events, in which each interaction uses a different ligand and receptor. The resulting pattern of cell fates also changes the focus of patterning from parasegment to segment. There are now external markers, as the *engrailed*-expressing cells become the most posterior cells of each segment.

THE HOMEOTIC SELECTOR GENES

Patterns of Homeotic Gene Expression

After the segmental boundaries have been established, the characteristic structures of each segment are specified. This specification is accomplished by the homeotic selector genes. There are two regions of *Drosophila* chromosome 3 that contain most of these homeotic genes. One region, the Antennapedia complex, contains the homeotic genes *labial* (*lab*), *Antennapedia* (*Antp*), *sex combs reduced* (*scr*), *deformed* (*dfd*), and *proboscipedia* (*pb*). The *labial* and *deformed* genes specify the head segments, while *sex combs reduced* and *Antennapedia* contribute to giving the thoracic segments their identities. The *proboscipedia* gene appears to act only in adults, but in its absence, the labial palps of the mouth are transformed into legs. The second region of homeotic genes is the bithorax complex. There are three protein-coding genes found in this complex: *ultrabithorax* (*ubx*), which is required for the identity of the third thoracic segment; and the *abdominal A* (*abdA*) and *Abdominal B* (*AbdB*) genes, which are responsible for the segmental identities of the abdominal segments. The lethal phenotype of the triple-point mutant Ubx^-, $abdA^-$, $AbdB^-$ is identical to that resulting from a deletion of the entire bithorax complex. The chromosome region containing both the Antennapedia complex and the bithorax complex is often referred to as the homeotic complex (Hom-C).

Because these genes are responsible for the specification of fly body parts, mutations in them lead to bizarre phenotypes. In 1894, William Bateson called these organisms "homeotic mutants," and they have fascinated developmental biologists for decades. For example, the body of the normal adult fly contains three thoracic segments, all of which produce a pair of legs. The first thoracic segment does not produce any further appendages, but the second thoracic segment produces both a set of legs and a set of wings. The third thoracic segment produces a set of wings and a set of balancers known as halteres. In homeotic mutants, these specific segmental identities can be changed. When the *ultrabithorax* gene is deleted, the third thoracic segment (which is characterized by halteres) becomes transformed into another second thoracic segment. The result is a fly with four wings—an embarrassing situation for a classic dipteran. Similarly, the Antennapedia protein is usually used to specify the second thoracic segment of the fly. But when flies have a mutation wherein the *Antennapedia* gene is expressed in the head (as well as in the thorax), legs rather than antennae grow out of the head sockets. In the recessive mutant of *Antennapedia,* the gene fails to be expressed in the second thoracic segment, and antennae sprout out of the leg positions.

These major homeotic selector genes have been cloned and their expression analyzed by in situ hybridization. Transcripts from each gene can be detected in specific regions of the embryo and are especially prominent in the central nervous system.

INITIATING THE PATTERNS OF HOMEOTIC GENE EXPRESSION

The initial domains of homeotic gene expression are influenced by the gap genes and pair-rule genes. For instance, the expression of the *abdA* and *AbdB* genes is repressed by the gap gene proteins Hunchback and Krüppel. This inhibition prevents these abdomen-specifying genes from being expressed in the head and thorax. Conversely, the *Ultrabithorax* gene is activated by certain levels of the Hunchback protein, so that it is originally transcribed in a broad band in the middle of the embryo, and the transcription of *Antennapedia* is activated by Krüppel. The boundaries of homeotic gene expression are soon confined to the parasegments defined by the Fushi tarazu and Even-skipped proteins.

Maintaining the Patterns of Homeotic Gene Expression

The expression of homeotic genes is a dynamic process. The *Antennapedia* gene (*Antp*), for instance, although initially expressed in presumptive parasegment 4, soon appears in parasegment 5. As the germ band expands, *Antp* expression is seen in the presumptive neural tube as far posterior as parasegment 12. During further development, the domain of *Antp* expression contracts again, and *Antp* transcripts are localized strongly to parasegments 4 and 5. Like that of other homeotic genes, *Antp* expression is negatively regulated by all the homeotic gene products expressed posterior to it. In other words, each of the bithorax complex genes represses the expression of *Antennapedia*. If the *Ultrabithorax* gene is deleted, *Antp* activity extends through the region that would normally have expressed *Ubx* and stops where the *Abd* region begins. If the entire bithorax complex is deleted, *Antp* expression extends throughout the abdomen. (Such a larva does not survive, but the cuticle pattern throughout the abdomen is that of the second thoracic segment.)

As we saw above, the gap gene and pair-rule gene proteins are transient, but the identities of the segments must be stabilized so that differentiation can occur. Thus, once the transcription patterns of the homeotic genes have become stabilized, they are "locked" into place by alteration of the chromatin conformation in these genes. The repression of homeotic genes appears to be maintained by the Polycomb family of proteins, while the active chromatin conformation appears to be maintained by the Trithorax proteins.

REALISATOR GENES

The search is now on for "realisator genes," those genes that are the targets of the homeotic gene proteins and which function to form the specified tissue or organ primordia. In the formation of the second thoracic segment, for example, *Antennapedia* is expressed. Casares and Mann have shown that Antennapedia protein binds to the enhancer of the *homothorax* gene and prevent its expression. Homothorax is necessary for producing a transcription factor critical for antenna formation. Therefore, one of Antennapedia's functions is to suppress those genes necessary for antenna development.

The Ultrabithorax protein is able to repress the expression of the *Wingless* gene in those cells that will become the halteres of the fly. One of the major differences between the appendage-forming cells of the second and the third thoracic segments is that Wingless expression occurs in the appendage-forming cells of the second thoracic segment, but not in those of the third thoracic segment. Wingless acts as a growth promoter and morphogen in these tissues. In the third thoracic segment, Ubx protein is found in these cells, and it prevents the expression of the *Wingless* gene. Thus, one of the ways in which Ubx protein specifies the third thoracic segment is by preventing the expression of those genes that would generate the wing tissue.

Another target of the homeotic proteins, the *distal-less* gene is necessary for limb development and is active solely in the thorax. Distal-less expression is repressed in the abdomen, probably by a combination of Ubx and AbdA proteins that can bind to its enhancer and block transcription. This presents a paradox, since parasegment 5 (entirely thoracic and leg-producing) and parasegment 6 (which includes most of the legless first abdominal segment) both expressUbx. How can these two very different segments be specified by the same gene? Castelli-Gair and Akam have shown that the mere presence of Ubx protein in a group of cells is not sufficient for specification. Rather, the time and place of its expression within the parasegment can be critical. Before *Ubx* expression, parasegments 4–6 have similar potentials. At division cycle 10, *Ubx* expression in the anterior parts of parasegments 5 and 6 prevents those parasegments from forming structures (such as the anterior spiracle) characteristic of parasegment 4. Moreover, in the posterior compartment of parasegment 6 (but not parasegment 5), Ubx protein blocks the formation of the limb primordium by repressing the *distal-less* gene. At division cycle 11, by which time Ubx has pervaded all of parasegment 6, the *distal-less* gene has become self-regulatory and cannot be repressed by Ubx.

THE GENERATION OF DORSAL-VENTRAL POLARITY

In 1936, embryologist E. E. Just criticized those geneticists who sought to explain *Drosophila* development by looking at specific mutations affecting eye colour, bristle number, and wing shape. He said that he wasn't interested in the development of the bristles of a fly's back; rather, he wanted to know how the fly embryo makes the back itself. Fifty years later, embryologists and geneticists are finally answering that question.

The Morphogenetic Agent for Dorsal-Ventral Polarity

Dorsal-ventral polarity is established by the gradient of a transcription factor called Dorsal. Unlike Bicoid, whose gradient is established within a syncytium, Dorsal forms a gradient over a field of cells that is established as a consequence of cell-to-cell signaling events.

The specification of the dorsal-ventral axis takes place in several steps. The critical step is the translocation of the Dorsal protein from the cytoplasm into the nuclei of the ventral cells during the fourteenth division cycle. Anderson and Nüsslein-Volhard isolated 11 maternal effect genes, each of whose absence is associated with a lack of ventral structures. The absence of another maternal effect gene, *cactus*, causes the ventralization of all cells. The proteins encoded by these maternal genes are critical for making certain that the Dorsal protein gets into only those nuclei on the ventral surface of the embryo. After its translocation, the Dorsal protein acts on cell nuclei to specify the different regions of the embryo. Different concentrations of Dorsal protein in the nuclei appear to specify different fates in those cells.

The Translocation of Dorsal Protein

The protein that actually distinguishes dorsum (back) from ventrum (belly) is the product of the *dorsal* gene. The RNA transcript of the mother's *dorsal* gene is placed in the oocyte by her ovarian cells. However, Dorsal protein is not synthesized from this maternal message until about 90 minutes after fertilization. When this protein is translated, it is found throughout the embryo, not just on the ventral or dorsal side. How, then, can this protein act as a morphogen if it is located everywhere in the embryo?

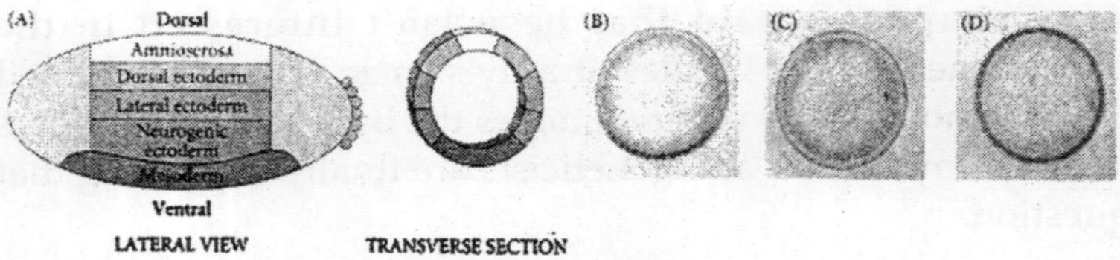

Fig. Translocation of Dorsal protein into ventral, but not lateral or dorsal, nuclei. (A) Fate map of a cross section through the Drosophila embryo. The most ventral part becomes the mesoderm; the next higher portion becomes the neurogenic (ventral) ectoderm. The lateral and epidermal ectoderm can be distinguished in the cuticle, and the dorsalmost region becomes the amnioserosa, the extraembryonic layer that surrounds the embryo. (B-D) Cross sections of embryos stained with antibody to show the presence of Dorsal protein (dark-stained area). (B) A wild-type embryo, showing Dorsal protein in the ventralmost nuclei. (C) A dorsalized mutant, showing no localization of Dorsal protein in any nucleus. (D) A ventralized mutant, in which Dorsal protein has entered the nucleus of every cell.

In 1989, the surprising answer was found. While Dorsal protein can be found throughout the syncytial blastoderm of the early *Drosophila* embryo, it is translocated into nuclei only in the ventral part of the embryo. In the nucleus, Dorsal binds to certain genes to activate or suppress their transcription. If

Dorsal does not enter the nucleus, the genes responsible for specifying ventral cell types (*snail* and *twist*) are not transcribed, the genes responsible for specifying dorsal cell types (*decapentaplegic* and *zerknüllt*) are not repressed, and all the cells of the embryo become specified as dorsal cells.

This model of dorsal-ventral axis formation in *Drosophila* is supported by analyses of mutations that give rise to an entirely dorsalized or an entirely ventralized phenotype. In those mutants in which all the cells are dorsalized (as is evident by their dorsal cuticle), Dorsal protein does not enter the nucleus in any cell. Conversely, in those mutants in which all cells have a ventral phenotype, Dorsal protein is found in every cell nucleus.

THE SIGNAL CASCADE

Signal from the Oocyte Nucleus to the Follicle Cells

If Dorsal protein is found throughout the embryo, but gets translocated into the nuclei of only ventral cells, then something else must be providing asymmetrical cues. It appears that this signal is mediated through a complex interaction between the oocyte and its surrounding follicle cells.

The follicular epithelium surrounding the developing oocyte is initially symmetrical, but this symmetry is broken by a signal from the oocyte nucleus. The oocyte nucleus is originally located at the posterior end of the oocyte, away from the nurse cells. It then moves to an anterior dorsal position and signals the overlying follicle cells to become the more columnar dorsal follicle cells. The dorsalizing signal from the oocyte nucleus appears to be the product of the *gurken* gene. The *gurken* message becomes localized in a crescent between the oocyte nucleus and the oocyte plasma membrane, and its protein product forms an anterior-posterior gradient along the dorsal surface of the oocyte. Since it can diffuse only a short distance, the Gurken protein reaches only those follicle cells closest to the oocyte nucleus. Mutations of the Gurken gene in the mother (and thus in the oocyte) cause the ventralization of both the embryo and its surrounding follicle cells. Mutations of this gene in the mother (and thus in the oocyte) cause the ventralization of both the embryo and its surrounding follicle cells. (If the mutation is in the follicle cells and not in the egg, the embryo is normal.)

The Gurken signal is received by the follicle cells through a receptor encoded by the *torpedo* gene. Molecular analysis has now established that *gurken* encodes a homologue of the vertebrate epidermal growth factor (EGF), while *torpedo* encodes a homologue of the vertebrate EGF receptor. *Maternal* deficiency of *torpedo* causes the ventralization of the embryo. Moreover, the *torpedo* gene is active in the ovarian follicle cells, not in the embryo. This was discovered by making germ line/ somatic chimeras. Schüpbach transplanted germ cell precursors from wild-type embryos to embryos whose mothers carried the torpedo mutation. Conversely, she transplanted the germ cells of the torpedo mutant embryos to the wild-type embryos. When mated to wild-type males, the wild-type eggs produced ventralized embryos when they developed within the torpedo mutant mothers' follicles. The torpedo mutant eggs were able to produce normal embryos if they developed within a wild-type ovary. Thus, unlike the *gurken* gene product, the wild-type *torpedo* gene is needed in the follicle cells, not in the egg itself.

Signal from the Follicle Cells to the Oocyte Cytoplasm

The activated Torpedo receptor protein inhibits the expression of the *pipe* gene. As a result, the Pipe protein is made only in the ventral follicle cells. The Pipe protein (in some as yet unknown way) activates the Nudel protein, which is secreted to the cell membrane of the ventral embryonic cells. A few hours later in development, the activated Nudel protein initiates the activation of three serine proteases that are secreted by the embryo into the perivitelline fluid. These three serine proteases are the products of the *gastrulation defective* (*gd*), *snake* (*snk*), and *easter* (*ea*) genes. Like most extracellular proteases, they are secreted in an inactive form and become activated by peptide cleavage. It is thought that the activated

Nudel protein first tethers and activates the Gastrulation defective protein. This protease cleaves the Snake protein. This cleavage activates the Snake protease, which in turn cleaves the Easter protein. This cleavage activates the Easter protein, which cleaves the Spätzle protein.

The cleaved Spätzle protein is now able to bind to its receptor in the oocyte cell membrane, the product of the *Toll* gene. Toll protein is a maternal product that is evenly distributed throughout the cell membrane of the egg, but it becomes activated only by binding the Spätzle protein, which is produced only on the ventral side of the egg. Therefore, the Toll proteins on the ventral side of the egg are transducing a signal into the egg, while the Toll receptors on the dorsal side of the egg are not.

Separation of the Dorsal and Cactus Proteins

The crucial outcome of signaling through the Toll protein is the establishment of a gradient of Dorsal protein in the ventral cell nuclei. How is this gradient established? It appears that the Cactus protein is blocking the portion of the Dorsal protein that enables the Dorsal protein to get into nuclei. As long as this Cactus protein is bound to it, Dorsal protein remains in the cytoplasm. Thus, this entire complex signaling system is organized to split the Cactus protein from the Dorsal protein in the ventral region of the egg. When Spätzle binds to and activates the Toll protein, the Toll protein can activate the Pelle protein kinase. The activated Pelle protein kinase can (probably through an intermediate) phosphorylate the Cactus protein. Once phosphorylated, the Cactus protein is degraded, and the Dorsal protein can enter the nucleus. Since the signal transduction cascade creates a gradient of Spätzle protein that is highest in the most ventral region, there is a gradient of Dorsal translocation into the ventral cells of the embryo, with the highest concentrations of Dorsal protein in the most ventral cell nuclei.

The process described for the translocation of Dorsal protein into the nucleus is very similar to the process for the translocation of the NF-κB transcription factor into the nucleus of mammalian lymphocytes. In fact, there is substantial homology between NF-κB and Dorsal, between IκB and Cactus, between the Toll protein and the interleukin 1 receptor, between Pelle protein and an IL-1-associated protein kinase, and between the DNA sequences recognized by Dorsal and by NF-κB. Thus, the biochemical pathway used to specify dorsal-ventral polarity in *Drosophila* appears to be homologous to that used to differentiate lymphocytes in mammals.

Effects of the Dorsal Protein Gradient

What does the Dorsal protein do once it is located in the nuclei of the ventral cells? A look at the fate map of a cross section through the *Drosophila* embryo at the fourteenth division cycle makes it obvious that the 16 cells with the highest concentration of Dorsal protein are those that generate the mesoderm. The next cell up from this region generates the specialized glial and neural cells of the midline. The next two cells are those that give rise to the ventral epidermis and ventral nerve cord, while the nine cells above them produce the dorsal epidermis. The most dorsal group of six cells generates the amnioserosal covering of the embryo.

This fate map is generated by the gradient of Dorsal protein in the nuclei. Large amounts of Dorsal instruct the cells to become mesoderm, while lesser amounts instruct the cells to become glial or ectodermal tissue. The first morphogenetic event of *Drosophila* gastrulation is the invagination of the 16 ventralmost cells of the embryo. All of the body muscles, fat bodies, and gonads derive from these mesodermal cells. The Dorsal protein specifies these cells to become mesoderm in two ways. First, Dorsal activates specific genes that create the mesodermal phenotype.

Three of the target genes for Dorsal are *twist,snail,* and *rhomboid*. These genes are transcribed only in nuclei that have received high concentrations of Dorsal protein, since their enhancers do not bind Dorsal with a very high affinity. The Twist protein activates mesodermal genes, while the Snail protein represses particular nonmesodermal genes that might otherwise be active. The *rhomboid* gene is interesting because it is activated by Dorsal but repressed by Snail. Thus, *rhomboid* is not expressed in the most ventral cells (i.e., the mesodermal precursors), but is expressed in the cells adjacent to the mesoderm that form the presumptive neural ectoderm. Both Snail and Twist are needed for the complete mesodermal phenotype and proper gastrulation.

The sharp border between the mesodermal cells and those cells adjacent to them that generate glial cells (mesectoderm) is produced by the presence of Snail and Twist in the ventralmost cells, but of only Twist in the next cell up. In mutants of *snail,* the ventralmost cells still have the *twist* gene activated, and they resemble the more lateral cells.

The Dorsal protein also determines the mesoderm directly. In addition to activating the mesoderm-stimulating genes (*twist* and *snail*), it directly inhibits the dorsalizing genes *zerknüllt* (*zen*) and *decapentaplegic* (*dpp*). Thus, in the same cells, the Dorsal protein can act as an activator of some genes and a repressor of others. Whether the Dorsal protein functions to activate or repress depends on the structure of the genes' enhancers. The *zen* enhancer contains a silencer region that contains a binding site for Dorsal and a second binding site for two other DNA-binding proteins.

These two other proteins enable the Dorsal protein to bind a transcriptional repressor protein (Groucho) and bring it to the DNA. Mutants of *dorsal* express *dpp* and *zen* genes throughout the embryo, and embryos deficient in *dpp* and *zen* fail to form dorsal structures. Thus, in wild-type embryos, the mesodermal precursors express *twist* and *snail* (but not *zen* or *dpp*); precursors of the dorsal epidermis and amnioserosa express *zen* and *dpp* but not *twist* or *snail.* Glial (mesectoderm) precursors express only *snail,* while the lateral neural ectodermal precursors do not express any of these four genes. Thus, as a consequence of the responses to the Dorsal protein gradient, the axis becomes subdivided into mesoderm, mesectoderm, neurogenic ectoderm, epidermis, and amnioserosa.

Axes and Organ Primordia: The Cartesian Coordinate Model

The anterior-posterior and dorsal-ventral axes of *Drosophila* embryos form a coordinate system that can be used to specify positions within the embryo. Theoretically, cells that are initially equivalent in developmental potential can respond to their position by expressing different sets of genes. This type of specification has been demonstrated in the formation of the salivary gland rudiments.

First, salivary glands form only in the strip of cells defined by the activity of the *sex combs reduced* (*scr*) gene along the anterior-posterior axis (parasegment 2). No salivary glands form in *scr*-deficient mutants. Moreover, if *scr* is experimentally expressed throughout the embryo, salivary gland primordia form in a ventrolateral stripe along most of the length of the embryo.

The formation of salivary glands along the dorsal-ventral axis is repressed by both Decapentaplegic and Dorsal. These proteins inhibit salivary gland formation both dorsally and ventrally. Thus, the salivary glands form at the intersection of the vertical *scr* expression band (second parasegment) and the horizontal region in the middle of the embryo's circumference that has neither Decapentaplegic nor Dorsal gene products. The cells that form the salivary glands are directed to do so by the intersecting gene activities along the anterior-posterior and dorsal-ventral axes.

A similar situation is seen with tissues that are found in every segment of the fly. Neuroblasts arise from ten clusters of four to six cells each that form on each side in every segment in the strip of neural ectoderm at the midline of the embryo. The potential to form neural cells is conferred on these cells by the expression of proneural genes from the achaete-scute gene complex: *achaete* (*ac*), *scute* (*sc*), and *lethal of scute* (*l'sc*). The cells in each cluster interact to generate a single neural cell from the cluster. Skeath and colleagues have shown that the pattern of *achaete* and *scute* transcription is imposed by a coordinate system.

Their expression is repressed by the Decapentaplegic and Snail proteins along the dorsal-ventral axis, while positive enhancement by pair-rule genes along the anterior-posterior axis causes their repetition in each half-segment. The enhancer recognized by these axis-specifying proteins lies between the *achaete* and *scute* genes and appears to regulate both of them. It is very likely, then, that the positions of organ primordia are specified throughout the fly through a two-dimensional coordinate system based on the intersection of the anterior-posterior and dorsal-ventral axes.